GEORGE WASHINGTON'S WAR

Books by Robert Leckie

HISTORY

None Died in Vain: The Saga of the American Civil War
Delivered from Evil: The Saga of World War II
The Wars of America: Updated and Revised, 1609–1991
American and Catholic: The Catholic Church in the U.S.
Challenge for the Pacific: The Struggle for Guadalcanal
With Fire and Sword (*edited with Quentin Reynolds*)
Strong Men Armed: U.S. Marines Against Japan
Conflict: The History of the Korean War
The March to Glory: 1st Marine Division's Breakout from Chosin

AUTOBIOGRAPHY

Helmet for My Pillow
Lord, What a Family!

BELLES LETTRES

These Are My Heroes: A Study of the Saints
Warfare: A Study of War
A Soldier-Priest Talks to Youth

FICTION

Ordained
Marines!
The Bloodborn
Forged in Blood
Blood of the Seventeen Fires
The General

FOR YOUNGER READERS

The Battle for Iwo Jima
The Story of Football
The Story of World War Two
The Story of World War One
The War in Korea
Great American Battles
The World Turned Upside-Down
1812: The War Nobody Won
The Big Game
Keeper Play
Stormy Voyage

GEORGE WASHINGTON'S WAR

★ ★ ★ ★ ★ ★ ★ ★ ★ ★ ★ ★ ★

The Saga of the American Revolution

ROBERT LECKIE

HarperPerenial
A Division of HarperCollins*Publishers*

A hardcover edition of this book was published in 1992 by HarperCollins Publishers.

HarperCollins books may be purchased for educational, business, or sales promotional use. For information please write: Special Markets Department, HarperCollins Publishers, Inc., 10 East 53rd Street, New York, NY 10022.

First HarperPerennial edition published 1993.

Designed by Alma Hochhauser Orenstein

The Library of Congress has catalogued the hardcover edition as follows:

Leckie, Robert.
George Washington's war: the saga of the American Revolution/Robert Leckie
p. cm.
Includes bibliographical references and index.
ISBN 0-06-016289-9 (cloth)
1. United States—History—Revolution, 1775–1783. I. Title.
E208.L439 1992
973.3—dc20 92-52607

ISBN 0-06-092215-X (pbk.)

09 10 11 RRD H 30 29

To My Three Red-Haired Grandsons:
Danny and Billy Salvas
and Alex Leckie

CONTENTS

MAPS

ACKNOWLEDGMENTS

I would like to express my appreciation to the staff of the New York Public Library; to Major Herbert Nath and the staff of the Daniel Library at the Citadel in Charleston, South Carolina; to Mrs. Richard Sawyer and her staff of the Free Public Library of my hometown of Rutherford, New Jersey; to my editors M. S. "Buz" Wyeth and Daniel Bial for their customary courteous criticisms and suggestions; and, finally, to my dear wife, who typed this manuscript with such splendid bad grace, filing a friend-of-court protest that the only persons on earth able to read—not to say interpret—my horrid, labyrinthine copy are herself and the makers of road maps.

—Robert Leckie
Polliwog Pond
Byram Township
Andover, New Jersey

August 2, 1991

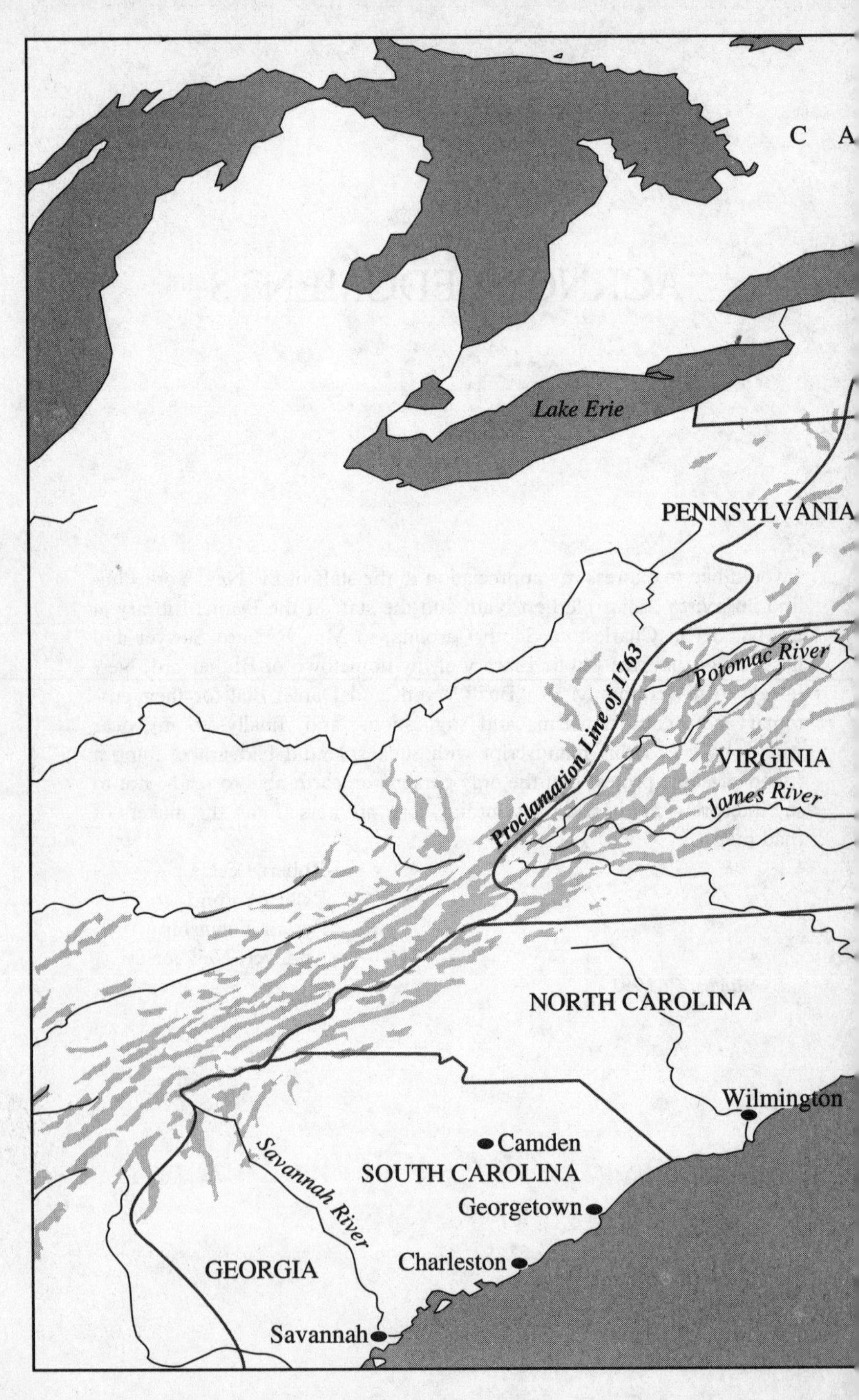
C A
Lake Erie
PENNSYLVANIA
Potomac River
Proclamation Line of 1763
VIRGINIA
James River
NORTH CAROLINA
Wilmington
Camden
SOUTH CAROLINA
Savannah River
Georgetown
Charleston
GEORGIA
Savannah

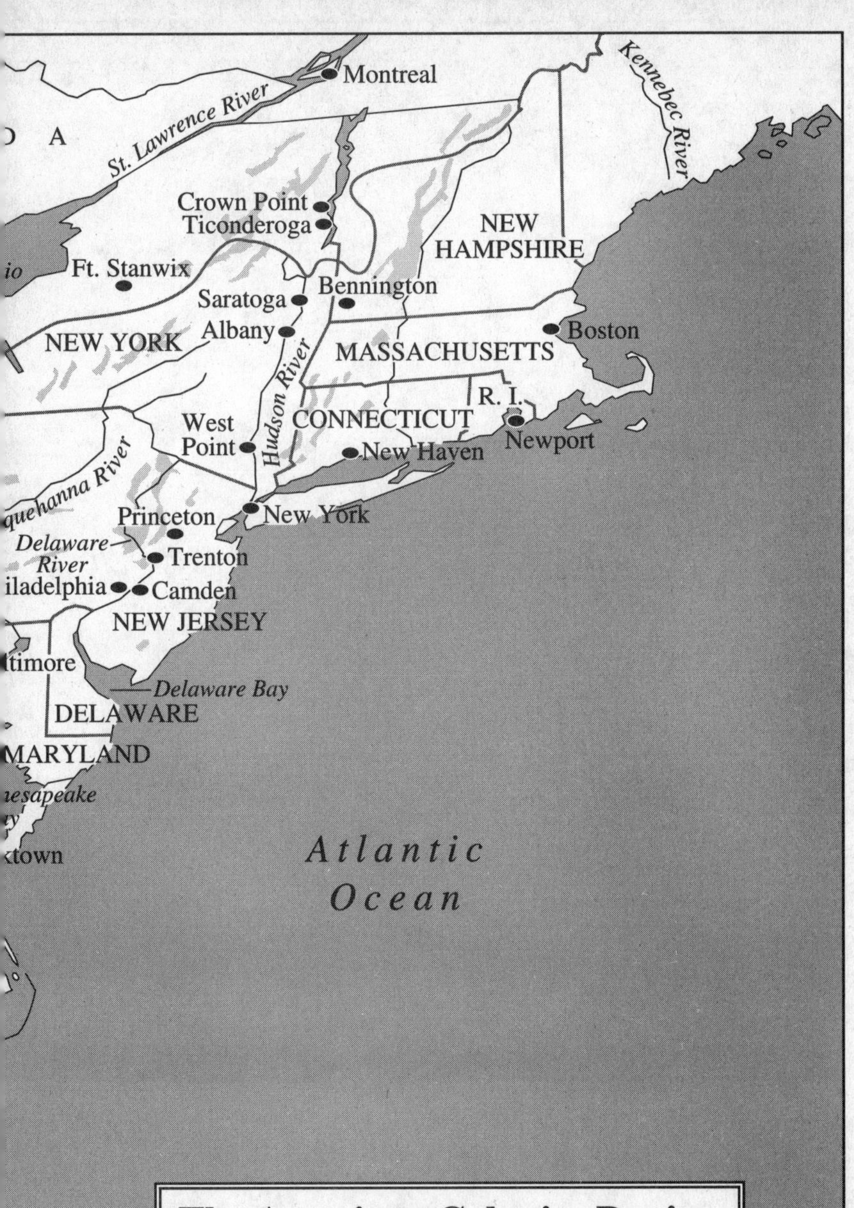

The American Colonies During the Revolution

★ 1 ★

THE FALL OF QUEBEC

During the early days of September 1759, General James Wolfe sank deeper and deeper into the dark night of despair. Only a few months previously, he had come sailing up the broad St. Lawrence River toward Quebec in a mood of the highest optimism and exaltation. To him, at only thirty-two years of age, had gone the chief command of William Pitt's three-pronged campaign to end the 150-year-old Anglo-French struggle for North America. While the veterans Lord Jeffrey Amherst and General John Prideaux were to capture Montreal and Fort Niagara, respectively, Wolfe, a mere colonel during the American campaign of a year earlier, had been chosen to crack the hardest nut of all: Quebec. The selection had provoked bitter criticism both in the army and in the ministry. The Duke of Newcastle complained to King George II that Wolfe not only was too young to command such an important expedition, but was also slightly demented. "Mad is he?" the old king growled. "Then I hope he will bite some others of my generals."

But James Wolfe was not insane, only insanely ambitious. When the British fleet arrived in the great basin below Quebec on June 26, his heart beat wildly when he beheld the beautiful white city on the cliff above him. If it were his, Niagara and Montreal would fall like rotten fruit and North America at last would be the king's. What, then, of James Wolfe? A peerage? James Wolfe, first Earl of Quebec? Why not? Dukedoms had been granted for less. Coming back to earth, Wolfe saw immediately that this clifftop city would be a tough nut to crack, indeed. He knew that it held 14,000 enemy soldiers against his 8,500, of whom many were those Americans whom he despised as "the dirtiest, most contemptible, cowardly dogs that you can conceive." Yet it was the American Rangers—forty of them—whom he quickly ordered ashore to capture the Island of Orléans, across the basin from Quebec. Here, he built his base camp, hastening a few days later to the island's tip to study Quebec's fortifications.

Wolfe held his telescope delicately. A soldier standing near noticed the marks of scurvy on the backs of his thin white hands. Here was no "normal" British general. Tall, thin and awkward; pallid in complexion; given to picking nervously at his cuffs with his long, tapering fingers, he seemed more a sissy than a soldier. He did not even wear the customary military wig or powder his bright red hair, but let it grow loose and long, pinning it together at the back of his head like any jackanapes. Yet James Wolfe's bulging blue eyes were hard, blazing now with a zealous fire and then with wonder while he studied his objective.

High, high above him, beautiful and white in the sunlight, was the city. He could see the stone houses, the churches, the palaces, the convents, the hospitals, the forest of spires and steeples and crosses glinting beneath the white flag whipping in the breeze. Everywhere he saw thick square walls and gun batteries, even along the strand of the Lower Town, straggling out of sight to his left beyond Cape Diamond. To his right as he swung his glass slowly like a swiveling gun, Wolfe perceived the entrenchments of Montcalm. He saw the sealed mouth of the St. Charles and the thundering falls of the Montmorency guarding the French left flank. He saw the little town of Beauport and the mud flats before it beneath the grape and muskets of Montcalm's redoubts. From left to right he saw steep brown cliffs, scarred with the raw red earth of fresh entrenchments; the stone houses, with windows reduced to firing slits by piles of logs; and behind them, the tops of the Indian wigwams and the white tents of the regulars. If Wolfe could have seen beyond Cape Diamond to his left, he would have been appalled by natural obstacles that were more formidable than Montcalm's fortifications. Here for seven or eight miles west to Cape Rouge rose steep after inaccessible steep, ranges of cliffs atop which a few men might hold off an army, all ending at another river and waterfall like the Montmorency.

Each time Wolfe thought he detected a flaw in the enemy's fortifications, he paused, studying the area eagerly, searching for a likely landing place, each time shaking his head petulantly and moving on. At last he snapped his telescope shut in exasperation and returned to his camp to notify William Pitt that he had gazed upon "the strongest country in the world."

Louis Joseph, the Marquis de Montcalm, had commanded in Canada since 1755 and had proved himself a veritable thorn in the side of

William Pitt and his luckless, feckless generals, from the unimaginative Edward Braddock to the listless Lord Loudoun to the willy-nilly and artless James Abercrombie, known to his contemptuous troops as "Mrs. Nanny Cromby." Montcalm was also a gentleman of high principle and deep religious convictions and a scholar. He was extremely proud of those fortifications that had so dismayed James Wolfe, having erected them over the objections of Pierre François Rigaud, the Marquis de Vaudreuil, governor of Canada and son of an earlier governor of the little colony of sixty thousand souls along the mighty St. Lawrence. Vaudreuil seems to have studied corruption under his father, learning how best "to clip and cut and rob the king." Vaudreuil's objections to spending money to fortify the capital of the colony were based, in part, on his jealousy of Montcalm's victories—which he often reported to Versailles as his own—and, in part, on his awareness that Montcalm had informed Paris of Vaudreuil's connivance in the colony's corruption. "Everybody appears to be in a hurry to make his fortune before the colony is lost," Montcalm had written, "which event many perhaps desire as an impenetrable veil over their conduct."

Nevertheless, Montcalm had persevered in his determination to make Quebec impregnable. His confidence remained unshaken even after the appearance of the British fleet carrying Wolfe's army. "Let them amuse themselves," he said calmly. "Two months more, and they will be gone."

At first, James Wolfe made no impatient or impetuous assault upon this "strongest country," but rather attempted to lure Montcalm out of his fortifications. First, he deliberately divided his army into three dispersed forces, hoping Montcalm would seize this seeming opportunity to defeat him in detail, but relying on the British fleet to concentrate his separated army at any given point. Montcalm refused the bait. Next Wolfe ravaged the countryside, calculating that the French general would be so enraged that he would come rallying to the rescue of his tormented countrymen. Again Montcalm sat still. Finally, goaded into indiscretion, Wolfe launched an incredibly ill-conceived and badly executed amphibious assault in which boated troops crossed the river to disembark under enemy fire and attempt to storm a fortified height above them. Here—without harming a single Frenchman—he lost 443 men killed and wounded, together with the respect of his staff, his three brigadiers and Admiral Charles Saunders, commander of the fleet. Enemy sniping had also thinned his ranks, so that by the end of August he had lost 850 men killed and wounded, an alarming 10 percent of his entire force. Disease and desertion further reduced his strength, while the general himself was gripped by an indecision that was nearly as destructive of discipline as was his constant feuding with his brigadiers. Then, on August 20, Wolfe himself fell ill of a fever that was probably malaria. For a week he lay in a French farmhouse, his thin body racked in an oven of heat. Recovering, he assembled his brigadiers and asked them how best to attack the enemy.

As they had done before, the brigadiers recommended that he seize a position on the opposite shore somewhere between Quebec and Montreal upriver. To their surprise, instead of peremptorily rejecting this advice, as he had done before, he not only accepted it, but proposed to climb the inaccessible heights beneath the high plateau of the Plains of Abraham under the very walls of Quebec. Montcalm, cut off from assistance from Montreal, would have to come out and fight.

Here, it seemed to the startled brigadiers, was a desperate solution born of despair and their commander's dread of defeat, of going home to face "the censure and reproach of an ignorant population." Here also was a resolve strengthened on September 10, when Admiral Saunders informed him that with ice floes beginning to form on the Gulf of St. Lawrence, he would have to leave. Alarmed, Wolfe told Saunders that he was going to send 150 picked men up a secret path leading to the Plains of Abraham. If they could overpower the light guard posted there, his main body would follow. If they could not, Wolfe would agree to return to Britain.

Wolfe is said to have discovered this path while studying the cliffs west of Quebec. Examining a little cove called the Anse-du-Foulon—Fuller's Cove—he is said to have discerned outlines of a trail winding up the steep cliffside, and observed that only a few white tents were visible at the top. But because this assumes much too much and because Wolfe deliberately destroyed the September entries in his diary, it is not too speculative to suggest that treachery, rather than the implausible pretext of seeing the path "through a glass darkly," had revealed to him Montcalm's Achilles' heel.

Montcalm knew of the path and had said to Vaudreuil: "I swear to you that a hundred men posted there would stop their whole army." He did post a hundred men there, under the trustworthy Captain St. Martin. On call behind them on the plains themselves was another thousand, the crack Guienne Regiment, commanded by a capable colonel. But unknown to Montcalm, Vaudreuil ordered Guienne back east to the St. Charles River, replacing St. Martin's command with one under the chevalier Duchambon de Vegor, a close crony whose corruption was rivaled only by his cowardice. Unlike St. Martin, who had refused to allow his men to go home to help in the harvest, Vergor granted leave to forty of his own, provided that they also put in hours on his farm. So there were sixty men—not a hundred—guarding the cliffside path, and the supporting regiment designed to destroy any momentary penetration of their position was out of the impact area. Finally, the false Vergor was in command.

Thus the possibility of treachery seems to outweigh the romantic legend of the desperate young commander on the riverbank suddenly espying the chink in Montcalm's armor. However Wolfe discovered it, he made masterly preparations for exploiting it, his indecision and despair being blown clean away by this cleansing wind of good fortune. First, he had part of the fleet drift upriver with the flood tide and down with the ebb, thus compelling the French to march and countermarch themselves into exhaustion while remaining abreast of the enemy ships. Next to delude Montcalm further as to the point of attack, he had Saunders deploy his main fleet in a demonstration off Beauport. Finally, from two deserters he learned that a convoy of provisions from Montreal would be coming downriver the night of September 12. Although this operation was canceled, no one informed the sentries below that the familiar store ships were not coming. So Wolfe decided to have his own ships, loaded with 4,800 troops, precede this customary traffic of French supply vessels, hoping that the sentries would mistake Wolfe's ships for their own.

On the night of September 12 all was in readiness. The stars were visible, but there was no moon as the British transports drifted upriver on the flood tide. Commodore Louis Antoine de Bougainville, in command west of Quebec, weary of the enemy's nautical promenading of the past few days, ignored them—confident that they would drift downriver again with the ebb. Besides, he was to spend the night with the accommodating Madame de Vienne. Below Quebec Admiral Saunders had begun to bombard Montcalm's position while lowering boats filled with sailors and Marines.

At two o'clock in the morning of September 13, 1759, the tide turned to the ebb. A lantern with its light shrouded from the Quebec shore was hoisted to the main topgallant masthead of the *Sutherland*. It was the signal to cast off, and the boats of the British began drifting silently downstream.

General James Wolfe stood in one of the foremost boats, surrounded by his staff. Softly he began to recite Gray's "Elegy in a Country

Churchyard." Finishing, he said: "Gentlemen, I would rather have written those lines than take Quebec." There was an embarrassed silence. Wolfe said no more, perhaps reflecting on the possibly prophetic line:

> The paths of glory lead but to the grave.

Unchallenged and ignored, the boatloads of soldiers had been drifting downstream for a full two hours. Now the tide was bearing the lead craft with Wolfe's "forlorn hope"—twenty-four volunteers who were to surprise Vergor—toward the dark and towering shore. A sentry shouted:

"Who goes there?"

"France!" shouted Simon Fraser, a young Highland officer who spoke French. "And God save the king!"

"What regiment?"

"*De la Reine*," Fraser replied, aware that the Queen's Regiment was with Bougainville.

Satisfied, the sentry allowed them to pass. But another sentry repeated the challenge, and a second French-speaking Highlander, Captain Donald McDonald, gave the answer. "Provision boats!" he hissed, disguising his accent with a hoarse whisper. "Don't make such a bloody noise! The British will hear!" The sentry waved them on.

Now the boat rounded the headland of the Anse-du-Foulon with the current running strong. Its sailors broke out their oars and rowed desperately against the tide. Fraser and McDonald and their men leaped ashore. They clambered up the cliff face. Suddenly the figure of a sentry became visible out of the gloom. "Who goes there?" he shouted down at them. Still hissing his hoarse whisper, still climbing, McDonald replied that he had come to relieve the post. The sentry hesitated—a moment too long—and twenty-four shadowy figures charged him with blazing muskets. Captain Vergor came dashing out of his tent, barefooted and in a nightshirt. He fired two pistols wildly into the air and turned to lead his rapidly departing troops in the race for Quebec, until a bullet pierced his heel and he fell screaming.

Below, James Wolfe heard the firing and for one slow desponding moment he despaired again. But then he heard the huzzahs of his men and was seized by a fierce wild joy. Quickly he gave the order for the following boats to land, and soon the cliff face was crawling with redcoats and kilted Highlanders. Among them was James Wolfe. Diseased, weakened by bloodletting, never strong, he was climbing on his magnificent will alone, and as he reached the summit, the empty boats of the first wave were already returning to their ships for the men of the second wave. By dawn the last of Wolfe's 4,800 soldiers had reached the undefended Plains of Abraham and were forming a mile distant from the western walls of Quebec.

That was how the Marquis de Montcalm saw them as he rode out of the city in a drizzling rain.

"This is serious," Montcalm said to an aide when he saw those rows of redcoats on the plateau that had once belonged to a French pilot named Abraham Martin. Almost at once he found himself in an atmosphere of distrust and dislike. Governor Vaudreuil refused to release more than three of his twenty-five cannons and would not send him the troops stationed at Beauport. Eventually, Montcalm conferred with his officers. Should he attack now or wait for Bougainville to strike the British rear? If he attacked immediately, he would have to do so without Bougainville and the troops withheld by Vaudreuil, but he might also strike the enemy before they had time to dig in. Attack now, his officers counseled, before Vaudreuil can appear with more hamstringing orders—and so Montcalm ordered his soldiers out to the Plains of Abraham.

Out they marched to the last battle of New France. All that was French, all that Samuel de Champlain had planted 150 years before on the cliff above the river, was to be defended here this day. Golden lily and gilded cross, dream of an empire stretching to the Rockies, fervor and faith and feudalism, all that had nourished or corrupted the martial and colorful little colony along the great river was at stake on the plains beyond. Through the narrow streets they thronged, white-coated regulars in black hats and gaiters and glittering bayonets, troops of Canadians and bands of Indians in scalp locks and war paint; out of the gates they poured, the battalions of Old France and the irregulars of the New, the victors of Fort Necessity, the Monongahela, Oswego, Ticonderoga and Fort William Henry, tramping to the tap of the drum and the call of the bugle for the last time in the long war for a continent.

With them rode their general. He had never seemed more noble to his officers and men. Mounted on a dark bay horse, he was a splendid figure in his green-and-gold uniform, the Cross of St. Louis gleaming above his cuirass. "Are you tired?" he cried. "Are you ready, my children?" They answered him with shouts, and as he swung his sword to encourage them, the cuffs of his wide sleeves fell back to reveal the white linen of his wristbands.

In splendid composure, the English watched the French arrive. Since dawn, when the high ground less than a mile away had become suddenly thronged with the white coats of the tardily arriving Guienne, the redcoats had been raked by Canadian and Indian sharpshooters. After Montcalm's three cannon had begun to punish them, Wolfe had ordered them to lie in the grass.

James Wolfe had put on a new uniform: scarlet coat over immaculate white breeches, silk-edged black tricorne on his head. He walked gaily among his reclining men, making certain that they had loaded their muskets with an extra ball for the first volley. The desired battle had arrived, and Wolfe was exalted. His voice was steady, and his face shone with confidence.

At about ten o'clock the French and their Canadians began to come down the hill. Wolfe ordered his men to rise. Onward came the enemy, shouting loudly and firing once they came within range. The British stood silent and still. Gradually the Canadians' habit of throwing themselves prone to take aim and fire disordered the French lines. But they still came on, firing as they came—and then, from forty yards away, the silent British lines erupted in flame and black smoke. A second volley followed. Now the redcoats could hear screams and cries of terror and then, through the lifting smoke, could see the field littered with crumpled white coats and the mass of the enemy turning to flee.

"Charge!"

Cheers and the fierce wild yell of the Highlanders rose into the air, and the pursuit was begun. Redcoats with outthrust bayonets bounded after the fleeing enemy. Highlanders in kilts swinging broadswords overhead leaped forward to decapitate terrified fugitives with a single stroke.

James Wolfe joined the charge. He had already taken a ball in the wrist and had wrapped a handkerchief around it. Now, leading the Louisbourg grenadiers, he was wounded again. He pressed on, but a third shot pierced his breast, and he sank to the ground. He was carried to the rear. He was asked if he wanted a surgeon.

"There's no need," he gasped. "It's all over with me."

He began to lose consciousness, until one of the sorrowing men around him shouted, "They run! See how they run!"

"Who run?" Wolfe cried, rousing himself.

"The enemy, sir. Egad, they give way everywhere!"

"Go one of you to Colonel Burton," Wolfe gasped, "and tell him to march Webb's regiment down to Charles River, to cut off their retreat from the bridge." Turning on his side, he murmured, "Now, God be praised, I will die in peace!" and he perished a few moments later.

The Marquis de Montcalm was also stricken. His horse had been borne toward the town by the tide of fleeing French, and as he neared the walls a shot passed through his body. He slumped, but kept his seat, rather than let his soldiers see him fall. Two regulars bore him up on either side. He entered the city streaming blood in full view of two horrified women.

"*O mon Dieu! O mon Dieu!*" one of them shrieked. "The Marquis is dead."

"It is nothing, it is nothing," Montcalm replied. "Don't be troubled for me, my good friends."

But that night he was dying. His surgeon had told him that his wound was mortal. "I am glad of it," he said, and asked how much longer he had to live. "Twelve hours, more or less," was the reply. "So much the better," Montcalm murmured. "I am happy that I shall not live to see the surrender of Quebec." He died peacefully at four o'clock the next morning.

Wolfe had fallen, knowing that he had won an important skirmish; Montcalm perished, aware that his army was routed and demoralized, but neither knew that all was won and all was lost.

Another year passed before the seal of final triumph was placed upon the Battle of Quebec as the decisive victory in the 150-year struggle for wordwide colonial supremacy. This occurred in the spring of 1760, when Montreal fell to the British army led by Lord Jeffrey Amherst. Even before then French sea power in the Atlantic was shattered by Admiral Sir Edward Hawke's victory over Admiral de Conflans at Quiberon Bay.

Canada had been conquered, and the French and Indian War was over. A few years later the Peace of Paris ended the Seven Years' War in Europe. France ceded her colony on the St. Lawrence to Britain, retaining in America only that vast though vaguely defined region called Louisiana. France had emerged from the conflict a wreck: only five towns in India remained to her, her navy was gone and her finances were in the ruin that was to produce the French Revolution. Britain and Prussia were all-powerful: the one to rule the waves, the other to rack Europe.

Britain had beaten France, and she had won an empire. Yet she was already in danger of losing the fairest jewel in that imperial crown. As the Count Vergennes had warned:

> Delivered from a neighbor they have always feared, your other colonies will soon discover that they stand no longer in need of your protection. You will call on them to contribute toward supporting the burden which they have helped to bring on you, they will answer you by shaking off all dependence.

This they would do, indeed.

★ 2 ★

THE AMERICANS

Whence came they, these "Americans," these "new men," and whence derived that spirit of independence so fierce that it was an absolutely new phenomenon in the history of mankind?

In the main they came from the Western Islands—England, Scotland, Wales and Ireland—what came to be known as Great Britain or the United Kingdom, although not too many of those bellicose Celts—Scots, Welsh and Irish—took too kindly to the designation "British." At first they came mostly as fugitives from religious persecution: the Puritans of New England fleeing the mild persecution of the Anglican Church, and Quakers of Pennsylvania fleeing harassment from the same quarter; Catholics of Maryland fleeing rigid Protestant discrimination; and French Protestants (Huguenots) of the South fleeing persecution in Catholic France. After them came the Germans, avoiding military service and the harsh rule of their petty princes and electors; then the Lutheran Swedes, settling in Delaware; and finally the hard-bargaining, opportunistic Dutch, supposedly buying Manhattan Island from the Indians for a few strings of beads.

Here was the first of those astonishing real estate deals in which these land-hungry Europeans fleeced the trusting red men out of their hunting grounds. Of the aboriginals to whom Columbus had mistakenly given the name Indians, there were only a few hundred thousand occupying this marvelous land, so vast that its length and breadth were immeasurable and its natural riches so incalculable that even to think of exploiting them staggered the imagination. So these few tens of thousands of Europeans settled along two thousand miles of seacoast that were eventually to be organized into thirteen little seagoing republics that would receive additional hundreds of thousands of fugitives—again chiefly from the Western Islands—risking the terrifying, long ocean voyage and seeking sanctuary for different reasons.

William Bradford led his Separatists to New England to found a New Jerusalem that was based solely on the Bible, thereby laying the foundation of that grim Congregational church, which installed a theocracy more intolerant than the faith the Separatists had fled. When Cromwell and his Roundhead Puritans defeated and beheaded King Charles I, many of the king's Cavalier followers sought refuge in Virginia and New York. Upon the restoration of the Stuart monarchy under Charles II, those now-proscribed Puritan regicides fled to New England. After them came the Scottish Covenanters, or Presbyterians, rebelling against the autocratic Charles's attempt to impose Anglicanism on them, only to be crushed in 1679 at the Battle of Bothwell Bridge. Military disaster also overtook a fiercer breed of Scot, the Highland followers of Bonnie Prince Charlie, who sought to restore the Stuart dynasty by wresting the British throne from its Hanoverian kings, only to be utterly crushed at the Battle of Culloden in 1746. For these once-proud warriors, now outlaws, dispersed and hunted down like rabbits in their Highland warrens, America was the only hope; they found their refuge on the western frontiers of the Carolinas. The west of Pennsylvania and Maryland attracted the Catholic Irish, seeking sanctuary from Cromwell and Charles II, while fleeing the famine and poverty imposed by their rent-wracking Protestant masters. From the Protestant north of Ireland came the Scotch-Irish, militant Presbyterians so-called either because they were the "Plantation Irish," transplanted to lands seized from their Catholic owners by the persecutions of King James I of Britain or Cromwell, or because en route to the colonies as fugitives from the bitter conflicts dividing their homeland, they had stopped in Ireland under the protection of its British army of occupation. Finally, there were the Welsh, many of them Quakers, who found sanctuary in William Penn's colony of Friends.

These were the first arrivals, of whom the overwhelming majority were English. They were bound together by a common Christianity and a single English language, even though they had also brought with them the divisiveness of sect and race. For the most part, then, they were noble human beings—which could not exactly be said of the second wave of immigrants arriving in the eighteenth century.

Britain of that time was a nation of 10 million souls, almost evenly divided between the haves—nobility, gentry, professionals, freeholders of land, merchants, craftsmen and petty officials—and the have-nots—laborers, paupers, clerks, apprentices, servants, soldiers and sailors, criminals, homeless and prostitutes. Forty-seven percent of the population belonged to the upper classes, and 53 percent to the lower. Of these dregs of British society it has been estimated that there were 50,000 beggars, 80,000 criminals, 10,000 vagrants, 100,000 prostitutes, 10,000 rogues and more than 1 million on parish relief. The remainder of the lower classes lived a cruelly hard and generally short life. They worked from six in the morning until eight at night for a pittance that barely sustained them. They had no holidays except Christmas and Easter or public hanging days, when rich and poor, exploiter and exploited, rubbed elbows in glee at the sight of those wretches kicking and jerking at the end of a rope because they had stolen a handkerchief or a loaf of bread. Orphans, legitimate or otherwise, abounded. They were sent to workhouses or to parish orphanages, where, it was estimated, only seven out of a hundred of them survived their third birthday.

Of this population—half happy, half despairing—there was no need or purpose for any of the upper classes to migrate to America, but among those of the lower classes who were still young and healthy enough to endure a long sea voyage, the tales they heard of the freedom and opportunity in the New World and of the colonies' crying need for cheap labor made their hearts leap with that stranger joy of hope. And land! They could own their own *land!* At first this vision was just that: a dream. How could a young maid who hated her mistress, and whose only affordable solace was in gin and animal rut, possibly save enough money to finance a transatlantic trip? Eventually, however, the growing demand for labor produced the system of indentured slaves. Indentured servitude was based on the ancient custom of apprenticeship. Agents paid for the passage of men and women who contracted themselves to work for a specified number of years to pay off the costs of their voyage.

Such a system—like bounties for military enlistment—lent itself to abuse. Crimps and "spirits"—for "spiriting away"—abounded "like birds of prey along the Thames, eager in their search for such artisans, mechanics, husbandmen and laborers" whom they could sell to a merchant for shipment to America. Tavern owners and innkeepers found such kidnaping a profitable sideline, for a drunken or sleeping patron was an easy victim. One spirit boasted that he had been spiriting people away for twelve years at the rate of five-hundred a year. He would pay twenty-five shillings for a likely candidate and immediately sell him or her to a merchant or shipmaster for fifty. Not all these spirits were as depraved as the imaginary ones whom mothers used to frighten their children into obedience, and many of them helped young men and women to emigrate against the wishes of their parents or employers. These may indeed have been "the poorest, idlest and worst of mankind, the refuse of Great Britain and Ireland," but they did supply the colonies' demand for labor, and most of them prospered alongside those first arrivals, whose purpose and means of migration might have been nobler. Here, indeed, is a study in sociology: proof, indeed, that it is poverty and exploitation, not choice or heredity, that produces the so-called dregs of humanity. Through indenture—crimps and spirits included—tens of thousands of the British and Irish poor were able to make their way to the New World, where they became known as indentured "servants," the word *slaves* being used only to describe black bondsmen.

At the end of their service the indentured servants were freed and provided with enough money and clothing to make a new start in life. In some colonies they received land at the end of their terms. In North Carolina fifty acres of land and three barrels of Indian corn plus two suits of clothing worth five pounds were provided. Kind masters might allow the most industrious of their indentured servants to go free before the expired term, or at least allow them to grow their own crops and keep their own livestock while they were indentured. Conversely, a cruel master, just like a cruel slave owner, could make the term of indenture a sacrament of hell, as many letters sent back home suggested.

There is no doubt that not all those who arrived on the shores of America were prodigies of morality and industry. The crimp's net was as likely to catch a criminal as a law-abiding citizen, and old Mother England did not hesitate to empty her jails for the transportation of hardened criminals to the New World, thus transferring the expense of caring for them and the risk of being murdered, raped or robbed by them to their beloved cousins across the sea. Three or four times a year the convicts to be so transported were marched in irons from Newgate Prison through the streets of London to Blackfriars, in a form of entertainment almost as popular as hanging day. Hooting, jeering mobs gathered on either side of the street to form a gantlet of derisive contempt to which the felons responded with appropriately pungent obscenity and blasphemy. These convicts could be—and often were—an unwelcome trial to the colonists: yet many of them did establish themselves as respectable citizens. It is therefore possible that some of those staid and superpatriotic Daughters and Sons of the American Revolution, so proud of their heritage, may discover, on tracing their ancestry back to its beginnings, that they have descended from pickpockets or prostitutes.

One of the chief reasons for British victory in the triangular British-French-Spanish competition for possession of North America was that whereas the French sought furs and the Spanish gold, the British coveted land. Neither the pursuit of precious metal or of animal skins conferred permanence like the clearing and cultivation of land, and permanence meant community, with social organization and a division of labor. Land, as it was gradually acquired from the Indians, also meant a growing population, but that steady acquisition—so often obtained by trickery and deceit—also meant conflict with the Indians.

At first the American aboriginals had greeted the British colonists with a friendship and generosity that, exploited by the white men, ultimately weakened them. They taught the colonists how to plant corn and tobacco and the other crops native to America: peas, beans, squash, pumpkins, melons and cucumbers. They showed the colonists how to harvest maple sugar, how to make canoes or use fish for fertilizer, how to hunt and trap. Because they had no experience of private property but held land in community—that is, as a tribe, not as an individual brave—and because they were guided by the spirit of an agreement or the sacredness of a promise, rather than by the letter of those contracts so dear to the colonists or the legalisms that often were intended to deceive, they were at first willing to make treaties ceding their land. In their simple, letterless society, trickery was not esteemed, which is why they were enraged to discover that they were constantly being swindled.

The shabbiest instance of so-called hard bargaining by the colonials was the infamous Walking Purchase of Indian lands in Pennsylvania. The Indians accepted an offer for an area of land that a man could walk around in a single day, which, at a normal pace, would come to about twenty square miles. But the colonists used relays of runners to cover an area many times larger. To the outraged Indians, this was plain deceit and trickery, to the colonists a clever ploy to obtain more land for the money. No wonder Pocahontas could say that the British "lied much" or that they "spoke with a forked tongue." No wonder that more than a century later, the great Tecumseh could point to thousands of such treaties violated by the false and devious white man. Not only were the Indians gradually becoming uneasy at the steady encroachment upon their ancestral lands, they were also infuriated by the arrogance and intolerance of the Puritans' imposition of the white man's customs and religion upon them. In Massachusetts, Indians as well as whites were liable to the death penalty for blasphemy, interpreted to be the denial of the existence of God or deprecation of Christianity, while in Plymouth, no Indian was permitted to hunt, fish or carry burdens during the Sabbath day. To a proud though savage people, such as the American Indians, such provocation could be just as intolerable as the shrinking boundaries of their homelands, and together they produced a hatred that finally erupted in King Philip's War of 1675–76.

King Philip's bizarre name came to him after his father, the sachem Massasoit, asked the British to give English names to his sons, Wamsutta and Metacom. Recalling the ancient kings of Macedon, the colonists named the former Alexander and the latter Philip. After Massasoit died in 1661, Alexander became the sachem. Distrusting the colonists, he tried to rule independently of them and was dragged into Plymouth and subjected to a humiliating interrogation. While there he died of a fever. King Philip succeeded him, now fired by an insatiable thirst for revenge that he kept in check by a remarkably patient attempt to bind twenty thousand Indians of different tribes into a single whole. It took twelve years, but by 1675 he was ready—hurling this force against the forty thousand whites then in New England.

Philip meant to paralyze the colonists by a campaign of terror. Massacre followed massacre from Massachusetts to Rhode Island. Of New England's ninety settlements, fifty two were attacked and twelve were destroyed. It seemed that all the northern colonies would perish. But Philip, though a splendid leader, had no understanding of organization for war. His tactics were those of primitive warfare: pounce and withdraw. He had no solid base of operations to which he might return if he were defeated or in need of supplies, there to regroup and replan. He had no stores. His war parties lived off the land. Conversely, the New England colonies had their militia, which hurriedly assembled to come to the rescue of their brethren in Plymouth, the first colony to feel Philip's revenge, while the very hideousness of his tactics provoked in them a ferocity that, because it was organized and disciplined, was more than the equal of their enemy's. Indian scalps were taken, bounties were offered for Indian heads and captured Indians were sold into slavery in the West Indies. On December 19, 1675—a cold, snowy day—a force of a thousand colonists hurled themselves upon Philip's three thousand Indians, who were holding a fortified village in a marsh known as the Great Swamp. The red men were routed, and Philip was chased into hiding. One by one Philip's tribal allies left him until, on August 11, 1676, he was betrayed and killed in a skirmish at his ancestral stronghold on Mount Hope.

Thus ended King Philip's War, the opening struggle in a racial conflict that was to rage intermittently for another two centuries until it ended with the final defeat of the embattled Indians on the western Plains. Although it is certainly true that the gradual extinction of most of the Indians and the seizure of their lands remain the sorriest episodes in the history of the United States, it would be sentimental to believe that, granting the imperfect nature of humanity, when a more sophisticated, technologically advanced society comes into conflict with a primitive one, any other conclusion could have occurred. But most significant for this study of these early Americans is that for the first time, they had been compelled on their own—without the help or protection of the Mother Country—to organize for war and to make a successful defense of their farms and villages.

King Philip's War, then, may be regarded as the first challenge to bring forth that unique, unifying spirit of independence that the rulers of Britain were to find at once so mystifying and infuriating. From fighting Indians, the Protestant colonists of New England would soon turn to fighting their "natural enemies"—the Catholic French in New France.

In American folklore the myth of "the most peace-loving nation in the world" still persists. But the truth is that American history is not only concurrent with the annals of American arms, but is as firmly woven into it as a strand of hemp in a rope. Probably it could not have been otherwise, for the birth of both the British and French colonies in the New World is simultaneous with the birth of modern warfare.

Even before America was colonized, the Spanish had revolutionized war by introducing an improved matchlock musket and fielding units of professional foot soldiers called infantry. (The name *infantry* is derived from the custom of adopting Spanish princesses, or *infantas,* as the honorary colonels of various formations.) With their new but clumsy six-foot-long muskets, the Spanish infantry were invincible, and their advent opened the age of modern infantry tactics. Deployment and maneuver on the open plains supplanted siege warfare.

However, the true maturing of modern warfare probably occurred during the Thirty Years' War (1618–48), a horrible religious conflict during which the Catholics and Protestants of Europe were at each other's throats, and its true parent was the Swedish captain, Gustavus Adolphus. It was this warrior-king who placed the modern emphasis on infantry firepower. He saw that the real arbiter of battle was the foot soldier carrying the handgun. Therefore, he shortened and lightened his muskets to increase the number of his musketeers and to reduce the number of his pikemen. Gustavus Adolphus also introduced modern military discipline into his army and organized the service of supply. He was the first to make widespread use of artillery in the field, using bombardments to soften the enemy for the shock tactics of his cavalry. After Gustavus Adolphus, the ponderous Spanish infantry became obsolete, and European commanders everywhere adopted the Swedish soldier's light and mobile battalions.

None of these changes had much effect on far-off America until 1689, when New France delivered its first blows against New England in the first New World offshoot of war in the Old World. Known as the War of the Grand Alliance, it was called King William's War in the colonies, and the reason is significant. As much as Americans are fond of pretending that the religious intolerance that erupted in the Thirty Years' War had failed to infect the forefathers of America, the fact is that the doctrinal disputes that sundered Christendom were, from their very beginning, a powerful influence on American history. It may be that the true motives underlying the wars of these European kings and nobles were the not-so-noble passions of pride, prejudice and greed, but the fact is that when the Catholic French from Canada struck the Protestant British of New England, it was to punish the heretic while their enemy fought back to chastise the idolator. The War of the Grand Alliance, then, was "King William's" to the colonists because William of Orange (Holland) was a Protestant prince, who had sworn to guarantee Protestantism in Britain, while the deposed King James II of Britain was a Catholic Stuart, who had attempted to restore his faith in his kingdom. War erupted in 1689 when the Catholic King Louis XIV of France tried to restore his friend James to the throne of Britain.

Fighting began after Louis de Buade, the Count Frontenac, the first professional soldier to serve in the New World and at seventy a crusty, audacious old war dog, sent war parties south to ravage British settlements there. There then occurred the massacre of many of the sleeping Dutch inhabitants of Schenectady in New York, after which the village was put to the torch and burned to the ground. Outraged as they had been by the depredations of King Philip, the colonists of New York and New England outfitted an expedition against Canada under Sir William Phips, a burly and opportunistic treasure hunter. Phips captured Port Royal by summation on May 11, 1690, but his later and larger expedition to capture Quebec was repulsed, and King William's War ended in 1697.

Four and a half years later the War of the Spanish Succession broke out. It was called Queen Anne's War in America because King William had died from a fall from his horse and his sister-in-law Anne ascended the British throne. It began because King Louis of France coveted the crown of Spain for his grandson, Philip of Anjou. King Louis's claim was justifiable, especially because if the crown had gone to Austria, France's ancient fear of being encircled would have been realized. But when the Sun King committed unwarranted aggressions and excluded British merchants from the Spanish colonial trade in support of his claim, the war began.

It brought a return of the scalping horrors to the borders between New England and New France. In 1704 a band of French and Indians sacked the sleeping village of Deerfield in western Massachusetts. Once again the colonies reacted with horror and outrage, and even New Jersey and New York contributed money and men to help New England punish the barbaric French. Pennsylvania, ruled by pacifist Quakers, sent only money—£3,000—with the quaint proviso that it should not be used to kill anybody. An overly ambitious campaign to capture both Montreal and Quebec had to be scaled down to another attack upon Port Royal, which failed. But a third assault upon the capital of Acadia was successful, and the entire province passed into the permanent possession of the British Crown. Americans also participated in the third attempt to take Quebec, this one organized in Britain with an invasion force of twelve thousand men under the command of an armchair British admiral and an amateur British general. As might have been expected, this Tory attempt to eclipse the glory of the great Whig soldier, the Duke of Marlborough, ended in a fiasco.

It was the new Kingdom of Prussia that provoked the third war to affect the colonies. Prussia had been proclaimed a nation in 1701 by the Margrave of Brandenburg, who became known as King Frederick I. The king's son, King Frederick William I, infected Prussia with a demonic spirit of militarism, while becoming notorious for his obsessive fondness for his army, especially his tall grenadiers, who were kidnapped from every corner of the world—even a giant Italian priest was taken while saying mass—and mated with tall women, who were similarly enslaved. But it was not he who again convulsed Europe and the New World, but his son, Frederick the Great, who swung the sword his father had forged. Frederick aimed at beautiful young Empress Maria Theresa of Austria, who had been bequeathed her possessions in her father's will. Like jackals, many of the kingdoms of Europe rushed to despoil her, especially Spain, and the conflict became known as the War of the Austrian Succession. In Britain it was given the quaint name of the War of Jenkins's Ear because a sea captain of that name had his ear cut off by the Spanish and was sent contemptuously back to Britain with the ear preserved in a jar of seawater. America called it King George's War because Britain had entered on the side of Austria and to protect King George II's possessions in Hanover.

The first blow struck for King George in America came from the new colony named for him: Georgia. In the summer of 1740, James

Oglethorpe, Georgia's founder, sought to evict the Spanish from St. Augustine. But he was foiled when the enemy reinforced the city from Cuba, and Oglethorpe's two thousand whites and Indians sailed back to Georgia sunburned and hungry. In retaliation, Don Manuel de Monteano sailed out of St. Augustine and up to St. Simon's Island off the Georgia coast, hoping to defeat Oglethorpe there and annex Georgia—perhaps even the entire South—to Spain. But the audacious little Oglethorpe—known as the "Stormy Petrel" after he threw a drink in the face of an insulting royal duke—sailed out of his stronghold to begin to chew Monteano up piecemeal, finally frightening him off by planting a bogus letter on him warning of the approach of a huge British fleet. Thus the only fighting between Britain and Spain in North America ended in a stalemate.

Up north 4,200 raw Massachusetts militia, under Sir William Pepperell, sailed to Cape Breton Island in hopes of capturing the fortress of Louisbourg, "the Gibraltar of North America." Surprisingly enough, they did—after suffering hideous hardships, but finally compelling the French bastion to haul down its flag.

For eight years the crowned heads of Europe remained at peace with one another, although an undeclared Anglo-French war was actually begun in the Ohio Valley in 1754. French troops from Canada had begun to build forts in what is now western Pennsylvania, but was then claimed by Virginia. Alarmed, Governor Robert Dinwiddie sent Major George Washington, a twenty-one-year-old giant, to demand that the French return from whence they came. They refused. Dinwiddie then built a fort at the forks where the Allegheny and Monongahela rivers joined to form the great Ohio. The French captured the fort, replacing it with a larger one of their own called Fort Duquesne. About 110 miles southeast of Duquesne, Washington, with a party of militia and Indians, heard of the disaster and began to push northwest to establish a forward base to receive promised reinforcements and artillery. Halfway to Duquesne (now the city of Pittsburgh), he encountered a formation of French. A firefight ensued in which the French leader, the sieur Jumonville de Villiers, and nine other Frenchmen were killed. Here was the spark that was to set battlefields ablaze in Europe, America and India. The Seven Years' War (French and Indian War in America) was the final round in the great Anglo-French colonial struggle. It did not immediately erupt, for both sides were not yet ready to renew hostilities, although Britain did send a force of 1,200 regulars and 450 Virginia militia under Major General Edward Braddock to recapture Duquesne. The British force was ambushed and routed on July 9, 1755, at the Battle of the Wilderness, in which young Washington again distinguished himself. In the following year the general conflagration began, culminating in America with the seizure of Quebec and Montreal and ending in 1763 with the Peace of Paris.

In all these struggles, covering almost a full century, the American colonists had shown a surprising aptitude for war. True enough, the indifferently trained militia were never really the equal of the professionals of both sides. As free men, they could never accept the brutal discipline of the royal armies, and it is discipline—together with the ability to endure adversity—that makes the good soldier. They had also shown that they could raise armies on their own and organize for war: two skills that contributed to their growing sense of self-reliance. Moreover, the soldiers of most of the colonies met and mingled with each other, respecting one another and becoming conscious of being American—as different from the British as American forest fighting differed from the European wars of mass and maneuver.

One other factor contributing to the American spirit of independence was the Albany Congress of 1754, called by the British Lords of Trade to discuss the conduct of Indian affairs. Commissioners from all the colonies but New Jersey, Virginia, Connecticut and Rhode Island conferred with representatives of the Indian Five Nations known as the Iroquois. Here Benjamin Franklin presented his famous "Plan of Union." Although adopted with some minor modifications, the plan was never really put into execution if only because it went too far for both the Mother Country and the colonies themselves. It spoke of a "general government" of all the colonies, which would consist of a president-general, appointed by the Crown, and a Grand Council, chosen by the colonial assemblies. The general government would have the power to raise armies and pay soldiers for the common defense, "make laws, and lay and levy such general duties, imposts, or taxes as shall appear to them most equal and just. ..." Neither Britain nor any colony was prepared to surrender such power to a general government: the Crown because it prized its prerogatives, as did the colonies, and the colonies more so because the Plan of Union spoke of "negotiations" with the Indians over expansion, a word that was anathema to colonial land speculators, most of whom—eventually including George Washington—were also political leaders. But the word *union* had been spoken, just as three other plans besides Franklin's made similar proposals, suggesting that although no one at the Albany Congress entertained the slightest desire for a break with Britain, the persistent spirit of independence under the presence of growing grievances with the Mother Country could become the catalyst for an outright rupture.

And there were grievances, both during and after the colonial wars. Americans who gloried in their share of the success of British arms also bitterly resented the haughty British soldier's unconcealed disdain for their fighting prowess. British officers—supercilious to a man—had nothing but contempt for the militia, and George Washington never forgot or forgave those regulars who were his juniors, who not only refused to serve under him but also blocked his advancement. Conversely, the British minimized the colonial contribution, calling it niggardly and never made without the grant of some political concession. Such unfair criticism only reflected the ingrained British conviction that the American colonists—though so self-consciously proud of their Britishness—were actually only some kind of second-class subjects or, at best, junior partners in the business of empire. Indeed the very nature of the economic theory of mercantilism suggested that they were.

★ 3 ★

MERCANTILISM/BIRTH CRY OF AMERICAN FREEDOM

Shooting wars among the great sea powers of the day—Britain, France, Spain and, to a lesser degree, Holland—were also trade wars. Colonies were the weapons, which, in mercantilist theory, were to be completely subordinated to the mother country. British colonies were founded to give the Mother Country a favorable balance of trade, as well as to develop a merchant marine that was supreme on the ocean and a reservoir of seamen for the navy in time of war.

These colonies were to produce raw materials to be shipped to the Mother Country in British ships, there to be manufactured into finished products, some of which would be shipped back to the colonies, thus providing a second profit to British shipping interests. Meanwhile, severe legislation, such as the Trade and Navigation Acts, would discourage any trade with the rival mercantilist powers, thus having the two-edged effect of enriching Britain while impoverishing its rivals.

In 1660–61 Parliament began to dictate its restrictions on colonial trade. Captains and three-fourths of the crews of ships carrying goods to and from the colonies must be British, while certain commodities could be shipped only to Britain or other colonies. Thus Dutch vessels could not carry Virginia tobacco to Britain and French carriers could not bring sugar from the West Indies to a British port. When molasses was added to the restricted list, the intention was to keep British molasses from the West Indies away from the French and Dutch while encouraging British everywhere to drink rum made from molasses and thus severely cripple the French wine and brandy trade.

In 1707 Parliament decreed that nothing could be imported by the colonies from Europe unless it were first landed in Britain and then shipped to its destination in British bottoms. In 1733 the final nail was driven into the mercantilist coffin with the passage of the Molasses Act setting stiff import duties on French West Indian rum and all foreign sugar or molasses. It was a tax intended to bail out planters in the British Sugar Islands at the expense of the American colonists. Because the tax made it plain that trade laws could be manipulated to enrich particular British who were in favor "at home," it enraged the Americans. This resentment, together with the incredible inefficiency of the Board of Trade and Plantations, the agency charged with enforcing these regulations, produced a veritable explosion in smuggling along the Atlantic seaboard.

Before 1733 smuggling had been common enough, but after that date, it became endemic to America. Many, indeed, were the fortunes made by merchants turned smugglers, among them John Faneuil, the French Huguenot who built the famous Faneuil Hall in Boston, which would become the center of King George III's "sad nest" of sedition, and John Hancock. Now the Americans could take a dual delight in continuing to buy imported goods cheap and in thumbing their noses at the Mother Country. Here was another grievance provoking a typical response of that growing spirit of independence.

Soon these wily Americans, realizing that the Board of Trade was so ponderous and slow in its dealings with them that it might take years for it to reply to a query or a petition, deliberately began to pass short-term laws that they knew would be unacceptable to the Crown. Thus, by the time notice of the law's veto came back across the ocean, the law would have expired and a new one enacted in its place. Such tactics made the colonial assemblies masters of parliamentary maneuver. And if the royal governors should desire to veto these willfully evasive laws, the colonial assemblies had ways of dealing with them: harassment, social ostracism—even bribery. It was also tempting for the royal governors to keep the peace in their colonies by allowing the Mother Country to bear the onus of a veto.

The royal governors were almost always a source of grievance to the Americans. They were drawn from the military, members of the upper classes or sometimes the colonies themselves. All, of course, had to be in the Crown's good graces and owed a favor. A governorship, then, was actually a form of political patronage. Most recipients treated their appointments either as a sinecure—remaining in Britain while sending a lower-paid lieutenant in their place—or as opportunities to enrich themselves by such means as land speculation or the aforesaid bribery. There were indeed able governors who understood the Americans' problems and sympathized with them—but not many.

Another grievance was the governor's control of the courts. The governor appointed the judges, usually to serve in "good behavior"—meaning as long as the judges brought in verdicts favorable to the Crown. If the judges didn't, they didn't last long. Admiralty courts, which heard alleged violations of the Navigation Acts, had no juries. Moreover, the judges' salaries were financed by the fines they imposed. Obviously, an American who appeared before any of these political toadies—pompous and patronizing in their white wigs and black robes—had little hope of justice.

Mercantilist theory, then, was the evil mother of this brood of grievances that were so irritating to the proud American soul; yet, because the agencies charged with imposing and enforcing it performed so inefficiently, the colonists were able to evade its restrictions for a century. If the administration of the Navigation Acts had been more capable, it is possible that the American Revolution might have come sooner—even without the removal of the Canadian menace to the north.

Such evasion had become so ingrained in the American merchant's character that the attempt in 1761 to enforce the Navigation Acts by introducing "writs of assistance" provoked a storm of outraged opposition that made a stupefied Mother Country finally realize how fierce indeed this American spirit of independence had become. Armed with these writs, a customs agent could, without showing cause, search not only a ship suspected of smuggling, but "any house, shop, cellar, warehouse or room." Indignation was particularly violent in Boston, where the merchants called upon the brilliant lawyer James Otis to attack these blanket search warrants.

At thirty-one, this bull-necked giant was the foremost lawyer of the colony. A prodigy of immoderation, with his burning brain like a blacksmith's forge melting ideas into slogans and his great body consuming food and drink in Brobdingnagian quantities, when he was "up" in the courtroom, the gallery was packed. As Otis himself predicted, he would eventually go insane and then sink into alcoholism as well. No respecter of persons, he wore no man's collar, and though he was to give the American Revolution its creed and its rallying cry, it was not so much independence that he sought with all his magnificent passion but, rather, the triumph of justice over tyranny. Otis's theories moved more toward the formation of a commonwealth of nations, such as the one that was to evolve out of the British Empire.

As advocate-general, Otis had the duty of representing the government, but he resigned and took up the cause of the people in a flaming and eloquent oration against the writs of assistance as a violation of the natural laws of mankind. At one point he electrified the packed courthouse with the declaration: "Taxation without representation is tyranny!" Here was the birth cry of American freedom, but it passed unheeded except for an impressionable young lawyer named John Adams, and in the end Parliament's right to issue the writs was upheld. Here was another grievance, and although the colonists still resented being made commercial pawns in a mercantilist war, while in London they were generally regarded as a crowd of stubborn, scheming, deceitful ingrates, not even the detested writs were capable of reversing a mutual spirit of goodwill begun the previous year upon twenty-two-year-old King George III's ascension to the British throne.

⋆ 4 ⋆

KING GEORGE III

If any argument were needed against the institution of monarchy, one of the most compelling could be found in the careers of the first three Georges of the Hanoverian kings of Great Britain. Except for the third of that name—a family man of pious though dull disposition—the others seemed possessed of every minor vice in the entire catalog of human frailty. None was a bad-hearted or intrinsically evil man, the sort of ruler who could build his towers of skulls like Tamerlane or pronounce a death sentence on entire populations like Genghis Khan or, in our own time, like Adolf Hitler or Joseph Stalin. But all of them were decidedly unfit to reign, chiefly because of their preoccupation with themselves; that is, they were more mindful of their mistresses than of their ministries, their own fortunes than of the public weal, their own German lands than of the land they ruled, as it was with the First and Second Georges, or with himself as king by divine right, as it was with George III. And every one of them was mad, touched or crippled by that disease of the nervous system known technically as neuropathy, which produces manic depression.

The disease had begun among the rulers of Hanover—that tiny electorate of about fifteen thousand square miles that is now an eastern province of Germany—as long ago as William the Younger, born in 1535, dying in 1592 at the age of fifty-seven, hopelessly insane and held incompetent to rule during the last eleven years of his life. In varying degrees of virulence, this affliction remained on the paternal side of George III's family until it manifested itself most notably in the neurotic behavior of his great-grandfather, George I, who imprisoned his wife; in his grandfather, George II, a neurotic little dandy who hated his son Frederick Louis and wished to see him dead; and in Frederick Louis himself. On his mother's side, it was manifest in an uncle who probably committed suicide; a psychopathic first cousin, Christian VII of Denmark; two distant cousins—Ludwig II and Otto I of Bavaria—who were also probably schizophrenics; and two mentally deficient nephews in the House of Brunswick. George III's own family included two sons—the decided psychopath George IV and the emotionally unstable William IV, one of whose sons, the Earl of Munster, committed suicide. This was the family tree of this royal brood, which was imported from Prussia to continue the "Glorious Revolution of 1688," which decreed that, henceforth, after the final defeat of the Scots and Catholic Stuarts at the Battle of the Boyne in 1690, none but a Protestant might sit upon the throne of Britain.

The first of these Hanoverian kings was George I, the second Elector of Hanover, born in 1660. At twenty-one he married his sixteen-year-old cousin, Sophia Dorothea of Zelle. Charming, vivacious and witty, she fell in love, at age twenty-six, with one of her courtiers, Count Königsmark. In 1693, Königsmark vanished, presumably murdered. A year later George divorced Sophia and imprisoned her in a castle in which she spent the last thirty two years of her life, her children taken from her by her former husband. In 1698 George took possession of his Hanoverian throne and seemed moderately happy as the first frog in his little pond. But then in 1714 Queen Anne of Britain died. Despite seventeen pregnancies she left no heir, and the Whig leaders of Britain demanded that George, as a grandson of James I the rightful heir to Queen Anne, who had indeed so named him in her will, must accept the throne of Britain. With great reluctance, George complied.

George reigned for thirteen years, always a German prince, uncaring to learn either the customs or the language of his subjects. When he conversed with his ministers, who spoke no German, it was in a kind of imperfect Latin. Lord Chesterfield described him thus: "George the First was an honest, dull, German gentleman as unfit as unwilling to act the part of a King, which is to shine and to oppress, lazy and inactive even in his pleasures, which were therefore lowly and sensual … [he preferred] the company of wags and buffoons. Even his mistress, the Duchess of Kendal, with whom he passed most of his time, and who had all influence over him, was very little above an idiot. Importunity alone could make him act, and then only to get rid of it. His views and affections were singly confined to the narrow compass of his Electorate; England was too big for him." Chesterfield added: "The King loved pleasure, and was not delicate in his choice of it. No woman came amiss to him if they were very willing and very fat.... The standard of his Majesty's taste made all those ladies who aspired to his favor, and who were near the suitable size, strain and swell themselves like the frogs in the fable to rival the bulk and dignity of the ox. Some succeeded, and others burst." Stubborn and suspicious, stingy and crude, "so cold that he changes everything to ice," after hearing of the death of his former wife Sophia, he sank into a melancholy from which he never recovered, dying suddenly of apoplexy in 1727.

George II was no improvement. Again it was Chesterfield, who knew him for forty years, who described him: "He had not better parts than his father, but much stronger animal spirits, which made him produce and communicate himself more. Everything in his composition was little, and he had himself all the weaknesses of a little mind, without any of the virtues, or even the vices of a great one. He loved to act the king but mistook the part.... Avarice, meanest of passions, was his ruling one; and I never knew him deviate into any generous action."

Short and stout with, the puffy, gargoylelike features of a true Hanoverian, he was honest and brave like his father; at the Anglo-German victory over the French at Dettingen, though sixty years old, when his horse shied during an attack he leaped from it and led a charge forward on foot. He was also dapper, neat and orderly, neurotically concise and exact in his records. Although he spoke English with a German accent, like his father he preferred life in Hanover, to which he constantly repaired, leaving his extremely capable wife, Queen Caroline Wilhelmina of Anspach, to rule. His disdain for his subjects was best expressed in his declaration that "no English cook could dress a dinner, no English confectioner set out a dessert, no English player could act, no English coachman drive, no English jockey ride, nor were any English horses fit to be ridden or driven. No Englishman could enter a room and no English woman dress herself." Though he pretended to have a love for the arts, when Hogarth dedicated a painting to him, he cried in his German accent: "Damn the Bainters, and Boets, too!"

A miser, he was always counting and recounting his money, leaving vacancies at court unfilled so that he could save the money. He did give Queen Caroline a gift of a team of Hanoverian horses, but used them mostly himself while charging her for their fodder. To his great prime minister, Sir Robert Walpole, whom he admired for his financial acumen, he gave a single present: a cracked diamond.

For all these petty vices and peccadilloes, unredeemed by either punctuality or abstemiousness in food and drink, his neuropathic nature is nowhere more evident than in his unnatural and undying hatred for his firstborn son, the Prince of Wales, Frederick Louis. It is true that Fred was small, frail and ugly, his face the perfection of all those repulsive Hanoverian features: the low, receding forehead, the bulging eyes with their baggy eyelids, the thick long nose and pouting mouth above a flabby, swinging double chin, yet listen to his father: "My dear first-born is the greatest beast in the whole world, and I most heartily wish he were out of it." And from his mother: "Fred is a nauseous beast and he cares for nobody but his nauseous little self."

In Caroline's defense it may be said that after her husband evicted Fred and his new wife, Princess Augusta of Saxe-Gotha, from Kensington Palace, refusing ever to speak to him again, when they met infrequently, Caroline would allow Fred to hold her hand, but would not look at or speak to him. In response, the despised Prince of Wales joined his father's political opposition and made open allies of such degenerates as Sir Francis Dashwood, whose cronies met semiannually at his estate for week-long sexual orgies. Even when his beloved Caroline lay dying, George II prohibited his son from seeing her, and when she did gasp her last after an excruciating ten-day ordeal, the epitaph for both her and her husband's reign was pronounced by a placard posted on the Exchange declaring:

O Death where is thy sting—
To take the Queen and leave the King?

Less than seven months later—on June 4, 1738—a boy named George was born to the Princess of Wales.

This infant, who was to rule from probably the world's most powerful throne, was so puny at birth that, fearing death imminent, his parents had him baptized at midnight, waiving the custom of having him suckled by a noble wet nurse, relying instead on Mary Smith, a low-born laundress who was handy. Mary's affection and care so quickly restored the child to health that within a month he could endure the ordeal of public baptism. As a child George grew rapidly, developing those Hanoverian features that were far less repulsive in him than in his father, and was so carefully sheltered from reality in his nursery that by the time he was eleven, he was still unable to read English.

His education, if it may be called that, was a disaster. So many noble families quarreled over the right to be his governor or tutor that there was a rapid turnover among these guardians who were eager only for place or profit; thus nothing resembling a systematic curriculum was installed. George received no training for any position or calling whatsoever, and because he was lazy, he never acquired the habit of study or even of reading. In a word, he was hardly less ignorant than the day he was born. Yet, his mother, Augusta of Saxe-Gotha, the Princess of Wales, daily assaulted his ears with the admonition, "George, be a king!" and this, together with her ardent hope that through some miracle he would be, was the extent of her contribution to his preparation for the throne.

Augusta did, of course, rely to some extent on her husband, who was ever a loving father to their nine children, but in March 1751 Frederick was taken from her when, in a fittingly freak accident, he was hit in the head by a tennis ball. Thereafter she sought the counsel of such living freaks as Bubb Dodington, an outrageously rich, fat, ugly, aged and dull-witted fellow who had befriended Frederick in the hope of gaining a peerage. Bubb loved to play cards with the dowager princess's children, and after they had been put to bed, would offer his advice, which, invariably, was: "Teach him to know men! Teach him to know the world!" Indubitably, and the way to grow rich is to buy low and sell high, but how it is to be done is quite another thing, of which the doddering Dodington knew nothing, and he was shortly replaced by another, subtler favorite: John Stuart, the third Earl of Bute.

This Scots nobleman literally began playing a hand in British history when Frederick Louis found that while sitting at his royal tent at Egham waiting for rain-delayed races to begin, a game of whist was proposed as a diversion. Frederick was irked because there was no one of sufficiently high rank to play a vacant hand at his table. But then Lord Bute was found. Handsome, cultivated and courteous, Bute was celebrated for his acting in amateur theatricals and for his fine legs, which were so admired by the ladies of the upper class. He fascinated Frederick, as well as Augusta, so much so that her husband encouraged her to flirt with Bute while he attended to one of his mistresses. Although Augusta was not beautiful or gracious, but plain with a long neck and awkward long arms, she was nevertheless well endowed with an amplitude of Germanic charms, both before and behind. She could not resist Bute's deep, solemn voice and the masculinity so lacking in Frederick, and the two became lovers. According to the Earl de Waldegrave, another of George's governors, besides his voice and bearing, "the sagacity of the Princess Dowager had discovered other accomplishments, of which the Prince her husband may not have been the most competent judge." It was thus that this softly ingratiating peer—following a route from the backstairs to the bedroom to the nursery—became the paramount preceptor of this impressionable young Heir Apparent. In letter after pathetic letter, young George appealed to his "Dearest Friend" to direct him on the proper path to kingship.

There was another source of instruction, and this was Viscount Bolingbroke's *Idea of a Patriot King,* published when George was seventeen. It is ironical that this brilliant and revolutionary libertine, exiled by George I and repatriated only upon payment of a bribe of £12,000 to the king's mistress, should have written a decidedly moral essay that would exert such a powerful influence on this essentially moral youth. Bolingbroke argued that the monarch should be above all influences, including party or profit; the monarch's only concern should be the welfare of his people. Corruption should be stamped out, whether in court or in Parliament. Here was the antithesis of James Madison's practical remark, "If men were angels, there would be no need of government," and it was perhaps unfortunate for Great Britain that it should be read and reread and cherished by a youth whose most outstanding characteristic was a simple—not to say naive—piety.

George did indeed desire to satisfy his mother and be a king. Now he would be a Patriot King, manifesting in his person all those noble graces and edifying tenets of the Anglican Church of which he would one day be the head. He would be orthodox to the bitter end and brook neither innovation nor compromise in his zeal to create an immaculate kingdom of righteousness that would one day be his. *His* is the proper word, for Bolingbroke had inflamed him with an unshakable faith in the Divine Right of Kings, making him ever ready to declaim: "The character and government of a Patriot King can be established on no other [basis], if his right and office are not always held divine and his person always sacred." The realm was his, the colonies, the armed forces, the subjects—both highborn and low—all *his*. Finally, there comes from the perceptive if profligate Lord Waldegrave, probably the least liked of all Prince George's preceptors, an astonishingly penetrating insight into the result of this attainted Hanoverian blood, this contradiction and confusion emanating from George II's disdainful treatment of Prince George's parents—especially his father—the smothering love of his mother so misguided in her dreams of the power she would one day share with him, the absence of any intellectual discipline or systematic learning in his so-called education, and even the sense of inferiority he always felt when in the presence of his rude and brutal grandfather, the king.

"His parts," wrote Waldegrave, "though not excellent, will be found very tolerable, if they are ever properly exercised. He is strictly honest, but wants that frank and open behavior which makes honesty appear amiable. When he had a very scanty allowance, it was one of his favorite maxims that men should be just before they are generous; his income is now very considerably augmented, but his generosity has not increased in equal proportion. His religion is free from all hypocrisy, but it is not of the most charitable sort; he has rather too much attention to the sins of his neighbors. He has spirit, but not of the active kind; and does not want resolution, but it is mixed with too much obstinacy. He has great command of his passions, and will seldom do wrong, except when he mistakes wrong for right; but as often as this shall happen, it will be difficult to undeceive him because he is uncommonly indolent and has strong prejudices... He has a kind of unhappiness in his temper, which, if it be not conquered before it has taken too deep a root, will be a source of frequent anxiety. Whenever he is displeased, his anger does not break out with heat and violence; but he becomes sullen and silent, and retires to his closet; not to compose his mind by study or contemplation, but merely to indulge in the melancholy enjoyment of his own ill humor."

"This prophetic paragraph," wrote Manfred S. Guttmacher, M.D., in *America's Last King, An Interpretation of the Madness of George III,* "has great significance. Here we have the picture of a prince of twenty showing a striking degree of emotional infantilism—a sullen child, sulking in the corner, sucking his thumb. Clinically, we know that such individuals are peculiarly liable to profound emotional upsets, often developing into frank mental disorder."

There indeed is another prophetic picture, boding direful consequences for Britain and America, for two years after Waldegrave made his appraisal—on October 25, 1760—the old king died, and his neurotic grandson succeeded him at the age of twenty-two.

The society that young George now ruled was a fixed one of about 10 million people. At the top was the aristocracy, living—not to say wallowing—in an extreme of comfort, privilege and conspicuous consumption not to be repeated or even rivaled in any subsequent age. Obliged by the complaisance of the established Church of England, the clerical ranks of which were frequently filled by the younger sons of the nobility who chose the altar rather than the battlefield, and possessing a complete monopoly of political power, the aristocracy looked upon this happy situation as divinely ordained, and if they did not believe themselves beyond the reach of both God and the law, they clearly acted that way. Certainly, no one reproached them for their indifference to the Ten Commandments, and in that very year, 1760, there was an almost universal cry of outrage when the Earl Ferrars was convicted of murdering his own steward. Even the sheriff who dispatched him apologized for having to perform such a distressing duty.

The self-indulgence of this class—in unrestrained and often unchaste sensuality, in food and drink, in gambling, in racing, in dancing, and in every other form of "riotous living" or in the equippage of their stables or the splendor of their homes—was beyond comparison with any age, and perhaps best expressed in the finery of their dress. The brilliance of the aristocratic male during the early reign of George III may be compared to the plumage of the male bird ranged alongside his less brilliant mate. The men's coats, of every color and shade—blue and green, scarlet and yellow, violet and pink—were lined with ermine or white satin, were laced with gold and silver thread and had brocade sleeves. Their waistcoats were similarly elegant, blooming with embroidered flowers or birds, and upon every button was a family crest in gold or silver or a miniature of the wearer's latest love. Their breeches, of contrasting silk or satin, were worn with silk hose of every color; on their shoes were buckles of precious metal, and on their heads, powdered wigs.

As much as the male might outshine the female, the ladies were only less varied in the brilliance of their attire. Their billowing gowns and sacques, spread over lace petticoats upheld by vast hoops of whalebone, conferred upon them a daintiness and feminine allure that actually was more likely to excite a man's imagination than the raw sex and unadorned female body of the modern age. Upon these flashing, rippling gowns were embroidered flowers and baskets of flowers, fruit and grain or gilded foliage, golden seashells or silver branches. Jewelry made living sunbursts of them. Each head seemed crowned by a tiara, all bare white arms gleamed and glittered with bracelets studded with precious stones, while at the waist was laced "the stomacher," almost solid with diamonds and other stones.

This pursuit of pleasure was undergirded by a monopoly of political power in Parliament. It was not enough that a patent of nobility guaranteed membership in the House of Lords; the House of Commons was also dominated by the presence of their sons. Popular elections were rigged or simply bought. Never to have appeared in one's district was no deterrent to election. In 1761, twenty-three sons of peers were returned to Parliament, most of them under the age of twenty-six. Although the merchant middle class was rising through its rapid accumulation of wealth, it as yet had no true power base in Parliament, while the lower classes, who owned no property, had no representation at all.

Until the appearance of the Methodists, with their high-minded horror of the wretchedness of the common people, there was no organized philanthropy to alleviate the suffering of the lower classes. Certainly, no Anglican curate would stand in the pulpit before the lord of the manor to berate him for his calloused indifference to their plight. It was not even that, as a class, the aristocracy either conspired in producing the misery of the poor or was wickedly indifferent to it; it was merely that this was society as God meant it to be. To suggest any alteration in the strata of society was to flout the divine will. Thus, in the grip of hopeless poverty, the British poor—especially those in the cities—reached for a glass of gin. As little as two pence could buy a dram—an eighth of an ounce—of that delightful drink that makes you forget. No matter that it also destroys, both physically and morally. Even a quick death might be better than a life in death.

Thus, the consumption of gin and other hard liquors rose from 3.5 million gallons in 1727 to 11 million gallons in 1751. With this increased consumption came a corresponding increase in crime—just as in our day the high cost of drugs has made the streets of our cities unsafe—followed by the propagation of a barbaric penal code pronouncing death by hanging for as little as the theft of a handkerchief or a hat. But the judges who were charged with enforcing this pitiless law might as well have been King Canute commanding the tide to halt. So far from ceasing, the wave of crime by people crazed by drink or seeking the wherewithal to buy it continued unabated until the Methodists, undaunted by the hatred of the very people they sought to save, joined by the rise of philanthropy, the opening of hospitals and the growing awareness of the Church of England, finally contained and reduced it. But it was still raging in all its abominable forms when George III ascended the throne.

More hopeful for the young king, the middle class was still expanding. Industry was booming and international trade had increased, making George's kingdom perhaps the wealthiest commercial nation in the world. Although the great economist Adam Smith had not yet published his *Wealth of Nations,* the seminal book that was the basis of modern democratic capitalism, the abhorred and mocked bourgeois merchant or industrialist—the upstart nouveau riche—was getting richer and richer and would soon destroy the barren system of mercantilism that was embraced by most European powers and upon which the whole rotten structure of society now rested. The middle class indeed might not dare to ape the manners or the elegance of the aristocracy—and certainly had no intention of imitating their morals—but their very respectability could have given young George a stability upon which to begin building the new and immaculate kingdom of the Patriot King. For their part, the middle class welcomed his coronation. It seemed to them that he embodied in his person all the qualities that they admired: virtue, sobriety, piety and love of family. To them, he would be the ideal king, their king—and so it appeared.

At first.

At twenty-two King George III was said to be a handsome man, tall, well built, gray eyed and dignified, and even those puffy, pudgy Hanoverian features seemed to be attenuated by his large face beneath the powdered wig he always wore in public. George dearly desired to be a king, and in him the renewal of popular royalty seemed likely. His grandfather and great-grandfather had both been German princes wedded to Germans; bound to Germany by their concern for their electorate; indifferent, if not hostile, to British ways. Rather than beloved, they were tolerated as interlopers, who at least had had the good sense not to meddle too much in the affairs of the empire. Such complaisance was also expected of the popular young king. But George III was not about to cooperate in the steady encroachment of Parliament upon the powers of the sovereign that had begun during the days of William and Mary and continued through the reigns of Queen Anne and the first two Georges. Parliament's very act summoning George I to the throne was indicative of its power, as well as of the fact that the legislature, not the throne, was running the empire. By the time of George III's ascension, that control was almost complete.

But George III was determined to show his realm and his mother that he would indeed be a king. He was determined to reclaim the royal powers and to restrain the arrogance of the great Whig families. He would do so not by open political warfare with Parliament, but by court influence, pensions, bribery—especially by the brightest bribe of all, a peerage!—personal loyalty and political management. To attain his ends, he would be as corrupt as the corrupt institution he sought to correct. He would become what he was fighting. He had fallen prey to the most common mistake of mankind: that the end justifies the means. But as the Patriot King, this contradiction never occured to him. His crusade would be a moral one, and thus on October 21, 1760, at the end of his first week on the throne, he hoisted his holy flag with his singular—if not astonishing—proclamation, "For the encouragement of Piety and Virtue, and for preventing and punishing of Vice, Profaneness and Immorality." On the Sabbath all forms of gambling were prohibited and the worship of God was to be enforced "on pain of our highest displeasure, and of being proceeded against with the utmost rigor that may be by law." During divine service, all taverns or coffeehouses and other places of congenial assembly were to remain closed, while all officers of the armed forces were to exhort their commands to prayer and worship.

To the pious and the simpleminded, this moral manifesto was received with great enthusiasm: evil and corruption were to be banished, and the Reign of the Good begun under the scepter of George the Good. To the aristocrats and other sophisticates, it was an ephemeral novelty by an honest, naive boy who would soon learn that a nation would be moral only when its men were moral and that, in any case, morality could be neither commanded nor legislated. So they dwelt instead on the favorable impression he was making—"He rises every morning at six to do business, rides out at eight to a minute, returns at nine to give himself up to the people"—feeling no rebuke in his piety and high-mindedness, but preferring to find charm in his good manners, his resonant voice and his simple dignity. None of these chosen people seemed to notice—or wished to notice—that he really intended to clean out corruption and change the government.

Nor were they immediately aware that he had brought to the throne an unrivaled set of hatreds and prejudices. Chief of all, he despised Frenchmen and Catholics, although it is highly unlikely, granted his sheltered childhood and youth, that he had met a member of that race or religion. He could not abide criticism or disagreement, however honest, always regarding its author as at best disloyal and at worst a traitor. It was only gradually, however, that these unlovely traits became evident, just as his determination to rule rather than reign was not immediately apparent. Besides, in those early days, his most pressing problem was to find a suitable wife.

The Patriot King had already been in love. He had fallen for Lady Sarah Lennox, an adorable, charming, vivacious girl, the youngest daughter of the Duke of Richmond and a descendant of Charles II, but also the sister-in-law of Henry Fox, the skillful if unscrupulous manager of Parliament, who was anathema to the Tories and especially to George's mother and Lord Bute. When George asked these two what they thought of the match, both were adamantly against it. Without the will to challenge either—especially Dearest Friend—George became disconsolate, a dangerous attitude, granting his affliction, declaring: "So intensely do I love this lady, that I fear my mind will not be able to bear up against the shock of disappointment." But neither Bute nor the dowager princess would retreat, and George acquiesced—another dangerous precedent suggesting how thoroughly these two lovers-conspiratorial could dominate him.

It was decided that George must marry a Protestant princess, but since his kingdom had none to offer at that moment, a hunt was begun in Germany, where there was an abundance of such eligible young ladies. It ended at the court of the Duke of Mecklenburg-Strelitz, in the person of Princess Charlotte, the duke's youngest daughter. Charlotte was a short, thin, decent and well-educated girl of eighteen, whose plain looks were not improved by a wide mouth with which the cartoonists of the political Opposition would one day have such cruel fun. She became betrothed to George in the summer of 1761, when she knelt beside a Mr. Drummond—the king's agent—and then was lifted upon a sofa upon which Mr. Drummond placed his bared foot as a symbol of the invasion of her bed. Charlotte arrived in London in early September, dismayed to learn that she was to be married that night. But she was charmed and delighted by the appearance of her bridegroom, who met her in the garden of the Palace of St. James, pausing momentarily as though taken aback, but then gallantly advancing to embrace her. They were married sometime between ten and eleven o'clock that night, amid the brilliance of that decorative age, but "did not get to bed till two." Few royal unions, if any, were quite so productive. Every year, it seemed, the queen gave birth to a new prince or princess, so that eventually George found himself the proud and happy father of no less than fourteen healthy children. George and Charlotte were crowned on September 22 in Westminster Abbey, ablaze with light, blaring with bugles and splendid with the combined traditions of throne and altar. Suitably weighted with crowns, orbs and scepter (a rod for the queen), they were dismayed at the conclusion of the ceremonies, when a horse trained to back away from the royal couple instead advanced upon them rump first.

In all that brilliant company in attendance, it was observed that William Pitt was not present. In the following month the Great Commoner resigned, and the way was now clear for the Patriot King, eventually to be assisted by Dearest Friend as prime minister, to install his own government.

After the departure of Pitt and the rise of Bute, it appeared that King George had at last found the opportunity to work his revolution and to seize control of the government—but at what a price. The Patriot King, who had vowed to select none but "persons of piety and virtue" to serve him, to complete the rout of both Whigs and Tories and to place the "King's Friends" in power, now found himself doing business with such scoundrels as Henry Fox, while Dearest Friend had found it necessary to make that depraved prince of eroticism, Sir Francis Dashwood, his chancellor of the exchequer. Fox succeeded in bringing Parliament to the king's side, but only by the tried-and-true method of corruption. So, George's new broom sweeping clean eventually became as dirty and splintered with placemen and bought elections as had its predecessors. Moreover, his alliance with Bute quickly caused the evaporation of his popularity. In those days, Englishmen still detested Scotsmen—witness Samuel Johnson's definition of oats as, "In England a food for horses, in Scotland a food for men"—and Bute was not only scorned as one born above the River Tweed, but hated as the scandalous lover of George the Good's widowed mother. Together, Bute and the dowager queen were despised as the "Little Junto," with the Patriot King either under Bute's spell or his mother's petticoats. Bute was so thoroughly detested that he could go nowhere without a bodyguard of armed bruisers, and once a rioting crowd pelted his coach with stones and mud.

While George was gaining control of the government, he was also cleansing his court—once again by command. In 1762 when a page announced to George the arrival of his lord chamberlain, the duke of Devonshire, the king growled, "Tell him that I won't see him." The astounded page hesitated, and George angrily repeated: "Tell him that I won't see him!" Devonshire left in a rage, and shortly afterward all the incumbent lords of court resigned. George's replacements apparently were personally screened for the slightest suspicion of wit or merriment and then, perhaps, given shoes two or three sizes too small for them so that they could creep into the royal presence with their faces screwed into those expressions of pain that passed with their benefactor for piety. Although the new court pleased the bourgeoisie, it was greeted with hilarious contempt by the great aristocratic families, who, whether Whig or Tory, were still the foundation of loyalty to the Crown.

Even so, by the spring of 1763 George believed that he was securely in command. The Peace of Paris in February had ended the "bloody and expensive" Seven Years' War, and the use of the royal purse and prerogatives, by which Parliament was bribed, elections were bought and allegiance was secured through the dangling of the peerage bait, had put both Tories and Whigs into disarray and the Patriot King and "friends" solidly in the saddle. But then there appeared on the streets of London another Opposition newspaper edited by a Whig member of Parliament named John Wilkes.

Looking backward, Lord Byron wrote that John Wilkes was a "merry, cock-eyed, curious-looking sprite." So he may have seemed to that growing number of disillusioned Britons who transmuted their hatred of George and Lord Bute into an astonishingly loyal affection and devotion to this political adventurer and sham champion of freedom. However, John Wilkes was not a cock-eyed sprite, but a cross-eyed gnome, slight of build and ugly, with a huge, prognathous jaw, perpetually squinting eyes and a forehead so high that it was only a few millimeters short of idiocy. He was indeed merry, bawdy and frequently and delightfully obscene. Wilkes was the son of a distiller and had married a woman much older than himself for her money, an expedient not uncommon then or now. He lost most of her money, for he was a rake and a gambler, as well as an improvising member of the Dashwood set, to which he introduced such revels as the stripping and "ravishing" of prostitutes dressed in nuns' habits. John Wilkes could always be counted upon for proposing an entertaining new way of producing the old pleasure of sexual orgasm.

A devotee of Pitt—"I am Pitt-bitten"—he was outraged, along with many other Britons, at the easy terms given the French by the Peace of Paris, conditions even more generous than those angrily repudiated by Pitt a few years earlier. Holding George and Bute responsible, he attacked them with a bitter rancor that eventually brought down Bute on April 8, after which the now disenchanted Patriot King sat coldly silent while Dearest Friend vanished into opulent obscurity. But Wilkes had never dared to attack the sovereign, until on April 23, in issue No. 45, he launched a scathing attack on George's Speech from the Throne, concluding with the warning: "The prerogative of the crown is to exert the constitutional powers entrusted to it in a way, not of blind favor and partiality, but of wisdom and judgment.... The people too have *their* prerogative."

The last sentence, so suggestive of revolt, infuriated the king. Any attack on the government, he believed, was an attack on him because he was the government, and he ordered that Wilkes be prosecuted for libel. Wilkes was seized and confined in the Tower of London, his house was searched and his papers were confiscated. A week later he was freed on the grounds of Parliamentary immunity and next won a judgment of a thousand pounds for the improper seizure of his papers. Vindicated, Wilkes attacked the government with renewed vitriol, reprinting No. 45. Then he wrote an "obscene and impious parody" of Pope's *Essay on Man,* entitled *Essay on Women,* which, though received with delight by his adoring adherents, was found so odious by Parliament that he was expelled from the Commons in January 1764.

Nevertheless, what seemed to be the "persecution" of this twisted little twister made him the idol of all those who believed that British freedom—particularly of the press—was at stake, and in America he was hailed as a hero. For the king and his ministers, l'affaire Wilkes ended in ignominious defeat, a sad conclusion that might not have occurred had George been less sensitive to "personal attack." In fewer than three years, George III had dissipated almost all of the good will that had warmed his ascent to the throne. Yet, there were stormier days ahead, especially now that George Grenville, the prime minister who had succeeded Bute and who had so badly bungled the prosecution of Wilkes, was preparing to retire the incredibly enormous debt of nearly 140 million pounds incurred during the Seven Years' War by the unprecedented policy of directly taxing the American colonies.

★ 5 ★

THE STAMP ACT AND SAMUEL ADAMS

George Grenville was a descendant of an old and powerful British family that was prominent in politics and that included both earls and dukes. Finance was Grenville's passion, thrift his creed. Of him it was said that he would consider "a national savings of two inches of candle as a greater triumph than all of Pitt's victories." The Anglo-Irish historian W. E. H. Lecky described him as a man who "possessed ordinary qualities to an extraordinary degree." Lecky also wrote: "He was a conspicuous example of a class of men very common in public life, who combine considerable administrative powers with an almost complete absence of political sense—who have mastered the details of public business with an admirable competence and skill but who have scarcely anything of the tact, the judgment, or the persuasion that are essential for the government of men." If Grenville had been born in a modern socialist state, he would have made an excellent commissar: honest; diligent; blindly devoted to the Communist cause; calmly confident that the future belonged to the command society, no matter how grievously its people might momentarily suffer; and never for a moment doubting the economic wisdom of charging as much for a product that cost fifty cents to manufacture as one that cost a hundred dollars. But all these skills and virtues were canceled out and made minus by an enormous defect that is common to all commisars and mandarins: the failure to comprehend or care for human nature. Thus crippled, this unabashed servant of big business, aware of the crushing burden of taxation already imposed upon a nation in which almost everything in common use was subject to imposts—beer, salt, soap, cider, even window panes—decided that some other source of revenue must be found.

To George Grenville this source was the American colonies.

Grenville was shocked by what he considered to be a manifestly unfair distribution of the burden of paying for the Seven Years' War that favored the colonies, to him the chief beneficiary of the struggle. He calculated the colonial cost at eight shillings per person, while in Britain it was eighteen pounds a head, about $1.60 to $90.00 in modern dollars. Also, salaries for British customs agents amounted to $40,000 a year, but the agents had collected only $10,000 in duties. Obviously, the Navigation Acts had to be strengthened, and he began to do that in 1764 with passage of the Revenue Act, called the Sugar Act in the colonies because it was aimed at ending the smuggling of sugar and molasses.

By halving the tax on molasses, Grenville sought to give a conciliatory tone to his measure, but the colonists knew as well as he did that the molasses duty was seldom *paid,* whereas the new impost, though lower, would be *collected.* Smugglers and evaders, who were accustomed to the old, unenforced Molasses Act, were in for hard times. So was the colonial distilling industry, which was so huge that in 1750, Massachusetts alone had sixty-three distillers. American rum—the popular drink of the ordinary man—was distilled from molasses. Obviously, both maker and drinker were opposed to price increases that would follow any collectable duty. They swore they would not pay the new one, and one colonial hooted that Britain's attempt to stop smuggling would be as foolish and costly as "burning a Barn to roast an Egg."

Moreover, the new law transferred smuggling cases from colonial courts, with juries that were customarily friendly to the defendants, to a new Vice-Admiralty Court in Halifax, Nova Scotia, where there would be no juries but only an informer—or accuser—and a Crown judge, both of them hostile and standing to profit from a conviction. To these injustices must be added the costs and time lost in a journey to Nova Scotia.

In its preamble the Sugar Act stated that it was enacted to help pay the costs "of defending, protecting and securing" America. It was a *taxing* measure. This, the colonists, particularly the Yankees of New England, found abhorrent. A committee of the Massachusetts House of Representatives, under the redoubtable Otis, challenged Parliament's very *right* to tax the colonies, declaring that such measures had "a tendency to deprive the Colonies of some of their most essential Rights as British Subjects, and ... particularly the Right of assessing their own Taxes."

Where or when the colonists got this novel idea was immaterial.

What mattered was that they now had a cause: taxation without representation is tyranny. Parliament, not King George, was the tyrant. The colonists were as loyal subjects of the British Crown as any Britisher, but they, not the British Parliament, would impose their own taxes. This was the idea that such artful propagandists as Samuel Adams were spreading abroad while the colonists evaded the Sugar Act, and an attempt to enforce the long-disobeyed Navigation Acts, by bringing the techniques of smuggling to a state of near-perfection.

In 1765 Britain countered with the Stamp Act. Once again Parliament thought that it was asking the colonies only to share a burden already borne at home. Britishers had long been accustomed to buying revenue stamps to be affixed to all legal documents, commercial paper, ships' charters, bills of lading, titles, and even newspapers, pamphlets and playing cards. But the Americans had not. They were infuriated to be informed that if they did not purchase stamps, all their transactions would be declared illegal and their press would be closed. This, a taxing act undisguised, simply could not be accepted, and the bellow of protest that followed the Stamp Act made the uproar against the Sugar Act seem comparatively a bleat of dissent.

In Virginia, the House of Burgesses met in the lovely rose-brick-and-white town of Williamsburg to hear the fiery backcountry lawyer, Patrick Henry, suggest that just as Caesar had had his Brutus and Charles I his Cromwell, some good American should stand up for his country. There was a cry of "Treason!" and Patrick Henry quickly apologized to the Speaker, vowing that he was ready to shed his last drop of blood for George III.

Still, an open defiance of the Crown had been spoken, and Patrick Henry was in the forefront of the radicals who were pressing for passage of the famous Virginia Resolves. Even though the most inflammatory of the Resolves were eventually killed, they were reprinted throughout the colonies as though they had been passed in their entirety and so increased the uproar against the Stamp Act that Massachusetts called for a congress of colonial representatives.

In October 1765, the Stamp Act Congress convened in New York. It expressed its loyalty to the Crown and "all due subordination" to Parliament, but firmly stated that since the colonies had no representatives in Parliament, they could not be taxed by that body. Only their own legislatures could tax them, the colonies continued, adding the practical argument that the stamp taxes were so heavy that they precluded the buying of British goods and would thus be harmful to British trade.

Into this atmosphere of defiance and distrust there stepped Samuel

Adams, a poverty-stricken and discredited former tax collector, who was also a born revolutionary.

Few men in American history have been as controversial as Samuel Adams. He has come down to us either as "Sam Adams, the rabble rouser" and organizer of street gangs to terrorize Crown officials; or as Samuel Adams, the devoted defender of the charter of Massachusetts Bay Colony, whose public stance of legal precedents and constitutional rectitude would never have permitted him to violate the rights of person and property that he held sacred. But there is another possible perception of this complicated man that is, perhaps, an amalgam of the first two: Samuel Adams, the genuinely dedicated defender of American liberty by a process of peaceful protest and resistance who, under the pressure of such Crown encroachments as the Stamp Act, became an actual but unintended rebel. Aware that an omelet cannot be made without breaking eggs, he did resort to violence and terrorism when he saw that this was the only way to bring on the revolution, and thus the separation that he considered the only solution to the British-American quarrel.

Like many revolutionaries, Samuel Adams was born into a well-to-do family. The date was September 16, 1722, and the place was Boston. His father, also named Samuel, was called "Captain," a title derived from his service in the militia. But Samuel, Senior, was better known as "the Deacon," from his years of service at Old South Meetinghouse. He traced his ancestry to Henry Adams of Barton St. David in Somerset County, Britain, who came to Massachusetts with his eight sons and settled in Braintree (now Quincy) in 1638. Joseph Adams, Henry's seventh son, was the great-grandfather of both Samuel, Junior, and his cousin and fellow revolutionary, John Adams.

Deacon Adams had prospered in the business of making malt for brewers, becoming even wealthier after he married Mary Fifield, the only daughter of the rich merchant Richard Fifield. He and Mary had twelve children, of whom only three survived: Mary, Joseph and Samuel. While the Deacon's wealth enabled the family to live in comfort, his wife's grim Calvinism transmitted to her children the stern religious principles of the early Puritans, almost an anomaly in those "enlightened" days when the theocratic nature of Congregational society was on the wane. Samuel was especially impressed by her inflexible beliefs, and she, in turn, hoped that he would become a minister. That is why the boy was sent to Harvard College.

Harvard's records show little of Samuel's activities, except that he was once rebuked for oversleeping and missing morning prayers and fined for "drinking prohibited liquors." Drink itself was not yet the bête noire of the Protestant fundamentalists in America, among whom the steady drinking of wine or beer was common and acceptable, so it must have been that young Samuel put away some rum. Actually, he would always be temperate in both food and drink.

Like the young cousin who would follow him to Harvard thirteen years later, Samuel came under the spell of the great English political philosophers: Thomas Hobbes, John Milton, Sir Algernon Sydney and, most of all, the incomparable John Locke. Locke's great trinity of "life, liberty and property" was forever enshrined in Samuel's heart. While his father became active in local politics and those of the General Court—the colony's legislature—his son was swallowing theory on a much broader scale, especially the relationship between the ruler and the ruled, the people and their sovereign.

Like his classmates and the colonial leaders of the time, he was a loyal subject of King George II. But he accepted without question Locke's theory that men were born equal, with life, liberty and property their natural rights. Their only ruler was a just God, who had conferred upon kings their so-called divine right. But the sovereign must be responsible to the legislature chosen by the people. If he were a tyrant, the people could and should depose him. Furthermore, upon a king's death they need not accept the traditional principle of heredity and accept the king's son as the ruler, but could choose another. Most of all, there drummed in the back of this perceptive young man's brain—like the recurrent notes of a fugue—the precept that Parliament could not interfere in a colony's charter, which was a covenant between the Crown and its subjects there. The loss of a single—even the slightest—right was the beginning of enslavement.

This was the basis of Samuel Adam's commencement paper, a support in Latin of the thesis: "Whether it be lawful to resist the Supreme Magistrate if his commonwealth cannot otherwise be preserved." It has been said that such a provocative, if not treasonable, position must have outraged the royal governor and his council, who always attended Harvard graduations, but although the paper was written and turned in to the master of ceremonies, it was never delivered. The fact that it disappeared may suggest that it was quietly destroyed. In that year of 1743 "seditious" writings were not yet popular among the Patriots, the Seven Years' War had yet to be fought and at twenty Samuel Adams was far from being the fiery exponent of colonial rights that he would become over the next two decades. Samuel Adams also did not realize, being three thousand miles from the seat of government and never having crossed the sea, how deeply Parliament had encroached upon the power of the king. Thus his reverence for the charter, particularly the colony's right to impose its own taxes, was not shared in London.

So he returned to his books during a three-year course of study at home, after which Harvard granted him a master's degree. By then his passion for political theory had driven from his mind all thought of the ministry, much to his mother's grief. He spoke to her of the law, but Mary, distrusting and disliking all lawyers—an attitude then prevalent in New England—did not wish her son to become one. There was then really nothing that twenty-three-year-old Samuel could do. He did possess that deep grasp of the proper operation of society, a talent that in troubled times would be of great value to one side or the other. But these were tranquil times. To quote Samuel Johnson: "Uncommon parts need uncommon times for their exertion." Of course, young Samuel might well teach political philosophy at Harvard, except that his father was a hard-headed businessman who had no patience for such learned trivia. There were three routes to success: the church, the law and the counting-house, and since the first two were not acceptable, the third had to be. Samuel Adam's career would be in business.

But the Deacon, perhaps already suspecting that his bookish son had no head for commerce, did not immediately take his son into the family concern. Rather, he prevailed upon a merchant friend to try Samuel at the ledgers and was not surprised when he was told that Samuel cared for nothing but politics. But the Deacon still refrained from hiring his son, lending him £1,000 instead to set himself up in business. That money quickly vanished, half of it in a loan to a friend. Though exasperated, the Deacon finally put Samuel on the payroll. That's all it was: a salary, not a job—for Samuel's head was still crammed with political theory.

In 1748, the Deacon died after a brief illness. His fortune and possessions were willed to his wife Mary, after which his three children would divide the estate, Samuel to be minus the thousand-pound advance he had frittered away. Now he was in charge of the business, and it rapidly began to deteriorate. Most of thc young man's time was spent with a political discussion club or in writing articles for the *Independent Advertiser,* which he and his friends founded in 1748, or in courting Elizabeth Checkley, daughter of the minister who had baptized Samuel. He and Elizabeth were married on October 17, 1749, and had five children, of whom only two—a boy and a girl—survived.

By the time he was forty, Samuel Adams was living in poverty. His clothes were as shabby as his house on Purchase Street, and in appearance he could be described as "Mr. In-Between." Middling in everything—height, weight, station—except for that constantly turning brain within that great, sideways-canted, palsied head, which in moments of excitement would shake while his long thin hands trembled. To many Bostonians it seemed that Samuel Adams was always excited, buttonholing friends or likely candidates for the Patriot cause everywhere—at church, in the taverns or Masonic Lodges or on the streets—to warn them of the Parliamentary plot to enslave the American colonists. But though he might seem agitated, he was never offensive or bullying. He was extremely likable, neighborly and always anxious to help someone in trouble—in a word, a born politician.

Samuel had learned much about politics from his father, including the art of making something prepared in advance seem spontaneous. Thus he had known for many years of the Boston Caucus, a secret and exclusive political club to which his father belonged. "There," according to Samuel's cousin, John, "they smoke tobacco till you cannot see from one end of the garret to the other. There … selectmen, assessors, collectors, wardens, firewards and representatives are regularly chosen before they are chosen in the town." It was in this first "smoke-filled room" that Samuel Adams was chosen in 1756 to be a tax collector—an office for which his monumental indifference to money and his good heart eminently disqualified him.

For about a half dozen years Adams had little difficulty producing the receipts that the five collectors were assigned to collect, their private fortunes serving as a bond for failure to do so. But then in 1763 the city was ravaged by financial disaster, followed by a dreadful smallpox epidemic that not only severely reduced its population but provoked a mass exodus to the country. Many of those who fled were merchants, who closed their establishments and took their goods with them. By 1765 there was an arrears in tax collections of almost £10,000, of which about £7,000 was owed by Samuel Adams.

Although he still had enough friends among the Patriots to reelect him, the Tories saw an opportunity to discredit this man, who had by then become a troublesome Patriot leader. They did succeed in getting him into court, but the prosecutor, Adams's good friend James Otis, failed to convict him, although Otis won an appeal that was taken to the Tory-filled Superior Court. In the end, the court's order for Adams to make up his arrears in nine months came to nothing, and in 1769 Adams was able to persuade the Boston town meeting to free him from his obligation by settling for a trifling sum. Not at any point in this unpleasant experience—not even from the Tories—was there ever a suggestion of dishonesty. It was a combination of a depression and a plague, plus Adams's woeful incompetence, that produced the deficit.

But as a revolutionary this friendly man with the forgiving heart was a competent, relentless organizer, indeed. It was he who created the ubiquitous, secret organization known as the "Sons of Liberty." The name came from the debate on the Stamp Act in Parliament in 1765. Charles Townshend, speaking in support of the act, had patronizingly described the Americans as "children planted by our care, nourished up by our indulgence ... and protected by our arms." Isaac Barré, a friend of the colonists, along with Pitt, Edmund Burke, Wilkes, Charles James Fox and others, leaped to his feet in indignation to deliver a stinging rebuke in which he spoke glowingly of the Americans as "these Sons of Liberty." The phrase had a magnetic quality that attracted all Patriots everywhere who opposed the Stamp Act. In Boston, under the guidance of Adams and Otis, they would gather to march to the "Liberty Tree," a huge elm under which they held their meetings. Eventually the Sons of Liberty became the organ by which the lawyers and merchants of the North and the planters of the South guided the movement toward independence.

In Boston, to fill the prescription for violence without which no revolution can remain healthy, the Sons of Liberty also drew into their midst street gangs, such as the North and South End mobs who were notorious for their "Pope Day" brawling.

Pope Day was November 5, the anniversary of the 1605 Gunpowder Plot in Britain when a group of Catholics, led by Guy Fawkes, sought to blow up the king and Parliament. It was called Guy Fawkes Day in Britain and celebrated with parades and anti-Catholic speeches, but in Boston it was Pope Day—a date on which the Calvinist Protestants visited their scorn upon the pope of Rome by an unceremonious battle between these two gangs.

The North Enders were led by Samuel Smith, a Harvard graduate and lawyer with a fondness for combat, and the South Enders, by a shoemaker named Ebenezer McIntosh, a born revolutionary who affected a gorgeous blue-and-gold uniform, together with a speaking trumpet through which he barked his orders. Each gang built an elaborate float featuring popes and devils, and each float was the other gang's objective. To capture each other's floats, the gangs fought some notably bloody fights, once they collided with each other in the heart of the city. There was nothing religious or political about these contests; they were just a bonny opportunity for a darling fight and the chance to tear down fences or commit other jolly acts of vandalism in a drink-nourished explosion of high spirits that also produced the next day the kind of hangovers that "go out only by prayer and fasting." It is not known when these donnybrooks began, but the last of them was in 1764, the year before the Stamp Act was passed, and Samuel Adams and the Sons of Liberty enlisted both gangs in the crusade against the stamps.

Meanwhile, up and down the American seaboard, the Sons of Liberty went into action. They were particularly well prepared in Boston, where they moved against Andrew Oliver, the newly appointed stamp distributor for Massachusetts. If his appointment were not enough to draw the Patriots hatred, Oliver was also the brother-in-law of Lieutenant Governor Thomas Hutchinson, despised as an inveterate dispenser of nepotistic office and detested as a native-born collaborator with British tyranny. It is not exactly known who unleashed these former Pope Day brawlers on Oliver, although it is almost certain that Adams knew that they were on the rampage and against whom. Blacksmiths and cartwrights, tavernkeepers and fishermen and some "mechanics," whose soft white hands suggested a readier acquaintance with quill and ink than with turnspit or tar, they gathered in the glare of torches and lanterns and went roaring off to Oliver's house. They smashed his windows, shook his doors, and hanged him in effigy. Glad to get away with his life, Oliver quickly resigned his commission. That same month mobs burned the records of the Vice-Admiralty Court—destroying all evidence of smuggling that had been tolerated in the past—and sacked the office of the comptroller of customs, finally moving against the fine mansion of Governor Hutchinson. In a frenzy of rage, misdirected against a man who had spoken and written against the Sugar and Stamp Acts, the mob wrecked his splendid dwelling, destroyed his furniture, defaced his paintings and ruined the finest collection of books and manuscripts in America by burning most of them or scattering the pages through the streets.

In New York City violence erupted with the arrival of a shipment of stamped paper. Old Cadwallader Colden, the acting governor and scholarly correspondent of Linnaeus, Benjamin Franklin and Dr. Samuel Johnson, was nearly frightened out of his wits and shut himself up in Fort George while the howling mob reduced the gilded splendor of his coach to a pile of smoking ashes. Then the mob rushed uptown to the home of the fort's commander, breaking into the wine cellar to nourish their "patriotism" before falling upon the house in a paroxysm of vandalism.

So it went from Maine to South Carolina, and as barbaric as the mobs might have been, they quickly achieved their purpose of intimidation: stamp officers resigned in droves. Came November 1, 1765, the day the act was to go into effect, and the American seaboard went into mourning.

Flags flew at half-staff, minute guns were fired and muffled bells tolled a dirge. No one bought stamps, and all business was at a standstill. Political or economic death was not the goal of the colonists, however, and soon unstamped newspapers appeared and business was resumed as usual—without stamps.

★ 6 ★

GEORGE'S FIRST SEIZURE/STAMP ACT REPEALED

American opposition to the Stamp Act, which King George had called a "wise regulation," shocked the young sovereign. He was bewildered by the storm of violence that greeted the arrival of the stamps in the colonies and was shaken once again when the colonists, in a campaign to have the law repealed, organized a boycott of British goods. The boycott worked, for America was Britain's chief customer. With British factories and mills closed and thousands out of work, Parliament began debating a possible repeal—and it was then that the overwrought king showed the first symptoms of the family ailment.

Failed by Bute and his mother, opposed by Pitt, rejected by his subjects, reviled as a simpleton by that seditious monster Wilkes, George began to yearn for the quiet pleasures of a workshop, where he could turn soldiers' buttons upon a lathe, study the mechanisms of clocks, fiddle with locks and delight in every conceivable kind of ingenious device or tool, rather than have to impose the will of an honest man upon a world of evil. Occasionally, at first, the distraught young king began to perspire in the presence of his ministers. He was hesitant, then he began to gabble, complaining that his head ached so horribly that he had to have his hair cut off. In January 1765, in his twenty-seventh year, George III's "alarming illness" was plain to everyone about him. It was a fever with pronounced mental disturbance that lasted until April. George was kept quiet, was bled and saw no one but his physicians and members of his family. "The King sees nobody whatever," Grenville complained, "not even his brothers."

Queen Charlotte did her best to keep ministers, even Grenville, away from her husband, while Princess Augusta sought to keep Charlotte from her husband's bedside. Eventually, George recovered, but his ministers thereafter were most cautious about presenting their monarch with anything that might provoke a recurrence. It was observed that the king avoided people who might disagree with him or engage him in serious conversation. He preferred the company of elderly ladies or decorous clergymen. Terrified of obesity, he lived on potatoes and water. He sought relief in exercise, chiefly riding, or the soothing influence of cheerful or pious music. As a result of this first attack of insanity and those that would follow, King George III placed himself—or was placed—beyond the slightest familiarity with his people.

He did not abandon—would never abandon—his deep and disastrous belief in his divine right to rule. What he really wanted was a prime minister who would do his bidding without offering some irritating objection or proposing some annoying alternative. That was why he hoped for better things when the volatile Charles Townshend succeeded Grenville as chancellor of the exchequer in 1766, to become the real power in Britain after the repeal of the Stamp Act brought its author into disfavor.

Repeal of the Stamp Act had brought joy to America. It was succeeded by an outburst of gratitude and loyalty that lasted about a year and might have had much to do with King George's recovery from his first seizure. But the growing influence of Townshend soon ended this era of goodwill. Known as "the champagne Charlie of British politics" for his fondness for a glass of bubbly, and feared by his enemies for his ready and acerbic wit, Charles Townshend was one of the many British officials who had never crossed the sea to study those "contumacious" Americans at first hand and thus learn how the frontier life that depended upon self-reliance and decades of self-rule had nourished their stubborn spirit of independence, or how deeply they loathed standing armies as a threat to their cherished liberty. Never a friend of Americans, the bumptious Townshend still claimed that he "understood" them. The Americans, he thought, objected only to "internal taxes," such as the Stamp Act, but would not oppose "external taxes," such as duties on imports. So the famous—or infamous—Townshend Acts were passed. These acts imposed duties on imports from England of glass, certain painters' materials and tea. The proceeds were to be used to pay the salaries of the colonial governors and judges, who had been paid heretofore by colonial legislatures and had therefore been beholden to them. Writs of assistance were also revived, and provisions were made for a reorganized and vigorous customs service that would be directly responsible to the British Crown.

The Townshend Acts proved how thoroughly their author misunderstood the Americans. The colonists made no fine distinctions between external and internal taxes; they hated all taxes with a fine fervor that was fortified by their recent "victory" over the Stamp Act. Those writs of assistance that had called forth Otis's immortal cry were still anathema to them, and they were not going to cooperate in the death of smuggling. From Massachusetts came a circular letter urging concerted action again. Britain responded by ordering the colonial governors to force all legislatures to drop all opposition to the Townshend Acts under pain of dissolution. Such steps were taken in half the colonies and only succeeded in stiffening opposition.

But then in September 1767, Townshend unexpectedly died, and the odious acts that bore his name conferred upon him a dubious immortality. His death also created a new government crisis in Britain. Out of the shadows stepped Frederick, Lord North, the childhood friend of George III who had already been brought into the government to please the king. With Pitt now absent, there was no one to restrain the hard-line ministry installed by the pliant North upon the insistence of his friend George, and relations between the colonies and the Mother Country deteriorated steadily, especially when North sought to enforce the Townshend Acts.

With both sides now intractable, there sailed into this impasse, with an impact that actually redoubled mutual animosity, the smuggler sloop *Liberty,* owned by John Hancock. Hancock was an active Son of Liberty, though only thirty-one years old in that momentous spring of 1768. He was handsome, spoiled, peevish and vain, with an ambition far outrunning his capabilities, but for all this, he was possessed of that saving grace that, in the eyes of New Englanders, redeems all defects: enormous wealth. Though the son of a parsimonious parson, he was also the nephew of Thomas Hancock, the merchant prince of a colony of merchant princes. When John's father died, his childless uncle took him into his sumptuous mansion on Beacon Hill and adopted him. When Thomas himself "shuffled off this mortal coil," he left young John a fortune that in today's inflated dollar would be worth at least $100 million. It was a wealth so immense that when Samuel Adams was able to recruit Hancock for his Sons of Liberty, he rejoiced in the knowledge that all the order's bills would now be promptly paid. And they were, for John Hancock was generous and ardent in the Patriot cause. Governor Francis Bernard considered him one of the most dangerous men in the colony.

As a Boston merchant, Hancock was ipso facto a smuggler. He did not, of course, evade warships or deceive customs agents himself; this was done by the masters of his vessels. Thus in May 1768 Hancock's sloop *Liberty* tied up at a Boston pier. The captain declared a cargo of twenty-five pipes of Madeira wine—about 3,150 gallons. Joseph Harrison, Boston's chief collector of customs, considered this cargo far below the *Liberty's* capacity and was deciding whether or not to seize, condemn and sell the ship—even if it was owned by the wealthy, influential and popular Hancock—when two British warships entered the harbor before he could act.

The two ships were the *Romney* and the *St. Lawrence.* Both were shorthanded. Captain Corner aboard the *Romney* sought to bring his crew up to strength by the time-honored tradition of seizing American seamen and impressing them into service. That impressment of seamen in American waters had been illegal for one hundred years had never bothered British captains, than whom in those days there was no creature more arrogant, haughty or bloody minded. If the seaman refused to serve, the captain had it in his power to hang him. So the *Romney*'s press gang of sailors went to a waterfront tavern—the customary place of "recruitment"—and seized an American sailor named Furlong. An angry crowd surrounded the British, showering them with stones and invective and rescuing Furlong. Enraged, Captain Corner sounded general quarters aboard his ship and prepared to fire on the crowd.

Now Boston really seethed. First illegal impressment, now the threat to shoot those who opposed it! In this ugly atmosphere, customs collector Harrison decided on June 10 to seize *Liberty.* To this unwise move—if such a euphemism can describe such a prodigy of imbecility—he added the insult of doing so under the protection of a boatload of armed *Romney* sailors. Before a crowd could assemble to stop the *Romney* longboats, *Liberty* was seized and towed beneath *Romney's* guns. Upon this news, a huge throng assembled—some or even many of its members not quite sober. Harrison, his son and customs collector Benjamin Hallowell were seized and brutally beaten. Young Harrison was knocked down and dragged by his hair through the streets. His father, though battered, managed to escape, while Hallowell was left bleeding and unconscious in an alley.

Now the Sons of Liberty sought to calm the mob. Patriot leaders everywhere pleaded with its aroused members to disperse. They did, but only after they had broken the windows in Hallowell's and Harrison's houses, and broke one hundred more in the home of John Williams, inspector general of customs. Meanwhile, all frightened customs officials and their families took refuge aboard *Romney,* and while they gathered there, Samuel Adams and James Otis requested Governor Bernard to order Corner's warship out of the harbor. In his reply Bernard said he would do his best to stop impressment, and a few days later Captain Corner promised not to seize any more Bay Colony seamen. Now the customs officials, beginning to realize that they had acted with rash arrogance, asked the Patriot leaders to allow them to return to their duties. In reply, Hancock, unwilling to let them off the hook, said he would prefer that the entire affair be allowed to run its course—that is, in the courts.

So after *Romney* departed and the customs people were transferred to their second sanctuary in Castle William, a trial was held: Otis and John Adams for Hancock, Jonathon Sewall as Crown prosecutor. Sewall, in sympathy with the town's general indignation and aware that, in a modern lawyer's phrase, he had "a leaky bag," was not exactly zealous in the service of the king, and in March 1769, the case was dropped.

But the Crown had lost another round in its continuing duel with Massachusetts, and perhaps more important, the Sons of Liberty had shown, by their circumspect handling of an ugly and highly inflammable situation, that they were to be regarded no longer as rabble-rousing manipulators of street mobs, but rather as determined, experienced and responsible leaders of a genuinely popular movement for freedom.

Predictably, the Crown reacted with the customary angry face and clenched fist—sending two regiments of infantry into rebellious Boston. The regiments landed in October 1768, and their proud, disdainful hosts refused to quarter or supply them. Two more regiments that arrived in later months received the same treatment. As much as the commanders of all four might exposulate with Hutchinson or curse the damned insolence of the upstart Yankees, they found that they had to rent their own quarters and purchase provisions. They were also vilified as "foreigners" and the soldiers derided as "lobsterbacks"—a reference to the bloody floggings with which the British army enforced its brutal discipline. Again and again there were nasty confrontations between the detested redcoats and the despised townsmen. Epithets and obscenities were exchanged, and when the townies' insults were followed by barrages of rocks, the soldiers leveled their bayonets and threatened to draw blood. Although two of these four regiments were removed in late 1769 and early 1770, their removal did little to ameliorate this steadily growing mutual hatred. Sooner or later blood would flow, and when the town bells began to clang on the clear cold night of March 5, 1770, both soldiers and civilians realized that the dread moment had come.

★ 7 ★

THE BOSTON MASSACRE

About a foot of snow lay on the ground. Where it had melted during the day, it turned to ice. Private Hugh White shivered as he stood guard duty in the sentry box beside the Customs House. Several wig-maker's apprentices began baiting him. One, named Edward Garrick, declared that White's company commander was a cheat who had not paid his master for a wig. White challenged the youth to show his face, and when he did, struck him with his musket butt. Garrick cried out in pain and staggered away, pursued by a sergeant with bared bayonet. White joined him and struck Garrick again. The boy's cries brought a half-dozen youths running to his aid. The youths surrounded White, cursing him: "Lousy rascal! Lobster son of a bitch! Damned rascally scoundrel lobster son of a bitch!" Pelting feet and angry cries could be heard in all the streets leading to the Customs House. The crowd grew, many of its members armed with palings torn from picket fences or clubs that once were the legs of produce stalls. Private White was now thoroughly terrified. He backed up the Customs House steps, loading his musket and pointing it with its glittering bayonet at the crowd. Burly Henry Knox, a Boston bookseller, warned him that if he fired, he would perish. "Damn them!" White cried. "If they molest me I will fire!" More and more angry Bostonians joined the throng. White tried to get inside the Customs House, but the door was locked. Now snowballs flew at him, some striking him. Then chunks of ice, or whatever debris could be scraped up from the streets and hurled at him. In the dim, flickering light provided by a pale moon, tavern lamps and the waving torches of the mob, White could see that his tormentors were mainly waterfront toughs or members of the street gangs. Soon level-headed, respectable Boston citizens began arriving. Some sought to dissuade the infuriated mob from violence. The mob's reply was to scream more threats. "Kill him! Kill him! Knock him down!" Jeers and taunts followed: "Fire, damn you, fire! You dare not fire!"

Shortly it appeared that much of the male population of the town was on the streets. Some members of the crowd threatening White ran about shouting, "Town born, turn out! Town born, turn out!" Another noisy, infuriated crowd gathered in front of the Main Guard Barracks in a converted sugarhouse. They yelled at the British officers, "Why don't you keep your soldiers in the barracks? Are we to be knocked down in the streets? Are we to be murdered in this manner? We did not send for you. We will not have you here!"

With faces as white as their powdered wigs, the officers sought to soothe the throng, explaining that they were doing all possible to control their men. But just then, a redcoat rushed out of the barracks, kneeling in the street to aim his musket at a crowd gathered in an alley. "God damn your blood!" he screamed. "I'll make a lane through you all." Two officers quickly knocked him down and drove him back inside. But another cursing soldier ran outside and leveled his musket at another knot of Bostonians. Again it was an officer who knocked him down with the flat of his sword and tore his weapon away. Obviously, the officers were doing all possible to calm their men, just as some of the leaders of the Sons of Liberty roamed the streets appealing to the mobs to disperse, for everyone to go home.

But the clamor of the bells excited the Bostonians, many of whom hearing the cries of "Fire! Fire!" actually turned out with leather buckets to help fight a conflagration, or pushed pump engines toward the Customs House or the Main Guard Barracks. A man named Benjamin Davis, seeing his friend Samuel Gray rushing by with a bucket, called out, "There's no fire. It's the soldiers fighting!" "Damn it," Gray replied. "I'm glad of it. I'll knock some of them on the head!"

Meanwhile the besieged Private White began shouting for help from the Main Guard, and Captain Thomas Preston, the officer of the day there, soon received word of White's danger and the ugly mood of the crowd menacing him. At forty, Preston was a veteran soldier, cool and courageous. He quickly buckled on his sword and ordered a rescue party formed. Then he carefully began weighing his options. He realized at once that an armed rescue party might be the spark that would ignite an explosion of violence, and yet, one of his men was in need of help and could not be sacrificed to a mob. He also knew that he could not go to the defense of the Customs House without orders from a city official, and yet, how could he hope to find one at nine o'clock at night among a hostile, near-rioting populace in time to save White's life? If he did rescue White, should he leave the Customs House defenseless among throngs of infuriated Bostonians who had already shown what they could do to public property when aroused? And could his rescue party succeed in getting through to White? Such were the considerations that came to mind as Captain Preston calmly awaited the formation of the rescue detail. In the end, as he probably suspected from the beginning, there were really no options but only one imperative: as an officer, he must go to White's assistance. So he led the relief party—Corporal William Wemms and Privates Matthew Killroy, Hugh Montgomery, William Warren, William McCauley, John Carroll and James Hartegan—all grenadiers except for Wemms—toward the Customs House.

Upon Preston's arrival, Henry Knox rushed up to him and cried: "For God's sake, take care of your men. If they fire, they die!" Preston nodded, replying in a calm voice, "I am sensible of it." He was indeed "sensible" of the tinderbox he had stepped into. The crowd was huge and unruly, surging back and forth in front of the beleaguered White on the steps, vapor puffs shooting from their mouths as they screamed their insults and taunts. The wonder was that this terrified young man had retained his self-control and not done anything foolish, for the crowd was clearly out for blood, months of indignity—real or imagined—feeding their fury, the incessant clamor of the bells and the fact that their intended prey was clearly at their mercy nourishing their mob courage. Momentarily stunned by the appearance of Preston and his redcoats, the crowd fell silent, and in this moment of opportunity, Preston ordered White to fall in with his detail.

With this order, a roar of protest broke from the crowd, which surged forward to prevent the escape of their prey and his despised comrades. An impasse ensued. Unable to penetrate the crowd, Preston ordered his soldiers to form an arc from the sentry box to a hitching post. There they stood, receiving the snowballs and epithets hurled at them. "Damn you, you sons of bitches, fire! You can't kill us all!" Again and again, it came, the maddened mob of three or four hundred men chanting, as though in suicidal supplication: "Fire! Why don't you fire? You dare not fire!" But the taunt was not actually suicidal, for each time the challenge passed untaken, it only strengthened the mob's conviction that they—not the armed redcoats—were the masters of the situation.

Preston thought that the arrival of Justice of the Peace James Murray to read the Riot Act might subdue the mob, but Murray was driven off by a barrage of snowballs and chunks of ice. The incident further inflamed the crowd. Now the bolder spirits surged forward to displace their more timid comrades and confront Preston and his men. Richard Palmes, a merchant who had tried to calm the mob at the barracks, asked Preston: "Are your men loaded? Are they going to fire?" Preston shook his head. "By no means, by no means." His men would not fire unless he gave the order to fire, and because he stood in front of them that would mean that he "must fall a sacrifice."

Just then a club came spinning out of the crowd, striking Private Montgomery and knocking him down. Montgomery arose in a fury, cocking his musket and shouting in bitter mimicry, "*Damn you, fire!*"—and pulled the trigger. But the shot hit no one. Still, the merchant Palmes, at last losing his self-possession, struck at Montgomery with his own club, hitting him on the arm, and then at Preston's head. Missing, Palmes fell down, and Montgomery lunged at him with his bayonet, missing again but driving him off. Now the crowd fell back, but both attempts to draw blood had pushed both sides over the brink. At once Private Killroy raised his musket, pointing it at Edward Langford and Samuel Gray. Langford cried, "God damn you, don't fire!" but Killroy squeezed the trigger, and Gray fell with a hole in his head. Another musket roared—apparently double loaded—and two slugs struck the breast of Crispus Attucks, a huge, forty-year-old freed black from the Bahamas, who also was believed to be part Indian. Attucks fell dead. More shots came. Robert Patterson was struck in the wrist of his left hand, and Patrick Carr—an immigrant from Ireland—was mortally wounded in the hip and backbone. Samuel Maverick, a kegmaker's apprentice, who was running for home, was struck in the chest by a richocheting bullet and killed instantly.

Suddenly the crowd fell silent, shocked and incredulous. Its members stared in disbelief at their fallen neighbors. All along, it appeared, they had believed that the redcoats' muskets were loaded with powder only, which may explain their indiscreet taunts. But then they pressed forward again, and the soldiers, having reloaded, lifted their weapons. At once Preston moved among them, knocking up the barrels and shouting, "Don't fire!"

In the dim, fitful light a man named Benjamin Burdick stepped up to Preston and his men, peering at them and murmuring: "I want to see some faces that I may swear to another day." He and Preston exchanged challenging glances, and the captain replied softly, "Perhaps, sir, you may."

★ ★ ★

That was not the end of the dreadful episode that has gone into history as "the Boston Massacre." Massacre it was not—unless the death of four men and the wounding of two others out of a throng of three to four hundred men may be so described—but even as early as 1770, Boston had such clever propagandists as Samuel Adams and Dr. Joseph Warren to break into print with emotional, inflammatory words. If there were to have been any real massacre that fateful night, it might have been among the British garrison. Even as Captain Preston marched his redcoats back to the Main Guard, he could hear the town drums beating a summons for the militia to form, along with cries, "To arms!" Reports reached him of an army of four or five thousand infuriated Bostonians forming to attack his soldiers, and he promptly ordered his guard to deploy for "street firing," that is, to prepare for street warfare. In fact, there were only about a thousand aroused citizens hastening to the beat of the drum, but if they were armed and understood the rudiments of combat—as they were and did—they could, indeed, overwhelm his command. When Preston next heard the town's bells tolling dolorously, as though clanging a dirge in advance, he ordered his own drums to beat "To arms!" and alerted the entire Boston garrison. Those who were scattered in the town on errands of pleasure had difficulty returning to their units. Two ensigns were beaten and knocked to the ground, and a captain was struck in the face and his sword was torn from him. Thus the unhappy Preston was not displeased when he saw Governor Hutchinson and his aides hurrying through a crowd toward him, even though Hutchinson's face was dark with fury.

"How came you to fire without orders from a civil magistrate?" Hutchinson burst out angrily.

"I was obliged to, to save my sentry," Preston replied, provoking one of the governor's aides to shout: "Then you murdered three or four men to save your sentry!"

Calm as ever, Preston turned to the governor and said: "Pray, sir, do you go up to the Guard House." Hutchinson hesitated. "I don't think it prudent for me to go to the Guard House," he replied warily. Another aide, fearful for the governor's safety, suggested instead that he "go into the Council Chamber and speak to the people." Hearing this, members of the crowd began crying, "To the Town House! The Town House!" while gathering around the governor and hurrying him off in that direction. But when Hutchinson saw the huge throng assembled there, he decided to speak from a balcony, rather than from inside. He spoke of his own sorrow at the bloodshed and promised a full investigation and swift justice, to be followed by punishment for those found guilty. "The law shall have its course," he declared. "I will live and die by the law." His words had the effect of calming the crowd, and many departed for home. Others still insisted that they would not leave until the governor ordered the soldiers back to their barracks. Instead of issuing a command, Hutchinson suggested to Lieutenant Colonel Carr, the senior officer present, that it should be done—and it was. With this, the crowd dispersed.

Now Hutchinson kept his word, immediately summoning justices of the peace, as well as the British commander, Colonel Dalrymple, to his presence. Witnesses were rounded up and testimony was taken, while the sheriff was dispatched to arrest Preston. The weary captain was brought before the justices at two o'clock in the morning, and after several witnesses testified that they heard him give the order to fire, he was jailed. The next day the eight soldiers involved were also imprisoned.

So ended the Boston Massacre, a tragedy that would never have occurred if the obtuse British Crown had not sent armed troops into a town that was celebrated throughout the civilized world for its love of freedom and hatred of standing armies. But for the discipline of the British soldiery and the coolness of Captain Preston, as well as the calming influence of the Patriot leaders and Hutchinson's quick intervention, it could have ended in a hideous bloodbath that there and then could have provoked a revolution and a war.

As might be expected, Preston and his men were indicted on a charge of murder, and after a long delay finally brought to trial. Representing them were probably the two finest young lawyers in the colony, Josiah Quincy and his friend and cousin, John Adams.

★ 8 ★

JOHN ADAMS

John Adams could trace his lineage back to those sturdy Puritans who, rejecting the "persecution" of the Church of England though not repudiating the Established Church itself, founded the colony of Massachusetts Bay in the 1630s. His great-grandfather was Henry Adams, who migrated from England to Braintree (now Quincy) just outside Boston in 1638. His father was John Adams, a farmer and cordwainer (a trade that included the making and repair of shoes, harnesses and leather breeches), a solid, simple man; wise from experience rather than from books; and for many years a Braintree selectman and a deacon of the Congregational Church. The forebears of John's mother, Susanna Boylston Adams, were of the same stock, although a bit more illustrious, as she constantly reminded her husband, in the person of Uncle Zabdiel Boylston, a physician who, with Cotton Mather, introduced smallpox inoculation in Massachusetts during the dreadful epidemic in 1721.

Young John was born in 1735, the first of three sons. He had a happy childhood and youth, in his old age describing it in the third person: "Fifteen years he spent at schools male and female, grammar and A.B.C. When he played truant, and when he did not, he spent all his mornings, noons and nights in making and sailing boats, in swimming, skaiting, flying kites and shooting, in marbles, ninepins, bat-and-ball, football, etc., quoits, wrestling and sometimes boxing, and what was no better running about to quiltings and huskings and frolicks and dances among the boys and girls!!! These fifteen years went off like a fairy tale. Apply such a 15 years to his present age and it will make 93."

Curiously, this catalog of youthful joy and pleasure suggests that old John Adams, like so many autobiographers, was unconsciously leaving out misery. Only poets seem to remember (along with Buddha) that life is an alternating rhythm of joy and sorrow, pleasure and pain. For one thing, that fifteen-year fairy tale also was flawed by the steady presence of an ogre: the hated and dreaded Papists across the border in French Canada. To young Johnny, it seemed that fear of the French was a condition of life in Massachusetts. Of course, there had been the marvelous interlude of joy after the colony's militia in 1745 had stormed the fortress of Louisbourg seemingly ending forever the threat from the north. But then in the following year, the menace was renewed with sightings of an enormous French invasion fleet under the great warrior-admiral, the Duc d'Anville, sent by King Louis XV to recapture Louisbourg, burn Boston and strike the British West Indies. At ten, young Johnny had stood on his father's sloping pastures gazing apprehensively toward Boston Bay, where the smoke from the campfires of six thousand Massachusetts militia—many of them veterans of Louisbourg—curled upward from Boston Common, and then out to sea waiting for the dreadful moment when the white sails and detested golden lilies of France should heave above the horizon. How frightened Johnny had been when the somber-faced men of Braintree had gathered one evening in his mother's kitchen and he had heard many of them urging flight into the interior, but then how proud he had been when his own father arose, walked to the chimney to knock out his pipe, and said:

"I am fifty-four. I have seen other French wars. Two of them, and lived through them. They did not frighten my father out of Braintree, or my father's grandfather. The French were fighting us to the northeastward in ninety-one, the year that I was born. They came to York with their Indians on snowshoes, killing and burning. My father's cousin saw it. We fought them again before I was twenty. Am I to leave now because French ships have been sighted four hundred miles to the eastward?" John's father turned and spat contemptuously into the fire. "I stay where I am, and take in my apple harvest until the French cut down my trees."

Growls of approval arose in the kitchen. Chairs scraped. Someone said, "Neighbor Adams has the right of it." Tears of pride rolled down Johnny's cheeks as the men of Braintree clumped out the door. Weeks later Johnny shed tears of joy with the arrival of Governor Shirley's sloop the *Rising Sun* bearing the news of the destruction of the French fleet. D'Anville was dead, supposedly having poisoned himself after a violent storm sank two of his finest ships and crippled and scattered the rest and an outbreak of pestilence reduced the invasion force from seven thousand to one thousand able-bodied men. *Deliverance!* It was a miracle, and all Massachusetts—Episcopalians and Dissenters alike—fell on their knees to thank God for the storm and sickness with which He had cursed the Popish fleet. It seemed to these exultant Yankees that not even the passage of the children of Israel through the Red Sea and the destruction of the pharaoh's pursuing host could surpass this marvelous intervention of the Almighty on the side of the Chosen People of America.

Johnny's love of history and country was matched by his passion for freedom: freedom to revel in the joys of nature, to ride bareback over his father's pastures—oh, unspeakable joy when his father promised him Polly's next colt!—or to go shooting in the woods with his uncles. He seemed to sense when a hunting expedition was in the making, suddenly appearing at a run—he never walked—shouting breathlessly that he knew where the partridges were feeding and if he could come along, he would show them. Laughing uproariously, Great Uncle Peter would hand him a fowling piece with one hand and clap him on the back with the other. No one bothered to ask why Johnny was not in school.

He was not in school because he hated it. Bright boy though he was, with a memory like a sponge soaking up every sight and sound and insight that came his way, he could not abide the dull and deadly regimen at the Braintree Free Latin School, run by Mr. Joseph Cleverly. It was not that Mr. Cleverly was one of those monstrous schoolmasters with a cane, given to spattering the walls of his study with boys' blood. Actually, he was a mild man, known among the livelier spirits of Braintree as very good company, even if he was an Episcopalian. But he had no real talent and didn't own a farm, and because he had to eat like anyone else, he had taken to schoolteaching. He hated the crushing boredom of this eight-hour routine as much as any of his students—even Johnny Adams—and yearned for the release of the five-o'clock bell just as desperately. As an Anglican, he felt no fondness for the New England school rules that prescribed twice-weekly doses of the Westminister Catechism, that very soul of the region's grim Calvinist faith. With a sigh he would reach for his own catechism and ask in a tired voice: "*What is the misery of that estate whereinto men fell?*" Back came fifty shrill, equally bored voices chanting in singsong unison: "All mankind by their fall, lost communion with God, are under His wrath and curse, and so made liable to all the miseries of this life, to death itself and to the pains of hell forever."

It was not that young John questioned this sacred book. He was a Congregationalist—a true Dissenter—body and soul. He took his faith for granted in the same way that he accepted the farmhouse he lived in, the plentiful food and warm clothing, the beautiful green pastures with their grazing sheep sloping away to a breathtaking view of the bay. It was just that there was so much of it! Even worse, so much more of Lily's *Latin*

Grammar. Did all learning consist of conjugating Latin verbs and parsing Latin nouns? And if he went to Harvard College, as his parents—especially his mother—desired, would it be more of the same with Greek and Hebrew parts of speech thrown in?

What of the earth? Johnny loved nature with a passion: the sight of the wide blue bay dotted with the sails of the fishing skiffs or the high white canvases of the great ships entering and leaving the port and the feel of the dew-wet grass under his bare feet or of the cow's soft warm hide as its breath rose and fell against his cheek at milking time. Rather than sit on his hard bench and listen to Mr. Cleverly's monotonous voice intoning the soulless Latin, he would prefer to be in the swamp hunting turtles or lying on his back in the warm grass, the sun falling on his closed eyelids like a benediction, his nostrils filled with the mingling scent of pine and salty sea. Or even listen entranced to Uncle Peter fiercely denouncing the Stuart kings, pointing his finger at him while reminding him to thank the Lord for making him a freeborn Englishman, free to worship and speak his mind without interference from the Crown or clergy. It was because of this love of freedom, of nature and of history, compared to the dessicating boredom of the schoolroom, that Johnny was so frequently late for classes or played hooky so often or begged to stay home for the haying. Mr. Cleverly did not fail to notice Johnny's increasing truancy, but being a man who did not enjoy confronting angry parents, he said nothing.

Susanna Adams, meanwhile, had observed in her beloved firstborn—indeed, her secret favorite—a slow but perceptible change in personality. Talkative, obliging Johnny—who gaily chattered his head off while carving pegs for her kitchen, bringing in the milk, making linen kites for his brothers Peter and Elihu or teaching them how to skate when the creek froze—had become morose and silent. He had withdrawn into himself. Worse, he seldom studied. Yet, he could hardly wait until supper was over to dash out the door and go gallanting with the girls. Try as she might, Susanna Adams could not fathom what had come over the boy. And he never confided in her anymore. All that she knew was that if he continued this way instead of going to Harvard College, he would be married at eighteen and doomed … yes, doomed … to a … to a farmer's life. Yet, for two heartbreaking years, she never revealed her fears to her husband. He had enough to worry him, she thought, what with the farm and the shop, politics and the church. But then, a few months before Johnny turned fifteen, John mentioned casually that if they sold the Stony Acres, they would have enough money to finance the boy's education at Harvard.

"Stony Acres!" Susanna exclaimed in an explosion of scorn that startled her husband. "*Harvard?*" For ten minutes she poured out her grief, what she had seen since Johnny turned thirteen. John was crushed. Taking his cold pipe from his mouth, he humbly apologized for his negligence. "I have favored the boy too much, perhaps," he said slowly, and strode out the door toward the barn where Johnny was playing bat and ball with his brothers. Motioning Johnny to him, he watched the boy approach and saw in his face for the first time that stubborn look Susanna had described.

"Your mother tells me you are behind in your studies. Very far behind. Is that true?"

"Yes, sir."

John Adams gasped. "So!" he cried in anger. "If you won't study you can't go to the college."

Johnny's blue eyes clouded, and his round face reddened. "Sir," he replied, his voice rising. "I hate school. I hate Mr. Cleverly and his books. I don't want to go to the college."

John Adams was breathing hard. "And what … what *do* you want to do?"

"I want to be a farmer," Johnny said simply.

John Adams was incredulous. "No!" He was almost shouting. "No! The farm is for your brothers. My will is made, my testament inscribed. You are to be a clergyman, a scholar. Don't you know your duty?"

Johnny remained silent. But he did not lower his eyes.

"A *farmer!*" his father cried in scorn. "What do you know of farming, beyond galloping your colt around the pasture, scaring the sheep." He paused. "I'll show you what it is to be a farmer."

John Adams was true to his promise. For the next few weeks of vacation time, he introduced his son to the farm's dirtiest, most miserable work. Johnny shoveled stinking cow flop until the blisters on his hands broke. No matter, he was next given a spade and told to dig a cattle pond by the brook channel. Then there was dead wood to be gathered and split for winter fuel, and one dreadful day, standing knee deep in marsh mud among clouds of stinging mosquitoes, there was grass to be cut for roof thatch. All the while his father worked soundlessly beside him, speaking only to give orders. Perhaps worse were the silent suppers under the reproachful eyes of his mother and brothers. After the meal there were harnesses to be cleaned and oiled, farm tools to be sharpened. One night an exhausted Johnny left the table to sit on the settle—and fell instantly asleep, exhausted. His secretly pleased father shook him awake. "Well, John, are you satisfied being a farmer?"

"Very well, sir," Johnny muttered, and staggered off to bed.

But when he awoke next morning, he realized that he had been defeated. He could not go on like this, driven like a yoked beast, his body in torment, his soul stultified, his heart aching at the unspoken rebuke in the eyes of all his loved ones. But what could he do? The answer came to him after breakfast, when he was surprised to find himself alone with no chores to do. He would go back to school, but not to Mr. Cleverly. Rather, he would go to the school kept by Mr. Joseph Marsh.

Johnny Adams was aware that his father disliked Joseph Marsh. His father was forever reminding his mother that Marsh had failed as a preacher and failed as a physician, yet Marsh was always telling other people what to do. Marsh was stuck up, pronouncing Canadian place-names with a French accent. He knew nothing about the land or anything that grew out of it. When did anyone ever see him at a town meeting? Oh, yes, John Adams would concede condescendingly, Marsh did have a knack of getting boys into Harvard.

That last remark, Johnny thought, walking down the road to Mr. Marsh's house—was the tack to take if Mr. Marsh agreed to accept him. Johnny realized that if he told his father that he would go back to school, but at Mr. Marsh's rather than at Mr. Cleverly's, his father's passionate desire to see him at Harvard, together with his grudging admiration for Marsh, would gain his consent. Johnny was shrewd enough to foresee that there would be no winner or loser in the confrontation between him and his father. It would be a trade-off. And that was what happened. On July 6, 1851, at the age of sixteen, Johnny Adams successfully passed the examination to enter Harvard.

Harvard College then consisted of three tall red brick buildings forming a quadrangle that opened on Cambridge Common. Here some ninety boys lived and studied. Cambridge itself was no larger than Braintree, but this little town, meandering along the Charles River, was famous throughout the colonies, and even known in Europe, for the quality of education available there. Harvard's soul was Puritan and its regimen monastic. All students were to behave themselves blamelessly and to follow a day beginning at five in the morning and ending at nine at night, with respite from studies granted only for meals and an hour or so on the playfield. It would seem that the customs, fines, bell ringing, rules and admonitions that enforced this Spartan existence would be like a fence around the freedom that Johnny Adams prized so highly, except that this young man was so happy to be beyond the constraints of home and too exhilarated by intellectual excitement to protest. Indeed, if the five o'clock bell awakened him in the cold dark, he was accustomed to arising in the cold dark. If the food was plain, it was plentiful. There was linen on the tables, and the plates, bowls and mugs were of pewter—in Johnny's eyes elegance, indeed. For breakfast Johnny could consume an entire loaf of bread soaked in beer and do similar justice to the boiled meat and vegetables served at the other meals. John still had a farm boy's gargantuan appetite, shorn of a farm boy's energy-consuming chores, and it was thus inevitable that his muscular body—he had reached his full height of five feet, seven inches—would gradually approach the pudgy. The hair on his bulging, belligerent forehead was already beginning to thin, and he would eventually be bald.

In his sophomore year Johnny Adams began to read so voraciously (two books a day) that the librarian dryly inquired if he could remember on Tuesday what he had read on Monday. Johnny laughed. Nothing could squelch this impetuous enthusiast, and soon he developed a reading skill that enabled him to discover at a glance what he sought on any page. He plunged through translations of the Greek historians and playwrights, gulped down Newton, Shakespeare, Dryden, Pope.... When he read *Natural Philosophy* by Willem Gravesande, Sir Isaac Newton's Dutch pupil, he made a discovery that opened his mind as though it had been bombed. "*The properties of Body cannot be known a priori: we must therefore examine Body itself.*" Inflamed by this insight, he rushed into the laboratory of the science instructor, Dr. John Winthrop, eager to share his find. For ten minutes he stood on tiptoe, as though preparing to charge, pouring out a cascade of commentary on what he had discovered. Winthrop sat on a stool, gravely studying him. Though he had experienced such scenes before, he found in this boy a passion to communicate that was almost unique. When Johnny finally fell silent, Winthrop arose and said, "What you have discovered today Adams, is your own mind."

Gravesande's practical insight had shaken Johnny Adams because it challenged the beliefs held by the Congregationalists of New England that man was born knowing, with ideas stamped upon his mind. When Johnny encountered this perception again in the great English philosopher John Locke—*All that we know, we know from experience*—he began to question what he had been taught at home. He remembered his father and his deacon-uncles in Braintree dodging a difficulty in religion or politics by disqualifying it with a text, but never questioning it or examining it for truth or falsehood. How many Congregational ministers he had known had been prone, in Locke's phrase, to "cram their tenets down all men's throats," without logic or proof. Johnny was not yet questioning his faith—although he had begun to wonder if the world had really been created in 4047 B.C., or if it really mattered—but doubting if he actually wanted to become a minister. That reservation turned to a negative conviction after his dogmatic uncles and others like them hounded the Reverend Lemuel Briant, the youthful, thoughtful minister of the Braintree Congregational Church, out of the ministry, so thoroughly slandering him and breaking his spirit that he died within a year of his departure. When John Adams was graduated from Harvard in July 1755, he had decided to become a teacher.

John Adams was shocked when he arrived in Worcester to take charge of the Congregational school for boys, not so much by the town itself, which was charming enough, with its lovely village green shaded with handsome great oaks and maples, its new courthouse—it was a county seat—and new jail, but by the gloomy boredom in which his choice of a career had engulfed him. His school was a one-room loghouse containing fifty boys aged five to fifteen, whose "intellectual" growth was to be nourished by a stack of dog-eared books that were almost exact replicas of those dull tomes used in Mr. Cleverly's school. His daily routine was also a duplicate of that once-hated place, eight to five daily—eight hours of unending, horrifying, stultifying tedium. His charges were uniformly dirty. All had colds, and most had running noses. The place smelled, and when the hearth fire was blazing, the woolen clothes they wore made it stink like an animal cage. In that heat the smaller boys fell asleep and had to be shaken awake and propped up. The older ones sought to escape the stifling atmosphere by constantly raising their hands for permission to visit the outdoor privy. Oh, just and deserving retribution for the things he had said of Mr. Cleverly! Could Mr. Cleverly, too, have been trapped in such "quiet desperation?"

Although the citizens of Worcester were kind and generous to John, always greeting him cordially or inviting him into their homes, he lived a solitary life, thrown back on himself with only books for companions. He kept a diary, confiding in it his hopes and fears, his nagging self-doubts, his contempt for a social system that placed birth above ability. Adams had always resented Harvard's system of grading pupils according to social standing, rather than academic achievement. Thus, first preference went to the son of a royal governor; second, to the lieutenant governor's son; then to the sons of members of the Governor's Council; and finally, to sons of judges and justices of the peace. Only then did academic excellence receive its reward. He could not keep his tongue—either in public or in private—off the hated "lace coats" of Massachusetts. Where there had been the Quincys of Braintree or the Hancocks of Boston to despise, here in Worcester it was the Chandlers. Exercising his wit at the expense of such people, he soon realized, quickly got him into disrepute—but until his dying day John Adams never could suppress his perverse skill in the alienating art of the wounding epigram.

Yet, there was one man in Worcester who appreciated both his humor and his growing erudition: the lawyer James Putnam. Here was probably the most respected and brilliant man in this frontier town of fifteen hundred persons. When he was trying a case, the courtroom was packed. Elegant in his light gray coat with silver lace and gleaming silver buttons, Putnam won his cases not by bullying or shaking or trickery, but by his deep knowledge of the law. Gentle and courteous in his cross-examination of opposition witnesses, his questions not only skillfully brought out his own side of the case, but led these witnesses into contradiction and confusion. It was said that he could have a man executed for petting his neighbor's cat.

John Adams was fascinated by James Putnam, eagerly awaiting the arrival of court week, consciously comparing Putnam's own high station in life with his own miserable estate. He was overjoyed when Putnam invited him to dinner at his fine house on the green. He became a frequent visitor. Soon his discontent with the schoolroom became transformed into a desire to shine in the courtroom. He asked Putnam to accept him as a law student in his office, and to his unspeakable joy, Putnam not only agreed but invited John to come live with him. Thus John Adams not only learned the law by daily studying such authorities on English jurisprudence as Coke and Blackstone, but was introduced to the practice of it during dinner discussions with his host and mentor and postprandial conversations over port and brandy at night. After two years of such an incomparable course of instruction, John Adams was ready to pursue a career in law. But in Braintree, and then in Boston, not in Worcester. On October 1, 1758, a bright, windy autumn day, he said his good-byes (but not to James Putnam, his benefactor, who was mysteriously elsewhere), mounted his horse and rode the seventy-odd miles eastward to the town of his birth.

★ 9 ★

TRIAL OF THE REDCOATS

It was indeed fortunate for Captain Preston and his men that their trial was delayed for two months because another murder trial preceded it. Otherwise the passions inflamed to fever pitch against them by those artful propagandists—Dr. Warren and Samuel Adams, together with a new recruit, the young silversmith Paul Revere—would have made a fair proceeding next to impossible.

Beginning with the funeral for the four slain men on March 8, when an incredible twelve thousand men and women marched behind the cortege while church bells tolled dolefully, an overwhelming majority of the townspeople openly and fiercely made it clear that they would settle for nothing less than a guilty verdict and a sentence of death. Even the transfer of the two British regiments to the sanctuary of Castle William out in the harbor, where the sight of their muskets and redcoats could no longer infuriate the populace, did little to moderate this burning thirst for revenge. Paul Revere made an engraving of a crude drawing showing Preston with raised sword ordering his soldiers to fire on cowering, innocent men. Hundreds of hand-colored prints were turned out with the inscription:

Shoulde venal courts, the scandal of the land,
Snatch the relentless villain from her hand,
Keen execrations on this plate inscribed,
Shall reach a judge who never can be bribed.

Preston and his men were denounced from podium and pulpit as "brutal banditti" or "grinning furies gloating over their carnage," while the

Reverend John Lathrop preached a sermon on the text, "The voice of thy brother's blood crieth unto me from the ground." The murdered men, Lathrop said, had fallen victims "to the merciless rage of wicked men."

And yet, not every voice was raised in irrational and bloodthirsty demands for revenge, rather than justice. There were some who pleaded for a calm, orderly and dispassionate trial, based on evidence, not on emotion. Among them was John Adams, who, in the dozen years since he had hung out his shingle in Braintree, had risen to the pinnacle of his profession in the colony. It was to Adams that James Forest, a Tory merchant and friend of Preston, came one day with tears streaming down his cheeks, begging him to become the captain's counsel. Forest said that Preston had found that no reputable lawyer would take his case, fearing popular displeasure. Only young Josiah Quincy, Adams's friend and cousin, had said that he would agree to defend Preston, but only if Adams would join him. John Adams at once consented, but not without a touch of that self-importance swollen in him by success. "Counsel ought to be the very last thing that an accused person should want [lack] in a free country," he said, and "this would be as important a cause as ever was tryed in any court or country of the world." It would also be under the scrutiny of the Heavenly Tribunal. Yet it did take considerable courage to accept such a case in the face of almost universal prejudice against his clients. However, John Adams was a leading exponent of the Patriot cause, and even though his cousin Samuel and others were collecting testimony that the British soldiers had deliberately shot down their victims in cold blood, his fears that his popularity would suffer proved to be groundless.

At the outset there was a difficulty. Preston's chief argument for acquittal would be to prove he had not given the order to fire, while the soldiers' case rested on their claim that he did in fact issue that order. But if Preston were to be found not guilty, that verdict would, in effect, contradict their position. So the soldiers petitioned the court for a simultaneous trial, only to have their plea denied. There were also numerous rumors prejudicial to either side. Chief among them was that if Preston were convicted, Hutchinson would deliberately delay Preston's execution until the verdict had passed under royal review, with the likely outcome of a pardon. Preston himself thought this view would harm him, since the jurors might feel free to convict him in the anticipation of his being set free. There were also frequent rumors that the more violent members of the Sons of Liberty planned to break into the jail to seize Preston and his men and hang them. This report was so persistent that Hutchinson ordered the sheriff to keep the warden's keys on his own person so that "if they should be demanded [of the warden] he will not have the power to deliver them."

Actually, although the populace was still almost wholly inflamed against the redcoats, both the prosecution and the defense were anxious for an acquittal, or at least no verdict of murder. If the soldiers were found guilty and then pardoned, the reaction in Boston would probably be more furious than the outburst succeeding the so-called massacre itself. Both sides were also eager to vindicate their city and were therefore zealous for a fair trial, one that would not suggest that the defendants had been sacrificed to popular prejudice or make a mockery of the Yankees' professed devotion to law and constitutional procedure. Thus both sides—though not joined in an actual conspiracy to thwart the law—had a common interest in a fair trial.

And the trial was indeed fair. Even Richard Palmes, the merchant who struck angrily at Preston and was standing beside him when the shooting began, testified that the captain never gave the order to fire. Three black men also helped Preston. One Andrew, "servant [slave] of Oliver Wendell," and Jack and Newton Prince, a freeman and pastry cook from the West Indies, testified to the ugly, baiting mood of the crowd and its abuse of the soldiers. Captain James Gifford of the Fourteenth Regiment said that if the command to fire had been given, it would have resulted in a concerted volley—which would certainly have struck Preston—not single sniping as occurred. Quincy and Adams used the occasion of both trials to deliver stirring lectures on the sanctity of the law. To establish the absolute imperative of a fair trial, Adams quoted from Sir Matthew Hale's *Pleas of the Crown:* "It is better that five guilty persons should escape unpunished, than that one innocent person should die." He thereafter proceeded to demolish point by point the testimony against his client. It was no surprise, then, that after both sides rested their case, the jury took only three hours to bring in a verdict of not guilty. What was truly surprising was the grudging calm with which the townspeople took the decision, perhaps because their quarrel actually was with the soldiers, not with their captain.

This hostility became apparent in the second trial, when Samuel Quincy, Josiah's brother, appearing for the prosecution, introduced voluminous testimony suggestive of soldierly abuse of the townspeople. Most telling was the report that Private Killroy had openly hoped to fire on Boston's inhabitants "ever since he landed."

None of the prosecution witnesses had any recollection of the events of March 5 as anything other than a peaceful gathering of mannerly citizens. No one spoke of rocks, snowballs, debris, clubs or sticks being hurled at the soldiers. However, on Adam's cross-examination, a sailor named James Bailey said he had seen Crispus Attucks waving "a large cord-wood stick" at the head of a party of "huzzaing, whistling" sailors. Samuel Quincy concluded, erroneously, that this evidence "fully proved" that the soldiers had deliberately opened fire on their own, informing the jurors that "you must pronounce them guilty."

Josiah Quincy, apparently unaware that he had been led off the scent by this red herring—addressing the relationship between redcoat and townie before the massacre, and not the events of the night of March 5 themselves—proceeded to introduce fifteen witnesses who testified to the persistent harassment of the redcoats since their arrival in Boston. This tactic dismayed his colleague John Adams, who told Quincy after a recess that he had taken the case to free the soldiers, not to indict the city of Boston. If Quincy continued in this vein, Adams said, he would have to retire from the defense. The real question at issue was what actually happened the night of March 5.

Quincy accepted this criticism and when the court reconvened, began systematically to build a powerful case against the crowd that harassed the soldiers on the night of March 5. Patrick Keaton testified that Crispus Attucks seized two four-foot logs from a wood pile and handed him one, while Andrew, appearing again as a witness, reported that the powerful Attucks, flailing the log about as though it were a mere ax handle, attacked a soldier who was compelled to parry his blows with his musket. Johnathon W. Austin, Adams's own law clerk, recited his fears that White would be carried off bodily at any moment, adding: "I thought if he came off with his life he would be doing very well." Most telling was the testimony of Dr. John Jeffries, a friend of Samuel Adams and an ardent patriot. Jeffries had attended the young Irish immigrant Patrick Carr as he lay dying. Dr. Jeffries recalled: "I asked him whether he thought the soldiers would have been hurt if they had not fired. He said he really thought they would be, for he heard many voices cry out kill them. I asked then … whether he thought they fired in self-defense, or on purpose to destroy the people. He said he really thought they did fire to defend themselves, that he did not blame the man, whoever he was, that shot him."

Self-defense, then, became the keystone of the defense's case. Both Quincy and Adams made dramatic and powerful perorations on that theme in their closing remarks to the jury, while the prosecution, in the person of Robert Treat Paine, who was ill and in any case convinced that he had "the severe side of the question," spoke at listless length as though he were the typical country lawyer "arguing for a fee." In two and a half hours the jury came in with a verdict of innocent for all the defendants except Killroy and Montgomery, who were convicted of manslaughter. Both pleaded benefit of clergy—an archaic ecclesiastical privilege by which the death sentence could be avoided and that really did not apply to soldiers—and each was branded on the thumb and discharged.

So ended in amity a near thing that could easily have triggered the escalating violence that so often ends in armed conflict. Rational people on both sides of the ocean breathed a sigh of relief, once they had caught this terrifying glimpse of the horrid face of Mars. A period of relative calm and mutual good will ensued. Even before the trial of Preston and his soldiers—in April 1770—the hated Townshend Acts had been repealed, not through the belligerence of Boston, but through the boycott of British goods. British exports to America had been cut in half, and all the late, unlamented Charles Townshend's "external taxes" except the levy on tea had been revoked. This gesture of conciliation did much to cultivate the spirit of quiescence spreading in America. Even the boycott sank into desuetude, attendance at Sons of Liberty meetings fell off—and Samuel Adams began to grieve for the slow death of the spirit of independence.

★ 10 ★

THE BOSTON TEA PARTY

Independence had not died. Like Lazarus, it was only sleeping, and it came bounding awake with the *Gaspee* Affair in Rhode Island.

Because of the geography of Narragansett Bay, the colony of Rhode Island had become the queen of the smugglers among all those thirteen seagoing sisters of the American seaboard. The bay, a large, protected body of water splitting Rhode Island in two, has many coves and inlets that were ideal as sanctuaries. By 1772 the Rhode Islanders had become so successful at evading payment of duties that the British Navy made a special effort to stop them. From his headquarters in Boston, the British fleet commander, Admiral John Montagu, an unusually efficient seaman, despatched the schooner *Gaspee,* under Lieutenant William Dudingston, also energetic and efficient, as well as arrogant and stiff necked, to patrol Narragansett Bay. Dudingston mortally offended the Rhode Islanders. They complained that he was "haughty, insolent, and intolerant, personally ill-treating every master and merchant of the vessels he boarded, stealing sheep, hogs, poultry, etc., from the farmers round the bay, and cutting down their fruit and other trees for firewood; in a word, his behavior was so piratical and provoking that Englishmen could not patiently bear it." Worse than all this, he had severely curtailed smuggling, so much so that Governor Joseph Wanton threatened to arrest him.

Hearing of this threat, Admiral Montagu warned Wanton that he was going to report him to the secretary of state for his "insolent letters" and that he had better not carry out his threat to send the sheriff aboard his ships. To this warning, Wanton replied: "I will send the sheriff of the colony at any time, and to any place … as I see fit."

While this battle of the "billets-doux" raged unchecked, Dudingston, aboard *Gaspee* on June 9, sighted a smuggler and gave chase, only to run aground on a sandbar a few miles from Providence. Overjoyed at this proof of their archenemy's putrid seamanship, as well as at a report that *Gaspee* would remain stuck until high tide, Sheriff Abraham Whipple sent a drummer boy to call surrounding residents to arms. A boarding party, drawn from the Sons of Liberty, was formed, and under Whipple's command a flotilla of small boats made for *Gaspee,* surrounding it.

Rushing on deck, Dudingston cried: "Who comes there?"

"I am the sheriff of the County of Kent, God damn you," Whipple answered. "I have a warrant to apprehend you, God damn you—so surrender, God damn you."

"I will admit no sheriff at this hour of night," Dudingston replied, and the boats closed in on *Gaspee,* approaching from the bow to avoid the ship's guns. They boarded, and the feeble resistance put up by crewmen roused from their sleep was swiftly overcome. While aiming a sword stroke at one of the boarders, Dudingston was struck in the groin by a bullet and had his arm smashed by a club that knocked him down.

"I am mortally wounded," Dudingston muttered, struggling erect, only to be knocked down again. "Damn it, you're not wounded," a boarder shouted angrily. "If you are, your own people done it." Actually, Dudingston was in severe pain, losing blood rapidly. He might have died if the boarders had not reluctantly ordered him carried below, where two surgeons patched him up. Carried on a blanket-stretcher, he was placed in a longboat and rowed toward Pawtucket, his progress over black glittering water illuminated by the flames of his ship, which burned to the waterline and was an utter loss.

News of the *Gaspee* Affair thrilled the Americans and infuriated the government of Lord North. A king's ship had been seized and destroyed in a bloody attack! No bolder, more insolent insult could be imagined, and a commission was at once formed in America to collect evidence. But to find among these friends and neighbors of Abraham Whipple and his sea guerrillas anyone foolish or disloyal enough to testify against them was as easy as discovering teardrops in a bucket of water, and the commission finally announced its inability to make a case.

But the enraged Crown had other arrows in its quiver. Lord North threatened to try the accused men—even though there were no accusers—in Britain. Here the most basic of British liberties—the right to be tried by one's peers, that is, by men of one's own community—was menaced. If this could be done in the *Gaspee* Affair, what of the Patriot leaders? Would they all be rounded up and deported to London, to be tried there for treason? Though the Crown wisely decided not to pursue the affair further, rather than give the hitherto slumbering colonies a cause célèbre, its change to a stance of conciliation was too late. The colonies had already been effectively aroused once more.

When Britain sought to influence the colonial courts by paying judges out of the royal treasury, Massachusetts countered with offers of higher pay. Next, Samuel Adams, alarmed by the danger to liberty implied in the threat to try the *Gaspee* offenders for piracy in Britain, organized the first Committee of Correspondence to act as an information network for all the towns of the Bay Colony. Other colonies followed suit, and an efficent chain of communication was established. Thus by 1773 the colonies were ready for the next intrusion upon their liberties, for the East India Company—a mercantilist creature of the North government—was by then begging Lord North to do something about the Yankees' refusal to buy its tea.

King George had kept the tax on tea because he believed "there must always be one tax" to maintain the right to tax. The Americans thought otherwise and gleefully evaded the odious duty by buying mostly smuggled tea. This evasion, together with the company's incredible corruption and arrogant exploitation of the subcontinent of India, had brought it close to bankruptcy. To understand the loathing that the intelligentsia and merchants of America felt for the East India Company, one need only read the judgment of the historian Lecky: "They defied, displaced or intimidated all native functionaries who attempted to resist them. They refused to permit any other traders to sell the goods in which they dealt. They even descended upon villages and forced the inhabitants, by flogging and confinement, to purchase their goods at exorbitant prices, or to sell what they desired to purchase at prices far below the market value.... Monopolizing the trade in some of the first necessaries of life, to the utter ruin of thousands of native traders, and selling those necessaries at famine prices to a half-starving population, they reduced those who came under their influence to a wretchedness never known before." Moreover, company officials spent more time enriching themselves than attending to business. It was because of the East India Company's reputation for exploitation and corruption, as much as for its high prices, that the colonists refused to buy its tea.

As a result some 17 million pounds of tea had accumulated in the company's London warehouses. Without quick access to the American market, much of it would become rotten—and that might be the last straw to break the East India Company's back. At this juncture Lord North came up with what appeared to be a clever idea. The company paid two taxes: one when it landed its tea in Britain for sale or transshipment, another of three-penny a pound when it landed the shipment in America. North decided to forgive the British tax and keep the smaller American duty, making East India tea even cheaper than the smuggled product. North knew that the Yankee cousins were inveterate tea drinkers and believed that tea so cheap would sweep away any scruples about tax while delighting their thrifty—not to say penny-pinching—hearts.

But it would not.

The Yankee cousins were by then sick and tired of being the milch cow on the British mercantilist farm. They wanted a farm of their own, a democratic farm in which, like George Orwell's *Animal Farm,* "all animals are equal." The fact that most of the tea was to be shipped to Tory merchants—usually relatives of that Prince of Nepotism, Thomas Hutchinson—may have been as big a blunder as North's crass conviction that the Americans would scrimp on anything—even their cherished liberty—to save a penny. It threw mostly moderate Patriot merchants straight into the arms of the Sons of Liberty. Together with dealers in smuggled tea, who were determined to prevent the introduction of cheaper tea into the colonies, they flocked to the mass meetings under the Liberty Trees. Once again political and economic forces were joined, and soon American ship captains were refusing to ship East India tea aboard their vessels. The astutely agitating merchants of Philadelphia had branded anyone who approved of the Tea Act "an enemy to his country," and "the whole country was in a blaze from Maine to Georgia." Like the stamp agents before them, the new tea agents hastily resigned, rather than risk a tar and feathering and a ride out of town on a rail. It remained now to prevent receipt of the tea.

The Patriots of New York and Philadelphia had compelled the masters of the ships carrying tea to their ports to turn about and head back to London. In Charleston, after tedious negotiation, the tea was landed but locked up in a warehouse and never sold. What, then, would Boston do? The answer to that question was what Thomas Hutchinson did. By then, unfortunately, for the Mother Country, the usually flexible Hutchinson had had enough of his tempestuous fellow Americans. What they had done to his splendid home and library would have been enough to disenchant the saintliest of men, and when to this was added the constant defiance and bickering of the succeeding decade he had become indeed embittered against them. Being bitter, he was thus obtuse and vengeful. He would not, like the other royal governors, stand aside and let the shipowners, captains and consignees meet with the enraged colonists to negotiate the question of allowing the tea to be landed. If he had, and a great procession of unloaded tea ships began streaming back to Britain, Lord North would have had no choice but to capitulate and try to save face. Certainly, His Majesty's first minister, mindful of the Boston Massacre, was not going to send redcoats overseas to compel the colonists to buy East India tea. Hutchinson, however, was not now as conciliatory as were his fellow governors. He may even have been hoping that he could provoke the Sons of Liberty to set in motion some new deviltry and thus call down upon themselves the unrestrained wrath of Parliament. So when the *Dartmouth* arrived in Boston Harbor with a cargo of tea, to be followed by *Eleanor* and *Beaver*, similarly loaded, he ordered Admiral Montagu to close the harbor mouth so no ship might return to Britain. He did so even though the owners of these three vessels had promised the Patriots that the ships would return unloaded.

Now it was up to the Sons of Liberty.

They had assembled at Old South Church when the colonist Captain Francis Rotch reported to them that the port was indeed under blockade. The leaders of the meeting—Samuel Adams and the lawyers Josiah Quincy and John Rowe—directed Rotch to appeal to Hutchinson to rescind the order. While awaiting his return, the crowd grew to an incredible seven thousand, both inside and outside the church. Adams, Quincy and Rowe seemed exceptionally calm—even preternaturally so—almost licking their chops like the cat that swallowed the canary. Obviously, they did have a plan, the nature of which was revealed when Rowe asked the throng: "Who knows how tea will mingle with salt water?" A great shout of laughter arose.

At six o'clock Captain Rotch returned to say that Hutchinson would not withdraw his order. At this news, Adams stepped into the pulpit and said: "This meeting can do nothing more to save the country." As though on cue, an Indian war whoop arose outside, and three troops of "Mohawks"—paint or dust-smeared braves with bright blue eyes—went racing down Milk Street to Griffin's Wharf. Fifty men to a troop, they clambered into boats and rowed across the darkened harbor to the three tea ships riding at anchor. George Hewes remembered that the troops were "ordered ... to board all the ships at the same time"—which was done. Aboard one of the ships, Hewes demanded that the captain give him the keys to the hatches and a dozen candles. "We were then ordered to open the hatches and take out all the chests of tea and throw them overboard, and we immediately proceeded to execute orders, first cutting and splitting the chests with our tomahawks, so as thoroughly to expose them to the effects of the water." Everything was done quietly, with none of the war whoops of Yankee mythology and no interference from the captain or crew. In three hours Boston Bay had been turned into a huge teapot, and the Mohawks returned to their bobbing boats and departed as silently as they had come.

Said Hewes: "There appeared to be an understanding that each individual should volunteer his services, keep his own secret and risk the consequences for himself. No disorder took place during that transaction, and it was observed at that time that the stillest night ensued that Boston had enjoyed for many months."

"No disorder" indeed, but John Adams, upon his return to Boston the following night, saw at once that the Boston Tea Party was to have consequences "so lasting, that I can't but consider it as an epocha in history." It was indeed, this bold and dramatic challenge to the most powerful nation in the world. It captured the hearts of the friends of America everywhere. In the House of Commons Edmund Burke arose with a reasoned and eloquent plea: "Leave the Americans as they anciently stood.... Let the memory of all actions in contradiction to that good old mode be extinguished forever. Be content to bind America by laws of trade; you have always done it.... Do not burthen them with taxes; you were not used to do so from the beginning."

But even the heartfelt eloquence of this master political pragmatist could not move hearts hardened by a decade in which condescension was added to misconception and hatred was piled upon prejudice, and in the hearts that counted most—those of George III and most of the members of Parliament—there burned a horrible ache for revenge. A member named Van seemed to speak for most of his colleagues when he came snarling to his feet with that ancient Roman cry of vindication: "*Delenda est Carthago!* Carthage is destroyed! I am of the opinion that you will never meet with that proper obedience to the laws of this country until you have destroyed that nest of locusts."

King George and Lord North were both enraged, and the king himself declared: "We must master them or totally leave them to themselves and treat them as aliens." Both Boston, that hotbed of treason, and Massachusetts, that schoolhouse of rebellion, were to be brought rudely to heel. Boston was to be closed as a port, leaving Marblehead and Salem the only ports in the colony, while Massachusetts was to suffer in its charter: its Assembly was to continue to function, but its upper chamber, the Council, was to be appointed by the king. Lesser judges, sheriffs and other officials were to be appointed by the governor, the king's man. Town meetings, the soul of self-rule in the colony, were to be held only once a year to elect officers, and otherwise only by permission of the governor. Anyone indicted for a capital offense connected with a riot or revenue laws was to be tried either in Britain or in another colony, and, finally, troops were to be quartered in Boston.

These were the four Coercive Acts, which the now-seething colonies decried as "the Intolerable Acts." Not every Briton approved them, nor were they passed by a unanimous vote of Parliament. One by one the Coercive Acts were opposed and denounced by the steadfast friends of America, led by Burke and Barré, who pleaded with customary eloquence for a policy of conciliation. But George was adamant. The royal rod was out, and the colonies were to be chastised. There would be no more indulgence of that cowardly argument that such a policy would only provoke American confederation and rebellion—perhaps even independence. The king's sole concern after passage of the acts was to find a man who was qualified to tame the Yankee troublemakers, a man of soldierly discipline and political acumen, who was also familiar with America—and he quickly found him in the person of Lieutenant General Thomas Gage.

★ 11 ★

THOMAS GAGE

Thomas Gage was born in 1721, the second son of an obscure noble family distinguished only by what their peers regarded as a curiously unyielding attachment to their proscribed Catholic faith. His father was the first Viscount Gage, a political dilettante and—what was worse in the eyes of his fellow aristocrats—hopelessly in need of funds until his oldest son married a wealthy Jewish heiress. Thomas's mother was suspected of sexual promiscuity, a not-uncommon activity among the noble matrons of the day, and one eminently more acceptable socially than her foreign creed or modest fortune.

But Thomas's appearance came much earlier than the introduction of great wealth into the family, so that, like most younger sons of the needier nobility, he found himself limited to following a career either in the church or in the army. After eight years at Westminster School, where he met and befriended the sons of more prominent earls and barons, he chose the military. By then his brother William, the future Lord Gage, had made his splendid marriage and was able to lend him the money to buy a commission, again the accepted practice of the day. William was also of use when he "inherited" the family seat in the House of Commons, so that after fifteen years of service—including combat against the French in Flanders and the Jacobites in northern Britain—big, handsome, genial "Tommy" Gage at thirty held the rank of lieutenant colonel. Through the influence of the Keppels—his friends at Westminster—he received a "pretty" appointment as aide-de-camp to their father, the Earl of Albermarle.

Such service could be of inestimable value to an officer on the make, and in 1755 it was to prove so for Tommy Gage. Gage commanded Braddock's three-hundred-man advance party that was ambushed and all but massacred at the Monongahela by the French and their Indians. Although Gage bravely strove to halt the rout, he could do nothing with his panic-stricken men, a fact ignored by modern historians who are critical of his conduct. There was not in His Majesty's armed forces a single officer—for that matter a single redcoat—who was familiar with the tactics of forest warfare in which the French were adept. Nevertheless, Gage did not show himself then, or at any time thereafter, the born commander who knows instinctively how to adjust to a surprising situation. Actually, he blamed his own defeat on his men, a rather ungallant attempt to escape responsibility; and when, hearing that the colonel of his regiment had been killed, he immediately asked, but was not given, promotion to the vacancy, even those fellow officers who shared his cynicism blushed.

Thereafter in his long service in America, Thomas Gage was to show that he was hardly more than a courageous plodder. His outstanding achievement in the New World was to raise and train a regiment of light infantry based upon the forest-fighting tactics of the American Rangers led by Robert Rogers, but without their tendency to indiscipline and riot. He led them in 1758 under General James Abercrombie in the unsuccessful assault on Fort Ticonderoga (French Carillon), but there is no record of any unusual contribution by Gage. When Lord Jeffrey Amherst ordered him to support Wolfe's attack on Quebec in 1759 with an assault on La Galette at the head of the St. Lawrence, he failed with the customary catalog of excuses or shifts of blame. Next he took command at Fort Niagara after the French had failed in their own foolish belief that bayonets could conquer a fixed, fortified position. But he learned nothing from this shocking sight of mangled corpses in white uniforms red with blood, just as he failed to profit from his experiences at the Monongahela, Ticonderoga and La Galette. During six years' service in America, he had acquired a reputation for, in Amherst's acid phrase, "finding difficulties where there were none." It might also have been that having finally gotten his own regiment, plus a brigadier general's star and the title of second in command in North America, Tommy Gage was content.

Certainly his financial fortunes had improved immensely through his marriage in the summer of 1758 to Margaret Kemble, daughter of a wealthy New Jersey family. Margaret was with him in 1760 when he became military commander of Montreal. There, relieved of the stress of combat with its terrifying imperatives of instant decision and rapid reaction, his qualities of intelligence, tact and patience came to the fore. His obvious desire to understand a people who had once been his enemies endeared him to them, and when he left Montreal to squelch an Indian uprising in 1763, they mourned his departure. Gage's campaign against the Indians in 1764, though successful and almost bloodless, owing more to the western tribes' failure to destroy the British garrisons at Detroit, Niagara and Fort Pitt the previous year, was also arduous and time consuming. After British victory in the Seven Years' War, the problem of preventing another costly Indian rebellion was foremost in Westminster's mind when it reorganized its forces in North America.

Fifteen regiments were to be kept on the mainland, strung out from Nova Scotia in the north to Florida and the Gulf Coast in the south. From his headquarters in New York, Major General Thomas Gage was to command this force of six-thousand men who were holding over a thousand miles of alternating civilization and wilderness. Such a costly garrison was to lead to the British Parliament's attempt to raise taxes in the colonies: the root cause of rebellion in America. Moreover, it was not exactly clear why it was needed, if only because there was nothing to fear from Canada again and the massive emptiness of the Florida and the trans-Appalachian regions certainly could not be policed by a few rustic garrisons. Any renewed incursion by France or Spain or both could be repulsed by British sea power. Rather, it seems more likely that this reorganization of 1765 was for the unspoken purpose of keeping the colonists "in due subordination." Vergennes's warning that the colonies would reward the Mother Country for ending the French menace to the north by seeking independence from her had fallen upon open ears in Parliament, and the riots succeeding passage of the Sugar and Stamp Acts had rung in them with the clang of alarm bells.

Yet, Tommy Gage never gave the aroused colonists the slightest hint of his deep distrust of them and his belief that the remedy for an unruly mob, as Napoleon was to sneer three decades later, was "a whiff of grape." In 1768 he wrote to Lord Barrington, secretary at war: "Quash this spirit at a blow without so much regard to the expense and it will prove economy in the end." And again: "If the principles of moderation and forebearance are again adopted ... there will be an end to these provinces as British colonies." Even after the Boston Massacre, in which he was able to maintain his image of moderation, Gage was still trusted. Patriot leaders, such as Dr. Joseph Warren, could consider him "a man of honest, upright principles." But then in 1773, to his immense relief, Gage was recalled to London. Whether the decision was his or Westminster's is not known, but it is likely that Gage had been unable to bear the galling strain of dissimulating to these arrogant, upstart Americans or the stress of dealing with a far-flung, poorly supplied, miserable and resentful army while whirling about like a weather vane under the flow of conflicting orders from the erratic government that had succeeded the great William Pitt. So he went home, probably hoping that his friend Barrington's influence with young King George III might fetch him a less trying governorship or even a profitable sinecure. Within a week of his arrival in London, he had an interview with the new sovereign, who was much impressed with his advice that the colonists "will be lions while we are lambs, but if we take the resolute part they will undoubtedly be very meek."

This was exactly the sort of bad advice that delighted the ponderous, slow mind of this Teutonic ruler of the English, Welsh, Scots and Irish, and he swallowed it with relish. In the following year, after George the German lifted his royal rod to chastise the rebellious Yankees, he recalled this little homily on lambs and lions, and Tommy Gage went sailing back to America.

⋆ 12 ⋆

GAGE TAKES OVER

A cold rain fell from a codfish sky on that momentous May 17, 1774, when Lieutenant General Thomas Gage arrived in Boston to take command of His Majesty's troops in America and to assume office as governor of Massachusetts Bay.

The enforcer of the Coercive Acts—for Gage's two hats, or sticks, had been given to him to beat both the port and province to their knees—met with a mixed reception. The Patriots who greeted him with chill propriety remembered that it was Gage's troops who had perpetrated the Boston Massacre, and they grimly deduced that he had come again to destroy their liberties. The Tories who joyfully welcomed him recalled his military service in America, as well as his marriage into the Loyalist Kemble family of New Jersey, and they rejoiced that the king had sent them just the man to make Yankee Doodle dance.

It was not long, however, before Gage realized that if Yankee Doodle did dance, he preferred to call the tunes himself. For weeks after Gage's arrival, church bells tolled dolefully, prayer and fasting were proclaimed and mourning badges were displayed. Gage's answer was to put the Boston Port Act into effect on June 1 with a sweeping totality that left the town paralyzed.

"Did a lighter attempt to land hay from the islands, or a boat to bring in sand from the neighboring hills, or a scow to freight to it lumber or iron, or a float to land sheep, or a farmer to carry marketing over in the ferry-boats, the argus-eyed fleet was ready to see it, and prompt to capture or destroy it."

Such Draconian thoroughness succeeded only in making a martyr of Boston. Though many abruptly unemployed people fled to the countryside, most of Boston's twenty thousand inhabitants remained within the city. And they did not starve, for the rest of the colonies rallied to Boston's side. Flour, cattle, fish and other foods came pouring into the blockaded city from all over New England. From the distant Carolinas came supplies of rice; from Delaware, money—and even Quebec sent a thousand bushels of wheat. Boston was abjured to stand firm, to refuse to ransom her economic life by paying for the destroyed tea.

Boston did not waver, and on June 17 the General Assembly of Massachusetts met in Salem to protest the removal of the capital to that place. Gage sent an order dissolving the assembly, but the doors were locked against his emissary. Inside, the aroused assembly made its historic proposal for a Continental Congress of the colonies and elected delegates to represent Massachusetts.

Shortly thereafter Gage's task of subduing these stiff-necked Yankees was made even more difficult. The Quebec Act had been passed by Parliament and signed into law by King George. It was probably the most statesmanlike measure of George's stormy reign, yet it came at absolutely the wrong moment for the American colonies. Extending the Province of Quebec to include the French-speaking settlements in the valley of the Ohio and the Illinois country, the law also recognized French civil law and the Roman Catholic Church in Canada. Thus the abhorred religion was to be guaranteed in the North and a fresh obstacle to colonial expansion was erected in the West. It was as though Canada had never been conquered, and the colonies saw red. Meanwhile, the Continental Congress met in Philadelphia.

No new nation a 'borning was ever blessed with such practical political midwives as those fifty-six delegates to the Continental Congress, who gathered in Carpenter's Hall in Philadelphia for their first session on September 5, 1774. Pragmatic men all, whether doctor, lawyer, farmer, miller, planter, carpenter or even shoemaker turned judge, they were in incredible contrast to the theoretical geniuses who assembled in Paris fifteen years later to chart the course of the French Revolution. Indeed, John Dickinson of Pennsylvania—known as "Farmer John" for his celebrated *Letters from a Farmer in Pennsylvania to the Inhabitants of the British Colonies*—set the policy to be followed with what was perhaps the Congress's most perceptive insight: "Experience must be our only guide. Reason will betray us." How drastically reason could mislead was demonstrated by the French thinkers, brilliant men like the Abbé Sieyes, able to turn out a new system every other day or two; always, like the Communists of the twentieth century, leaving out human nature so that the revolt in France, unlike the one beginning here in Philadelphia, ended in bloodbath and dictatorship.

All the delegates were middle-aged property owners, most of them in comfortable circumstances, some actually wealthy, only one poor—but even Samuel Adams was able to appear in Philadelphia in a handsome new suit and carriage. The legal profession, once held in low esteem, was now obviously among the most respectable, no less than thirty of the delegates being lawyers or jurists. Judge Roger Sherman of Connecticut made his cobbler's bench—at which he taught himself law—a step up to the judicial bench. Nine others were planters or farmers, while nine were merchants, three were millers, three were officeholders and one was a carpenter. All but one—born in Wales—were native born and could trace their family histories back from one to four generations to England, Scotland, Wales or Ireland. In the main they were at least as well educated as were the members of Parliament. In fact, twelve of them had been educated in Britain. Leading the list of schools were the Inns of Court—those ancient London law schools—with seven, Harvard with five, Yale with three, William and Mary with three, the College of Philadelphia (now the University of Pennsylvania) with two, the College of New Jersey (now Princeton University), King's College (now Columbia University) and Edinburgh University with one apiece.

Three days before the Congress convened, a meeting that was perhaps even more significant was held by the Massachusetts and Virginia delegates. Virginia and Massachusetts were the two oldest colonies, and while the Bay Colony was the northern axis of the opposition to the Crown, the Old Dominion was the southern axis. But it was only in these two situations that they were similar; in all else—in character, religion, economy and society—they were as dissimilar as simplicity differs from elegance, these Yankee Puritans and southern Cavaliers, and if they had failed to get along, it is safe to say that there might not have been an American Revolution, or at least not then.

Puritan Massachusetts was the birthplace of what has been called "the American work ethic" and the spirit of free enterprise, eventually to be known as democratic capitalism. Because it was democratic, it was sometimes jealous of excellence, or at least of social superiority, so much so that John Adams himself could declare that his fellow Calvinists were so disdainful of lordly people that, once in Heaven—to which they all believed themselves predestined—they would strive to limit the power of the Almighty. This was the "leveling spirit of New England"—the belief that "I'm just as good as the next man and maybe even a little better"—that the aristocratic Cavaliers of Virginia despised. The men whom the

Virginians greeted that day seemed to be the apotheosis of the Yankee, typical votaries of the money god Mammon: Thomas Cushing, the successful merchant-turned-politician; John Adams and Robert Treat Paine, flourishing county courthouse lawyers; and Samuel Adams, looking like a diffident clerk. But if the Southerners could have looked into Samuel's heart, they would have been shocked to see that it not only burned for liberty, but also beat—not for democracy—but for a theocracy similar to William Bradford's intolerant Plymouth Colony, alongside which Britain's "oppressive" rule would seem a paragon of permissiveness, indeed.

Conversely, these Puritans saw the Virginians as lovers of democracy who carried themselves like noblemen, for theirs was an agricultural and semifeudal society. The society of Virginia was rigidly structured, with these Cavaliers—the great planters—presiding over the pyramid from its apex, with the yeoman farmers, tradesman and merchants below them, the despised and impoverished "mudsills" of the frontier lower still, and the black slaves at the base. Because Virginia was aristocratic, it was able—like ancient Greece and eighteenth-century Britain—to produce men of outstanding ability. Present in the New City Tavern on this momentous September 2, 1774, was Peyton Randolph, Speaker of the Virginia House of Burgesses, who joined the ungentle political tactics of a ward heeler to the gracious manners of a grand duke. Richard Henry Lee was also there, a thinker and a man as tall and thin as Colonel Benjamin Harrison was wide and fat. Colonel Richard Bland was a subtle pamphleteer in the cause of liberty, striking John Adams as "a learned, bookish man."

It would seem almost certain that such disparate men would have distrusted each other on sight, or at least have been wary of working together; yet, because they shared such a common passion for American freedom, they formed the unlikely Yankee-Cavalier coalition that eventually was to control the Congress on the side of the radicals. When Patrick Henry arrived, the union was strengthened, for even though the New Englanders found him somewhat flamboyant, they saw that he was a solid Patriot with a practical grasp of the problems at hand. George Washington's impression upon "the Boston Gentlemen" was extremely favorable. His frankness and honesty, together with his direct and careful way of speaking, endeared him to them, while he, in turn, was pleased to find them hardheaded and shrewd politicians, rather than the band of wild-eyed rabble-rousers he expected to meet.

In the rough-and-tumble of politics, seemingly trivial disagreements often become the focal dispute that can set the tone of any gathering. Thus, at the outset a seemingly mild standoff ensued when Philadelphia offered the delegates Carpenter's Hall, while Joseph Galloway, the wealthy conservative from Pennsylvania, offered the State House, where he was the Speaker. The radicals opposed this proposal because it came from Galloway and because Carpenter's Hall had been built by the city's skilled workmen with their own labor, it would stand as a symbol of the Congress's democratic nature—and they won. In the choice of a secretary Galloway chose Silas Deane of Connecticut, seemingly a Son of Liberty, but actually a self-seeking trimmer. The radicals countered with Charles Thomson, "the Sam Adams of Philadelphia," who was chosen. Finally when Patrick Henry arose, looking like a clergyman in his suit of parson's gray, he sank Galloway into deep gloom when he declared, to thunderous applause: "The distinctions between Virginians, Pennsylvanians, New Yorkers and New Englanders are no more. I am not a Virginian, but an American."

This steady repulse of the conservatives—mostly from New York, New Jersey and Pennsylvania—continued when Galloway presented his plan of union. The plan's principal feature was continued allegiance to Britain through a British-American legislature that alone would possess taxing powers in the colonies, under the jurisdiction of a grand council and a president-general. Galloway's plan was essentially a diversionary tactic, calculated to appeal to timid spirits who were reluctant to make bold decisions. It also avoided any reference to what was to be done about Boston. As the historian Page Smith observed, if it did not give up "any one liberty" or "any one right," it certainly gave up Boston—and it was defeated under spirited radical attack led by Patrick Henry. Henceforth Galloway and his supporters were committed to bitter but ineffectual delaying action, which for Galloway would end in self-imposed exile in London.

At the very outset the delegates realized that they had no real constituencies, that whatever they did actually bound no one. As Patrick Henry would say: "We are in a state of nature." Nor did any of these delegates, whether radical or conservative, as yet envision a direct break with the Mother Country. John Adams, who eventually became the most influential and respected man at the Congress, spoke for all delegates when he said: "There is no man among us who would not be happy to see accommodation with Britain."

But then Paul Revere galloped into town, his saddlebags bulging with news from the north. Massachusetts had defied General Gage and set up its own Provincial Congress. The explosive Suffolk Resolves had been passed. They were read out before a hushed and thrilled Continental Congress: the Coercive Acts were "the arbitrary will of a licentious minister"; they were "murderous law," and because of them the streets of

Boston were "thronged with military executioners"; the Quebec Act was "dangerous to an extreme degree to the Protestant religion and to the civil rights and liberties of all America." Therefore the Suffolk Resolves advised that Massachusetts form its own government to collect taxes and withhold them from the royal government until the Coercive Acts were nullified. The people of the colony were to arm and form their own militia. The most severe economic sanctions must be brought to bear on Britain.

The hearts of the radicals lifted. The standard of implacable opposition was at last being raised. Moderates also were carried away. Swarms of shouting delegates engulfed the men from Massachusetts. Without changing a comma, the Congress adopted the Suffolk Resolves. Then, calling for the third and most stringent boycott of British goods, it served notice on Parliament that the colonies were no longer bound by its laws outside purely commercial regulations. The king was politely informed that his prerogatives must conform to the Americans' ideas of their liberties and his authority.

No one had yet spoken of rebellion or independence or an appeal to arms. But the American Revolution had begun. In Boston the war which was fought to preserve that revolt was beginning to sputter.

General Gage had been steadily accumulating troops. He called for workmen to build barracks. None came forward. Though unemployed, no one cared or dared to work for the "lobsterbacks." Gage sent to New York and Halifax for workmen, and the Bostonians began a campaign of sabotage. Brick barges were sunk, straw for soldiers' beds was burned, and wagons were overturned. Enraged, Gage countered by sending soldiers over to Charlestown and Cambridge to seize colonial powder and cannon. The troops carried out his orders, but their little foray gave Massachusetts an opportunity to carry out a dress rehearsal for the later reality of mobilization.

News of the seizure spread swiftly throughout the province. Details of the coup were so magnified that the Continental Congress heard the absurd news that Gage had bombarded Boston. Nevertheless, by the day following the seizure, some four thousand armed and angry men had come crowding into Cambridge, while all over New England other men were on the march. Gage blinked and took note. Now he began to fortify the narrow neck of land linking Boston to the mainland. The Provincial Congress replied by appropriating the huge sum of £15,627 to purchase military supplies. It called for the organization of "minutemen"; named three generals to command its militia; set up a Committee of Safety under Dr. Joseph Warren to take over its own duties once it had ceased to exist; and then, on December 10, having set up all the apparatus for rebellion, dissolved itself.

Gage too late proclaimed all the acts of the vanished Provincial Congress as treasonable. His attempts to undo its mischief were like the sound of a cannon trying to overtake the flash. Everywhere in New England men were drilling on the green. Guns and powder were being stolen from British forts. Colonial supplies were increasing. To counter American thefts of munitions, Gage sent a British expedition to Salem on February 26, 1775. The British met the colonial militia under Colonel Timothy Pickering at an open bridge.

Pickering refused to obey the British demand to lower the drawbridge. Finally, a Salem clergyman intervened. He persuaded the militia to lower the bridge on the British promise to march only thirty rods into the town and return. It was done, but the redcoats discovered nothing but the Yankee willingness to fight.

Marching home, the British passed through the town of Northfields, where a nurse named Sarah Tarrant called to them from an open window: "Go home and tell your master he has sent you on a fool's errand and broken the peace of our Sabbath. What, do you think we were born in the woods, to be frightened by owls?"

Stung, one of the soldiers pointed his gun at her, and Nurse Tarrant scoffed: "Fire, if you have the courage—but I doubt it."

A month later the fierce spirit of resistance sweeping through America caught fire in Virginia. There, Patrick Henry arose in the House of Burgesses to declare:

> There is no retreat but in submission and slavery! Our chains are forged. Their clanking may be heard on the plains of Boston! The war is inevitable—and let it come! I repeat it, sir, let it come!
>
> It is in vain, sir, to extenuate the matter. Gentlemen may cry, 'Peace! Peace!'—but there is no peace. The war is actually begun! The next gale that sweeps down from the north will bring to our ears the clash of resounding arms! Our brethren are already in the field! Why stand we here idle? What is it that gentlemen wish? What would they have? Is life so dear, or peace so sweet, as to be purchased at the price of chains and slavery? Forbid it, Almighty God! I know not what course others may take, but as for me, give me liberty or give me death!

The choice was not a month away, and by then the Patriots were ready. If General Gage tried to crush them, they had an arsenal and a militia, thanks in great part to Dr. Joseph Warren, and a spy system and courier service led by Paul Revere.

★ 13 ★

DR. JOSEPH WARREN AND PAUL REVERE

Joseph Warren was a descendant of one Peter Warren, a British sailor whose birthplace and birthdate are not known, but who probably arrived in the New World sometime in the 1650s, either as an immigrant or as a seaman who jumped ship upon his arrival in Massachusetts. In 1654 he was working for a fisherman named Matthew Cannedge on the lonely island of Monhegan off the coast of what is now Maine. After Cannedge was murdered in a quarrel with one Gregory Cassell who "was in drink … [and] struck him on the head with a hammer as he was about to mend his shoes," Warren migrated to Roxbury just outside Boston. There he became a minor official, married and founded the Warren family, from which was descended perhaps the most distinguished medical family in American history.

His great-grandson, Joseph Warren, was the first of these physicians. Joseph was born on May 29, 1740, a year to the day after his father, also named Joseph, at age forty-five married Mary Stevens, a comely woman seventeen years younger than he was. Joseph, Senior, became a prosperous farmer, although his affluence was no deterrent to his sending his son bare legged into the Boston market to peddle milk. Young Joseph had a happy childhood on his father's farm, climbing the apple trees to munch on the fruit or helping to pick it for sweet and hard cider, riding over the meadows and through the marsh on the farm's little black horse, milking, or hunting and fishing in the woods. Both recreation and farm chores were to confer on Joseph good health, exceptional strength and a fine physique: with his broad shoulders and deep chest, he stood somewhere about five feet eight or five feet ten inches in height. He was also handsome, with wide-set gray eyes and a face that, in repose, reflected an inner gentleness. He hoped to attend Harvard College, but the attainment of this ambition seemed doomed, or at least delayed, when his father fell from an apple tree and broke his neck. At fourteen, Joseph was now the head of the family, seemingly charged with a heavy responsibility that would end his education. However, his mother insisted that he continue it, taking over the farm herself and spending a substantial £266 to send Joseph to Harvard for four years. There he earned a reputation as an outstanding student, but no bookworm, lighthearted and given to pranks. His later political enemy Peter Oliver described him as a boy "possessed of genius which promised distinction."

That promise seemed to be fulfilled after Joseph, like John Adams, spent two years at home studying for his master's degree. Joseph's thesis was on medicine, for he had already decided he wanted to be a doctor, and it was fully as abstract and as abstruse as a classmate's paper on whether or not Adam had an umbilical cord and a belly button.

In those days only a few youths in the colonies could afford to be educated in the great medical schools of Europe. Instead, all but these few chose a preceptor, that is, an established physician under whom they would serve an apprenticeship, usually of five years. Joseph Warren chose Dr. James Lloyd, a renowned Boston physician who had not only completed such a novitiate himself, but had afterward gone to Britain to study under leading surgeons there. Lloyd came home to found a thriving practice in obstetrics and general medicine and to introduce the use of ligatures, or stitches, rather than searing to stop an incision from bleeding, as well as new techniques in amputation. Warren selected Lloyd because of his reputation and because he kept a large number of students in his home. It was a wise decision, for he learned the most advanced techniques of the European medical schools, while becoming an advocate of the smallpox inoculation introduced by Abigail Adams's uncle, Zabdiel Boylston. As an apprentice, he learned the practical side of his profession by practicing it. Because most doctors then were their own apothecaries, he also became expert in compounding drugs for Lloyd's patients. Clinical experience flowed from dressing wounds and an understanding of diagnois, from accompanying Lloyd on his rounds. But his opportunity to demonstrate his genius did not come until the dreadful smallpox epidemic of 1763.

Two theories of the cause of epidemics were then current in the colonies. One was that a disease was transmitted by air, food and water and that cure and prevention should emphasize sanitation; the other was that it was carried by contagion and could be controlled only by isolation. Because of the second theory, Boston had enacted laws placing incoming ships in quarantine and fences, red flags and guards around the homes of afflicted families. Inoculation, though introduced as long ago as 1721, still had no such acceptance as either of these two theories. Because it actually infected a person with a mild case of the disease to secure immunity to it, many private people were afraid to risk the needle, most clergymen found it a blasphemy upon the will of God and quite a few physicians either distrusted it or were not convinced of its efficacy. Thus the lower house of the General Court, or colonial legislature, refused to approve an inoculation hospital. But Joseph Warren and other advocates of the process, assisted by the governor and his council, were able to open two private hospitals, and it was at the one at Castle William in Boston Harbor that Warren and another doctor became resident physicians. For eight months, they stayed at their posts night and day, nursing their inoculated patients through their milder attacks of the disease, while across the harbor in Boston the epidemic created a panic causing many householders to pack their families and belongings onto wagons and head for the safety of the countryside. After the epidemic ended, the value of inoculation was conclusively demonstrated. Of 699 persons who were infected naturally, 124 died, while of 4,977 who were inoculated, only 46 perished.

From this triumph Dr. Joseph Warren emerged as one of Boston's heroes, and the practice he opened there became an immediate success. As it grew, his patients numbered some of the most famous names in town, almost all of them, like Warren himself, ardent in the Patriot cause: John and Samuel Adams, James Otis, John Hancock, the Quincys, Thomas Cushing and others. As his practice increased, so did his wealth. Eventually he would have thousands of patients either visiting his office or receiving him on house calls. Unknowingly, he was building a political base. His charm, gentleness, skill and scrupulous honesty endeared him to artisans, clerks, mechanics and laborers, as well as to the great names that might be in politics for sordid reasons. Dr. Warren, however, could be accused of no such motive when he entered politics. He also numbered among his patients the leading editors, lawyers and merchants of the city, and his circle of friends expanded after he joined the St. Andrew Lodge of Freemasons, eventually becoming its grand master. Most significant for him as a Patriot was his deepening association with Samuel Adams, and this unlikely pair eventually came to be regarded as the radicals of the radical. He regularly attended the monthly meetings of Adams's Sons of Liberty, held in a distillery a few doors from his home, and was a respected director of Paul Revere's mechanics group, which caucased in the North End.

In the summer of 1764 Dr. Warren, at twenty-four, met and fell in love with eighteen-year-old Elizabeth Hooton, said to be one of the most beautiful girls in Boston. Elizabeth was also wealthy, having inherited a "handsome sum" from her father, a deceased merchant. They were married September 6 of that year. Four children were born of the marriage, but Elizabeth died eight years later at the age of twenty-six. When Revere's wife died a week later, the two men became bound closer in their mutual grief, and both, probably seeking distraction from sorrow, plunged deeper into politics. During 1765, the year of the Stamp Act, Dr. Warren, in his relentless opposition to that despised piece of legislation, emerged as a consumate, if sometimes scurrilous, propagandist.

And so the rise of this amazingly popular energetic physician was steady: chairman of the Committee of Safety, president of the Provincial Congress. It was no wonder, then, that when General Gage prepared to execute King George's orders to arrest the members of the upstart Congress and seize its arsenal, one of his top priorities was to put Dr. Joseph Warren behind bars.

Late in 1715 or early in 1716, a "great" transatlantic ship of possibly three hundred tons crept slowly and with flapping sails into cold, windswept Boston Harbor. It carried a cargo of miserable fugitives from the Old World. Among them was a thirteen-year-old French boy named Apollos Rivoire. Apollos was one of thousands of Huguenots—Protestants with Lutheran tenets—who fled France after King Louis XIV in 1686 revoked the Edict of Nantes, which had granted them religious tolerance. Clutching his little bundle of belongings—the immemorial and pathetic emblem of the refugee—this slight, dark-skinned lad stood shivering on deck, his eyes full of awe as they contemplated the busy, bustling port, with its wharves, islands, forts and forests of masts. Away from the shore stretched the town, some seven hundred acres—no bigger than a large farm—but containing fifteen thousand souls. Apollos wondered what life would be like in Boston and what sort of man his master, John Coney of Anne Street, perhaps the most skillful silversmith* in all Boston, would be.

Apollos had left his native village of Riaucaud in the wine country of Bordeaux on November 21, 1715, bound for Guernsey, where his

*The craft is properly known as goldsmithing, but because of the value and scarcity of this most precious metal, the vast preponderance of the work is done in silver.

Uncle Simon lived. It was his uncle who paid for the boy's apprenticeship and had put him on the ship for America. Coney was at the wharf when Apollos came down the gangplank and led him off to his home, where the boy would become part of his household, sharing it with five girls—the survivors of twelve children—and Coney's third wife.

John Coney was a good man, quiet, religious, modest and industrious, but, perhaps because he was also a Yankee, he had shrewdly obtained the services of this youth for ten years, rather than the customary seven, for which he had received from the boy's uncle a considerable sum of money. True enough, Coney would have to feed, clothe and shelter him, but toward the end of his indenture, Apollos would produce revenue by what he himself could make. During this time he was not free to borrow money or marry without his master's permission, and it was Coney's obligation to make sure that Apollos became a decent citizen, having to give the town a bond for his good behavior.

There was no trouble with Apollos, however, which could not be said of all the apprentices who thronged the narrow, crooked streets of Boston. Many apprentices stole; seduced their masters' daughters; ran away; and got drunk, singing their rollicking songs or clawing and kicking each other as they rolled fighting in the gutters. For such transgressions—usually committed on Saturday night in the belief that no God-fearing master would desecrate the Sabbath by punishing his apprentice, and the hope that by Monday his temper would have cooled—they were flogged, either publicly or in private. Sometimes an apprentice might fail at one or another craft and then succeed in a third, as Benjamin Franklin flunked candle making and cutlery before he found his metier as a printer's devil. So Apollos Rivoire was not unhappy to put on his leather apron and those wide leather breeches that apprentices of the sedentary crafts wore, so they could be turned about after the seat was worn through. He knew that in ten years he, too, would be a master, just as John Coney had become one, and before him his master, and so backward through the centuries into the Middle Ages. Yet, his term did not last that long, for in August 1722 Coney died and Apollos was able to pay his estate forty pounds for the unexpired three and a half years of his indenture. How he raised the money is not known, but if he had not, he could have been sold to the highest bidder for that unexpired term. So at twenty, Apollos was regarded as a skilled artisan working in silver.

In those days silver service of all descriptions was the mark of a prestigious household and a reserve against financial ruin. There was no bank in Boston, and the fledgling stock market was as risky as those mercantile ventures that often cleaned out investors. Silver was safe, and after a hoard of silver coin had accumulated, it could be taken to a silversmith, who would make it useful and decorative. Unfortunately, as the supply of silver thus vanished from the market, specie became extremely rare, and soon London merchants would accept nothing else in payment, least of all the near-worthless colonial paper that began to flood the market. Coney himself had engraved the first plates for paper currency in America. But in 1722 the gathering dark clouds of financial crisis were not visible over the horizon, least of all to the young artisan on Anne Street.

Apollos by then had taken to calling himself Paul and then Revere, so "that the Bumpkins pronounce it easier." Whether he stayed in his deceased master's old shop or hired himself out as a journeyman is not known. But in 1729 he married Deborah Hitchbourn, whose father owned a wharf on Anne Street, and in the following year an advertisement appeared in the *Weekly News Letter* declaring: "Paul Revere, Goldsmith, is removed from Capt. Pitts at the Town Dock to North End over against Col. Hutchinson." It would be three years before the birth cry of a child would be heard in the North End home. It was a girl, born on February 6, 1733, and named after her mother. Two years later, on the last day of 1735, a boy was born and named after his father. Seven more children would follow, of whom five survived—a high percentage for those days.

Young Paul Revere was a cheerful child, happy in the riotous North End, a miniature replica of the streets of London, where elegance rubbed elbows with rags and filth, nabobs mingling with pickpockets and prostitutes, with the great difference that what was fixed in London was fluid in Boston. An artisan, such as Paul Revere, could live cheek by jowl with an aristocrat, such as Colonel Hutchinson, his tiny house and shop nestling beneath the colonel's fine mansion, with its gardens and stables, orchards and coach houses, and need not tug his forelock or in any other way acknowledge an innate superiority. The air of freedom that this fugitive from class and privilege cherished so ardently was sucked in unconsciously by his little son. Paul was always eager to help out in the twelve-by-twelve shop where the pungent charcoal smoke rose up the flue from the brick furnace in which silver coins and worn household utensils were melted and then annealed to make the mass malleable. Young Paul's velvety brown eyes would go big with interest as his father bent over his tools and anvil to shape and form a dragon's snout for a teapot spout or splay feet for a candy dish. Paul had been promised that one day he would learn this fascinating craft. But that did not come until after he had finished five years of schooling at the North Writing School, where the sons of most of the North End's artisans studied. It was at best a rudimentary education, designed to teach a boy enough so that he might learn more on his own, if he so wished—an intellectual waterwings, if you will, but nothing like North Latin, which was attended by the sons of the well-to-do who were destined for Harvard and the professions. At thirteen young Paul began to learn his craft, progressing so rapidly that it was clear to his father that he would not only soon surpass him, but eventually equal or even exceed the legendary John Coney. But the older Paul did not live to see that day, dying on July 22, 1754. At nineteen, Paul was the head of the house.

By then Paul Revere had reached his physical maturity. His height was medium, but everything else about him was stocky or even "square": his full face with its smooth dark skin, his forehead above deep-set brown eyes and square chin, his broad shoulders and powerful craftsman's hands. His cheerfulness made him immensely popular among the other artisans' sons, and he was thought to be bold by his refusal to decline any dare, be it to dive from the highest mast in the harbor or to ride the wildest horse in the Hutchinson stable, where he earned a few pennies exercising mounts or helping the grooms with their currying. But now he was a householder, responsible for his mother and six siblings, with the added difficulty of not being allowed to step into his dead father's shoes for four or five more years, no matter how skillful he might be. Probably, he either worked for other masters or, more likely, did the work assisted by his younger brother Tom, while his mother nominally continued her dead husband's trade, as was permissible. Whichever, he didn't last long on his own, for two years later—in February 1756—he joined Richard Gridley's regiment as a lieutenant of artillery to serve under Lord Loudoun—that prodigy of timidity—against the French at Crown Point.

It is possible Paul "jined up" for the wages: a handsome five pounds, six shillings, eight pence a month against one pound, six shillings for a private. It was also fortunate that the dilatory Loudoun was in command of the British regulars and New England militia, for Paul Revere saw no action. Indeed, the only fighting of the summer campaign of 1756 was during the loss of the small fort at Oswego to the French. Paul Revere returned to Boston, leaving behind him many comrades buried in shallow graves around Lake George, their brief military careers a melancholy testimony to the truism that in the America of the eighteenth century, more men died of disease in their filthy wilderness camps than ever perished among the smoke and roar of battle.

★ ★ ★

By the time the guns of the Seven Years' War at last fell silent in America, Paul Revere had completed his apprentice years and was a full-fledged master silversmith. By then, he had also taken a wife, Sara Orne, of whom little is known except that she gave him eight children, of whom only three died in infancy. Sara died in childbirth on May 3, 1773. On the following October 10 Paul married Rachel Walker, seemingly a hasty union but a common-enough practice in those days, when a widower rushed to find a mother for his children. It was said that a man might enjoy four wives, until his fifth—her youth outlasting his old age—finally buried him and inherited his fortune. Rachel Walker Revere also had eight children, of whom only two died in infancy.

Meanwhile Paul Revere was growing both in affluence and in popularity among the artisans of Boston. His influence among them did not pass unobserved by the shrewd Samuel Adams, who realized that he could depend upon these sturdy, religious, hardworking, often intellectual craftsmen to be his shock troops in defense of the sacred charter of Massachusetts Bay. Samuel's cousin John also befriended this stocky, smiling silversmith, and after Revere joined the Masons on September 4, 1761, he became acquainted with many brothers of Boston's two lodges, among them John Hancock and James Otis. Dr. Joseph Warren was a particularly close friend, and after Samuel Adams drew Warren away from the half-mad Otis, with his unquenchable love of the British Empire, and into membership in the Sons of Liberty, Revere went with Warren.

Meanwhile, as the gulf widened between the colonies and the Mother Country, Paul Revere's fame as a silversmith steadily grew in Boston, until in 1770 his engraving of the Boston Massacre made him a celebrity along the Atlantic seaboard. As art, the prints pouring off the press were not first class—the figures were stiff, awkward, and disproportionate and the overall effect was amateurish—but as propaganda, they were magnificent: the bloodthirsty lobsterbacks slaughtering innocent, defenseless Boston citizens! Nor was "The Boston Massacre" quite accurate or truthful: a little dog standing bewildered among the fallen Patriots was a nice touch, but nowhere was there evidence of the Boston rowdies baiting the redcoats or pelting them with rocks and snowballs. One may wonder what John Adams, that paragon of justice, thought of this twisting of the truth. Doubtless he saw its propaganda value and probably blinked at it in the interest of "the cause." Probably also the self-righteous Adams had by then learned that in this world of perpetual conflict, there is only one absolute, and his name is God. Whatever, under the watchful eye of Warren and the Adamses, Paul Revere was becoming a worthy ally in the quarrel with the Crown.

For himself, Revere was no thinker, but a simple, matter-of-fact man who left intellection and perception to the aforementioned trio, taking his politics without question, just as he accepted his Congregational faith. He could be depended upon for other things besides propaganda or organizing the artisans. One of them was his physical stamina, which made him an excellent courier. Since the days when he walked the Hutchinson mounts or helped out in the stables, he had been fond of horses, and even though he had no need of a mount, Boston being so small and all places of assembly so close to his home, he nevertheless had bought a mare of his own in 1773. Probably it was one of those smallish horses sired by "the Yankee Hero," standing usually only twelve hands (or four feet) high and no higher than fourteen hands. But these horses were wiry and hardy, and when the *Dartmouth*—the first of the tea ships—arrived in Boston Harbor, Revere, having stood guard over the tea ship that very night, was one of six riders who clattered out of Boston the next day to warn the other seaports of tea-ship arrivals in their own harbor.

Revere was also one of Samuel Adams's "Mohawks" who boarded the *Dartmouth* on a cold December night to dump its detestable tea into the harbor, and with his dark eyes and skin, he probably looked more the part than his blue-eyed and fair-skinned comrades. Again it was Revere who rode south to the First Continental Congress in Philadelphia in 1774, bearing those inflammatory "Suffolk Resolves" that so united the colonies. On his return only eleven days later, he was able to say with a grin that the tea spilled at Boston had washed ashore in Virginia and the Carolinas. It was no surprise, then, that when Revere learned through his spy system of Gage's intention to capture Hancock and Samuel Adams, as well as the Patriot military stores at Concord, it was he, along with William Dawes, who was chosen to "ride and spread the alarm, to every Middlesex village and farm."

⋆ 14 ⋆

LEXINGTON AND CONCORD

At Gage's request Lord Dartmouth, the colonial secretary, had been steadily reinforcing the Boston garrison until, by the spring of 1775, it stood at four thousand men. Naturally, a military force that large had a visible and abrasive impact upon a city of sixteen thousand souls, so that tension between the townspeople and redcoats was drawn even tauter than it had been before the Boston Massacre.

To their delight the soldiery had discovered how cheaply drunkenness could be bought in this city flowing with rum and beer, while their officers amused themselves either in the gaming room or in the boudoirs of obliging Tory damsels and in amateur theatricals in which the more effeminate of the officers sometimes quarreled over who should play female parts and wear dresses. Perhaps the chief source of pleasure was the spirit of mutual derision between soldiers, who collapsed with laughter at the spectacle of Yankee Doodle trying to appear fiercely martial at "milishy meetings" on the green, and farmers, who were similarly convulsed at the sight of British soldiers who practiced firing at targets on the bay. One farmer watched while an entire regiment shot at the target—and missed. He laughed so hard that an annoyed British officer asked him what was so funny.

"I laugh to see how awkward they fire," he replied. "Why, I'll be bound I hit it ten times running."

To call the bumpkin's bluff, the officer ordered five loaded muskets to be brought forward, but the grinning farmer said one would be enough if he could load it himself. He did, took aim at the left of the target and hit it, at the right and hit it and then hit it in the center. Grinning again, he turned to the astonished officer and his men and drawled: "Why, I'll tell you naow. I have got a boy at home that will toss up an apple and shoot out all the seeds as it's coming down."

Apocryphal as the story certainly was, it does truthfully reflect the American's contempt for the redcoats as marksmen, and such exaggeration also colored the British disdain for Americans as fighting men. The British believed that Yankee courage was of the bottled variety. "Without rum they could neither fight nor say their prayers." One volley from trained British regulars would put them to flight like rabbits. Said Major John Pitcairn of the Royal Marines: "I am satisfied that one active campaign, a smart action, and burning two or three of their towns, will set everything to rights." Such an instinctive sense of superiority was based neither upon reason nor upon experience, but was born of British class prejudice. Courage was a consequence of birth. The lower classes were cowardly clods, and only by training and discipline could they become reliable soldiers. The untrained Yankee rabble withstand British regulars? It is to laugh!

But that famous—or infamous—discipline was having a disturbing effect on these celebrated warriors. They were deserting in droves. Poor pay, rotten food and the lash, together with offers of land and a new start in life from many of the Yankee towns that were desirous of obtaining a professional for a drill sergeant, was having an effect so serious that Gage, with the obtuse insensitivity of most British commanders of the day, ordered severe punishment for those caught in the act or recaptured. Ordinarily they would have been hanged, but to execute so many would sharply deplete his strength, so the sentence was "reduced" to a thousand lashes, to be applied at the rate of 250 per week. Intended to cow the troops compelled to watch these bloody demonstrations of "discipline," the policy probably had the reverse effect of confirming them in their intention to desert.

The Patriots, meanwhile, were busily cleansing their own armed forces of Tories and other unreliables. It was done by stipulating that all officers, from lieutenant to captain, must resign their commissions, after which the towns elected new officers who were known to be a hundred percent patriotic, and these, in turn, elected field-grade officers. Generals, of course, were chosen either by Congress or by the colonies. At this time the militia was organized in companies of "fifty privates, at the least, who shall equip and hold themselves in readiness, on the shortest notice to march to the place of rendezvous." The shortest notice would be a minute, hence the birth of the minutemen. Some also organized "Alarm

Companies," composed of boys and old men who would protect the town while the minutemen were campaigning elsewhere.

Obviously, both sides were preparing for war.

King George and Parliament had ignored the petitions of the "illegal" Continental Congress, moving to subdue the "most daring spirit of resistance and disobedience" that existed in the colonies. More oppressive measures were passed, capped by the Fishery Act, which forbade New Englanders to trade with Britain, Ireland and the West Indies and banned them from the Newfoundland fisheries.

Infuriated beyond restraint by this dreadful blow to its economy, Massachusetts replied by reviving the Provincial Congress. The members met in chambers so cold that they kept their hats as well as their coats on and placed the colony on a virtual war footing. Then, again turning the military over to Dr. Warren and his Committee of Safety, the Congress once more adjourned.

That was on April 15, 1775, the day after Gage received his "get-tough" orders. Force was to be quickly applied to crush the rebellion before it spread. The leaders of the Provincial Congress were to be arrested. Gage realized that this last act would be difficult if not impossible. Although Dr. Warren was still in town, the others were out in the country, some of them, like the Adamses and John Hancock, on their way to the Second Continental Congress, which was due to convene in May. Samuel Adams and Hancock were near Concord, and John Adams was still farther away. At Concord, however, lay the Committee of Safety's arsenal. Gage had been kept minutely informed of its growth by none other than Dr. Benjamin Church. This urbane grandson of the old Indian fighter of the same name had fallen hopelessly in love with a lady, and because he needed money to keep her, he betrayed the committee's secrets to Gage.

Resolved to seize the stores of arms at Concord, Gage collected his best troops—the grenadier and light infantry companies—and placed them "off all duties 'till further orders" to learn "new evolutions." The Patriot spies, however, knew what Gage hoped to "evolve." Boston patrolmen, under Paul Revere, had seen the transports hauling up their whaleboats for repairs. They guessed correctly that an expedition was being prepared to go by boat from Boston to Cambridge and then to take the road to Concord, about twenty miles away.

The next morning Warren sent Revere riding to Lexington to warn John Hancock and Sam Adams to be ready to flee. Revere returned that night and arranged "that if the British went out by water we would show two lanterns in the North Church steeple; and if by land, one." This is the famous "one if by land, two if by sea" of Longfellow's poem, but Revere did not intend that "I on the opposite shore will be." The lanterns were to rouse the Charlestown countryside.

During daylight of April 18, Gage sent mounted officers out to patrol the Concord road and to keep it free of rebel couriers. That night his elite troops—from six hundred to eight hundred men—were awakened by sergeants shaking them and whispering to them. Startled, unaware of their destination, knowing only that their packs were full for a march, they slipped out of the barracks, unknown to their sleeping comrades. Having stolen away from their own quarters, they marched openly to Boston Common, where they formed ranks under the lackluster eyes of their commander, fat, slow-thinking Lieutenant Colonel Francis Smith. Fortunately for Smith, Major John Pitcairn of the Royal Marines was also coming along. Although Pitcairn has gone into some American histories as a profane and bloodthirsty boor, he was actually a gallant gentleman and a fine officer. At half-past ten the British were ready to move, and by then Dr. Warren had sent William Dawes and Paul Revere flying from Boston to warn the countryside.

Dawes took the longer land route over Boston Neck to Cambridge and thence to Menotomy (now Arlington) and the road west to Lexington and Concord. Revere, booted and swathed in a greatcoat, had himself rowed over to Charlestown. At eleven o'clock he sprang onto a waiting horse and clattered off.

Behind him two lanterns began to glow in the steeple of old North Church.

"The regulars are out!" Paul Revere cried, galloping along in the moonlight, cupping his hands to his lips to make his voice heard above his horse's hoofbeats. "The regulars are out!" He shouted at lighted windows, threw pebbles at darkened ones and then rode on, his mount's hooves ringing boldly in the darkness, the sweat on its hide forming puffs of foam.

At Lexington, Revere rode up to the home of Parson Jonas Clark. Samuel Adams and John Hancock, Clark's cousin, were staying there. Revere shouted to William Munroe, a militia guard, to open the door. "Please!" Munroe yelled back. "Not so loud! The family has just retired and doesn't want any noise about the house."

"Noise!" Revere roared. "You'll have noise enough before long. The regulars are out!"

Munroe hurried inside to awaken Adams and Hancock. They dressed while their horses were being saddled. "What a glorious morning this is!" Adams exclaimed. Seeing Hancock puzzled, he added: "I mean for America."

It was not such a glorious morning for Paul Revere. After Dawes arrived in Lexington an hour later, the two set out for Concord. Along the way they were joined by young Dr. Samuel Prescott, who was returning home from a long evening of courting. While Prescott and Dawes stopped at a house to arouse the family, Revere rode on. Seeing two British officers sitting their horses under a tree with pistols in their hands, he called for his two companions. Then he saw two more redcoats also armed. One of them shouted: "God damn you, stop! If you go an inch farther you are a dead man!" Revere halted. Dr. Prescott rode up. He, too, was detained. Both men were ordered into a pasture. As they entered it, they touched their spurs to their horses and broke for the fence at its end. Six more British riders intercepted them. But Prescott, riding over familiar territory, was able to get away, hastening to Concord where he warned the militia, while Dawes had already escaped. Riding up to Revere, the senior officer courteously asked his name.

"Revere."

"What? *Paul* Revere?"

"Yes."

Realizing whom they had caught, the mounted redcoats began crowding around their captive, cursing and denouncing him.

"Don't be afraid," the officer said reassuringly. "They will not hurt you."

Revere smiled tauntingly. "You've missed your purpose."

"Oh, no! We're after some deserters who've been reported on the road."

"I know better," Revere replied boldly. "I know what you're after. You're too late. I've alarmed the country all the way up. I should have five hundred men at Lexington soon."

Dismayed, some of the redcoats rode off, returning with the detachment's senior officer, a Major Mitchell. He put his pistol to Revere's head and ordered him to tell the truth or he'd blow his brains out. Under questioning, Revere revealed that the entire countryside was aware of Gage's expedition and would be ready for it. Thoroughly alarmed, Mitchell ordered Revere to mount, handing his reins to one of his men, and led the party toward Lexington. Going about a mile, he ordered Revere freed, probably because Revere was now of no use but an impediment, and turned about to lead his patrol back to Cambridge.

Relieved, Paul Revere rode to the Clark house, where he found Adams and Hancock, who were still uncertain about what to do. At once

Revere urged them to flee, accompanying them to a crossroads where the way seemed clear. Spurring their horses on, they began their journey to Philadelphia. Behind them the clear, cold dawn of April 19 fell faintly upon the long red British columns that were marching into Lexington.

Colonel Francis Smith's soldiers were fuming. It was bad enough being perpetually damp from the waist down because of that moist white paste called pipe clay with which they were supposed to keep their breeches impeccably white, but now those same pants were stained with mud and the men were sopping from the chest down.

The whaleboats had put them ashore at Lechmere Point in knee-deep water. Then, after their fathead colonel had kept them waiting two hours for rations, he had led them into a backwater of the Charles in which they had been forced to wade up to their chests. No sooner had they begun squishing and squelching away for the Yankee lair at Concord, than shots and ringing bells and scampering feet to either side of the road made it clear that there was to be no surprise. The only surprise that day would be if any of the officers knew any of the men they commanded. Their own officers were sick or on detached service. In their place were volunteers, thrill seekers and smooth-chinned subalterns out for a lark. Some of them did not even come from the crack "flank" companies but wore the silly cocked hat of the line.

At Menotomy there was a surprise. Alarmed by outriders' reports that the rebels had been warned, perhaps prompted by Major Pitcairn, Colonel Smith made a wise decision: he sent an express rider back to Boston with a request for reinforcements. It was then about three o'clock in the morning. The men had been on their feet for five hours, and they continued to slosh forward, burdened by perhaps sixty pounds of equipment—packs, belts, bayonet scabbards and cartridge boxes—hampered by stiff and awkward clothing, and still clutching their ten-pound muskets, the famous Brown Bess of England.

The guns' barrels and metal fittings were no longer brown, but brightly burnished like the socket bayonets fitted to their muzzles, and these rows of gleaming barrels and glittering blades were visible from afar to the handful of patriots drawn up on Lexington Green.

Captain Jonas Parker and about seventy men had formed on the green. They stood inside a triangle formed by three roads. The road to Concord was at its base. Parker's men stood about a hundred yards above it, and they could clearly see the steady, awesome approach of the British advance guard under Major Pitcairn.

"There are so few of us," one man said, "it is folly to stand here."

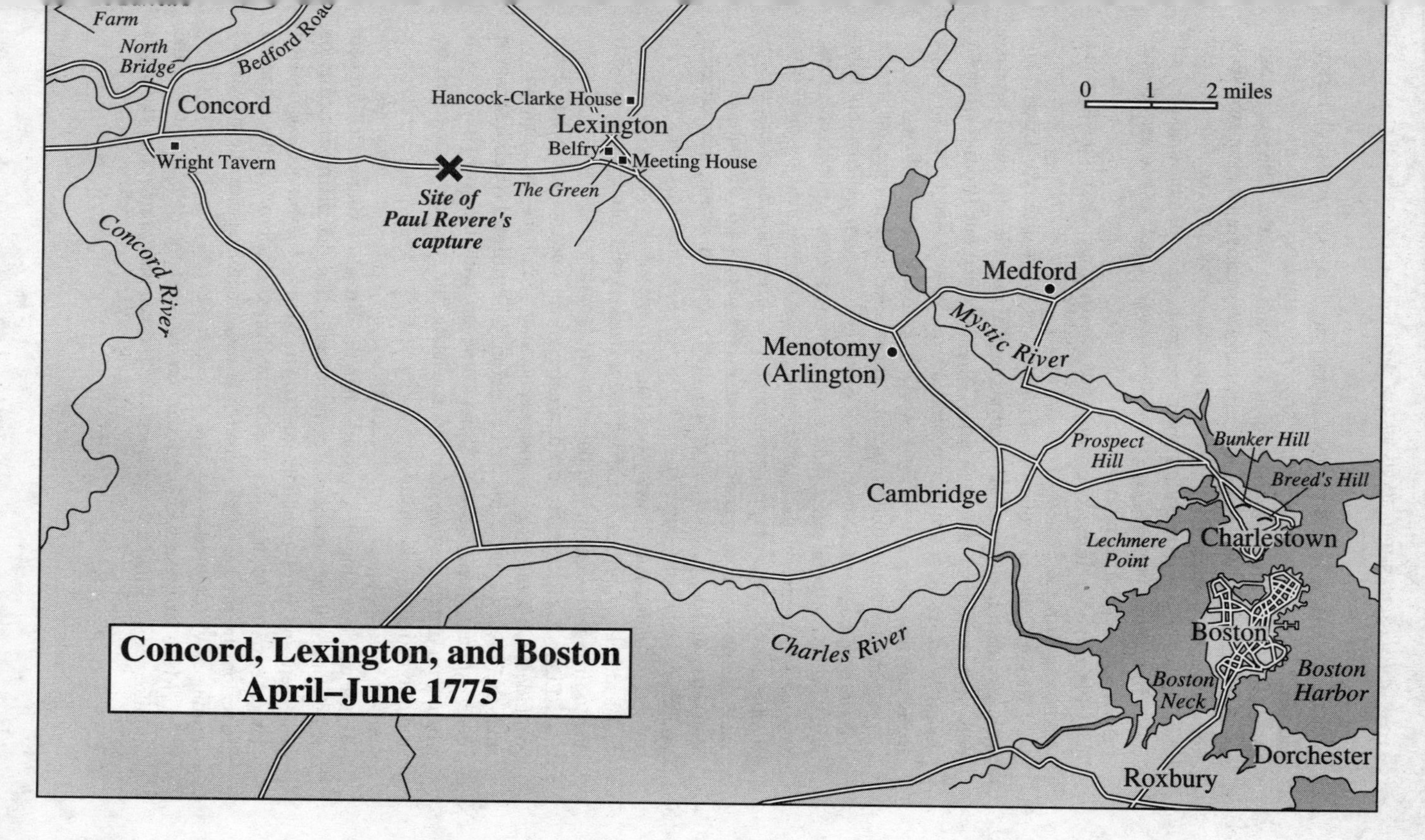

Concord, Lexington, and Boston
April–June 1775

"The first man who offers to run shall be shot down," Parker warned.

Major Pitcairn ordered his men into line of battle. The rear ranks ran forward at the double to line up with the others and form two sections, three men deep. They shouted and cheered as they ran.

"Stand your ground!" Parker ordered. "Don't fire unless fired upon. But if they want to have a war, let it begin here!" Some men shook their heads and drifted away.

Pitcairn rode forward crying, "Lay down your arms, you damned rebels, and disperse!"

Parker finally saw that this situation was impossible. He ordered his men to disband, taking their weapons with them. Pitcairn called repeatedly to them to lay down their arms. Shots crashed out (from the British on the road or from Patriots behind a wall, history will never know), a British soldier was wounded and two balls grazed Pitcairn's horse.

"Fire, by God, fire!" a British officer cried, and a volley of British ball tore through the Americans. "Soldiers!" Pitcairn called. "Soldiers, don't fire! Keep your ranks. Form and surround them." But the regulars, taunted for months in the Boston prison cage, driven mad by their frustrating march, were not to be checked. Pitcairn swung his sword downward as the signal to cease fire, but they replied with another crash of musketry, and then, after the rebels fired a ragged return, they cheered and charged with the bayonet.

The militia fled. Brave Jonas Parker stood alone. He had fired once and had been wounded. He stood like a stricken bull in the arena, reloading to fire again—and British bayonets cut him down.

Eight Americans lay dead on the green, and ten more had been wounded. Only the single British soldier had been hurt—and that was all that there was to the Battle of Lexington. The British officers re-formed their exultant men, Colonel Smith came up with the main body, and then, with drums beating and fifes squealing, the redcoats swung west on the last six miles to Concord.

The alarm bell rung in Concord after the arrival of young Dr. Prescott had brought three companies of minutemen and one alarm company of old men and boys tumbling into town. Many of them joined Colonel James Barrett hurrying over the North Bridge that crossed the Concord River on the road west to Barrett's house, where most of the province's munitions were stored.

Much of these had been sent farther west the day before, but the minutemen still had to lug barrels of musket balls, flints and cartridges into the attic and cover them with feathers. Powder was hauled into the woods, and a plowman dug furrows in which muskets and light cannon were laid while the earth from other furrows covered them.

Meanwhile, other militia companies from other towns and villages were arriving in Concord. Eventually they numbered about four hundred men, under the nominal command of Colonel Barrett. Most of these men were stationed on a ridge overlooking North Bridge from Barrett's side of the river. They stayed there, watching, while the British marched into town unhindered.

Colonel Smith and his staff went to a tavern to refresh themselves, carefully paying for all that they ordered, while four companies of light infantry crossed North Bridge and went up the road to Barrett's house. Behind them, three other companies of light infantry guarded the bridge, fanning out on both sides of the river. Inside Concord, the grenadiers, with a courtesy that should make the twentieth century blush, began searching houses. One huge grenadier retreated, red-faced, before a determined old lady brandishing a mop, and a grenadier officer in another house politely accepted the falsehood that a locked room was occupied by an invalid, when it actually contained military stores. Still, they found one hundred barrels of flour and sent them splashing into a millpond, followed by five hundred pounds of bullets. But the flour barrels were not stove in and the bullet sacks were not slashed, and almost all of these supplies were salvaged. However, gun carriages found in the Town House were set afire, and then put out after the grenadiers realized that they might also set the Town House blazing. Dragged outside, they were relighted—and that column of smoke spiraling lazily into the sky above Concord's elms and oaks was seen by Colonel Barrett's men on the hill.

"Will you let them burn the town down?" an officer asked Barrett, and Barrett replied by ordering the militia to march to the defense of the town and not to fire unless fired upon. In column of twos they came down, these "embattled farmers" of history, marching silently to the beat of drummer boy Abner Hosmer with Captain Isaac Davis, the Acton gunsmith, at their head.

At North Bridge Captain Laurie of the light infantry watched their approach in surprise. He sent back to town for reinforcements. Colonel Smith ordered a few companies of grenadiers forward, "but put himself at their head by which means he stopt 'em from being [in] time enough, for being a very fat heavy Man he wou'd not have reached the Bridge in a half hour tho it was not half a mile to it."

Suddenly Laurie was nervous. The long column of Americans was coming straight down the steep hill to the bridge. His own men were uneasy. There were no better troops in the world, but today they were strangely unruly. Unfamiliar officers were having trouble forming them after Laurie pulled his outposts back to the Concord side of the bridge. Lauric wanted the front-rank men to fire, peel off and run to the rear to reload, thus exposing the second-rank men who would do the same and so on. Smartly executed, it was a fine maneuver, designed to rake the approaching Yankees with a steady fire. But it was done clumsily that day. The first British shots fell short in the river. One of them whistled by the ear of Captain Timothy Brown.

"God damn it, they are firing ball!" Brown exclaimed.

They were, indeed, and now they had the range. Captain Isaac Davis was knocked down dead. Little Abner Hosmer toppled beside him with a ball through the brain. Two other Americans were wounded.

"Fire, fellow soldier!" an American officer pleaded. "For God's sake, fire!"

The first full American volley of the Revolutionary War crashed forth. Three redcoats—the first Britishers to die in that war—fell lifeless, and nine more were wounded. Then the Americans cheered, for the British were withdrawing! Leaving their dead and one wounded man lying on the road, they rushed back to town in disorder. They met and mingled with Smith's tardy grenadiers and were finally re-formed and faced toward the Americans.

But the undisciplined Yankees pursued for only a few yards before breaking ranks. Some went back across the bridge to carry off the bodies of Davis and the little drummer boy, but most of them returned to the ridge. Perhaps they were amazed by their own "victory" over the regulars. Perhaps also they did not want to be caught between Smith's force and the four companies of light infantry who might return from Barrett's house any minute.

Silence came over North Bridge. The Yankees stared at the crumpled red-and-white forms of the fallen foe. They saw a gangly farmer come over the bridge. He had an ax in his hand. One of the sprawled soldiers stirred. The farmer panicked, struck at him with his ax and ran off. The soldier sank back onto the road.

Now came the tread of marching feet. The light infantry was returning from Barrett's house. They had found nothing. They were disgruntled, then frightened to see their dead comrades and the "scalped" soldier. Their step quickened. They began running. They went tearing around the bend on the double, and the Americans on the hill to the left let them pass without firing a shot.

It was now ten o'clock, and in Concord Colonel Smith was preparing to leave. He hired carriages to carry his wounded, and at noon the silent columns trudged back the way they came.

Yankee Doodle went to town
Ariding on a pony,
Stuck a feather in his cap
And called it macaroni.

The Earl of Percy was marching to Colonel Smith's rescue with a force of one thousand men and two cannon, and his fifes and drums were derisively playing "Yankee Doodle" as they struck confidently over Boston Neck. Passing through Roxbury, they met a schoolboy, who is supposed to have laughed so hard at the tune that Percy asked him why. The boy replied with a mocking reference to a ballad that went:

To drive the deer with hound and horne
Erle Percy took his way.
The child may rue that is unborne
The hunting of that day!

On every side of the British column the Americans were gathering. Towns and hamlets too far away to fight at Lexington or Concord had sent militia hurrying to the scene. Some dispatched only a few dozen and others as many as three hundred men. In all, perhaps four thousand Americans were gathering along that sixteen-mile gantlet running back to Charlestown.

The Americans fired from behind stone walls or from trees. They took long-range potshots from houses or rushed boldly to within a few yards of the line of march and blazed away. Redcoat after redcoat slumped in the dust. Smith's hired carriages were piled high with wounded. But the Patriots did not escape unscathed. Smith sent his light infantry out on the flanks. They surprised groups of militia in the hollows and put them to rout. They doubled back on themselves and took the unsuspecting Americans in the rear. They cornered them in houses and shot them down or drove their slender bayonets into them. And because they had taken as much as men can be expected to endure, they set fire to the houses or wrecked them.

But the militia were hydra headed. Each time an American was killed or put to flight or merely quit the battle, two more arrived to take his place. And the galling fire from both sides of the road continued.

The fire not only tore British flesh; it fragmented British discipline.

Smith's column became a disorderly crowd of men. Soldiers broke ranks to ransack roadside houses or taverns for food and whatever they could carry off. Nearing Lexington, Smith halted and ordered Pitcairn to hold off the Americans while he re-formed his ranks. The Americans swarmed around Pitcairn's rear guard and opened fire. Riflemen lying behind a pile of rails blazed at Pitcairn, conspicuous on an elegant horse. The horse plunged, threw Pitcairn, and ran into the American lines, carrying off Pitcairn's set of fine horse pistols. The rear guard was driven in, and Smith was forced to renew the retreat.

Now the dreadful pace was killing. Men who had been on their feet for more than twenty hours were wilting. The light infantry were exhausted from the ordeal of covering the flanks. Some soldiers were breaking ranks in a stumbling run. Men continued to fall—from American musket balls or fatigue—and the redcoats' ammunition was running out. Entering Lexington, the British were on the verge of breaking into a rout. Officers had to stagger around their hurrying men to confront them with bayonets and warn them to slow down or die. And then, at three o'clock in the afternoon, they beheld the black hats, scarlet coats and white breeches of Percy's brigade formed in a hollow square. Too tired to cheer, they passed through their saviors' ranks and sank to the ground, "their tongues hanging from their mouths, like those of dogs after a chase." Percy's pair of six-pound cannon kept the Americans at a respectful distance while Smith's exhausted men rested.

Meanwhile, American reinforcements were arriving. General William Heath came to Lexington and so did Dr. Joseph Warren. Neither man saw the opportunity lying at hand. If a force could have been sent downroad while the redcoats rested, Percy's retreat could have been sealed off. A party of axmen could have been formed to fell trees across the British path. Neither tactic was adopted, although it must be said that the Yankee "army" was actually only a great crowd of armed and angry farmers, each fighting individually and entering or leaving the fight at his whim. Nor were they the crack shots of legend, either. When Percy resumed the retreat some time after three o'clock, the Americans again buzzed about his flanks like swarms of bees. The finest targets lay under the muzzles of their muskets, and even though that weapon's projectile falls harmlessly to the ground after 125 yards, they still should have been able to slaughter the defenseless enemy.

Still, they continued to torment the British all the way to Charlestown. And the British fought back. They were burning and ransacking every roadside house now, and at one point the flankers drove a party of Patriots into a house and bayoneted twelve of them to death. At

Menotomy forty Americans and forty British fell. At Cambridge a mile and a half of continuous battle was begun. Redcoats and men in homespun fought each other at close quarters, with bayonets and clubbed muskets.

Again and again Percy halted his column and unlimbered his little cannon. They spat, drove the Americans off, the gunners limbered up again, and the guns and carriages became covered with the scarlet coats of the wounded and fatigued. At last Percy's battered force crossed Charlestown Neck into Charlestown under the protecting muzzles of the British ships. The Americans fell back, darkness came and the bloody retreat from Concord was over.

British casualties were 73 killed, 26 missing and probably dead, and 174 wounded, a total of 273 out of about 1,800 men engaged. The Americans lost 49 killed, 5 missing, and 41 wounded, a total of 95. If a battle's importance were to be measured by its casualties, Concord and Lexington would have been trifling indeed. But the shots "heard round the world" had been fired, and the Revolutionary War—one of the most momentous in history—had been started.

Next day, Percy's troops were hardly safely across the Charles before the vanguard of thousands of armed New Englanders rushed into Cambridge. Works were thrown up outside the city, an army arose on the plain and the siege of Boston was begun.

★ 15 ★

ETHAN ALLEN AND FORT TICONDEROGA

The day after Lexington and Concord, a British ship arrived in Boston Harbor with Lord North's "peace proposal." The king's minister, realizing that he had been too harsh to the Americans, offered not to tax those colonies that voluntarily paid their share of the cost of empire.

His lordship, however, was too late with much too little. Americans were generally too enraged even to consider this evasion of the issue of the *right* to tax, and one of them exclaimed: "An armed robber who demands my money might as well pretend he makes a concession by suffering me to take it out of my own pocket, rather than search there for it himself."

Meanwhile, couriers from the Committee of Safety had gone galloping north and south ever since the first American perished at Lexington. At ten o'clock that fateful morning, Israel Bissell went pounding out of Watertown bound for points south. Two hours later the horse beneath him fell dead, but Bissell mounted a fresh horse and clattered on: New York … New Brunswick … Princeton … Philadelphia. Other express riders carried the news farther south, and before the month of April was out, it had spread across Virginia and was en route to South Carolina.

In Virginia a British major named Horatio Gates knew that Lexington meant war. Like Thomas Gage, now commanding in Boston, Gates had been wounded at the Monongahela. Gates, however, had left the service to become an American planter. He was definitely on the colonial side. So was another former British soldier, General Charles Lee. Thin, ugly and irascible, fonder of dogs than of men, this soldier of fortune was considered by many Americans to be the ablest military man in America. Charles Lee was certainly—as he would personally insist—more experienced than that Colonel George Washington whom he had just visited at Mount Vernon.

Washington also heard the news from the North, and it so affected him that he packed the old red-and-blue uniform he had worn under Braddock and took it to Philadelphia for the second session of the Continental Congress.

The Congress was due to convene on May 10, 1775, the day that Fort Ticonderoga was attacked by the Green Mountain Boys under Ethan Allen.

It was perhaps prophetic that on the night Ethan Allen was born—January 21, 1738—a howling northern wind blasted the little town of Litchfield, Connecticut, all but burying its tiny log cabins, and that the timber wolves in the surrounding woods howled back in a rising counterpoint, joined by the milder baying of the town dogs. For this strapping baby boy, the first of seven children to be born to Joseph and Mary Baker Allen, was to be, if nothing else, a howler and a shaker and an original of the first order.

He also was to be afflicted with the wanderlust that had infected the family since the first Allen arrived in Massachusetts in 1638. It was transmitted to him by his father Joe, who moved to the tiny frontier town of Cornwall shortly after Ethan's birth. Joe was also something of a maverick, forever baiting his Congregationalist neighbors for their stubborn belief in the Calvinist doctrine of predestination for the Elect of God, in which happy company, of course, they included themselves. Joe was an Arminian, a follower of Jacobus Arminius of Leyden, who insisted that Christ died for all men, bad as well as good, not just for those Chosen who were S-A-V-E saved. He was so persuasive that in 1754 his friend, the Reverend Solomon Palmer, actually declared to a shocked congregation that God was not a murderer who made some men for heaven and some for hell. With such a father, it would have been hard for young Ethan not to be a bit anticlerical himself.

Little is known of Ethan's boyhood. He probably fished, hunted and trapped like his friends and he certainly worked hard; by the time he was fifteen, he was strong enough to carry the grist to the mill at Woodbury, twenty-five miles away over a "road" that was nothing more than a blazed trail. At maturity he would be a giant, probably husky and certainly tall. How tall is not known, other than by the local tradition that he stood more than a head higher than the sixty-nine-inch fowling piece of the day, meaning at least six feet four inches and possibly taller.

As a boy Ethan was precocious, forever questioning his elders or burying his nose in a book. He read the Bible, of course, but every other book in Cornwall as well. He wrote down his thoughts before he was nine, so impressing his father that Joe sent him to a school in nearby Salisbury for preparation for college. But then Joe Allen died, and Ethan had to leave school to become the teenage head of the family. He became a good farmer, hardheaded but truculant. No neighbor or merchant tried to skin him, for fear of landing in his cow pond.

But then in 1757 the opening of the French and Indian Wars ended Ethan's domestic life. At the age of nineteen, Ethan turned the farm over to his brothers, shouldering a musket and marching off with a local regiment to the defense of Fort William Henry. He saw no action, for the fort had fallen before he could get there. But he had seen the world and would also be a confirmed wanderer.

After a four-year hiatus, during which nothing is known of his activity, he emerged about 1761 as an ironmaster. In these backwoods the only real industrial activity was the production of potash, which had to be done inside huge iron kettles. Iron for the kettles had to be smelted in a blast furnace, and there happened to be an abundance of the ore needed for this operation beneath a large Salisbury hill. Through his skill at trading, Allen obtained the right to mine this hill and to cut wood for fuel on a nearby tract. So prepared, he and his brother Heman built a blast furnace—which was an immediate success. Allen now decided that he needed a wife, and he rode to the mill at Woodbury to secure the hand of Mary, daughter of miller Brownson. Little is known of Mary except that she was deeply religious, humorless and illiterate—a fair description of most of the suffering housewives of the backwoods. Her cross grew heavier when her husband, after two years with the blast furnace, tired of such a pedestrian pursuit, however profitable, and began to think seriously of the more exciting—and more lucrative—occupation of speculation in real estate.

In the spring of 1765, Ethan and Heman sold the furnace to George Caldwell for the princely sum of five hundred pounds, after which this exuberant trio went on a twenty-four-hour bender that ended when Ethan beat up Caldwell. For doing so, Ethan was fined ten shillings. Next he became interested in a Woodbury lead mine. En route to inspect it, he encountered Caldwell with a man named Robert Braithwaite. An argument ensued, and Ethan belted Braithwaite; then, as Caldwell moved to restrain him, Ethan hit him on the head with a club. When Braithwaite grabbed at the club, Ethan whacked him again. Though arrested, Allen apparently escaped prosecution, journeying to Northhampton, where he decided to stay even though the lead mine had proved unattractive.

With the money from the sale of the blast furnace, he spent his time in Northhampton in "riotous living," meanwhile composing obscene jokes at the expense of local churchmen. Upbraided by the local parson, he persisted in this unseemly pleasure, whereupon in July 1767, the town selectman kicked him and his wife and child out of town. Thus a brooding Ethan Allen left his family with his brother Heman in Salisbury and set out for the New Hampshire Land Grants.

In those days royal governors were able to grant sections of land for a fee, and the New Hampshire Land Grants, which eventually became the state of Vermont, were actually a howling wilderness in which, in Kipling's phrase, "there ain't no Ten Commandments, and a man can raise a thirst." There were also only four hundred people living there: woodsmen and trappers, a few farmers and some old soldiers seeking surcease in the solitude of the woods. There was also an intercolonial dispute between New York and New Hampshire, the former claiming that the latter's grants were actually in New York. In 1768 this quarrel was still in abeyance before the Crown, but New York continued to insist that the New Hampshire settlers either pay a second fee or face eviction. Into this quasi-war came that hulking free spirit—Ethan Allen—and he very nearly didn't get there. When rain fell one night, his clothes froze on him. Then came cold and snow. Allen marked out a circle and walked and walked it all night long, fearing to fall asleep and freeze to death.

When Ethan Allen finally settled in the Land Grants, he took his family to the little settlement of Bennington. There he was elected colonel-commandant of a motley army of "ring-tailed roarers" who styled themselves the Green Mountain Boys. Their headquarters was the Catamount Tavern, where they gathered to drink rum punch or "stonewalls," rum laced with *undiluted* hard cider, and plot their responses to the latest outrages perpetrated on their brethren by the colony of New York. Surveyors sent from Albany would encounter bands of "Indians" with bark-stained faces, who would break their compasses and seize their chains and be warned by a towering "sachem" that, "If you come back, by God, we'll cut off your head." Enemy deputy sheriffs, hoping to collect the twenty-pound bounty placed on Allen's head, received similar treatment. Once Allen seized two of them, locking them in separate rooms of a farmhouse. In the morning he awakened both of them and told them to look out the window. Aghast, they saw a figure on a rope twisting in the wind. Chuckling, Allen left them with their doors open, and each, thinking the other had been hanged, skedaddled back across the Hudson.

Ethan Allen's legend grew. Like the mythical Paul Bunyan's, most of it was based on his great strength. It was said that he once encountered a New York sheriff with six henchmen and left all seven unconscious and bleeding on the ground, or that he picked a surveyor and his chainman off the ground, holding them at arm's length and beating their heads together. But there were true stories about his terrible wrath and prodigious profanity, such as the time he caught a New Yorker named Charles Hutchinson living in a cabin he had built on a New Hampshire grant. At once he ordered the cabin burned to the ground, and when Hutchinson protested, he yelled: "Complain to that damned scoundrel your governor! God damn your governor, your laws, your king, council and assembly."

"Colonel Allen," the pious and shocked Hutchinson replied, "you curse most horrible."

"God damn your soul," Allen shouted, "are you going to preach to us?"

Eventually, "Colonel" Ethan Allen commanded a not-inconsiderable force of three hundred "boys." When the call went out from the Catamount Tavern for them to assemble, these hardy woodsmen in buckskin would lay down their farm tools and take down their muskets from above their fireplaces. They idolized Allen, as much for his humor as for his bravado. They were fond of recounting the time when a party of British regulars from Crown Point came to the Catamount hoping to arrest Allen and collect the bounty. The big Yankee greeted them effusively and called for a bowl of punch. The British listened enchanted while Allen boasted of wrestling bears or running down deer or killing a catamount with a knife. More punch.... More.... At last a chuckling Allen stowed his "arresters" safely under the table. A year later he rode into Albany to nail to a tavern wall his own poster offering a twenty-pound bounty for the arrest of the governor.

With such a reputation, it was no surprise that Ethan's brother Heman should canter into the Catamount yard riding a winded horse, and eagerly inform Ethan that the Connecticut authorities in Hartford desired him to mobilize the Green Mountain Boys for an attack on Fort Ticonderoga.

Dawn of May 10 crept across Lake Champlain and the stone walls of Fort Ticonderoga. Ethan Allen realized that the fort would have to be rushed immediately if surprise were not to be lost. Turning to address his Green Mountain Boys, he stood just a bit forward of Benedict Arnold at his side to make it clear that he, Ethan Allen, by orders of the Connecticut Assembly, not Arnold, representing Massachusetts, was in command of the expedition.

"I now propose," Ethan Allen said, "to advance before you and in person to conduct you through the wicket-gate. For we must this morning quit our pretensions to valor, or possess ourselves of this fortress in a few minutes. Inasmuch as it is a desperate attempt—which none but the bravest of men dare undertake—I do not urge it on any contrary to his will." He paused. His great figure was growing more distinct in the half-light, and he seemed to dwarf the short, stocky Arnold. "You that will undertake," Ethan Allen called, "poise your firelocks!"

All obeyed, and they marched off, three ranks deep, toward the fort on a venture that was not actually that "desperate." Ticonderoga was held by only forty-odd British soldiers—most of them unfit for service—under Captain William Delaplace and Lieutenant Jocelyn Feltham. Still, neither Allen nor Arnold nor their eighty-three men knew this as they went charging toward the wicket.

A sentry saw them, pointed his musket and pulled the trigger, but it flashed in the pan, and the sentry ran back into the fort to sound the alarm. The Americans pursued, crying, "No quarter! No quarter!" Another sentry slightly wounded one of Allen's officers with a bayonet, and huge Ethan Allen lifted his sword to cut him down. Taking pity, he softened his blow to a saber cut on the face and went on up a staircase with Arnold.

At the top of the stairs stood Lieutenant Feltham clutching his breeches.

"Come out of there, you damned old rat!" Allen roared, and the astonished officer asked by what authority these men had intruded on the king's domain.

"In the name of the Great Jehovah and the Continental Congress!" Allen bellowed, waving his sword over Feltham's head. Then, demanding "the Fort and all the effects of George the Third" upon pain of a general massacre, Allen brought Captain Delaplace hurrying down the stairs. Delaplace promptly handed over his sword and Fort Ticonderoga.

The gateway to Canada, with all its priceless artillery, was in American hands.

★ 16 ★

CONGRESS CHOOSES A WAR CHIEF

Some delegates to the Second Continental Congress were not exactly enchanted or enthused when they heard of Ticonderoga. Lexington and Concord were, in their way, somehow excusable: embattled farmers had resisted the Crown's attempt to crush them and arrest their leaders. But at Ticonderoga a royal fort had been attacked and captured, the king's cannon, powder and ball seized, his soldiers imprisoned. It seemed to these timorous delegates that bellicose New England might be trying to stampede the other colonies into war. As debate began over such military matters as common defense, the fact that America was openly opposing Britain sank deeper into the minds of most delegates, and although reconciliation with the Mother Country was still an important consideration, the smell of gunpowder was in the air and was making some people nervous.

These timid souls, of course, did not include Colonel Washington, now visible daily in his uniform. Assigned to chair a committee "to consider ways and means to supply these Colonies with ammunition and military stores," he was delighted to hear that Ticonderoga had yielded sixty cannon and mortars. He was also pleased with reports of the Lexington-Concord fighting and assured John Adams that Americans could stand up to British regulars. Privately, Washington wrote to a friend: "Unhappy it is, though, to reflect that a brother's sword has been sheathed in a brother's breast and that the once-happy and peaceful plains of America are either to be drenched with blood or inhabited by slaves. Sad alternative! But can a virtuous man hesitate in his choice?"

Even though there were more than a few who would indeed hesitate, this second Congress with its new delegates was a more forceful body and guided more by a spirit of independence than was its predecessor. There were new arrivals, such as John Hancock, whose reputation as a Son of Liberty and the central figure in the *Liberty* Affair, put him in the president's chair. Benjamin Franklin was another newcomer. For fifteen years he had been a colonial agent in London, but now the chilling perspective of war clouds gathering had brought him home and into Carpenter's Hall as a delegate from Pennyslavania. Approaching seventy, he still possessed his faculties undiminished—including his practical wisdom, his wit and his insights so penetrating that he could have been called Mr. Heart-of-the-Matter. Author of *Poor Richard's Almanack*—that widely read storehouse of witty aphorisms—inventor of the Franklin stove, bifocal glasses and the lightning rod; a pioneer in the investigation of electricity; as well as the founder of what became the American Philosophical Society, of the Academy of Philadelphia (forerunner of the University of Pennsylvania), and of the Philadelphia Library, he had served also as deputy postmaster general for the colonies. Although Franklin had been born in Boston, where he learned the printing and publishing trade as a printer's devil, he migrated to Philadelphia and there opened a profitable printing house while publishing the Pennsylvania *Gazette.* Though a bachelor, Benjamin Franklin always had a lively eye for a pretty face, and from one of these unknown liaisons there issued his natural son, William, in whose rise to become the fiercely Loyalist governor of New Jersey he did not glory and from whom he was now bitterly estranged.

It was no surprise that this oldest delegate should almost immediately befriend the youngest: Thomas Jefferson of Virginia. Tall and red-haired, this wealthy Virginia aristocrat was the son of a backcountry yeoman who, as a surveyor in the tradition of George Washington, amassed a fortune in land that he later populated with black slaves. Franklin and Jefferson hit it off because both were philosophers who were interested more in political theory than in metaphysics, and although Jefferson had been graduated from the College of William and Mary, he was, in the main, a self-taught thinker like Franklin. "Tall Tawm," as he was called, was an English deist, like so many of the delegates in Carpenter's Hall, who believed that reason and nature suggested that a deity who created the universe might exist—indeed, even did exist—but that he was both unknowable and indifferent to his creation. From this belief flows the absolute rejection of the tenets of all revealed religion, and by 1775, Thomas Jefferson was already an implacable foe of the various established faiths then existing in the colonies, most especially the Anglicanism of his native Virginia. Finally, he was an uncompromising pacifist. He would fight for freedom with words and conclusions, but not with blood or bullets. While other delegates of or near his age of thirty-two actually took up arms to keep faith with the mutual pledge of "our lives, our fortunes and our sacred honor," Jefferson would retire to Williamsburg, where as governor of Virginia, he would hear no shots fired in anger.

Yet while conservatives, such as James Duane of New York, Dickinson and Galloway, were attempting to revive the spirit of conciliation with the Crown, Jefferson did not join them. He was drawn, rather, like the Cavaliers of the First Congress, to unite with Yankees such as John Adams. When a petition was received from the Massachusetts Committee of Safety asking Congress to adopt the New England army that had laid siege to British-held Boston, it was Adams who did his utmost—inside and outside Carpenter's Hall—to prevent the nine lower colonies from splitting from the northern four. He arose in Congress to warn of the common danger from the tried-and-true British policy of "Divide and Rule." If New England were to fall, then one by one the others would be enslaved, beginning with New York. Adams shocked many conservatives and middle-of-the-roaders by speaking bluntly of an "American army" recruited from all the colonies. He already knew whom he would recommend to command it. It should not be a professional, such as British-born Charles Lee, a general by grace of the King of Poland, but a native-born American. Should he be from the North, which had raised the army before Boston, or from the middle or southern colonies, which seemed to be wavering?

On June 14 Adams gave his answer. Ambitious John Hancock in the president's chair listened hopefully as his fellow Bostonian began to describe his candidate for American war chief: "—a gentleman from Virginia who is among us here, and who is—"

There was a stir. The tall man in uniform had risen quickly to his feet and bolted for the library.

"—George Washington of Virginia."

There was a swelling hum of voices, raised first in surprise, as well as, from New Englanders, some resentment. John Hancock's face fell farther when his old friend, Sam Adams, arose to second his cousin's motion. Washington, in the library, might have been a bit chagrined to hear Edmund Pendleton of Virginia say that although the colonel was a decent man, he had lost every big battle he'd been in.

Debate continued until the next day, June 15, when Washington appeared and heard Hancock say: "The President [of Congress] has the order of Congress to inform George Washington, Esquire, of the unanimous vote in choosing him to be General and Commander-in-Chief of the forces raised and to be raised in defense of American liberty. The Congress hopes the gentleman will accept."

The gentleman would accept, but with the modesty that was one of his finest traits, he said:

"Mr. President ... I ... declare with the utmost sincerity, I do not think myself equal to the command I am honored with. As to pay, Sir, I beg leave to assure the Congress that as no pecuniary consideration could have tempted me to have accepted this arduous employment at the expense of my domestic ease and happiness, I do not wish to make any profit from it."

He would keep an account of his expenses, which were all he asked Congress to pay.

After the selection of the leader came the choice of his lieutenants. Artemas Ward in command at Cambridge was, of course, the first of them as a major general; then Charles Lee; Philip Schuyler, the wealthy Hudson River patroon who was so influential in New York; Israel Putnam, to satisfy Connecticut; and finally, as a skilled professional adjutant to handle Washington's staff work, his neighbor from Virginia, Horatio Gates.

Meanwhile, George Washington prepared to leave next day for Boston.

★ 17 ★

GEORGE WASHINGTON

Although much has been made of George Washington's supposedly patrician forebears, the truth is that if the Washingtons—or Wessingtons—could boast of a family tree stretching back five centuries in Britain, they were neither high nor low: of the gentry, but not of the nobility, yet above the common people. After Henry VIII they were steady Anglicans and loyal Royalists, Cavalier adherents of King Charles I in the Civil War ending in his execution and in the triumph of Oliver Cromwell—the dictatorial Lord Protector—and his hymn-singing, sword-swinging Puritans, or Roundheads. Many of these despoiled Cavaliers fled to the friendly shores of Virginia, there helping to establish what was nothing less than a feudal society. It was a social pyramid rising from the broad base of black slaves in the field upward through indentured servants and other poor whites—all unlettered—higher to the despised though literate merchants and mechanics, and thence to the farmers and smaller planters, most of whom struggled and schemed to climb to the apex of the structure, where the grandees, owning thousands of acres of land, resided and ruled in almost regal splendor.

In such a society democracy did not flourish. There were few settled municipalities in this vast, sparsely populated province, unlike the northern colonies—especially those of New England—with their town meetings, where men might legislate for themselves, or sit together in the numerous taverns and discuss, over a glass of wine or mug of punch, how men who were weak individually might unite against the grasping strong. In Virginia the grandees had no difficulty controlling both the House of Burgesses and the Anglican Church. The only restraint upon their power was the royal governor, a true despot transplanted from the

Mother Country, who ruled with a council of his own choosing. But the governor, so often interested in enriching himself, could be persuaded. Such a society was most attractive to those bluebloods who were fleeing the bloody wrath of the regicidal Cromwell, so that between 1640 and 1670, Virginia's population rose from fifteen thousand to seventy thousand.

Among these arrivals was John Washington, who came to the Old Dominion in 1658 on a commercial venture and decided to stay. He was followed by a brother Augustine (the family was fond of naming its sons John, Lawrence or Augustine), and then a sister Martha. Eager to join the ranks of those seignurial families at the apex of the pyramid, John began to accumulate land and slaves. So did his son Lawrence and his grandson Augustine, the father of George Washington.

Augustine had married Jane Butler, who gave birth to four children, including two sons—Lawrence and Augustine—who survived him. On Jane's death in 1730, he married Mary Ball, a woman in her midtwenties, who, though barely able to write her name, was nevertheless self-willed and given to a perverse pleasure of reminding her husband of her common origins. Mary bore seven children, the first of whom was George, born on February 22, 1732. When George was three, the family moved to a plantation on Little Hunting Creek on the south bank of the Potomac. Later they took up residence at Ferry Farm on the north bank of the Rappahannock near Fredericksburg. Here Augustine died in 1743.

Because seven of Augustine's nine children survived infancy, something of a record in those days, his progeny were far too numerous for him to bestow any great legacy on each of them. So the bulk of his possessions went to Jane's sons—Lawrence and Augustine—both of whom had been educated in Britain. Lawrence received the estate on Little Hunting Creek, and Augustine, an older one on the Lower Potomac. George was given Ferry Farm, a few parcels of land elsewhere and ten slaves. He was eleven, and until he came of legal age, his mother was his guardian—meaning that she controlled the family finances.

Mary Washington took her guardianship seriously, seeing at once that there was simply no money to educate young George abroad like his older half brothers, or even for him to attend the College of William and Mary in Virginia. Uneducated herself, she set no store by such patrician fopperies and kept George at Ferry Farm to help with its management. So his schooling was local and brief and may not have equaled Abraham Lincoln's pathetic total of twelve months in a classroom. Of classical learning, then, George had none; he spelled badly, knew nothing of syntax and yet, where he could, he found books to educate himself. Thus he read *Don Quixote* and *Tristram Shandy,* developed a handsome, cursive handwriting, picked up a smattering of science and mathematics and became a good draftsman. But the literary work that had the utmost influence upon his life was a little pamphlet entitled *The Rules of Conduct and Politeness.*

It was composed in 1595 by the Jesuit fathers of La Fleche, intended for the sons of the nobility and ruling classes of France. It is a surprising document, for of its 110 maxims only one concerns God, one conscience and two kindliness, while no fewer than twenty-one are devoted to cleanliness and fifty-seven to politeness. But this, after all, is nothing less than the customary pragmatism of the sons of Ignatius Loyola, with their policy of adapting to the customs and social mores of their environment.

The success of this little pamphlet was enormous; it was translated into Latin, German, English and Bohemian. By the time it had reached George, the name of its authors had disappeared, and luckily so, for it is doubtful that the feudal lords of Virginia, most of whom were anti-Catholic Freemasons, would have allowed circulation of a work by such enemies of their Anglican faith. Young George treasured these admonitions, committing many of them to memory, for they clearly marked the path that he should follow to make himself amenable to the seigneurs of Virginia. Here were rules for proper table manners, dress, comportment in the presence of the mighty, sympathy for the unfortunate, modesty, moderation, pity for the guilty, fidelity, generosity and prudence, together with reverence for the Almighty, respect for parents and a resolve to be guided always by "that little spark of celestial fire called conscience."

To say that young George scrupulously obeyed all these admonitions would be to suggest that he became a combination of Machiavelli, Lord Chesterfield and the Second Person of the Holy Trinity—but he tried to. As a result he was most welcome at the estate of his half brother Lawrence, who took an interest in him. Upon his return to Virginia from London, Lawrence had served briefly in an unsuccessful British expedition against Cartagena in what is now Colombia. His admiration for his commander, Admiral Vernon, was so great that he named his plantation Mount Vernon. There he prospered, becoming adjutant general of the Virginia militia and a member of the House of Burgesses. His fortune and influence rose even higher upon his marriage to Anne Fairfax, daughter of the colonel of that name who owned Belvoir, a nearby estate. Colonel Fairfax was also a member of the governor's council and a cousin of Lord Fairfax, possessor of nearly 6 million acres of land. So young George found himself welcome not only at Mount Vernon, but at Belvoir and even at Lord Fairfax's home, Greenway Court. In a word, he learned to ingratiate himself with the First Families of Virginia, not by any exceptional wit or charm, which he did not possess, but by the quiet manners of a perfect gentleman, while keeping his own counsel and his mouth shut.

Even so, at the age of fourteen George encountered a crisis: his mother did not know what to do with him, whether to encourage him to follow the life of an obscure poor relative on Ferry Farm's infertile acres or take up the life of a land surveyor, at which he appeared adept. But then Lawrence suggested the sea. Mary Washington was sceptical, writing for advice to her half brother, Joseph Ball. Joseph's reply was a vigorous negative: British ships were floating hells, and George could not be promoted without influence in London; it would be better to apprentice him to a tinker than send him off to sea. Mary agreed and decided to permit George to continue to live at Ferry Farm while following the surveyor's craft.

This he did with great success, for he possessed a natural eye for land and the constitution and strength of a horse, being able to spend long hours in the saddle riding through the wilderness and in every kind of weather, his long legs encased in those protective cowhide chaps that, a century later, would be identified with the western cowboy. Being much in demand, his earnings were high, and he was able to accumulate more than 1,400 acres of land before he was twenty-one. By then Washington had matured physically. Accounts of his height differ, but he stood at least six feet tall, probably two or three inches taller. His shoulders were strong and sloping, his torso thick and his hips lean. His arms were long and muscular, his hair brown and his eyes a light blue that, in rare moments of rage, could blaze with anger or go cold and hard when challenged or displeased. Although his features were regular, his nose was long, with a slight leftward twist at the end, and his cheeks were pitted with the livid scars of the smallpox that afflicted him in Barbados, where he had gone with Lawrence, who sought to alleviate his pulmonary tuberculosis in a balmier climate.

During his surveying travels, he stopped frequently at inns or taverns for rest or refreshment and became known as a good companion. Though not witty, he had a good sense of humor, quick to laugh at a good joke or join a ribald chorus, and was ready to play billiards or card games, such as whist or loo, usually losing but always carefully marking the amounts in his notebook. He liked a glass—developing an iron head for wine or rum—and was extremely fond of pretty lasses. It is probable that Washington accepted the young southern bachelor's dichotomy of

"Good girl to court with, bad girl to play with," for the evidence seems to suggest that, like most of his peers, he was not averse to seeking surcease among girls who were, if not bad, at least obliging. On the first axiom, however, he seemed not so successful, either because of those uncomely scars on his cheeks, the perpetually serious air he had adopted from his *Rules of Conduct* or his treatment of genteel ladies as though they were the younger sisters of the Blessed Virgin Mary.

Yet behind those blue eyes that were so expressive of his moods, there seemed to be a screen, a shutter, shielding a boundless ambition, not so much to rise into the First Families of Virginia alongside his half brothers, but to shine with military glory.

Whence this secret passion for the profession of arms possessed George Washington is not exactly known. In his teens he had fenced with Jacob van Braam, a retired Dutch soldier who may have enchanted him with tales of warfare, or he might have felt a kinship for his great-grandfather, John Washington, a colonel of Virginia militia who led a punitive campaign against the Indians with such success that in admiration they called him "*Conocontarius,*" or "destroyer of villages." All that is known is that after he left his brother Lawrence still suffering from pulmonary illness in Barbados in December 1751 and returned to Virginia, he rode almost at once to Williamsburg to present Lawrence's letters to Robert Dinwiddie, the new governor of the colony. Dinwiddie was a canny Scots merchant who had made a fortune in West Indies trade and now, through his high office, was intent upon increasing it through acquisitions of land in the Ohio Valley. He invited his solemn young guest to dine with him and quickly became favorably impressed by him. What they discussed is also not known, but in the spring of 1752, learning that Virginia was to be divided into two military districts for the training of militia, Washington wrote to Dinwiddie asking to be made the adjutant of one of them. The request was granted, and in December of that year, Washington was commissioned major in command of the southern district with an annual salary of one hundred pounds. It was quite a plum for a young man not yet twenty-one, even though it was for the southern, rather than the northern district, which he desired. But this difficulty was quickly overcome, probably through the influence of Colonel Fairfax, his distant relative, on the governor's council. Next, Washington found a deputy to carry out his military duties for half the salary. Such sinecures were common, both in Britain and in the colonies, but for this young man to have moved so quickly to obtain one suggests a sophistication that does not quite conform to Parson Weems's cloying confection of the Perfect Little

Prig or the bewigged fussy old woman in men's clothing that Gilbert Stuart's wretched portrait of the Father of His Country has preserved for posterity—most notably on the one-dollar bill.

Another false image created that year was after Washington's induction into the Masonic Order in Fredericksburg. Washington the Ardent Mason simply never existed, nor does the mistaken belief among the Masons of France and Spain that Freemasonry in Britain and her colonies shared their political activism. In truth, Washington seldom attended Masonic meetings, and there is no proof that the order shaped his convictions or helped him to rise in the world. Rather, his twin benefactors were his brother Lawrence and Governor Dinwiddie. It was therefore a great shock to George when Lawrence returned to Mount Vernon in 1752 only to die of his affliction that July. It was as though he had lost a loving and wise father, ending an affectionate and almost adoring relationship that was never to be replaced by the attitude of a dutiful but not overfond son that he showed to his importunate mother. To fulfill his ambition, George Washington must now depend on Dinwiddie alone.

In 1752 it appeared that Washington's military ambitions would be confined to training militia, when and if he deigned to appear at any of its meetings, because the treaty of Aix-la-Chapelle in 1748 seemed to have ended the Anglo-French struggle for worldwide colonial supremacy. Both nations were exhausted, and their rulers—George II and Louis XV—were weary of the dreadful costs of war. To young Washington, no war meant no glory. Yet, the greed of the commercial upper classes of both nations had not been satisfied. When the French moved to rearm, the British did likewise. The prospect of a renewal of hostilities by these two leading powers—hostile in race as well as in religion—stupefied the rest of Europe. As Voltaire would write upon the outbreak of the Seven Years' War: "These two nations have gone to war over a few acres of snow in Canada, and, in it, they have spent a great deal more than Canada is worth."

In the spring of 1752, the French attempted to link their vast possessions along the St. Lawrence River in Canada with those to the south, in what would become known as Louisiana, by entering the disputed valley of the Ohio. If successful, they would contain the thirteen British colonies in America between the Allegheny Mountains and the sea. Even though the French numbered only 60,000 in North America, as opposed to about 1.2 million British colonists, by the nature of their militarist society and through their Indian allies and the assistance of a powerful French fleet blockading the Atlantic coast, they could eventually conquer the thirteen colonies, and the eastern seaboard, from being British and Protestant, would become French and Catholic.

Such, in effect, was the dire prophecy of impending disaster that Robert Dinwiddie transmitted to his superiors in London, once he learned that a body of French troops from Quebec had landed on the south shore of Lake Erie. The French built a fort at Presque Isle, now Erie, Pennsylvania, and another to the south called Fort Le Boeuf—on territory sacred to the British crown! Dinwiddie's alarm was not without personal and commercial considerations. He was a member of the Ohio Company, formed in 1747 by leading Virginians—including Lawrence Washington and sundry Lees and Fairfaxes—to settle and exploit the Ohio Valley. The project had been approved in London, and when Lord Holderness, the secretary of state for the colonies, learned that the French had invaded "our province of Virginia," he ordered Dinwiddie to evict them, if necessary "by force of arms." Meeting with his council on October 22, 1753, the governor decided to send a message to the commander of the French troops in the area demanding that they be withdrawn. Learning of the decision, probably from Colonel Fairfax, Major George Washington asked to be appointed the bearer of the message. His request was granted, and on November 14 Washington and his party of horses, baggage, four hostlers and orderlies, the frontiersman Christopher Gist and Jacob van Braam, the Dutch soldier who said he could speak French, Washington set out for the Ohio country.

It was a difficult journey over unfamiliar terrain and in the cold rains of a dying autumn that would soon be succeeded by the icy-iron hand of a western winter. But on December 4, Washington's command rode out of the dripping woods at Venango.

The French officers there greeted Washington with flawless courtesy. They also tried to lure his Indians to their side. Failing to do so, they suavely refused the young Virginian's message and sent him up French Creek to Fort Le Boeuf to their superior officer, Legardeur de St. Pierre. At Le Boeuf, Washington presented Dinwiddie's demand that the French leave the Ohio country. The demand was politely refused by St. Pierre. "He told me," Washington wrote later, "that the country belonged to [the French]; that no Englishman had a right to trade upon those waters; and that he had orders to make every person prisoner who attempted it on the Ohio, or the waters of it."

On December 16, bearing St. Pierre's reply, Washington and his party started downriver for Venango. They hurried, plying their paddles furiously, for the creek had begun to freeze. Leaving Venango, Washington discovered that their horses, which had been quartered there, were too feeble to carry riders. The party dismounted and began to walk. Snow was falling regularly. The temperatures fell. Some of the men were so frostbitten that they had to be left in a temporary shack. Washington pressed on grimly, eager to get the French answer to Dinwiddie as soon as possible. If he delayed, he might be snowed in until spring, when the French would be already on the move. Eventually, the young major struck out on foot with his guide.

"I took my necessary papers, pulled off my clothes, and tied myself up in a match coat. Then with gun in hand and pack at my back, I set out with Mr. Gist, fitted in the same manner."

They were shot at—and missed—by a false Indian guide. Attempting to cross the Allegheny River by a log raft, Washington was thrown into the icy water—saving himself only by throwing one long arm across the raft. But both men could not pole through the current to either shore, and they waded ashore on a little island, spending the night sheeted in ice. In the morning, to their inexpressible joy, they beheld the treacherous river locked in a silent white vise of ice. They crossed, and on January 16, 1754—exactly one month after his departure from Fort Le Boeuf—George Washington placed the French refusal in Governor Dinwiddie's hand.

At the age of twenty-one the Father of America had already entered his nation's history.

Robert Dinwiddie was an energetic and resourceful man. He saw at once that the fork of land (modern Pittsburgh) where the confluence of the Allegheny and Monongahela rivers formed the great Ohio was the key to the west. Washington had written: "The land in the forks I think extremely well situated for a fort, as it has the absolute command of both rivers. The land at the point is twenty or twenty-five feet above the common surface of the water; and a considerable bottom of flat, well-timbered land all around it, very convenient for building."

Eager to fortify the forks before the French could do so, Dinwiddie soon found, like all royal governors before and after him, that the colonies were hopelessly divided and that his own House of Burgesses was extremely jealous of its prerogatives. The burgesses made him a frugal grant of funds and placed it in the hands of a committee of their own. Dinwiddie's appeal for assistance to the other colonies was either ignored or rejected, except for North Carolina, which also had claims to western lands. Still, in February 1754, he was able to send a party of backwoodsmen to the Ohio forks under orders to build a fort there. Meanwhile, he bickered with the burgesses for more funds while he busily rounded up companies of British regulars that he joined to half the Virginia militia of three hundred men and sent this force, under George Washington, now a lieutenant colonel at twenty-two, moving westward to garrison the completed fort. But before he could get the other half of the militia moving, the French, demonstrating their capacity for swift movement, came bobbing down the Allegheny, seized the British fort by summons, demolished it and replaced it with a stronger one of their own.

Fort Duquesne now held the West for France.

Lieutenant Colonel Washington was just across the Alleghenies—perhaps 110 miles southeast of Duquesne—when he heard of the disaster. Immediately, he began pushing northwest to establish a forward base for the arrival of reinforcements and artillery. On May 28, 1754, halfway to Duquesne, he surprised an advance party of French.

Jumonville de Villiers, the French leader, was slain in the first volley. After Washington's Indians had brained and scalped the wounded, there were 10 French dead, 1 wounded and 21 captured, against Washington's losses of 1 wounded. It had been the youthful commander's first fight, and he was elated at the near-perfect result. In fact, his biggest difficulty came in keeping his fierce Indian ally, Half King, from killing and scalping his prisoners. Half King swore that he would be avenged on the French for allowing their Indians to kill, boil and eat his father.

But Washington dissuaded Half King, after which the young Virginian withdrew ten miles to a place called Great Meadows. Here he threw up a ramshackle stockade, aptly named Fort Necessity. Meanwhile, all Canada and later France seethed with rage over the "murder" of Villiers by "the cruel Vvasington." The dead man's brother, the sieur Coulon de Villiers, came marching hotly from Montreal to avenge "*l'assassin.*" On July 3 Villiers's nine hundred men clashed with Washington's four hundred at Fort Necessity.

The French quickly drove the British into rain-filled trenches and then carefully shot down every horse, cow or dog within the fort. In a half hour the English realized that their transport and meat were gone. By nightfall it was obvious that the British were beaten, and the disconsolate young Washington, certain that a glorious career had ended before it had barely begun, sent his old comrade Jacob van Braam out into the night to ask for terms.

The French were generous. They could not have known that van Braam had mistaken the French word for *assassination* for the word *death* and they were pleased that Washington was willing to acknowledge his crime of murdering Jumonville de Villiers. Unaware of a concession he would certainly never have made, Washington capitulated. The next day the British were accorded the honors of war.

Drums beating, colors flying, arms sloped, they marched out of the slime of Fort Necessity while the enemy Indians went rushing in to plunder all that had been left behind. Though the British attempted to show a proud face, they were weary and hungry, many of them carried wounded men on their backs, and they had barely enough powder and ball to drive off the hostile Indians who harried them along the sixty miles back to Wills Creek. A heartbreaking march had begun, and the youth who led it never forgot the day that it started.

It was the fourth of July.

George Washington did not return to a hero's welcome in Virginia. Although his friends among the burgesses stood by him, it was widely bruited about, both in the province and in the Mother Country, that he had admitted to "murder" to save his life. Washington indignantly denied the charge, trying to explain that he spoke no French and had relied on van Braam's supposed skill in that language. But now he knew that his Dutch friend was, at the least, exaggerating. Moreover, if he were guilty of murder, why was he not punished by Villiers? Obviously, the word "*l'assassin*" was of a political nature, and all Villiers wanted was an admission that a French officer had been slain on French soil. Furthermore, his friends argued, the young commander's reputation for integrity and bravery was so unassailable that he could not possibly be accused of cowardice.

Doubtless, but the stigma did not disappear, and when Governor Horatio Sharpe of Maryland—a former British officer—was commissioned to lead a force of a thousand regulars against Fort Duquesne in the autumn of 1754, Dinwiddie dissolved the Virginia militia and offered Washington a captaincy in this force. Disgusted, and certain that British officers of the same rank would insist upon being senior to him, the young colonel resigned. Although this campaign never materialized, he still headed north for Mount Vernon. There it is possible that he sought surcease from his disappointment among the ladies of pleasure in Alexandria. So it may be inferred from letters to him from companions in arms. Three years later his friend George Mercer, writing from South Carolina, complained that the ladies there lacked "those enticing, heaving, throbbing, alluring plump breasts common with our northern belles."

Washington did not protest.

Although the death of Jumonville de Villiers and the fight at Fort Necessity were the sparks that set battlefields blazing in Europe, America and

India, France and Britain did not renew their hostilities until 1756. In the meantime, they allowed their colonies in the New World to strike at each other in a sort of prelude to this fourth and final round in the great conflict for colonial supremacy—each side providing battle fleets and regiments of regulars to ensure victory. Thus while France prepared to send a fleet carrying three thousand soldiers to the New World in 1755, Britain countered by ordering Major General Edward Braddock to sail for Virginia with two regiments and to take command of all regular and colonial forces in America. Braddock arrived in February 1755.

Braddock's arrival excited the ardor for glory that slumbered in the breast of George Washington, and he informed Braddock of his desire to join the expedition forming against Fort Duquesne. He asked for a regular's rank of major, thus hoping to outrank those disdainful British captains who refused to serve under colonials. Washington was naively unaware of the need for powerful friends in the Mother Country to obtain such rank at the age of twenty-three or of the necessity of buying such a commission. Mentioning neither, he heard nothing until, in desperation, he offered to serve as a volunteer on Braddock's staff. This offer was immediately and gladly accepted, for his experience and knowledge of the terrain and its Indians would be of great value. So he joined Braddock at Frederick, Maryland, and journeyed with him to the staging area at Wills Creek.

Edward Braddock was a short, stout man congenial although sometimes choleric, as brave as he was bullheaded, but with little experience of battle. Except for Washington, whom he came to like, he condemned most colonials as a crowd of ignorant sloths, reserving a special contempt for colonial troops and deriding their officers as a pack of "General Buckskins."

Braddock was schooled in the tactics of European warfare that had been developed since the turn of the century. After the flintlock had replaced the firelock, and with the development of the socket bayonet, infantry tactics had been simplified. Four kinds of infantry—pikemen, musketeers, fusiliers and grenadiers—were now reduced to one general type of foot soldier, armed with a bayoneted flintlock. The foot soldier was drilled incessantly and subjected to a barbarously brutal discipline, which made him, in effect, a battlefield automaton.* He fought in the open against other automatons, who were also taught to wheel and to dress ranks amid the very smoke and stress of battle, to load and advance,

*In 1712 a British guardsman was sentenced to 12,600 lashes and nearly died after he received the first 1,800.

to fire and reload—and to drive home the assault with the bayonet under the smoke of the final volley.

A musket's killing range was only a few hundred paces, and firing was not accurate; in fact, the British fire drill of the period did not include the order "Aim." The object was not so much to riddle the enemy as to frighten him and pin him down for the shock action of the cavalry. Such tactics, adjusted to terrain and weapons as tactics always are, were almost the opposite of American bush fighting, in which the forests imposed a premium upon dispersion, cover and accuracy. To say that Braddock could not or would not see this difference is only to say, after all, that he was an ordinarily competent commander, but not gifted with the insights of genius. New wars are always being fought with the fixations of the old, and Edward Braddock was no exception to that dreary axiom as he reached Wills Creek on the tenth of May to take command of his army.

Braddock had a fourfold plan for evicting the French from the New World: he would personally capture Fort Duquesne, another force would take Fort Niagara on Lake Ontario, a third would reduce the French bastion at Crown Point on Lake Champlain and a fourth would capture Acadia. For his own operation he had more than 2,000 men, divided among 1,400 redcoats, perhaps 450 of the despised Virginia militia, 300 axmen to clear roads through the wilderness and a handful of Indians. In early June the expedition left Wills Creek.

George Washington, down once again with "the bloody flux" and what was probably malaria, had been compelled to ride in a covered wagon. Agonizing over the column's slow pace of two miles a day, fearful that such slow progress would give the French time to reinforce Duquesne, he staggered from his wagon to advise Braddock to divide his forces for speed. An advance body of about 1,500 men, shorn of its wagons and heavy equipment, could move swiftly against the fort, while the remainder of the army under Colonel Arthur St. Clair could follow at a slower pace. Astonishingly enough, Braddock agreed to this violation of the cardinal rule of concentration of forces. He took command of the advance body while Colonel Thomas Dunbar followed with the second contingent.

Still feverish and weak from dysentery—though pleased by Braddock's decision—Washington returned to his wagon.

The sieur de Contrecoeur Duquesne ordered Captain Daniel Beaujeu to ambush the approaching British. Leading a mixed force of about nine hundred French, Canadians and Indians, Beaujeu marched to a point seven miles below the fort where he knew the enemy would have to recross the Monongahela River. It was a rocky, woody, murky place made for ambuscade, and even though half his Indians had deserted him, Beaujeu was confident of victory.

So was George Washington, moving with the advance force. Though barely able to walk and still in agony, he had left his wagon to strap a pillow to the saddle of his horse, painfully clambering onto it to ride forward. En route he was dismayed to see how conspicuous the scarlet coats of the regulars were against the tender spring green of the wilderness. Braddock had crossed the Monongahela and was preparing to recross when Washington overtook him. Lieutenant Colonel Thomas Gage had already moved across the stream with his covering force to protect the main body. Cries of exaltation succeeded the successful recrossing. Duquesne was only seven miles away!

Suddenly the guides in front of the column came sprinting back to shout that they had seen the French. A white man in Indian dress with a gorget around his neck came running toward Braddock's men. It was Beaujeu. Catching sight of the redcoats before him, he waved his arms to the right and the left. His still-invisible men parted, moving to either side of their enemy. Blood-curdling war whoops came from the woods, then explosions, smoke, bullets—and the screams of stricken redcoats.

Gage's troops wheeled into line almost immediately. Shouting "God save the King!" they discharged volley after volley. They killed Beaujeu and sent his Canadians flying away in fright. Captain Dumas, now in command, rallied the Indians, who had stood their ground. They hid behind trees or fallen trunks, they crouched in gullies or ravines, and thus invisible they poured a heavy fire into the close-packed redcoats of the British soldiery.

Soon the British fell silent. In their ears was a frightful cacophony. The endless yelling of the Indians, the screams of their own stricken, the rolling musket fire of the battle, all were picked up and sent reverberating through the encircling gloom of the forest. Rare was the British regular who saw his enemies, and rarer still was the survivor who ever forgot that whooping and screeching.

Only the despised Virginians seemed capable of fighting back. A party of them, led by Captain Thomas Waggener, dashed for a huge fallen tree. They threw themselves down behind it and began picking off red men flitting from cover to cover or darting to the road to scalp a dead or wounded soldier. But the British regulars mistook their only friends for foes and opened fire on the Virginia rear, killing many colonials and forcing the rest to withdraw.

Now from a hill to the British right came a plunging fire. Demoralized and then terrified, the redcoats fired volley after volley into thin air. They riddled the trees and chipped the rocks. Some of them tried to take cover like the colonials, but their officers would not allow them. The officers yanked the men erect or away from trees and strode among them with bared swords, crying angrily: "Stand and fight!" Back came the pitiful plea: "We would fight if we could see anybody to fight with." And so, rather than disperse, they stood fast; they huddled together, shrinking from the bullets that swept among them, presenting to their tormentors larger and ever larger targets of red.

Suddenly the rumor spread that the French and Indians were attacking the baggage train in the rear. Gage's men turned and ran. They thundered over St. Clair's second echelon, abandoned their cannon to the enemy, and came tumbling eastward into the ranks of the British main body even as General Braddock led these soldiers forward.

Now both British regiments were mixed, and confusion reigned unchecked. The towering fury of Braddock riding among them failed to rally this disorganized mass. How could it have? Braddock beat his men with the flat of his sword rather than allow them to adopt the "cowardly" cover that is the only way to fight in a forest. He refused George Washington's request to allow him to take the provincials against the hill on the right in Indian style. Instead, he ordered Lieutenant Colonel Ralph Burton to storm the height with dressed ranks. Burton obeyed. He rallied a hundred regulars, who followed him until he fell wounded, after which they melted away.

Gage was also wounded, as were Horatio Gates and Braddock's two aides, Robert Orme and William Morris. The carnage among the officers was frightful. Mounted, resplendent in laced regimentals, the British leaders were choice targets. Sir Peter Halkett was shot dead. So was young William Shirley, son of the Massachusetts governor. Of eighty-six officers, sixty-three were killed or wounded.

Washington himself had four shots through his clothes, and two mounts were shot from under him. Braddock lost four horses, mounted a fifth—and took a musket ball that passed through his right arm and pierced his lung. He fell gasping into the bushes beside the road.

It was then that the retreat that Braddock had ordered became a frenzied rout. The British simply turned and fled for the river in their rear. Some of them were scalped by pursuing Indians even as they plunged into the ford. Washington saw that it was useless to attempt to rally them on the right bank of the Monongahela. Instead he hastened to Braddock's side and found him mortally stricken. Braddock would live long enough to exclaim, over and over, "Who would have thought it?" and to curse his regulars and their officers for firing on each other, while praising Washington and his Virginia "blues." He died after Washington successfully re-formed his broken army and led it fifty miles to the rear at Dunbar's camp and thence, after he had buried the British bulldog, to Wills Creek.

Behind the retreating British, howling hideously, their scalping knives unsheathed, Beaujeu's Indians took possession of the field.

Colonel George Washington returned to Williamsburg like a conquering hero. No matter that Braddock was defeated and dead or that only the Acadian campaign out of the fourfold plan of conquest had succeeded; the Virginians, under their youthful commander, had alone stood up to the enemy, and but for them and their leader, total disaster might have befallen the British in this sorry Battle of the Wilderness. An exaggeration, yes, but this was the attitude of Dinwiddie, down through the jubilant members of the House of Burgesses, who voted Washington three hundred pounds in recompense for his losses during the campaign, while the governor placed him in command of a new regiment of one thousand men to serve on the frontier.

George Washington spent three years on the border, protecting settlers there against the incursions of the Indians unleashed by the French at Duquesne, learning much about wilderness warfare, while suffering anew under the onslaught of his twin afflictions of malaria and dysentery, plus a new source of pain from the deterioration of his teeth. Throughout this ordeal he steadily sought a commission in the British Army, and even though he had a staunch ally in Governor Dinwiddie, his campaign for royal rank was never successful. His friendship with the governor also cooled, chiefly because of Washington's youthful arrogance and his alliance with members of the House of Burgesses who were hostile to Dinwiddie. Nevertheless he did have the satisfaction of gazing upon the destruction of Duquesne. In November 1758 he was with General John Forbes, a Scottish veteran, as commander in chief of the Virginia militia, when Forbes led the final expedition against the French. Approaching the fort with an overwhelming force, he found that its commander, with only five hundred men to defend it, had blown it up. Thus on November 25 George Washington gazed in satisfaction upon the ashes and charred timbers of the fortification that had been for so long one of the objectives of his young life. Another commission—of field rank in the British Army—was denied, and Washington shortly thereafter resigned from the Virginia militia.

During four years in uniform, George Washington had shown himself prone to all the arrogant vices of a young man in high command. He had quarreled with his benefactor, Dinwiddie, and played politics in Williamsburg, while dissembling to British generals in hopes of receiving a commission. His hasty and rash attack in which Jumonville had died had triggered the greatest colonial war, and he had been rudely chastised for it at Fort Necessity. Only his self-possession at the Battle of the Wilderness had rescued him from the reputation of a bungler. Yet he had shown—by his unrivaled physical and moral courage, by a steadfastness in adversity that always redeemed his habit of complaint, joined to an astonishing durability and determination in hardship, ill health and filthy weather, along with a simple dignity endearing him to his officers and the stern but fair discipline that made him beloved of his men—that here, indeed, was a chief. With this reputation to sustain him, he retired to a planter's life in Mount Vernon.

Although Lawrence Washington in his will had confirmed the arrangements made by his father—that his half-brother George would receive Mount Vernon—he also provided that his wife, Anne Fairfax Washington, would have the use of the estate for life. However, Anne quickly remarried and ceded this right, or usufruct, to George for an annual payment of fifteen thousand pounds of tobbaco. Upon her death in 1761 that payment ended, and George held the property free and clear.

Washington enjoyed life as a planter and was on good terms with his neighbor George William Fairfax and his charming and vivacious wife Sally. Sally sought to cure the dysentery that still tormented him by prescribing a diet for it. The diet was not successful, yet Washington's frequent rides downriver to Belvoir to consult with Sally soon brought him under her spell. She flirted with him, discreetly, especially after her husband departed for London, and Washington fell in love with her. He wrote her letters that were models of how, in a hideously involuted style, a man hopelessly infatuated does not dare to say plainly—and thus perhaps damningly to eyes other than Sally's—that avowal of eternal love that his heart demands but his head rejects. The result was a compound of halfhearted confusion. That he should have written anything to his friend's wife is surprising, and that she should have preserved these letters is incredible. Still, Sally had the good sense to hold him at arm's length. Perhaps she suspected that, given the mores of the day, such a liaison, once it was inevitably discovered, could end only in a duel. Moreover, at Belvoir she and her husband could remain on good terms with Washington and the lady he had married.

This was Martha Dandridge Custis, a widow whom Washington had been formally courting while composing those stuttering letters. Finding Sally inaccessible—although it might have been that Washington was proposing a platonic liaison, which would have been in contradiction to his virile nature—he married Martha.

Martha Custis Washington was a delightful little dumpling. Barely literate, only five feet tall, plump, with a hooked nose and large baby blue eyes, if she had been taller and shapelier she still would not have been sexually exciting. But she was very sweet and very gentle—and also very rich. The fortune she had inherited upon the death of her merchant husband, Daniel Parke Custis, went to Washington upon her marriage to him, in accordance with the law and made him one of the wealthiest men in Virginia.

Having been elected to the House of Burgesses in 1765 and reelected four years later, Washington was now a man not only of great possessions but of political power. His happiness was real, even though he sired no children, probably because of his own sterility, inasmuch as Martha had born four in her previous marriage, of whom a boy and a girl survived. Washington took these stepchildren to his heart and was a loving and caring father to them.

He now occupied himself with expanding his estate, so that he soon presided over more than seven thousand acres, while his work force of a hundred slaves was greatly expanded by purchase and propagation. He was a good businessman, shrewd but honest, and an agricultural innovator, shifting from the tobbaco that so swiftly exhausted land to farming of food crops, experimenting with varying degrees of success with grains and fibers. Under the relaxing influence of a happy marriage, his health improved remarkably, and he was eventually as robust and hardy as the high-hearted youth who had survived the ordeals of the Venango mission.

In his political life, George Washington gradually came to be considered one of the outstanding members of the House of Burgesses. He shared the convictions of most of its members: perpetuation of the feudal status quo in the province and opposition to Parliament's harsher and harsher taxing measures. Although not a gifted orator in the manner of Patrick Henry or Richard Henry Lee or a thinker of the perception of James Madison or Thomas Jefferson, he was nevertheless forthright and forceful. To him the Stamp Act was a "direful attack" upon colonial liberty. When Britain in 1768 prohibited white settlements beyond the Appalachian divide, ostensibly to protect the Indians, Washington bitterly attacked the decision as actually a measure to contain the colonies. Charged by his critics with a venal ulterior motive—that is, his holdings behind that line—he replied that these were long-term investments, and no matter what the cabinet might decree, its line would eventually be breached—as it was.

His dislike of the British, planted in him by those arrogant regular captains who refused to serve under him, then nourished by his failure to obtain a royal commission, was made to bloom by the London merchants who overcharged him for goods that were often of poor quality. Thus, with his friend George Mason, he was a leading author of Virginia's nonimportation agreement. After King George III lifted the royal rod to chastise Boston, "that nest of sedition," and Massachusetts with his Coercive Acts, Washington rose from his seat in fury to ask: "Shall we, after this, whine and cry for relief, when we have already tried it in vain? Or shall we supinely sit and see one province after another fall a prey to despotism?"

From Lexington and Concord came the fiery reply, and so it was that when the Second Continental Congress convened on May 10, 1775, among those Virginia delegates who rode north to cross their Rubicon at the Potomac River, wearing his old blue uniform, was George Washington of Mount Vernon.

★ 18 ★

THE BATTLE OF BUNKER HILL

During the two months succeeding Lexington-Concord, a steady stream of New Englanders flowed into Cambridge and adjacent towns to form a besieging force holding the British army in Boston at bay. It was not a very military formation, for these arrivals from Rhode Island, Connecticut and New Hampshire were even less warlike in their appearance and professional in their bearing than were the smirkingly superior minutemen of Massachusetts. All told, they numbered close to 10,000 men, with the Nutmeg State providing about 2,300, Rhode Island and New Hampshire roughly the same between them and the remainder coming from the Bay Colony. Their commander, Major General Artemas Ward, had served as a colonel of militia in the French and Indian War, but was now ill with "the stone," as any affliction of the kidneys or bladders was then called. Ward had risen from a sickbed to ride to Cambridge. He divided his "Army of Observation," so-called because even the bellicose Yankees were still reluctant to appear to be making war on Britain, into three divisions. He held the center at Cambridge with fifteen regiments; John Thomas was on the left, and Nathanael Greene of Rhode Island was on the right at Roxbury.

Greene, with Benedict Arnold, would one day become the most able field soldier in the Continental Army. The son of a Quaker preacher, he had been raised to regard the Bible as the source of all wisdom. Instead, the gimpy-legged Greene had gravitated more toward mathematics, political theory and—above all—military history. For this last un-Quakerish avocation, and his professed belief that war to resist tyranny was not only acceptable but imperative, the pacifist Society of Friends read him out of meeting. Joining the Rhode Island militia as a private, he went to Boston in 1773 to buy himself a gun, becoming friendly there with the bookseller Henry Knox, another devotee of military history. Upon his return he brought with him a life of Henri Turenne, the great French general, and a British deserter to drill his company. Greene did not rise to a general's rank because of his political activity, like Dr. Joseph Warren, but because of his native intelligence, grasp of military theory—even though of the textbook variety—and an air of confidence joined to one of quiet authority.

It was these three men who were to oppose the British "triumvirate of reputation" that sailed into Boston Harbor aboard *Cerberus* on May 25. These three major generals—King George III's unhesitating choice of George Washington's "sad alternative"—were William Howe, John Burgoyne and Henry Clinton. Howe was the senior officer.

William Howe was born in 1729, the third son of the Irish peer, the second Viscount Howe, and his wife, Mary Sophia, the daughter of Baroness Kielmansegge, who had been one of the mistresses of King George I. This connection with the Teutonic House of Hanover has often been advanced as an explanation of the meteoric rise of all three Howe brothers in the Royal Army and Navy, but there is little evidence to support it—other than how their own bulging features, it was maliciously whispered about, were so distinctly Hanoverian. Actually, all three rose on their own merits, rather than from royal favor.

In 1746, at the age of seventeen, Howe purchased a cornet's commission in the Duke of Cumberland's light dragoons, and within a year was a lieutenant serving in Flanders during the War of the Austrian Succession against the forces led by Marshal Saxe of France. After the war ended he served with the 20th Foot with James Wolfe, who became his close friend.

Within a few years Howe's military career became closely associated with America. In 1758, after the outbreak of the Seven Years' War, he served under Wolfe in command of a regiment at the second siege of Louisbourg, earning Wolfe's high praise for his gallantry in leading an amphibious invasion of beaches held by the heavily armed French. The capture of these positions outflanked the enemy, and eventually the Bourbon lilies dipped to the British Union Jack for the second time. Much of Howe's elation, however, was sobered by grief when, in July of that year, he learned of his brother's death in Abercrombie's ill-fated assault on Ticonderoga. Lord George Augustus Howe, the third viscount of that name, was the one British officer for whom the colonists had both love and respect. He neither despised nor derided them, adopting their customs—even their buckskin dress—and was so eager to learn the tactics of forest fighting that he chose to serve with the Rangers of Captain Robert Rogers. With Major Israel Putnam of Connecticut, Lord Howe had gone forward with a scouting party. A sharp firefight ensued, and Howe fell dead in Putnam's arms. With one shot the French had saved themselves, for then, as Major Thomas Mante wrote, "the soul of General Abercrombie's army seemed to expire."

William Howe's greatest feat of arms was to take place at Quebec the following year, when he led his regiment up the precipitous path in a fighting ascent that turned Montcalm's flank, bringing on the decisive battle of the Seven Years' War. In 1760, as a brigadier general, Howe distinguished himself in the taking of Montreal. Returning to Europe, he fought in the siege of Belle Isle off the French coast and in 1762 was the adjutant general of the British army that captured Havana from Spain.

William Howe was now a famous general, and his reputation was enhanced when, taking a page from Gage's book, he gave the British Army a mobile striking force by introducing companies of light infantry, elite troops lightly equipped and trained to move with great celerity. The innovation was a huge success, and all line regiments soon had light companies of their own.

After the war Howe was the nominal governor of the Isle of Wight, a sinecure that failed to keep him far from the gay life of London, where he had every opportunity to indulge his fondness for cards, a glass and a lass. Although Howe was not an inveterate libertine, and certainly never in the field or in combat when he was every inch an alert and able soldier, he did succumb to the soldier's vices whenever he entered a period of inactivity. His indulgence in food and drink might have made him corpulent if his height of about six feet and strong build had not enabled him to carry it off as merely stout. He had a prominent nose and brooding black eyes. His complexion was dark, and he suffered from the Howe family's fits of gloom.

This alternating rhythm of a Spartan and Sybaritic life was probably best described by Charles Lee when, as Howe's prisoner in Philadelphia, he wrote with customary causticness: "He is naturally good-humored, and complacent, but illiterate and indolent to the last degree, unless as an executive soldier, in which capacity he is all fire and activity, brave and cool as Julius Caesar. His understanding is … rather good than otherwise, but was totally confounded and stupefied by the immensity of the task imposed upon him. He shut his eyes, fought his battles, drank his bottle, had his little whore, advised with his counsellors, received his orders from North and Germain … shut his eyes and fought again."

No such belittling estimate had reached the ears of the Crown, when, in 1758, Howe first appeared in London after being elected to the seat from Nottingham made vacant by the death of his brother George. Howe was no political dynamo, having entered politics because, as Lord Chesterfield observed, "it was the known way to military preferment." Indeed it was common: in the election of 1761 no less than sixty-four army officers won seats in the House of Commons.

Inactive though he might have been politically, Howe was openly and avowedly on the side of the colonists in their estrangement from the Mother Country. But not on the floor of the House. Much of his sympathy for the Americans derived from his service in America and the fact that after his brother George fell, the Massachusetts Assembly in its grief erected a monument in George's honor in Westminister Abbey. Neither he nor his brother Richard, now an admiral and the fourth Viscount Howe, ever forgot this gesture and this, more than their opposition to the Tory government, accounted for their attitude. But General Howe did oppose the Coercive Acts aimed at the Bay Colony, and in the winter of 1774–75 informed his Nottingham constituents that if an American command were offered to him, he would not accept it.

But then in February 1775, he changed his mind, much to the dismay of his notoriously pro-American electorate. In explanation he said he was going to America because the king had ordered him to do so. "A man's private feelings," he said, "ought to give way to the service at all times." Many other army and navy officers disagreed, among them General Amherst and Admiral Keppel, preferring to sacrifice their careers rather than their scruples. Indeed, Burgoyne, admittedly no friend of Howe's, insisted that he actively sought the assignment.

It is possible that William Howe believed that he would come to America as a negotiator, rather than a conqueror. Like many other Englishmen, he was convinced that the bulk of the colonists were loyal to the Crown and that the firebrands were a distinct minority, who, if they rose in rebellion, could be easily brushed aside, after which he would, through a policy of magnanimity, bring the remaining Patriots to their senses.

There is no doubt that the king and Lord North sought Howe above all other generals. Reporting from America, Major Philip Skene had told North that he had served with Howe and found him to be "unsurpassed in activity, bravery and experience, and beloved by the troops." Even Lord George Germain, who later became Howe's superior—as well as his enemy—while secretary of state for the colonies, declared in June 1775 that no one in high command understood the difficulties of American forest warfare better than did William Howe. Germain considered Gage to be timid and disinclined to act on his own, but thought that Howe—though three thousand miles away from the source of his orders—was capable of independent action. But Howe, the brilliant and daring colonel, was about to become the commanding general in what was then to be the most momentous war in his country's history. The war was his to win, and no one else's. What a chief's complete responsibility can do to a soldier makes the difference between an officer of ordinary competence and a unique great captain. Thus when William Howe stepped ashore in Boston at the age of forty-six, the opportunity to rise to greatness lay before him.

Henry Clinton, the next general in seniority, was a colorless career soldier, the sort of "regulation" officer who "never takes his finger off his number." He was the only son of an admiral and former governor of New York, having been born and raised there. His military career began at the age of thirteen, when he purchased a lieutenant's commission. He was a lieutenant colonel at twenty and a major general at thirty-four—à meteoric rise explicable only in terms of influence. Three years later he boarded the *Cerberus,* chosen for his reputation as a planner.

John Burgoyne's reputation was of a different order. Gentleman, wit, playwright, member of Parliament and bon vivant, he shared William Howe's passions for the gaming table and the boudoir. He was a good soldier, inclined to treat his troops more as human beings than as flesh-and-blood automatons. Unfortunately, his sharp tongue got him into trouble before he arrived. Having heard that five thousand British regulars were held at bay in Boston by a force of raw militia only twice their number, he exclaimed: "What! Well, let us get in and we'll soon find elbowroom." Coming ashore on May 25, Burgoyne was not pleased to hear saucy apprentices and street urchins crying: "Make way for General Elbow-Room."

All three generals were dismayed to learn that Gage's complaints about the situation in America were far from being exaggerated. Even with the arrival of reinforcements, subduing the Patriots would be difficult. As for Massachusetts, the countryside was actively hostile. Many Tories were still loyal to the Crown there, but they stood in such fear of the Sons of Liberty that they would be good for nothing more than entertaining and acclaiming a victorious army. Unable to forage in the countryside, Gage's army became that much more dependent upon a supply line three thousand miles long. Next, the chance for maneuver in the traditional European style was made almost nil by the wilderness behind the seaports, with its poor roads and multiplicity of rivers. Troops who were trained to march and countermarch would not easily adjust to the tactics of forest fighting. Third, even though British sea power gave Gage the advantage of being able to move rapidly anywhere among the coastal colonies, there was no single great capital, the fall of which usually brought capitulation, as it did in Europe. In effect, there were thirteen different subcapitals, each so far removed from the others that any attempt to gather them all in simultaneously would be like a farmer trying to sweep up all his geese in one armful.

All London's witty contempt for the Yankee "cowards," so drolly relayed by General Burgoyne, would not raise the siege of Boston. King George's arrogant proposal of a criminal amnesty for this "army of thieves and vagrants" was not likely to bring Yankee Doodle to his knees in repentant tears. Generals such as James Grant might taunt Benjamin Franklin that all he needed was one regiment of grenadiers "to go from one end of America to the other and geld all the males," but Grant and others like him would soon discover that even before a thousand burly grenadiers, moving under the weight of their heavy equipment, could traverse just this wild seaboard—let alone the entire continent—both they and their castration knives would have been worn clean away. Thus the bombast, which always fills the air when the bombs aren't working. What was needed that June was neither—just a little fresh beef.

By then the British in Boston were on lean rations, indeed. As one of Gage's officers wrote home: "However we block up their port, the rebels certainly block up our town, and have cut off our good beef and mutton. At present we are … subsisting almost on salt provisions."

Gage had directed Howe to destroy the American army, and Howe quickly designed a bold plan of attack. Because it was intended to be a rapid and crushing blow, it seems to bear out the possibility that Howe had come to America with just such a course in mind, after which the humiliated rebels would be quick to come to terms with the Crown. His objective would be the colonial command and supply headquarters at Cambridge. Howe himself would lead an amphibious invasion at Dorchester Point, to the right of Cambridge, while Clinton would land at Willis Creek to the left to secure the high ground at Charlestown. Both landings would be under the protection of British naval cannon. Then both Howe and Clinton would roll up the American flanks to converge on Cambridge and victory.

Word of the plan came to the Committee of Safety through its efficient spy network. At first the plan was understood to be an assault upon Dorchester Heights. At once, with remarkable celerity for these supposed amateurs, a council of war was called by General Ward. It was proposed to beat the British to the high ground by seizing and fortifying Bunker Hill, just behind Charlestown to the north and across the water from Boston. This act would bring the enemy within range of American cannon. The decision was not made easily. Both Artemas Ward and Dr. Joseph Warren—now a major general himself, but not yet holding the commission—opposed such an operation. Ammunition was low, and there were only eleven barrels of powder in the entire American camp. Moreover, Bunker Hill, out on the Charlestown Peninsula between the Charles and Mystic rivers, was exposed to the guns of the British fleet riding in the bay. It could be easily cut off at Charlestown Neck to its rear, and its garrison lost.

These were intelligent criticisms, but they were swept away by the rhetoric of Major General Israel Putnam, who assured the council: "The Americans are not at all afraid of their heads, though very much afraid of their legs. If you cover these, they will fight forever." Perhaps, but even if both were covered, they would also not be able to do much fighting if they were cut off in the rear and bombarded at their front. Nevertheless, the council agreed, even though no one asked Putnam how troops were to "fight forever" once their ammunition ran out. But then, few people dared to challenge "Old Put."

At fifty-seven years of age, Israel Putnam was still a commanding figure, with his bear's body, his bull's voice and his great round owlish head. It was he who had caught Lord Howe's dying body at Ticonderoga, had narrowly missed being burned at the stake by Indians, had been a prisoner of the French at Montreal and had been shipwrecked while leading an expedition against Havana. Such was his great courage and capacity for inspiring men that no one dared to suggest that Old Put seemed to specialize in narrow escapes from avoidable traps. On the night of June 16, however, he sat his splendid horse in Charlestown, Major John Pitcairn's fine horse pistols in his saddle holsters, surrounded by wagonloads of picks and shovels, empty barrels to be filled with earth for fortifications, as well as supplies of fascines—bundles of sticks woven together to absorb the impact of cannon balls. Putnam awaited the arrival of Colonel William Prescott with about 1,200 men.

Although Putnam was a major general and outranked Prescott, he commanded Connecticut militia on Massachusetts soil, and because the vast majority of the men marching to Charlestown were minutemen, it was decided to give the command to a local man. Colonel Prescott, a farmer from Pepperell, had fought at Louisbourg during the French and Indian War, so well in fact that he had been offered a commission in the

British army. But he preferred to return to the plow, until Lexington-Concord. Prescott was a lean, taciturn man, with light blue eyes and the born leader's habit of coolness. He was as practical and careful as Old Put was impetuous and sometimes rash, and he was well served in having Colonel Richard Gridley along as his engineer.

Gridley had shown his engineering talent at the Plains of Abraham, getting two vital cannon up there from the Anse-du-Foulon below and personally directing a galling fire that helped turn the tide of battle. In gratitude the Crown had made him a colonel at half-pay in the British army, awarding him three thousand acres of land in New Hampshire and possession of the Magdalen Islands in the Gulf of St. Lawrence. A few months earlier he had been asked if he would serve the Mother Country again in the impending hostilities, and he replied: "I have never drawn my sword except on the side of justice, and justice lies, I believe, with my countrymen." At sixty-five he was easily the oldest man in the American armed forces, and his mission was to fortify Bunker Hill once it had been occupied.

The force that Prescott commanded arrived in Charlestown about nine o'clock at night. Dressed mostly in homespun, dyed in the tan and brown colors of local oaks and sumac, wearing broad-brimmed farmers' hats and clutching hunting muskets or old Brown Besses from the Colonial Wars, with here and there an ancient Spanish fusee or firelock, they marched silently through the little town's deserted streets and into the hills beyond. There Prescott, Gridley and Putnam began to reconnoiter the ground, searching for Bunker Hill, the height they were to occupy, but finding three hills instead. Moulton's Hill, the lowest of the three, was quickly disqualified.* There remained Breed's Hill and Bunker Hill, to its rear. But Breed's Hill could be far more easily held. Yet, Prescott insisted that his orders were to hold Bunker Hill, and an argument ensued. Gridley and Putnam maintained that the hill that they stood on—Breed's—was the best one to fortify and they did not really care what it was called. It took them a valuable hour to convince Prescott that this should be done, and as a result the critical fight on Charlestown Peninsula has entered most history books as the Battle of Bunker Hill, when it was in fact fought on Breed's Hill.

For any other troops but American militia, that lost hour might have been decisive. But these were iron-armed farmer-soldiers, better farmers than they were soldiers, and after Gridley had marked out the lines of a redoubt 160 feet long and 80 feet wide and gave the order, "Dig!" they

*Also called Morton's Hill and Morton's Point.

sent the earth flying with a vigor and in a volume that would have exhausted a European soldier within an hour. They dug with such astonishing fury that a Marine sentry aboard the *Lively,* staring through the dissolving mists of the hot moist dawn of June 17, started in disbelief at the sight of the raw, red earth of the Yankee position. It was as though it had sprung up overnight at the command of some martial genie. At once his excited cries brought Captain Thomas Bishop leaping from his bunk and rushing to the quarterdeck. Following the Marine's pointed finger, Bishop saw what he had not seen when he had retired the night before: a fortification six feet high and one foot thick, about fifty yards in length, commanding the city of Boston. And it was no amateurish redoubt thrown together helter-skelter by a pack of country clods. It was professional, indeed, with a redan to shelter cannon jutting out from it and sally ports at either end.

Bishop quickly ordered the drums to beat general quarters, and the ship resounded to the noise of pelting bare feet pattering on wooden planking as the *Lively's* crew of 130 hands raced for their battle stations. "Commence firing!" Bishop roared, and ten starboard guns spouted flame and smoke, sending red blobs arching toward the insolent Yankee fort.

Aboard his flagship the *Somerset* Admiral Samuel Graves heard the repeated roar of the broadsides and began dressing in a livid rage. Who gave the order to fire? Certainly not he! Informed that *Lively* was firing upon some Americans atop a hill on Charlestown Peninsula, he snapped: "He has no such orders. Tell him to cease fire immediately." *Lively* fell silent, until the irritated Graves emerged on deck and strode in silent anger to the starboard rail. What he saw through his leveled glass—though incredible, confounding all his contempt for Yankee Doodle—caused him to roar: "Order all ships to commence firing immediately!" Ten minutes later the entire fleet was booming away with 168 guns.

General Gage had called a council of war. Henry Clinton was the first to arrive, trying to hide the I-told-you-so smirk on his schoolmaster's face, but with a huge lack of success. Next came John Burgoyne, his sharp features full of inquiry. William Howe was fourth, his full face full of worry. Two brigadiers entered: the first, the Earl of Percy, the cocky and competent son of the Duke of Northumberland who had done so much to save Gage's expedition to Concord from disaster, followed by Robert Pigot, a short, stocky man with a reputation for hard fighting. These two remained mostly silent while the four major generals conferred.

Clinton at once proposed a plan to cut off the rebels on Bunker Hill by seizing Charlestown Neck. He proposed to land five hundred men at Charlestown and occupy the neck, thus sealing off the Americans' escape while the fleet battered them into submission from the water.

Gage pondered a moment, then slowly shook his head, murmuring: "We must remember, gentlemen, the enemy has troops stationed at the neck. How many we do not know. To put 500 men between two enemy forces, each of which may outnumber them, seems very dangerous tactics to me."

Howe agreed. An expert in amphibious warfare, whereas Clinton was not, he observed that there was little equipment available for such an operation. He did not mention another impediment to amphibious warfare in Boston: the bad blood existing between Admiral Graves and Gage. It had begun years ago in a heated argument between Graves and Gage's father, continuing in Boston with Graves's flat assertion that he took orders from no one but the Admiralty in London. Gage's troops, as well as the Tories, hated Graves for making a handsome profit from black-market meat sold in Boston. The admiral's ships were the only means of transporting meat from the harbor islands and seacoast towns and were suspected of regularly landing there in search of cattle. Thus the price of meat in Boston was an astronomical guinea a pound! Finally, when Howe had proposed his double-envelopment amphibious assault, scheduled for the following day, Graves had shown a spectacular lack of enthusiasm.

Deferring to Howe's superior amphibious experience, Clinton still protested vigorously against a costly frontal assault. An army as small as the force in Boston simply could not stand heavy casualties. Gage agreed, but he also felt that political considerations were overriding at this point. The Americans must be chastised, must be used very badly. What better way to crush the rebellion than by routing Yankee Doodle on a battlefield of his own choosing? This was Howe's thinking, had always been his thinking, and he quickly outlined his own plan of battle.

Morton's Point, at the tip of the peninsula, was the ideal place to land troops. For almost a half mile from the water's edge to the American position, there was no cover available for an ambushing force. Any foray attempted from the rebel fort could be broken up by the guns of the fleet. Howe's proposal was to land there and send a flying column of light infantry along the open shore of the Mystic River to turn the Yankees and get into their rear. Nothing demoralizes raw troops more than the knowledge that the enemy is behind them. Once the Americans were routed, Clinton could join him for the assault on Cambridge that was envisioned in the earlier plan set for the next day. In a sense, the American occupation of Breed's Hill had given the British a splendid chance.

Scatter them there, drive them in panic into the headquarters at Cambridge where they would infect the enemy main body with their terror, and the rest would be easy.

Clinton had one last objection: what if the Americans chose to fight inside their fort? "Unlikely," Howe drawled deprecatingly. "Anyway, I do not see how the works could be more than a redan. Never in my experience have I heard or even seen regular troops capable of building a complete redoubt in a single night's work." Moreover the hill was "open and easy of ascent" and could "easily be carried."

That clinched it. Gage approved the plan. On the basis of political expedience and contempt for the enemy's fighting prowess—not always the soundest considerations for forming a battle plan—together with only reluctant support from the Royal Navy and without detailed topographical maps or the kind of thorough reconnoitering that would prove that the Mystic shoreline was indeed passable, the plan was proposed and accepted by the two British officers in America who should have known better.

When *Lively* opened up on the American redoubt, Prescott's men dove for the shelter of its six-foot walls. But when it ceased fire on the orders of an infuriated Admiral Graves, Prescott ordered them back to work on a breastwork he was eager to build from the fort down to the Mystic River. Clutching their tools, beginning to sweat under a bright sun rising slowly into a cloudless blue sky, they streamed out of the fort and began to dig. It was then that Graves ordered his entire fleet to commence firing. A sudden roar rose from the harbor. Cannon balls—"solid shot," there were as yet no explosive "shells"—came whistling down on the fort. Once again the near-exhausted Yankees dove for its shelter. Some of them peered longingly at kegs of rum and one keg of water left on the hill exposed to the cannonade. A ball smashed the keg of water. Fearful that their cherished rum might suffer likewise, a few of them ducked outside between salvos to roll the rum inside the redoubt. They sampled it, and that, of course, made them thirstier. They thought wistfully of the smashed water keg, until someone suggested drawing water from one of Charleston's wells.

At once these exuberant young plowboys—"soldiers" only in name—began trooping down the hill, led by brawny, cheerful young Asa Pollard. A cannon spoke below. Pollard wavered. His head was gone, torn off by a solid shot. Blood pumped from the gaping hole where his neck had been like water from a spout. His comrades were horrified. Some of them screamed. Prescott came rushing over. He stared narrowly at the white-faced men around the twitching corpse. At any moment, now, panic could contaminate his entire command.

"W-what sh-should we do, sir?" a sergeant asked in a quavering voice.

"Bury him," Prescott snapped, deliberately curt, watching his men warily, before ordering them back to work. "There's a whole breastwork waiting to be finished down there on the other side of the hill." The men retrieved their tools and hurried downhill. But the sergeant was more persistent. "Without prayers, sir?" he asked, aghast.

"Without prayers," Prescott said softly, but then, seeing the agony in the young man's eyes, he drew his sword and jumped up on the parapet, striding fearlessly up and down it among the shower of shot. He *had* to calm them. He could not let them break. *Now!* "It was a one-in-a-million shot," he yelled. "See how close they come to hitting me!" But they didn't come close, and Prescott gave a huge sigh of relief to see his soldiers make the dirt fly once more, plugging that gaping hole in the Patriot line, extending it down toward the river shoreline that William Howe so confidently expected to find open.

At about ten o'clock the American artillery at last reached the redoubt. Prescott stared at it in dismay. Four guns. Pathetic little four-pounders up against King George's mighty twenty-four-pounders. They had been taken from the British ship *Diana* in an earlier fight at Noodle Island.* General Ward had larger guns but refused to relinquish them. Worse, the men who manned them were infantrymen with little or no experience with ordnance, and their officers hardly more. Prescott almost hoped they did not open a suicidal fire on the mammoths of Graves's fleet or the British artillery battery across the channel at Copp's Point.

What Prescott didn't realize—although it did not diminish his heroic inspiration of his men—was that all British fire was falling short. The ships could not elevate their guns high enough to reach the fort without withdrawing to a distance that would also put them out of range. The battery was simply too far away. Yet British balls were bounding and rolling over the hillside like ninepins, and these still-naive young Yankees were chasing them with wild whoops, eager to claim the small rewards offered for enemy shot. Again, they just couldn't imagine the weight of iron as opposed to the wood of ninepins, and many lads had their legs and feet mangled. Aaron Barr had his leg torn off and was borne dying from the hill.

*Some sources say Noodle, others Noddle.

"Colonel!" a soldier cried, running up to Prescott and pointing across the channel. "There's troops mustering in Boston! Artillery, too!"

It was six hours before General William Howe could collect his force of 2,300 men for their waterborne trip across the bay and the assault. First there was the British officer's passion for "tidying up the lines." There was going to be one of those military pageants so dear to their hearts, and it must be done "regulation" with the last boot properly blacked and the last belt pipe-clayed white. The men were also in full marching order with their packs full of cooked rations or ammunition, which, together with the weapons and ammunition and other equipment, totaled an incredible 125 pounds! How could such veteran officers as Howe and Clinton expect their men to fight in such heat with such weight upon their backs? No matter, that was the British Army's way, and, by God, that was how it was going to be done!

While the men were being broken out of their barracks, couriers were rushing throughout Boston rousing missing soldiers—both officers and men—from their sleep or from the arms of protesting wives or those of less licit companions screeching like fishwives for their unpaid honoraria. When all were rounded up, the various formations were inspected. Finally, the row barges that were to carry them across the water had to be requisitioned, made shipshape and inspected, while the sailors who would be at the oars were assigned to their benches, after which the barges had to be towed to Boston.

Most distressful for Howe that morning was his conference with Admiral Graves aboard *Somerset.* Because Howe's older brother—Richard ("Black Dick"), Viscount Howe—was already a famous admiral and the general himself was skilled in amphibious warfare, William Howe knew what was required for a waterborne operation, if only shore to shore over a few miles of open water. To each of his requests Graves answered no. No, he could not use *Somerset* to support Howe's landing because it was too big and the water too shallow. His big ships could lend only men and equipment to the smaller ones. When Howe asked for support from a big ship of the line (modern battleship) from the Mystic, Graves replied that because he knew nothing of the river's mud flats or shoals, he could not risk it. He had been in command of the American station for a year in that same port of Boston, yet had failed to chart the waters around him. Finally, Howe had hoped to transport his troops in those crude but effective landing boats developed by the British during the Seven Years' War. These boats had sides of thick raised planks to protect the men from enemy fire and flat bottoms taking very little water. But not a single one was available in Boston, so Howe had to be content with less maneuverable barges that made his soldiers perfect targets for those Yankee marksmen. That was why he chose Moulton's Point as the landing site: because it was so far from the Breed's Hill fort. There were not even enough of these barges to move his brigade in one crossing, so he would need two crossings—another complication.

But by one o'clock in the afternoon Howe and his 2,300 redcoats were ready.

Prescott and Putnam had seized upon the six-hour delay to strengthen the redoubt further. Prescott drove his men relentlessly. They were hungry and thirsty and wilting in the heat, but he refused to let up on them until the breastwork was complete.

On Bunker Hill to the rear, Old Put was in a rage of command. He was everywhere along the line, putting units into place, stiffening the spines of the unvaliant, trying but failing to get cannon out to Prescott's redoubt. Twice Putnam rode his horse across shot-swept Charlestown Neck to ask for reinforcements, and twice Ward refused him. Eventually, at the urging of the Committee of Safety, Ward sent out the New Hampshire regiments of John Stark and James Reed.

Colonel John Stark was the true commander of this force of about 1,200 frontiersmen. Though they were splendid sharpshooters, they had no ammunition. On the spot in Cambridge they were issued two flints apiece, a gill of powder and a pound of lead cut from the organs of a Cambridge church. Stark sent them back to quarters, where they made up fifteen cartridges apiece. Men with bullet molds made musket balls, men without them hammered out slugs of lead.

Leading his men on the four-mile march to the front, Stark took them through enemy naval shelling at such a deliberate pace that young Captain Henry Dearborn of the leading company suggested that he rush the cadence.

"Dearborn," Stark said calmly, "one fresh man in action is worth ten fatigued men."

At Bunker Hill, Stark paused to survey the battlefront.

With raving fifes and rattling drums, brilliant in the bright sun with their red coats and immaculate white breeches, the sunlight dancing on the tips of their bayonets, Howe's soldiers landed without opposition at Moulton's Point. Howe immediately began studying the American position. He saw at once that he could not turn Prescott's left so easily. The Yankee commander had built a breastwork out in that direction. Moreover, Howe saw numerous bodies of men farther back on Bunker Hill and mistook them for an American reserve. Then he saw a column of men—Stark's sharpshooters—come marching along the ridge to Breed's Hill and decided to call for reinforcements of his own.

In that second delay, Prescott again improved his position. The sight of the British forming on Moulton's Hill made it clear to him that there was still a gap yawning between his breastwork on the left and the Mystic River. So he sent some Connecticut troops and two cannon back to a stone-and-rail fence about two hundred yards to the left rear of the breastwork. The fence ran down to the Mystic bank, and it seemed good enough to block Howe's flanking attempt.

Colonel Stark did not agree. Coming up to the rail fence, Stark saw that it ended on the bank of the river, but that beneath it was a narrow strip of open beach along which four men might pass abreast. Taking his best shots, Stark put them on the beach behind a barricade built of stones. Then he posted the rest of his force along the rail fence. Now Prescott had about 1,400 men holding positions: the redoubt, the breastwork, the rail fence and the beach wall. Suddenly, to his surprise, Prescott saw Dr. Warren enter the redoubt.

Warren was a dashing sight in his white satin breeches, his pale blue waistcoat laced with silver and his carefully combed blond hair. Because he had just been appointed a major general, Colonel Prescott saluted him and offered him command.

"I shall take no command here," Warren said. "I came as a volunteer with my musket to serve under you."

The fiery young revolutionary mounted the firing platform alongside the men who had flocked to his standard of rebellion.

With his reinforcements Howe now led about 2,500 soldiers, evenly divided between himself on Moulton's Point and Sir Robert Pigot on the left in the town of Charlestown. Pigot was to storm the redoubt, while Howe was to burst the breastwork and rail fence to get in the Yankee rear. Because seizure of the beachhead—the most dangerous part of a waterborne operation—had been bloodless, the British commander had relaxed, laughing and joking with his staff, even taking a glass of wine proffered by his batman. Suddenly to his left he heard shouts and angry cries. Turning he saw Pigot's short figure advancing toward him. Beside him were five terrified soldiers being driven in his direction at bayonet point.

"What is it?" Howe asked impatiently.

"Deserters, sir," Pigot replied. "They broke out of ranks and ran for the American lines."

Howe stared sternly at the white-faced men. They swallowed and licked their dry lips. "The morning orders said: 'any man who shall quit his rank on any pretense will be executed without mercy.' You knew this?"

They nodded dumbly, their eyes pleading.

"I would like to hang all five of you," Howe murmured. "But we need men." Pointing to two men in the center, he ordered: "Hang those two."

The doomed men sank to their knees, begging for mercy. But they were dragged to a nearby oak, blossoming with the tender green of the late New England spring. A sergeant plaited the hangman's nooses and flung the ropes over a sturdy low-hanging branch. Then the men were hoisted screaming into the air, the noose was tightened around each neck, and before the eyes of their mournful comrades standing at attention, the screams ceased, their bodies jerked, their legs kicked, and they began to turn slowly in the baking sun....

Their comrades marching to form for the attack lowered their heads to avoid this grisly sight. Howe spoke to them, exhorting them to "behave like Englishmen," adding: "I shall not desire any one of you to go a step farther than where I go myself at your head."

Howe ordered his artillery to commence firing. It did, and suddenly fell silent. The guns' side boxes contained twelve-pound balls instead of six-pounders. Howe's fieldpieces were useless.

On the British left, American snipers in the houses of Charlestown began whittling the redcoats. General Pigot complained to Admiral Graves, who sent orders to burn the town.

Ships in the harbor and batteries planted on Copp's Hill in Boston began showering Charlestown with red-hot ball and "carcasses," hollow iron balls pierced with holes and filled with pitch. Within a few moments Charlestown caught fire, to the great delight of Johnny Burgoyne, who stood on Copp's Hill watching the scene with Henry Clinton.

Charlestown was one great blaze. Whole streets of houses collapsed against each other in walls of flame, ships on the stocks began burning, the high steeples of the churches were like great flaming spears, and everywhere was the hiss of flames and the crash of timbers.

On the British right, Howe was changing his formations. He drew off his light infantry and put them in columns of four along the Mystic beach. There were about 350 of them, and they were to storm the Yankee beach wall at bayonet point.

Opposite Howe's main body behind the breastwork and the rail fence, burly Israel Putnam rode up and down the lines roaring the immortal words: "Don't fire until you see the whites of their eyes! Then, fire low."

Behind the Mystic wall Colonel Stark went Putnam one better, dashing out about forty yards to nail a stake into the ground. "Not a man is to fire until the first regular crosses the stake," he yelled.

The attack commenced.

Pigot's men climbed steadily toward the redoubt. Some nervous Americans opened fire before they were in range. Prescott swore he would kill the next man who fired. A young Yankee officer ran along the parapet kicking up the leveled muskets. Pigot's redcoats came steadily up the slope.

On the right Howe's men marched down Moulton's Hill, across a lowland, and up the slopes of Breed's Hill against the silent breastwork and rail fence. It was hot. Neither the tall bearskins of the grenadiers nor the cocked hats of the line had brims to keep the sun out of the men's eyes. The regulars stumbled in thick grass reaching to their knees. A brick kiln and adjacent ponds broke their ranks, and they had to reform. Sweat began to darken the armpits of their scarlet coats. Men began to gasp beneath burdens of sixty pounds and more. Still they came on.

Along Mystic beach the light infantry—Howe's favorite troops—were trotting to the attack with outthrust bayonets. In the front were the dreaded Welsh Fusiliers.

Now all was thunder and flash and flame, Charlestown blazing, batteries crashing, naval guns roaring, echo and reverberation rolling over water and earth, while overhead—now exposing, now concealing—drifted the billowing black clouds of gun smoke.

The light infantry were running now.

The Welsh Fusiliers went slanting past Stark's stake, and the little wall ahead of them exploded in a crash of musketry.

The Fusiliers swayed and went down. Great rents were torn in the attacking column, but the King's Own Regiment swept forward to fill them. They ran on, while behind the fence the Yankee sharpshooters with empty muskets gave way to men with loaded ones.

Another dreadful volley crashed out, and the King's Own went down in heaps.

Now the picked flank troops of the Tenth Regiment were called upon. Officers ran among the reluctant, beating them with swords. Surely it would not be possible for the rebels to fire a *third* volley in so short a time. Once again the lines of scarlet and sun-tipped steel slanted forward, and there *was* a third volley—and that was all on Mystic beach.

Ninety-six dead redcoats had been left sprawled upon its blood-clotted sands, and even though his plan was wrecked at the pivotal point, Howe pressed his charge forward. Two ranks of men, grenadiers in front, came at the breastwork and the rail fence. Flame and smoke belched forth, and tightly dressed ranks of red and white were instantly transformed into little packs of stunned and stricken men. Again and again the American weapons spoke, and the men spun and toppled or went staggering away, streaming blood. Every man in Howe's personal staff was either killed or wounded. It was a wonder that the general himself, in the forefront as he had promised, was not scratched. But he was mortified to see his vaunted regulars sprawling in heaps under the guns of ignorant peasants, and then, when he heard that Pigot was also thrown back in what was little more than a feint against the redoubt, there came upon the heretofore invincible William Howe, as he was to write later: "*A moment that I never felt before.*"

He recalled his troops, sent for more reinforcements and began re-forming.

The Americans were exultant. They had met and beaten the finest troops in the world with but little cost to themselves. Colonel Prescott went among them, praising them and reminding them that the battle was not over. He encouraged them to stand fast, keeping to himself the fact that a steady trickle of desertions had drained his forces like a leaking pipe. The redoubt was down to 150 men.

There were many more men to be had back on Bunker Hill, but they refused to come forward. Putnam stormed among them, sometimes beating reluctant soldiers with the flat of his sword, but he got only a few to follow him back to Breed's Hill.

Worse, he got no ammunition.

A quarter hour after his first bloody repulse, Howe was attacking again.

His plan now was to avoid the beach wall. The light infantry had rejoined Howe's main body. They were to attack the rail fence while Pigot and Howe threw all that they had against the redoubt and the breastwork.

On the left, Pigot depended chiefly on John Pitcairn and his Marines. They got to within a hundred feet of the silent Yankee fort, and then the wall of flame gushed forth again. Pitcairn sank to the ground mortally wounded. His son, also wounded, held his dying father in his arms. "I have lost my father!" he cried in anguish, whereupon the Marines are said to have echoed: "We have lost our father!"

On the right before the breastwork, the regulars were also being sickled to the reddening earth, and the shaken Howe called for a bayonet charge. An incessant stream of fire poured from the American lines. The

British light infantry was riddled. Some thirty-eight-men companies had only eight or nine men left. A few had only four or five. On the left Pigot was staggered and actually retreated. For the second time, Howe withdrew.

Reinforcing regiments had been sent to Prescott, but Putnam found the men of one of them scattered on the safe side of Bunker Hill. Fat Colonel Samuel Gerrish lay flat on the ground; he told the livid Putnam that he was "completely exhausted." Old Put snarled that he was, rather, completely cowardly—and ran among Gerrish's shrinking violets, knocking some of them to the ground with his sword.

Two companies, however, did arrive in time to give some comfort to Prescott. But for every man he got, he lost three. Whenever a wounded man had been taken to safety, there were, in a cowardly dodge as old as arms, as many as twenty "volunteers" to carry him.

Most men had enough ball to repulse a third assault, but there was precious little powder. Cannon cartridges had to be broken open and their contents distributed.

Re-forming below Prescott, the British had reinforcements and all the necessary ammunition. Four hundred Marines and regulars had responded to Howe's call for fresh men. Henry Clinton had crossed the river to collect all the guards and walking wounded he could find and join Pigot's force. Cannon were brought into play. A demonstration was made against the rail fence, while Howe hurled himself against the breastwork in the center and Pigot-Clinton struck at the redoubt on the left.

"As soon as the rebels perceived this," Lord Francis Rawdon wrote to his uncle, the Earl of Huntingdon, "they rose up and poured in so heavy a fire upon us that the oldest officers say they never saw a sharper action. They kept up this fire till we were within ten yards of them. They even knocked down my captain, close beside me, after we had got into the ditch of their entrenchment."

But the redcoats had reached the ditch, and after the American fire "went out like a spent candle," they leaped down from the parapet into the open redoubt. From three sides they came. Little General Pigot, too small to leap into the fray, climbed a tree outside and swung himself into it.

Still the Americans fought, most of them without bayonets of their own.

"Twitch their guns away!" Prescott roared. "Use your guns for clubs."

Barehanded or with clubbed muskets, the Americans actually tore guns out of the hands of the regulars. But more and more redcoats were pouring over the walls, and Prescott shouted: "Give way, men! Save yourselves!"

Prescott fought on himself, his sword clanging against bayonets and gun barrels. His loose linen coat probably saved him. The bayonets cut it into tatters, but missed his flesh. Prescott was finally borne out of the rear gateway on the tide of retreating Americans. As he left, he passed a figure in a blue waistcoat steadily directing a covering action for the withdrawal. Outside, Prescott joined Putnam in conducting a running fight from one fence or wall to another, until their force had crossed Bunker Hill and gone across Charlestown Neck onto the mainland.

Nevertheless, it was in this retreat that Americans suffered most of their casualties. One of them was found at the redoubt exit. The body had been stripped of its waistcoat, but from the quality of the blood-stained ruffled shirt, it was obvious that the dead man had been a person of importance. A British officer rolled the body over and gasped in surprise.

Dr. Joseph Warren was dead.

⋆ 19 ⋆

BRITISH SHOCK AND CHAGRIN

British casualties at the Battle of Bunker Hill had been staggering. Of 2,400 engaged, 1,054 had been shot, of whom 226 were killed. It is doubtful if British regulars had ever before suffered in such proportions, and this at the hand of a rabble in arms.

Although William Howe was not a physical casualty, he was certainly a spiritual one. He never forgot that moment he had never felt before. The curtain never came down on that bloody tableau at the back of his brain, and William Howe, having formed his military character on the ardor and daring of his mentor and idol, James Wolfe, turned slow and cautious.

American casualties totaled about 450—most of them during the retreat—of whom about 140 were killed. The Battle of Bunker Hill had been a distinct Yankee victory, even though Howe's troops occupied the field. The sense of shock in the British Army was beyond description. Howe himself, though unscathed, had been in the forefront of the fight, his leggings streaked with blood where he had walked in the tall grass stained with the blood of his soldiers. But he had lost all his aides and most of his officers. Henry Clinton wrote in his diary: "A dear-bought victory, another such would have ruined us."

What neither side realized was that Bunker Hill had been a momentous turning point in the history of warfare, ushering in the era of modern arms. It was fully as great a military milestone as the Battle of Agincourt in 1415, when the British longbow slaughtered the flower of French chivalry, ending the battlefield reign of mounted knights in armor. At Bunker Hill the change was not one of weaponry but of fighting style.

If the minutemen had fought as they and the redcoats had been trained to do, loading and firing upon the orders of their captains, one forward line firing while a rearward one loaded, and so on, they would have been defeated early and easily because of the lapse of time between volleys. But the Americans were simply too individualistic to fight like automatons. Captain John Chester of Connecticut, whose company entered the battle late in the day, explained what was happening: "Here we lost our regularity, as every company had done before us, and fought as they did, every man loading and firing as fast as he could." This produced a steady relentless fire without those intervals between volleys that would have permitted the enemy to draw closer with each delay. Thus improvisation, the knack at the very soul of the Yankee spirit of independence, had come upon the battlefield. It was the ability to respond on the spur of the moment and individually to a new and dangerous situation without waiting for orders from an officer as "regulation" and trained "by the book" as the robots he commanded. And the bitter chagrin that some British officers and Tories felt at being "murdered" by a crowd of ignorant peasants who broke the rules of war was evident in the lament of a Tory lady, grieving over the death of gentlemen "of noble family" who fell at the hands of "despicable wretches" of whom "not one has the least pretension to be called a gentlemen."

At Bunker Hill, then, not only had the automaton and the self-reliant individual clashed, but democracy had met and conquered aristocracy. True enough, it would not seem so for most of the eight despairing years remaining in the war just begun, when all the advantages seemed to be in the possession of a militarist nation organized for war as no race had been since the Romans. But along with the improvising individual, spirit and love of liberty had also come upon the battlefield: henceforth each time the flame of the War of the Revolution appeared about to sputter out, it flared full and bright anew, as the Tory lady's "banditti of the country," under the inspiring leadership of the indomitable George Washington, fought the great fight for home and hearth that was to nourish other noble hearts around a world weary of oppression and exploitation. Strangely enough, an explanation of this new spirit came not from a great military or political leader, but rather from a cleric, Cardinal John Henry Newman, who said: "Most men will die upon a dogma; few will be martyr to a conclusion."

Thomas Gage and William Howe, the chief victims of that latest demonstration of mankind's unquenchable thirst for freedom, had not been so obtuse as to mistake it for a fluke. Gage wrote to Lord Barrington, secretary of state for war: "These people show a spirit and conduct against us they never showed against the French, and everybody has judged of them from their former appearance and behavior when joined to the King's forces in the last war, which has led to many mistakes. They were now spirited up by a rage and enthusiasm as great as ever people were possessed of, and you must proceed in earnest or give the business up.... I have before written your Lordship my opinion that a large army must at length be employed to reduce these people, and mentioned the hiring of foreign troops. I fear it must come to that."

Howe was not quite as chastened as Gage, although he was aware of the resentment against him among both his officers and men. He knew that many of the malcontents were writing home of their displeasure and that within a month there would be talk against him all over Britain. One officer wrote: "From an absurd and destructive confidence, carelessness or ignorance, we have lost a thousand of our best men and officers and have given the Rebels great matter of triumph by showing them what mischief they can do to us." There is no doubt that Howe, perhaps in his overwhelming desire to deliver that one crushing blow, had gone into battle overconfident. True enough, Admiral Graves had been the soul of reluctance, but there was no excuse for that six-hour delay and the failure to reconnoiter thoroughly. The delay did not affect Howe's own plans, for he had had plenty of daylight even after he entered the redoubt. But it did give Prescott and Putnam extra time in which to fortify. To have found twelve-pound balls in the side boxes of six-pound cannon was an error as common to battlefields as that of friendly troops firing on each other, but he should have suffered another delay in the interests of obtaining the proper ammunition. Without artillery, he could not hope to subdue the stone-and-rail fence that wrought such havoc among his men.

Howe had also erred in concluding that the redoubt was the Yankees' most formidable position, choosing instead the fence and the beach held by Stark's sharpshooters. In fact both the fence and the beach were impregnable, given the accurate firing of their defenders, and could have held him off all day, whereas the redoubt fell upon the first sustained assault, although admittedly only after its garrison ran out of ammunition. To choose the turning movement was not really a mistake: the error was to order it forward without careful reconnaissance. If Howe had really known what awaited him beside the Mystic River, he almost certainly would have changed his plans to a careful probing of the redoubt or wait for the proper ammunition to clear the fence. He did, of course, eventually shift his attack to the redoubt, with the help of Clinton and his cannon, but by then the awful slaughter forming that dreadful tableau at the back of his brain had taken place.

The tableau was still there when Howe made his perceptive report to Lord George Germain, now secretary of state for the colonies. Boston was unfit as a base for suppressing the rebellion, he wrote. It would be better to send 12,000 soldiers to sieze New York for a drive up the Hudson River to split the colonies in two. Another 3,500 men were needed for garrison duty. "With this force of 19,000 rank and file, an end to this now formidable rebellion might take place in one campaign.... With a less force than I have mentioned, I apprehend this war may be spun out until England shall be heartily sick of it."

Ominous words. From Gage the unthinkable suggestion of hiring foreign mercenaries to fight *British subjects!* From Howe, talk of 19,000 regulars when originally 4,000 were believed sufficient! Truly these insolent Yankees were placing an unanticipated and perhaps unbearable burden on King George III's war machine.

⋆ 20 ⋆

GEORGE III'S WAR MACHINE

At the outbreak of the Revolutionary War, the British Army consisted of about 48,000 men, of whom about 39,000 were infantry or foot soldiers, 6,000 cavalry or mounted troops and 2,500 artillerists or cannoneers. Of these, approximately 15,000 were in Britain, 12,000 in Ireland and 8,000 in America. The remainder were spread throughout the globe.

An infantry regiment usually comprised about 470 men, divided into ten companies. It was commanded by a colonel assisted by a lieutenant colonel or a major, plus a chaplain, an adjutant and a surgeon with his mate. Each company was led by a captain, 2 lieutenants, 2 sergeants and 3 corporals, with 38 privates and a drummer. Cavalry regiments were about half as large, usually 230, making up six troops. A colonel commanded, assisted by a lieutenant colonel and a major, together with a chaplain, an adjutant and a surgeon. A troop was led by a captain, 1 lieutenant, 1 cornet, 1 quartermaster, 2 sergeants and 2 corporals, with 37 privates and 1 hautbois, or oboe, player. The artillery regiment comprised four battalions, each of which was commanded by a lieutenant colonel with eight batteries led by a captain, and including a captain lieutenant; 2 first lieutenants; 2 second lieutenants; 4 sergeants; 4 corporals; 9 bombardiers; 18 gunners; 73 matrosses, or assistant gunners; and 2 drummers, for a total of 116. The preponderance of officers and noncommissioned officers in an artillery battery was probably due to the extensive technological nature of this arm. Finally there were specialists in each infantry regiment: grenadiers and light infantry. Grenadiers were originally introduced into the army in 1677, their function being to hurl hand grenades among the enemy at close quarters. The weight of the missile required throwing strength, so that grenadiers were usually big men. By 1775 such grenades were obsolete, but the grenadiers remained, becoming the flower of the army. Next came the light infantry, introduced after the Seven Years' War by William Howe. They were marksmen and although not as strong as the grenadiers became agile and resourceful skirmishers. Grenadiers and light infantry came to be known as the elite of the regiment and because they usually were placed on the flanks or at danger points were also called "flank companies."

These, then, were the regiments of the line, the ordinary formations of the army. In addition to them were the "household" regiments, that is, the King's Own, in effect his bodyguards. There were three regiments of Foot Guards—the First, or Grenadier; the Second, or Coldstream; and the Third, or Scots, plus three regiments of Horse Guards. Although regarded as the crème de la crème of British arms, being stationed in London or Westminster to protect the sovereign, they were sent to America not as units, but as a "Brigade of Guards," formed by selecting fifteen men from each of their sixty-four companies.

Thus the organization of the British Army of the late eighteenth century, a force together with its redoubtable navy, considered the most awesome in the world, but also one of remarkable contrasts and strange contradictions. It imposed a brutal discipline on its men, but in its officers tolerated almost every eccentricity or vile habit in the long catalog of human vice. Supposedly ordered by an efficient chain of command, it actually marched—and the navy sailed—to a confusing welter of conflicting commands and countercommands that were issued by powerful politicians with no experience of war—and certainly none of combat—guided, as politicians usually are, by considerations of party and personal profit before service to their country.

At the heart of this ponderous war machine was the cabinet, which planned, and the secretaries of state, who executed. The cabinet determined what expeditions were to be mounted and when, what troops and ships were likely to be sent abroad and when, where, how and in what number, as well as which of the services—army or navy—was to take precedence or to be in command. These decisions being transmitted to the secretaries of state, it was their duty to issue orders to the Treasury, the Admiralty, the secretary at war (army) and ordnance (maker of weapons).

The cabinet was composed of eight or nine major ministers, chosen by the prime minister almost always from the ranks of his own party. An average of six to eight ministers met for weekly dinners, and after the table was cleared and the port was poured, those who were still awake decided on the conduct of the war. Their decisions were then transmitted to the three secretaries of state: for northern Europe, southern Europe and the West Indies and North America, or colonies. The secretaries' own resolutions were carried to the king, who sat at the top of this rickety pyramid of command as the captain general. With the king's approval, these resolutions were next conveyed to the various departments in charge of service and supply. It was thus the secretaries of state who ran the war machine. But they had no real control over the agencies that were supposedly empowered to carry out their instructions.

The Treasury which was charged with provisioning the army in America, was hamstrung by tardy and vague requisitions that arrived from the commanders there and by the absence of ships that were detained in American ports without authority. New warships that were ready to put to sea might wait weeks or even months for their guns to arrive, and when they did it was sometimes discovered that vital parts were missing. Ordnance, hidebound as ever and still grossly inefficient, moved with infuriating slowness, taking months or even years before a requisition for weapons or clothing was filled. The Admiralty was so independent and so powerful—"With us," said a British field marshal in World War II, "the Admiralty is *everything*"—that it could become a master of obstruction, torpedoing any operation it opposed by feigning ignorance, by delay or by declaring that there were no bottoms available, just as when it approved, it reported an abundance of tonnage. What was needed to power this stalled and backfiring war machine was a single, skillful driver.

But there was none, none like the single great director William Pitt became when he conducted the Seven Years' War from his office as secretary for the Southern Department. There was only Lord North, the king's choice as prime minister, a man eminently disqualified for conducting a war. Lord North's appearance alone could not have been more unwarlike. Fat and clumsy, his large nearsighted eyes rolling in his great head as he talked, his thick tongue blurring his speech while spraying his listeners with saliva, his movements suggested a country yokel hawking hens at a county fair, rather than a descendant of one of the oldest and most illustrious families in Britain charged with leading his country during one of the great crises in its history. Bumpkin, of course, he was not, but a civilized and cultivated man, personally charming, extremely kind—especially to those of lower station—in a word, a true English gentleman. Yet, for all his parliamentary skill, political acumen, and dogged defense of his ministry, he was not the dominating, driving, ruthless leader of a nation at war—a chief of extremes who could reward victory with a peerage and punish defeat with disgrace and impoverishment. Lord North was a man of peace, a dove with the reins of a war chariot in his teeth. Unfortunately for his own health, he knew it, and this self-knowledge deepened his melancholia and hypochondria, together with his secret disapproval of the king's American policy.

North should have resigned, if the king would have let him, but George would not have let him, even though he realized North's inadequacy. "I fear," the king wrote, "his irresolution is only to be equaled by a certain vanity of wanting to ape the prime minister without any of the requisite qualities." So King George kept North, probably because of North's financial sharpness and the political difficulty of replacing him, as well as his own ability to dominate him.

The first inadequacy of this supposedly mighty armed force was that there were then no military or naval colleges, such as Sandhurst or Annapolis. True, Woolwich Academy, founded in the 1740s, trained officers for the engineers and artillery, but young infantry or cavalry officers aspiring to glory and high command disdained these arms as dead ends. Thus these officers had no professional training, and naval officers least of all, many of them going to sea between ages nine and twelve and with the barest rudiments of an education. Young officers learned their craft by reading military history or the memoirs of famous generals or admirals or in the "dear school" of experience. And they bought their commissions. During the Revolutionary War, the lowest rank in the army—an ensign in the infantry or cornet in the cavalry—went for £400. This amount was more than members of the lower gentry could earn in five years or the lower classes could make in a lifetime.

A wealthy young officer could not, of course, simply buy his way up the chain of command. He had to serve a certain amount of time in his rank and wait until a vacancy occurred above him, either in his own regiment or somewhere else. Even if promoted, he still had to buy his higher new rank. Thus a lieutenant colonel who commanded a regiment of infantry usually paid £3,500 for the rank; in the cavalry, he paid £5,200; and in the foot guards, £6,700, this last amount being equal to the combined annual salaries of the first lords of the Treasury and Admiralty.

Who received this money? Customarily the officer who was either retiring or moving higher. When new regiments were raised, the money went to those who were organizing them, either the Crown or a private person. For the private party his first task was to convince the secretary at war that he could do it cheaper than the king. If given approval, he hired officers to do the recruiting, designed a uniform that, given the royal approval, he then contracted out to tailors, and finally found a place to locate and train his command. His profit came from the fact that all the officers wishing to join his regiment had to buy their commissions from him. He also received from the War Office an annual stipend to maintain his formation, from which he directed a certain percentage into his own coffers, together with his colonel's pay. He was thus both the commandant and the proprieter, unlike the colonel of a king's regiment, who was only the commandant. Moreover, he need not actually command his troops; he could delegate that task to an officer of lower rank, sometimes a lieutenant colonel but usually a major, who was cheaper. As a result many British regiments were commanded and owned by an "officer" who need not inspect them more than twice a year and who was actually an aristocrat or a rich man or someone with high connections. There were officers of modest means in the army—even "rankers," former enlisted men—but they rarely rose very high because they simply could not afford it. Because an officer had to pay for his own uniforms, food, wine, servants and horses, he could not stand the increased costs of such "necessities" that were attendant upon a higher rank, even if he could afford the promotion. There is on record a man who had borrowed money to buy a cornet's commission in 1723, staying at that rank for forty-two years until 1765, when he was retired on half-pay as a debt-ridden old man. Thus promotion went to the wealthy and influential—both usually being embodied in the same men, more often than not peers—and it was these people who rose rapidly to high command.

If British officers came from the British upper crust, then British enlisted men issued from its lowest dregs. They were runaway fathers, poachers, thieves, drunks, village idiots or silly lads who took "the king's shilling" upon sight of a scarlet coat and the sound of a drum. And the king's recruiters were either judges, who offered a convicted criminal the sorry choice between a British jail or a British camp, or gangs of recruiters, whose fields of operation were taverns, doss houses, debtors' prisons or waterfront slums. Because they received a bounty for each man recruited, rival press gangs from the army and navy frequently fought each other for possession of a likely candidate. Nor were they exactly scrupulous in their methods, sometimes ordering some sorry specimen to stand on tiptoe so that he might reach the minimum height of five feet, six and a half inches notched on the sergeant's halberd. If a youth could not make it even then but showed promise of further growth, he was taken anyway. As the war continued and the army rose from 48,000 to 110,000, the minimum height was lowered to five feet three inches, and Roman Catholics were granted the privilege of fighting for their Protestant sovereign.

Grogshops were the chief sources of recruits. Treated to drinks by a friendly sergeant, serenaded by a band, enchanted by tales of glory and romance in distant lands and the chance to wear that gorgeous uniform, few youths so befuddled and beguiled had the sense to resist. So they signed an oath swearing that they were Protestants and had no "ruptures or fits." For this oath they were to be paid the princely sum of eight pence a day, or twelve pounds, three shillings, six pence a year. The jolly recruiter, of course, neglected to mention that there would be "charges" against these emoluments to pay for food, clothing, pipe clay, medicines, shaving gear, repair of arms and fees to the paymaster, the surgeon, and the hospital, so that in the end if "Tommy" wound up with his famous "tuppence" a day, he was a lucky soldier, indeed.

Moreover he probably did not know that he had enlisted for life, to be discharged before death only upon the onset of old age or disability caused by wounds or disease.

Misery was his daily companion. The uniform that had bewitched him, though splendid indeed, with its scarlet coat, white belt, white breeches, knee-high gaiters and cocked hat, nevertheless had to be brushed and pipe-clayed daily, while his weapons and equipment had to be cleaned against the chance of a surprise inspection.

On the field he was subjected to a brutal discipline while learning how to load and fire his musket, form ranks or swing smartly into line or column, responding instantly on the word of command. During battle those commands would come to him by drumbeat, and he had to learn to obey the drum as well. Oddly enough, in an army that prided itself on its precision, there was no uniform drill. Each regiment, the basic tactical unit, maneuvered according to commands and evolutions installed by its commander. Thus it was difficult to compel any larger formation such as a brigade—two regiments with artillery and cavalry—to conform to any single standard. Again and again the Hanoverian kings, who loved their troops as boys love toy soldiers, sought to "draw up a methodical exercise to be practiced throughout all forces," but the generals merely grunted, shelved the orders and continued to muddle through in typical British style.

All military discipline is instilled by the threat of punishment, and the British system was cruel, indeed. Fear of the lash or the noose compelled British redcoats to stand firm under a raking enemy fire or to rescue a desperate situation with a wild bayonet charge. For as little as failure to obey orders on the parade ground, a soldier could be sentenced to five hundred lashes across the bare back with the cat-o'-nine-tails, to a thousand if he struck or insulted an officer or to the gallows for looting, cowardice or desertion. To have avoided infractions of discipline was almost impossible, for these "lobsterbacks," as the colonists called them for their scarred and bloody backs, were everywhere hedged and hemmed in by regulations. In peace or war they could not leave their camps to visit towns and taverns, they could not gamble or, in America, to augment their meager rations "weavilly, … full of maggots, mouldy, musty and rotten" by foraging. For their pampered, spoiled and often effeminate officers to expect these miserable creatures to risk their flesh against an enemy they did not hate without the occasional consolation of a glass or a lass or a game of cards was selfish, heartless and cruel to an incredible degree. No wonder the lobsterbacks broke the rules, chased women, shirked work, stole and sold tools, collected "souvenirs"—a euphemism for looting—drank whatever and whenever they could, sang boisterously, complained incessantly and deserted in droves.

Yet, in another contradiction, the British allowed their soldiers to marry and even allowed the wives to live in camp and accompany their men into battle. Enduring the hard life of their soldiers, the camp followers became as hard as the men. They did the washing, cooking and mending, and they were also liable to the lash for any infraction. "Women who follow a camp," said one of Burgoyne's officers, "are of such a masculine nature they are able to bear all hardships." Their devotion to their men was legendary—caring for the wounded, fetching water for them under fire. Probably the most determined wife was the pregnant young girl who followed Burgoyne's army from Canada through the American wilderness. Stopping at a forest cabin to have her child, she gathered up her baby in the morning and trudged on until she found her soldier at Ticonderoga.

Except for the grenadiers and those numerous big, gullible farm boys recruited in Ireland, most of these redcoats were of medium or slight physique; yet with monstrous indifference, their officers sent them into battle in stiff, heavy, uncomfortable clothing and carrying up to 125 pounds. That was the weight of their packs, filled with personal effects, extra clothing, cleaning and blacking equipment, a blanket and a fifth part of a tent, plus a haversack filled with rations, a canteen, a cartridge box with sixty cartridges, a short sword, a bayonet and a musket. The musket was the famous—or infamous—Brown Bess, dating back to and named for Queen Elizabeth I. Said to have a killing range of 300 yards, a ball from a Brown Bess fell harmlessly to the ground at 125. It was of little use in a storm when the wind might blow the powder out of the pan or whip the flash out of the touchhole into a man's face or eyes, or the rain would wash away the powder or make it so wet it would not ignite. In such weather not one shot in four would go off.

Five feet long and weighing about fourteen pounds, the Brown Bess fired a round leaded ball weighing about an ounce. It took a soldier twelve motions to fire it. First, he must remove a paper cartridge containing powder and ball from the cartridge box, then tear the cartridge open with his teeth, sprinkling a few grains of powder into the firing pan, ramming the rest down the musket barrel with a ramrod, followed by the bulk of the powder, the wadded cartridge and then the ball—after which he could fire the musket.

It was said that a good marksman could fire five times a minute, but this is absurd, even if he were standing or kneeling. He could not fire so rapidly while advancing, and certainly not if he were prostrate to offer the enemy the smallest target. At best a good soldier might fire twice a minute, and even this frequency would be difficult if the bayonet were fixed to the musket muzzle and thus blocking the ramrod. Sometimes soldiers would load powder and ball without ramming, but this untamped charge fell quickly to the ground. Actually, many officers frowned on rapid fire. Wolfe remarked: "There is no necessity for firing fast; a cool, well-leveled fire with the pieces carefully loaded is more destructive and formidable than the quickest fire in confusion." Notice that Wolfe said properly "loaded," rather than "aimed." Indeed, the word *aim* did not appear in the British manual of arms, and the Brown Bess had no rear sight!

The Brown Bess was prized not for its firepower, but as a noise-and-smoke-making machine. The true arbiter of battle was still the bayonet. A volley was designed to frighten the enemy, and its drifting cloud of black smoke was the cover from which the bayonet charge would be launched; and the frightened enemy would be terrified by the sight of these redcoats yelling—"Hurrah!" or "God save the King!"—bursting out of the smoke with leveled, gleaming bayonets. Throughout their history, blundering British generals had been saved by the bayonet charge, and they still relied on it during the American Revolution—and with reason: American militia were terrified of it. Burgoyne prized it, ordering his officers "to inculcate in the men's minds a reliance on the bayonet. Men of half their bodily strength and even cowards may be their match in firing; but the onset of bayonets in the hands of the valiant is irresistible."

What the British redcoat feared most was not battle but the hospital, often a leaking, listing transport converted into a hospital ship: poorly lighted, filthy, stinking, reeking of blood and urine and filled with diseased and wounded men pleading pitifully for help from surgeons with neither the time nor the assistants nor the medicines to succor them. A ticket to a hospital was regarded as a sentence to a firing squad. On the battlefield many wounded were left to die because the surgeon believed they had no hope of recovery or because a retreating force could not allow the wounded to slow its flight. Throughout their miseries and ordeals, though, the British redcoat like so many famous soldiers never lost his sardonic sense of humor. It was his mainstay, like a crutch to bear him up, and also his own subtle little whip with which to flog unpopular officers. A captain sailing to Quebec with a load of recruits overheard one of them making light of a terrible storm:

> One of my recruits coming upon deck, not observing anyone there, and the sea so tremendous, immediately went below and cried out to his companions: "Oh by my soul, honeys, the sea is very dreadful, and we are all sure to be drowned, for the ship's a'sinking. However, I have this consolation, that if she goes to the bottom, the captain must be accountable for us when we get to Quebec."

Thus the hard-nosed, high-hearted British lobsterback, whom Rudyard Kipling would immortalize, more than a century later, as "Tommy Atkins":

> Oh it's Tommy this, and Tommy that, and please
> to walk behind.
> But it's "The thin red line of heroes" when
> there's trouble in the wind.

★ 21 ★

WASHINGTON'S YANKEE DOODLES

George Washington was still en route to Cambridge when he heard the great news of the Battle of Bunker Hill. Raw Yankee recruits had stopped the world's finest troops! Although they had retreated, they had given better than they got! But when he arrived in Cambridge on July 3 and took command, his elation turned to dismay when he realized that these raw militia believed that their "victory" had proved that all they needed to do to defeat trained professionals anywhere was to get their Yankee Doodle dander up and grab their muskets. This fallacy had blithely ignored the fact that the Americans were behind fortifications while the British were out in the open and was based on the assumption that the great carnage among Howe's troops was due to superior Yankee marksmanship. There had indeed been some sharpshooters at Bunker Hill, especially among Stark's frontiersmen, but even the most near-sighted neophyte could hardly have missed packed scarlet ranks at fifty feet. No, the invincible minuteman, except for the hunter and trapper of the frontier, was seldom a crack shot. He was a plowboy or a clerk or a mechanic and was too far from the wilderness to develop prowess with firearms.

From the standpoint of discipline, a rueful Washington discovered, the minuteman was also a slovenly soldier. He was imbued with what his commander in chief always excoriated as "the New England leveling principle," the belief that "I'm just as good as the next man and maybe even a little better." It was perhaps the defect of the virtue of democracy, the region's distrust of the military as an enemy of liberty, born of town meetings and a fierce spirit of independence. Privates who had "listed" in the crusade for freedom would not be awed or organized by officers whom they had elected, and who in civilian life might have been either their customers or employees. Officers so chosen did not dare to push their constituents about, and it was not uncommon at Boston to see a captain shaving a private or a lieutenant fixing a corporal's musket. A colonel who was the army's chief engineer was seen carrying a ration of beef to his tent to cook it himself "to set the officers a good example." Such leaders, elevated by nothing other than popularity contests, were too frequently beguiling, smiling schemers more eager for profit and promotion than for discipline or glory. Washington moved swiftly and harshly against such incompetents, reporting to Congress in August:

> I have made a pretty good slam among such kind of officers as the Massachusetts government abound in … having broke one Colonel and two Captains for cowardly behavior in the action on Bunker Hill—two Captains for drawing more provisions and pay than they had men in their company—and one for being absent from his post when the enemy appeared there and burnt a house just by it. Besides these, I have at this time one Colonel, one Major, one Captain and two Subalterns under arrest for trial.

He also strove to introduce some semblance of order into a camp that appeared to be a huge, smoking, stinking hobo jungle in which the men cooked their own messes and the latrines ("necessary houses") were constructed next to sleeping quarters. The Reverend William Emerson, grandfather of Ralph Waldo Emerson, found the camp's very variety to be a thing of beauty, observing:

> Some [tents] are made of boards, some of sailcloth, and some partly of one and partly of ye other. Others are made of stone and turf, and others again of birch and other brush. Some are thrown up in a hurry and look as if they could not help it—mere necessity—others are curiously wrought with doors and windows done with wreaths and withes in ye manner of a basket.

Gradually, the inflexible and sometimes irascible gentleman from Virginia produced a measure of order and cleanliness in the camp. Old latrines, with their black clouds of buzzing, disease-carrying flies, were filled up and new ones dug. Offal and carrion were burned. Company messes were set up and inspected regularly, loose women were run out of camp and drunken or defiant soldiers flogged. Although Washington seems to have discouraged some of the more barbarous punishments then in vogue, he was, like every other commander of the time, a believer in corporal punishment—to wit, the whip. He asked Congress to raise the number of allowable lashes from the biblical maximum of thirty nine to five hundred, or half the British limit, but the gentlemen in Philadelphia wisely lowered that figure to one hundred. Even more than the British redcoats, these Yankee Doodles were amazingly stoical. Inveterate offenders would stand with folded arms and a bullet clenched between their teeth, while being flogged by those drummers and fifers whose odious duty it was to ply the cat-o'-nine-tails, uttering not a whimper, eyes fixed on the drum major in charge of the lashing and calmly defying him to do his worst. Another punishment was running the gantlet. The men of the culprit's outfit would be drawn up in two lines facing each other while he ran between them to be struck by the switches they held. If he were unpopular, his bare back turned quickly red; if he were well liked and fleet of foot, his passage would be quick and almost painless. To prevent a quick passage, another soldier might be ordered to slow his progress by retreating slowly before him with leveled bayonet.

Desertion, one of the Continental Army's greatest problems, was punishable by death. A condemned man, his coffin borne before him, the doleful notes of the "Dead March" in his ears, would be paraded in front of his comrades while his sentence was read aloud. Approaching a freshly dug grave, the soldiers would lay his coffin beside it. Kneeling alongside, usually with a chaplain beside him, the condemned man would join the chaplain in prayer, until he was left alone and a firing squad of twelve soldiers came forward to end his life. Usually one of the muskets was unloaded, so that no one soldier could be sure he had killed his comrade. Also, this melancholy scene could end in soldierly shouts of joy when, at the last moment, a messenger rushed up with a reprieve. But for one soldier convicted of deserting seven times, each time reenlisting to claim the bounty of twenty-five dollars, there was no reprieve.

Washington's problem was unique, probably never faced by any commander before or since: to form and train an army on the battlefield with one hand while attempting to raise a new one to replace it with the other hand. Constant recruitment was necessary because the American militiamen believed in going home after the battle. They had short-term enlistments, usually for six months and sometimes for as few as three months. The Yankee Doodles at Boston claimed their enlistment expired January 1, 1776—some said December 1, 1775—and they had withstood every attempt to make them reenlist. John Adams, that shrewd, intuitive observer who understood the Yankee temperament better than most men, bluntly declared that a regiment might be procured in New England but only "of the meanest, idlest, most intemperate and worthless, but no more. We should have trademen's sons and farmer's sons, or we should be without defence, and such men certainly would not enlist during the war, or the long periods, as yet. The service was too new; they had not yet become attached to it by habit. Was it credible that men who could get at home better living, more comfortable lodgings, more than double the wages, in safety, not exposed to the sicknesses of the camp, would bind themselves during the war? I knew it would be impossible."

It very nearly was impossible, and Washington had to accept the melancholy fact that the army he was molding would melt away by the end of the year before he could raise another. His recruiting problems were made more difficult when each of the colonies began fielding militia armies of their own, raising their enlistment bonuses higher and higher until the zenith was reached by Virginia's $750 plus land, compared to the Continental Army's paltry $25. Then there was the reluctance of the more southern colonies, such as Georgia and the Carolinas, to contribute troops to the Continental Army at all.

Moreover, in those early years many brave men, full of patriotism and the love of adventure—plus loot—were drawn off by the numerous privateers who were commissioned by Congress to prey on the British merchant marine. Clever advertisements extolling the rich spoils taken in the West Indies drew off as many as ten thousand skilled sailors from New England. These privately owned warships did indeed twist the British lion's tail so tight that he howled horribly at his sea losses, and they protected the seacoast towns against British marauders, but a dismayed John Paul Jones deplored their monopoly on seamen who might otherwise have joined the fledgling American navy.

Yet Washington did succeed in developing a regular military organization that was based on the "lines" to be recruited from the various colonies. Its basic formation was a 720-man regiment consisting of eight companies, each company having one captain, two lieutenants, one ensign, four sergeants, four corporals, two "Drums and Fifes" and seventy six privates. There were as few of these regiments as two in the New Hampshire Line and as many as six in the Pennsylvania Line. No lines were forthcoming from Georgia and the Carolinas. Men who joined the line regiments enlisted "for three years or the war" and were given a bonus of $20. Privates were to be paid $6.67 a month, or 40 shillings, compared to the redcoats' 30 shillings. The money was supposed to be payable in silver, but it seldom was. Eventually, inflation made the Continental dollar sink so low in value that Yankee Doodle found that while his supposedly lower-paid enemy was paid regularly in specie, he was paid irregularly in paper "not worth a Continental."

On September 16, 1776, Congress authorized a Continental Army, to be composed of eighty-eight battalions mostly in the line regiments, with some militia. It added to the enlistment bounty a grant of a hundred acres of land, to be provided by the colonies if the man were killed in action. A soldier's arms, clothing and other necessities were to be provided by the colonies, the cost of the clothing to be deducted from his pay. Though simple on paper, this plan produced the inevitable complications. Men who had already served a term of enlistment, especially those with families, were reluctant to reenlist, while Congress refused to raise the soldiers' pay to lure them back, and it was then that the colonies were drawn into a bonus-bidding war to fill their quotas. Drafts were also introduced, but with so many exemptions for men living in seaboard towns, schoolteachers, artisans, the unfit, students, farmers and workers in powder mills or other war-related manufacturies that the manpower pool shrank alarmingly. Eventually, the colonies stopped using army officers as recruiting agents and appointed their own recruiters, to be paid eight dollars per enlistee and five dollars per deserter who was returned to duty. In the end, according to figures provided by Henry Knox, an estimated 232,000 American men served in Washington's army at one time or another, a figure that most students of the subject consider low.

Although freed blacks had fought at Bunker Hill, the problem of whether or not they should be enrolled in the Continental Army had been evaded by both Washington and Congress, until in November 1775, Lord Dunmore in Virginia proclaimed that all slaves and indentured servants would be freemen if they would join the British Army. Washington countered in December with an edict permitting the recruitment of free blacks, but Congress compromised by permitting only those who had served at Cambridge to reenlist. Despite later Congressional efforts to exclude them, blacks continued to serve as soldiers, so that in August 1778, Washington's returns showed an average of fifty-four blacks in every full-strength brigade of about 1,500 men. Southerners naturally opposed the recruitment of slaves, the work force of their agricultural economy, although Colonel John Laurens of South Carolina, admiring the blacks' soldierly qualifications, sought without success to dissuade them from that policy.

Poorly paid, Yankee Doodle was also badly clothed. Although much has been written of "the blue and buff" uniforms supposedly worn by

Continental soldiers, in actuality very few were issued such garments because cloth in the proper colors was not available. At Boston, Washington's men were dressed either in buckskin, homespun or British uniforms left over from the colonial wars. Serviceable wool was in such short supply that Washington adopted a hunting shirt or long loose coat of tow cloth, spun from flax, hemp or jute, with a pair of knee-length breeches of the same material to which were attached short gaiters held down by straps under the shoes. That is, if the men had shoes. It would not be long before Washington's men were naked or half naked in that dreadful northern winter. A gentleman, writing from Ticonderoga on December 4, 1775, observed:

"For all this Army at this place, which did consist of twelve or thirteen thousand men, sick and well, no more than nine hundred pair of shoes have been sent. One third at least of the poor wretches is now barefoot.... The poor creatures (what's left alive) is now laying on the cold ground, in poor thin tents, and some none at all, and many down with the pleurisy. No barracks, no hospitals to go in ... I paid a visit to the sick yesterday in a small house called a hospital. The first object presented to my eyes, one man laying dead at the door; then inside two more dead, two living lying between them; the living with the dead had so laid for four-and-twenty hours."

Like the redcoat, Yankee Doodle dreaded being sent to a hospital, or to what passed for one, a converted church, town hall or schoolhouse. Overcrowded and short of medical stores, the hospitals were actually charnal houses. Often with no straw available, the wounded lay on the floor, or else the straw might remained unchanged until four or five occupants had bled and died on it. Very few towns or villages welcomed the location of a hospital inside their borders. The arrival of a wagonload of wounded would provoke groans and cries of protest from the populace. Sentiment against the hospital could be so strong that as soon as the patients were able to walk, they were ordered to return to their units by foot, begging from house to house for their sustenance. British prison hospitals were even worse. The patients were not mistreated there but, rather, allowed to starve slowly to death. One man, driven to madness by his hunger, was said to have gnawed his fingers up to the first joint of his hand before he died. Others chipped mortar and stone from the prison walls and swallowed it, to their eventual extinction. Some of these reports may have been exaggerated, but there were enough of them to suggest that if these horrors were not widespread or systematic, they occurred.

Even worse were the British prison ships. As many as five hundred American prisoners might be herded aboard a rotting, leaking vessel that was fit to hold no more than a hundred. Fed four moldy biscuits and a bit of rancid butter daily, with an occasional bit of meat and a canteen of water—"meals" that were often missed—lying below decks in their own filth or squeezed together gasping in the foul, fetid air, half naked and often delirious, ravished by smallpox or attacked by ghoulish guards wielding cutlasses, their nights made hideous by the piteous crying and groaning of the stricken, their days darkened by despair, freezing in winter in unheated holds and suffocating in summer in the airless dark, they died at the rate of four or five a day. Indeed, a quick death was their only hope, unless they chose to escape by serving King George. To swim to freedom was not possible, even when they were allowed above decks, for they were simply too weak to go very far, and hence drowned or were recaptured. It is possible that British prison ships killed more Americans than did British rifles, for some seven or eight thousand perished aboard them.

Thus the ordeals faced by Yankee Doodle. And yet, though the men fought naked or in rags or stained the snow with blood from their shoeless feet, and though many of these Continentals might desert, in the main most of them never lost faith in their cause. When, two months before Yorktown, two Spanish ships arrived with cargoes of clothing, when the men found that the coats were of British red, they refused to wear them. Nor did they ever lose their gallows sense of humor, laughing with the comrade who wryly prophesied: "if the war is continued through the winter, the British troops will be scared at the sight of our men, for as they never fought with naked men, the novelty of it will terrify them."

Yankee Doodle was just as sardonic about his wretched food, or the lack of it. He was supposed to have received the daily ration similar to the one authorized by the Provincial Congress on June 10, 1775:

> A pound of bread, half a pound of beef and half a pound of pork, and if pork cannot be had, one pound and quarter of beef; and one day in seven they shall have one pound and one quarter of salt fish, instead of one day's allowance of meat; one pint of milk, or, if milk cannot be had, one gill [four ounces] of rice; one quart of good spruce or malt beer; one gill of peas or beans, or other sauce equivalent; six ounces of butter a week, one pound of good common soap for six men per week; half a pint of vinegar per week per man, if it can be had.

Such a ration—a veritable repast in the eyes of Yankee Doodle—was never issued, not even in the early days at Boston, when the Patriot farmers were not hamstrung by the absence of hired hands and sturdy sons in the Continental Army and the harvests and slaughtering suffered accordingly. Profiteering was also rampant, producing that ruinous inflation that helped shrink the soldier's pay of $6.67 to an actual buying power of a few shillings. Everywhere British specie outbought Continental dollars, so that the enemy, either in Philadelphia or New York, was always amply supplied with grain, as were profiteering American civilians throughout the colonies. If Yankee Doodle went naked because merchants in Boston would not move cloth off their shelves for anything less than profits ranging from 1,000 to 1,800 per cent (in specie), his belly also shriveled and growled with hunger because Connecticut farmers refused to sell meat livestock at anything near state prices.

Washington's men also suffered from a great shortage of vegetables. Because such perishables could neither be preserved nor carried on the march as readily as could meat, soldiers were afflicted by those diseases rising from a steady diet of meat. Fresh milk was also difficult to acquire, especially from avaricious farmers demanding outrageous prices. Eventually, some thirty men and an officer were drawn from each regiment to collect cows and to provide milk for the army, just as some colonels, whenever it appeared that their units would go into camp for some months, detailed men to plant and grow vegetables. Salt and vinegar, which might have been an antidote to the meat diet, were just as difficult to obtain, as were beer and cider. Rum, it seems, was usually available in quantity. It was drunk daily and on any pretext—a victory, the cold weather, a case of the blues. There were frequent drinking contests. Two soldiers at Cambridge challenged each other to see who could drink the most, and the winner died. A Continental named John Coleman was widely celebrated in the army for having downed three pints of hard cider at one draught. Two youths who had gotten drunk on hard cider got into a fistfight and were taken to their captain, who stared at them sternly, and said: "You are ordered for punishment to drink together a mug of cider." Shouts of laughter succeeded this "sentence," and the two culprits left the captain's tent arm in arm.

But there was not much merriment when Yankee soldiers had to go as many as four days at a stretch without a single scrap of food and were reduced to chewing on bits of bark or leather for sustenance, as Joseph Plumb Martin wrote in *Private Yankee Doodle,* a narrative of his experiences in the Connecticut Line. Company messes eventually became things of the past, and the men themselves cooked whatever underweight ration they received or could forage. Thus Martin: "The flour was laid upon a flat rock and mixed up with cold water, then daubed upon a flat stone and scorched on one side, while the beef was broiling on a stick in the fire." After four days without food, "except a little black birch I gnawed off a stick," he saw "several of the men roast their old shoes and eat them, and I was afterwards informed by one of the officers' waiters, that some of the officers killed and ate a favorite little dog that belonged to one of them."

It was not always the profiteering or inflation or undermanned farms or bungling quartermasters that produced such dreadful shortages in food and clothing in the Continental Army, but rather the simple ineluctable fact that Congress possessed neither the funds nor the sophistication nor the enforcing power to establish a smoothly functioning service of supply. There was no central purchasing-and-distributing agency comparable to the British War Office and secretaries of state. These dedicated Patriots, so many of them political theorists of the first order, did not realize that war requires much more organization than does peace. The British war machine might be unwieldy, but it was still an engine of parts fitted together, and better than no machine—which is what the colonists possessed. The Patriots perhaps did not also perceive that their chief advantages were negative: they were fighting at home, whereas the British must maintain a supply line over three thousand miles of often-tempestuous ocean to subdue them, and there was not a single major American city the capture of which would end the Revolution. But they did have one positive asset: Yankee Doodle. In rags and in hunger, deficient in every want of war save his steady ardor and allegiance, he would continue to deny victory to an enemy better trained, led, fed, clothed and—most important in combat—better armed.

Five days before Lexington and Concord, the military stores held by the Patriots in Massachusetts and what is now Maine numbered 21,549 firearms, 17,440 rounds of powder, 22,191 pounds of lead balls, 144,699 flints, 10,108 bayonets and 11,979 cartridge pouches. There is no mention of the amount of coarse gray paper needed to make cartridges or of artillery. Presumably there was none at that time and very few cannon. Moreover, of those 21,549 firearms, many were undoubtedly pistols, fowling pieces or antiquated blunderbusses. Still it was a surprising arsenal for a people who were forbidden to manufacture anything—least of all, arms. The remainder were either handmade muskets fashioned by the village gunsmith or Brown Besses carried during the colonial wars. These were personal firearms, and after the short-term soldiers went home, they took their muskets with them, vastly diminishing the army's stock.

Still the Continental Congress decreed that each soldier was to be armed with a good musket, with a barrel three and a half feet long firing a one-ounce ball; a steel ramrod; worm; priming wire with brush; bayonet; cutting sword or tomahawk; a cartridge box containing twenty-five cartridges; twelve flints; and a knapsack. If a soldier provided some or all this equipment, he was given credit for it. Eventually, after a gun factory was established at Lancaster, Pennsylvania, and a gunlock* plant at Trenton, the standard shoulder weapon was a replica of the Brown Bess, with that weapon's short range and slow loading disability.

Even so there was a scarcity of firearms in Boston, so much so that Benjamin Franklin advocated the use of pikes or bows and arrows, claiming that four arrows could be launched for every bullet. There was some merit to this suggestion, for an arrow fired at night is silent and cannot be traced to its source and during the day emits no telltale and choking smoke. The discovery of gunpowder came so fast upon the development of the English strong bow that the worth of that formidable weapon was never fully appreciated. And it was not appreciated in Cambridge, either. Nor were the spears suggested by a colonel. Washington's solution to the shortage of firearms was to order soldiers returning home who owned their weapons to sell them to the army. He also authorized regimental commanders to buy whatever guns the militia units were willing to sell. But by early 1776 the army still needed two thousand flintlocks. In May of that year one regiment was down to ninety-seven muskets and seven bayonets. In New York militiamen without arms were ordered to bring to camp either a shovel, a spade, a pickax or a rude spear made of a straightened scythe fastened to a pole. Other colonies ordered collections of firearms from private citizens. Such a multiplicity of muskets made it difficult to supply each soldier with the proper caliber bullets until a single mould embracing all calibers was developed.

Unlike the lobsterbacks, Yankee Doodle was trained in marksmanship, taught the drill for loading, aiming and firing even in those days of gun and powder shortages. Not every Yankee became a crack shot, but there were plenty of hawkeyes in the western wildernesses of Pennsylvania, Maryland and Virginia. When Virginia decided to recruit five hundred sharpshooters, so many men came forward that it was decided to select them in a shooting contest. A chalk outline of a nose was traced on a board one foot square and nailed to a tree 150 yards from the firing

*A lock was a musket's firing device. Although Yankee Doodle still called his weapon a "firelock," which ignited the powder by a burning cord, he actually carried a flintlock. The flint striking a steel "battery" ignited the powder.

line. Those who hit it or came closest were to be chosen. The first forty or fifty shots cut the nose out of the board!

Some 1,500 of these backwoodsmen—"remarkably stout and hardy men, many of them exceeding six feet in height"—arrived at the Cambridge camp. They had had to march four hundred to seven hundred miles to reach the camp. Old Daniel Morgan, still bearing the scars of the flogging he had received under Braddock, put his men on horses and rode them six hundred miles in twenty-one days. Not a man was lost by sickness on the way.

These men in leather hunting shirts and moccasins carried a new weapon: the Kentucky rifle. It was the long, slender and graceful gun that German and Swiss gunsmiths in Pennsylvania had designed for the American frontier. Whereas a musketman rarely could hit a man beyond 60 yards, a rifleman could put ball after ball into a seven-inch target at the range of 250 yards.

If the rifle had not been so slow loading and if it could have been fitted with a bayonet and placed in the hands of a marksman who would accept discipline, the American arsenal would have been augmented in truly splendid style. However, the endless pop-popping of unruly frontiersmen at British redcoats who were far out of range drove George Washington to distraction, to say nothing of the riflemen's custom of freeing any of their comrades who were confined in the guardhouse for misdemeanors. The riflemen were of use later in the Revolutionary War, but not at Boston, and Washington wished that they had never come.

Because the Continental Army actually was a child of the British Army, it was natural that the so-called Norfolk Discipline, developed in 1757 in Britain to train militia, was adopted. This was a simple drill, designed for men who would exercise but one day a week. Embraced by New England in 1768, it would be used to train the Continental Army until the arrival of Baron von Steuben in 1778. The British Army's complicated procedure for loading and firing a musket was also used, sometimes with tragic or near-tragic results. One man forgot to shut his powder horn, so that when he touched off his pan powder the entire horn flared, burning nearby soldiers. Another Continental lowered his musket to recock it, and when it went off the butt kicked him in the breast, killing him. In one of those common I-didn't-know-the-gun-was-loaded accidents, a soldier in barracks pulled the trigger, and the bullet pierced a double partition of inch boards and passed through a bunk and then through the breast of a man to hit a chimney and leave a mark.

Eventually the Yankees, consummate smugglers that they were, resorted to that tactic to eliminate the gun shortage. Ships carrying cargoes of guns or gunpowder arrived regularly from St. Eustatius in the Dutch West Indies, while warships in the French ports were under orders to protect American vessels entering or leaving their harbors.

Throughout the war gunpowder was the crying need, unrelieved by the efficient smugglers sailing back and forth from the West Indies, leading Washington, who rarely complained or boasted, to exclaim at Cambridge: "To maintain a post within musket-shot of the enemy without powder, and at the same time disband one army and recruit another within that distance of twenty-odd British regiments, is more, probably, than ever was attempted." To produce powder, civilians were implored to save niter and sulfur, while the Congress in Massachusetts drew up instructions for the manufacture of saltpeter and sent them to every town and village in the province, promising to purchase all that was made. Powder manufacturing in the Bay State improved when a "simple countryman" sauntered into the House carrying half a bushel of saltpeter that he had made by extracting it from earth taken from beneath old houses or barns. He said he could make more in eight months than the province could buy. How much his contribution helped is not known, although the gunpowder shortage was never really alleviated until France began sending covert material assistance to the colonies.

Lead for bullets was more easily obtained. There was enough lead in New York's pulled-down statue of King George and on its housetops to supply the campaign of 1776, while the operations in 1777 were based on bullets moulded from the leaden spouts and window weights of Philadelphia. Flints were also in short supply. Ordinarily a sturdy flint could last for sixty rounds of fire, but the custom of using "snappers" during drill to preserve the flint had the counterproductive effect of wearing out the flint sooner. The discovery of a prodigious vein of finc black flintstone at Mount Independence near Ticonderoga was a great boon to the Continental Army.

All these shortages were not really eliminated until France, Spain and finally Holland intervened in the war on the side of the colonies.

⋆ 22 ⋆

LORD GEORGE GERMAIN

One of the belated and unforeseen consequences of the Battle of Bunker Hill was that it placed the conduct of the war in America into the hands of the most despised man in Britain: Lord George Germain. As one contemporary historian wrote: "The most odious of tasks was assigned to the most odious of instruments," for Lord George Sackville, as he was named at his birth, only to change it later to Germain to claim an inheritance, had been a soldier convicted of cowardice and sentenced never again to serve His Majesty in a military capacity. And yet, on November 10, 1775, he became, as secretary of state for the colonies, the minister responsible for running this most momentous war.

Such high office was nothing unusual in the history of this clan of earls and dukes. Nor was any family in British history more devoted to the theory of the Divine Right of Kings—or its corollary, the Divine Right of the Elite—than these Sackvilles, whose long and illustrious career began in 1066 when a Norman knight named Herbrand de Sackville crossed the English Channel with William the Conqueror. Through ardent and unswerving pursuit of gain and a succession of profitable marriages, the family prospered until in the late 1500s Thomas Sackville was made "Earl of Dorset, Baron of Buckhurst, Knight of ye Noble Order of ye Garter," by a grateful Queen Elizabeth I. With these honors went the magnificent mansion Knole, the most famous house of Britain, built, it was said, on Roman foundations, occupied by Pembrokes and archbishops of Canterbury, until Thomas Cranmer, then archbishop, under pressure from an admiring Henry VIII, reluctantly gave it to his most gracious and avaricious noble lord, the king. Thereafter Edward VI gave it to the Earl of Warwick; Queen Mary, to Reginald Pole, Catholic theologian, cardinal, almost a pope and later Papal legate to the queen; and Queen Elizabeth, to the aforesaid Thomas.

Here in this veritable palace—for such it was, with its stone towers, mullioned windows, vast rolling deer park, fruit orchards and huge rectangular gardens—there dwelt for two centuries the successive earls of Dorset with their families: brave, arrogant, willful men, convinced that as night follows day, so also was the inevitable innate superiority of Sackvilles over other human beings. Knights of the Garter, High Stewards of Britain, warriors, wastrels, dissolutes and ambassadors, before they were any of these they were Sackvilles. It was to Knole, then, that the seventh Earl and first Duke of Dorset brought his small third son, born June 26, 1716, in the family town house in Haymarket.

Here Lord George Sackville grew to manhood, surrounded by a breathtaking elegance, an opulence so constant that it might have been found suffocating to any human being other than a Sackville. But young Lord George took it for granted. With his two older brothers and three sisters, he actually explored this edifice covering four acres, verifying the number of its staircases at fifty-two; the number of its rooms at 365, exactly duplicating the days of the year; but probably finding uncountable the number of its portraits, by masters ranging from Van Dyck to Reynolds and Gainsborough; coats of arms; china; silver—and perhaps even counting the number of huge Renaissance fireplaces, with their mantels of colored Italian marble. Here young George could also ride the white rocking horse, ridden by four generations before him, or even shout with glee to discover a bewildered deer that had wandered through the enormous wide-open oak doors fronting on the park.

For young George perhaps the liveliest time of the year was spring planting time. Like his forebears, the Duke of Dorset was a great planter, especially of trees. When George was seven, the duke's gardeners planted 300 crabapple, 200 pear, 500 holly, 200 cherry and 700 hazel trees, along with "1,000 holly for ye kitchen garden … 200 small beeches in ye Park … 10,000 seedling beeches for my Lady Betty." Lady Betty was the widowed Lady Betty Germain, who had come to live at Knole with her great friends, the duke and duchess. A gentle, generous lady, with great wit and invincible good humor, she became especially fond of young Lord George.

And with reason, for among all those Sackvilles there had rarely been one who combined a stable personality and brilliance of mind with the customary family obstinacy. But George possessed all three, to which were added charm, diligence and common sense—all yoked to and driven by a galloping ambition. Moreover, the connections of his father, the Duke of Dorset, Knight of the Garter and Lord High Steward of Britain, were hardly to be paralleled in the entire realm, not to mention his friendship with the sovereign lord of that domain, King George II, who had not only consented to be Lord George's godfather but had actually attended the christening, holding the baby in his arms and resting his royal corpulence that night in the same huge four-poster in which the burly Henry VIII had slumbered. All that was missing was wealth, and although the duke had enough revenue for himself, there was certainly not enough ready cash available to stake out a political career for his third son. Yet, in Lady Betty Germain there was indeed a fairy godmother very much inclined to leave most of her fortune to her beloved George. Indeed, then, everything seemed ready to fall into place for this aspiring young man, including a fairly good education at Westminster, where George, always cherishing nothing for itself but always as a means to an end, took from his studies only what he thought would help him most in life. It was the same at Trinity College in Dublin, when, at fourteen, he accompanied his father to Ireland as the new lord lieutenant there.

At Trinity, said to be "half beer garden and half brothel," Lord George joined other young noblemen in riotous living, drinking, wenching and preparing for the duels that were not uncommon by practicing pistol fire in their rooms. Even so, Oxford and Cambridge were no better, and Lord Chesterfield went so far as to declare: "The Irish schools and universities are indisputably better than ours." After receiving a master's degree at eighteen, Lord George became his father's secretary, showing a skill in the political arts of bribery and deception that, though not exactly applauded by his infinitely more honorable father, was nevertheless of great help to the lord lieutenant. But Lord George's arrogance and highhandedness were not quite so highly appreciated by the hot-tempered Irish, who were jealous of what privileges had been left to them by their conquerors. By this time, the young nobleman had matured physically. He was tall, rawboned, heavy but not corpulent, with a sloping forehead, dark complexion, full lips and a large nose. Not at all a handsome man, and in later years, his detractors would say he was "rather womanly."

After his father's term ended, George accompanied him to France on a diplomatic mission in 1736, but was back in Dublin the following year as an aide to the new lord lieutenant, the Duke of Devonshire. Here he served as a captain in the duke's regiment and was beginning to show a fondness for the military, long ago observed by his maternal grandfather, the old Marshal Colyear. Here his godfather, the king, was somewhat helpful, making him a lieutenant colonel at the age of twenty-five. Just like the old king, the young lord distinguished himself at Dettingen, for which service his godfather made him a royal aide-de-camp. He also fought at Fontenoy, where the French and Irish troops of Marshal Saxe defeated the British. At Fontenoy he was severely wounded, shot in the breast, and it is possible that some of Saxe's Irish rejoiced to hear that their arrogant and disdainful classmate at Trinity was lying near death in the tent of the King of France. But Lord George recovered, though slowly and with much pain. He saw no more campaigning until "the Forty-five," the year in which Bonny Prince Charlie raised the Stuart standard of rebellion and was utterly crushed at the bloody Battle of Culloden. Later campaigning against the scattered Stuart remnants in the Highlands of Scotland, Sackville earned high praise from the British commander, the Duke of Cumberland.

As was customary with many British soldiers when there was no fighting, Lord George was elected to the House of Commons as a member from Dover—one of those Cinque Ports of which his father was now the Warden. Defeat in Dover was thus unthinkable, but if it had happened, no matter; the Sackvilles also controlled two other seats near Knole. Momentarily, he seemed destined by success in politics to duplicate his glory in war. But then, when Lord George was thirty-four, his father was once more appointed Lord Lieutenant of Ireland, and Lord George again accompanied him to the Emerald Isle, not only as his indispensable right hand, but also as secretary for war for Ireland.

The Irish—that is to say, that small portion of the population not disfranchised by the infamous British Penal Code prohibiting a Catholic, among other things, from hearing Mass, voting or owning a pistol or a horse worth five dollars—were pleased upon the return of the amiable Duke of Dorset, and they would show their affection by naming Dublin's chief thoroughfare Sackville Street. But they were not quite as enthusiastic about the return of his son.

Battle had not mellowed Lord George. Rather, his unbroken success had exaggerated in him an air of easy confidence that could easily be taken for conscious superiority, if not insufferable arrogance. In his effort to control Irish affairs, both through his father and his own office, he outraged the entire country. He had begun by declaring that the Crown need not consult the Irish Parliament in the use of any unassigned surplus Irish revenue. By this single act of arrogance, he united a people who ordinarily took perverse delight in division and dissent. When Sackville attacked Hugh Boyle, for twenty years the Speaker of the Irish House, the people formed a solid phalanx behind Boyle. And then, relying as usual on the subtle art of bribery, Sackville secretly offered Boyle a peerage and a pension of £1,200 a year if he would drop his opposition. Boyle's reply was public: "If I had a peerage, I should not think myself greater than now that I am Mr. Boyle; for t'other thing, I despise it as much as the person that offers it." With this, Sackville had sunk his lordly spurs deep into the proud Irish soul, provoking such a storm of rage and violence that both Whitehall and Westminster became alarmed at possible rebellion, while the Sackvilles—father and son—fearing for their very lives, fled to London.

At first George II sought to protect his friend the duke by permitting him to serve out his term as lord lieutenant from London. But public opinion in Britain was so great against Dorset that the king had to replace him, ordering him never to return to the Emerald Isle. In consolation the king awarded Dorset the office of Master of the King's Horse. Dorset's son, meanwhile, in typical defiance and disdain, placed the blame on those rebellious and inferior Irish. Here was another of Lord George's unpleasant traits: his ability to find fault everywhere, but in himself. As though in reward, five days after his father was dismissed, he was promoted to major general.

After his return to London, Lord George began courting Diana Sambrooke, a descendant of the Earl of Salisbury, but with no title or great funds of her own. Most of Sackville's friends believed he could have found someone more helpful to his career, but apparently Lord George actually fell in love with her. They were married August 5, 1754.

Sackville now busied himself with politics. Aware that the king was aging, he began flirting with Leicester House, the home of the Prince of Wales and headquarters of the Opposition gathering around him; the prince's wife, Augusta; and Lord Bute. His overtures were muted, for if Lord George wished to ingratiate himself with the next king, either Frederick Louis himself or his son George, he also had no intention of provoking the choleric King George II. For a man of his domineering temperament, he showed rare skill in intrigue—not to say changing horses—deciding to follow Pitt after the Great Commoner returned to power. Lord George cogently reasoned that Pitt would prosecute the war with France more vigorously, which would mean the chance of military advancement for himself. He was right, for Pitt, in gratitude, made him a lieutenant general and second in command of a raid on St. Malo on the French coast.

In this operation Lord George's imperiousness earned him the enmity of two rising officers in the king's service: the Howe brothers. William Howe was an infantry commander, then famous as a man who did his talking at the cannon's mouth, while his brother, Lord Richard Howe, commanded the naval squadron for the St. Malo expedition. Both lords needed but to meet to know that they disliked each other, but Sackville's constant criticism of Captain Howe was so public and unrestrained and so devoid of understanding of a seaman's difficulties—the tides, the current, the wind, shoals and reefs, even the height of the waves on the landing beaches—that this mutual distrust soon escalated into open hatred. No wonder so many of Sackville's officers could wish that they knew as much about *anything* as Lord George pretended to know about *everything*. In such an atmosphere the miracle was that St. Malo was merely a failure, rather than a disaster. For the first time Sackville's reputation was tarnished. Horace Walpole said: "If they send a patch-box to Lord George Sackville, it will hold all his laurels." It was even suggested that he had led his men in the wrong direction, or that the bullet that felled him at Fontenoy had also crippled his courage.

Yet, there was no criticism of the fiasco: the ministry could not attack Sackville because Pitt had chosen him; the Opposition could not either because Lord George was its friend. Still Sackville was disturbed, vowing that he would go on no more "buccaneering" excursions. His heart was now set upon the war against the French in Germany. Here, more than in America or in hit-and-run incursions on the French coast, real glory was to be had. So he hoped to become second in command once more under the Duke of Marlborough—so amenable to his ideas and domineering personality—who now headed the British Army serving under Prince Ferdinand in Germany. Because Pitt had not lost confidence in George and because the Opposition, so far from objecting to him, actually was grooming him as their top military man upon Frederick Louis's ascension to the throne, his wish was granted.

Traveling to Munster, Sackville found the complaisant duke now under the spell of Prince Ferdinand and no longer so ready to seek Lord George's counsel. For this defection, he merely hated the prince, and poured out a constant stream of criticism of him to London. His criticism became even sharper after the duke died and Sackville was chosen to succeed him. At the age of forty-three he now held the highest active command in the British Army. But that army was not a happy one under his constant interference with his staff; his contempt for his second, Lord Granby, whom everyone else admired; his bickering with such juniors as William Howe; and his feud with Prince Ferdinand, carried on while writing reassuringly to Pitt of Ferdinand's "attention and goodness to me." And then, on August 9, 1759, came the Battle of Minden.

Prince Ferdinand's allied army was drawn up on a lightly wooded slope opposite Minden, in which Marshal the Marquis Louis Georges Contades's French army was concentrated. Behind Ferdinand on a nearby ridge stood the British and German cavalry, commanded by Lord George Sackville. Early in the morning the French attacked. Four times Contades's cavalry and foot troops hurled themselves upon the British and German infantry, and each time they were repulsed. Ferdinand's forces counterattacked, throwing the French into disarray. Here was the moment for a cavalry charge that would shatter the retiring enemy, perhaps even destroy them, and with this single decisive victory perhaps end the Seven Years' War. Eagerly aware of his opportunity, Ferdinand sent two separate aides hastening to Lord George Sackville with orders to attack at once. But Sackville did not. A half hour passed before the Allied horse moved out, but by then the French had regained their fortifications in Minden and the golden moment passed unexploited. By his infidelity Lord George had saved the French from "the greatest defeat of this century," and although Minden was an Allied victory, it was not a decisive one.

In the Allied army that night criticism of Lord George Sackville was bitter and unrestrained, yet he dined with Prince Ferdinand and his officers with such outward composure that the prince exclaimed: "Here's a man so much at ease that you would think he had worked wonders!" Later Ferdinand wrote a personal account of Minden to his cousin, George II, declaring: "His behavior on the first [of the month] was such that neither the men in general nor I in particular was happy with it. The situation was on the brink of disaster, and yet our success on that day was not as it could have been, since he had everything he needed for victory easily within his reach."

King George exploded when he read those lines, and when Lord George unwisely demanded a court-martial, the king gleefully consented. The trial began March 7, 1760, and ended a month later, with a clear verdict of guilty to the charge of having disobeyed the orders of his commander in chief. But the sentence, never again to serve the king in a military capacity, was comparatively light. He might have been forbidden to serve in *any* capacity, or even been executed, like the unfortunate Admiral John Byng who had been shot the previous year. George II was all but apoplectic when he read the sentence, and he showed what he thought of it by the zeal with which he rewarded those who testified against Sackville and punished those who had defended him. Nevertheless Lord George Sackville was in complete disgrace. Horace Walpole, who wrote that only he and two other men dared to speak or sit by Lord George in public places, pronounced his epitaph: "So finishes a career of a man who was within ten minutes of being the first man in his profession in the kingdom."

Hidden among Lord George's many defects were the sturdy, practical virtues of patience and a thick skin, both eminently suitable to withstanding a siege of social ostracism. He had not only not read his epitaph, he would not have believed it if he had. Almost immediately after his conviction, he began his campaign for rehabilitation—although his irrepressible arrogance almost aborted it at the start. This incident occurred in November, when young George III held his first levee. A gasp broke from every gilded throat when Lord George approached the throne and knelt to kiss the king's hand. William Pitt never forgave Lord Bute—the instigator of this enormous faux pas—for this offense against the memory of the dead George II, and Lord George was forbidden ever to come to court again.

It would seem that now Sackville was really finished, but, like Lazarus, he was not dead but only sleeping. Within a few months he cooly sauntered into the House of Commons, where he was received with cold and silent contempt—yet not expelled. He showed himself at the theater and the opera and the races, impervious to the glacial silences, raised eyebrows or turned backs that greeted him. Always his gracious wife was with him, and Lord George discovered in the Lady Diana a surprisingly valuable and subtle ally. Lady Diana possessed that magical quality of popularity and was so well liked by her society friends that they simply could not bring themselves to snub *her.* Under Diana's influence, the Sackvilles gradually were able to be received in the great houses as well, and even to welcome the great names into their own. Lady Sarah Lennox, who but for the hostility of George III's mother and Lord Bute might have been queen of Britain, wrote in her diary of playing cards at the Sackvilles. And Lord George did return to court in spite of the king's prohibition, and he continued to come, just as he continued to rise in the House to earn himself a reputation for sagacious and cogent speeches, especially on those military matters he was supposed to shun, eventually almost literally making his enemies weary of disdaining him. Yet, his power and influence grew, until in late 1765 he felt himself completely rehabilitated when he received one of the lucrative vice-treasuryships of Ireland. But on July 30, 1776, his implacable enemy William Pitt came out of retirement to join the Rockingham Cabinet, and on that very day Sackville was "rather cruelly removed" from his post.

Once again the end seemed near, but Lord George simply would not accept defeat, writing to a friend: "A garrison never surrenders at discretion until deprived of every means of offense and defense. Thank God as yet I have some ammunition left and plenty of provisions." He did, indeed, for in 1769 Lady Betty Germain died and left Lord George her great estate at Drayton—with all its possessions and rentals—plus £20,000 to maintain it. Lady Betty's only condition was that Lord George assume the name of Germain. This he did with alacrity, probably because it rid him to some degree of the stigma of Minden.

So Lord George did have "some ammunition left and plenty of provisions," along with that inexhaustible patience and uncommonly thick skin. Thus when Lord North became the king's first minister and began looking around in 1775 for an able politician with a knowledge of war to become secretary of state for the colonies, he conceded that he could conceive of no candidate better equipped for this vital post than Lord George Germain.

And of America itself? Germain's remark calling for "fire and sword against the Bostonians" had endeared him to the king, who felt the same way. At last the man and the mission had met. Since his childhood and youth in Knole, the scion of wealth and privilege, he had been instructed in a simple catechism: the Divine Right of Kings and of the elite. At last he was to serve his only superior—the king—in suppressing the insolent rebellion of that mass of wretched commoners, his divinely ordained inferiors, across the sea. Just as Attila the Hun had been the Scourge of God, Lord George Germain would be the Scourge of George III.

★ 23 ★

THE LURE OF CANADA

Congress had taken charge in America. Although as yet there was no true American government with a chief executive and Supreme Court and the Continental Congress had no legal foundation for its actions, the legislature was in fact running the country. Later, in September 1775, when Georgia sent its delegates to Congress, all thirteen colonies would be represented at Philadelphia.

Congress's most important measure was to assume responsibility for the conduct of the war. In this it had adopted the New England Army as its own, naming George Washington as its commander and appointing its chief officers. It next drew up a military code, set up a postal service under Benjamin Franklin, named commissioners to deal with the Western Indians, issued paper currency and, finally, found itself incapable of resisting the Canadian magnet.

At first, Congress attempted to coax Canada—still populated in the main by French Catholics—into joining the rebellion. But the Canadians refused, chiefly on the advice of their bishops and clergy, who were content with the generous provisions of the Quebec Act. Having felt the military wrath of their neighbors to the south and read some of their fulminations against their faith, the Canadians realized that they could expect nothing more than second-class citizenship from the colonies, which—with the exception of Maryland—still banned Catholics from holding office.

Upon this rebuff, Congress decided to conquer Canada. Those two incompatible comrades of Ticonderoga—Ethan Allen and Benedict Arnold—had already been to Philadelphia with schemes to do just that, but the delegates, while adopting their advice and plans, somewhat ungratefully chose General Philip Schuyler instead.

It was a bad choice. An able aristocrat and a truly ardent Patriot, Schuyler was a man skilled more in counsel than in command. Fortunately, his second in command was Richard Montgomery, the dashing Irish officer who, at forty, was one of the youngest general officers in the Continental Army. Tall and handsome, forceful, with that passion for speed that is the mark of the born soldier, Montgomery had served in the British Army during the French and Indian War. Leaving that service, he settled in America, marrying into a wealthy family. Throughout the spring and summer of 1775, the impetuous Montgomery had been urging the dilatory Schuyler to move rapidly down the lake-and-river chain into Canada to capture Montreal.

At last, in September, Schuyler was ready to move. But then he was called back to Albany for an Indian parley. Before departing he received word from General Washington that Washington had authorized another, eastern expedition into Canada under Benedict Arnold. Quebec was the objective, and thus this double-pronged invasion would be mutually supporting. At this point, Montgomery, now in command, received reports that an enemy expedition was being prepared to sweep Lake Champlain and recapture the forts at Ticonderoga and Crown Point. He thus set out at once by himself, embarking a force of about one thousand men on Lake Champlain and notifying Schuyler that "I don't like" moving without his orders, but that "the prevention of the enemy is of the utmost importance."

With him were Ethan Allen and a regiment of Green Mountain Boys.

After his capture of Ticonderoga, Ethan Allen returned to Bennington looking for a Roman triumph replete with everything except captive enemy kings "to grace in chains his chariot wheels." His arrival, according to legend, was on a Sunday on which the Reverend Jedediah Dewey, an iron-lunged preacher of marathon sermons, was to thank the Lord for the fall of Fort Ti. Colonel Allen allowed that he would attend meeting that day, perhaps in hopes of hearing a kind word or two about his own role in that celebrated event. But after listening to two hours of effusive gratitude toward none but the Almighty, Colonel Allen drew his great body erect and growled: "Parson Dewey, aren't you going to tell the Lord about me being there, too?"

"Ethan Allen, thou great infidel," the parson bellowed—"be quiet!"

Enraged, the "great infidel" stomped out of the church. But the bruise that Parson Dewey had placed upon his ego was as nothing compared to his dismay when the Green Mountain Boys, meeting to elect their leader for the new campaign, "diselected" Ethan Allen, replacing him with his friend, Seth Warner. It was small comfort that Ethan's brother Heman was chosen captain, for Allen himself received not a single vote. What had happened was that the balloting was not done by regular Boys—or the "Bennington rioters" as they were called—but by about fifty of the more sober and pious farmers of the Grants' towns. These farmers had had enough of Ethan Allen's godlessness and parson baiting, and they considered Seth Warner to be more reliable and less inclined to rashness. There was some consolation for Allen when many of the Boys he recruited refused to serve without him, but to his credit he did not encourage them to stay home or join other units in New York or Connecticut. Instead, he went to General Schuyler and persuaded the general to let him join the expedition—but without a commission, only as a scout and advance man charged with inducing the French Canadians and their Indians to join the Americans, or at least not fight them.

It was not a wise decision.

Guy Carleton, governor and captain general of the Province of Quebec, commanded at Montreal. He had more than three hundred regulars and Canadians and probably could have raised a force of two thousand Indians if he had not regarded them as untrustworthy. Carleton was Scotch-Irish, having been born in County Down in the North of Ireland in 1724. He was an ensign at eighteen, serving under James Wolfe at Quebec and again elsewhere in Canada, Europe and against the Spanish in Havana. Carleton's insistence upon adhering to the Quebec Act earned him the affection of the French Catholics and the enmity of the British merchants, many of whom openly sympathized with the Americans.

Aware in May 1775 that Congress had authorized an expedition for Montreal, Carleton left Quebec and hastened to that threatened city. Although his garrison was small, the American delay in organizing gave him at least three months in which to strengthen the fort at St. John's on the Richelieu River. On September 5 the Americans sailing down the Richelieu could see smoke rising from the fort.

Montgomery realized that St. John's was the key to lightly defended Montreal, and it was there that he began his siege. Stationing his gunboats in the river to protect his own rear, he sent Ethan Allen and a lawyer-soldier named John Brown around the British flanks—Allen to take command of a body of rebellious Canadians waiting downriver, Brown to strike the enemy supply line.

While increasing cold and disease delayed Montgomery at St.

John's, Allen and Brown met in the enemy rear—where Brown proposed that they take Montreal on their own. Allen was delighted. It was just the sort of wild adventure that appealed to his rash nature, and, of course, he took no account of how reliable his force of about 110 men and Brown's force of 200 would be in combat nor of what resistance he might meet. Their "plan," if it may be thus described, was for both to cross the broad St. Lawrence—with Allen to strike below the town and Brown above it. As Allen moved out, he took pleasure in being told that a report that "Ethan Allen, the Notorious New Hampshire Incendiary" was approaching the city's gates had thrown the town "into confusion."

This, to say the least, was an exaggeration. Carleton had remained calm, and after Allen crossed the St. Lawrence and Brown failed to appear, he sent a force of about 250 regulars, volunteers and Indians out the Quebec Gate to attack the invaders. Upon their approach, the Canadians on Allen's flanks fled into the woods. A short but not very bloody fight ensued—"I never," complained Allen, "saw so much shooting result in so little damage"—and Allen, down to thirty-seven men, was compelled to surrender.

Just as he handed over his sword, he was attacked by a huge Indian, who sought to sink a tomahawk into his brain. Another redskin joined the first, and Allen seized a British officer, using him as a shield until "an Irishman came to my assistance with a fixed bayonet, and drove away the fiends, swearing by Jasus he would kill them." Colonel Richard Prescott of the British garrison had the same idea when the giant American was marched into his presence. He also wanted to shoot the Canadians who had been captured, but Allen bared his breast and demanded that he be killed instead. "I am the sole cause of their taking up arms," he said.

"I will not execute you now," Prescott muttered, "but you shall grace a halter at Tyburn, God damn you." To that end he ordered Allen bound in irons and sent to London for trial as a traitor. The giant swashbuckler of the Catamount Tavern was not executed, but was later exchanged for a British prisoner. However, his military career definitely did expire after the debacle at Montreal. Now it was up to Richard Montgomery to redeem that failure.

Montgomery's men were now paying the price of the delays that had sent them into Canada at the onset of a cruel northern winter. Snow had not yet fallen, but the incessant rains were cold and soaking, causing chills and sometimes pneumonia. Montgomery wrote: "We have been like half-drowned rats crawling through the swamp." Food and powder were in precariously short supply. Perhaps worse was the habit of the New England soldiers to vote on accepting or rejecting their general's tactics. When Montgomery sought to move a battery of light guns within range of the St. John's fort, they objected with such obvious hints of mutiny that he changed his mind.

While holding St. John's in check, Montgomery sent some cannon downriver to Chambly, a little fort held by about one hundred Welsh Fusiliers, but also containing 124 barrels of precious powder. A bombardment compelled its surrender. Montgomery next returned to the attack on St. John's, persuading his reluctant artillerymen to move their guns closer to the fort. A cannonade shook the garrison, but did not induce Colonel Prescott—now commanding there—to run up the white flag. Prescott held out, hoping for reinforcements from Carleton. Carleton tried to relieve him with a pickup force of Canadians, Indians and a few regulars, but Seth Warner's Green Mountain Boys ambushed and repulsed them. Now a huge mortar called "the Old Sow" arrived in the American camp. Its shells were so devastating that on November 2, 1775, Prescott surrendered.

Among the British who marched out of the fort under terms of the surrender was Captain John André. Like his men, he was warmly clothed, much to the anger of the Americans who were shivering in their rags. The Americans demanded the enemy's reserve supply of clothes, to which Montgomery would not consent. "There was no driving into their noodles that the clothing belonged to the British," he wrote.

Now his soldiers pleaded to go home. They had suffered cruelly in every imaginable shortage and in the worst weather, now a combination of snow and ice. But their resolute commander would not turn about; rather, he faced north once more to march to Montreal. With their clothes freezing to their bodies, their spirits rose at the report that the city had been abandoned. It had been, when Carleton escaped to Quebec, and the victorious Americans were overjoyed to discover that Montreal contained an abundance of food and clothing.

Promising the residents to pay for all that they seized and to respect their religion, Richard Montgomery now awaited word from Quebec and the eastern expedition under Benedict Arnold.

★ 24 ★

BENEDICT ARNOLD AND QUEBEC

By an ironic quirk of fate the name Arnold is derived from an Old English word meaning "honor." It is believed to have been borne by a Welsh prince of the twelfth century whose descendants settled in Warwickshire, England. One of these descendants—William, born in 1587—a dissenter fleeing the persecution of the Anglican Archbishop Laud, crossed the ocean to settle in Boston. But he soon found the stern theocracy of the Massachusetts Puritans even less to his liking and followed the banished Roger Williams to his new colony of Rhode Island, building a home on the Pawtuxet River in 1636. His son Benedict moved to Newport, where he became both wealthy and governor of Rhode Island for several terms. Benedict's son, also named Benedict, was not as successful, so that his son—the third Benedict—was reduced to apprenticing himself to a cooper. But when he set up his own business, he chose to locate it in Norwich, Connecticut.

Abandoning his prosperous cooperage for the sea, Benedict became a captain and then a merchant and shipper with a brisk trade on Long Island Sound and in the West Indies. On November 8, 1733, he married Hannah King, the pretty widow of another captain-shipper. They had six children, of whom only two survived: a girl Hannah, and a boy, born January 14, 1741, the fifth Benedict, who was given the same name of a deceased older brother. During the worldwide turmoil provoked by the War of the Austrian Succession (King George's War), a severe depression seized the seafaring New Englanders, and the senior Benedict Arnold's business suffered so severely that this once-respected constable and selectman sought recourse in the bottle. As a result he was unable to restrain his wild and willful young son, who was well on his way to becoming the prince of all "the fresh kids" in Norwich when, at the age of about eight or nine, his anxious mother placed him in a school in nearby Montville. At eleven, she sent him to the Reverend Dr. James Cogwell's school at Canterbury, fourteen miles up the Quinebaug River. Here he did well in his studies, excelling in Latin and mathematics and perhaps laying the foundation for his knowledge of French, probably gained later during his career as a trader. At the age of fourteen, with the family's fortunes declining in exact proportion to the senior Arnold's growing dependence on drink, Benedict was withdrawn from Cogswell's school.

He was now free to do as he pleased. Although he would stand no taller than five feet seven inches at maturity, he was broad shouldered and deep chested, with great strength for his size and a marvelous agility, matched only by an irrepressible belligerence. To these traits were added an inexhaustible energy. Bounce and brilliance best described this daring young man, given to cartwheels and handsprings, climbing a rope hand over hand, sliding down a shroud with the speed of the ablest-bodied seaman or diving off a ship's crow's nest and coming down gracefully with outspread arms and pointed toes. In all these acts Benedict sought the approval of his peers, the outward expression of his inner lust to dominate. To be their leader, he reasoned, he must do things none of them would dare attempt.

Thus, en route to a gristmill with corn to be ground, he stupefied his comrades by suddenly seizing one of the mill wheel's arms, shouting with laughter as it carried him on high and then silenced him by breathless descent to drag him through the waters of the millstream. He emerged dripping—and once again laughing. Or again, to celebrate a British victory over the French, he led his gang of yelling boys to the green, where they swarmed over the cannon, upending it so that Benedict could pour a horn of powder down the muzzle. But the boys were not prepared when he ended the escapade by plunging a flaming torch on top of the powder, thus, but for the stoutness of the cannon, ending everyone's career then and there. Next he and his followers decided to celebrate Thanksgiving Day by building a bonfire of barrels on the green, and when a constable arrived on the scene to squelch this irregular outburst of gratitude to the Lord, Benedict tore off his coat and challenged him to a fistfight. Startled at first, the constable recovered his composure by collaring this brash and burly boy and dragging him home to his mother. Mortified, Hannah Arnold finally put a period to her high-spirited son's adventures by apprenticing him to her cousins, Daniel and Joshua Lathrop, who ran an apothecary shop in Norwich.

The Lathrops' shop was no small concern, but among the largest of its kind, dealing not only in medicines and surgical equipment, but in dried fruits, wines and other amenities as well, being thus a forerunner of the modern American drugstore. To Benedict the shop was a bird cage. Even though he was learning to be a pharmacist, he was bored and frustrated—especially after the outbreak of the Seven Years' War brought the sound of squealing fifes and shouted commands drifting up from the green. In 1758 he finally ran away from home, walking to New York, where enlistment bounties were higher than in Connecticut and joining a company in Westchester County. But his redoubtable mother, through the good offices of a clergyman, soon "dislisted" him and returned him to the dreary apothecary routine. Still, he had tasted the so-called glamor of war, but not enough to realize that it is, for the most part, indigestible. Thus when a fever of recruiting swept the colony in 1759 for the grand campaign against the French in Canada, he persuaded his mother to allow him to enlist, joining another New York company on March 16.

Here, as his outfit began to train for Lord Jeffrey Amherst's expedition against Ticonderoga and Montreal, he came to the unhappy conclusion that a soldier has more use for a shovel than for a musket. Thus disenchanted, his receipt of word in May that his mother was seriously ill was all that was needed to send him sneaking out of camp, bound for home. In a word, he deserted, but was probably unaware of the gravity of his crime. It may also have been that he knew he would get no furlough once the campaign began and was eager to see his mother before she died, after which he would return to duty. That was what happened. Hannah Arnold died on August 15, 1759, and a few months later Benedict was back in uniform—but by then Quebec had been captured, and his active service again was short. In 1761, after Benedict had sailed to the West Indies as a supercargo and been to London to buy merchandise for the shop he planned to open, his father died of alcoholism. Perhaps eager to escape the stigma of his father's vice and ignominious end, as well as in search of a larger town than Norwich, he decided to locate his business in New Haven.

At twenty, Benedict Arnold had reached his full height, and the burly boy was now a powerfully built man. His dark brown hair was thick and his chin was sharp and determined, his nose was long and hawkish, his skin was dark and his eyes were of such a hard pale blue that those who felt that glance in anger could never forget it. He was also something of a dandy, sheathing his handsome, muscular legs in the finest white silk stockings. He could afford such clothes, for he had sold his father's home for £700 and his shop in New Haven was an almost immediate success. Besides a stock ranging from medicines to jewelry to maps and rum, he carried a large inventory of books: bibles and religious tracts, philosophical works, plus Latin, Greek and French grammars for the students at Yale, all suggesting that his mind was inquiring and his tastes were wide. As his business grew, he decided to call upon his sister Hannah for help. Hannah was not eager to come to New Haven, for her little brother, finding her being courted by a French Catholic, a race and faith he detested, like most New Englanders, frightened her suitor off by firing a pistol shot over his head. At last Hannah was persuaded to leave Norwich, after which her brother was free to become a sea captain and shipper, trading in Canada and the West Indies.

Arnold's reputation as a shrewd but not always scrupulous businessman grew, along with his notoriety for trying to resolve all disputes with his fists or his pistol. In the Bay of Honduras, being busy loading his ship, he ignored an invitation to dine with an English captain named Croskie, but on the following day, he came aboard to apologize and explain. "You damned Yankee!" Croskie shouted. "Have you no manner?" At once Arnold challenged him to a duel. They met on a small island. Croskie's shot missed, and Arnold's plowed a furrow in the Englishman's arm. After the wound was dressed and the pistols reloaded, Arnold glared at Croskie with his hard cold eyes, snarling in his rasping voice: "If you miss this time, I shall kill you!" With this threat, Croskie allowed that he had been a mite too hasty, and Arnold accepted his apology.

Arnold was not so lenient with one of his seaman, Peter Boles, during the Townshend Ministry's determination to enforce the law against smuggling. Boles had demanded higher wages, which Arnold refused to grant, even upon the threat of being denounced as a smuggler. So Boles went to the authorities, and Arnold, enraged, cornered him and compelled him to sign a confession admitting his attempted blackmail, undertaken "at the instigation of the devil." But once freed, Boles reneged, taking sanctuary in the home of a tavern keeper. At the head of a gang of the Sons of Liberty, Arnold broke into the house, dragged Boles out, stripped him and tied him to a tree on the green, where Boles was given forty lashes with "a small cord"—if that can be believed. Then the gang drove Boles out of town. For this incident, Arnold and his accomplices were brought to trial.

The Boles incident created a furor in New Haven, as the town divided between the conservatives loyal to the Crown—being wealthy and in possession of most high offices—and the more radical Patriots led by Arnold. Arnold's mobs roamed the streets, hanging and burning the jurors and judge in effigy, screaming that informers, rather than honest businessmen such as Arnold, should be on trial. Undeterred, the court brought in a verdict of guilty, and Arnold was fined fifty shillings.

If anything, the incident installed Benedict Arnold as a leader of the radicals in Connecticut, a prestige in which he exulted, regularly attending meetings of the Sons of Liberty to deliver scathing denunciations of the Mother Country. His reputation grew, even after a shortage of specie in the colony drove its businessmen deeper into debt with the London merchants. Like many other traders, Arnold tried to beat the exchange rate, but was caught by the London agent in America and made to accept his true obligation. Such sharp practice did nothing to diminish Arnold's popularity, if it did not actually increase it, nor did it deter his suit for the hand of pretty Margaret Mansfield, daughter of Sheriff Samuel Mansfield. He and Margaret were married February 22, 1767, and Arnold remained so devoted to her that as his fortune grew, he surrounded her with luxuries and built for her one of the finest mansions in New Haven overlooking his wharves and ships and with a fine view of the harbor and Long Island Sound.

At this time Benedict Arnold's very success involved him in another duel. His ferocious energy had never made him popular in the West Indies, where he drove hard bargains, rarely honoring the social amenities in his eagerness to unload and load his ships so that, being first in port, he could command the highest prices. It was this arrogance that had annoyed Captain Croskie, and in 1771 Croskie's friend, an English shipmaster named Brookman, similarly insulted Arnold for refusing to pay a courtesy call to his ship. Given his choice of weapons, the skilled swordsman Brookman understandably chose the blade. To his astonishment, Arnold, known only as a marksman, by his strength, agility and supple wrist disarmed and humiliated him—and this second success in the Bay of Honduras provoked the envious circulation of scurrilous stories insinuating that the duel was over a woman or that Arnold had contracted venereal disease in the bay. Although these tales infuriated Arnold, there was little he could do to stop them, except, perhaps, what he could never do—adopt a conciliatory attitude toward his fellow sea captains.

The very virtues that had enriched Benedict Arnold possessed defects that were bound to provoke envious enmity in those who were not quite so fortunate. Thus the dark side of his self-confidence was arrogance; of his indomitable will was ruthlessness; of his quick intelligence impatience with others; and of his unswerving sense of the virtue or sacredness of his own cause—or at least could be—hypocrisy. Few other than his beloved Peggy and their three sons could love Benedict Arnold—his enemies would be legion.

In 1774 the Boston Tea Party completed the bifurcation of New England into "Tories" or Loyalists and Patriots. In Hebron, Connecticut, a Tory clergyman named Samuel Peters denounced the Boston "Mohawks" as thugs and enemies of the Crown. An angry band of Sons of Liberty searched his house and later roughed him up, forcing him to leave town, eventually finding sanctuary in New Haven in the home of the Reverend Dr. Hubbard. Upon receiving word that Benedict Arnold and the Sons of Liberty were marching toward them, Hubbard and his family fled, while Peters collected twenty muskets to distribute among his family and servants. When Arnold and his radicals arrived, Arnold ordered Peters to unbar the gate. Leveling his musket, the cleric replied: "The gate shall not be opened this night on pain of death!" The challenge enraged Arnold's followers, who demanded that he break down the gate. So Arnold called for an ax. Hearing him, Peters again aimed his weapon and shouted: "Arnold, so sure as you split the gate, I will blow your brains out, and all that enter this yard tonight!"

Momentarily hesitating, Arnold withdrew. To those who taunted him with cowardice, he calmly replied: "I am no coward, but I know Dr. Peters's disposition and temper. He will fulfill every promise he makes, and I have no wish for death at the present."

Strangely enough, by this surprising prudence Arnold the impetuous solidified his position with the Sons of Liberty and other radicals, so that when General Gage closed the port of Boston, sixty-five New Haven "gentlemen of influence and high respectability" met on December 28, 1774, to form a military company eventually called the Footguards; and on March 15, Benedict Arnold was elected its captain. A month later, "the shot heard 'round the world" was fired in Concord. Two days later Israel Bissell galloped into New Haven with the incredible news: Gage's redcoats had been routed!

Almost at once Benedict Arnold sent out calls for his Footguards to assemble. They did the next day—fifty of them—gathering in full military regalia for a march to Cambridge, where the Massachusetts Army was assembling. Arnold, accompanied by his wife, three sons and Hannah, led the Footguards toward the green. They made a great red splash against the tender green grass of spring, in their scarlet coats trimmed with silver buttons, buff facings, white ruffled shirts, waistcoats and breeches, and black half-leggings. Arnold paraded his Guards before an enthusiastic crowd, putting them through the manual of arms. Then he sent a message requesting powder and ball from the selectmen who were meeting in a nearby tavern. When the selectmen refused, an infuriated Arnold marched his company to the tavern, where he repeated his request with the threat to break into the powder house. To the mediator sent outside to dissuade him, he roared: "None but Almighty God shall prevent my marching!" In a few moments, the keys to the powder house were surrendered to him.

With their muskets loaded and their cartridge boxes filled, the company formed ranks again. Above them floated the colony flag, with its motto emblazoned in gold letters, *Qui Transtulit Sustinet* (He who brought us across [the ocean] sustains us). Drums rolled, fifes squealed, the crowd cheered, and with yelling small boys and yapping dogs running alongside, the proud Footguards of New Haven stepped out for Cambridge. Ahead of them—his head high, his chin lifted—strode the short, sturdy figure of Benedict Arnold.

Arriving in Cambridge eager for glory, Benedict Arnold was somewhat dismayed to find that he and his Footguards were just another one of the units forming the Patriot army besieging Boston. Chafing at the boring camp routine, he conceived a daring plan to capture Fort Ticonderoga and persuaded the Massachusetts legislature to authorize such a campaign with himself as its leader. But when he appeared on the shores of Lake Champlain, he was chagrined to find Ethan Allen and his Green Mountain Boys there before him. Nevertheless, he agreed to serve as Allen's second, and it was he, not the giant Vermonter, who organized the fort's defenses after its capture. But then he received word that his wife Margaret was dying, and he hurried back to New Haven only in time to bury her. Next there came a series of embittering setbacks. First, Massachusetts questioned the honesty of his military accounts; next the Bay State sided against him in his dispute with Ethan Allen over command at Ti; and finally, Congress, having accepted his advice and plans for the invasion of Canada, conferred command of the Montreal campaign on General Schuyler instead.

Enraged, he hastened to Cambridge where he immediately requested and was given an interview with General Washington. The American commander was so impressed with Arnold's bearing and fire that he authorized him to lead a second, complementary invasion of Canada.

He was to go up the Kennebec River and then down the Chaudière to assault the old fortress of Quebec while Montgomery engaged Carleton at Montreal. Hundreds of musketmen and riflemen, bored with the siege of Boston, volunteered for the expedition. Altogether Arnold had about a thousand men, among them nineteen-year-old Aaron Burr and Captain Daniel Morgan, when he began, in late September, a march that ranks as an epic ordeal in American history.

First, the bateaux that were to carry them up the Kennebec from Fort Western (present-day Augusta, Maine) were made of green wood and badly built. They came apart. Often they had to be carried or hauled upriver against boiling rapids. Going down the swift-running Chaudière, some smashed into rocks and the men aboard were lost. Floundering, stumbling against one another, the men waded for days over one stretch of nearly 180 miles.

After the provisions gave out, the Americans ate soap and hair grease. They boiled and roasted their bullet pouches, moccasins and old leather breeches and devoured them. They killed and ate the dogs that accompanied them. There were dropouts and slow death and mass defections along the way. At one point Lieutenant Colonel Roger Enos refused to go on and withdrew his division of three hundred men. Undaunted, Arnold pressed forward. On November 9 his ragged band burst from snow-cloaked forests onto the south bank of the St. Lawrence. They marched upriver to Point Lévi on the Isle of Orleans. They were ragged and bearded. Their feet were shod in raw skins. Their clothes hung in tatters over bodies that were but bags of sticks. There were only six hundred of them. They had taken forty-five days, not the estimated twenty, to cover 350, not 180, miles. But they had arrived, and they were going to attack Quebec.

For all his doggedness, events were thwarting Arnold. He had collected canoes and dugouts to make a night crossing of the St. Lawrence and ascend the cliffs to the Plains of Abraham, as James Wolfe had done. Quebec was held by a mere handful of Marines and regulars and a weak body of about four hundred militia. Arnold was certain he could not fail. But for two straight nights the winds blew so strongly that he could not cross. In the meantime, Lieutenant Colonel Allen Maclean had arrived in Quebec with about one hundred veteran soldiers. Their coming heartened Quebec's defenders and raised their number to about 1,200.

Arnold still thought that in a stand-up fight his hardy band could scatter the militia and overwhelm the remaining regulars. At nine o'clock on the black night of November 13, the first detachments began crossing to the Anse-de-Foulon, now Wolfe's Cove. They landed and kindled a fire to revive a lieutenant who had fallen overboard and been towed through the ice-cold river. The rest of the Americans crossed on the following night.

Now Arnold led his men up to the Plains of Abraham, routing a force of militia there. He sent a flag of truce to Quebec to demand its surrender. His emissaries were routed by a cannon ball. Then Arnold was driven off as the frigate *Lizard* sailed upriver to cut off his rear, and Maclean prepared to attack with eight hundred men.

Miserable again, with many of their number barefoot, the invaders retreated to Pointe aux Trembles. Here, on December 2, they saw with elation the topsails of a schooner coming downriver. It was Montgomery with reinforcements of three hundred men.

Montgomery had brought with him captured British clothing: great white blanket-coats with caped hoods, heavy blue overalls, sealskin moccasins and fur-tailed caps. Arnold's freezing men joyfully damned the reinforcements for their tardiness and donned the winter clothes. Then, about a thousand men strong, the hardy little American army marched back to Quebec.

Once there, it became plain to Montgomery and Arnold that they could not conduct a siege. They had no heavy guns to batter Quebec's walls, and they could not possibly endure an entire Canadian winter encamped outside the city's gates. Smallpox had broken out, food was short, and worst of all, the enlistment of Arnold's New Englanders expired at the year's end. They decided to attack, even though Sir Guy Carleton had entered the town and raised the number of its defenders to 1,800 men. On the first snowy night they would storm the Lower Town, Arnold attacking from the north, Montgomery from the south.

On the afternoon of Saturday, December 30, snow began falling. It thickened. The wind rose. By early morning of the thirty-first, a blizzard was howling about Quebec. Snow mixed with hail whistled into the faces of the Americans moving to their positions. They ducked their heads and shielded their firelocks with their coats. At some time after four o'clock, signal rockets burst red in the blackness above them, and the Americans began marching.

Within Quebec drums began beating and bells tolled. Officers ran through the streets shouting, "Turn out! Turn out!" Guy Carleton's formidable barricades in the Lower Town were quickly manned.

On the left of the American pincers, Montgomery's division was slipping and sliding down the slopes toward the road from Wolfe's Cove to Cape Diamond. Men carrying unwieldy scaling ladders could barely struggle through drifts six feet deep.

On the right Arnold's force of six hundred men left the suburb of

St. Roche and stole silently past the Palace Gate. They veered right, and a sudden blaze of musketry from the ramparts above raked them. Men fell. They moved on, Arnold leading an advance party of about twenty-five men, including Daniel Morgan. Behind them came forty artillerists dragging a six-pounder on a sled, and behind them came the main body.

Arnold and Morgan came to a narrow street that was blocked by a barricade. They called for the six-pounder. It had been abandoned. A gun in the barricade fired but did no damage. Arnold ordered a charge.

Out of the snow the Americans came, yelling, rushing to the barrier, and firing through its gun ports. The British fired back. Arnold fell with a ball in his leg. Bleeding freely, he was helped away while huge Daniel Morgan took command. The Old Wagoner mounted a ladder set against the barrier, calling upon his men to follow. A blaze of fire tumbled him back into the snow. He had a bullet through his cap and another through his beard. Shaking himself, Morgan leaped erect, climbed the ladder again and jumped over the parapet. Others followed. The defenders fled. The Americans were inside the Lower Town. Another barrier lay ahead, but the Americans did not attack it. Instead, they decided to halt to await the arrival of Montgomery.

Richard Montgomery's force had also come to a barricade. Soldiers began sawing at it. Montgomery and his officers tore at half-sawed posts with their hands. They pulled the barricade down and passed on, no more than sixty or seventy of them, the remainder of the division having been disorganized and scattered by the storm.

Now a blockhouse confronted them. Inside were about fifty men and four little three-pounders charged with grape. The British blew on their slow matches and awaited the American approach. Montgomery came on. His men faltered. He called to them through the storm, "Come on, my good soldiers, your General calls you to come on."

Montgomery, Aaron Burr, a few other officers and about a dozen men rushed forward. They were within a few paces of the blockhouse when a sheet of flame and a hail of grape and musket balls raked them. Another burst, and it was all over.

Montgomery lay dead. So did most of his officers. Only Burr and a few men got away.

To the north, inside the Lower Town, the Americans under Morgan were fighting desperately. Carleton had sent a force of two hundred men and cannon out the Palace Gate to take them in the rear. Morgan's men were trapped. They began to surrender. Morgan fought on. He set his back against a wall. Tears of rage and despair flowed down his face as he stood there, his sword uplifted for his last blows. His men implored him to give up. He shook his head. Then Morgan saw a clergyman in the crowd and called: "Are you a priest?" The man nodded, and Morgan handed him his blade with the words: "Then I give my sword to you. But not a scoundrel of these cowards shall take it out of my hands."

Two bursts of gunfire, an able maneuver by Carleton, and the attempt to storm Quebec had been repulsed.

The total American casualties at Quebec were devastating: 48 killed, 34 wounded and 372 captured, probably more than half the small force engaged. And yet, Montgomery and Arnold might have succeeded, had not the death of the former and the wounding of the latter simply demoralized their valiant troops. They had also been unbelievably durable, especially the survivors of that incredible march from Fort Western. No other troops in the world could have endured such an ordeal, and no other commander than Arnold could have led it. Cold, hard and ambitious though he might be—and to be thus might describe every great captain in military history—he was nonetheless an indomitable driver who captured the hearts of his men by example, rather than by precept. As he lay in pain on his hospital cot in the hospital at the suburb of St. Roche, he was still determined to take Quebec. Hearing that Carleton was coming to destroy him and the remnant of his command, he ordered his pistols loaded and placed on his bed, along with his sword. As he had always vowed, he would fight to the end and take with him as many redcoats as he could.

Next he wrote to his friend and fellow townsman, General David Wooster, now in command in Montreal, begging him for all the men and arms he could spare so that the attack could be renewed. But Wooster replied that he could send very little help, lest he weaken Montreal and thus provoke an uprising by the inhabitants. Moreover the refusal of the New York regiments there to reenlist also severely reduced Arnold's chances for a successful renewal of the assault. Yet Arnold was able to maintain a siege, and Wooster, openly marveling at his ability to keep the city embattled, managed to dribble down to him what supplies and men he could spare. It was inevitable, then, that when a huge British force under the command of Lieutenant General John Burgoyne sailed up the St. Lawrence in the spring to the relief of Quebec and to prepare for an invasion of New York intended to split the colonies in two, Arnold's little besieging force had to withdraw.

Before then Brigadier General Arnold—a grateful Congress had promoted him—was compelled to move to Montreal. Beginning to ride again, his horse had slipped on an icy road, and in falling Arnold had reinjured his wounded leg. Although reluctant to leave, he was consoled somewhat by his general's star, and also was pleased to be present when a congressional commission to Canada arrived in Montreal. The commission's were Benjamin Franklin and three Marylanders: the resolute Samuel Chase, the Reverend John Carroll and his brother Charles Carroll of Carrollton, perhaps the richest man in America. Father Carroll had been a Jesuit priest until the papacy, under pressure of King Louis XV of France, encouraged by Voltaire and other anticlerical intellectuals, had suppressed the Society of Jesus, the formal name for the Jesuits. He then became a secular priest and would one day be America's first Catholic bishop. The purpose of the commission was to impress upon the Canadians how much their interests coincided with those of the Americans in the struggle against British tyranny, and to assure them that in such a union they would enjoy full religious and civil liberty. Evidently the repulse at Quebec had induced Congress to drop the stick and reach for the carrot again, more hopefully this time by sweetening the carrot with the presence of two Catholics on the commission, one of them a cleric. But this embassy was no more successful than the first one, and Canada remained unconquered and unconvinced.

Without Montgomery and Arnold, the American forces were compelled to retreat. General Wooster could not duplicate the military ability he had shown against France; General John Thomas who succeeded him had none to begin with; and General John Sullivan, a New Hampshire lawyer and politician of whom Washington had complained of his vain lust for popularity, recorded the first of his remarkable record for consecutive failures by a defeat at Three Rivers on June 7, 1776. With Montreal already abandoned, the remnants of Montgomery's and Arnold's once-proud and fierce commands washed back on the shores of Lake Champlain the following July. Although this most ambitious American campaign of the Revolutionary War had ended in humiliating defeat, it remained imperishable proof of how well Americans could fight if they were also well led.

And the man who, with the slightest nod from the gods of war, could have led them on to victory—General Benedict Arnold—was the last man to leave the mainland of Canada. He had bequeathed to the pursuing British a trail of scorched earth and made a smoking desert of St. John's. On the night of June 18, with Captain James Wilkinson, he stood by his horse—listening. From the woods behind him came the unmistakable sounds of a great body of troops on the move: the muffled tread of many shod feet, the rattling of wagon wheels, the cries of the teamsters and the steady tap of many drums. Behind him Arnold saw scarlet coats flashing through the tender-green leaves of the late northern spring. It was Burgoyne's advance guard. Arnold dismounted, removing his horse's saddle and bridle and placing them in a canoe being steadied by Wilkinson. Then he shot his mount, climbed into the canoe, seized a paddle and was off upriver to America—defiant to the last!

★25★

TOWARD AN AMERICAN NAVY

Not only had the United Colonies, as they were still called, had the effrontery to challenge the Mistress of the Seas, they had done so without a navy of their own; yet, they did it successfully through the combination of their seamen's audacity and skill and the surprising inefficiency of the Royal Navy.

If after the Seven Years' War Britannia ruled the waves—as she certainly did, just as, in her treatment of her American colonies she was inclined to waive the rules—it may well be wondered how badly King Louis XV had been served at sea. From top to bottom, from John Montagu, Earl of Sandwich, one of the more innovative eroticists of the infamous Dashwood set, who was then First Lord of the Admiralty; through that prodigy of inaction Admiral Samuel Graves, commander of the British fleet with headquarters in Boston; down to the lowliest of British seamen, the Royal Navy within fewer than a dozen years had become a broken reed in the hands of King George III. It was under the steadily avaricious hand of Sandwich that the British Navy went into its rapid deterioration after the great, war-ending victory at Quiberon Bay. Traditionally believed to be the inventor of the sandwich from his habit of feeding on pieces of meat between two slices of bread while seated at the gaming table, Montagu was also known as "Jemmy Twitcher" for the unabashed celerity with which that same hand could twitch away a bribe. His contribution to the success of the American sea wolves was his unfounded contempt for their fighting prowess and his conceited reliance upon a derelict and deficient Admiralty that his own corruption had made powerless to sweep the upstart Yankees from the seas. In 1775, when he had that opportunity, Sandwich proposed to reduce the number of seamen for the navy by two thousand fewer than the previous year. Such a First Lord was well served by admirals such as Samuel Graves.

Of Graves it has been well said by Page Smith that he "reacted so slowly to every emergency that one might conclude that his own bottom was as encrusted with barnacles as the bottoms of the vessels under his command." And if he cared little for his ships, he cared less for his sailors. In their miserable lives—a compound of "rum, sodomy and the lash," as another First Lord, Winston Churchill, was to say almost two centuries later—was reflected the corrupt base upon which British military glory rested. If commissions were bought and sold on top, then on the bottom human beings were seized by press gangs roaming the waterfronts of the principal British ports and summarily herded aboard ship for life. It was no wonder that so little was done for the health and well-being of sailors so easily procured. Their malnutritious diet made them the victims of scurvy and dysentery, and thus susceptible to every kind of contagious infection. Nor could an inexhaustible issue of grog ever compensate for a miserable existence, alternating between the blaze of battle in the cockpit of a man-of-war or a night of homosexual love in foul, stinking, rat-infested holds so far below the waterline that there was no hope of rescue should the ship founder in a storm.

Yet these pitiful human beings were supposed to perform prodigies of valor for commanders such as Graves, who regarded them, as Wellington so ungallantly described his own soldiers, as "the scum of the earth." But the derision that this vain, vindictive, venal and cowardly admiral directed toward those despicable Yankees of New England was answered by them with a contempt for both his person and the king's property so infuriating that even Graves found himself, in that ingenious style of doublespeak for which he was justly celebrated, hard-pressed to report failure as success.

His first rebuff came when the whalers and fishermen of the Boston area burned lighthouses right beneath the admiral's nose: Cape Ann Light on Thatcher's Island and Boston Light in the harbor. Then about three hundred whaleboats issuing from the rivers, coves and inlets above and below the city converged on the harbor islands to seize livestock and grain that were sorely needed by Gage's garrison in Boston.

Graves sent a party of Tory carpenters to repair the Boston Light under a guard of Marines. But the guards got so drunk that a party of rebel raiders had no difficulty surprising them. While the terrified carpenters took refuge in the unfinished lighthouse, the lieutenant commanding the Marines put them aboard boats and made for a British schooner anchored offshore. But the ship ran aground after hoisting anchor and was seized by the Patriots. In this skirmish fifty-three British were either killed or captured, against one American killed and two others slightly wounded.

The admiral was again embarrassed in Bristol, Rhode Island, when Sir James Wallace, commanding a fleet of sixteen vessels—including three men-of-war—demanded two hundred sheep and thirty cows under pain of bombardment. The town officials named a committee to negotiate with Captain Wallace, and while they talked and stalled, proposed and delayed, Bristol was busy evacuating the town and driving all livestock into the countryside. When the exasperated Wallace at last opened fire, not many targets were hit, for the gunnery was as poor as the powder, an event celebrated in the ditty:

> They fire low, they fire high,
> The women scream, the children cry,
> And all their firing and their racket,
> Shot off the topmast of a packet.

Probably the first true naval battle of the American Navy-to-be occurred in June 1775 in the seaport town of Machias, Maine, then part of Massachusetts. A Boston Tory named Ichabod Jones sought to supply the city with desperately needed wood. With two supply sloops escorted by the armed schooner *Margaretta,* Jones appeared off Machias and began to "negotiate" with the townspeople for a supply of lumber. But his arrogant demands so infuriated them that they took him prisoner while the Sons of Liberty seized his sloops. Next the midshipman commanding the *Margaretta* threatened to bombard the town unless Jones were freed. But as he sailed inshore to carry out his threat, he ran aground. Working himself free, he tried to escape from the harbor, but the Sons of Liberty, led by Jeremiah O'Brien and Benjamin Foster, boarded his schooner, capturing it in a fierce fight while killing its commander. Jubilant, O'Brien and Foster proceeded to outfit Jones's sloops as privateers, taking as their first prize a British surveying vessel that had sailed into the harbor to take soundings. With this success, O'Brien and Foster and other enterprising Maine seamen opened a merry—and profitable—guerrilla warfare against Gage's supply ships and were joined by privateers from Rhode Island, Connecticut and South Carolina.

General Washington also discovered that the best means of supplying his ragtag army in Cambridge was from the holds of captured British ships. Although he had no authority to organize a Continental Navy, he did have the power of granting commissions, which he used to create a fleet of sea wolves that preyed on British ships sailing to and from Boston. Though his sailors were successful, Washington found them even more difficult to discipline than his soldiers and was not at all enchanted to be told that they would not put to sea unless promised a third of the value of all enemy shipping and cargo seized. Even so, he could hardly complain when such prizes as *Nancy,* loaded with 100,000 precious flints and 2,000 muskets with their bayonets and cartridge boxes, were brought into Gloucester. Nor could he refuse a glass of punch from *Nancy's* huge, sixteen-inch brass mortar, which an exuberant Israel Putnam christened "The Congress."

Congress itself was sharply divided after Rhode Island proposed that it establish a Continental Navy. The timid souls still clung to the flabby conviction that economic sanctions, such as the nonimportation and nonexportation agreements, would bring the Mother Country round, but the fire-eaters, such as John Adams, scoffed at their arguments as wishful thinking. "Why should not America have a navy?" Adams asked. "No maritime power near the sea coast can be safe without it. It is no chimera. The Romans suddenly built one in their Carthaginian war."

Eventually Congress decided to form the nucleus of a navy, ordering the construction of four and then eight warships. Before the ships could be completed, Admiral Graves ordered the destruction of the port of Falmouth at the end of 1775, in retaliation for Yankee "insolence" on the high seas. It was both a wanton and vindictive act, which had no parallel in the limited naval warfare of the day, and, through bitterness and a thirst for revenge, it did more to strengthen than to weaken the Patriot cause. Thus by February 1776 the fledgling little American fleet, under Ezek Hopkins of Rhode Island, was ready for war on the waves with the Mistress of the Sea.

★ 26 ★

CHARLES LEE AND CHARLESTON

Although Lord Germain would later insist that the operation against Charleston, South Carolina, had been planned by his predecessor, Lord Dartmouth, the fact is that he did approve it and anticipated great things from this appeal to the loyalty of his "people of the South"—the Tories. In this decision he might have been influenced by the early success of the operations conducted in Virginia by the governor, John Murray, the Earl of Dunmore.

Dunmore had been driven from Williamsburg to the safety of a ship anchored in Norfolk Harbor. From this refuge he was able to make the port city a sanctuary for Loyalists, chiefly British and Scots merchants active in the tobacco trade. From his Norfolk base he made frequent raids on the vulnerable plantations strung out along the tidewater, so that on November 7, 1775, he felt strong enough to proclaim a condition of martial law, ordering every loyal citizen to support the Crown. He also offered freedom to those slaves of rebel planters who joined him in fighting their masters. It was not a wise move, and even though the response among the blacks was surprisingly strong, that very fact only helped to inflame the hearts of most Virginians with a unifying hatred of Dunmore.

The governor's plan was to raise a mixed force of Indians, slaves, Tories and a detachment of British regulars from Detroit. With this he would destroy the Patriot plantations throughout the colony. Discovering the scheme through the capture of one of Dunmore's agents, the planters appealed to the Virginia Convention for help, so alarming the delegates that they requested Congress to pay and supply the troops that they raised. They also issued a promise of pardon to any slave who returned to his master, and Washington himself wrote to Richard Henry Lee: "If

[Dunmore] is not crushed he will become the most formidable enemy America has."

It indeed seemed so after Dunmore, using a nucleus of two companies of regulars, put together an army that easily routed a smaller Virginia force of militia and a few hundred volunteers. The way to ravage the plantations seemed clear, except that William Woodford, the rebel commander, rallied his beaten troops at a bridge below Norfolk. Dunmore, still contemptuous of the "Shirtmen," as he called the Virginia marksmen in their buckskin hunting shirts, ordered a charge across the bridge supported by artillery.

If he had learned from Howe at Bunker Hill, Dunmore would have found the silence at the other end ominous, rather than a sign of enemy retreat—for once the redcoats and their allies were within fifty yards of the rebel breastwork, a volley of musketry killed their leader and riddled their ranks. Another volley sent them reeling backward. Counterattacking, the Shirtmen put them to rout and spiked their guns, and the Battle of Great Bridge ended in defeat for Dunmore, whose followers took refuge aboard the ships in the harbor while the pursuing rebels occupied Norfolk.

Dunmore's next decision—full of spite and vengeance—was to order the town bombarded and set on fire. Parties of Shirtmen, who repulsed a British landing party that was ordered to set fire to buildings and warehouses along the shores, motivated by their own spite and vengeance, took up the soulful task of setting Tory homes ablaze, so that the fire burned for three days and Norfolk was left a smoking ruin.

Although Norfolk had been destroyed, so had the power of the Earl of Dunmore, and news of this success arrived in Philadelphia simultaneously with reports that Lord George Germain had ordered an expedition to capture Charleston. Alarmed, Congress placed the defense of that vital southern port in the hands of Major General Charles Lee.

Born in Dernhall, England, and baptized on February 6, 1731, Charles Lee was the scion of both arms and wealth. His father was Major General John Lee, an ardent Whig who would transmit his liberalism and wit to his son, and his mother Isabella Bunbury Lee, daughter of an extremely rich family with French blood in her veins. From her Charles would receive little love, much criticism and more money. Both houses were of the high middle class, the near-nobility, what today might be called the landed gentry. There were knights on both sides, one bishop and a single earl, all of whom were thoroughgoing Tories whom the mature Charles thoroughly despised.

Charles's education began in the King Edward VI Grammar

School, one of the finest in England, his entrance there coinciding with his being enlisted in his father's regiment, the famous Forty-fourth Foot. At fifteen, still studying there, pursuing a lifelong love of the classics—especially Shakespeare—he was commissioned an ensign. Not yet in uniform, he spent his late teens in a Swiss academy, becoming fluent in French and finding other literary loves in Rousseau and Voltaire, whose hatred of royalty and privilege and passion for freedom he made his own.

In 1751 Lee's father died, naming his son executor of his will. It was not a wise choice, for Charles had no head for business, yet it did provide a large sum for his sister, Sidney, and a splendid trust for his mother. With his own legacy, Lee purchased a lieutenant's commission in the Forty-forth Grenadiers, just in time to join Edward Braddock on his campaign to evict the French from the Valley of the Ohio. He bade his sister good-bye in a letter, but said or wrote nothing to his mother. He had done something mysterious of which she disapproved, and they parted company forever.

Charles Lee was by then twenty-three, standing about five feet eight inches, of slender build—not to say scrawny (he detested sports)—blue eyed and light haired, if not ugly at least unattractive, with his sharp face and slovenly dress. His wit was ready and often wounding, yet yoked to a courtly charm upon which he drew at will. Self-willed and self-confident in the extreme, he was consumed by an ambition nourished by a seemingly boundless vitality. To his friends he was an eccentric genius, to his detractors a graceless boor. Both were appalled by the troop of yelping, yapping poodles that accompanied him almost everywhere he went. Lee adored dogs, actually preferring their company to that of men. A guest invited to dinner in his home might find a place set for several dogs, the host caressing them, kissing them, conversing with them or sharply rebuking those servants who did not show them the proper deference. Lee's best friend was a little Pomeranian named Mr. Spada, a sort of canine major domo, whose duty it was to put the pack through the tricks taught them by their master.

The dogs were with Lee when he arrived in America. To his dismay, he was detached to a supply command, and thus did not accompany the Forty-forth on the march toward the French outpost at Fort Duquesne. But this assignment also spared him the humiliation of Braddock's defeat at the Monongahela or the news that a massacre had been averted only by the quick action of "General Buckskin."

In June 1756 Charles Lee purchased a captain's commission for the sum of £900. He was then on garrison duty north of Albany, enchanted by the grandeur of the American wilderness and also by the charms of the daughter of the Seneca chief, White Thunder. Having been made a blood brother of the Mohawks, he now became the husband of this copper-skinned beauty, who eventually presented him with twins, a boy and a girl. But the blare of battle bugles soon ended this conjugal union, and Charles was ordered to join the assault on Louisbourg. Like the people of Massachusetts, he was incensed when his "stupid superiors" returned the vital fort to France in exchange for that post in far-off India. He was also disgusted when a new "stupid superior"—the inept Earl of Loudoun—took command of His Majesty George II's forces in North America.

To Lee's mind, Loudoun did little more than have the men plant cabbages to ward off scurvy, and he was even more nauseated when James Abercrombie, another stupid superior, succeeded him. But Lee was delighted by the presence in Abercrombie's army of Lord George Augustus Howe, the gallant young Irish peer who was the very soul of the force attacking Fort Ticonderoga. Lee was with Lord Howe on patrol when a French musket ball dropped Howe dead in the arms of Israel Putnam. Later in a foolish bayonet charge ordered by the "Booby-in-Chief," Lee was knocked unconscious by a shot that broke two of his ribs. Recovering both his health and his venom in an Albany field hospital, he wrote to his sister explaining that Abercrombie had decisively demonstrated how the obtuseness of a single commander could snatch defeat from the jaws of victory. "Fortune and the pusillanimity of the French had crammed victory into Abercrombie's mouth, [but he] contrived to spit it out again."

Lee was with Lord Jeffrey Amherst in the conclusive British victory at Montreal during the summer of 1760, after which he sailed home to besiege Westminster for promotion. None came until his friend Lord Pembroke put in a word with Field Marshal Lord John Ligonier: "You can have no real objection to him, unless he is too honest." At thirty Charles Lee was a major. But not for long. Having distinguished himself against the Spanish in 1762, he returned home a hero—until the Peace of 1763 retired him at half-pay! There was nothing to do but steep himself in military history and attend meetings of the American Club, presided over by Amherst or Lord Richard Howe, who had succeeded his lamented brother in the peerage. From conversation in the club, and his own American experiences, Lee developed some farsighted prescriptions for placating those stiff-necked American colonists: settle the Ohio and Wabash valleys with Protestant immigrants from Germany and Switzerland and encourage those sturdy New Englanders to cross the Alleghenies and establish water links with the Mississippi to keep the Indians and the Spanish to the south in check.

But once again those Westminster "blockheads" would not listen, especially when Lee insisted that happy Americans would be of as much value to the Crown as angry ones would be inimical. Regarded now as an erratic crackpot posing as a visionary, Lee lost all hope of advancement. Momentarily he toyed with the notion of standing for Parliament or seeking knighthood. But he did not have the money to pursue either, having wasted so much of his substance in "riotous living." But then his mother died in 1766 and he was a rich man again. Now he remembered that he was no politician, but a warrior: a soldier-scholar, wealthy enough to pursue the delightful career of a soldier of fortune. So he crossed the Channel, hurrying toward the sound of cannon. But the guns had been stilled, and he had to be satisfied with a most gratifying interview with Frederick the Great and the friendship of King Stanislaus of Poland, who made him his aide-de-camp.

Stanislaus was a hail-fellow-well-met, fluent in English and a devotee of Shakespeare. He would listen by the hour to this ebullient, itinerant professional soldier quoting such dangerous minds as Voltaire and Rousseau, saying not a word when Lee spoke gleefully of the impending harvest of the crowned heads of Europe. Stanislaus even made Lee a major general and decorated him with the Order of St. Stanislaus. Delighted, Lee wore the medal on all ceremonial occasions, unaware that the bright red ribbon with its gleaming silver star seemed to accentuate the food spots and wine stains on his general's white uniform edged in red. It was Stanislaus who satisfied Lee's yearning to fight the Turks in the Ottoman Empire's war against Catherine of Russia. The king took him to the frontier, but Lee saw no action, merely witnessing Catherine's Cossacks being driven across the Dniester by the Grand Vizier's Tatar horsemen. Once again he wrote to his sister of the blockheads on both sides who gave war such a bad name.

One more fling of exotic travel: to Malta, Calabria, Sicily, Gibraltar and Minorca, but the sounds he was hearing now were not gunpowder explosions, but the outraged outcries of indignant Americans inflamed by young King George III's unbending policy of tyrannous taxation.

Bearing a letter of introduction from Benjamin Franklin, Charles Lee boarded ship for New York City in midsummer 1773. He had put aside his uniform and was dressed in shabby civilian clothes, a change that has led some historians to believe that he was fleeing possible prosecution as the likely author of the "Junius letters," those anonymous and vitriolic attacks on George's corrupt Tory government, or at least for his own criticism of the Crown's handling of the American situation. Actually, he was just fed up with Britain, to him a barren, hostile soil in which his libertarian ideas would never flourish. In America he expected to find the world's first sanctuary for liberty and freedom of speech. He did not, however, expect to participate in any rebellion; rather, he wanted to discover how much the colonies had changed since he had campaigned there nearly twenty years before.

Arriving in New York three months later, Lee found it a Tory city. Men who had served with him were now prosperous merchants or publishers, who, almost to a man, were staunch supporters of the status quo. So he headed south with his luggage containing his general's uniform, a brace of Polish pistols and his Order of St. Stanislaus. Mr. Spada was also with him, and three other dogs. He found Philadelphia much changed physically, not only prosperous but a growing cultural and intellectual center. In Wilmington, Delaware, the wife of a tavern keeper was mystified by this strange, nervous man, his cultivated manners and speech so much at odds with his worn leather jerkin, greasy vest, frayed deerskin breeches, old and dirty jackboots and a big, broad-brimmed beaver hat crammed down to his pointed nose. In Dover, Delaware, he met the Rodneys, Thomas and his more famous brother, Caesar. "Our people are but peasants," Tom Rodney told him, "unarmed and naked before mighty foes." But they are freemen, he continued, who will "defend their liberty and country!" Charles Lee's heart sang when he heard these fiery phrases. "I shall aid them with all my skill," he said. "Liberty I adore … where she lives, that is my country."

Lee was in Williamsburg when Lord Dunmore dissolved the Virginia Assembly, and it is likely that he might have helped write the inflammatory protest which that decision provoked among the burgesses. Rebellion was in the air, and it exhilarated Lee. He also found talk of nonconsumption and nonimportation rife in Boston, where he was thrilled to meet Samuel Adams. By then Charles Lee's presence in America was well known and well received. His coming was hailed as a gift from the gods of war. A major general and a veteran of so many campaigns! Wherever he went an admiring circle formed around him to hear him allude casually to his acquaintance with Frederick the Great or his friendship with King Stanislaus. His easy chatter about turning movements or tactical withdrawals or the correct use of such esoteric fortifications as redans or fleches or chevaux-de-frise awed them. What American soldier could equal Charles Lee?

Although Lee, of course, was not a delegate to the First Continental Congress in 1774, he was certainly welcomed there, and when the Second Continental Congress assembled in May 1775, he was again in

Philadelphia to hear that George Washington—whom he had twice met at Mount Vernon—was to command the rebel army in Boston, with Artemas Ward his second in command and none other than Charles Lee to be the third.

To everyone's surprise, Lee seemed reluctant to accept. Some of his friends were convinced that he was angry because first or second place had been denied him, although everyone knew that Artemas Ward was too old and too sick to take the field and that third was thus tantamount to second. Actually, Lee feared that to serve in the rebel army might bring confiscation of his fortune in England and thus impoverish his sister Sidney. But he did accept, and he served Washington loyally and well when the two major generals arrived in Cambridge. His zeal in the cause of freedom, together with his stinging attacks on King George, led Congress to place him in command of another expedition north to Canada. John Adams wrote to him: "I wish you the laurels of Wolfe and Montgomery, with a happier fate." But then, as Germain prepared his expedition to "the people of America," his orders were changed, and Major General Charles Lee rode in the opposite direction to Charleston.

Germain's approval of the Charleston operation was based upon his conviction that the South was full of Tories who would flock to the king's service once the Union Jack were unfurled above this fine seaport below Baltimore. General Sir Henry Clinton was to command this combined military and naval force. His orders were to reestablish British authority in Virginia, the Carolinas and Georgia, after which, having placed reliable Loyalists in charge there, he was to rejoin Howe for northern operations to commence "as soon as the navigation of the northern coasts of North America became practicable."

Clinton left Boston in late January 1776 with two companies of light infantry, heading for the Cape Fear River in North Carolina, where he was to be joined by a fleet under Admiral Sir Peter Parker that was sailing from Cork in Ireland with two regiments commanded by Lord Charles Cornwallis. Assistance was also expected from the fierce Scottish Highlanders of the North Carolina western frontier, men who hated the seaboard aristocracy. The Highlanders' mission was to capture the North Carolina ports.

Trouble in Ireland and contrary winds delayed the departure of Parker's fleet—but in North Carolina the kilts came out on schedule.

Governor Josiah Martin of North Carolina had pronounced the Patriots to be in "most horrid and unnatural rebellion" against their rightful sovereign, summoning the Highlanders to crush them in battle. In

February the clans began gathering. With bagpipes skirling, tartan kilts swirling in the wind, muskets on their shoulders, Claymores at their hips and dirks tucked into their argyle stockings just below their wind-reddened knees, the McDonalds and McDowells and the Campbells and the Camerons were marching under General Donald McDonald toward the port city of Wilmington.

There were about 1,500 of them, and out to meet them came some thousand Patriots under Colonels Richard Caswell and John Lillington. Coming to Moore's Creek Bridge, the rebels crossed it and began to fortify the opposite bank—until they realized the folly of fighting with a river at their back. Returning to the other side of the stream, they dug in afresh.

The soft fresh dawn of February 27 broke with the faint sound of the pipes skirling in the distance. Then McDonald's Highlanders became visible, raising a great shout when they came upon the empty trenches on their side of Moore's Creek Bridge. *The rebels had fled!* Still shouting, they rushed the bridge—and were shredded and struck to the ground by a single crashing volley. Now the Patriots rose up to counterattack, to shatter the kilted ranks and slaughter them in merciless pursuit. Many of the Highlanders sought to escape by jumping off the bridge, only to drown or be picked off by musket fire.

Moore's Creek Bridge was a Tory disaster. North Carolina remained firmly in the rebel camp, Georgia and South Carolina stiffened their opposition to the Mother Country—and Sir Henry Clinton found no jubilant army of triumphant Loyalists ready to welcome him when his little fleet dropped anchor off the Cape Fear River.

Clinton did not immediately learn of the disaster at Moore's Creek Bridge; rather, he was at first delighted by the abundance of delicious vegetables and game he discovered upon coming ashore. Such food was a blessing to both the sailors and the soldiers, who were accustomed to an unrefreshing and unhealthy diet of salt pork and salt beef. The men also marveled at the array of unfamiliar beasts and birds they found in the fragrant pine woods and swallowed whole the local fiction of the "whipping snake" that could flay a man even more cruelly than the practiced floggers of the British Army. Two of them, it was said, could kill a horse.

But then the "melancholy tidings" of McDonald's defeat arrived, together with reports that the Tories of South Carolina had been similarly handled, with all their leaders captured. To a man of Clinton's pessimistic nature, this was depressing news, indeed, and his melancholy was not improved by a wait of fifteen weeks—from late February to the end of May—before all Parker's ships arrived. By then Clinton had lost his normally minimal enthusiasm for the Charleston operation. He tried to persuade the admiral to change the objective: forays into the Chesapeake, where bases could be established to recruit and organize the Tories there. But Sir Peter insisted that the great South Carolina port was a bigger and truer target, and Clinton, as easily dissuaded as discouraged, acquiesced. On May 31 the British fleet hoisted anchor and headed south for Charleston, almost immediately encountering bad weather again.

While Sir Peter Parker's ships plunged south, two conspiring gentlemen met secretly in Paris. One was Charles Gravier, the Comte de Vergennes, foreign minister of King Louis XV; the other, Pierre Augustin Caron de Beaumarchais, the famous author of the plays *The Barber of Seville* and later *The Marriage of Figaro*. Vergennes was driven by a passionate hatred of Britain and all things British, Beaumarchais by an equally intense love of liberty and all things American.

Vergennes did not yet advise his royal master to make war upon King George III, if only because he was aware that the time was not yet ripe, and that France was not fully recovered from the costs of the Seven Years' War. Instead, he sought to harm the detestable *Anglais* by helping those admirable Americans. In secret he had invited Spain to join him in this pleasurable pursuit, and was much pleased when King Charles III accepted. A secret fund of one million livres was set up by both kingdoms. In May the firm of Hortalez et Cie, under the able management of Caron de Beaumarchais, began "acting" for the Americans by supplying them with munitions. During 1776–77 as much as 80 percent of the gunpowder used by the Continental Army came from Hortalez and Beaumarchais. It was excellent gunpowder, made by a famous chemist named Antoine-Laurent Lavoisier.

South Carolina had been aware for some time of the approaching British invasion fleet, and had already mustered six regiments for the defense of Charleston, together with three volunteer artillery companies, two thousand raw militia recruited from the interior and seven hundred Charleston militia, famous for the splendor of their uniforms, if not yet for fighting prowess. This force was increased after Congress ordered Virginia and North Carolina to send a Continental regiment apiece to Charleston.

Neither the colony nor the city was particularly alarmed at the impending crisis, having already calmly elected a new state government replete with a bicameral legislature and a supreme court, as Congress had been urging all colonies to do. John Rutledge was elected the first president of South Carolina, with Henry Laurens vice president, and William

Drayton became chief justice. The government was inaugurated with a festive military parade in Charleston "amidst the heart-cheering plaudits of the people" and the firing of artillery salutes at the battery and from the ships in the harbor.

In the meantime the harbor had been fortified under the energetic supervision of Colonel William Moultrie, a veteran of the expedition against the Cherokees during the French and Indian War. To the south of the harbor lay James Island, guarded by Fort Johnson. Across the harbor mouth was a sandbar and outside the sandbar, the perilous Five Fathom Hole. Inside the harbor on the mainland guarding the city were batteries at Haddrell's Point. To the north of the harbor was Sullivan's Island, with a formidable redoubt of palmetto logs, which was to gain Colonel Moultrie's name. Farther north across a narrow strip of water called the Breach lay Long Island (now Isle of Palms), unoccupied and undefended.

Fort Moultrie on Sullivan's Island was obviously the key to Charleston, and Moultrie had taken pride in its walls of palmetto logs enclosing a fill of earth sixteen feet thick. He believed that the soft and fibrous palmetto wood, backed by so much smothering dirt, could soak up British cannon balls like a huge sponge. Moreover the fort was armed with thirty guns, ranging in caliber from nine- to twenty-five pounders, manned by a crew of 450 men, who were actually confident and eager for action. Powder, however, was in short supply. In all, there were about six thousand men in Charleston holding what was nothing less than a fine and bristling series of fortifications, although they did not seem to satisfy General Charles Lee when he finally arrived in Charleston on June 4—about sixteen weeks after Congress had directed him to move south.

Lee was satisfied with nothing that had been done before his arrival. He found Moultrie's position on Sullivan's Island untenable, and his fort "a slaughtering stage" that "could not hold out half an hour." Unable to persuade President Rutledge to abandon the fort, he transferred many of its troops and much of its sorely needed powder to Haddrell's Point, a sector least likely to be attacked. Surrounded by his yapping dogs, Lee darted about like a querulous rooster, giving orders, cursing, criticizing—and horrifying the elegant Charlestonians with his rude manners and uncouth clothes. He badgered Moultrie like a hectoring schoolmaster: "For Heaven's sake, sir ... exert yourself...." Fortunately for the Patriot cause, the good-natured Moultrie, though miffed, ignored him, calmly clinging to his own plans and completely prepared when, three days after Lee's arrival, the sun-gilded sails of the British fleet appeared off the bar.

★ ★ ★

Clinton saw at once the importance of Fort Moultrie. His plan was to land his troops on undefended Long Island and to cross the Breach onto the land side of the fort while Parker's ships bombarded it from the sea. He was certain that the Breach could be easily waded at low tide. Why he thought this is not known. Either he was purposely misinformed by some Patriot posing as a Tory, or else he simply did not bother to explore the bottom of this narrow strip of water. In fact, the Breach was full of potholes, some of them seven feet deep, which his unfortunate light infantry and grenadiers—especially the heavily encumbered grenadiers—discovered when, on June 28, they attempted to ford it. Many of them simply vanished. Clinton next called for boats, only to find to his "unspeakable mortification and disappointment" that the Breach was half deeps and half shallows and thus impassable. Dismayed, Clinton sent a message to Parker asking how best to retrieve and deploy his troops to support the seaward attack. The admiral, more aggressive than the general and probably delighted that the whole show was now his, replied that he could do it all himself. Thus reduced to the role of crestfallen specator, Clinton watched glumly while the battle for Charleston became a fight between a fleet and a fort.

The bomb ketch, *Thunder,* began the British fleet's attack by hurling shells at the fort. Then the rest of Parker's fleet sailed to battle stations. Close inshore of the fort were *Active,* 28 guns; Parker's flagship *Bristol,* 50; *Experiment,* 50; and *Solebay,* 28. Stretched farther offshore eastward were *Actaeon,* 28; *Sphynx,* 20; *Syren,* 28; *Thunder;* and the armed ship *Friendship* with 28 guns.

The British were highly confident. The wind was right, it was a clear day, and the fort seemed to be answering weakly. Then *Thunder* realized that her bombs were falling short. Rather than come in closer and perhaps foul the other ships, she increased the powder charges in her mortars. The first supercharged shots broke the mortar beds, and *Thunder* was of no further use.

Now the American guns were replying with a slow and awful accuracy. *Bristol's* cable was shot away. She lay end on to the fort and was raked horribly. Twice her quarterdeck was cleared of every person except Parker, and Sir Peter, to his lasting mortificiation, had the seat of his trousers shot off and his behind singed. *Experiment* suffered just as badly.

Within the fort, sweat-drenched Americans were scorched by a hot southern sun and sometimes by the muzzle flashes from thirty cannon in continual blaze. Colonel Moultrie cheered his gunners on, while men with fire buckets full of grog darted along the fire platforms to refresh the thirsty. Gradually the artillery duel rose to such a frightful roar that even the veteran General Lee, who had come over to the island, was astonished. Once a combination of three or four British broadsides struck the fort with such force that Moultrie feared another such salvo would shake it down.

When it came, a British ball disemboweled a Sergeant McDaniel. As he lay dying he gasped: *"Fight on my brave boys. Don't let liberty expire with me today."* His words were passed along the firing platforms, inspiring the men toiling away in the fierce heat, their blackened faces singed with powder. Then the fort's flag was shot away. British sailors could be heard cheering, while a great groan arose from the crowded shoreline of the surrounding islands and the mainland. Inside the redoubt, Sergeant William Jasper cried out to Moultrie: "Colonel! Don't let us fight without our flag!"

"What can you do?" Moultrie replied. "The staff is broke."

Jasper's reply was to run outside the fort; seize the flag; and then, fixing it on a sponge staff, set it upright again while British shot and shell crashed around him. A cheer arose from Charleston as the blue flag with its white crescent and the word "Liberty" whipped in the breeze again.

Now three of the British second line of ships upped anchor and tried to move around the western end of the island. They wanted to batter the fort on its flank and bring their guns to bear on a plank bridge behind the island. All three ships ran aground. *Actaeon* and *Sphynx* fouled each other, *Sphynx* losing her bowsprit. Eventually, two ships worked free, but *Actaeon* was immovable.

As night fell the jubilant Americans could hear their shots crashing into her, and eventually she was set afire.

Night also marked the end of the battle. At eleven o'clock, horrified at the carnage aboard their ships, mortified at having been so mauled by the tiny American fort, the British slipped their cables and stole off into the night.

Charleston had held, the glory of Fort Moultrie had entered American history, and it was two years before Lord George Germain would think again of "the people of America" who dwelt in the South.

★ 27 ★

HENRY KNOX AND THE GUNS OF TI

By New Year's Day 1776, General Washington's Continental Army had melted away to about 10,500 men.

A month previously the Connecticut regulars had set the example of home-going, insisting that their enlistments expired December 1, rather than at the end of the year. All attempts to dissuade them failed, including the perverse performance of General Charles Lee, who had not yet left for Charleston.

"Men," Lee roared, after "entreating" them with curses and insults, "I don't know what to call you. You are the worst of all creatures."

The troops merely laughed, and at the appointed time they marched home, ignoring the hisses and groans of the comrades they left behind, the showers of stones and the mocking blandishments of the women of the camp. Even Washington lost his temper and wrote of the "dirty, mercenary spirit" of the men "upon whom I reckoned" and who now had "basely deserted the Cause of their Country."

In fairness to these men, however, it must be made clear that they *had* enlisted for eight months only, that the practice of enlisting for specified short terms—for the "campaign," as it was called—was customary, and that very few ranking officers, the wealthy Washington in particular, were called upon to make sacrifices comparable to those demanded of most of the junior officers and all the enlisted men. While they served, their farms went uncared for or their trades were gobbled up by stay-at-homes. They had served long enough, they argued, and now it was someone else's turn.

Fortunately for Washington, thousands of men in the Massachusetts and New Hampshire militias decided that it was their turn. They poured into Washington's camp while the time-expired regulars jeered at them as "Long-faced People" and marched home. The new arrivals did not intend to stay long, either, but they at least gave Washington a respite in which to recruit men and rebuild his army, and they were numerous enough to keep Howe contained in winter quarters.

Actually, Washington might well have attacked at this time, and he would regret not having done so. The British army was in dreadful condition. Smallpox was spreading and food was short. Howe, who assumed command after Gage returned to London, strove to maintain order and discipline, but never so desperately as to forego the charms of blond Betsy Loring, whose complaisant husband not only condoned the liaison but encouraged it in the interests of his steady acquisition of abandoned Patriot property. Howe's officers were bored, amusing themselves by turning Old South Church into a riding academy, and dramatic plays—heretofore banned in Boston—were performed at Faneuil Hall. *The Blockade of Boston* was a burlesque of Washington and his Yankee Doodles, and the American commander was invited to attend and fashion his own noose. Washington replied by raiding Bunker Hill on opening night. British officers dressed as women rushed off to battle in petticoats.

While the British and the Tories played, the Patriots dug—so diligently that Gage complained before he left that "they have fortified all the passes and heights round this town from Dorchester to Medford and Mystic." Still the British clung to the hope that Yankee Doodle might be losing his ardor for war, until a red flag, hoisted above modern Somerville, disabused them of that notion. The familiar combined crosses of St. George and St. Andrew could be seen, but this Union Jack was only a miniature inset in a corner of a flag covered with thirteen alternate red and white stripes. It was the first American flag, and its appearance and a thirteen-gun salute celebrated the birthday of the Continental Army.

Although the Americans obviously were not quitting, George Washington still hesitated to attack. His greatest shortage was in artillery, and without the guns to support an assault, he simply could not risk it. But then Henry Knox, the Boston bookseller who had become his artillery chief, suggested bringing the captured guns of Ticonderoga to Boston, and Washington gave the proposal his enthusiastic approval, with Knox himself to command the venture.

★ ★ ★

Some biographers of Henry Knox suggest that he was a descendant of John Knox, the great—and grim—Scottish reformer who organized the Presbyterian Church in his native land. Actually, Henry's ancestor was John's older brother, William, the Laird of Gifford near Edinburgh. Both brothers died long before there was a British colony in Massachusetts Bay. During that interval, James VI of Scotland and later James I of England uprooted the Catholic Irish from Ulster—as the six northern counties of Ireland are still called—replacing them with fellow Scots who came to be known as Scotch-Irish. Henry's father William was one of them, migrating from Derry, Ireland, to Boston in 1729 and, on February 11, 1735, marrying Mary Campbell in the "Church of the Presbyterian strangers," as those even grimmer Congregationalists described these newcomers of a stranger creed. On July 25, 1750, Henry Knox was born at 247 Federal Street, the seventh of William Knox's ten sons.

Henry's father was a shipmaster and owner of a small wharf. But in 1756 he failed in his business. Three years later he left his family, seeking his fortune in St. Eustatius in the West Indies, where he died in 1762 at the age of fifty. Because only four of the ten Knox boys grew to manhood, and because two of them—John and Benjamin—went to sea never to return to Boston, it was up to nine-year-old Henry to support his widowed mother and his younger brother. So Henry left Boston Latin Grammar School, where he had been an exemplary student, and went to work for Wharton & Bowes's Book Store.

Henry was a genial, bright and obliging boy, who showed promise of becoming an uncommonly big man. Thus he took pride in his name, meaning "hill" in Gaelic, and sometimes in a metaphoric sense, "stout." He was indeed stout, in heart, head and body, and at maturity would stand over six feet tall and weigh more than 250 pounds. His calm gray eyes were keen and his round face shone with good humor. But it was his inquiring mind that astonished his employers, especially Nicholas Bowes, who acted as a father toward him, instilling in him a deep moral sense and an attachment to the Protestant work ethic of New England. Henry read incessantly. No customer entering the shop ever found him alone there without a book in his hand. He read the Greek and Latin classics in translation, but his favorite subjects were military history and the science of fortification.

Little is known of the young man's recreation, although it seems likely that such an exuberant spirit would take part in whatever sports that did not detract from his work or studies. Henry was an exuberant member of the South End gang of street brawlers and made himself famous one Pope Night. He was leading the chief float in his group's procession, and when a wheel fell off, he stooped to seize the axle, holding the vehicle upright while urging his comrades forward in his deep, booming voice.

Henry's energy and ingenuity were later directed into more serious efforts, when he joined an artillery company formed in the South End and known as "the Train," a play on the phrase of train of artillery. Its members were young mechanics and clerks like Henry, usually brawny fellows as cannon cockers usually are if they are to manhandle heavy guns and cannon balls. They drilled regularly, looking smart in their bright uniforms. When a British company of artillery passed through Boston in 1766 bound for Quebec, its officers mingled with those of the Train, giving them sound professional advice.

Four years later Henry was on not-so-friendly terms with the redcoats during the Boston Massacre, and then, in another year he had turned twenty-one and decided to open his own bookstore. It was a picturesque place, where not only books, but patent medicines, musical and mathematical instruments, telescopes and wallpaper were sold. It became a favorite haunt of British officers, drawn by Henry's large stock of military histories and memoirs and by his still-growing knowledge of strategy and tactics. Behind his counter Henry was an affable figure, quickly assimilating the genteel manners of his aristocratic customers. A dapper dresser as well, Henry did not resemble the British stereotype of the vulgar and crude Bostonian, and he was soon on equal social terms with his dandified cousins from across the sea.

Prominent Patriots who visited the shop included Paul Revere, John Hancock and Nathanael Greene, a blacksmith from Rhode Island. Henry was at first surprised to see Greene, who was dressed in somber Quaker clothes, go limping rapidly about his shop, but when he began to talk about guns and battles the two became fast friends.

One frequent visitor who found Henry fascinating was Lucy Flucker, the vivacious and pretty—though plump—daughter of Thomas Flucker, royal secretary of Massachusetts Bay. Lucy always seemed to arrive when the shop was empty, and Henry spent long hours with her, discussing books, and sometimes, by fixing her with ardent looks from his keen gray eyes, bringing a charming flush to her cheeks. Henry was delighted by Lucy's perceptive mind, and the fact that she was a bit chubby could certainly not repel a man who was already stout. But Henry was a devoted Patriot, and even if Lucy sympathized with his convictions, she was the child of unbending Tories. It was not long before Thomas Flucker made it plain to his daughter that he disapproved of her growing intimacy with this rebel firebrand.

Henry Knox was no incendiary such as Samuel Adams, but he was indeed prominent in the rising spirit of militarism that had seized Boston after the massacre. When Captain Joseph Pierce, assisted by Henry, formed the imposing new "Boston Grenadier Corps," an offshoot of the Train, he made Knox a lieutenant and second in command. No man in this company stood less than five feet ten inches, and Lucy Flucker was thrilled to watch big Henry striding down the street ramrod straight at the head of his stalwarts, resplendent in his uniform, his bandaged left hand (to conceal the loss of two fingers in a hunting accident) resting on his sword hilt. But by 1774, Henry Knox was growing impatient with his true love. On March 24 he wrote to her: "What news? Have you spoken to your father?" She had, and the answer was a resounding no. Knox was not only a damned rebel whom General Gage had put on his most dangerous list, but was also a low tradesman far beneath the notice of aristocrats such as the Fluckers. Lucy was shaken, but not dissuaded. They were married in June 1775, a few days after the Battle of Bunker Hill.

Now the Fluckers attempted to woo their unwanted son-in-law away from his foolish Patriot allegiance. Lucy's brother, a lieutenant in the British Army, spoke to him glowingly of the future he might have wearing a red coat. Through his father's influence, he offered Henry a commission. Knox refused the offer, and a few days later on a dark night he and Lucy rode in a carriage past Gage's sentries and into Cambridge, leaving Henry's bookstore—failing because of his Patriot sympathies—and Lucy's family behind them forever.

The following November, when George Washington, accompanied by Charles Lee, arrived in Cambridge to take command of the New England army adopted by Congress, both generals were immensely impressed by the fortifications built by Henry Knox at Roxbury. As a result, Knox was made a colonel, replacing Gridley as commander of American artillery. Here began Knox's extraordinarily close association with the commander in chief, and when Washington complained to him of his force's dangerous dearth of big guns, it was then that Knox suggested bringing the captured British guns to Cambridge.

En route to Ticonderoga, Knox stopped at Fort George, about a mile below his objective. There he was assigned a small cold room with a large fireplace where he met Captain John André, still a prisoner—and one of the most interesting men the young colonel had ever encountered. The two young officers immediately became good friends, staying awake all night lying before the fireplace to discuss their remarkably common interests in literature, history, the theater—and most of all, military history and artillery. That they were enemies occured to neither of them, and when they parted the following morning—André on parole headed south for Pennsylvania and exchange, Knox bound over Lake George for the fort—it was with affectionate farewells.

At Ticonderoga Knox was delighted to find fifty-nine serviceable guns, ranging from four- to twenty-four pounders, including howitzers, or high-angle fire cannon, and mortars, vertical angle weapons. There were also a few coehorns, named for their Dutch inventor, Baron von Coehorn—small brass mortars with handles at either side. These guns ranged from one foot to eleven feet in length and from 100 to 5,500 pounds in weight, for a total of 119,000 pounds. There was also a barrel of those precious flintheads from that excellent black flint mine near the fort, as well as twenty-three boxes of lead. To carry all this down Lake George—not yet frozen, although skim ice had formed on its shores—Knox hired three vessels: a scow, a piragua and a bateau, the last two being two-masted light-bottomed craft designed for lake sailing. Also shipped aboard were the oxen, horses and sleds necessary for the land segment of the journey. On December 9, 1775, the little flotilla, with its teamsters and soldiers, shoved off—and almost immediately ran into what appeared to be a disaster suggestive of the dreadful ordeal that lay ahead.

The scow skippered by Knox's brother William ran aground on a sunken rock. Fortunately, and by sheer luck, not the nautical skill of Knox's brother, it slipped off, and the journey was resumed until the wind died down and then, with characteristic deviltry, rose to blow hard against them. For four hours Knox's men rowed hard against the wind, and when night fell, beached their craft on the shore. A huge bonfire was built, and the exhausted men fell asleep in the biting cold, their feet turned inward to the fire lest they freeze.

Thus began an ordeal rivaling Arnold's march to Quebec, for on the following day the scow actually sank and a horrified Knox despaired of the heavier guns aboard it. But then came a message from William cheerfully reporting that the scow had been close to the shore and sank only up to the gunwales. It had been raised, and William would soon join Henry. Once off Lake George, the guns were transferred to sleds to cross snow-covered hills and valleys and frozen rivers. Sometimes the ice broke and the guns sank, having to be laboriously grubbed up. At the Hudson River Knox and his men spent New Year's Day 1776 cutting holes in the ice to strengthen it by flooding the hole and let more ice thicken it. Snow fell and coated both struggling beasts and their human masters in white, or roads "never used before and never to be used again" turned to ice so that Knox's "noble train of artillery" often slid or spun out of control. Over the Taconics the column toiled, up and down the Berkshires, men shouting warnings as the heavy sleds began to gather momentum like juggernauts rumbling down the snow slopes, or the horses and oxen began to pant and wheeze as they struggled upward hauling their precious cargo. Sometimes the poor beasts perished in the traces, but there were always replacements to be found along the way.

There were also refreshment and festive welcome to be found along the way as the column drew closer to Cambridge. Warm dinners and hot buttered rum were available in the roadside inns and taverns. At Westfield, Massachusetts, the entire town turned out to greet the column with cheers and mugs of cider and punch and glasses of rum or whiskey. Like children at a circus, the townspeople gaped at the guns and fondled them as though they were live creatures. Even the gunners themselves, growing light hearted and light headed from their emptied glasses, hugged and kissed their iron pets. When the crowd surged marveling around a big twenty-four-pounder—that very same "Old Sow" that Montgomery had used to batter St. John's into submission—Henry Knox, never a man to forego a frolic, had a charge of powder placed inside its breech. When the charge exploded with a monster bellow, the people of Westfield blinked and recoiled momentarily, before emitting a great roar of their own. And so it was an eventually happy column that lurched into Cambridge on hissing runners in mid-January. The movement of the guns had not taken two weeks, as Knox had anticipated, but six.

★ 28 ★

HOWE EVACUATES BOSTON

George Washington was delighted with the number, weight and variety of the guns, and he gradually had them installed in his fourteen-mile line besieging Boston. He knew, now, that he need not attack his enemy but merely bombard him into evacuating the city. Twice before during the seige, Washington had called councils of war to poll his generals on the wisdom of attacking Howe, and both times the generals had advised against it. Councils of war, usually the recourse of timid generals anxious to shift blame for possible defeat, were not in the character of the combative Washington, although he might have called them to instill in his commanders the spirit of attack, rather than the torpor of static defense.

But now with the guns of Ticonderoga, he could seize and fortify Dorchester Heights as he had planned. A battery there would look down Howe's throat by cutting his communications with Boston Neck, while battering both the town and the British ships in the bay. Howe had learned of his opponent's plan and had sent a company of grenadiers and light infantry to the peninsula to "destroy the houses and every kind of cover wherever." They had done so, but Howe had not occupied the scorched earth, perhaps inviting Washington to seize it so that Howe could avenge the disaster at Bunker Hill.

Washington did just that, but with that maddening alacrity and diligence with which these wildly digging Americans so often amazed their enemies, who never seemed to realize that they were not fighting professional soldiers but embattled farmers whose calloused hands were born of hoes and shovels, rather than of Brown Besses. First, because the ground was still too frozen for digging, Washington ordered portable wooden frames for gun platforms to be made, broken down, and then carried to Dorchester Heights in darkness, there to be reassembled and filled with hay. For barricades barrels were crammed with earth and rocks. On the night of March 2, Washington ordered Knox to begin a diversionary bombardment of the town. The bombardment was carried out with great skill and accuracy, so much so that a British officer wrote to Lord Bute: "Our lines were raked from the new battery they had made, and though we returned shot and shell, I am very, very sorry to say with not quite so much judgment."

At dark an advance party of some eight hundred soldiers swarmed over Dorchester Heights to take up defensive positions. They were followed by twelve hundred men under General John Thomas and with more than three hundred carts filled with fascines, barrels, rocks and pressed hay. They began to do what they did best—dig, favored by the noise of the Continental cannonade smothering the sound of their labors and a wind blowing the noise inland. Two hours before midnight they had erected two forts capable of protecting them from grapeshot or small-arms fire. Fresh working parties relieved them at three in the morning, and the work continued at a feverish pace. Although the night was mild and a bright moon was visible, a low-hanging mist on the harbor shielded them from British eyes.

In the light of dawn the British were even more astonished than they had been at Bunker Hill. One engineer said only a force of from fifteen to twenty thousand men could have built such fortifications so fast. Another officer opted for magic: "an expedition equal to the genii of Aladdin's lamp." Magic or muscle, William Howe was dismayed. He could not permit the upstart Yankees to improve these already formidable positions and immediately began planning to attack them. Even though by March 4 the Dorchester Heights fortifications were made much more complete and forbidding than those of Breed's Hill, Howe still intended to strike the next day, the first anniversary of the Boston Massacre. Washington fully expected that he would, telling a group of soldiers: "Remember it is the Fifth of March, and avenge the death of your brethren."

Howe's plan was wildly unrealistic: a nocturnal amphibious invasion. No operation is more fraught with danger and difficulty. Indeed, his redcoats seemed to sense a fresh debacle impending, clambering into their boats "pale and dejected." Fortunately for them, a violent storm broke, raising such high white caps on the bay that Howe quickly called off the operation. Actually, it is doubtful that the British chief was going to risk another and fiercer gantlet of death. He knew that if he were repulsed, Washington would most likely counterattack, and if he were victorious, the war might have been ended then and there in British defeat. Moreover, even before the troops had embarked, Howe's generals at a council of war had recommended evacuation. Howe was said to have agreed, explaining that he had ordered the assault only for "the honor of the troops." Indeed? Tuppence-a-day Tommies thirsting for the honor of being lead soldiers storming a hot stove? No. Howe had no such intention. At best he might have planned a reconnaissance-in-force or at worst a simple feint and withdrawal that would have satisfied someone's "honor"—but not that of his simple soldiers. The hurricane, then, provided an excuse.

On March 17, 1776—St. Patrick's Day, forever more in Boston to be joined to Patriot's Day—the last of Howe's soldiers and about one thousand dejected Tories sailed from Boston Harbor for Nantasket Harbor. Ten days later this woebegone fleet of perhaps 170 vessels set sail for Halifax.

Triumphant, the Patriots rushed into the city that had been the center and the symbol of the rebellion. Now it was Tory property that went under the auctioneer's hammer. Now it was Tory homes that sometimes went up in flames while the owners were stripped, tarred, feathered and ridden out of town on a rail. No one hates more than hostile brothers, and even the British themselves were not hated as venomously as were those Loyalists whom Howe was forced to leave behind.

From Maine to South Carolina the Loyalists were lashed through the streets, pelted with rotten eggs or forced to go down on their knees to damn the king and his ministers. One Tory is on record with the quaint lament that he "had the misfortune to affront one of the Committee men, by not giving His Daughter a kiss when I was introduced to her. This has offended the old man so much, that ... he has several spys to watch my actions. Sorry I did not give the ugly Jade a kiss." Washington himself wanted the more notorious Tories hung as an example to the rest, and Governor William Livingston of New Jersey said: "A Tory is an incorrigible Animal: And nothing but the Extinction of Life will extinguish his malevolence against liberty." Before the war was over the Patriots were forcing all secret Tories to declare themselves by imposing oaths of loyalty to the United States. Those who refused were fined, imprisoned, deprived of civil rights or, as the new states seized upon this handy means of raising revenue, dispossessed.

Witch-hunt though this was (although it never led to stake or gallows), it is difficult to see how the Patriots could have acted otherwise. The Tories were a dangerous fifth column. They were nearly as numerous and fully as able as the Patriots, and they were so inimical to the Revolution that Lord George Germain would never abandon his belief that the war was to be won by a Tory uprising.

★ 29 ★

TOM PAINE AND *COMMON SENSE*

Persecution of the Tories and the ouster of royal governors, together with the establishment of independent governing bodies in the colonies, naturally enough brought the Americans closer to the final step: independence, the severance of the umbilical cord from the Mother Country. And yet, as this spirit grew more unabashed and belligerent, it was always directed against Parliament or the "ministerial" government—almost never against King George III.

This was because the colonists stubbornly—almost pathetically or with fatuous nostalgia—clung to the concept of a wise and benevolent monarch who would heed the stream of petitions flowing from Philadelphia and eventually triumph over his scheming, evil ministers to free his beloved Americans from the chains being forged for them in Whitehall. Such a sentimental fiction was possible because so few Americans crossed the sea to Britain, and of the handful who did, few were ever privy to the king's furious and abiding determination to give the Americans "a few bloody noses." The king's hostility was uncompromising and was repeatedly made plain to his ministers. "Every means of distressing America must meet with my concurrence." "Before I will even hear of any man's readiness for office, I will expect to see it signed under his hand that he is resolved to keep the empire entire, and that no troops shall be subsequently withdrawn from America, nor independence *ever* allowed." Thus ignorant of their beloved monarch's true state of mind, the Americans would even speak of the armed forces sent to quell the rebellion as "the ministerial army," rather than the king's soldiers or sailors. Gradually, however, the inexorable march of events began to strip the camouflage from this pleasant myth, and the king could be seen as a relentless ruler who was prepared to negotiate with his unruly subjects only after he had knocked them down. Newspapers that openly editorialized the inevitability of independence began to print comments critical of His Majesty. The young Patriot poet Philip Freneau could fume at "pirates sent out by command of the king/To plunder and murder, but never to swing" and, more forcefully:

> From the scoundrel Lord North, who would bind us in chains,
> From a dunce of a king, who was born without brains …
> From an island that bullies, and hectors, and swears
> I send up to heaven my wishes and prayers
> That we, disunited, may freemen be still,
> And Britain go on—to be damned, if she will.

Into this atmosphere of thickening hatred of King George III, there stepped a born revolutionary and sworn hater of royalty named Thomas Paine.

Tom Paine was born in 1737 in the little market town of Thetford, about seventy miles northeast of London. His father was a Quaker whose income as a staymaker was implemented by the revenue from a small farm, while his mother, an Anglican, was the daughter of a local attorney. Although somewhere below the middle class in the rigidly stratified English society of the day, Tom's parents still had sufficient income to afford to send him to a local grammar school for seven years. It was here that the foundations of his literary skill were laid, for even such a short period—which certainly included four years of Latin—at one of those excellent schools in which the country then abounded was enough to drill the basics of the language into any bright young boy. And Tom was bright, even precocious, always asking questions, some of which were dangerously embarrassing. Thus he was dismayed when his father took him out of school at thirteen to become an apprentice in the craft of making stays for corsets from whalebone, the elastic horny substance found in the upper jaws of certain whales.

Tom detested staymaking from the start. It was physical work requiring strength, which Tom never liked. He preferred to make his way by education or native intelligence, and thus for three years his hand may have been on the corset but his heart and head were in the classroom. He also was a proud youth, who was not disinclined to flatter or fawn over the fat women who came into the shop. But it was not until he was sixteen that he ran away from home to serve aboard a British privateer during the

Seven Years' War. However, his life as a sailor was brief, and in 1756 he came ashore for good to resume his staymaking career in London.

The great city of the empire was all the education that this nineteen-year-old youth sought so fervently. It abounded in libraries and societies dedicated to the intellectual and moral edification of working-class people, together with scores of stimulating discussion clubs that met in taverns and alehouses. Tom Paine frequented all these places, listening enchanted to lectures on science. Science, not literature, was then his first love. In later years he would study the causes of yellow fever and experiment with smokeless candles and a kind of internal combustion engine, as well as design an iron bridge. Yet, as one student of the period has remarked of these lectures: "What began as scientific curiosity, often ended in political and moral speculation."

A new class of articulate and thoughtful men—self-educated artisans and small-shopkeepers, many of them Dissenters or freethinkers—had appeared in the Britain of the mid-eighteenth century. This new reading public devoured the novels of such writers as the famous nonconformist Daniel Defoe and the political pamphlets of Jonathan Swift, Joseph Addison and Sir Richard Steele. They read John Locke and the newspaper articles of the mysterious Junius—whose identity is still debated—bitter attacks on the unabashedly corrupt Tory government of young King George III. Tom Paine was part of this astonishing revolution in political debate among these Tory-hating Whigs, this astounding growth in numbers and influence of printers and booksellers, but only as a listener—not yet as a lecturer himself. Because of this, and the need to eat, he remained a staymaker, moving to another shop in Dover in 1758, and then opening his own in the nearby town of Sandwich. Here he met and married Mary Lambert, a maid for the wife of a local merchant. A few months later they moved to Margate, where Mary died after less than a year of marriage.

Because of the influence of Mary's father, an officer in the Customs and Excise Service, Tom Paine now sought to become an excise officer, and he returned to Thetford to study for the examination, which he passed easily. In 1762 he was appointed a collector of excise taxes in Alford, Lincolnshire. There passed three blank years in this unexalted—even despised—occupation, ending with his dismissal for "stamping the whole ride," the minor but common offense of filing a report without actually examining the commodities involved. After a brief but half-hearted attempt to resume staymaking in Norfolk, Paine became an English teacher in a local academy for half the salary he earned as an excise officer. After three years on these starvation wages, Paine swallowed his pride and wrote a letter of humble apology to the Excise Board, begging for restoration to his old job. It was granted, and he landed in the market town of Lewes, fifty miles south of London. Here he boarded with a tobacconist named Samuel Ollive, and after Ollive died in 1771, Paine married his daughter, taking over the shop while remaining in his excise post.

Now there began to coalasece in the mind of this seemingly shiftless misfit all those influences of his youth and later experiences that were to culminate in the shaping of a radical. From his Quaker father he had absorbed a detestation of hierarchy—either in church or state—as well as a crusading zeal against such abominations as slavery and dueling. He abhorred the laws prohibiting Protestant Dissenters from holding public office or positions in the universities or the professions, and advocated the separation of church and state. But he did not persevere in his father's belief in God, for he was by then an avowed freethinker, who would later scoff at the deistic phrase, "I am Who am," with the remark, "A truth that large ought to be written on the sun." There burned in his heart not so much a love of liberty as a hatred of oppression.

Royalty and nobility were an abomination to him, and he could sneer with Rousseau: "Who ever heard of King Adam or the Emperor Noah?" Paine the atheist could never believe that if there were a God, He had decreed that the rich should exploit the poor. He cherished the remark of Sir Algernon Sidney—so often mistakenly attributed to Thomas Jefferson—that it was not divinely ordained that most people were born with saddles on their backs and a few others booted and spurred to ride them.

Because he had been poor, he sympathized with the downtrodden; because he had had to crawl before the Excise Board and beg for his daily bread, he despised bureaucracy; and because of what he experienced in Lewes, he hated King George's rubber-stamp Parliament of handpicked "placemen." Paine also resented the unjust excise taxes on such common articles as ale, beer, soap and salt, imposts that he was sworn to enforce and that in Lewes gave rise to sympathy for smugglers and hatred of excise officers, who were frequently beaten. In Lewes a fierce spirit of political independence also flourished, so that in 1734 there was a movement for universal manhood suffrage, squelched when Parliament ominously issued the warning that only householders could legally vote. Lewes was also a stronghold of the Duke of Newcastle, and just before Paine arrived there, the duke's toadying candidate for Parliament suffered a humiliating defeat. Enraged, the duke ordered his agents to evict all tenants who had voted the wrong way, and to "call in the bills of such tradesmen of Lewes, who have been employed by me, and did not vote as above, and not employ them again on my account."

Such rigging of the sacred electoral process infuriated Paine, thus fanning to higher heat his hatred of a corrupt establishment based on royalty and nobility and the exploitation of the common people. By then also Tom Paine had probably become an active political pamphleteer and orator himself. Although this is not certain, it does explain why his fellow excise officers chose him to write their petition for higher pay. The movement, of course, was doomed to failure, probably because, as one contemporary dryly observed, "a rebellion of excisemen, who seldom have the populace on their side, is not much to be feared."

Paine had spent the winter of 1772–73 in London agitating for this impossible petition, and because he had left his post in Lewes without authorization, he was again dismissed from the excise service. Next his tobacco shop failed, and he and his wife separated. At the age of thirty-seven in the year 1774, it appeared that Tom Paine was about to drink again the dregs of an embittered, impoverished existence. He did, however, have a little money from a separation agreement with his wife, and he did have a letter of introduction from Benjamin Franklin, having met and impressed Franklin at his London "Club of Honest Whigs." Paine had for years been keeping abreast of events in America, and Pennsylvania's astute agent in London believed that this remarkable and fiery friend of freedom might be of use to his Patriot associates in Philadelphia. So Paine took ship for the City of Brotherly Love.

So little is known of Tom Paine as a human being that it is difficult to portray him as someone other than the Great Pamphleteer, a creature of pen and paper, rather than of flesh and blood. There is, however, a painting of Paine hanging in London's National Portrait Gallery that provides at least a minimal insight into his character. Fortunately for posterity the painter was a consummate artist. He shows a man in his forties with a long head and high forehead crowned by a thatch of thick wavy dark hair streaked with gray. Paine's nose is long, sharp and pockmarked, the beak of a wit or a baiter. It is in the mouth, bitter lipped and twisted, disdainful, even mocking, and the watchful, wide-set, dark eyes beneath heavy eyebrows that one may perceive the inner demon that drove this man:

Hatred of kings.

The Philadelphia in which Paine arrived in the fall of 1774 was the leading metropolis of America. Its population of thirty thousand was the largest among the colonies, and its population of Quakers, Anglicans and

Catholics of English origin, as well as Scotch-Irish Presbyterians and a sprinkling of German and Irish Catholics, made it also the most cosmopolitan. That Irish-German leavening was constantly growing: during the decade beginning in 1764, some 215 ships left German and Irish ports bearing immigrants to the New World.

By modern standards the city was tiny, covering no more than one square mile of an area of seven blocks along the western shore of the broad Delaware River. In the countryside surrounding the city stood the splendid estates of Philadelphia's wealthiest merchants and shippers. Yet for all its diminutive size, the City of Brotherly Love was the indisputable financial and commercial center of the colonies, as well as its cultural leader in the arts, theater and educational institutions.

Tom Paine was delighted to find so many Philadelphians interested in science, and, just as in London, so many artisans eagerly attending so many lectures, and so many bookstores offering the works of his favorite political thinkers. At Aiken's Bookstore, where rebel literature was sold, he found a company of congenial Patriots, among them young Dr. Benjamin Rush, a fiery radical. Rush and Paine instantly discovered themselves of one mind, but the good doctor—one of Philadelphia's most successful physicians—found that his new friend's foaming hatred of royalty was perhaps a bit too venomous, even though he, himself, was composing an essay on independence.

Rush was also not sure that the time was propitious for such a radical proposal. More to the point, publication of an inflammatory pamphlet under his name might alienate all those wealthy conservatives and outright Tories who were his patients. So he suggested to Paine that he undertake the project, and was delighted when—with equal enthusiasm—Paine agreed. From this fortitious union of the hesitant lover of liberty and the bold hater of royalty, there was born the pamphlet *Common Sense,* beyond doubt the most influential political pamphlet ever written, and published in an age that had brought that particular art form to a high peak of perfection.

Common Sense was really not very sensible or logical, especially not so in those passages in which Paine blames the calamity of war on kings alone, as though every form of leadership in both government and religion did not bear some of the guilt for mankind's greatest evil, or as though there were never such a conflict as a just war. Fortunately for the Patriot cause Tom Paine was not a thinker, but a passionate man whose angry prose flowed from a heart wounded again and again by injustice and discrimination, but was never quite soured or embittered by all those years of frustration. *Common Sense* was written for the common man. It was the cry of a crusader out to destroy a selfish society dominated by a few gluttons of power, privilege and possession. True enough, in his political theory Paine was a devotee of Locke and those other writers who were the ideological fathers of the American Revolution. But Tom Paine's intended audience was not those thoughtful politicians, such as John Adams and Jefferson and the other solons of Philadelphia, but the ordinary men who would shed their blood—not expend their ink—in the rebellion that was impending. And it was because of this audience that his attack on kingship was a stroke of genius. To have argued logically and calmly against the excesses of Parliament or the cabinet would only have been to imitate those reasonable, educated men who were so much better fitted for the halls of counsel. But logic will not so enrage a man that he will reach for the musket over the fireplace. And Thomas Paine did indeed fling out as dogma rather than logic a new one denying the old and accepted doctrine of the divine right of kings: that there was simply nothing in nature or Scripture maintaining that some people were born to be kings and others to be subjects. The accident of birth did not give anyone the right to every priority and pleasure at the expense of those born to wait in line, to suffer and endure.

Even more than monarchy Paine detested the hereditary right of succession as "*an insult and imposition upon posterity. For all men being originally equals, no one by birth could have a right to set up his own family in perpetual preference to all others forever.... One of the strongest natural proofs of the folly of hereditary right in kings, is that nature disapproves it, otherwise she would not so frequently turn it into ridicule by giving mankind AN ASS FOR A LION.*" Again: "*How impious is the title of Sacred Majesty applied to a worm, who in the midst of his splendor is crumbling into dust.*" Finally: "*Of more worth is one honest man to society, and in the sight of God, than all the crowned ruffians that ever lived.*"

Having had at George III—"the royal brute"—Paine swung hard at the suggestion of reconciliation. "*To be always running three or four thousand miles with a tale or a petition, waiting four or five months for an answer, which, when obtained, requires five or six more to explain it in, will in a few years be looked upon as folly and childishness. There was a time when it was proper, and there is a proper time for it to cease.*"

Paine closed by scoffing at the notion that all would yet end well. "*Ye that tell us of harmony and reconciliation, can ye restore to us the time that is past? Can ye give to prostitution its former innocence? Neither can ye reconcile Britain and America. The last cord is broken.... There are injuries which nature cannot forgive.... As well the lover forgive the ravisher of his mistress, as the continent forgive the murderers of Britain.*"

"*O ye that love mankind!*" he cried in final passion. "*Ye that dare oppose not only the tyranny but the tyrant, stand forth! Every spot of the old world is overrun with oppression. Freedom hath been hunted around the globe. Asia and Africa have long expelled her. Europe regards her like a stranger, and England hath given her warning to depart. O receive the fugitive, and prepare in time an asylum for mankind!*"

Thus *Common Sense* in essence, not just the most successful political pamphlet of all time, but in its effect as inspiring and liberating as Lexington-Concord and Bunker Hill combined—and in its reach worldwide. *Uncle Tom's Cabin* may have had the same influence in provoking the American Civil War, but its message stopped at the ocean's edge, whereas after its publication in Philadelphia on January 9, 1776, *Common Sense* not only was republished and read in all the colonies, with copies passed hand to hand until they became dog eared and sweat stained, but also crossed the sea to be translated into French, Dutch and German. It was even published in London, but with all the "treasonable" strictures against the king omitted. Paine himself estimated that within three months it sold a staggering 120,000 copies, but its actual readership was much, much more: probably as many as a million people, or half the literate population of America.

It changed many minds, among them George Washington, who never again proposed a toast to the king at official meals. John Adams might smile, as he did, at its naive political theorizing, but he saw at once what a powerful force it was toward independence. *Common Sense* had destroyed the awesome father figure of the king in the minds—even the hearts—of the American colonists. In a few deadly paragraphs, like the strokes of a surgeon's scalpel, he had stripped away all the awe-inspiring habiliments of monarchy—crown, scepter, orb and robes, at the head of nobles, judges, troops and ships—all designed to produce fear, subordination and dependence in the hearts of ordinary men, and shown that the man who possessed them was no more remarkable than a chimney sweep, with nothing but the accident of birth to sustain him. *Common Sense* killed the concept of kingship in America.

After *Common Sense* independence was king.

★ 30 ★

THE DECLARATION OF INDEPENDENCE

By that momentous spring of 1776 the spirit of independence was so pervasive in the colonies that a person could scarcely breathe without sucking it in. And in London, as might have been expected, King George and his Parliament in their effort to supress it, actually gave it the firmest shove toward realization.

Parliament began by voting an army of fifty-five thousand men to be raised to crush the rebellion, but the king's subjects did not rally to the cause. Among the officers of the Royal Army and Navy there was much sympathy for the Americans, and many of them—led by General Jeffrey Amherst and Admiral Augustus Keppel—simply refused to serve against the Americans. The British yeomen were even more disinclined to bear arms against their cousins overseas, and those stout "hearts of oak" of song and story had never fancied the poor pay and brutal discipline of the king's armed forces. Those press gangs, judges and tavern keepers who had always been His Majesty's chief recruiters were thoroughly chastened by the general hostility to their practice of persuading drunks, drifters, idiot boys and runaway fathers to take the king's shilling; and even if they had not been, they could never have found enough victims to flesh out an army of fifty-five thousand. Faced with universal disenchantment, King George III went looking for hirelings.

He found them in the principalities of Germany: Brunswick, Waldeck, Anhalt-Zerbst, Anspach-Bayreuth, Hesse-Hanau and Hesse-Cassel. Eventually some thirty thousand German mercenaries were hired for the American war, and because more than half of them were supplied by the Landgrave of Hesse-Cassel, they were all called Hessians.

Britain agreed to pay all expenses of the Hessians, as well as $35 to their prince for each soldier killed, $12 for each one wounded and over $500,000 annually to the Hessian Landgrave alone. Thus these subjects of the German princelings, not to say human chattels, were worth more dead than on the hoof.

The decision to "Search every kingdom that breeds the slave," as it says in the Irish song of rebellion, was George III's last fatal blunder. He had rejected the colonies' Olive Branch Petition that sought reconciliation, he had used harsh language in describing them as being in a state of rebellion, his navy had wantonly burnt Falmouth and now His Majesty was sending foreign mercenaries against his own subjects, as though they were his foreign enemies. With this last act, he convinced most Americans that there was nothing left to do but cut the umbilical cord and declare their independence.

Nine of the thirteen colonies could be counted upon to vote for independence, but both the New York and Pennsylvania delegations had been instructed by their assemblies to oppose it, while South Carolina was hesitant and Maryland was "on the fence." Try as they might, both John Adams and Richard Henry Lee—master politicians trained in such disparate schools as the town meeting and the county parish—could not secure the unanimity they considered necessary. All that could be obtained was to name a five-man committee to prepare a declaration that would conform to the famous Virginia Resolves: "That these United Colonies are, and of right ought to be, free and independent states." The committee's members were John Adams, Benjamin Franklin, Roger Sherman, Robert Livingston and Thomas Jefferson.

The selection of Jefferson as chairman was a distinct surprise. Except for Livingston, a member of a wealthy and conservative family of New York who opposed independence and was on the committee solely as a sop to that faction; and Roger Sherman of Massachusetts, whose literary style was as blunt as the shoemaker's hammer he had dropped to assume a judge's gown and the presidency of Yale, Jefferson was the least likely choice to draft this all-important document. At thirty-three he was among the youngest of the delegates at Philadelphia, and although he was known as an ardent Patriot and regarded as a clear thinker and fine writer, he was an indifferent orator and so-so politician whose reputation could not compare to that of Adams or Franklin.

Either Adams or Franklin would seem to have been the natural choice for chairman and drafter of the declaration. Both were senior to

Jefferson in years, experience and fame. Both were renowned as writers, Franklin on both sides of the Atlantic, Adams so highly regarded that he was at first believed to have been the author of *Common Sense*. Both, of course, were vain—and Franklin was inclined to be facetious. But if they could be taxed with vanity, why, then, did they allow the creation of what was to be one of the most famous documents in history to pass by default to a comparatively unknown neophyte? The answer seems to be that neither Adams nor Franklin suspected that the declaration would become immortal. After all, the vote for independence itself would be the true revolution. Its declaration was almost an afterthought—and to some conservatives who opposed it, nothing more than a political tactic to undermine them and weaken their strength. It is also true that Franklin, who was inclined to be lazy, did not covet such an apparently thankless literary task and that Adams, the true author of independence if any single delegate at Philadelphia can be so designated, did not wish to allow such a trivial assignment to interfere with his incessant politicking for the Great Cause. It was only after Jefferson's genius turned a routine document into a splendid expression of mankind's deepest and noblest aspirations that Adams realized he had passed on immortality. No doubt he was chagrined, and it was in later years that he concocted the charming story of how he and Jefferson were strolling in a garden when the young Virginian suggested to him that he ought to compose a draft of a declaration of independence. Adams said he declined, and a surprised Jefferson asked him, "What can be your reasons?"

"Reason first—you are a Virginian," Adams said he replied, "and a Virginian ought to appear at the head of this business. Reason second—I am obnoxious, suspect and unpopular. You are very much otherwise. Reason third—you can write ten times better than I can."

"Reason third," in its coy submission to Jefferson's supposedly superior writing skill, makes an unlikely charade of the entire scene, for John Adams wrote very well, and he knew it. In fact, the declaration went to Thomas Jefferson by default.

Jefferson's great document was not entirely original, based as it was on George Mason's famous Virginia Bill of Rights, which, in turn, relied almost entirely on John Locke. Mason's preamble declared: "That all men by nature are equally free and independent, and have certain inherent rights, of which, when they enter into a state of society, they cannot by any compact deprive or divest their posterity; namely, the enjoyment of life and liberty, with the means of acquiring and possessing property, and pursuing and obtaining happiness and safety."

Jefferson renders—the word is deliberate—these fifty-eight words in thirty-five of his own: "We hold these truths to be self-evident, that all men are created equal, that they are endowed by their Creator with certain inalienable rights, that among these are life, liberty and the pursuit of happiness." Here is the genius of compression that commands attention while with its marvelous rhythms it charms the ear and with its insight excites the mind. In all, Jefferson compressed Mason's first three articles of 170 words to 86 of his own, almost exactly in half. But he also substitutes for the Lockean trinity of life, liberty and property Mason's "pursuing and obtaining happiness," which, in his own happier prose, he changes to "the pursuit of happiness."

As he well knew, happiness is not a right and certainly is not an equivalent of life and liberty, although it can be an aim of government to create the climate of freedom in which it may be pursued without hindrance, if never actually attained. "Property" is more incisive than "happiness" because it is in the sanctity of his property or home that a man may resist the intrusion of government, while happiness, though certainly desirable, offers no such sanctuary against oppression. Stylist that Jefferson was and consciously sought to be, he may have preferred "pursuit of happiness" for its rhythm and because it was a phrase more harmonious and felicitous than plain "property." To Jefferson's credit he never pretended that his declaration was original, but explained that his sources were "the harmonizing sentiments of the day," that is, the insights of Locke, Sidney and other political theorists to be found "in conversation, in letters, in printed essays, or in the elementary books of public right."

Jefferson's modesty was again apparent when he took what he called a "rough draft" to Adams and Franklin for their criticisms and suggestions. Forty-eight changes were made, mostly by Franklin and a few by Jefferson himself. Perhaps the happiest emendation was to change "We hold these truths to be sacred and undeniable" by replacing "sacred and undeniable" with "self-evident." Adams was deeply impressed by the language of the declaration, while Franklin, perhaps because he proposed the most changes, sought to mollify the somewhat chastened Jefferson with the story of a hatter who, about to open his shop, thought that he needed a sign that was to read, "John Thompson, Hatter, makes and sells hats for ready money." In criticism his friends declared "Hatter" superfluous because there was a picture of a hat on the sign, "makes" not necessary because the buyers could care less about who made them and "ready money" obvious because no one bought hats on credit. Only "John Thompson sells hats" was left, and these words also vanished after it was argued that "sells" was redundant because no one gives hats away and "hats" was not needed because of the picture. So nothing was left.

Whether the story comforted Jefferson is not known, but he certainly must have been a bit chagrined when Congress made a wholesale deletion of his tirade against King George III as the patron of chattel slavery. Congress was right, of course, for the normally calm and evenhanded Jefferson lost his balance in this vituperative, turgid and unfair indictment. It may be that as a great slaveholder whose anguish over the evil source of his wealth was often made manifest, he had unconsciously transferred this unbearable burden of guilt to a person who, under the influence of his friend Tom Paine, he had come to hate. He could also, by the savagery of his language, create a distraction from the obvious hypocrisy of a proclamation of freedom written by a slaveholder and up for approval by a Congress that was filled with owners of bondsmen. Many delegates saw through this ruse at once and would have none of it. Others were embarrassed by it, although a few sanctimonious Northerners were ready to swallow it. So it was cut, as were some harsh words directed against the British people. But for these minor objections, the great Declaration of Independence sailed through Congress on a tidal wave of enthusiasm. It now remained for the actual vote on the resolution for independence to take place.

John Adams arose on the morning of July 1, 1776, confident that the vote on declaring the colonies "free and independent" that was to follow debate on the resolution would pass unanimously. But a canvass showed that there were still only nine colonies in which a majority of the delegates supported the measure. Maryland had swung toward it, but South Carolina had defected under pressure from Edward Rutledge, while Delaware was evenly divided with Caesar Rodney, known to be a friend of independence, home at the bedside of his ailing wife. That night Thomas McKean, a proindependence delegate from Delaware, sent a courier riding ninety miles to Rodney's home with the plea to be in Philadelphia the next day to cast his crucial vote. New York, its delegates still claiming their instructions were to oppose independence, abstained from voting. Pennsylvania, no longer similarly bound, nevertheless was in opposition by a vote of four to three. The Quaker ruling class, battling against the challenge of an alliance of merchants, artisans and frontier radicals, apparently was still in the saddle, and Pennsylvania was crucial—not for passage, which was assured, but for the unanimity so necessary for the powerful effect of a united front.

But then Richard Henry Lee of Virginia persuaded Rutledge to drop his opposition if both Delaware and Pennsylvania voted approval. Next a deal—typical of Adams or Lee, or both—was made. Benjamin Franklin, of course, supported independence, along with James Morton and James Wilson. John Dickinson still opposed it, as did Robert Morris, but when these two agreed not to take their seats officially the next day, Pennsylvania would be in the affirmative, three votes to two.

On July 2 Congress again convened, spending the morning on routine business. But there was tension among the delegates, many glancing anxiously at the rain-lashed windows, either in hopes of seeing Caesar Rodney gallop up or reassured by the sight of an empty street. Rodney had it in his power to swing Delaware to the side of independence, and it was rumored that he was on his way. After lunch, he did appear, flinging himself off his horse, splattered with mud and soaked to the skin, the cancer sore on his small round face—hardly bigger than a large grapefruit—livid from his ordeal. Hastening into the chamber, he put Delaware in the affirmative column, after which Pennsylvania followed suit and South Carolina came back aboard. Although New York still abstained, the colony's assembly notified Congress on July 19 that it now favored independence, and the unanimity sought so passionately by John Adams as though it were the Holy Grail was finally achieved.

By then, on the Fourth of July, all the delegates to Congress who were present except John Dickinson approved the Declaration of Independence. John Hancock, as president of the Congress, signed first—with a great bold flourish that was to make his name synonymous with the flamboyant signature, declaring: "There, I guess King George will be able to read that!"

One by one, the others signed; radicals, moderates and conservatives, all united in their determination to be "Absolved from all Allegiance to the British Crown." There were the Adamses of Massachusetts, openly jubilant now that "the river is passed and the bridge cut away"; there was the wealthy Marylander, Charles Carroll of Carrollton, a Catholic island in a Protestant sea, signing because "I had in view not only our independence of England, but the toleration of all sects professing the Christian religion." The Lees of Virginia signed, one before and one behind a beaming Thomas Jefferson. So did Benjamin Franklin, his wise old eyes still twinkling over his quip, "We must all hang together, or assuredly we shall all hang separately." After the Pennsylvanians came Caesar Rodney, his eager small face relaxed and the cancer sore now barely visible. Now all argument was done. Fifty-six delegates from twelve colonies signed, New York still abstaining, pledging to each other, "Our Lives, our Fortunes and our Sacred Honor." Four days later—on July 8—the Declaration of Independence was published. Philadelphia heard for the first time those noble ideals and ringing phrases that still have the power to move hearts. But Philadelphia took the news calmly. After all, the debates had been common knowledge for some time. But it was different elsewhere in this new-born country. Savannah burned King George in effigy. New York pulled down his statue, and Connecticut melted it down for bullets, while Boston tore George's coat of arms from the statehouse and burned it along with every other memorabilia of His Majesty that could be found.

Thus it was an exultant and defiant United States of America, not thirteen cowed and submissive colonies, that greeted Admiral "Black Dick" Howe when he arrived in New York Harbor empowered to talk of peace.

★ 31 ★

THE BATTLE OF LONG ISLAND

Lord Howe's "peace" overtures began with a letter to "Mr." Washington, which the American commander coldly refused to accept. Next Admiral Howe sent a letter to "George Washington, Esquire," as well as an emissary who claimed that both Howes had been specially nominated as peace commissioners by the king. Washington received the emissary, but discovered that all that the Howes had power to do was to grant pardons. Since no fault had been committed, Washington said, no pardon was needed—and he coolly dismissed his guest.

After this exchange, the Howes decided to attack New York. The general had come down from Halifax to Staten Island with a large body of regulars, the admiral had come from Britain with the Hessians and Henry Clinton and Sir Peter Parker soon came limping up from Charleston with their men and ships. General Howe now had an army of 32,000 superbly armed and equipped troops to hurl against 19,000 ragged, untrained Americans in New York. His brother led a fleet of ten ships of the line, twenty frigates mounting 1,200 guns and hundreds of transports. Britain had never before sent out such an armada. She had spent the staggering sum of £850,000 to organize and supply it.

On August 22 the troops began landing on Long Island.

Washington clearly understood the importance of New York. "It is the Place that we must use every Endeavour to keep from them," he wrote to its commander, Brigadier General Lord Stirling.* Control of New York

*William Alexander, "Lord Stirling," is probably the only peer in American history, although his claim to the earldom of Stirling was rejected by the House of Lords.

City meant command of the Hudson and access to the lake-and-river chain to Canada. If the British held it, they could cut off New York City and New England from the rest of the colonies.

But Washington did not yet appreciate British sea power. He believed New York could be held against it, when, actually, Manhattan Island and the other islands clustering around it were highly vulnerable to amphibious attack.

To defend it Washington divided his force into five divisions under Israel Putnam, Nathanael Greene, William Heath, Joseph Spencer and the garrulous John Sullivan of New Hampshire. One division held the northern end of Manhattan Island, where King Bridge linked it with the mainland; three held the southern end, where the mile-square town of New York was located; and the fifth, under Greene, was across the East River on Long Island.

Greene built works on Brooklyn Heights, which rose one hundred feet above water and commanded New York. But then he came down with malaria and was evacuated to New York. Command passed to John Sullivan, who was in charge when Howe began landing twenty thousand troops at Gravesend Bay, Staten Island.

Great white sails flooded the bay. Longboats, galleys and flatboats, crowded with scarlet coats and green-clad Hessian jaegers, rowed away from them toward shore. The sun made a million points of light on bayonets and burnished buckles, on flashing white oars and on the instruments of the bands playing lively marches to spur on "Black Dick" Howe's bluejackets. By noon Howe had fifteen thousand men ashore—a feat that modern amphibious commanders with motor-powered ships might well admire. Three days later Howe received another five thousand men and now outnumbered Sullivan about four to one.

George Washington was quite aware that the British appearance on Staten Island opened a new and ominous phase in the War of the American Revolution. It signified that the British had at last come to their senses militarily, abandoning chauvinist convictions that the Yankee rabble would run the moment they saw the approach of a battalion of redcoats, and preparing with grim realism for a major campaign in which its best ships and regiments, commanded by its ablest officers, would crush the rebellion in a single battle. This would be no Lexington-Concord or Bunker Hill, which had actually been little more than minor actions in which the Americans had chosen their own ground in mainly defensive situations where their skills in fortification and marksmanship more than compensated for their lack of training and discipline. Now the poorly trained and outnumbered Yankee Doodles, with their wretchedly inadequate service of supply, would have to meet the splendidly trained and supplied British regulars, commanded by His Majesty's finest tacticians, on the enemy's own terms. The best that Washington could hope for was a standoff, the worst a decisive defeat in which his army would be destroyed and the Revolution crushed. It is not known if the American commander sensed so early in the war that in such an uneven contest he could never, until he felt strong enough, risk his army in decisive battle—that he must always save his army, for that army was the Revolution. He must, then, be another Cunctator, a delayer, like the great Fabius, whose cautious tactics against Hannibal enabled Rome to recover its strength so that Scipio could finally destroy Carthage at Zama.

Certainly the true power of Great Britain was made manifest to Washington by that forest of masts in the waters between New Jersey and New York. So, too, was a dawning respect for sea power. Yoked to this awareness was a growing irritation with his commanders on Long Island. Sullivan, as Greene's replacement, was woefully inadequate. He was a man made of bombast and conceit, whose messages reflected an almost total inability to grasp a military situation. On August 22, when Howe began landing at Gravesend, his report of a clash between his soldiers and a probing patrol of Cornwallis's concluded: "We have driven them a mile from their former station. These things argur well for us, and I hope are so many preludes to a general victory." Washington in New York could see at once what this tiny action signified: the enemy probers, finding opposition, had returned to base to report it. And Sullivan magnified the gnat into an eagle! Furious, Washington immediately replaced Sullivan with Israel Putnam.

Here, too, he would not be well served. "Old Put" had developed a Bunker Hill psychosis. He was forever looking for "the whites of their eyes." Inside his round owlish head stood the embattled farmers again and again mowing down the serried ranks of redcoats, who were still obligingly mounting frontal assaults on entrenched troops. He was, of course, much more energetic than was his predecessor, but because he knew nothing of Long Island's terrain or its troops, he continued Sullivan's dispositions. On the American right were about 1,700 men under Stirling. On the left was the main body commanded by Sullivan. To the rear, guarding Brooklyn, were the works on Brooklyn Heights held by Putnam's reserve. Because Washington had begun to send him reinforcements, Putnam's force had risen from about 5,000 to 8,000 men. Unfortunately, although Putnam had posted troops to watch the roads, he had not covered all of them—probably because he was unwarrantably confident that Sullivan was blocking the vital Jamaica Pass into Jamaica Road leading to his rear. Perhaps his frontal-assault mentality did not permit him to consider that William Howe had had enough of the glorious charge and might try to turn him and get in his rear.

Whatever, the Jamaica Pass, where such a turning movement could be blocked for hours, was not covered by Sullivan.

Among the reinforcements Washington sent across the East River was the Connecticut Line, in which seventeen-year-old Private Joseph Plumb Martin of Milford marched. Martin had been on a work detail when a sergeant major rushed up to him and his comrades to order them to fall in for movement to Long Island. The men—raw recruits all—exchanged nervous glances. They could see the tiny black puffs of artillery smoke across the water, but the wind carried away the sound of the explosions. Such a sudden summons to the crucible of combat, Martin mused, was not exactly the way to end training, but, "Although this was not unexpected to me, yet it gave me a rather disagreeable feeling, as I was pretty well assured I should have to snuff a little gunpowder."

But the fears of private soldiers in every army since Agememnon's are usually somewhat assuaged by food, and when Martin and his comrades marched past an opened cask of sea-bread, they fell gleefully on these tasteless biscuits "hard enough to break the teeth of a rat," stuffing them inside their jackets and filling their knapsacks with them. Once across the river they began climbing the cliff to Brooklyn Heights. Coming down were wounded men on stretchers, "some with broken legs and some with broken heads." Martin wrote: "The sight of these a little daunted me, and made me think of home." Below him he could see British and American soldiers skirmishing, like puppets on a string—but those smoke puffs and the now-audible explosions made it clear that when the tiny figures fell, it was all too real. Next an officer in Martin's company lost his nerve, dashing wildly about "snivelling and blubbering, praying each one if he had aught against him, or if he had injured any one, that they would forgive him, declaring at the same time that he, from his heart, forgave them if he had offended him.... A fine soldier you are, I thought; a fine officer, an exemplary man for young soldiers! I would then have suffered anything short of death rather than have made such exhibition of myself; but as the poet says, 'Fear does things so like a witch/ 'Tis hard to distinguish which is which.'"

When Martin and his fellow foot-sloggers finally took up their positions on the American line, they soon discovered a few more miseries in the life of a combat soldier: hunger, thirst, exposure to the elements, rain-filled trenches—and, of course, that ever-present companion: fear.

William Howe did indeed plan a turning movement. It would be around the American left, held by Sullivan, and down the vital Jamaica Road into Sullivan's rear. Tories had informed Howe of the existence of the unguarded Jamaica Pass. Howe's plan of battle was to place the American-hating Colonel James Grant on his left with orders to strike Stirling and hold him in place. The center, composed of Hessians under General Philip de Heister, was to strike at Sullivan and the American main body. Meanwhile, Howe's main body would slip through the Jamaica Pass and follow the Jamaica Road into Sullivan's rear.

At nine o'clock on the night of August 26, Howe's main body under Clinton, Percy and Cornwallis began moving out. Tories led them to the pass. At dawn the British stole through and turned left down the road to Sullivan's rear.

To the left, Grant had begun attacking Stirling, who had reminded his men that the general opposing them had boasted he would geld every male in America. Stirling's men fought valiantly. They not only repulsed Grant's regulars, but also tried to seize a British-held height. Grant, however, was content with keeping the Americans engaged.

So was Heister with the Hessians in the center. He waited until two cannon shots signaled the successful turning of Sullivan's position. The shots came, and the Hessians lunged forward, bands playing, some of them singing hymns. The Americans met them with the oaths and profanity characteristic of all English-speaking troops since the "Goddams" who fought Joan of Arc. Resistance was fierce, at first. But then came reports that Howe's main body was in the American rear, and Sullivan's troops panicked and ran.

The Hessians moved among Sullivan's troops mercilessly. They had been told by their English officers that the Americans gave no quarter, and they spitted many of the ragged rebels on trees or slaughtered entire groups of men who had laid down their arms.

Caught between two fires, the American main body was completely routed, and Sullivan himself was captured trying to rally his troops in a cornfield.

On the right, Stirling's men fought on. They were now surrounded on three sides. Lord Cornwallis had come down the road to attack their rear, Grant charged them on the right, and the Hessians hit them in the front. Too late, Stirling ordered a retreat. Many of his men who were

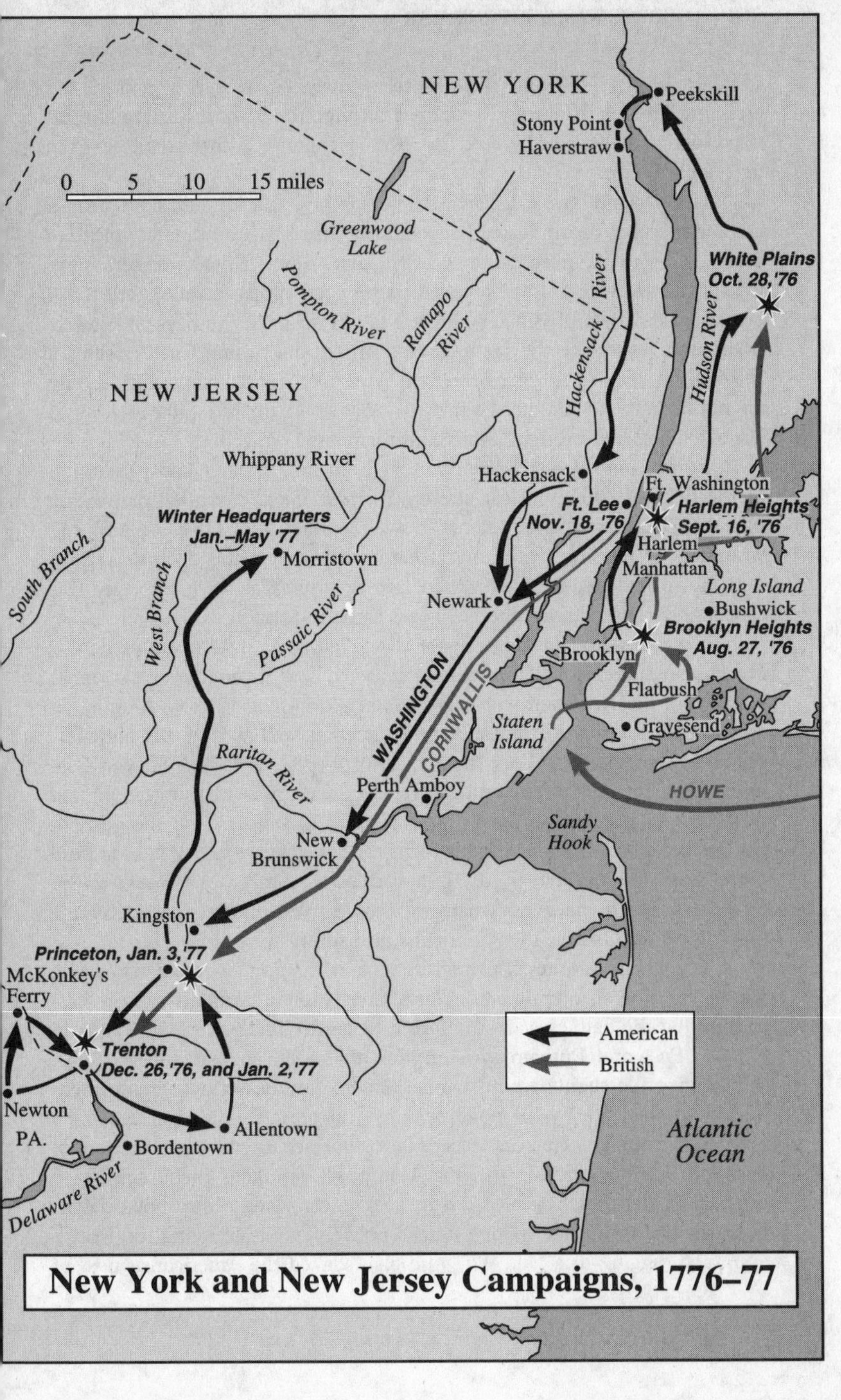

New York and New Jersey Campaigns, 1776–77

trying to escape through the Gowanus marshes were drowned in the attempt. The rest broke and scattered through the woods. Stirling himself then deliberately surrendered to the Hessians, rather than to the detestable Grant.

Long Island was a decisive British victory, and it could have been a greater one if William Howe had consented to his subordinates' pleas to storm the American redoubts at Brooklyn. Some British officers were livid with rage when Howe ordered their eager troops to retire. But those crumpled redcoats of Bunker Hill still lay in heaps at the back of Howe's brain, and he would not again assault Americans behind fixed positions. Instead, he decided to take Brooklyn by regular approaches, thus missing an opportunity to end the war with one blow, for Washington was at Brooklyn and had brought over reinforcements.

Long Island was a British victory both in casualties and possession of the field. Washington lost about 970 men killed, wounded or missing plus 1,079 taken captive, against Howe's casualties of 63 killed and 337 wounded or missing. But Long Island was not yet the decisive victory that Howe had expected. It would not be until Washington's army was thoroughly routed and scattered, never to be re-formed.

Nevertheless, Washington was dismayed by the extent of his defeat. He had lost almost half the troops engaged and a quarter of his entire command. Perhaps even worse, he was in a trap, cut off from Manhattan by the East River and Admiral Howe's fleet, as well as from the New Jersey shore and the New York mainland north of Long Island. He was positive that General Howe would not repeat the blunder of Bunker Hill and powerless to prevent him with his artillery and sappers and the guns of his brother's fleet from taking his fortifications apart stone by fascine until there was nothing left to do but surrender. Moreover, time was on Howe's side. He need not rush and could even, again assisted by the blockading fleet, starve the Americans into submission.

Yet when George Washington took command on the Heights, he wasted no time on recriminations or attempts to fix blame. It was obvious to him that the battle was lost before it began by Sullivan's failure to hold Jamaica Pass and Putnam's assumption that Sullivan had done so. Nor did he give the slightest hint of his concern for the serious predicament he was in. Instead, by his powerful physical presence alone, he gave his men new courage. He was everywhere, overseeing the construction of new fortifications, visiting the guard outposts, speaking encouragingly to his men in the trenches. Nor did he seek cover when a fortuitous downpour made any further enemy attacks unlikely, while bringing the British approach digging to a halt. The rain also soaked the Americans, most of whom were without tents, making it impossible to cook their food or keep their powder dry. Through this ordeal General Washington remained the calm, confident commander they had learned to respect, if not exactly revere, while proving how necessary it was for a chief to have the sort of iron constitution that can endure physical hardship and adversity. On August 28 the arrival of General Thomas Mifflin, with the Pennsylvania regiments of Colonels John Shea and Robert Magaw and the seagoing soldiers of John Glover's Marblehead Regiment, raised Washington's strength to about nine thousand men.

Next day the rain was intermittent, and the British resumed their digging. Soon they would have their guns within range. By then Washington had made up his mind to withdraw and quietly began collecting boats. Still acting as though he planned to continue the defensive, he surprised his generals at a council of war that evening by asking them to approve his retreat. He did not, of course, being the decisive commander that he was, ask them for a vote on the alternatives, as so often occurs in such councils that are called by timid chiefs who are anxious to transfer blame, but simply put forth his proposal forcefully and requested their approval—which came.

To get across the East River to safety, George Washington was relying on luck, darkness and bad weather to immobilize Admiral Howe's fleet—and on John Glover's regiment of seagoing soldiers.

They were called infantry, these men of Marblehead, but they had the look of men of the sea. They marched with a sailor's rolling gait. They wore cocked hats of the line, but also the short blue jackets and loose white trousers of the sailor. Their faces were grizzled from salt and their hands curled from oar and line. They spoke a language of their own: a stern man was "hord-horted," a barrel of tar was a "tor-borrl" and a useless man was a "froach." Their colonel, stocky John Glover, was happier to obey than to command when he was on land, but on this dark night of August 29 he and his men were on water.

With similar men of the Salem regiment they took charge of the small boats that Washington had wisely collected in advance. They brought them bobbing up to the Brooklyn ferry landing. Men bent beneath loads of baggage and equipment came marching silently down to the waiting boats. No lights were shown. No words but softly whispered commands were spoken. Then the wind blew northeast against the Americans. The ebb tide ran so strong that even the Marbleheaders could not make the crossing. Suddenly, the wind veered to the southwest, lessened and subsided. All seemed well.

But all was not well. At about two o'clock in the morning Washington, standing on the steps of the landing silently watching his men moving quietly aboard the boats, ordered aide-de-camp Colonel Alexander Scammell to hurry the remaining units to the ferry so that all would be boated before daylight. Scammell by mistake told General Mifflin, who commanded the covering party that was to delay the British if they attempted to pursue, that he must withdraw. Mifflin objected, but Scammell insisted—and Mifflin ordered Colonel Edward Hand to move out. Hand also objected, saying his men needed time to collect their equipment.

"Damn your pots and pans!" Mifflin burst out. "I wish the Devil had them. March on!"

Hand had barely started before Washington rode up in the darkness on his gray horse. Astonished to see his rear guard leaving its post, Washington angrily asked why. "I did not abandon it, sir," Hand replied in an injured tone. "I marched by order of my immediate commanding officer."

"That's impossible!"

"I trust that if I can secure General Mifflin's word that he ordered me to withdraw, that will clear me, sir, of any imputation of cowardice?"

"Of course, I should not blame you if you can prove you acted under orders."

At that moment Mifflin rode up, annoyed that Hand's troops had halted. To his astonishment the tall figure of Washington stepped out of the darkness, crying angrily: "Good God, General Mifflin! I am afraid you have ruined us by so unseasonably withdrawing the troops from the line."

"I did it by your order!" Mifflin retorted with equal force.

"That, sir, is impossible!"

"By God, I did. Did Scammell act as aide-de-camp for the day, or did he not?"

"Yes, he did."

"Then I had orders through him."

"Well, I gave no such orders. Colonel Scammell misunderstood."

Hoping in anguish that the British had not discovered Mifflin's rear-guard post abandoned, Washington quickly gave the order for Hand to return to his station—and a staff officer's blunder that truly could have "ruined" Washington's army and the Revolution as well was corrected and the evacuation continued smoothly.

Toward morning and the daylight that would reveal the boats to the guns of the British fleet, a fog set in. The fog enabled Mifflin's covering force to the withdrawn without mishap. Not until then did the British take note of the strangely silent Yankee trenches. When they opened fire and charged, they found the trenches empty.

Out on the water a young Connecticut lieutenant named Benjamin Tallmadge peered through the swirling mists of the fog and saw the last man step down the slippery steps of the landing into a boat. He was very tall and wore a blue sash across his breast.

★ 32 ★

"PEACE" TALKS/ALEXANDER HAMILTON/KIP'S BAY

Although the brothers Howe were chagrined at Washington's "escape," they still rejoiced in a comparatively easy victory suggestive of a crusher not long in coming. It seemed to them that with Congress chastened and Washington's army demoralized, the Americans might be more tractable. Both men had seen how awed—not to say humbled—the captured General John Sullivan had been by the power of British arms. Invited with General Stirling to dine with Lord Howe, Sullivan showed himself immensely pleased at such a signal honor, almost fawning on his famous host. Quickly the Howes saw that Sullivan was just the man to carry their request for the renewal of peace negotiations to Congress, and they sent him to Philadelphia for that purpose.

Congress was less than enthusiastic at the appearance of the defeated general, listening coldly to his message. But after four days of debate, it finally appointed a committee consisting of Benjamin Franklin, John Adams and Edward Rutledge to confer with the Howes at the general's headquarters on Staten Island.

Lord Howe met the delegation at the landing, exuding that grace, charm and good humor for which he was celebrated, careful to make the Americans aware of his friendship for them and of his reluctance to accept his present command against them. Because the Americans had been warned to be wary of his lordship's persuasiveness, they were on their guard. Thus when the admiral declared, in Adams's recollection, "that such was his gratitude and affection (for America) … that he felt for America as a brother, and, if America should fail, he should feel and lament it like the loss of a brother," Franklin, with that mocking bow and sly smile for which he was also famous, replied: "My Lord, we will do our utmost endeavors to save your lordship that mortification."

His affable manner somewhat bruised, Howe quickly pointed out that he could not receive his guests as representatives of Congress, for "upon the restoration of legal government" that body would, of course, cease to exist. He also assured the Americans that Britain coveted not her wealth but "her commerce, her strength, her men." At this, the frequently facetious Franklin, in a lamely joking allusion to the prolific American birthrate, responded: "Ay, my Lord, we have a considerable manufactory of men."

His lordship was not amused, quickly asking: "Is there no way of treading back this step of independency, and opening the door to a full negotiation?"

Franklin said there was not. Britain had decided to punish the Americans for trying to protect their liberties, and with this act, "all former attachment was *obliterated*" and only the force of arms would compel a return to the embrace of the Mother Country. Franklin also asked Howe if the Americans should make propositions to Great Britain would Howe be able to transmit them. Howe shook his head. He had no authority to treat with Congress or any Americans except in the character of British subjects. But the king and Parliament "were very favorable toward redressing the grievances and reforming the administration of the American colonies."

The delegates exchanged glances. Indeed? After a brief consultation, they told Howe through Adams that theirs was a "complete revolution" and that only the force of arms could induce them to accept British government again. With this, his charm all but vanished, Howe expressed his regrets, and his visitors withdrew.

If this limping conference had done anything, it had placed a severe strain on Lord Howe's affection for America, while delaying his brother's pursuit of George Washington.

Washington had saved his army, moving it safely to Manhattan in one of the most brilliant feats of his career. But in simplistic America a successful retreat under pursuit was still a defeat, and not, as a few military sophisticates, such as Nathaniel Greene and Henry Knox, might insist, the most difficult of military maneuvers. Congress was deeply alarmed, as were many of Washington's officers. As John Haslet, the capable colonel of the excellent Delaware Regiment, wrote to Caesar Rodney: "Would to heaven General Lee were here is the language of officers and men."

The commander in chief himself somewhat ungallantly placed much of the blame for the loss upon his men. "The militia," he wrote to Congress, "are dismayed, intractable and impatient to return home. Great numbers have gone off, in some instances by whole regiments … with the deepest concern I am obliged to confess my want of confidence with the generality of the troops."

Actually the men had fought much better than Washington had a right to expect, and if there were any fault to find, it should have been with their officers. True enough, the general could not point his finger at the officers without alienating commanders who were so badly needed and without further alarming a Congress that, henceforth in the war, would show a truly alarming propensity for flight, rather than fight. What Washington needed most was reliable staff officers. Colonel Scammell's near-disastrous misunderstanding of his chief's orders to General Mifflin had shown that clearly enough. What were needed were bright and brave young men, sturdy enough and healthy enough to go without sleep or shake off a cold and blessed with that rare, single-minded devotion to their chief. And even as Washington's spirits rose when his muster rolls showed that despite his losses at Long Island he still had about twenty thousand men at his command, he found the sort of aide-de-camp he sought in the person of Alexander Hamilton.

The pompous John Adams called him "the bastard brat of a Scots peddler," a well-known journalist named Callender scorned him as "the son of a camp girl" while Thomas Jefferson, who would be notorious in later years for his black mistress, branded him "a foreign bastard." Despite the hypocritical horror of these so charitable gentlemen, however, it was, as they well knew, a fact that the circumstances of Alexander Hamilton's birth were far from being unique during a morally indifferent age when bastardy was common on both sides of the Atlantic and matrimony even less sacred on the carefree islands of the West Indies in between.

Hamilton's mother was a French Huguenot named Rachel Fawcett, who, after three or four years of unhappy marriage to a Jewish merchant named John Levine on the island of St. Croix, fled to her parents' home. There she met James Hamilton, the son of a renowned Scottish family. Hamilton's personal charm was rivaled by his inability to earn a living, yet the beautiful Rachel became his lover. They took up residence on Nevis in the Leeward Islands, struggling on a small allowance from her parents, and on January 11, 1757, a son was born to them and named Alexander. A few years later another son named James was born. That was enough for his father, who quickly vanished, presumably still seeking that fortune that always eluded him. Crushed, Rachel and her two children returned to St. Croix to throw herself upon the merciful charity of her relatives.

The husband she had left was not quite so lenient. When Alexander was two, Levine obtained a divorce from Rachel on the grounds of abandonment and "profligacy" and was therefore, under Danish law, free to marry again, whereas Rachel, for her illicit union with Hamilton, was not. But abject poverty was not to be the little family's portion. Perhaps because of Rachel's striking and exotic beauty, she and her two little sons enjoyed the hospitality of two wealthy planters who were friends of her mother. Here Alexander grew up in the easy and gracious society of the Caribbean Creole aristocracy, and it was in these surroundings that this exquisite manners were formed. He also quickly astounded his schoolteacher—the Reverend Hugh Knox, a disciple of the celebrated Reverend Aaron Burr of the College of New Jersey in Princeton—by the quickness of his mind and his retentive memory. Always, it seemed to Knox, this little boy, with the noble forehead, reddish-sandy hair and large, violet eyes had his head bent over a book, and when he lifted his head, it sometimes seemed that he knew the book by heart. Quickly Knox conlcuded that he had been blessed with a prodigy. And so among the sighing palms and murmuring blue sea, in sun-kissed days and moonlit nights, happy with his books and schoolboy companions, Alexander's idyllic life continued—until suddenly, in February 1768, his mother died.

Alexander was crushed. At eleven years of age his world seemed to have ended, especially after merchant Levine successfully brought suit to recover Rachel's small fortune for "her legally begotten heir, Peter Levine." Now he was penniless, and quite aware of how his peculiar status might haunt him for the rest of his life. Yet, being small—at maturity he would stand about five feet, five inches—he was accustomed to taunts and challenges and had never yet retreated. Too proud to depend any longer on his grandmother's friends, he left school and went to work as a clerk in a trading company owned by Nicholas Cruger. The speed of the boy's perceptions and the rapidity with which he adapted to the shipping business, but, most of all, his calm and unshakable self-confidence, astounded Cruger. Like Knox, Cruger quickly realized that he had hired a prodigy. Alexander had also developed a keen insight into human nature. Some of his judgments of the characters of Cruger's ship captains were far from charitable, a cynicism not exactly pleasing in one so young. Yet, of one skipper who was about to sail through Spanish waters made dangerous by the presence of filibusterers and pirates, he told Cruger: "You cannot be too particular in your instructions to him. I think he seems to want experience in such voyages."

But even after he became Cruger's most valued employee and was proud to know that he could support himself and his brother, young Hamilton's ambitions soared high above the roof of a warehouse or the mast of a ship. He wanted to see something of the big world and to seek a bigger role in it—and his chance came after one of the most violent hurricanes in memory on August 31, 1772, cut a destructive path through the Virgin Islands, especially St. Croix. While others were bemoaning and bewailing their misfortune, Alexander seized his pen and composed a long and powerfully evocative account of the disaster, describing its endless roar and shriek, the flash of its lightning, the crashing of the trees and collapsing houses, the misery thereafter afflicting its victims who were left homeless and without food or water or the funeral corteges for those who lost their lives. The article was published in *The Royal Danish-American Gazette* of Christianstadt as the letter of an unknown correspondent, and its fame spread throughout the Virgin Islands, so that when the author's identity became known, a subscription was raised by the governor-general to send this worthy and precocious fifteen year old to America for an education he could never obtain in the islands. Thus, before the year was out Alexander had packed his belongings—including a box of books from Knox—and gone aboard one of Cruger's ships for the six-week voyage to Boston.

For this young Creole with the warm blood and the genteel airs, Boston's climate was too cold and the manners of its prim and proper Puritans too frigid, and he lost little time in journeying south for the more equable tempers and temperatures of New York City and New Jersey. His first stop was as as lodger in the New York home of a Cruger agent with the improbable name of Hercules Mulligan. But the atmosphere of trade no longer excited Hamilton, and he quickly followed the advice of Knox's friends to enroll in Dr. Francis Barber's grammar school in Elizabeth, New Jersey. There, with customary zeal and insight, he absorbed all that Barber had to offer within less than a year and by autumn of 1773 considered himself ready for Princeton. But that institution refused to permit Hamilton to move through classes at his own speed, as he requested, observing that a similar petition from little Aaron Burr at the age of eleven was rejected even though Burr's father was the college president. In a huff, Hamilton enrolled instead in King's College (now Columbia). New York.

At first, he was shocked and repelled by the ferment the Mother Country's taxing measures had produced. Above all, young Hamilton believed in law and order, and he could not abide the spectacle of the

Sons of Liberty, high on rum or beer, parading the streets in boisterous song, terrorizing Tories and sometimes doing violence to their persons or homes. Hamilton was too much of a conservative, satisfied with a settled order of things, to be revolutionary. He could not see, like Samuel Adams, that a revolution needs a mob. Gradually, however, as he listened to the litany of American discontent, he came to realize that the colonists were truly contesting tyranny. The arrival of General Gage with an army intended to ram British imperialism down colonial throats, with a bayonet if needed, put him solidly alongside the Sons of Liberty. Putting aside Locke and Aristotle, he studied books on military theory and tactics and organized a student corps at King's College. After Bunker Hill he was committed without reserve to the rebellion, and on March 14, 1775, at the edge of eighteen, he was selected captain of the New York Provincial Company of Artillery.

Zealous as ever, he trained his sixty-three men and four officers—all older than he was—like the martinet that a man of his orderly single-mindedness can often become, even spending the last of his subscription money for uniforms and equipment. When Washington marched into New York at the head of the Continental Army that had evicted Howe from Boston, he was among the ecstatic throngs that cheered the tall, powerfully built Virginian in the blue uniform. And soon after that, he, too, was marching with the Continentals.

Washington used the respite granted him by the peace talks to reorganize his army again, this time into three divisions. The first division, assigned to protect New York City, went to Israel Putman. Putman's obvious incompetence in assuming the Jamaica Pass had been blocked was overlooked by Washington, if only because "Old Put" had at least not got himself killed or captured. With Greene not yet recovered from malaria, command of the second, or middle, division was given to Joseph Spencer, a Massachusetts militia general whose only distinction seems to have been his pique at Congress for having voted him only one star while two went to Putman. Enraged, Spencer went home, but was persuaded for no better reason than the honor of the Bay State to return to service. Spencer's mission was to occupy Harlem at the northern end of Manhattan to prevent a British landing there. Another Massachusetts militiaman—William Heath—commanded the third division, assigned to hold King's Bridge, also at the northern end of Manhattan, and thus to keep open Washington's line of retreat. Heath's self-description "of middling stature, light complexion, very corpulent and bald-headed," does indeed suggest modesty, but he was still an amateurish general come only recently to the study of military history. He had been at Lexington, and with Dr. Joseph Warren, had failed to grasp the golden opportunity of cutting off the British retreat.

Putnam urged Washington to abandon New York City and concentrate on blocking the Hudson so that Admiral Howe could not transport his brother's army upriver. General Greene went further, wisely arguing for burning the city to deny the British winter quarters. But Washington was reluctant to abandon the city without at least the pretense of a fight, even though, as his grasp of the importance of sea power grew greater, he realized that its vulnerability to attack from water made it impossible to hold against a powerful fleet such as Howe's. But he knew that Congress would not take kindly to such a suggestion, especially the delegates from the middle colonies.

Then, as the weeks passed with General Howe still indolent across the East River, Washington undertook a shrewd letter-writing campaign, deliberately playing on the skittish nerves of Congress. Far from being the saintly chief of popular history who would rather suffer noble defeat than gain ignoble victory, he deliberately exaggerated his predicament, just as he had consciously belittled his soldiers as though to ensure his reputation against defeat or to magnify it in the event of victory. Certainly his position was most vulnerable. The British controlled both the Hudson and East rivers and could land at any point before Washington could concentrate against them. Now, in the interests of gaining approval to evacuate, he wrote: "It is now obvious that they mean to enclose us on the Island of New York, by taking post in our rear, while the shipping secures the front, and thus oblige us to fight them on their own terms, or surrender at [their] discretion." On September 8, in a masterful explanation of the kind of delaying war, never risking destruction, that circumstances compelled him to wage, he wrote: "On our side, the war should be defensive: it has been called a war of posts; we should on all occasions avoid a general action, and never [be] drawn into a necessity to put anything to risk. Persuaded that it would be presumptuous to draw out our young troops into open ground against their superiors in numbers and discipline, I have never spared the spade and pickaxe.... I am sensible that a retreating army is encircled with difficulties; that declining an engagement subjects a general to reproach; but when the fate of America may be at stake on the issue, we should protract the war, if possible. That the enemy mean to winter in New York, there can be no doubt; that they can drive us out, is equally clear; nothing seems to remain, but to determine the time of their taking possession."

Back came a complaisant if not puling reply from Congress: It was not Congress's intention "that the army or any part of it should remain in that city a moment longer than he shall think it proper." Washington had his carte blanche. He could retreat without "reproach" and, by extension, fight that delaying war that would one day earn him the sobriquet "Cunctator American."

On the other side of the East River criticism had also mounted against General William Howe. The same junior officers who were enraged by his failure to finish off Washington's beaten and demoralized army on Long Island were now openly urging him to move quickly so as not to lose his advantage over his still-reeling opponent. Among his sharpest—and most sarcastic—critics was Sir George Collier, commander of the frigate *Rainbow,* who, in addition to sneering at the "generous, merciful, forbearing" Howe, also said: "For many succeeding days did our brave veterans, consisting of twenty-two thousand men, stand on the banks of East River, like Moses on Mount Pisgah, looking at their promised land, a little more than half a mile distant." Others insisted that Howe's procrastination was born of their chief's native indolence or his sympathy for the Americans, and many modern historians have indeed made much of that statue to his dead brother in Westminster.

But neither of these charges was true. Howe's career had repeatedly shown his capacity to seize an advantage, and as a professional soldier seeking glory and promotion, it is highly unlikely that he would deliberately damage his reputation to satisfy some supposed fondness for the enemy. Moreover, the fiasco of the "peace conference" had dissipated whatever vestiges of his sympathy that had remained after Bunker Hill and his forced evacuation of Boston. No, William Howe was a loyal officer of the king, and what was perceived as his dilatoriness was only the reluctance of a professional who was schooled in the careful and cautious warfare of the eighteenth century. He would fully agree with a contemporary who wrote: "Battles have ever been the last resort of good generals.... The fighting of a battle only because the enemy is near, or from having no other plan of offense, is a direful way of making war." Howe had been trained in the war of maneuver, in which possession of territory or capitals was of more value than the destruction of enemy armies. For even in victory, the victor suffers. He loses men and arms—highly expensive military commodities—sometimes more than the loser, and thus battle is to be avoided. This was because these European wars were "the sport of kings," conflicts of dynasties seeking larger dominion or over boundaries. They were the "rosewater wars" that the great Clausewitz derided in the next century, regulated struggles with rules, precedents, traditions, the "proper" conduct of which was to maneuver for position, to occupy strategic points, to avoid battle unless success cheaply bought was certain—and, above all, to preserve one's army.

But unknown to both sides, the American Revolution had ushered in a new kind of conflict: the ideological war. Ordinary subjects or citizens—"the people"—were no longer indifferent bystanders or unhappy victims of the old kind of war but actually participants. They fought for an ideal: in this case, freedom. To achieve this shining goal, they suffered prodigies of misery and hardship that no professional European soldier would ever endure. Granted that in the customary military comparisons of training and discipline, arms and equipment, quarters and transport, they were woefully deficient. But they had a *spiritual* purpose, they were *motivated,* they had *morale,* and, as Napoleon said, in war the moral or spiritual is to the material as three is to one. Untrained and slothful soldiers, they would surely run, but most of them would always come back—something that could not be expected of the regular who was driven to desertion by fear of the noose and the lash. They were indeed a rabble in arms, but what a cause it was that ennobled them!

To ask William Howe to understand this would be asking too much of him and his top commanders and his successors. He simply did not understand what kind of a war he was fighting, that his own reluctance to seek decisive and costly battle exactly dovetailed with Washington's splendid insight into the necessity of a defensive stance: to survive and grow stronger and await that blessed day when Britain's traditional enemies—France and Spain—made common cause with America. True enough, for the Bourbons to do so would set loose the dreadful genie of democracy in Europe, but whoever said that the desire to injure a fellow king was not stronger than the will to make a mutual defense of monarchy? So William Howe, not even aware that he was fighting this new kind of war that would engulf Europe in another decade, had no precedents and no experience from such to guide him, simply because it had not occurred to him that they were needed. Why, then, relentlessly pursue a ragtail-and-bobtail army that obviously was about to burst at the seams? Why risk his precious soldiers to subdue a falling foe, why expose them to the rigors of warfare in a wilderness with a climate that was an alternating hell of heat and cold? Why not, rather, wait for the moment when a slight push, rather than a strong shove, would be all that was needed to topple this army of straw men? So Howe bided his time, meanwhile collecting flatboats until he had about eighty of them. By mid-September he was ready.

★ ★ ★

On September 13, four or five British frigates sailed up the East River, followed the next day by a half dozen more. Under their protection an amphibious assault force of about three thousand or four thousand redcoats was ferried from Long Island to Montressor's Island in the East River, and on Sunday the fifteenth, three more British warships sailed up the Hudson to cut off any American retreat. Washington, meanwhile, left Putnam with four thousand men to hold lower Manhattan while he set up his headquarters on Harlem Heights, where he expected the main enemy blow to fall. Other points also were fortified, one of them Kip's Bay in the vicinity of modern Thirty-fourth Street. Among the troops there was Private Joseph Martin.

Martin was not enchanted by the so-called line that his regiment was assigned to defend. It had obviously been scratched out as an afterthought. Nor did he welcome the order to leave his pack in a wood, knowing full well that he would never see it again. Burrowing in this ditch on the American left, he heard throughout the night, without any sense of assurance, repeated sentry cries of "All is well," preferring to believe the shouts of British sailors crying, "We'll alter your tune before tomorrow night!" At dawn he saw with awe the packed ranks of Hessian soldiers on the Long Island shore looking "like a clover field in full bloom." For some reason he decided to explore an abandoned warehouse, and as he browsed among the litter on its floor, "all of a sudden there came such a peal of thunder from the British shipping that I made a frog's leap for the ditch, and lay as still as I possibly could, and began to consider which part of my carcass was to come first." He had little time for such consideration, for with his comrades he rose and fled before the enemy in their approaching boats could put foot on New York soil.

General Washington, who had galloped to Kip's Bay the moment that he realized that it was the enemy's objective, rose in his stirrups in a fury at the flood of rear-bound men around him. "Take the walls!" he cried to his fleeing troops. "Take the cornfield!" But only a few obeyed. In a paroxysm of rage, Washington dashed his hat on the ground and bellowed: "Are these the men with whom I am to defend America?" He snapped his pistol at them, he beat them with his cane—privates, officers, even a colonel and brigadier general. But they kept running, flinging away muskets, knapsacks, even their coats and hats—anything that could slow down their flight from troops they had not even seen.

Washington sat his horse blinded with rage and despair. He paid no attention to a party of Hessians within eighty yards of him. He would have been killed or captured had not an aide seized his bridle and hurried him away.

Howe now had another opportunity. He might cut off Israel Putnam and four thousand men to the south if he plunged straight across the island. But he moved slowly again, not, as a charming legend suggests, because Mrs. Robert Murray beguiled him and his officers with cakes and wine while Putnam made his escape, but because he had obtained his first day's objective and was satisfied.

He had been right. The rabble would not fight. They would fly rather than face British regulars. Next day he would move north and bag or break them all.

★ 33 ★

THE RABBLE AROUSED/NEW YORK BURNS/NATHAN HALE

On September 16 Washington prepared to defend Harlem Heights against Howe, who had swung right, or north, to attack those entrenchments. The American commander had recovered his calm and was jubilant at the sight of so many of his soldiers flowing into his fortifications. He had feared that he had seen the last of many of them. Joseph Martin was among them, still sheepishly trying to forget his panic at Kip's Bay. He had headed inland and then swung north. Like his comrades, he was hungry and frightened, feeling his energy draining from him in the moist midday heat. They had to move cautiously, for there were British scouting parties everywhere, seeking to kill or capture the American stragglers. He trudged through the customary litter of battlefield retreat: "The ground was literally covered with arms, knapsacks, staves, coats, hats and old oil flasks," used to carry wine. At a small stream he knelt to drink, shocked to find that a man next to him drinking with his head in the water was actually cold and dead. Nearing Harlem, he took heart at the crowds of American soldiers converging on the position. The closer they came to General Washington, the more their drooping heads seemed to rise and their dejection to vanish, and it was the sight of them that raised the spirits of their chief.

Just before daybreak, Washington had sent Lieutenant Colonel Knowlton on a scouting mission with 150 Connecticut Rangers. At dawn the Rangers ran into two battalions of British light infantry and a unit from the famous Black Watch regiment. To the enemy's surprise, the American rabble did not flee but knelt to fire volley after volley into them.

Hearing the musketry, Washington sent his adjutant general, Colonel Joseph Reed, forward to investigate. Reed returned to report that Knowlton was successfully holding off a large enemy force. He suggested reinforcements and volunteered to lead them. Delighted, Washington consented.

While Reed advanced, Knowlton, seeing the Black Watch in their kilts trying to work around his flank, wisely withdrew. As he did, Reed saw the enemy's point advancing and heard the taunting bugle notes of a fox-hunter's call burst forth "in a most insulting manner." His men, who understood the contemptuous call, also reacted in rage. Reed led about 150 of them forward in a counterattack, aiming at the point of the enemy regiment, while with three companies of Virginia riflemen he sought to turn their flank. A fierce firefight ensued, bullet for bullet among the rocks and gullies and bushes. Now Washington fed in another eight hundred soldiers. They rushed eagerly forward and, said the amazed Reed, "Finding there was no stopping them, I went with them the new way—and in a few minutes our brave fellows mounted up the rocks and attacked them."

And the British ran!

They fled with the mocking American cries of "Halloo! Halloo!" resounding in their ears. Exhilarated, the Yankees pursued them, driving them backward like cattle thrashing through the brush. For a moment it seemed that the redcoats would be killed or captured. Some of them made a stand in a buckwheat field near present-day West 120th Street between Broadway and Riverside Drive. They would have been routed but for the arrival of a company of Hessian jaegers armed with two three-pound cannon. Firing off about sixty rounds, the Hessians saved the British light infantry from destruction. But once their ammunition was exhausted and they began to withdraw, the cocky Americans still pressed forward. In their exuberance the Americans might have charged full tilt into a large body of British reinforcements hurrying north under Lord Cornwallis. At that point, their delighted commander ordered them to withdraw into their own lines.

As battles go, Harlem Heights was but a skirmish, with about a hundred casualties on the British side and an unknown but far fewer number among the rebels. Among the dead was Colonel Knowlton, who died in Reed's arms speaking proudly of the bravery of his men. More important than the favorable casualty count was the psychological effect upon Washington's troops. The sight of their senior officers *leading*—not *urging*—them into battle had so inspired them that they had rushed bravely against the redcoats and sent them scrambling backward. The officers had done this consciously, realizing at last that "Follow me!" was a far more animating command than "Forward!" Even the British spoke openly of their surprise, a captured soldier admitting how shocked he had been when the Yankees did not flee as they had the day before. And a young British naval officer who had witnessed the two-hour battle returned to his warship gloomily convinced that now that the rebels were actually fighting, it would take years to subdue them.

Just as important in its effect upon the esprit of Washington's soldiers was the fact that Harlem was a *national* victory: all the troops from all the engaged colonies fought well, and for once the Southerners and Pennsylvanians stopped sneering at the "dastardly, cowardly" New England soldiers.

After that action, a shocked William Howe, still neglecting the opportunity to get onto the mainland to cut off Washington's army, contented himself with accepting the tumultuous acclaim of New York's numerous and overjoyed Tories.

The moment the redcoats marched into the town at the foot of Manhattan Island, they were overwhelmed by throngs of weeping, shouting Loyalists. Women as well as men carried British officers around on their shoulders. The rebel standard was torn down and trampled under foot and the king's hoisted in its place.

Then the witch-hunt began. Rebels or suspected rebels were rounded up, especially those who had been overheard to vow that they would set fire to the town rather than allow the British to occupy it.

In the early morning of September 21, by accident or design—history does not know—New York *was* burning. By the time the alarm was given, the fire was out of control. Whipped by high winds, flames believed to have begun in a shed near Whitehall Slip howled through street after street. Hovels went up, fine mansions, Dutch houses dating back to Peter Stuyvesant, wharves, churches—all collapsed and were consumed. Frenzied women and children were driven from house after house, until finally they could only lie down on the common, mingling their screams and shrieks with the cries and curses of the citizens and soldiers who had spilled outdoors to fight the blaze. But buckets were few and the supply of water was scanty, and the holocaust continued to spread, engulfing Trinity Church. Soon the church's steeple was "a lofty Pyramid of fire." Flames ate away the outer shingles, exposing timbers that quickly began to burn themselves. Finally, with a great hissing roar and a shower of sparks, the entire structure came crashing down.

Meanwhile, mob frenzy had overcome the Tories. They seized suspects and strung them up without trial. Some suspects were even thrown screaming into the flames.

At last, the wind changed and the fire was brought under control. What Nathanael Greene had wished and Congress had forbidden had come to pass. New York was gutted and of very little use to William Howe. Next day the angry general confronted an American officer who was accused of being a spy. The American had been captured on Long Island the night of the fire. His name was Nathan Hale. He was about twenty-four, well educated and completely composed as he admitted to Howe that he had been observing British troops movements for General Washington.

Howe curtly ordered him hanged without the grace of a trial. Hale asked for a clergyman. He was refused. He requested a Bible. He was turned down. A gallows was erected at what is now Fifty-second Street a bit east of First Avenue. The noose was slipped around Nathan Hale's neck. He stood there calmly, his light blue eyes betraying no inner fear, and said: "I only regret that I have but one life to lose for my country."

Then the noose tightened, and life passed from the body of the first martyr to the American fight for freedom.

★ 34 ★

THE BATTLE OF WHITE PLAINS

After Harlem Heights Washington again reorganized his army, this time into seven divisions under Generals Charles Lee, Greene, Heath, Putnam, Spencer, Benjamin Lincoln, Sullivan and Stirling, the last two having been exchanged and returned to duty. Lee commanded the largest division and, once again, much attention from his legion of admirers. He had been recalled from South Carolina by Congress and ordered to join—if the word was not actually "rescue"—Washington in New York.

Given credit for the successful defense of Charleston, over which he had excercised distant and minimal command, he was also admired for the brisk and thorough suppression of the Cherokee uprising on the Carolina and Virginia frontiers, another operation that he did not actually direct but that crowned his brow with laurels. Unknown to most members of Congress and Washington, however, the hawk had become a dove. He had astonished Senator Charles Carroll of Maryland—whom he had privately derided as a pussycat—by advising him to sue for peace, and told other influential politicians that they should send delegates to the Howes to talk peace. But Lee was still the darling of Washington's army, one officer writing his wife that the British soldier of fortune was worth ten thousand men. There were, however, a few dissenters from the Lee cult, among them an officer who wrote: "General Lee is hourly expected as if from heaven, with a legion of flaming swordsmen." Upon his arrival he did achieve the customary impact, striding everywhere breathing fire and advice while followed by the familiar pack of yapping dogs.

Lee began by urging Washington to abandon Manhattan Island and encouraging him to threaten Congress with his resignation if it continued to interefere with his plans—interesting advice when it is realized that the successor to the Virginian would doubtless be Charles Lee. Lee also persuaded a council of war to vote for retreat, even though Congress was firmly in favor of keeping the Hudson closed to enemy shipping. But Congress's position was made absurd after British warships successfully ran the batteries at Fort Lee on the New Jersey shore and Fort Washington on the New York side, also penetrating a famous blocking system of chains, booms and sunken hulks. With this setback, Washington decided to move north to the mainland in what is now Westchester County, leaving General Greene in Fort Lee with 3,500 to 4,000 men and Colonel Robert Magaw in Fort Washington with 1,500. With his main body of 14,500 soldiers, he began his northward march—and here once again he presented General Howe with an opportunity to destroy both him and the Revolution.

Even the best of armies is at its most vulnerable while on the march, with all the attendant confusion and close packing of troops and facing the extreme difficulty of deploying swiftly to meet an attack. Washington's retreat into Westchester County was a nightmare march conducted at a crawl. Without enough horses to haul wagons and guns, many cannon had to be pulled by hand. Even for so short a movement there was not enough food, and hunger was added to an ordeal already aggravated by the advent of colder weather.

Private Joseph Martin has left a graphic record of what the cooler nights meant to a rebel foot-slogger still dressed in thin summer clothing: "I have often while upon guard lain on one side until the upper side smarted with cold, then turned that side down to the place warmed by my body, and let the other side take its turn at smarting.... In the morning the ground was white as snow with hoar frost. Or perhaps it would rain all night like a flood; all that could be done in that case was to lie down (if one could lie down), take our musket in our arms and place the lock (firing device) between our thighs and 'weather it out!'"

Thus suffering and weary, Washington's long, exposed line of Continentals had to march past General Howe's powerful army, encamped only six miles away at Eastchester. And Howe did not move! In a single day he could have smashed the Americans beyond hope of putting the pieces together again. He might even have forestalled his opponent by moving to take possession of the high ground at White Plains. Instead, he marched languidly from Eastchester to New Rochelle, where he wasted three days, and then wasted another four at Mamaroneck, a bare two or three miles away, so that when he arrived at White Plains at the end of October, reinforced by 4,000 Hessians and 3,400 British under the German General William von Knyphausen, he found Washington holding all the high ground. In exasperation the British historian Trevelyan was to write: "The sun had set and risen more than forty times since General Howe broke up his cantonments on Staten Island. In seven weeks—with an irrestible army and a fleet which there was nothing to resist—he had traversed, from point to point, a distance of exactly thirty-five miles."

Howe was startled to find Washington so strong. It may be that he was following the American army at such a snail's pace because he was convinced that the men's misery and the psychological impact of a retreat would hasten its dissolution. Or he could just have been making certain that the enemy was fleeing north, thus leaving to him the rich granary of those plump Westchester farms with which to feed his army during the approaching winter quarters. Whatever the purpose of his deliberate speed, he was indeed displeased to find the Yankees so firmly entrenched above him.

The Americans, with their customary "magic" at the ends of their picks and shovels, had constructed a formidable position, about three miles of high ground with the left flank anchored on rough terrain and the right flank on the narrow valley and stream of the Bronx River. To the rear was the higher ground of Newcastle, to which Washington could retreat and that he blocked the enemy from seizing. And yet, because the position was so strong, and because Charles Lee and Israel Putnam were predicting disaster for Howe if he should attempt to storm it, the Americans were afflicted once again with a bad case of Bunker Hillism. Here again was to be that single culminating clash, that biblical Armageddon so dear to the hearts of all these Jonathans and Sauls, Seths and Samuels, these fierce Christian warriors out of the Old Testament, that Adjutant General Joseph Reed could write to his wife: "The business of this campaign, and probably the next, may probably be determined this week." Evidently, Howe's turning movement at Long Island had been completely forgotten, and the Americans once again expected him to do what they wanted him to do.

But then the Achilles' heel in the American defense was noticed by General Lee: Chatterton's Hill, a height about a half mile to the right, or east, of Washington's right flank across the narrow valley and stream of the Bronx River. It was a ridge about three-quarters of a mile long, rising 180 feet above the river and dominating the White Plains line so completely that if it fell to the British, that position simply could not be held. It was defended by about 1,600 men, including Haslet's fine Delaware Regiment, commanded by General Alexander McDougall. Even so, Lee felt it needed heavy reinforcements. Without them, he said to Washington, pointing to the higher Northcastle hills north of White Plains: "Yonder is the ground we ought to occupy."

Of course, but there was now no way that Washington could disengage in front of Howe's regulars of about equal strength, and before he could reluctantly reinforce Chatterton's Hill and thus weaken his main line, Howe, with about a third of his force of roughly fourteen thousand men, began attacking Chatterton's on October 27.

A preliminary artillery bombardment against the Americans almost won the day before the assault could begin. The first volley wounded a militiaman in the thigh, and the sight of blood spouting from his wound like a roman candle, together with the screams of the stricken soldier, so unnerved his comrades that they turned and fled. Fortunately, the gallant Haslet and his officers ran among the men, rallying them and leading them back to their lines. Now the oboes blew and the British and their hymn-singing Hessian allies swept up Chatterton's. It seemed that they would quickly overrun the Yankees, until cannonballs from two light artillery pieces directed by Alexander Hamilton fell among them with intimidating affect. Colonel William Smallwood's regiment sallied downhill to delay the enemy further. But the British were far from being halted, merely stopping to regroup and probe the American strength.

Private Joseph Plumb Martin, with his regiment supporting Haslet's, could see the British building a short bridge over the Bronx River, which was hardly more than a rivulet at that point. Soon the British wagons and artillery were moving over the bridge. Martin, crouching behind a stone wall, could see the enemy firing from the cover of an orchard about a hundred yards below him. Their musket balls spatted sharply against his protecting stones, sending splinters into the air—but harming no one. Each time one line of redcoats fired, they withdrew to lower ground to reload while another wave replaced them. It did not seem like very terrifying warfare, until the mournful oboes blew again and the green-coated Hessians came marching up the hill on the American left—their bayonets glittering in the sunlight, their high miters making them seem seven feet tall. Seeing themselves outnumbered, the Americans retreated. They did not flee or panic, as they did when that first enemy ball struck down their comrade, but they did move off rapidly "in a great body, neither running nor observing the best order." And that was the end at Chatterton's Hill. Howe's triumphant troops spent the night digging in at the height's summit, and watching their artillery fire plunge into the discomfited Americans below them. Solidly on Washington's flank, to an officer and a man, they expected to roll up the enemy in the morning and end the war.

But they stayed where they were. Colonel Charles Stuart, whose regiment helped take Chatterton's, was crushed: "We were ordered to encamp, to our astonishment, as the hill we had taken commanded the Rebel position. Moreover, not a shot was fired." The rebels, meanwhile, were suffering hideously and could have easily been swept aside. Lying on wet ground in the open and in their thin summer dress, without food or water, pelted by rain and then an early wet snow, many of them came down with severe colds—among them Joseph Martin. From his description of alternating seizures of chills and fever, it might be that he actually had malaria.

For three days Howe did nothing but construct batteries while awaiting reinforcements, presumably, like the Bunker Hillist Yankees, confident that his opponent would remain in place. But on the night of November 1, the "Old Fox," as Washington was beginning to be called, gathered his stores, his sick and wounded, and slipped away to Northcastle five miles to the north. Howe's chagrined officers were beside themselves with frustration as their foe marched clean away almost in plain view. Colonel Stuart wrote: "Is it through incapacity or by design of our Commander that so many great opportunities are let slip? I am inclined to adopt the latter." Another officer lamented: "O thou spirit of the Great Wolfe, the more I see, the more I think of thee, and the more I revere thy most sacred memory."

There was much more gnashing of teeth the following day after Howe remained immobile. His aide Lord Francis Rawdon explained his chief's failure to pursue as a wise decision based upon the well-known fact that the Yankees were "indefatigible in fortifying" a position. But Howe had not even bothered to reconnoiter Northcastle. If he had, he would have been incensed to find that the rebels were running a bluff: their "impregnable" fortifications were nothing more than heaped-up cornstalks covered with loose earth. So Howe lingered at White Plains for three more days, after which he led his army to Dobbs Ferry, on the east bank of the Hudson. There British ships, having broken the Yankee blockade of the Hudson, were able to supply him. Washington had once again saved his army, and this time, in an improvement over Long Island, his troops had been steadier and more responsive to his generalship. They had given more than they got: 130 Continentals killed and wounded against British losses of 230 killed and wounded.

Meanwhile, the generalship of William Howe received no accolades in London. Dismay that the decisive year of 1776, in which the most powerful army Britannia had ever assembled, supported by one of her most powerful fleets, was to crush forever this abominable Yankee impudence, was like its predecessor, ending in frustration, brought the brothers

Howe under much vilification, from which the word "treasonable" was not omitted. Years later, when he was asked by a House of Commons committee why he had not attacked the American right flank on October 28, he replied that he had "political reasons, and no other, for declining to explain." Cornwallis, a Whig like Howe who was there, concurred in this response. Was there, after all, another motive for William Howe's restraint? His tactics, as at Long Island, were flawless—like a boxer probing for his opponent's weakness. But then, finding it, there came no knockout punch. Could he as a Whig have hoped to exult in Tory defeat and the loss of the American colonies? Once again there is no certain explanation of his conduct. All that a historian can do is to ask the unanswerable question:

And Howe?

⋆ 35 ⋆

DISASTER AT FORT WASHINGTON

Although relieved by Howe's decision to return to New York, George Washington began to ponder his opponent's next move. He decided that Howe was going to invade New Jersey and perhaps also strike Fort Washington in northern Manhattan, the post across the Hudson opposite Fort Lee. So he divided his forces, leaving 11,000 men in Westchester under Charles Lee and marching with another 2,500 soldiers into New Jersey.

But he was still concerned about Fort Washington, with its garrison of two thousand men under Colonel Robert Magaw. Now known as Washington Heights, the fort had been christened Mount Washington by its defenders. Flanked by steep cliffs frowning above the Hudson and Harlem rivers, it was 230 feet high and about a mile long. Below it ran the road to Kings Bridge and mainland New York. Presumably its guns could command the Hudson and guard the rich produce of the Westchester farms. Actually, the British fleet had long since demonstrated its ability to traverse the Hudson with impunity, and Howe's army clearly could pick off Westchester whenever it chose—and Fort Washington along with it.

For all its strategic value and supposed strength, the fort was a military millstone around Washington's neck. It possessed no well, and water had to be hauled up from the Hudson. There were no bomb-proof trenches and no fuel, and sanitation was primitive at best. At first Washington decided to abandon it to save its men and valuable military stores, and he so informed General Greene, who commanded it, along with Fort

Lee. But then, in rare vacillation, he told Greene "to give such orders as to evacuating Mount Washington as you judge best."

It would seem that the clear-sighted Greene, having earlier given his chief the sagacious advice of not allowing himself to be trapped in New York City, would also have seen that the fort was untenable. But Greene in Fort Lee had been dubious about the reliability of his own Pennsylvania and New Jersey militia and thought that to abandon the post across the river would be construed by these jittery soldiers as another retreat—inducing many of them to head for home. So he decided to hold the fort, clinging to this resolution even after General von Knyphausen effectively surrounded it with six battalions of Hessians. Instead of trying to draw off his isolated garrison with all its precious arms, he reinforced it to a strength of about 2,600 men. On November 9 he told Washington: "I cannot conceive the garrison to be in any great danger. The men can be brought off at any time."

Washington, meanwhile, with his skimpy 2,500-man share of his army, had attempted to cross the lower Hudson into New Jersey, but was compelled by the presence of the British at the ferries there to march farther north to cross. This took three days, so that he did not arrive in Fort Lee until November 13. There he was dismayed to discover that the 5,000 Jersey militia he had expected to receive were actually no more than a handful. Greene's 3,500 and his own 2,500 now constituted his entire army—making the possible loss of those 2,600 cooped up in Fort Washington too great a risk to contemplate. But Greene was still eager to defend the fort, apparently, with all his practical sense of what was possible in war, having fallen under the influence of that Bashaw of Bunker Hill, Israel Putnam.

William Howe, meanwhile, was indeed preparing to assault the fort. He had detached three brigades under Lord Hugh Percy to assist Knyphausen in the attack, and had carefully laid his plans on information supplied by an American traitor—William Demont, an ensign in Colonel Magaw's Fifth Pennsylvania Regiment. Demont's motives in going over to the enemy are not exactly known, but he did furnish Howe with detailed plans of the fort. Howe saw that the east side of the redoubt had the skimpiest defensive positions, since the fort had been built to command the Hudson to the west. The north side was similarly weak, guarded by a hastily built position called Cock Hill Fort. What impressed Howe most was the disposition of Magaw's troops, now about three thousand soldiers crammed into a space designed for one third that number. Demont also told the British chief that the garrison had been ordered to fight "to the last extremity, having therein two months provisions, many cannon and plenty of ammunition"—a report that whetted Howe's appetite for booty.

So Knyphausen was ordered to take his Hessians against the fort from the weakest points: the east and north. Supporting attacks were to be launched by Lords Percy and Cornwallis from the south using both British light infantry, the Black Watch and more Hessians. On November 15, Howe sent an officer to the fort under a flag of truce to demand its surrender lest the entire garrison be "put to the sword." Magaw replied that he was determined to defend his post to the bitter end, rebuking his opponent's bloodthirsty terms with the remark: "I think it rather a mistake, than a settled purpose of General Howe, to act a part so unworthy of himself and the British nation."

Magaw also sent word of Howe's ultimatum to Greene and Putnam, bringing the generals rowing furiously across the river to inspect the post's defenses again. Strangely enough, they found them excellent. Upon their return they met Washington at midriver and assured him that "the troops were in high spirits and would make a good defense."

At dawn next day Washington, Greene and Putnam, along with General Hugh Mercer, again crossed the Hudson and struggled up the heights, only to hear the sound of bombardment and then the ragged rattle of musketry. The British attack had begun, there was now no chance to withdraw the garrison, and the four generals returned to Fort Lee.

As was worthy of a tactician as skillful as William Howe, the assault was a masterpiece. Actually it was an amphibious operation, some thirteen thousand soldiers having to cross both the Harlem and Hudson rivers in flatboats or transports before they could begin clawing their way up the heights. Knyphausen's Hessians, although striking at the weakest point, had to move over the most difficult terrain. At first they faced near-vertical cliffs. When Colonel Johann Rall shouted to his men, "All you that are my grenadiers, march forwards" the oboes blew once more and the Germans swept forward eagerly chanting their hymns. Gradually, the music and song subsided until it was no longer audible, for the attackers could not waste their breath while clutching at stones and bushes for handholds as they struggled upward under a withering fire. Even Knyphausen had to endure this ordeal. Most of the American fire came from Pennsylvania riflemen at the clifftops. At first the riflemen took a terrible toll, but then their fire slackened, for their beautiful hunting rifles with their narrow tapering barrels were not designed for sustained fire, and the sharpshooters from the Keystone State, without the hunter's customary leisure to clean his weapon, soon were fighting with clogged rifles. Gradually, the

Germans prevailed, easily turning Cock Hill Fort and then, with Knyphausen and Rall converging, moving against the main American position at the top of the ravine. Americans trying to surrender were granted no quarter but the cold steel of a Hessian bayonet.

Percy's and Cornwallis's forces successfully landed in the south from British transports in the Harlem River. Militia posted to defend the riverbank fled after their commander was killed. But other rebels on Laurel Hill resisted with heavy fire—only to be driven back into the Fort Washington redoubt. With Howe's three-sided front moving inexorably against almost three thousand Americans packed into their fort like cattle in a pen, Knyphausen decided to demand the fort's surrender. He ordered a captain to tie a white handkerchief to a musket barrel and advance upon the fort waving this flag of parley preceded by a drummer boy. And the Americans fired upon them! Luckily the Yankees were poor shots, for if they had cut down these unarmed emissaries whose persons were sacred under all the rules of war, it is likely that Fort Washington would have become the bloody graveyard of its garrison.

Colonel Magaw was very much aware of his peril when confronted by the enemy captain. Planning to escape that night with most of his men, he asked for a five-hour truce. The captain said no. A half hour. That was all. Otherwise the massacre would commence. With a sigh, Magaw surrendered. All his survivors—American losses were only 130 killed and wounded against 128 for the British and 326 for the Hessians—so that Howe's bag was nearly 3,000 soldiers, 161 cannons, 400,000 cartridges, two months' provisions and, of course, the rebel soldiers' weapons.

The Americans very nearly lost their own lives and then their uniforms, after the Hessians, enraged by their heavy losses, came at them with their bayonets. The Germans were restrained only with difficulty, and even then, the prisoners had to be detoured around these loot-seeking mercenaries—one of the conditions of their employment—to keep their clothes on their backs. Why their allies sought to strip these ragged "soldiers" puzzled the British, who could not look upon their captives—many of them boys and old men—without laughing aloud.

And so George Washington, so often a decisive war chief, was forced, by his vacillation, into a battle he should never have fought, losing precious men and munitions at a time when his army had sunk to its nadir in numbers and esprit. True enough, Greene had always been clear sighted, but his fears of what his jittery troops would think of another abandoned post clouded his judgment, while Putnam's bravado led him to fall another victim of Bunker Hillism.

Probably the most corrosive consequence of Fort Washington was the loss of confidence in Washington among his most valued officers. That same Adjutant General Joseph Reed, himself infected with the Bunker Hill virus, wrote to General Charles Lee in Westchester: "I do not mean to flatter, nor praise you at the expense of any other, but I confess I do think that it is entirely owing to you that this army, and the liberties of America so far as they are dependent on it, are not totally cut off. You have decision, a quality often wanting in minds otherwise valuable."

Reed's letter was like balm on Lee's bruised ego, still smarting from an unpleasant confrontation with his Massachusetts militia. Claiming their enlistments had expired, they said they were going home, but Lee, in his customary abusive and bullying style, sought to dissuade their leaders by calling them "enemies and pests to their country." Not surprisingly, they led their men back to the Bay State—leaving Lee bereft of half his command. Reed's missive also suggested to Lee that the time might be ripe to peel George Washington a bit, and he wrote to Congressman Benjamin Rush: "The affair at Fort Washington cannot surprise you in Philadelphia, more than it amazed and stunned me. I must entreat that you will keep what I say to yourself; but I foresaw, predicted, all that happened. ... My last words to the General were—Draw off the garrison, or they will be lost." Next, having chipped away at his chief, he sought to inflate himself with the words: "Had I the powers I could do you much good—might I but dictate one week—but I am sure you will never give any man the necessary power—did none of the Congress ever read Roman history?"

At his headquarters in Hackensack near Fort Lee, a soul-sick Washington was engaged in writing a litany of lamentation to his brother Jack, beginning: "I am weary almost to death with the retrograde motion of things." There followed a dolorous recital of the wrongs done to him: Congress had not listened to his complaints about the quality of his soldiers and had given him feckless scarecrows to command, his officers had ignored his advice or had ill-advised him, the various states were quarreling over commissions and nominating as officers men "not fit to be shoeblacks" and within two weeks he would not have more than two thousand regulars on the New Jersey side of the Hudson to oppose Howe's mighty host "and very little more on the other to secure the eastern colonies and the important passes leading through the Highlands to Albany."

Although Washington's catalog of complaints was intended only for the private eyes of his brother, it is still not pretty for posterity to behold. But then, only the statue of marble and bronze given us by some of the great man's pious hagiographers could have been indifferent to the unmitigated march of disaster begun with his unwise decision to follow Congress's mandate to defend New York. Nearly 4,500 Americans had been taken captive, thousands more—the exact number is not known since most were militia—died of disease and another 600 had been killed or wounded. Worse, from a commander in chief's viewpoint, were those thousands of militiamen—most of them from Massachusetts, Connecticut and New York—who had simply quit the war, going home to recite their own doleful jeremiads and thus infect their neighbors with their defeatism and conviction that the worst place a man could be was in the ranks of the Continental Army. Losses in matériel were just as daunting: 219 cannon captured, along with thousands of tents, entrenching tools and other military equipment that, given the low state of Yankee industry and a foolish attempt to try to finance a war with printing presses, could not be replaced. All that remained of the defenses of New York was the pathetic earthwork, once called Fort Constitution but then renamed in honor of the great man from England: Charles Lee. However, there were still men and arms of some value there, and the still-vacillating Washington, probably despairing of informing Congress of still another retrograde movement, waited three days before ordering its evacuation, thus giving William Howe the opportunity to demonstrate that he was not always a dilatory commander. The day after the fall of Fort Washington, he sent Cornwallis with six thousand men across the Hudson to take Fort Lee.

Nathanael Greene had begun to carry out Washington's withdrawal orders, when, early on the morning of November 20, an excited farmer burst into his headquarters to report that strong British force had crossed the Hudson at Dobbs Ferry and was marching on the fort. At once Greene sent a messenger galloping off to Washington to ask what to do. Back came Washington himself, even more excited than the farmer, but now at last the decisive leader of old. Form your men, he told Greene, and retreat—instantly. If the British seize that one bridge over the Hackensack, we are all lost. Do not tarry, the chief said, calm and confident in demeanor again. There is no time to strike a tent or douse a fire. Let the men take from their pots what they can, and let nothing go onto the wagons but arms and ammunition.

Now the militiamen of New York and Pennsylvania—especially the Keystone Staters who had lost so many friends at Fort Washington—turned surly. They didn't like missing a meal. Ignoring the orders to fall out, perhaps three or four hundred of them broke into the fort's rum supplies and got rapidly and hopelessly drunk. Washington ignored them. He formed a column and left them behind, heading for the Hackensack Bridge. En route they passed through the waving tan fox tails of the Jersey Meadows and saw a herd of thousands of moo-ing cattle coming toward them. They came from farms in eastern Pennsylvania and West Jersey and were intended for the Fort Lee garrison. But they would feed the British instead.

A few hours later Nathanael Greene rode back to Fort Lee to round up the drunks. He ordered them to fall in and head for the bridge. Most of them did, but about a hundred of them ran into the woods. Some of them staggered back to camp in search of more refreshments. When Cornwallis's light infantry burst through the fort's gates with leveled bayonets and loaded muskets, they found a dozen of these intrepid Yankee Doodles lying on the ground—dead drunk.

In command of himself, as well as of his army at last, George Washington became living proof of Napoleon's dictum that adversity is the school of the good soldier. Grim faced and silent, he led his escaping column slowly south through New Jersey. Moving in slow misery, they slogged over roads that cold and heavy fall rains had turned into a slop of mud. Again and again Washington got off despatches to Lee in Northcastle, urging him to join him with the main body. Desertions were melting his force like powder in the rain. He was down to barely three thousand men. If Lee could come down and gather up intervening units, Washington might have ten thousand men—at least on paper. But Lee, for reasons of his own, did not move.

Onward, in alternating fury and despair, Washington led his wretched scarecrows. With the oncoming raw cold of a northern winter they suffered more. Through the Watchung Mountains they trudged, into Newark, out of it ... into New Brunswick, and away again with Cornwallis nipping at their heels. Behind them, the numerous Tories of New Jersey were breaking out their British flags and welcoming their "saviors" in red coats. Into Trenton the rebels dragged their long tails of retreat. Washington began collecting all the boats on the Delaware, even as Congress prepared to flee from Philadelphia to Baltimore.

It was Howe who was on Washington's heels now, and he was dallying as usual. He might have gotten to the Delaware ahead of Washington, but his men did not enter Trenton until the last Americans were crossing the river.

Safe on the other side, George Washington fired off letter after imploring letter to Charles Lee. All depended on Lee bringing his troops south from New York. In another few weeks enlistments in the Continental Army would expire. The outlook was at its darkest. Pennsylvania had sent him only a few thousand men and New Jersey almost none. If the army was not quickly replenished, the general wrote to his cousin Lund Washington, "I think the game will be pretty well up."

★ 36 ★

"ADMIRAL" ARNOLD SAVES THE CAUSE

George Washington's decision to march south not only left what is today called the New York Metropolitan Area in the hands of General Howe, it also presented the British commander with the opportunity to march farther north to meet Generals Sir Guy Carleton and John Burgoyne coming down from Canada. If the three generals were to join in Albany, the junction would probably take New York State, with its numerous Tories, out of the war and isolate New England from its sisters to the south, so that unable to support each other, the colonies would be subdued one by one. In a word, the Revolution would be crushed.

There were only about 3,500 soldiers in northern New York between Carleton—as governor-general of Canada the overall commander—and this fatal linkup. But these were mainly the ragged scarecrows who had survived the disastrous invasion of Canada in 1775. As Colonel "Mad" Anthony Wayne said of his Pennsylvanians, they were still "destitute of almost every necessary fit for a soldier," and of his original command of two thousand, barely nine hundred were still alive. Even worse this army of ragamuffins, gathered around Fort Ticonderoga, was riven by dissension at the top.

Congress had named Major General Horatio Gates to command the Canadian army, replacing the feckless John Sullivan. But Major General Philip Schuyler, who was in charge of the northern department, insisted that he was senior and Gates was now second in command. Between the two men there was really little to choose. Schuyler, scion of one of those immensely wealthy Dutch patroon families of the Hudson

River Valley, was an aristocrat possessed of real organizing skill and business acumen, but a man fit more for the counsel table than for command on a battlefield. Gates, a large man who had served in the British Army, was perhaps proof that the Almighty is a practical joker, creating such compounds of consummate ambition and limited capacity. Between Schuyler and Gates, their feud divided this pathetic army. Schuyler as a wealthy New Yorker was unjustly suspected of Tory sympathy, Gates was justly suspected of intrigue and currying favor. Both were severely criticized for the retrograde movement from Crown Point to Ticonderoga, each insisting that the decision to retreat was born in the other general's brain. Of the two Schuyler was undoubtedly the most honorable—although he protested his devotion to it perhaps a shade too much—and he did bring off the diplomatic coup of persuading the Iroquois, the most powerful and warlike confederation of Indians in North America, to forsake their British allies and remain neutral in the coming struggle. He did so by entertaining the sachems of the Five Nations—as they were also known—at German Flats with lavish gifts, mountains of food and rivers of rum.

The alarmed British responded by enrolling in their cause Joseph Brant, an influential half-breed of the Mohawk Nation, who was believed to be the bastard son of the late Sir William Johnson, the powerful Indian agent who was also known as "the Great White Father" of the Iroquois. In 1776 Brant had gone to London to protest Carleton's humane policy of refusing to enlist the Iroquois and the Canadian tribes in the war against the Americans. Carleton's experience with Indians had taught him that their primitive tactics of pounce and withdraw might qualify them for ravaging border settlements, but gave them no stomach for conventional or "civilized" warfare, with its artillery, forts, casualties, discipline—and no scalps. But Lord George Germain, hating Carleton with his customary ferocity, quickly embraced Brant as a means of discrediting his detested Canadian chief, introducing him to a fawning cabinet, presenting him to a smiling king, showering him with gifts and having him painted in full warpath regalia by George Romney and Sir Joshua Reynolds. Returning home, Brant aroused the Iroquois villages with his bloodthirsty speeches in which he attacked Americans as the enemies of all Indians. Thus, to the Patriots' fear of that fatal Albany linkup between Howe and Carleton was added the return of that recurrent dread of the midnight raid, the war whoop—and the tomahawk in the brain.

However, this was also a unifying terror that had the effect of compelling the quarrelling American chiefs to put aside their vendetta. When they did, they realized that control of Lake Champlain meant the difference between victory or defeat in the north. Throughout the summer the British, with their unrivaled understanding of the importance of sea power, had been building a fleet for just that purpose. Carleton was aware that the 135-mile-long Lake Champlain was a straight, watery road to Fort Ticonderoga at its foot. For a modern army to march along its rocky, forested, swampy shores was just not possible. So the obvious solution was to build a fleet, one so powerful that it would sweep the rag-tag-and-bobtail American landlubbers off the lake. And Carleton had the money and the Royal Navy to help him do so. From the British fleet on the St. Lawrence he would receive the skillful craftsmen to build his ships and the veteran seamen to sail them. Also, at his shipyard at St. John's he had Captain Thomas Pringle of the Royal Navy to supervise construction using seasoned timber shipped inland from Montreal and Quebec, together with the necessary naval stores and guns. Carleton sought absolute superiority: no less than 24 gunboats, each armed with a single but heavy gun, ranging from 9- to 24-pounders; 2 schooners, the *Maria* and the *Carleton,* mounting 14 and 12 6-pounders, respectively; the huge raft *Thunderer,* armed with 6 24-pounders, 6 12-pounders and 2 howitzers; plus the full-rigged *Inflexible,* built expressly for maneuver on the narrow lake. *Inflexible* mounted no less than 18 12-pounders. To this fleet was added 680 batteaux or flatbottom boats to transport nearly sixteen thousand troops.

Who could resist such an armada? Certainly not the forces at the command of Schuyler-Gage: a woebegone army of 3,400 shadow-soldiers motivated by a spirit of defeatism—and no fleet. But someone had to attempt it, and Gage and Schuyler finally agreed that there was only one man in that army bold enough, brave enough, determined enough and salty enough to undertake it. He might also be the most hated man in that army, but there was no one else—and that was how Brigadier General Benedict Arnold became an "admiral."

Arnold was not only an admiral without a fleet; if he were to build one, he would have no sailors to man it. One of his first acts had been to send agents into New England to recruit seamen. But they returned with only a few sorry specimens and the explanation that anyone under sixty who was familiar with rope or sail and the smell of salt had shipped aboard or was shipping aboard a privateer where his share of the prize money would make him quickly rich. For seamen he had to draft soldiers from the Ticonderoga army, few of them, he growled, "ever wet with salt water." His "Marines" for the fighting tops were worse: "the refuse of every regiment."

But the men had the virtue of being there, whereas the wherewithal to build ships was not. There was absolutely no seasoned timber available at Arnold's shipyard at Skenesborough (now Whitehall) on the southern shore of Lake Champlain. Only green lumber from trees recently cut—wood that would warp and leak—could be had. Also wanting was every available kind of naval stores: sailcloth with twine to sew it, tar, sheepskins for sponges and two hundred swivel guns, as well as 9-, 12-, 18- and 24-pounders with their ammunition. All these stores were forwarded by the hardworking Schuyler, whose practical businessman's sense proved to be invaluable. From him also came a stream of blacksmiths, carpenters and shipwrights, along with the tools of their trade. There was even a contingent of fifty carpenters from Rhode Island, who had actually been ordered to Skenesborough by the Continental Congress. More persuasive than the delegates at Philadelphia was their daily pay: an astronomical five dollars a day, but in specie, not Continental paper—for without hard money the Rhode Islanders threatened to go home.

Arnold was everywhere at Skenesborough, energetic and driving, ingenious and innovative as ever. Each crisis seemed to make his hard blue eyes harder. Like a true leader of men, he seemed to thrive on adversity. His eyes never swerved from the objective of denying the enemy the lake and Ticonderoga, and in the single-mindedness that is another virtue of the gift of command, he rode roughshod over everyone who did not share his dedication. In this, the defect of his virtue of determination was the vice of ruthlessness, and so he made many more enemies who would combine to oppose him in the distant future. But for the moment in that momentous summer of 1776, he was the admiral, and he not only built his own fleet, but designed his own ships. These were gondolas and row galleys that might well have been modeled on those ancient galleys of Spain and Ottoman Turkey that fought the great Battle of Lepanto in 1570, when Don Juan of Austria saved Judeo-Christian civilization from being destroyed by the Moslem Turks of Süleyman the Magnificent. Crude and primitive, they were intended for a special place and time: narrow, shallow Lake Champlain and for battle before the November storms could sink them. There were the "gundelos," or gondolas, flatbottom, open boats, fifty or sixty feet in length and fifteen feet in the beam. Power came from two square sails on a sixty-foot mast and eight oars to a side. A single twelve-pounder was mounted on the bow with a nine-pounder on each side amidships. In the stern was a ten-foot platform for officers and helmsman. The row galleys were longer, up to seventy-two feet. Each had two masts, rigged with a high-pointed lateen sail. With six to eight cannon and twenty-eight oars, they required a crew of eighty sailors. By September Arnold had a total of five new galleys and eight gondolas constructed, and to them were added three schooners and a sloop captured from the British.

At first Arnold sailed to the head of the lake to take up a battle position across its mile-wide channel. British artillery forced him to retreat a few miles. But then, with typical forethought, he sent out patrols to discover just how powerful a fleet he was challenging. From two captured British soldiers he learned, to his dismay, that the enemy was assembling the broken-down parts of a warship so heavily gunned that it alone could blast his little green-wood flotilla into matchwood. This was the *Inflexible.*

A supreme realist, Arnold saw at once that he must assume a defensive stance, and he retreated down the lake, searching for a natural bastion in which to deploy his fleet. He found it at Valcour Island, about halfway down Champlain and close to its mainland shore near present-day Plattsburg. Valcour was rocky and heavily wooded, with a channel between it and the mainland about three miles long. At its northern end rocks and shoals made it impenetrable by warships, but to the south its waters were clear and deep. With the north end thus closed to the British, Arnold positioned his fleets across the channel's southern mouth. Thus his rear was protected and there was no chance for double envelopment. Carleton must strike his front. With his knowledge of Champlain's winds, Arnold knew that the British must sail into the prevailing north wind. So he ordered his captains to devise a network of anchor cables that would enable them to maneuver rapidly, so that as the British struggled ship by ship against the wind, they would blunder into this system and be destroyed piecemeal. Fearing that sharpshooters from the close western shore might riddle his seamen, Arnold had shields of pine and cedar planking built around their decks. Thus he did everything in his power to reduce the enemy's advantage of a superior fleet, while Carleton, through his innate caution, made just one mistake that was critical enough to diminish it further.

Carleton's officers were most anxious to close with Arnold in September, before an early winter could end the campaigning season. If they struck in September, there might be as many as sixty days in which to take Ticonderoga and move on to Albany. If they waited, "General Winter" would whittle their superiority with storms, ice and snow. All their ships were ready but *Inflexible,* and mighty though she might be, she was not worth waiting for. The available ships and guns could easily handle the upstart little American fleet. Carleton refused to move. He thought

Arnold's fleet was stronger than his officers calculated. He was also, like the Howes, reluctant to crush the Americans. His policy was to reestablish the authority of the Mother Country and wait for the rebels to ask for negotiations. How much this attitude influenced his decision to wait until *Inflexible* was ready to sail is not exactly known, but it certainly had to have affected his judgment. If Burgoyne had been in command, he certainly would not have delayed, but Carleton waited four weeks until *Inflexible* was put together, and thus it was not until October 5 that the British fleet sailed.

Led by this powerful ship, the armada slipped down the Richelieu River, past Ile-aux-Nois into Lake Champlain. It was followed by hundreds of Indians in war paint, paddling huge birchbark canoes holding thirty braves apiece. Next came the soldiers in 680 flatbottom boats, the white and scarlet of their uniforms bright against the riotous foliage of the early northern autumn. At dawn of October 11, 1776, they were off Valcour Island.

Shivering in an icy northern wind, the Americans at Valcour gasped at the sight of the powerful enemy fleet approaching, their sails whipping in the wind. Then, to their astonishment, the enemy ships sailed right by! They had not seen them! To Arnold, the moment of opportunity had come. As soon as *Inflexible* and the formidable gun raft *Thunderer* were well past the mouth of the channel, he ordered the schooner *Royal Savage* and three row galleys to attack the lesser British ships. As the American ships moved cautiously out of the bay, Arnold, standing on the deck of his flagship *Congress,* began counting enemy gunboats. He was shocked. Twenty-four of them! Three or four times as many as he had anticipated. So many of them could surround his ships like a pack of snarling dogs and rip them apart. Concerned, Arnold signaled for a return to the channel. The row galleys obeyed, but *Royal Savage* was also having trouble coming about in that hostile wind. A dozen gunboats came baying at her, so terrifying her crew that they ran her aground on Valcour's southern tip, jumping overboard to swim or wade for the safety of the island shore.

Hearing the cannon fire, Carleton and Captain Pringle put about with *Inflexible* and *Thunderer,* making for the helpless *Royal Savage.* But they made little progress, sailing into that bitter downwind with wildly flapping sails. *Maria* was also crawling. Only *Carleton* could close to within firing range. Her commander, Lieutenant James Richard Dacres, was a typically arrogant British naval officer, so contemptuous of the Americans that he presumed to take on their entire fleet. The Americans pummeled his ship, cleverly making use of their anchor cables to embrace him in a deadly arc. *Carleton* was staggered, and Dacres was knocked unconscious by a falling spar. Only the brave and heady intervention of nineteen-year-old Midshipman Edward Pellew saved the *Carleton* from sinking. Pellew crawled out on the bowsprit amid flying lead and steel to fashion a jib sail. Still his ship gained no power, and it was only after hawsers were thrown to him from approaching longboats that *Carleton* could be towed out of danger.

In the wind, clumsy *Thunderer* was about as maneuverable as a loggerhead turtle. Unable to bring her within range of *Royal Savage,* her infuriated sailors piled into longboats and rowed to the American ship, clambering aboard her. At that point *Royal Savage's* crewmen on Valcour splashed out to their vessel to board her and rout her British conquerors. Next cannon balls from the British gunboats drove the Americans ashore again. Again the Americans sought to recapture their ships, but another boarding party from *Maria,* wielding cutlasses, drove them off once more.

Aboard *Congress* Benedict Arnold was in a fury of command. His hair was singed, his face blackened by gunpowder, yet he dashed limping from gun to gun, aiming and firing his nine- and twelve-pounders. No one else helped him because no one else knew how to fire a cannon. Now the ferocity of the battle rose in crescendo, the roar of the guns reverberating around Valcour's rock cliffs 180 feet high to create such an iron clanging that many of the dazed seamen of both sides thought that their heads were encased in a giant kettledrum. *Congress* was rocked again and again by British twelve-pound balls. Her decks were slippery with blood, while the screams of her stricken crewmen seemed to counterpoint the pounding of the kettledrum like wild violins. Running beneath the symphony were the howls and whoops of the British Indians on the mainland.

For six hours—from half-past twelve until dark—the battle raged, with scarcely an American ship that still had half its officers active. Exposed as they were on their platforms, they were easy targets. Aboard the galley *Brigadier General Washington,* David Waterbury was the only officer still on his feet. Faint cheers arose from the Americans when a lucky shot hit a gunboat's ammunition locker and blew the ship apart. But there was only silence when *Inflexible* at last came within range. Her first broadsides were aimed at *Congress,* staggering her and leaving her decks awash in blood. The gondola *Philadelphia* seemed to be sinking, and *Washington* was barely able to stay afloat. But then the light began to fade from the autumn sky. Within a few swift minutes, the guns fell silent—and the first phase of the Battle of Valcour Island came to a close.

★ ★ ★

That night Sir Guy Carleton was confident that on the morrow quick victory would be his. The American ships were floating wrecks and needed but a few more balls to put them under. Moreover, his troops and Indian allies had occupied not only Valcour Island itself, but the Champlain shore as well: even if the Yankees abandoned their ships, they could not escape overland. To prevent the American ships from slipping out of the channel, Captain Pringle had formed his ships in a crescent around its mouth.

At a council of war aboard *Congress,* the rebel cause seemed bleak, indeed. From every ship came reports of near-exhausted supplies of ammunition and powder. *Philadelphia* had sunk. Aboard the gondola *New York* every officer but the captain was dead. Even as the Americans conferred, they could hear the chilling cries of Carleton's Indians issuing out of the dark. Suddenly that darkness erupted in flashing light followed by a terrible roar. The British, fearing that the Americans might reboard *Royal Savage,* had sent a demolition party to blow her up. Flickering flames were now visible, but then, gradually, they were obscured by a fog rising from the lake. As it thickened, a desperate plan formed in the mind of Benedict Arnold. Escape! Speaking rapidly, he convinced his captains that under cover of the fog they could slip through the British blockade. They agreed. Hooded lanterns in canvas sacks were hung at the stern of each ship. Oarlocks were greased and muffled with rags. Every rope passing through blocks and pulleys was also greased. With the galley *Trumbull* leading and *Washington* and *Congress* bringing up the rear, the battered fleet made silently for open water on the British left.

Through the fog the tense Americans could see the eerie glow of the burning *Royal Savage.* They heard the wham of hammers and the whine of saws as the British ship's carpenters worked desperately to repair their battered ships. Mercifully, there were no other sounds. No hoarse challenges, no strident warnings as the unseen rebels moved slowly through the gap and downlake eight miles to Schuyler's Island, where they anchored to repair their own wrecks.

When the mists of a foggy dawn were finally shredded by a north wind at the mouth of the channel, incredulous British seamen stared at the empty waters of the channel. The bird had flown! Aware that the fleeing Yankees certainly would not be heading north, even if they could sail against that stiff wind, Carleton at once upped his anchors and bore south. They very wind was now his ally, sending his vessels skimming down the lake while his prey was delayed by a southerly breeze.

In dismay the stalled Americans watched their enemy, led by mighty

Inflexible, bearing down on them inexorably. At eleven o'clock the British opened fire. Arnold ordered his helmsman to come about and signaled *Washington* to join him. Together Arnold and General Waterbury bravely held off the entire enemy fleet, hoping to gain time for the other ships to escape. *Washington* was pounded so severely that Waterbury was at last compelled to strike his colors. Now Carleton's fleet turned on *Congress.* She could not possibly survive such a fierce rain of metal. Yet Arnold fought on, limping from gun to gun, bellowing orders and pulling lanyards. Long-range support came from four gondolas that were too waterlogged to get under way. Then a providential hole opened in the British ring. Arnold made for it, signaling to the gondolas to follow. Forced once again to sail against the wind, the British could not pursue, and the Americans rowed safely to Buttonmould Bay, ten miles from Crown Point. Here they put arms and ammunition ashore and burned their ships, Arnold personally putting the torch to *Congress.* Burying their dead, they shouldered their wounded and struck off through the forest until they joined their five remaining ships at a point opposite Crown Point, after which they crossed the lake, where Arnold ordered the buildings that were still standing in the abandoned fort burned to the ground.

Finally, exhausted, they staggered into the sanctuary of Ticonderoga. They were not warmly greeted, for they seemed to be the survivors of a beaten fleet. Arnold was pilloried by those colonels he had alienated as an incompetent blunderer who was responsible for all the northern disasters, of which Valcour Island was the most recent proof. Of his gallantry and perseverence, the Patriots to the south heard little, nor did they hear of the bravery of his ragtag-and-bobtail soldiers. But the true proof of their valor and their actual success was contained in a report from Sir Guy Carleton to Lord George Germain: "The season is so far advanced that I cannot yet pretend to Your Lordship whether anything further can be done this year." In fact, nothing was done, much as Burgoyne and other officers might fume and argue heatedly that Ticonderoga must be taken and a march to Albany begun. Carleton knew the north too well. Even though he did move toward Ticonderoga, coming within three miles of it on October 28, he did not submit to Burgoyne's insistence that he at least probe its defenses. Within a few days the fierce November storms might be lashing the lake into a fury of white caps into which no canoe or open boat could venture. Next would come the snow and then the ice, and so Sir Guy Carleton, with all his ships, soldiers, sailors and Indians, turned about and sailed north to Canada.

There would be no junction between him and Howe in 1776, and

Benedict Arnold, though suffering a tactical defeat, had gained a splendid strategic victory. He had prevented the British from cutting the colonies in two, while gaining a precious year in which the Revolution could be rallied to gain the alliance of France and Spain.

In his valorous delaying action at Valcour Island, "Admiral" Arnold had saved the Revolution.

★ 37 ★

THE CAUSE COLLAPSING/ THE PERFIDY OF CHARLES LEE

White Plains ... Fort Washington ... Fort Lee ... Washington's retreat across New Jersey ... All these in the eyes of General Howe and his officers added up to the growing dissolution and eventual decay of the rebellion. Lord Francis Rawdon wrote: "I think that one may venture to pronounce that it is well nigh over with them."

Yet the prospect of quick victory renewed the running dispute between General Howe and General Clinton over how to apply the crusher. Clinton was furious with his chief for ignoring his every recommendation since Long Island, and he unwisely told General Cornwallis: "I cannot bear to serve under him and had rather command three companies by myself than hold my post." Cornwallis, ever eager to move up the chain of command like most British officers, artfully repeated the remark to Howe, who thereafter refused to listen to anything Clinton might suggest. If he had, the Revolution might have been ended before Christmas; but instead of heeding Clinton's plea to take six thousand men up the Delaware or Chesapeake to capture Philadelphia, or to land him on the New Jersey shore in the same strength to cut off Washington, take Philadelphia, scatter Congress and end the war, he ordered Clinton to assault and occupy Newport, Rhode Island. Though the occupation of Newport would give his brother Lord Howe a warm-water port from which to operate during the winter, it had no other value—except, of course, to occupy Clinton elsewhere.

In the meantime Howe ordered Cornwallis, who was pursuing Washington, to advance no farther than New Brunswick because he knew that Cornwallis was an aggressive soldier who might do something rash and thus upset his own plan for ending the war. This was nothing less than a public renewal of the policy of reconciliation that was so dear to the hearts of the Howe brothers. Riding from New York to join Cornwallis, who had notified him of the amazingly balmy weather he had encountered, Howe distributed copies of a proclamation ordering the dispersal of all armed groups and the submission of Congress. He also offered a pardon to all who appeared before a British official during the next sixty days to pledge their obedience to the king, in return for which they would be guaranteed against any "forfeitures, attainders and penalties" for previous conduct.

This last offer enraged Howe's officers and many Loyalists, who had been looking forward to obtaining rebel estates, or, in the case of the Tories, had hoped to attend the hanging of those Patriot neighbors who had terrorized them. But the Howes were adamant. They thought that they had perceived a distinct waning of enthusiasm in New York and New Jersey—especially in the Jerseys—and they were absolutely correct. The Garden Colony, as it was called even then because of its lush farms, was divided into two districts: East and West Jersey. Possession of them, along with the farmlands of Westchester County in New York, would permanently solve Howe's food-supply problems. The Jerseys were also politically ripc for thc plucking, the entire colony having been enraged by the arrest, abuse, trial and imprisonment of the popular Governor William Franklin, a leading Tory and estranged natural son of Benjamin Franklin. A strong pacifist streak among the Dutch settlers of the north along the Hackensack River, as well as among the Quakers and Germans of the west, more than offset the Patriot character among the Yankees of the south. Recent historical research has demonstrated the sagacity of the Howes' insight: at least half the colony's residents were either secret or active Loyalists.

If the Jerseys could be detached from the rebel cause, New York and Pennsylvania would certainly follow; the rebellion would be dismembered and separated into the South and New England, each of which could be subdued at leisure. To do so, Howe had already informed Germain that at least fifty thousand soldiers would be needed, and he confidently expected to get them. Except for New England, there were already signs of disaffection elsewhere. Delaware's Loyalists and anti-independence moderates had already unseated the colony's two foremost Patriots—Caesar Rodney and Thomas McKean—as its delegates to the Continental Congress, while two-thirds of the colony's newly elected judges and officials were faithful adherents of King George III. In New York, Long

Island was gone, and in Westchester and Dutchess counties secret companies of Tory militia were being organized. Pennsylvania seemed to be expiring of ennui. There was no fierce devotion to either side apparent anywhere, and John Dickinson was openly advising his anti-independence friends not to accept Continental dollars as payment for anything, while Joseph Galloway had crossed the Delaware to join the British Army. In Philadelphia—where an uneasy Congress was giving signs of preparing to bolt to Baltimore, as it eventually did—the financier Robert Morris was lamenting the demise of the American spirit of independence, declaring that at the outset of the rebellion "every man was a bold Patriot … but now, when we are fairly engaged, when death and ruin stare us in the face … those who were foremost in noise shrink cowardlike from the danger and are begging pardon without striking a blow."

Begging for pardon was almost endemic in New Jersey, of which General Alexander McDougall could write on December 22: "This state is totally deranged, without government or officers, civil or military, in it that will act with any spirit." Everywhere roving bands of armed Tories were harrying leading Patriots, forcing them into hiding in the snow-filled woods, terrorizing their wives and children or destroying their property—tactics, of course, that were only the exact duplicate of those embraced by the rebels when they were in the ascendancy. Counties once firmly in the Patriot camp now appointed Tories to act as commissioners to accept the pleas for pardon of all able-bodied men between sixteen and fifty. For those who did not submit, the most fiery of the Tories were recommending halters, although there is no record of any actual hanging. To George Washington, "The conduct of the Jerseys has been most infamous," especially now that the men upon whom he had mistakenly relied for the defense of the colony were, in great part, flocking to the Loyalist—not the Patriot—militia.

Washington, already dismayed by the defection of the New Jersey militia he had hoped to enroll upon his retreat south, now faced the appalling prospect of losing most of his troops when their enlistments expired on New Year's Day. His imploring letters to Charles Lee, almost begging him to march south with his division of from seven to nine thousand men, had either elicited evasive replies or gone unanswered. Washington knew that he could not hope to hold Philadelphia without Lee, or at least without Lee's troops. Yet, for some reason still inexplicable, he hesitated to order Lee to his side. Although the American war chief had indeed recovered his confidence since his successful retreat, he still seemed in awe of his second in command. In an almost fawning deference not exactly admirable in a commander in chief, he would always "entreat" or "request" Lee to march south from Westchester. Perhaps he was aware of the continued adulation of Lee among many of his officers and among some Congressmen or feared to alienate him with so much riding upon his obedience.

But then on November 30 he discovered why his deputy was refusing to join him. A sealed letter had come to headquarters from Lee addressed to Adjutant General Reed. Colonel Reed was one of Washington's most trusted subordinates, who was then in New Jersey seeking to persuade the colony's militia to join Washington's army. He was the same man who had secretly written to Lee to praise him as the only possible savior of the Revolution, and to lament his chief's "indecisiveness." Thinking Lee's letter was an official missive, Washington broke the seal and read it. Lee joined Reed in excoriating Washington for "that fatal indecision of mind which in war is a much greater disqualification than stupidity or even want of personal courage." With incredible condescension, he added: "The General recommends in so pressing a manner as almost to amount to an order to bring over the Continental troops under my command." This, he said grandly, "throws me into the greatest dilemma." Indeed? Was he planning to cross a Rubicon? *Almost to amount to an order.* What *cheek!* General Buckskins so to importune Charles Lee—a *British* officer?

George Washington was shocked. Not by General Lee, for he had already seen enough of him to distrust him as an adventurer and a hopeless eccentric. But this from Joseph Reed? This disloyalty, not to say perfidy? Quietly and sadly, he resealed the letter and forwarded it to Reed, together with a note explaining how he had come to open it by accident. Thereafter, George Washington was a different man, even though he still would not issue a direct order to Lee. Nathanael Greene could bluntly advise him to do so, but he still hesitated. Once in a report to Congress he wrote: "I have wrote to General Lee and ordered him to come over with the Continental regiments immediately under his command." But on reflection he deleted the phrase "and ordered him." Nevertheless that letter had been the final piece of adversity that can and did confirm the resolution of a great leader.

Washington came to realize finally that he was all alone, and on him alone depended the success or failure of the Revolution. He had allowed Putnam and the usually reliable Greene to mislead him at Fort Washington. Now the trustworthy Reed was in secret correspondence with the plotter—yes, plotter—Charles Lee. Thereafter George Washington read Lee's letters, it may be hoped, with a quiet amusement and a growing sense of having this man in his power. In his own letters to Congress he no longer dissembled or apologized or equivocated. With blunt realism he told Philadelphia that with his present force he had no hope of stopping the British advance. Without Lee's troops there was no chance. Now Congress became alarmed, instructing Washington to send an express rider to Lee to determine his actual strength. Washington obliged, writing "the sooner you can join me with your division the sooner the service will be benefited." Still no direct order. Still no confrontation. Was the noble Washington deliberately permitting his deputy to hang himself? Certainly Lee's private remarks to his officers and his ensuing letters were fashioning his own noose.

On December 3, Washington received a letter from Lee reporting that he was bringing "four thousand firm and willing people" into New Jersey, apparently to attack an enemy of his own choosing. Therefore, he told his chief, "I could wish you would bind me as little as possible." Indeed, "detached generals cannot have too great latitude." With incredible insolence, Lee was telling his chief that he not only did not intend to rally to him in his hour of need, but was proposing an independent command for himself. In private he could say to his still-spellbound officers: "Good God, have I come from gathering laurels in many other parts of the world to lose them in America?" Or else he would, with the professional's customary disdain for volunteers, recommend drafting the militia to flesh out the Continental regiments, for volunteers were "composed in general of the most idle, vicious and dissolute part of every society." Presumably, under his whip he would make real soldiers of them, and they, in turn, of course, would make of him a military dictator.

Unknown to Washington, Lee had already begun to try to make his division stronger. After refusing to comply with Washington's first requests in late November, he had ordered General Heath, then guarding the Hudson at Peekskill with four thousand men, to send half the men to him. Heath refused, declaring that he could not detach a man without express orders from Washington. Then in December, after General Schuyler had obeyed Congress's order to reinforce Washington by ordering General Gates south with about one thousand men, Gates was urged by the New York Council of Safety—the enemy of Washington and friend of Lee—to march instead to the British general's command. Wily as ever, his roving eye still wary for the grand chance, Gates refused. In spite of this refusal, Lee wrote to Washington on December 4, saying he was about to take command of Gates's troops, urging his chief "to communicate this to the corps immediately under your command. It may encourage them." How thoughtful! Finally, he explained that on his march through New Jersey he planned "to clothe my people at the expense of the Tories, which has a double good effect—it puts them in spirits and comfort, and is a correction to the inequity of the foes of liberty." Here, indeed, was a charming means of unifying a dividing cause: Lee's largely New England army was to be permitted to plunder the people of New Jersey.

At last Charles Lee did get his division moving south into New Jersey. For what purpose is not clear, although he did write Washington to say he could do him "more service" by striking the enemy's rear. He might also have entered the Garden Colony because it was just across the Delaware and the Congress in Philadelphia. Had not Joseph Reed suggested in his letter that "as soon as the season will admit I think yourself and some others should go to Congress and form the plan of a new army." Conspicuously absent from this delegation of martial experts was the name of George Washington. By December 9 Lee had reached Morristown, about a third of the way to Washington across the Delaware. But he was not thinking of joining Washington; rather, he was thinking big thoughts for Charles Lee, describing them in a letter to Heath: "I am in hopes to reconquer (if I may so express myself) the Jerseys." At the same time Washington was once again pleading with Lee to cross the Delaware: "I cannot but request and entreat you and this, too, by the advice of all the general officers with me, to march and join me with all your whole force."

This was to be the American war chief's last unseemly entreaty, for within four more days all his problems with this insolent, insubordinate military adventurer were to be solved for him by the honorable enemy.

Lord Charles Cornwallis was well aware that Lee was moving through New Jersey, and he yearned to take him to Howe in chains. On December 11 he ordered Lieutenant Colonel William Harcourt, commanding the Seventeenth Light Dragoons—Lee's old regiment—to find and capture the renegade. With twenty-five troopers and a red-haired oak stump of a cornet (second lieutenant) Banastre Tarleton, Harcourt rode out in search of Lee.

Along the way Tory sympathizers told them that Lee was indeed in the vicinity, and they rode to within a mile of his encampment, actually capturing two American sentries "without firing a gun," proof, if anymore were needed, that the Yankees knew nothing about fighting. Threatened with death by the burly, bullying Tarleton, these two sentries revealed that Lee was sleeping in a tavern somewhere in Basking Ridge, four miles away. Next an American horseman, carrying a letter from Lee to Sullivan, his second in command, was taken prisoner. If anyone would know where their quarry was it was he! At once the gentle Tarleton drew his saber and ordered the prisoner to reveal Lee's whereabouts or face decapitation. "Fear of the saber," as Tarleton expressed it, loosened the terrified soldier's tongue, and Harcourt learned that his old companion in arms was staying at Mrs. White's inn in nearby Basking Ridge.

Jubilant and with jingling spurs, the British horsemen rode off toward Mrs. White's

It was early in the morning of Friday the thirteenth of December 1776, and Charles Lee, having consumed Mrs. White's hearty breakfast, was sitting at a table writing to Horatio Gates. Although Gates had declined Lee's earlier invitation to join him, Gates was, after all, a former British officer like himself, and something of a born conspirator as well. Lee's aide, James Wilkinson, destined to outdo both men in the subtle art of treason, was standing at the window watching the snowflakes drift down and listening to the scratching of his chief's pen.

"*The ingenious manouevre of Fort Washington has unhinged the goodly fabrick we had been building. There never was so damned a stroke. Entre nous, a certain great man is most damnably deficient—*"

Ending his letter with another veiled slam at his chief and another forecast of doom, Lee was preparing to sign it, when Wilkinson whirled from the window and shouted: "Here, sir, are the British cavalry!"

"*Where?*" Lee cried in alarm, jumping erect.

"Around the house," Wilkinson yelled, watching with horror as Harcourt's dragoons neatly opened ranks and went trotting around the inn to surround it. Outside, Harcourt ordered a half dozen troopers to charge the sentries at the front door. Drawing their sabers to whirl them around their heads, screaming like cossacks—they rode straight for the terrified Yankees, who dropped their muskets and fled.

Inside, General Lee shouted: "Where is the guard? Damn the guard, why don't they fire?"

They didn't fire because as they came tumbling out of an adjacent outbuilding, the British horsemen came pounding down on them. Other riders galloped around the inn like Indians around circled wagons—firing into every door and window. An old woman burst out the front door and went on her knees in the snow before Tarleton screaming for mercy. The general was inside, she shrieked.

He was indeed, coldly rejecting a frantic maid's urgent offer to hide him under a bed. Wilkinson, meanwhile, had caught up his pistols, stuck Lee's letter in his pocket, and run outside in time to see the guard he sought to alarm meekly surrendering to the British. Shots were fired at him, and he ducked back inside. Then he heard Harcourt's voice, saying: "*If the general does not surrender in five minutes, I will set fire to the house.*" A few minutes passed, and Wilkinson heard another voice shout: "*Here is the general. He has surrendered!*" There was a loud shout of triumph. The assembly was sounded, and Lee, bareheaded, in slippers and blanket coat with open collar, was mounted on Wilkinson's horse that was standing saddled at the door. He was not at all charmed by the warmth of Harcourt's welcome back to the old Seventeenth Light Dragoons. And why should Harcourt not be friendly, not to say jubilant, as he rode off with a muffled clatter of hoofs striking snow—in his grasp the prize that would bring him his own general's star?

The date was Friday, December 13, 1776—the luckiest Friday the Thirteenth in the history of the United States of America.

★ 38 ★

TRENTON: WASHINGTON RALLIES THE REVOLUTION

It was the luckiest Friday the Thirteenth because the capture of Charles Lee removed forever the disastrous possibility that command of the American Army might fall to this eccentric egotist. Passionate patriot though he might have been, and his love of liberty genuine, neither ideal ever actually took precedence over his wild ambition. Under Lee the American Army would not have survived a second season of campaigning, for he was scarcely more fit to be a supreme commander than was his little Pomeranian, Mr. Spada, the major domo of his dogs.

Even more important, his capture removed his insinuating, intimidating presence from behind the shoulder of George Washington. The inexplicable diffidence that the American chief felt in Lee's presence, and which, worse, carried over to his correspondence with him, vanished just as Lee himself disappeared into captivity. Having already realized that the War of the Revolution was his alone to win among the Americans, Washington now was the true supreme commander who could accept, but not solicit or depend upon, the assistance of other foreigners who were eager to fight for freedom.

On that lucky Friday the Thirteenth Washington received another boon, the capitulation of Congress in all matters military. It was embodied in a resolution declaring: "Until the Congress shall otherwise order, General Washington [shall] be possessed of full power to order and direct all things relative to the department, and the operation of the war."

And the snow that fell on the Thirteenth convinced William Howe that in such weather he could not cross the Delaware. Although it is generally accepted that Howe decided not to attempt to cross the wide river because of Washington's wise forethought in collecting all boats on either side of it, actually, Washington himself knew that the British could cross to Philadelphia whenever they chose. They could easily have brought their flatboats on wagons to Trenton from New York or built them in the Trenton area. A hardware store and three blacksmith shops existed within the town, and there were already forty-eight thousand feet of cut boards a few yards from Howe's headquarters. With his engineers and the fleet's corps of carpenters, Howe would have had no trouble building his own flotilla, or even wading across at any of the eight fords within a day's march of Trenton. No, Washington's real purpose in collecting boats was that even before December thirteenth, he had begun to think offensively.

He had begun to think so because the capture of Lee, the only general that the British really respected, led Howe to dismiss Washington's army as a military skeleton. An intercepted letter of Washington's had already informed Howe that most of the American soldiers would vanish after their enlistments expired on New Year's Day. Moreover, New Jersey had been completely pacified, thanks to the carrot of his brother's pardons and the stick of his own army. The memory of the lovable blond Betsy Loring, awaiting him in the warmth and comfort of New York City, also convinced Sir William—he had just been knighted for his summer victories—that it was time to enter winter quarters. So Howe distributed his forces along a chain of posts on the New Jersey side of the Delaware, from Burlington to Trenton, while garrisoning points in nine other towns. Major General James Grant commanded the network from headquarters in New Brunswick. On December 17 Howe, accompanied by Cornwallis, returned to New York, and on the twentieth he reported his decision to Lord George Germain with the remark: "The chain, I own, is rather extensive."

It was, indeed, and Yankee Doodle was not really dead or dying or even only sleeping—but was awake and active again.

Having learned of Howe's chain of posts, Washington resolved to strike one of them, finally settling on Trenton. He *had* to do something, *had* to rally the dying rebel cause, *had* to shake and even stagger the enemy before the Delaware froze and became passable, before the disease of defection spread from New Jersey into Pennsylvania and elsewhere, before his army melted away on the first day of 1777. So he began a kind of guerrilla war against the Hessian outpost at Trenton, hoping to intimidate the enemy into withdrawing within a small perimeter and thus—

without far-ranging patrols—be easier to approach and surprise. Day after day Yankee patrols crossed the Delaware to strike German outposts around Trenton. Dragoons carrying despatches were so often ambushed and then captured, killed or wounded that Colonel Johann Rall, in command at Trenton, at one point detailed a cannon and a hundred soldiers to protect a letter to Brigadier General Alexander Leslie at Princeton. The twenty dragoons at Trenton were so frightened that they would not venture forth without infantry protection "for they never went out patrolling without being fired upon, or having one wounded or even shot dead." As Washington desired, they were thus rendered useless as scouts.

Gradually the Hessians' morale sank to a dangerous low. After a long sea voyage and an arduous campaign in which they had distinguished themselves, they had been eagerly anticipating the customary months of relaxation and revelry in winter quarters. Instead, they were in constant danger. Just for a few of them to appear on the Trenton shore would provoke a blast of artillery from the Pennsylvania side. They and their junior officers began to fear a surprise attack. But Colonel Rall belittled their worries. He ignored Colonel Carl Emil Kurt von Donop's instructions to fortify the town and refused to allow his men to build redoubts on their own.

Like General James Grant, who had boasted of how he would castrate every American male, Rall believed he could "keep the peace in New Jersey with a corporal's guard." He despised the Yankees and was pleased when Grant wrote to him to tell him how destitute they were. When a junior officer requested permission to fortify the Trenton ferry, Rall shouted at him angrily: "Let them come! We want no trenches! We'll go after them with the bayonet." After a leading Tory told him that a black slave reported the Americans were drawing several days' rations, which suggested a prolonged march, he blustered: "This is all idle! It is woman's talk!" Fine fighter that he was, Rall believed that winter quarters were for wine, women and cards—and he addressed all three with true Germanic efficiency. Thus, contemptuous of his enemy, overconfident in his own ability, he was just the sort of opponent the desperate Washington was seeking.

To be sure that Rall did not take undue alarm, Washington devised a little scheme to disarm him further. He called into service a former British soldier named John Honeyman, a Loyalist pretending to be a Tory spy. He instructed Honeyman to go to Trenton to declare his intention of suing for pardon and to tell Rall that he was a butcher and a dealer in cattle. Honeyman did so, and the Hessian commander was delighted to hire Honeyman to provide meat for him and his soldiers.

After spending about a week in Trenton memorizing the garrison's routine and the routes of their pickets, Honeyman wandered into the woods with a rope and a whip, ostensibly searching for cattle hidden by local farmers. Cracking his whip loudly as he strolled, he attracted the attention of a patrol of American soldiers, who held him at gunpoint, tied him up with that handy rope and took him across the river to Washington. Whether the patrol was in on the scheme is not known.

When Honeyman was brought into Washington's presence, the commander's face went black with feigned anger. So this was Honeyman, the notorious Tory spy! Washington would question him himself. Alone. The patrol left, and a half hour later Washington flung open his office door and called for the corporal of the guard to take the prisoner to the guardhouse and to shoot him if he tried to escape. In the morning Honeyman would be court-martialed and hanged.

But in the morning, Honeyman was gone, having opened his cell door with a key slipped to him by Washington. He also found a boat conveniently tied up on the Delaware and so returned to Rall in triumph. At once the colonel wanted to know the condition of the American army. Terrible, Honeyman replied. They were without every necessity. So many were shoeless that they could not possibly make a winter's march. Rall was pleased, thanked Honeyman—and returned in relief to wining, womanizing and cardplaying.

Across the river, perhaps smiling to himself at the success of his deception, George Washington added one more touch to his planned counterstrike. On December 23, he had his army formed into ranks to have the first issue of Tom Paine's *The American Crisis* read to them. Paine, who had been along on the retreat across New Jersey, was at his best: "*These are the times that try men's souls. The summer soldier and the sunshine patriot will, in this crisis, shrink from the service of their country; but he that stands it now, deserves the love and thanks of man and woman.*"

Words do not usually inspire soldiers, especially beaten men, such as these threadbare, hungry, shivering ragamuffins. But these words did. A thrill of patriotism and purpose ran through Washington's ragged ranks. They were ready for their general's great scheme, and that was simply to attack fifteen thousand Hessians under Rall at Trenton. In truth, the operation would be hardly more than a raid, yet Washington believed that its psychological effects could be equal to or greater than the British reaction after Bunker Hill. It was indeed a desperature venture, and if it failed, all might fail. That was why he chose such an ominous password: "Victory or death."

★ ★ ★

General John Cadwalader would cross downriver with about two thousand men to engage von Donop's Bordentown force and prevent reinforcements from being sent north to Trenton.

Brigadier General James Ewing would cross opposite Trenton with about nine hundred men to capture a bridge and seal off the Hessian escape route south to Bordentown.

The main attack, with 2,400 men, would be led by Nathaniel Greene, accompanied by Washington. This force would cross the Delaware above Trenton on Christmas Night and march downriver to make a surprise assault an hour before dawn.

As the daylight of Christmas 1776 began fading into a storm-tossed night, the American troops began to move toward McKonkey's Ferry. Here were gathered the boats Washington had collected, and at their oars were John Glover's blue-coated Marbleheaders. Snow mixed with sleet blew into the faces of the men.

Near the ferry, General Washington was preparing to mount his horse. Major Wilkinson presented himself with a letter from General Horatio Gates. "By General Gates?" Washington asked, astonished to hear that his Northern commander was in the vicinity. "Where is he?"

"I left him this morning in Philadelphia."

"What was he doing *there?*"

"I understood him that he was on his way to Congress."

"On his way to Congress!" Washington repeated. Without asking leave, the confidant of Charles Lee had gone hurrahing off to Baltimore to bask in the admiration of certain congressmen, who might also agree that "a certain great man is damnably deficient." Lee, a captive, and Gates … what? Without a word, Washington rode off to join his troops.

On Christmas Day Johann Rall awoke with the customary hangover. He dressed leisurely, listening to the serenade played by shivering Hessian bandsmen standing outside his window. He prepared to celebrate the Nativity in the hearty German manner.

At night, after the festivity, there was a minor scare when a roving American patrol shot up the picket guard. The troops were called to arms, but soon returned to quarters. Colonel Rall dropped in on a supper party at the home of a wealthy Trenton merchant. There was wine and cards. Near the middle of the night there was a knock on the door. A Tory had come with information for the colonel. Rall would not see him. The man wrote a note informing Rall that the American army was on the march. A servant delivered it. Rall stuck it into his pocket, unread. Eventually, his heart gladdened with wine, Colonel Rall went home to bed.

Outside his window the storm mounted in fury.

The Americans had been enjoined to silence. No soldier was to break ranks under pain of death. They stood huddled by the ferry landing, ducking their heads into their collars against the rising howl of the storm. Their firelocks were hopelessly wet, but Colonel Knox's artillerymen had kept the cannon touchholes dry.

The men entered the boats. Thin, jagged cakes of ice came floating downriver to strike the boats so hard that Glover's Marbleheaders had difficulty keeping afloat. Washington had hoped to have his troops on the New Jersey shore by midnight, but it was not until after three o'clock that Knox's booming voice announced that the crossing was completed.

Washington formed his forces into two divisions. John Sullivan would take his division—which included John Stark's sharpshooters—down the river road. Nathanael Greene's division, accompanied by Washington, would march on Trenton along a road two miles farther inland. Sullivan would hit the bottom of the town, Greene the top. The Americans began marching. The roads were slippery. Cruel ice cut through flimsy footwear and drew blood. In the morning, Major Wilkinson could follow the route by the bloodstains in the snow.

But down the roads they marched, steadily gaining on the still-sleeping enemy. With daylight, just before eight o'clock in the morning, both columns reached their destination—and both flushed Hessian pickets and drove them in.

"*Der Feind! Heraus! Heraus!*" the pickets shouted. "The enemy! Turn out! Turn out!"

Lieutenant Jacob Piel heard the shouts and rushed to alert Colonel Rall. He hammered on Rall's door. Rall, in his nightclothes, poked his head out the window. Piel told him he had heard firing. Rall withdrew his head and a few minutes later came rushing downstairs in full uniform. He formed his own blue-coated regiment on King Street. The scarlet-coated Lossbergs marched to the right to take over Queen Street parallel with King, while the black-coated Knyphausen Regiment made up the reserve. But at the top of both King and Queen streets stood the American artillery.

Two guns to a street, but would they fire? Captain Alexander Hamilton's gunners stuck their matches in the touchholes. The cannon roared and bucked. American cheers mingled with the shrieks of Hessian soldiers stricken by grapeshot. Rall's regiment was fragmented and driven back. The other brace of cannon cleared Queen Street, but the Lossbergs mounted their own cannon and fired back. The Americans charged. Captain William Washington—a distant relative of his chief's—and Lieutenant James Monroe led their men right into the cannon's mouth. They captured them, although both were wounded—a liability that eventually would be a political asset to President James Monroe.

Sullivan's men, at the bottom of the town, were attacking from the west. Greene's division extended its right flank to join Sullivan, while more of Greene's units worked around to the rear or the east of the town. If General Ewing had crossed to hold the bridge over Assunpink Creek, the Hessians were caught in a box.

Ewing had not crossed. The bridge lay open, and perhaps four hundred Hessians were escaping over it. The remainder, however, could not get away. Even with wet firelocks the Americans fought with conquering fury. "Use the bayonet," Washington ordered. "I am determined to take Trenton." Some Americans ran inside the houses to dry their pieces or pick the touchholes clear. They acted as snipers when Rall re-formed his shattered troops and tried to counterattack, and they sent two bullets into Rall's body. The Hessian commander fell from his horse, fatally stricken, and that was about the end of the battle.

Sullivan's troops now held the bridge, and the escape gap was plugged. One by one the Hessian regiments surrendered. In all, about 920 Hessians had been captured, about 25 were killed and 90 wounded. Two Americans had been frozen to death on the march, but not one was killed in the battle; two officers and two privates were wounded.

General George Washington stood radiant on the field. When Major Wilkinson rode up to him to announce that the last enemy regiment had grounded arms, Washington's face actually shone, and he extended his hand in thanks.

"Major Wilkinson," he said, "this is a glorious day for our country."

★ 39 ★

PRINCETON: CORNWALLIS'S "BAG" COMES UP EMPTY

It had been a glorious day. From the depths of despair the American people rose to the heights of exaltation. The rabble in arms had challenged, bested and taken captive an entire brigade of the world's most famous mercenaries. General Sir William Howe was stunned. He could not believe that "three old established regiments of a people who made war a profession should lay down their arms to a ragged and undisciplined militia." Even the supercilious General James Grant could no longer sneer, bleating instead in dismayed disbelief: "I did not think that all the Rebels in America would have taken that brigade prisoners." General Charles Cornwallis was the most crushed and crestfallen, for his baggage had already been loaded aboard the ship that was to take him home and to the bedside of his ailing wife. But Howe canceled that leave and ordered him into New Jersey to take command there, promising to join him later.

In New Jersey one of the surest signs of changing fortunes was reported by General John Cadwalader to Washington: as he led his brigade from Burlington to Bordentown the day after the Hessians there "skedaddled," he noticed Tories ripping down the pieces of red cloth they had nailed to their front doors as a sign of their allegiance to the British Crown. Meanwhile, on the last day of 1776 the captured Germans were paraded through the streets of Philadelphia before the city's ecstatic population. The contrast between the well-fed, warmly clothed Germans and their own emaciated heroes "in light summer dress and some without shoes" filled many eyes with tears. Some of the prisoners were a bit frightened by the crowd's enthusiasm, and one wrote in his diary: "Old women screamed fearfully and wanted to choke us because we had come to America to deprive them [of] their liberty."

On the day before, Washington, who had returned to Pennsylvania, again took his army across the Delaware into New Jersey. He was desperate to prevent the departure of those regiments whose enlistments would expire in two days. If only he could get them to stay with him for a few weeks! Six weeks would be long enough to allow him to reforge his force with men who had enlisted for several years or for the duration of the war. Yet, because most of the men whose enlistments would expire were from New England, he all but despaired of success. The Yankees had had enough of the insults of the Southern troops, most of whom never troubled to conceal their contempt for New Englanders as fighting men. Now this big Southerner on a big horse, who in the past had also spoken some harsh words against the Yankees, was pleading with them in his soft Southern voice to reenlist. "You have done all I asked you to do," he said, his voice throbbing with emotion, "and more than could be reasonably expected. But your country is at stake. Your wives, your houses and all that you hold dear." If they agreed to serve another six weeks, he promised, they would receive a bounty of ten dollars.

Continental dollars were not yet spurned in the phrase "not worth a Continental," and ten dollars compared to the six dollars they earned monthly was actually a handsome bonus that even this soft-spoken giant had regarded as "a most extravagant price." But when Washington asked for volunteers to step forward and the drums beat briskly, not a man moved. Washington rode down the line pleading again, "in the most affectionate manner." Something about this man touched their hearts. They could not name it, this mysterious, magical quality of leadership, but they could sense that he was asking nothing for himself but pleading for a cause bigger than all of them. It was not oratory, for Washington at best was a mediocre speaker. But his plea did issue from his soul, and these Bible-reading Yankees could see, as Christ had said of Nathanael: "Behold an Israelite indeed, in whom there is no guile." So they coughed and swallowed and exchanged glances, and at first one man stepped tentatively and then briskly forward. Another said to his friend, "I will stay if you will," and they, too, stepped forward, and as the drums resumed a joyful beating the entire regiment volunteered.

Washington did not so address all the regiments, leaving them to his subordinates, but in the end half the New Englanders volunteered. The Pennsylvanians did also, under the spell of golden-tongued Quartermaster General Thomas Mifflin, and the promise of a ten-dollar bounty, loot and a tongue-in-cheek assurance of the eventual appearance of food, warm clothing and reinforcements. Thus with fourteen hundred regulars, plus Cadwalader's men, Washington now commanded about five thousand soldiers, mostly militia and most of those Pennsylvanians who were still untried in the crucibile of combat. Nevertheless, to have resurrected his fighting force like a veritable Phoenix rising from its own ashes, and to have done so with the aggressive Cornwallis rushing to destroy him, was a feat of military presence perhaps unparalleled in history.

Next, Washington the soldier reverted to Washington the practical businessman, for he immediately called upon Robert Morris of Philadelphia, the Revolution's gifted and generous financier, to provide the money for the bounties as quickly as possible. Those hard-bitten New England Yankees might be moved by his sincerity, but they still preferred cash to promissory notes. Washington urged Morris to "borrow money where it can be done … upon our private credit. Every man of interest and every lover of his country must strain his credit upon such an occasion." He also asked for 150 pounds in specie to pay "a certain set of people who are of particular use to us," meaning, of course, his spies, such as Honeyman, for as the cynical Napoleon Bonaparte was to say, money is the true spy's only reward. Morris responded with alacrity, rushing 50,000 paper dollars to the commander in chief plus £124.7.6 for those particular people.

On the following day—the last of the year 1776 begun so auspiciously only to be sunk into the despairing rhythm of defeat and retreat before Trenton rescued it—Congress all but made a military dictator of George Washington. Without reservation it gave him "full, ample, and complete powers" to raise "in the most speedy and effectual manner" the sixteen extra battalions that he sought. It also bestowed upon him the power "to displace and appoint all officers under the rank of brigadier general" and "to take, wherever he may be, whatever he may want for the use of the army, if the inhabitants will not sell it" and "to arrest and confine persons who refuse to take the Continental currency, or are other wise disaffected to the American cause."

Charles Lee or Horatio Gates—or even Benedict Arnold, more deservingly—would have had this remarkable relinquishment of military power emblazoned on his uniform fore and aft like the lions of Richard the Lion-Hearted, but George Washington, a true soldier of democracy, replied that he would never feel himself "free from all civil obligations by this mark of confidence." Rather he would forever "bear in mind that as the sword was the last resort for the preservation of our liberties, so it ought to be the first to be laid aside when those liberties are firmly established." He said this amid the tide of adulation engulfing him, and he never broke that promise.

So exalted, he prepared to meet Cornwallis, who had reached Princeton on New Year's Day 1777.

Accustomed to the deliberate, slow movements of General William Howe, Washington was surprised at the speed with which Cornwallis moved toward him. General Cornwallis had at his command about seven thousand soldiers with artillery, having left three companies of light dragoons and three regiments of infantry behind at Princeton under Lieutenant Colonel Francis Mawhood. His hope was to pin Washington against the Delaware and destroy him.

Washington had not chosen a good position, deploying his main body on the east bank of Assunpink Creek across the bridge that Sullivan had closed to the fleeing Hessians a few days before. He had also posted a delaying force along the Princeton road under Brigadier General Mathias Alexis de Fermoy, a Frenchman born in Martinique, more skillful in persuasion than in battle, for he had induced Congress to give him the star he quickly disgraced by abandoning his troops. Fortunately, Colonel Edward Hand, a tough Pennsylvania Irishman, took his place to conduct a brilliant rearguard action with troops fighting so valiantly that Cornwallis imagined he was facing Washington's entire army. Deploying accordingly, Cornwallis was severely delayed in his approach to Trenton.

It was almost dark before Cornwallis reached Trenton and faced his quarry across the Assunpink. Nevertheless he sent out skirmishers to probe the enemy's defenses, and brought up artillery to bombard the Americans entrenched across the stream. His probers reported that the Yankee positions were indeed strong. He realized that his troops had been marching and fighting all day and needed food and sleep more than an order to do what British soldiers most dreaded doing in this topsy-turvy war: assault the rebels in fixed positions, and this time in the dark. So he told his staff he would "bag the old fox" in the morning. Brigadier Sir William Erskine demurred, remarking: "If Washington is the general I think him to be, he will not be there tomorrow morning." Cornwallis scoffed at the suggestion. He might move faster than Howe, but he was still a similar prisoner of his own professionalism: He had made his approach march and was exactly where he wanted to be, with Washington exactly where Cornwallis wanted him. Washington was between two streams, the narrow one at his front, the mighty one at his back. If he sought to retreat across the Delaware, Cornwallis would smash him; if he tried to escape into the southern end of New Jersey, he would still be in a trap. No, gentlemen, we will bag him in the morning.

On the face of it, it would seem that Cornwallis was right. Washington's position on high ground above the Assunpink was a cul-de-sac, from which only God could extricate him. Moreover, for him to attempt to escape by another one of those demoralizing retreats would at once tarnish the glory won at Trenton and restore to British arms its customary brilliance. Even if he did escape, Cornwallis would almost certainly pursue and bring him to the course he dreaded: decisive battle with a superior foe. If he retreated too far, Cornwallis could turn and cross the Delaware to take Philadelphia with a corporal's guard. These were the alternatives in the mind of this excellent tactician, who was schooled in Continental warfare. But none of them existed in the mind of his innovating, extemporizing opponent, who saw himself not in a trap but in position to improve on the glory of Trenton by another bold stroke—by an attack, not at Trenton but somewhere else.

That night of January 2 Washington saw nothing but unhappy faces at a council of war. One young lieutenant recalled: "The most sanguine among us could not flatter himself with any hopes of victory. The fate of this extensive continent seemed suspended by a single thread." All present knew that north of Trenton were several fords across the Assunpink that Tories had undoubtedly pointed out to Cornwallis. Just as at Long Island or White Plains, the British could employ their favorite maneuver: hold the Patriots in place with a frontal assault, while a strong force forded the creek to turn their flank and get into their rear. Washington was aware of this maneuver, but he also knew that the unguarded Quaker Bridge several miles beyond the British left flank led to the little-used Quaker Road to Princeton. So he did not ask his generals for advice; rather, he electrified them with his proposal to slip away in a night march, overwhelm the outnumbered garrison at Princeton and then turn to descend upon New Brunswick, Cornwallis's bulging supply depot and—best of all—his war chest of seventy thousand pounds. Now the lackluster eyes gleamed and color flowed back into all those wan faces. Such was the enthusiasm that this bold and confident chief now inspired that, when someone suggested that the muddy roads might make it impossible to move even light cannon, the warning was brushed aside by a general agreement that this was the cannoneers' problem. Yet, as the council broke up and the officers returned to their units, they found, to their delight, that the wind had shifted north, plunging the temperature to twenty-one degrees and almost guaranteeing hard-frozen roads.

As night fell, campfires were lighted and fed fast and furiously until there were dozens of bonfires blazing on the heights above the Assunpink. Baggage and guns were sent on ahead to the Quaker Bridge, the wagon wheels wrapped in rags to muffle the sound of their going. Regiments were quietly ordered to fall in, the low voices of their officers informing the men of what was happening—making the hearts of the soldiery leap. Four or five hundred men were left behind to feed the fires and—to lead the British to believe they were digging in deeper, as well as to keep warm—to make a racket with clanging picks and shovels. At last the silent columns moved out over blessedly frozen roads.

The night was utterly black and the weather bone-chilling cold. The columns slogged on, into a stretch of land called "the Barrens," full of stunted oaks in weird and grotesque shapes. Suddenly in this home of the harpies someone raised the cry that the Hessians were surrounding them. At this one thousand brave Pennsylvanians, who had been vowing to drive the British into the Hudson River, simply ceased to exist—bolting in a body that did not stop running until they reached Burlington, about ten miles to the southwest. Their defection left Washington with about four thousand men. From the Barrens the route followed a road full of tree stumps, making it difficult for the artillery horses. On the Quaker Road sheets of ice sent them slipping and sliding. Halts were frequent. Without the warmth of movement, the men cursed the cold that was holding them in its iron grip. Some sank to the road in slumber.

Dawn began to break as they neared Stony Brook bridge, about three miles from Princeton. It would be a fine day, but cold, a brilliant sun rising into a high blue sky. The sun's rays glistened on the trees and grass white and wet with frost, and glittered on the wavelets of the fast-running little brook. Across the bridge, Washington halted his troops in a field, warming their hearts and bodies with buckets of rum. Now he formed his force into two columns. John Sullivan's peeled off to the right to attack Princeton in its rear. Nathanael Greene, with Washington, made for the Post Road from Trenton, intending to make a frontal assault on the town.

But there were British troops on the Post Road, the Seventeenth and Fifty-fifth regiments, together with an escort of thirty dragoons, all commanded by Lieutenant Colonel Francis Mawhood of the Seventeenth. Mawhood was a fine professional officer, a bonny fighter. He was looking forward to joining the assault on Washington at Trenton when he left Princeton riding a small brown pony, his pet honey-colored spaniels scampering alongside him. Suddenly Mawhood started at the sight of the American advance parties marching up the Quaker Road. So did General Hugh Mercer, commander of the Yankee "brigade," who sighted Mawhood a few seconds later. It was a brigade in name only, a rag-tag, pickup force numbering at most 350 men. It included artillery—one of the few New Jersey militia companies that responded to Washington's pleas—and the valiant remnant of Colonel John Haslet's Delaware Regiment.

Mawhood thought that the slowly approaching Yankees were the fleeing survivors of Washington's army that was "defeated" at Trenton. But then he decided it was merely a patrol or some lost militia unit. Mercer likewise thought he beheld a small enemy force. But both men instantly grasped the significance of a nearby piece of high ground on which stood an orchard surrounded by a hedge fence, a farmhouse and a barn. At once they raced each other for possession of it. Mercer, cutting across fields to get onto the Post Road and put himself between the British and Princeton, got there first. But he had with him only about 120 men, while Mawhood had about 350 and two light cannons.

Taking cover in the orchard, the Americans began firing at the oncoming redcoats, delaying them only momentarily. In the interim, Mawhood's artillery opened fire, to be dueled by Captain Daniel Neil with his New Jersey militia gunners. Colonel Haslet also arrived puffing with his Delaware riflemen. Now the British regulars launched a bayonet charge with loud cries. Mercer's Pennsylvania riflemen could not fire and load fast enough to stop them. A few redcoats fell, but the main body came forward with slanting steel. The Yankees broke and ran. Mercer and Haslet tried to rally them, but the men paid them no heed. After a rifle butt drove Mercer to the earth, he arose with drawn sword to face a dozen howling lobsterbacks. Seven bayonets plunged into him, and he sank to the earth gushing blood. Haslet also was killed, with a bullet in the brain. Captain John Fleming with twenty Virginians tried to make a stand. They were among the few Americans with bayonets of their own, but they were stabbed to the earth. One of Fleming's lieutenants had thirteen bayonet wounds.

Now the routed Yankees were pouring back over the Quaker Road, washing around the big man on the splendid white horse who had come galloping up to the sound of battle. Waving his hat, he shouted to them, "Parade with us, my brave fellows!"—riding farther toward the advancing British as though expecting them to follow him. But no one did. Accompanied by Colonel John Fitzgerald, the American war chief rode among the demoralized rebels, urging them to re-form. The men still sulked, until the New England brigade went into line on the American right, holding fast to make that ten-dollar bounty perhaps the best investment in American military history. Then the Philadelphia militia joined them. Next came some of Sullivan's troops, followed by Mercer's men. Washington personally led them toward the approaching British. "Halt and fire!" he shouted, and as the Americans opened up so did the British. Washington was between both volleys, and Colonel Fitzgerald in horror put his hat over his eyes. When Fitzgerald lifted his hat, Washington was still there, calmly sitting his horse. In relief Fitzgerald rode toward his chief. "Thank God your Excellency is safe," he shouted. Taking his hand, Washington said, "Bring up the troops. The day is our own!"

The American troops did come forward, screaming battle cries, driving the astonished British down the road toward Trenton. Washington led the pursuit, crying, "It's a fine fox chase, my boys!" It was, indeed, the vaunted redcoats shedding knapsacks, canteens and even muskets as though they, not their pursuers, were the cowardly Yankees. Washington's face gleamed with a fierce wild joy so powerful that he almost rode into the arms of the British dragoons, who had turned about a mile below Stony Brook bridge to bare their sabers and cover Mawhood's retreat. Only the intervention of an aide induced Washington to gallop back to his troops.

There he learned with rising jubilation that Sullivan's force had swept a third British regiment out of Princeton. About half the British Fortieth had barricaded themselves in the College of New Jersey's famous Nassau Hall, but a single cannon shot from Captain Alexander Hamilton's battery had persuaded them to surrender. The rest of the unit and other redcoats made a brief stand outside the village, but then fled down the road to New Brunswick.

Before re-forming to march on the village, Washington ordered the Stony Brook bridge destroyed. It was, much to the consternation of Brigadier General Alexander Leslie's troops, sent by Cornwallis to overtake and destroy "the old fox," who had so impudently given him the slip. But by the time Leslie caught up with his soldiers and began to ford the stream, the Americans had thoroughly looted Princeton. Whether General Mifflin had meant it when he induced reenlistements by promising booty, the men took him at his word, stealing everything that was portable in the fifty-two-house village, Bibles as well as bottles of wine. Washington did not intervene, being too busy caring for his wounded and counting his captives. When he heard the sound of muskets to the south, he re-formed his army, set fire to British military stores and marched off for New Brunswick.

But by the time he reached Kingston, a few miles above Princeton,

Washington realized that his soldiers were shadow men, marched out and fought out. They were beginning to drop out, seeking warmth and sleep in barns and silos. If he attempted the nineteen-mile march to New Brunswick, no matter how grand the prize, he would arrive with hardly more than a color guard to seize it. So he decided instead to make for Morristown, where he would enter winter quarters, ready to strike at Howe's flank should he attempt to move on Philadelphia or up the Hudson.

It was a heartbreaking decision. As he later wrote to Congress: "Six or seven hundred fresh troops, upon a forced march would have destroyed all their stores and magazines" at New Brunswick, "taken … their military chest … and put an end to the war." Perhaps, but it did not happen—and the War of the American Revolution was far from being over.

★ 40 ★

THE TORIES SOUR ON "SAVIORS"/WASHINGTON ACCLAIMED

Lord Charles Cornwallis was indeed dismayed to awake that cold January 3, 1777, to find that the "old fox" had shown him his tail. He had been humiliated just as thoroughly as had Colonel Rall, although the Hessian commander at Trenton had had the good fortune to die before he could realize how completely he had been fooled. It was then that Cornwallis ordered a pursuit under Brigadeer General Alexander Leslie. Leslie's men arrived at Stony Brook bridge "in a most infernal sweat—running, puffing, and blowing and swearing at being so outwitted." But the Americans had destroyed the bridge and Leslie's advance guard had to mark time until their general arrived to order them to ford that icy swift stream. Always, it seemed to them, the Yankee commander managed to put something—a river, a creek, or an empty village—between himself and his pursuers.

They found that Princeton was indeed deserted, the rebels vanished and the residents hiding in their homes. Infuriated, the redcoats took out their frustration on the civilians. They wrecked Richard Stockton's beautiful home, Morven, throwing his furniture and his precious library onto a bonfire on his front lawn. By the time they took the road again, Princeton, according to one resident, appeared to have been "desolated with the plague and an earthquake."

Here was the beginning of the blind British policy of loosing their soldiers on American civilians in New Jersey, Tory and Patriot alike. The

Hessians, of course, could not care less which side their victims were on, being guided by the European mercenary's simple creed that whatever is portable should be stolen, whatever is permanent should be burned or blown up. If there was time, and the lady was not willing, rape could also be enjoyed. The Hessians also dressed their camp followers in the stolen finery of American women, and sent them sashaying down village streets to their immense amusement and the intense moral indignation of their victims.

Not all the indignities visited upon the Americans of New Jersey were the work of the German soldiery. British redcoats also proved themselves adept at the sport of "requisitioning" or "appropriation." Their fondness was for wood to burn to keep them warm. Thus they not only burnt up most of the available firewood wherever they passed or paused, but also tore the sides and roofs off homes and shops, cut down fruit and berry trees and chopped up fences—consigning all to the flames of their campfires—and what they could not remove, like sturdy mills or farmhouses, they set on fire. Whatever they coveted they stole: hats from heads; coats from backs; and horses, sheep, cows, hogs and dogs wherever they found them. One of the numerous Quakers of West Jersey was assaulted by a party of Hessians, who stole his hat, but this smallish man turned out to be a bellicose pacifist, indeed. These scoundrels were stealing *his* property and doing injury to *his* person, and here, it seems, doctrinal pacifism did not apply, and the ferocious little man counterattacked, knocked down a big Hessian, retrieved his hat and would have retired triumphant to the meeting-house had not more Germans entered the fray to subdue him and snatch the hat back again.

Not quite so humorous, the British also adopted a brutal, barbaric policy of mistreating American prisoners. It was done chiefly by neglect, although there were a few instances in which Yankee captives were "barbarously mangled and put to death." Mostly the American prisoners died of malnutrition or disease in makeshift prisons that, much to the horror of truly pious Christians, often were commandeered Protestant churches. Worst of all were the British prison ships, floating horrors in which men who were crammed into the foulest holds fought for food or for air: "some swearing and blaspheming, some crying, praying and wringing their hands and stalking about like ghosts and apparitions; others delirious … raving and storming; some groaning and dying—all panting for breath; some dead and corrupting." One prisoner who survived wrote: "The air was so foul at times that a lamp could not be kept burning, by reason of which three boys were not missed until they had been dead ten days."

According to Lord Francis Rawdon, it was necessary to ravage the countryside to teach a lesson to "these infatuated wretches." His lordship also found that the ravishing of American women was perhaps the most entertaining aspect of the sport. He wrote:

> The fair nymphs of this isle [Staten Island] were in wonderful tribulation, as the fresh meat our men have got here has made them riotous as satyrs. A girl cannot step into the bushes to pluck a rose without running the most imminent risk of being ravished, and they are so little accustomed to these vigorous methods that they don't bear them with the proper resignation, and of consequence we have most entertaining court-martials every day.

"Of consequence" also: fewer and fewer Tories were begging the king's pardon, many of them actually turning Patriots in repugnance to a policy of deliberate barbarity against civilians once supposedly warmly regarded as "our cousins across the sea." It may have satisfied the vengeful spirit seizing the British army after the twin humiliations of Trenton and Princeton, but it saddened Lord Richard Howe to see how it destroyed his dream of making New Jersey the first of the breakaway Yankee states to submit to the Crown. Howe reported to Lord George Germain that "I do not now see a prospect of terminating the war, but by a general action."

Lord Charles Cornwallis also wrote ruefully to Germain: "The unlucky affair of Rall's brigade has given me a winter campaign." And the atrocities of that winter campaign had also assured the safety of Washington's ragged army in its hill fastness at Morristown.

George Washington's pair of brilliant maneuvers had inflamed the hearts of his countrymen and earned him the admiration of Europe. Frederick the Great of Prussia, probably the leading soldier of his day, was unrestrained in his praise, declaring: "The achievements of Washington and his little band of compatriots between the 25th of December and the 4th of January, a space of 10 days, were the most brilliant of any recorded in the history of military achievements." In later years the distinguished Prussian military historian Friedrich Wilhelm von Bülow would acclaim him thus: "The maneuvers of the American general at Trenton and Princeton were masterpieces. They may be deemed models of the conduct of a general supporting a defensive war against a superior enemy."

Probably more satisfying to Washington himself than all this effusive praise was the drastic turnabout in America's relations with France. From being a secret belligerent and ally of the Americans, the Comte de

Vergennes had turned into a cautious neutral in the summer of 1776. Throughout the early months of 1776, King George and his ministers had been sunk in gloom, much to the pleasure of the British-hating foreign minister of France. Howe's evacuation of Boston, the defeat at Charleston and the suppression of the southern Indians suggested that the government of Lord North and ministers, such as Germain, all promising a quick end to the war, might not survive the year. Worse, Lord Richard Howe, being so preoccupied with supporting his brother's campaigns, could not afford ships to blockade America as anticipated. Consequently, the seas off the rebel strongholds were thick with privateers picking off British merchantmen.

Trade between the Yankees and the French and Dutch West Indies was growing alarmingly. As another harbinger of evil, it was well known that France and Spain were rearming and waiting only for the propitious moment to intervene on the American side. Naturally enough, none of these fears was conveyed to Paris by the North government, while Vergennes continued to supply the Yankees with munitions through the supplies provided through deception of Hortalez et Cie. Publicly these natural enemies professed an earnest desire for peace and friendship. But then came Long Island, White Plains, Fort Washington and Washington's tail-dragging retreat across New Jersey. These events were joyfully transmitted to Vergennes by the British ambassador Lord Stormont, thus introducing a new step in this Dance of the Friendly Enemies. Vergennes quickly suspended Beaumarchais's operations, ordering a halt to the sale of munitions to America and refusing to allow four ships stuffed with such supplies to leave France. Next, in that sweetly deceitful language characteristic of all two-faced diplomacy—a tautology if ever there was one—Vergennes wrote to Stormont:

> MONSIEUR
>
> I am indeed touched at the attention shown me by your Excellency in admitting me to share your joy at the satisfactory news of the success of British arms in Connecticut and New York. I beg your Excellency to accept my many thanks at this testimonial of your friendship and my sincere felicitations upon an event so calculated to contribute to the re-establishment of peace in that part of the globe. I shall impart the communication made me to the King, and now take it upon myself to assure you that His Majesty will always receive with pleasure news of whatever may contribute to the satisfaction and glory of the King your master.

News of Trenton and Princeton, however, led France's elated foreign minister to demonstrate his "friendship" for the British by canceling his prohibition against selling arms to the Americans and permitting Beauchmarchais's quartet of ships to sail. Spain, having paused in its rearmament, renewed it—much to the chagrin of George III, who, though he chose to ignore this ominous signal publicly, did much private pouting over this discordant note in the heretofore sweet music of the Friendly Dance.

Another result of Washington's successes was that Sir William Howe decided that without Tory cooperation he could no longer guarantee the security of his chain of garrisons. So he withdrew from Elizabeth, Hackensack and other communities, forming a defensive line along the Raritan River with heavy concentrations of troops at New Brunswick and Perth Amboy. So far from occupying the entire state, the British now controlled less than a quarter of it, and even inside this "safety zone" their troops were subject to raids or ambushes by New Jersey militia and parties of Rangers from Washington's base in Morristown.

Although the American chief had planned to stay in Morristown for only a few days, he was forced to remain there nearly five months. It was a cruel sojourn. On March 14, 1777, Washington reported to Congress that he had fewer than three thousand sick and starving scarecrows at his command. In desperation and dislike he used his dictatorial powers to commandeer provisions. However, he could not outlaw smallpox, which ravaged the camp.

But then the Patriot cause brightened. Vergennes's second turnabout had released the ships that brought twenty-two thousand muskets and other arms to the Continental Army. Eventually fresh troops to shoulder them also began to arrive, not in any spectacular flood, but rather in a steady small stream that was to be characteristic of Continental Army recruiting. By summer Washington's main body had risen to nine thousand men, not counting the army of the Northern Department with which Horatio Gates was guarding the lake-and-river chain from Canada. Veteran foreign officers were also rallying to the American cause, among them a German soldier of fortune who called himself the "Baron" Johann von Kalb, arriving in America as a member of the lesser French nobility named Jean de Kalb. Another was a tall, slender eager youth who was truly both French and noble. His name was the Marquis de Lafayette.

★ 41 ★

THE MARQUIS DE LAFAYETTE

As a youth the Marquis de Lafayette's astonishing ardor for soldierly glory and the service of mankind so impressed his friends that they spoke of him in amusement as "a statue in search of a pedestal." Some years later, his young, beautiful and devoted wife, hearing this description laughed in delight and clapped her hands. It was true. This scion of this noble and military family could trace his lineage as far back as A.D. 900, but neither he nor his ancestors ever made much fuss about their forebears. With the phlegm of the true Auvergnat, they took their blue blood for granted. Like them, Lafayette burned to serve his king against the enemies of France. Unlike them, he sided with those who sought justice for the common man, thus inevitably finding himself opposed to that same sovereign.

The infant who was to be this man of such seemingly conflicting aspirations was born on September 6, 1757, in the ancient Chateau Chavaniac in Auvergne amid the towering mountains of the heartlands of France, and given a name almost equally high: the Most High and Powerful Seigneur Marie Joseph Paul Yves Roch Gilbert du Motier de La Fayette. His father was the Marquis Gilbert de La Fayette, and his mother Julie de La Rivere, the beautiful daughter of a wealthy and powerful Parisian family with close ties to King Louis XV. They came to live in Chavaniac, where in April 1757, after the outbreak of the Seven Years' War, Colonel La Fayette was ordered to leave his pregnant wife and join his regiment. To his joy, he was allowed to return home twice in 1758 to see his newborn son, but in the following year at Minden, the same battle in which Lord George Germain disgraced himself, his head was blown off by a British cannonball. The little boy, not two years old, was now the Marquis Gilbert de La Fayette.

Throughout his life, Gilbert would cherish the memory of the father he could not really remember. From his grandmother and maternal aunts, as well as from his own widowed mother, he was daily indoctrinated in the exploits of the brave La Fayette soldiers, among them a marshal of France and companion in arms of Joan of Arc. There were so many of them that the little boy, so eager to emulate them, became pathetically overwhelmed and could not keep them straight in his head. But he was not an unhappy child, for life at the chateau in which he was born could be pleasant. The manor house was surrounded by fields of grain, vegetable gardens, pastureland, orchards and vineyards stretching past a fish pond toward the hazy blue mountains in the distance. Each of the chateau's windows was designed to give a different perspective of the Massif Central, the towering spine of France. There was also a billiards room, an intimate family dining room and larger ones with chandeliers designed for formal occasions. And, of course, for the growing boy—horses! Nowhere in France would there exist a better horseman than the young Marquis de La Fayette.

But life at Chavaniac could also be depressing for this lonely boy without siblings and only a girl cousin a year older than he to play with. Three widows dressed in black—his mother, his grandmother and his paternal aunt, Charlotte de Chavaniac, the mother of his playmate—plus another paternal but spinster aunt gave the chateau a somber and depressing atmosphere. Worse, his mother—who, by her love, could be expected to soften this routine of iron discipline and unquestioning obedience—spent only the summers in the Auvergne, preferring to live in winter at Versailles, where she could, by attendance at court, look after Gilbert's estates and also, perhaps, meet an eligible bachelor or widower. So the boy was left to the mercy of his grim grandmother and her two domineering daughters, from which he seemed to be rescued at the age of five by a Jesuit priest entrusted with his education.

From this remarkable preceptor Gilbert learned that intelligence and high principle could equal battlefield courage and, in the case of a sense of justice, even exceed it. But two years later, the papacy suppressed the Society of Jesus, and King Louis XV banished the black-robed sons of Ignatius Loyola from his realm. The Jesuit's successor—the Abbé Fayon—might have been totally unfortunate, with his violent prejudices, except that he was a stickler for mathematics, spelling, literature and fluency in English, even though he was a prounounced Anglophobe. The abbé's prejudices—against blacks and the "anti-Christ" Voltaire—produced an opposite reaction in his pupil. Strong-willed himself but not daring to break the apron strings of those grim La Fayette women, Gilbert deliberately came to the conclusion that blacks were as deserving of freedom as whites, however each was oppressed, and read all the works of Voltaire—the sworn enemy of Christianity—that he could find. This reaction was the beginning of a deep concern for the rights of human beings, a trait that distressed *Madame Grand-mère.* Finding him discussing crops with the peasants who paid his family's rents, she sharply inquired why he was lowering himself in such fashion, and he is supposed to have replied: "Because I care. When they have crops, we do well, too. When they starve, then we will starve." No better exposition of the theory of democratic capitalism—unlovely and selfish as it may seem—may be found anywhere.

When Gilbert was eleven, his mother suddenly took him to Paris to live. Gilbert was delighted, especially after being enrolled in the Collège du Plessis and enlisted in the King's Musketeers, the regiment that his grandfather had commanded. Two years later his mother died, and shortly afterward his grandfather, the Marquis de la Rivere, died as well. From both he inherited vast sums of money, the modern equivalent of many millions, together with his mother's estate and large holdings in Brittany and Touraine. The young marquis was now one of the wealthiest men in France.

But he showed no signs of changing overnight, like so many of his classmates might have done, from a sober, hardworking high-minded young man into a dedicated dissolute wastrel. Rather, he wrote the ladies at Chavaniac that he might buy a few fine horses, but otherwise was content to leave his huge fortune in the capable hands of his great-grandfather, the Comte de la Rivere the elder, who had been appointed his legal guardian. Otherwise he remained the outstanding student at the Collège du Plessis, leading everyone in studies, fencing and riding, showing himself a natural leader—and still aspiring with all his heart to be a soldier. His desire was so intense that it astounded his guardian, who had him transferred to the king's most prestigious regiment, the Black Musketeers. There he encountered the hostility of the young comte d'Artois, grandson of Louis XV. Artois had none of Gilbert's popularity and accomplishments, but because of his birth, he was automatically made the cadet captain. Being no diplomat, Gilbert instead of trying to ingratitate himself with his royal comrade, or at least of pretending to be pleasant to him, chose instead to ignore him—thus earning Artois's enmity. It was a trait that would make him many enemies over the years, but La Fayette—who now called himself Lafayette—simply could not be pleasant or polite to people he despised.

Unknown to him, his reputation had grown among the court families seeking a good marriage for their daughters. Gilbert had matured rapidly, like many of his ancestors standing six feet tall, at least a half foot higher than most Frenchmen of the eighteenth century. But he was not graceful, inclining toward fleshiness, and he was so awkward that the Queen of France laughed cruelly at his clumsy attempts to dance. He was not good-looking; although his features were refined, they failed to be symmetrical enough to form a handsome whole. His hair was reddish and seldom powdered, his skin freckled, his nose long and triangular and his eyes light blue. Most prominent of all was the sharp backward angle of his features, from uplifted chin to sloping forehead. However, this detraction may have been the result of European portraitists' fondness for painting their subjects in profile. The red-haired James Wolfe was similarly caricatured. But if Lafayette could be thought bumptious in his face and carriage, he was a fine horseman and—better than this to those match-making nobles—he was immensely wealthy.

The Duc d'Ayen—son of the Duc de Noailles, also a marshal of France—was the winner. Rich and powerful and the father of five daughters, he selected the fifteen-year-old Marquis de Lafayette to be the husband of his twelve-year-old daughter, Adrienne. But the duke's wife, unable to bless the marriage of a daughter not even in her teens, insisted that nothing would be said of the marriage to either party for a year and a half. Then two more years must pass, and thereafter the newlyweds must live with the Ayen family. Here, side by side with the corruption of the court of the Most Christian King of France was the faith of the Catholic nobility at its most conservative. So it was done, and after a stunning dowry of 200,000 livres was arranged for Gilbert, and Madame d'Ayen, charmed by the young suitor who had fallen deeply and shyly in love with her beautiful, tall, blue-eyed and blond daughter, had shortened the waiting period, they were married on April 11, 1774. The wedding was in the family chapel before a "modest" gathering of some four hundred guests, who had to be fed in two sittings with a meal so sumptuous and varied that each sitting took three or four hours to complete. Then, in the tradition of the day, the bridal couple was "bedded." Thirteen-year-old Adrienne and sixteen-year-old Gilbert lay in a huge four-poster while family and friends teased them, or nobles leered and matrons tittered, until the bride's father, horrified to see his daughter so upset by this vulgar custom that she threw herself into her husband's arms, hastily drew the curtains.

Whereupon the bridal chamber was evacuated, and the young couple was allowed to proceed with the pleasurable part of the purpose of marriage.

After his marriage the Marquis de Lafayette purchased a captain's commission in the Noailles Dragoons, named for the Duc d'Ayen's father. On his seventeenth birthday—September 6, 1774—he reported for duty at the fortress of Metz in Lorraine. Because there was no war, his life was a boring round of parades and reviews, relieved by invitations to dinners and dances. Now at his full height, his bucolic manners replaced by a charming grace, he became a great favorite with the ladies, although there is nothing to suggest any impropriety. Instead, he remained faithful to his young wife, who was already pregnant.

It has been said that when Lafayette rejoined his wife and journeyed with her to Paris, where they spent two days a week at court, he attempted to emulate his dissolute peers by choosing a mistress for himself. She was said to be the beautiful Aglae d'Hunolstein, the young and red-haired wife of Comte Philippe Antoine d'Hunolstein. But Aglae, already servicing another nobleman—the Duc de Chartres—is said to have rejected him. If so, it did not break Lafayette's heart, for he actually despised Versailles. Flattery—even of young King Louis XVI—was not among his skills, and he still preferred the battlefield to the boudoir. But then, to his disgust, he was assigned to the household staff of the king's younger brother, the Comte de Provence. It was like being banished for life to a ballroom. But then, at one of the weekly masked balls, Lafayette pretended not to recognize the comte, picked a quarrel with him and insulted him—for which transgression he was "punished" by being ordered back to his regiment at Metz.

It was there that he met the Duke of Gloucester, King George III's younger brother, who was then touring the Continent. Gloucester was an enthusiastic admirer of the Americans, whose rebellion against his brother had just begun. Lafayette listened eagerly to his glowing description of George Washington and his soldiers in homespun. It seemed to him that France could avenge herself on Britain by helping the colonists gain their independence. Here, too, was his chance to give more than lip service to his credo: "I am persuaded that the human race was created to be free and that I was born to serve that cause." With other young noblemen similarly on fire for the idealist cause of liberty, he formed a group of American sympathizers. In the fall of 1775 he returned to Paris to be with Adrienne when she delivered her first child (the first pregnancy had ended in a miscarriage) and to confer secretly with the American delegation there headed by Silas Deane of Connecticut. Deane offered Lafayette and his band of young nobles commissions in the American Army.

But then the Comte de Vergennes heard of Deane's offer. Vergennes did not believe France was quite ready for another war with Britain, and he ordered Lafayette and his followers not to accept the commissions.

This order only hardened Lafayette's resolve to cross the Atlantic to America—by himself, if need be, or at least with Jean de Kalb, in his own ship. The birth of his daughter Henrietta gave him the opportunity to transfer from active duty to the reserve, thus permitting him to be absent from France for some time without being charged with desertion. Then he sent an agent to Bordeaux to purchase a ship and to hire a crew. With officers he had recruited and de Kalb, he would sail to the New World. Lafayette was then only nineteen, but he so impressed Deane that he made both Lafayette and de Kalb major generals. Though delighted, Lafayette told no one—not even Adrienne—of the project. If word leaked out, the king would order him not to leave the country.

That was what happened. Even though Lafayette and his band boarded *La Victoire* in Bordeaux and sailed to the little Spanish port of Los Pasajes, a courier from King Louis overtook him there and handed him his sovereign's order to report at once to his father-in-law in Marseilles for a six-month tour of Italy. The Duc d'Ayen had triumphed over his headstrong son-in-law! Or so it seemed. But the Marquis de Lafayette did not go to Marseilles; he went to Bordeaux instead. There the governor sought to arrest him, an unfriendly gesture that led Lafayette to defy the king. Disguising himself, he hurried back to Los Pasajes and was greeted at the head of *La Victoire's* gangplank by a jubilant de Kalb, who had thought his friend had abandoned his scheme. Writing to his wife, de Kalb described his youthful chief's words to him: "I am an outlaw. I prefer to fight for the liberty of America rather than lose my own liberty and languish in a French prison. So, my friend, we shall be comrades in arms after all."

The voyage across the Atlantic lasted fifty-nine days, and it gave Lafayette a lifelong aversion to the "melancholy" necessity of traveling by sea. To amuse himself, he exercised daily, read books on military strategy and tactics and composed a marathon missive to his wife. On June 15, 1777, *La Victoire's* captain cast anchor near Charleston, South Carolina. With de Kalb and two junior officers, Lafayette had himself rowed ashore. He was astounded at the majesty of the lowland South's swamp forests. Everywhere were huge towering pines of astonishing height and enormous live oaks with great spreading limbs. Through the foliage could be seen water fowls of every size and color and those strange and horrible-looking beasts—the alligators—sunning themselves on the banks of creeks. He was also somewhat surprised at the hail of bullets that greeted them as they stumbled inland. Both he and de Kalb shouted their identification in English and the firing stopped. Out of the underbrush came a man who greeted them courteously. He was Major Huger of the South Carolina militia. Major Huger explained that his men thought they belonged to a company of German mercenaries who had deserted the British and were attacking local plantations. He took them to his home, where he served them a bountiful meal that Lafayette never forgot.

Next day Huger brought Lafayette and his band to Charleston, where they were instantly lionized. A man who could cross the ocean at his own expense to fight for liberty was indeed a hero. In turn, Lafayette was delighted to find so many Charlestonians of French extraction. Almost all of them were Huguenots who had come to America after the revocation of the Edict of Nantes. Eager to move on to Philadelphia, Lafayette quickly tired of the endless adulatory banquets, toasts and speeches, even the roving eyes of pretty girls. He bought wagons and horses for his band of sixteen officers and left Charleston on June 22.

If the sea voyage had been dismal and sometimes dangerous, the seven-hundred-mile trek by land was a miserable ordeal. Roads were few and primitive and inns far apart, while the weather alternated between drenching cloudbursts and scorching sun. There were frequent delays when wagons broke down and had to be repaired or horses had to be pulled from sloughs of mud. But since the woods and streams abounded in game and fish, there was no problem with food. It was cooked in the open, and many a night was spent under the stars. If some of Lafayette's men became discouraged, their young commander reveled in this new adventure. It seemed that every two hundred miles northward they encountered different flora and fauna, while animals, such as deer and squirrels, grew steadily larger. To his wife Lafayette wrote: "The United States is the most marvelous land on earth."

It did not seem so after they reached Philadelphia and descended on Congress, resplendent in their dress uniforms and bearing their commissions. Lafayette was told that Silas Deane had exceeded his authority. Congress, hard pressed for funds to pay its own army, not only could not afford foreign officers, but also feared to offend powerful politicians who were clamoring for promotions for their own protégés. Lafayette was politely urged to return to France. To this urging, he replied in a letter:

> After the sacrifices that I have made in this cause, I have the right to ask two favors at your hands: the one is, to serve without pay, at my own expense; and the other, that I be allowed to serve at first as a volunteer in the ranks.

Congress was impressed, and it was decided to let General Washington confer with this extraordinary and determined young man. Washington was also impressed, instantly perceiving that this youth, not yet twenty, was a natural leader of men, while Lafayette was surprised to find himself looking upward at a taller man. On Washington's recommendation, Congress confirmed the young nobleman's commission, requesting that it be considered merely honorary and thus not upset disgruntled American officers. De Kalb was likewise confirmed.

Major General the Marquis de Lafayette joined Washington's rag-tag-and-bobtail army outside Philadelphia, immediately endearing himself to his new comrades when he refused an invitation to make suggestions with the remark: "I am here to learn, not to preach or teach." He became very friendly with Colonel Alexander Hamilton, and again with burly Colonel Knox, who was delighted to find him well read in military art and history. Like Knox, Lafayette was an epicure, and they compensated for the army's plain food by discussing gourmet wines and dishes. Gradually, a father-and-son relationship developed between Washington and Lafayette—the one never having had children of his own, the other never having known his father.

The young French noble, a major general at the age of twenty, was riding beside the American commander in chief when Washington paraded his army through Philadelphia in late August 1777 as he moved to intercept General William Howe marching to capture the American "capital."

★ 42 ★

THE BATTLE OF BRANDYWINE CREEK

Sir William Howe was still smarting from those two humiliating setbacks delivered by the contemptible General Buckskins. As the spring of 1777 came and was nearly gone, he prepared to lure Washington from his hill fastness at Morristown into open battle on level ground and there destroy him and the rebellion as well. Sir William was aware that the British battle plan for 1777 did not prescribe just such a course. Instead, as Lord George Germain had informed him, he was to ascend the Hudson to make junction with John Burgoyne marching south from Canada. But Germain's language had sounded more like a suggestion than a direct order, and as General Henry Clinton could well testify, William Howe was a most "unsuggestible" man. Criticism he could not endure, and a suggestion he either ignored or followed its exactly opposite course.

In late May Howe was concentrated at Amboy with eighteen thousand disciplined and splendidly equipped regulars. Washington was still at Morristown with his nine thousand largely untrained troops. To Washington it seemed that his opponent was getting ready to capture Philadelphia. Fearing that Howe might make a swift descent on Princeton and then Trenton on the Delaware, on May 29 Washington marched his army twenty miles south to Middlebrook, about eight miles from New Brunswick, there taking up a strong position in the Watchung Mountains from which he could watch the Amboy–New Brunswick area as well as the road to Philadelphia. Here he built entrenchments and artillery posts and sent Sullivan with his division to Princeton.

On June 12 Howe began marching to New Brunswick. From there

Cornwallis led one column to Somerset, and Heister, a second to Middlebush. By these tactics, Howe hoped to lure Washington down from his commanding heights at Middlebrook and to cut off Sullivan at Princeton. Washington perceived Sullivan's peril and ordered him to retire to Rocky Hill, shifting him a few days later to Flemington, on the British right flank. He also stayed right where he was, realizing that he, not Philadelphia, was Howe's true objective.

Washington knew that his opponent was "marching light," having left his heavy baggage, his flatbottom boats and his portable bridge for crossing the Delaware at New Brunswick. This meant that Howe could not possibly be planning to attack Philadelphia and that, stripped down as he was, he was seeking decisive battle. That, of course, was exactly what the American did not want. In the words of Charles Stedman, Howe's perceptive aide, "The American general easily penetrated into the designs of the commander-in-chief, and eluded them all by his cool, collected and prudent conduct."

Howe next feigned retreat, moving secretly from Middlebush and Somerset on the night of June 19 "with marks of seeming precipitation." Washington nibbled on the bait, sending Greene with nearly five brigades to fall on the "retreating" enemy's rear. He also ordered Sullivan and General William Maxwell to cooperate with Greene.

Daniel Morgan's riflemen, who were leading Greene's advance, collided with Howe's picket guard of Hessians at the New Brunswick bridge at dawn the next day. They routed the Hessians and pursued, until they were blocked by the British rear guard. Here Greene and "Mad" Anthony Wayne came up to charge the redcoats, driving them as far as Piscataway. Here, if Sullivan or Maxwell, or both, had arrived as expected, was the chance to smash Howe or hurt him badly. Sullivan, as usual, was late, claiming he had not received his orders on time, while Maxwell said that he never received his. So Greene broke off the battle, and Howe continued his "retreat." Now Howe's soldiers, not customarily privy to a general's plans, became so enraged at this seemingly disgraceful flight from the Yankee rabble that they began to burn every house and barn that they passed. "All the country houses were in flames as far as we could see," an English civilian observed. But Howe continued his withdrawal, satisfied that his maneuver did have the effect of luring Washington down from his heights to a new position at Quibbletown (now New Market) to be "nearer the enemy." He also dispatched Stirling with a powerful detachment to Metuchen, midway between New Brunswick and Perth Amboy.

Howe now thought he had finally cornered his wily foe. At one o'clock in the morning of June 26 he departed Amboy in two columns: one under Cornwallis, moving to the east of Stirling at Metuchen, another under Lieutenant Colonel Joseph Vaughan, accompanied by Howe to the west of Stirling. The objective was to overwhelm Stirling before moving to block the passes back to Washington's abandoned high ground at Middlebrook. Washington would then have to fight on level ground.

It was a hot, humid day, the kind of enervating moist heat to which European soldiers are still unaccustomed. Howe's marching men, especially the Hessians with their heavier equipment, began to drop with sunstroke. Snipers raked them. As they neared Stirling's position, the two columns converged, launching a furious attack. Stirling, always a dogged fighter, tried to resist stubbornly, but then, seeing that Cornwallis was in position to cut him off, he retreated. Cornwallis pursued as far as Westfield, about eight miles northwest of Metuchen, but could not continue "on account of the intense heat of the day." In this engagement the British made the dubious claim of having killed or wounded one hundred Americans while capturing seventy, against seventy casualties of their own. But it was no victory, as they also insisted, for Washington had had time to retreat to the Middlebrook heights. Thus after three maneuvers, Sir William Howe found himself back where he had started at Amboy. Frustrated, he withdrew his entire army to Staten Island, so that by June 30 "the province of New Jersey was entirely evacuated by the king's troops."

There now ensued a kind of guessing game, comparable to a chess match, in which George Washington's side of the board had the customary chessmen standing among the checkered black-and-white squares and General Howe's side was the blank and opaque mists of the Atlantic Ocean. On July 23 Howe and his army vanished into those mists, leaving Sandy Hook aboard his brother's enormous armada of 260 warships carrying fifteen to eighteen thousand soldiers, innumerable horses, military stores of every description, together with artillery, and a vast supply of provisions that could feed this huge host for a month. The question was: where was it bound?

At first Washington was sure it was headed north to the Hudson and thence to Albany to meet General Burgoyne coming down from Canada with an army of eight thousand men. If not prevented, such a junction, long the dream of Lord George Germain, would effectively sever the colonies north from south. If this conjecture were true, Washington would have to strengthen his northern forces. But not with his entire army, for doing so would leave Philadelphia so naked to the enemy that it could be easily taken. When he was informed that the Howes had enough food aboard to last a month, he began to think that Charleston was once again the objective. Still he sent Sullivan north to the Ramapo Mountains. Bad news from the north—Arthur St. Clair, with 3,500 men, had abandoned Ticonderoga to Burgoyne without firing a shot!—made him forget Charleston. Reports that Burgoyne was advancing on Albany led him to guess that the Hudson was indeed Howe's destination, so he led his army north to the Ramapos west of the great river. But then on July 23 the mighty British host off Sandy Hook upped anchor and vanished.

Washington was shaken. Had he guessed wrong and left Philadelphia unprotected? It seemed to him that he had, and he began ordering his scattered formations south, eventually marching in that direction with his own army—positive now that Philadelphia via the Delaware River was Howe's objective. Howe certainly would be able to capture the city and sail back to New York in time to join Burgoyne at Albany. By the time Washington reached the Delaware—July 29—there were still no reports of the great fleet's whereabouts. It might have turned about and headed for the Hudson to join Burgoyne after all. So Washington decided to hold his forces on the New Jersey side of the Delaware, ready to move in either direction once he had a reliable sighting of the enemy armada.

That sighting came on July 31 from a pilot at Lewes, Delaware, who reported the fleet in sight at the mouth of Delaware Bay. At once Washington ordered his forces to cross the Delaware and march to Philadelphia. But then, on August 2, the same pilot reported that the fleet had disappeared to the east; "whether they are bound to New York or Virginia is not in my power to tell." Though distressed at having to conjecture with so much at stake, the American chief did guess again—and wrongly once more. Howe, he was sure, had been "practicing a deep feint." "There is the strongest reason to believe that the North [Hudson] River is their object." "I shall return again with the utmost expedition to the North River." But then, on reflection, he decided to wait until he had certain proof that the fleet had returned to Sandy Hook. Again changing his mind, he was on the march for the New Jersey side of the Delaware, when on August 10 he received the most startling intelligence of all: the great armada had been sighted off Sinepuxent Inlet in Maryland, thirty miles below the Delaware Capes! It was heading south! At once Washington halted his army and went into camp alongside Neshaminy Creek, thirty miles north of Philadelphia. There the puzzled American war chief asked himself: but why south? So he marked time beside the creek, still certain that Howe was trying to feint him away from his true objective and would soon return to either the Hudson or the Delaware. "Had Chesapeake Bay been his object he would have been there long since." Then a council of war held that same day came to the unanimous conclusion that it was Charleston after all that Howe was after. So certain were the generals that the enemy's objective was far, far from their power to prevent, that it was decided to march next morning for the Hudson River. But on that morrow came another express:

The Howes were on the Chesapeake "high up in the northeast part of it." Meaning Head of Elk.

Why, after reaching the Delaware Capes, did the Howe brothers decide not to sail up the broad river to a point within fifteen miles of Philadelphia, but chose instead to make a long, debilitating voyage south in the heat of an American summer to arrive at a point fifty miles from their objective? This is a question that has puzzled some able historians for two centuries, yet the answer appears to be simple: they were led astray by the pessimistic report of a veteran ship captain who should have known better.

After departing Sandy Hook on July 24, the British invasion fleet made the Delaware Capes six days later. There it was joined by the *Roebuck,* commanded by Captain Sir Andrew Snape Hamond. Coming aboard Howe's flagship, Hamond reported that navigation of the Delaware was intricate and dangerous. Great ships could pass certain places only at particular times of tide. Its shores were often marshy and laced with creeks. Between Reedy Island and Chester—the point within fifteen miles of Philadelphia—the channel was so narrow as to require four miles of anchorage for such a large fleet and was probably within cannon shot of the shore.

Almost all this ominous report was grossly exaggerated or absolutely false. Navigation was not so difficult or the current so strong because the flagship and twelve other large vessels were able to reach Chester in October. In November as many as one hundred ships were anchored in that supposedly narrow channel between Reedy Island and New Castle, while both Chester and New Castle were good landing places, the latter large enough to receive transoceanic ships.

Captain Hamond's assessment of the river's defenses was also overblown. The American "defending fleet" of one frigate, two xebecs, one brig and two floating batteries could no more defy Admiral Howe's massive armada than a minnow could challenge a whale, while the so-called channel obstructions were no more daunting than the sunken hulks and huge chains of the Hudson had been. It is not the fault of the Howes that they were thus dissuaded from the much easier landing at New Castle or Chester, although it is likely that General Howe, who seems to have favored the Chesapeake in the beginning, may have welcomed Hamond's pessimistic estimate as an excuse to return to his original plan.

Yet this decision did extend a projected voyage of, say, ten days to an actual thirty-two days, and this in buffeting winds causing much seasickness or in dreadfully still calms when the soldiery lay gasping in the heat like a live fish on a skillet. The long voyage also inevitably produced a shortage of fresh food, fresh water and forage for the horses. Anyone who has sailed aboard a troop ship for a month or more even in modern warfare can imagine the suffering endured by these men in the primitive facilities of two centuries ago. In eighteenth-century warfare, physical conditioning of the soldiery was not the sine qua non that it is today, so that the debilitation of the body that ensued from such a lengthy voyage must have been extreme. Men died, of course, but they were also made unfit to undertake prolonged marches upon reaching land. And the horses suffered horribly. Many of them perished and had to be thrown overboard. Upon reaching Head of Elk, the three hundred horses that survived were turned loose in a cornfield, where they so gorged themselves that half of them were felled by colic. How that affected the transport of Sir William's artillery, supplies and wounded is not known, but it could not have been otherwise than severe. There was not much chance to replace this shocking loss by requisitioning animals from the country around Head of Elk because most of the inhabitants "deserted their houses and drove off their stock." Those redcoated regulars and Hessians, for all their vaunted discipline, were almost unmanageable as well, landing full of resentment at their treatment aboard ship only to be struck by two days of unrelenting and violent storms, full of thunder and lightning, and then compelled to watch as two of their comrades were hung and five others flogged as punishment for plundering. So aroused, they defiantly looted the abandoned American farmhouses with the same fury that drove them to burn every house in sight on their June retreat through New Jersey. Thus the decision to shift to the Chesapeake from the Delaware, though based on what should have been reliable information, was flawed by all those intangibles and imponderables that are attendant upon any change in plan that extends an operation in time and distance.

Nevertheless, on August 28, 1777, three days after the Maryland landing, General William Howe's army was divided into two grand divisions—one under Cornwallis, the other led by Knyphausen—and began marching toward Philadelphia. Coming down to intercept him was George Washington, with a force variously estimated at 16,000 or 14,000 men, of which 11,000 or 12,000 were fit for duty. On September 11, 1777, the two armies collided at Brandywine Creek in Pennsylvania.

The Brandywine's depth was uneven, with crossings at numerous fords or shallows. Washington, holding the east bank of the stream, chose to guard most of them. His left rested on Pyle's Ford, held by Pennsylvania militia, his center was at Chad's (sometimes also spelled Chadd's) with two brigades under Greene and his right between Painter's and Brinton's fords, guarded by the divisions of Sullivan, Adam Stephen and Stirling, in that order, left to right. Smaller forces watched other forces higher up, but Trimble's Ford, seven miles north of Chad's Ford was neglected. And Cornwallis, accompanied by Howe, was making for Trimble's.

As much as Sir William might lack strategic acumen, he was indeed a brilliant tactician. Seeming to sense that Washington was always deployed to receive a frontal assault, he was preparing to repeat his flanking movements at Long Island and White Plains. He had ordered Cornwallis to take two-thirds of the British on a march of seventeen miles on a sweeping "end run" around Washington's right flank and into his rear. As he did, Knyphausen, opposite the American center under Greene at Chad's Ford, was to hold the rebels in place with constant cannonading; then, upon hearing the eruption of battle to the north as the signal of success in Howe's turning movement, he was to attack Greene.

Washington sat calmly still for the knockout blow. As on Long Island, he was braced for a frontal assault. And then, in the forenoon, there came to him a pair of conflicting messages: one warning that Howe's main body was making for Trimble's, the other, from Sullivan, insisting that no such movement had been detected. The first message was from Lieutenant Colonel James Ross, who wrote at eleven o'clock that "a large body of the enemy, from every account five thousand, with sixteen or eighteen field pieces, marched along the road just now. ... I believe General Howe is with this party." Ross's report thus put Howe on the west side of the Brandywine, and Washington at once ordered John Sullivan to cross to the west bank and attack him. But then came a dispatch from Sullivan reporting that Major James Spear, who was assigned to watch the fords, had been to several taverns in the west and had heard nothing of any movement of the enemy.

Here was Sullivan at his worst, dilatory and indisposed to check conflicting reports himself. In any such situation, where one man sights the enemy and another sees nothing, a commander's presumption must heavily favor the man who sees "something," not the one who sees nothing, if only because one normally does not see something that is not actually there. In Sullivan it was derelict not to confirm personally the truth of the situation. For him to act as though the British were not there was to expose the American army to destruction. If he had only pondered a few moments, he would have seen that Colonel Ross's report put the enemy where Major Spear could not possibly have seen them and that Spear's report was based on barroom hearsay. But Washington acted on Spear's report, countermanding his own orders for Sullivan to cross the Brandywine and for Greene to attack Knyphausen. In this, ironically, Sullivan's dereliction might actually have saved Washington's army from utter ruin, for Sullivan's division alone was certainly no match for Howe and Cornwallis together, with two-thirds of the British army. Greene might indeed have crushed Knyphausen at Chad's Ford, but the hole left in the American right flank by the destruction of Sullivan would have spelled disaster. Thus, by his very ineptness, Sullivan might have saved Washington.

Though puzzled by these conflicting reports, Washington was not vexed or apparently even anxious. His left, held by the Pennsylvania militia, evidently was in no danger; his center, under Greene was steady; and his right, with Sullivan, Stirling and Stephen, was not menaced. But then a hatless, coatless, bare-legged American farmer named Thomas Cheyney was brought to his headquarters. The British were across the Brandywine, Cheyney shouted. He had seen them and they had fired on him and chased him. Washington's staff smiled superior smiles. Obviously the man was a Tory out to deceive them. Cheyney turned on them wrathfully. "I'd have you know I have this day's work as much at heart as e'er a blood of ye!" he yelled.

Cheyney dropped to his knee and drew a map in the dust, marking the exact place where he had seen the British. Washington shook his head in disbelief.

"You're mistaken, General!" the farmer cried. "My life for it you're mistaken. By hell, it's so! Put me under guard till you find out it's so!"

Washington was torn by doubts, actually immobilized by them. *What to do?* Then another courier came clattering into camp on a foam-covered horse. Another dispatch from Sullivan. It read:

> Colonel Bland has this moment sent me word that the enemy are in the rear of my right about two miles coming down. There is, he says, about two brigades of them. 2 of clock PM he also says he saw a dust rise back in the country for above an hour.

There was no longer any doubt! Howe was again doing what he had done on Long Island and White Plains. While Washington sat still, once more calmly awaiting another Bunker Hill, Howe had awakened two-thirds of his army at four o'clock in the morning and, with Cornwallis, had led them fifteen miles to Osborne's Hill, in position either to roll up the entire Yankee line on the east bank of the Brandywine or to drive deep behind Washington's right to rout it and then pin the rest of Washington's forces against the Brandywine and destroy them. Other reports stated that the enemy had halted at Osborne's Hill to rest. The British troops had been marching for more than ten hours on a swelteringly hot day and had not eaten. They needed both food and rest, and they took both, lying sprawling in the grass while the countryside flocked around them in curious groups. A twenty-year-old Quaker youth named Joseph Townsend strode among them and recorded how he was awed by their bright uniforms and shining bayonets. He saw Cornwallis. "He was on horseback, appeared tall and sat very erect. His rich scarlet clothing loaded with gold lace, epaulets, etc., occasioned him to make a brilliant and martial appearance." Townsend thought that most of the British officers were "rather short, portly men, well-dressed and of genteel appearance, and did not look as if they had ever been exposed to any hardship, their skins being as white and delicate as is customary for females." He also saw Howe "mounted on a large English horse, much reduced in flesh. … The general was a large, portly man, of coarse features. He appeared to have lost his teeth, as his mouth had fallen in." In a moment, the sergeants were dashing about bellowing orders, the men arose, brushing the crumbs from their uniforms, formed ranks—and resumed their southward march.

Now that he knew his peril, George Washington moved decisively. He ordered his entire right wing—all three divisions under Sullivan—to march north at once to oppose Howe coming south. He was to seize and fortify the terrain around Birmingham Meeting House. At Chad's Ford Wayne, with two brigades and artillery, was ordered to hold Knyphausen. Greene's division of two brigades was detached from Chad's Ford as a reserve to march to the assistance of either Sullivan or Wayne. Washington remained with Greene. Waiting … Waiting … Waiting for the eruption of the sound of battle either to the north of him at Birmingham or to the west at Chad's Ford.

At half-past four it came with a roar that could be heard in Philadelphia. The main battle had begun at Birmingham. To the west at Chad's Ford, Knyphausen, having heard the signal, opened a bombardment preliminary to attack. Washington hesitated momentarily, but then, deciding that Wayne would have to handle Knyphausen by himself, he ordered

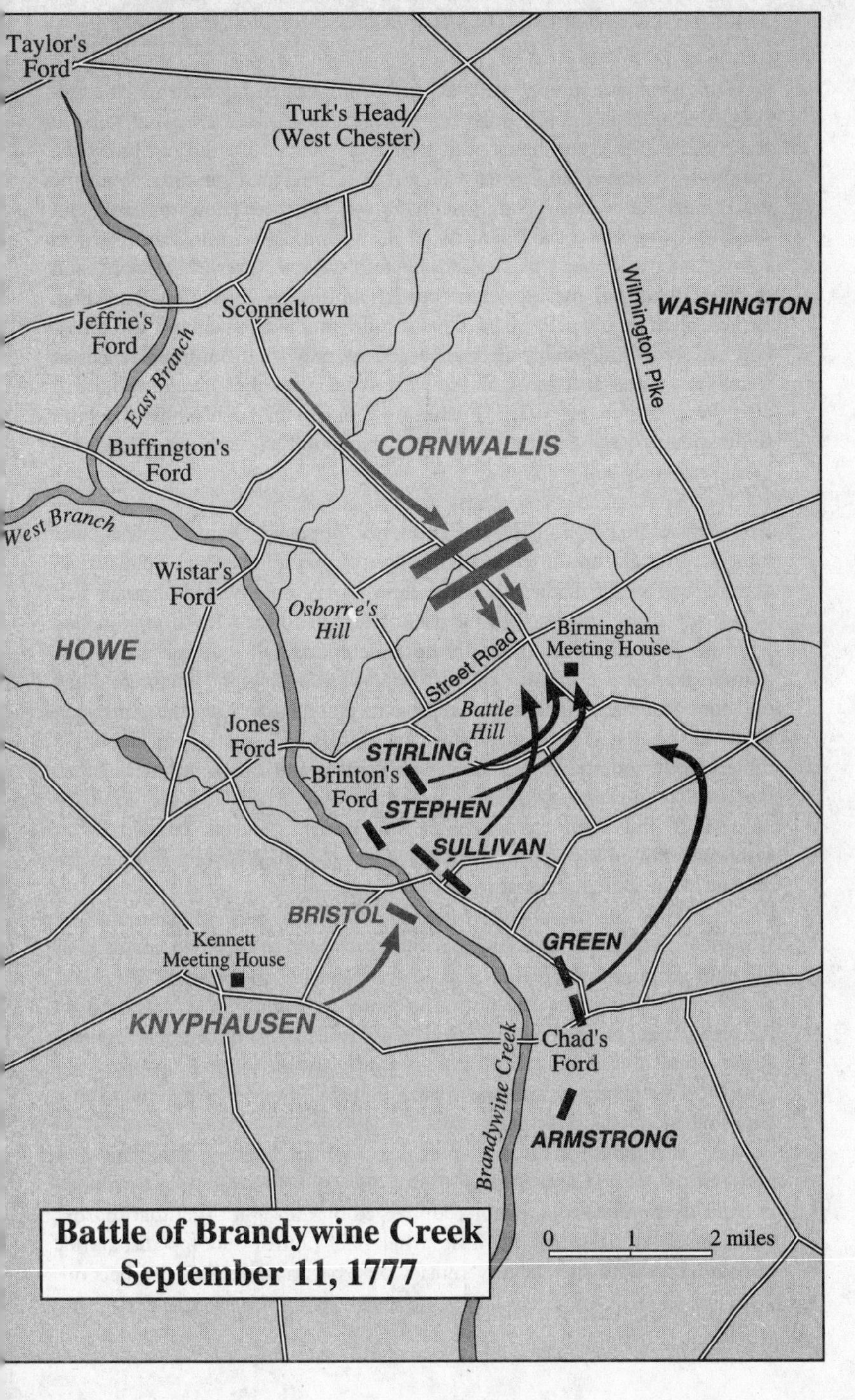

Battle of Brandywine Creek
September 11, 1777

Greene north to reinforce Sullivan and to hold open the road to Philadelphia. Washington himself must follow Greene because he wanted to be at the scene of the grand battle. But how to get there? He did not know the country! Seeing an old farmer among the countrymen standing about, he asked him his name. It was Joseph Brown. Yes, he knew the way; but when Washington asked Brown to lead him to Birmingham, Brown refused. At once an aide leaped from his horse, drew his sword and threatened to run the old man through unless he consented. Nodding, Brown allowed himself to be hoisted into the saddle—taking off cross-country for Birmingham, three miles as the crow flies, jumping fences at a gallop, up hill and down dale, while the big Yankee general pounded after him, crying furiously: "Push along, old man! Push along!" Behind them streamed the general's staff, and the sound of battle grew louder—then ominously still.

The American position, on an eminence opposite Osborne's Hill, was faulty. Stirling's and Stephen's divisions were joined, but Sullivan, in coming up on Stirling's left, was nearer to the enemy and about a half mile away from Stirling. Falling back, Sullivan formed his troops in line with the other divisions, but with the undefended half-mile space still separating them. Then he rode off to confer with Stirling and Stephen. They told him that the British apparently were planning to turn the American right and that he, Sullivan, should move in that direction to present a united front and the whole force would then shift farther right to block the turning movement. Sullivan agreed and returned to his division to move it to the right. At this point, the British attacked, coming down Osborne's Hill in a bright mass of color and glittering bayonets, the bands playing "The British Grenadiers."

Crossing the road between the two heights in perfect alignment, the British forces began climbing the hill in a silent, disciplined mass, with the light infantry and Hessian and Anspach jaegers in the lead. With loud cries but no shots, they fell upon the American right, which was held by the three regiments of Marylanders commanded by the French General Prudhomme de Borre. The sight of those outthrust steel tips was too much for the Yankees, and they broke and fled into a nearby wood, thus exposing Stephen's right flank.

At this point Sullivan's troops were marching to close the gap between themselves and Stirling's left. They moved directly in a column in front of the oncoming enemy. Unnerved by the sight of all that martial color approaching them; of those cruel steel points; and the disdainful, arrogant sound of the military music, they began to straggle, to become fragmented into groups. Sullivan was not there to rally and re-form them, for he had gone to his center to direct his artillery. Now thoroughly panicked, his men sought to return whence they came. Sullivan, riding up at last, sought to restrain them, but they paid him no heed, and so the American left was also swept clean away. Shorn of its wings, the American center, with Stirling's division and what was left of Stephen's, fought valiantly against the pride of European militarism. There were three thousand of them, and their generals—Sullivan, Stirling, Stephen and the French-Irishman Thomas Conway—moved among them shouting encouragement. Galloping into the fray, ardent for battle, came the young French nobleman, the Marquis de Lafayette—fighting on after being wounded in the leg. Five times the rebels were driven off that hill, and five times they returned to evict their tormentors. Though shaken, the British regulars and their Hessian allies, twice the number of the Yankees opposing them and backed up by four twelve-pounders, were not to be denied. All seemed lost for the American army and the new American nation. Its best troops fighting their best fight in the young country's brief history were giving way, tumbling back downhill—but marching up the road to their rescue came Greene's division, the brigades of Colonel Peter Muhlenberg and Brigadier General George Weedon.

Opening their ranks, the fresh Americans allowed their exhausted comrades to stagger through and re-form—closing their ranks again to confront the flower of Europe. At first they held them, backed up by artillery. But the British pressure was too great, and Greene began a slow, fighting retreat. Coming to a narrow defile, flanked on both sides by thick woods, the Americans turned again—holding off their pursuers with a steady fire. Still the enemy pressed forward, resorting for the first time to regular volleys of musketry, launching repeated bayonet charges. The fighting raged so close, sometimes hand to hand, that the Anspachers recognized their old comrade, Colonel Muhlenberg, who had fought with them as an enlisted man. "*Hier kommt Teufel Piet!*" they cried in delight. "Here comes Devil Pete!" But the Americans doggedly held the pass for forty-five minutes. At last the sun went down, and Greene skillfully drew off his entire division. Exhausted, the British and Hessians made no attempt to follow.

The Battle of Brandywine Creek did not end at Birmingham Meeting House. At Chad's Ford Knyphausen attacked furiously behind an artillery bombardment. Wayne's Americans held stubbornly at first, but gradually gave way after the allies, with Knyphausen personally leading, moved across Pyle's Ford below Chad's and launched an attack in the face of artillery and musket fire. With this assault, Wayne's left gave way, losing its artillery—after which Lady Luck, so often the true arbiter of battle, waved her wand over Knyphausen. Cornwallis's guards and grenadiers, who had pursed Sullivan's fleeing soldiers, became lost in the woods and by accident blundered upon the exposed flank of Wayne's center, and the entire American line fell back. With this and the advent of darkness, the Battle of Brandywine Creek came to an end.

It had been a fierce fight, and although Howe was victorious, the Americans for the first time showed a tenacity and discipline that surprised their enemies. British losses were 90 killed, 480 wounded and 6 missing. American casualties were never accurately computed, although Howe—with the victor's customary exaggeration—estimated them at 300 killed, 600 wounded and "near 400" taken prisoner. If they had been anything near that number, there would have been no American army and no American nation. A third of 1,300 would have been nearer the truth. But Howe was undoubtedly the victor. He had again outmaneuvered Washington, just as for the fourth time in succession, he had failed to deliver the crusher. And so George Washington had saved his army once more. Nor were his men downcast. Some of them, as they retreated to Chester and then to Germantown, were actually proud of how they had held off the regulars in a stand-up fight. Many of them were actually saying, "Come, boys, we shall do better another time."

Actually they did worse. In the early morning of September 21, British forces, under Major General Charles Grey, surprised Anthony Wayne's division at Paoli's Tavern. Grey had ordered his men to march with unloaded muskets, removing their flints to guard against accidental discharges. "No-Flint" Grey's men caught the Americans silhouetted by the light of their own campfires and routed them with a fierce bayonet charge. Some 300 Americans were killed or wounded, 100 more were captured, and reports of so-called atrocities at the "Paoli Massacre" caused fleeing congressmen to dig their spurs into the hides of horses that were carrying them from threatened Philadelphia to the safety of York, Pennsylvania.

On September 26 Howe entered Philadelphia. He received a liberator's reception and became convinced that he had come at last to the Land of the Tories. Notifying Mrs. Loring to join him—escorted by her husband, of course—Howe relaxed his vigilance. He divided his army, keeping one force in Philadelphia and a larger one in the unguarded suburb of Germantown.

Washington, seeing his chance, eager to silence a rising storm of criticism, prepared to attack.

★ 43 ★

THE BATTLE OF GERMANTOWN

Deeply disappointed at the Brandywine, dismayed by the Paoli Massacre, Washington was further discouraged when Howe, by a series of skillful maneuvers, marched triumphant into Philadelphia without firing a shot. Moreover, the plaudits of the delirious Tories hailing their British liberators were in sharp contrast to the barrage of criticism and complaint aimed at the American commander in chief.

When John Adams could cry, "O, Heaven! grant us one great soul!" Washington could shrug it off as the plaint of the typical armchair amateur, who was even then leading his congressional cohorts in flight from Philadelphia to York. But he could not so dismiss the disaffections of Gates, Conway and other disenchanted officers. Even Nathanael Greene was saying that his chief was again showing the hesitation he had shown at Fort Washington, conveniently forgetting that it was he who had advised defending that indefensible slaughter pen. Timothy Pickering, the new adjutant general, said to Greene: "Before I came to the army, I entertained an exalted opinion of General Washington's military talents, but I have since seen nothing to enhance it." To this, the usually loyal Greene replied: "Why, the general does want decision. For my part, I decide in a moment." Jean de Kalb wrote: "Washington is the most amiable, kindhearted and upright of men; but as a general he is too slow, too indolent and far too weak. Besides he has a tinge of vanity in his composition, and overestimates himself. In my opinion, whatever success he may have will be owing to good luck and the blunders of his adversaries, rather than to his abilities. I may even say that he does not know how to improve upon the grossest blunders of the enemy."

Surprisingly, in all this chorus of criticism, there was no exact catalog of specific failures, no where and when, and even Greene's "want of decision" was not exactly fair. Certainly no one could have been more decisive than Washington when he realized that his right was being turned. To have abandoned almost the entire line of the Brandywine by sending Sullivan with three divisions to Birmingham Meeting House actually blunted Howe's flanking maneuver, while to have left Wayne alone to contain Knyphausen at Chad's Ford while forming Greene's brigades into a rescue reserve was masterful. These maneuvers did not avert defeat, but they avoided disaster. Washington's most obvious shortcomings at the Brandywine and elsewhere appear to have been a tendency to prepare for battle on the basis of what he expected the enemy to do, rather than what he had the ability to do, as well as an indifference to thorough reconnaissance. True enough, watching the roads in their sectors was the responsibility of the division commanders, but Washington's army as yet had no reliable corps of cavalry upon which to rely for information.

Washington was keenly aware of what was being said about him, but he also could do nothing about it except to resign—which he also knew was exactly what some of his ambitious generals desired, especially Conway and Gates. He certainly could not offer excuses. To publicize the deplorable state of his own army, now down to less than half of Howe's, with more than a thousand of them shoeless, would be to give aid and comfort to the enemy. He also at this point, when the "savior of Trenton" had become "the bungler of the Brandywine," could not despond. He had to take counsel from his confidence, not his fears, to see in the Brandywine not the despair of another defeat, but in the performance of his soldiery there more proof that his faith in their ultimate ability to face British regulars on even terms was justified. Most of all, he could not falter in the heartless, thankless task of replenishing his always-vanishing army with new levies of ardent young Patriots able to fire a musket and dig a trench. In his tireless devotion to this basic but not glamorous achievement—the true miracle of his tenure as commander in chief—he refutes de Kalb's unfounded charge of "indolence," and in his repeated exposure of his person to hardship, danger and death, he also makes one wonder how another soldier could call him "weak." But Washington's near-despair gradually gave way to a renewal of hope with the steady arrival of more troops: A thousand militia from Virginia, about as many from New Jersey and Alexander MacDougall's brigade from New York, as well as Heath's Massachusetts line and Morgan's riflemen, made his army strong enough for him to think of striking Howe once more.

★ ★ ★

Washington was at Pennypacker's Mills when he informed Congress on September 28 that he had eight thousand Continentals and about three thousand militia, an army nearly as large as the one that marched through Philadelphia to the Brandywine. At a council of war he proposed leading this force against Howe at Germantown, but the proposal was rejected ten votes to five. Rather, it was decided to move "within about 12 miles of the enemy" and to await fortuitous events. A pair of short marches on September 29 and October 2 put the army within sixteen miles of Germantown. There it was learned that Howe had detached three thousand men to guard supply trains that were moving up from Elkton, Maryland, because he dared not bring them by water past the Delaware forts and obstructions. In Philadelphia Cornwallis had two battalions each of British and Hessian regulars, but had sent a good part of this force into New Jersey to capture the fort at Billingsport. This left Howe with only about nine thousand men in Germantown. A second council of war decided that conditions to attack him were now favorable.

Germantown was a village of houses each enclosed by a rail fence, stretching for two miles along the Skippack Road, the thoroughfare from Philadelphia to Reading. Other roads led to the village from Washington's camp. Washington decided to use the Skippack and three others for a four-pronged night march and dawn attack.

On the night of October 3, 1777, a quartet of American columns struck south for Germantown. On the right were the militia, then Sullivan, then Greene, then more militia. Sullivan and Greene in the center, with the bulk of the Continentals, packed the main punch. After they struck the British main body and rolled it back, the militia to either side would crumple the enemy's flanks. All four columns were to arrive at their jumping-off positions at two o'clock the next morning, to rest there for a few hours or to await the arrival of stragglers, and to attack precisely at five with a bayonet charge. Here at the outset was evidence of imperfect scrutiny of the proposed battlefield. All those rail fences would certainly fragment any such bayonet charge, if not make it impossible.

It was an elaborate plan for a great pincers movement, nothing less than a duplication of the famous double envelopment by which Hannibal of Carthage destroyed the Roman legions at the Battle of Cannae nearly two thousand years earlier and that has since proved so fatally attractive to many military commanders. But there were two great differences: first, Hannibal arranged his forces with his weakest units in the center and his strongest on the flanks, and he was *receiving* not *delivering* an attack. Thus as his weak center deliberately fell back before the advancing Romans, his powerful jaws swung shut behind them to annihilate them. Thus Hannibal did not have to contend with the debilitating, disorganizing effect of a long, nocturnal approach march over four separate roads by four attacking columns traversing unfamiliar terrain and needing to be coordinated in the dark. Contrary to Alexander Hamilton's dictum that in war the attack "has a three-to-one chance of success," it is rather true that the assault without possessing at least a three-to-one superiority has more difficulties to overcome than does the defense. Moreover, in attacking, Washington had placed his stronger Continentals in the center and his weaker militia on the critical wings. Finally, these were green troops—even the Continentals were mostly raw recruits. And they were led by relatively amateur officers, who were expected to march sixteen miles in perfect alignment and timing over four routes, six or seven miles apart, through rough, broken terrain without communication between them and then fall upon and defeat an army equal in number but better trained and led, and fighting from prepared defensive positions. If one of these columns failed, the entire operation would fail. Yet, in the face of such obviously insurmountable difficulties, the wonder is that Washington very nearly pulled it off.

Sullivan's column, marching down the Skippack Road, included Conway in the advance brigade, followed by Wayne, Stirling, Maxwell, and Washington himself. Its mission was to reach the British outposts at Mount Airy before dawn. But because of the roughness of the country they were traversing, they did not reach their objective until a misty sun was risen. At once Captain Allen McLane, of the Delaware light horse, charged the enemy pickets, driving them back—but not before they had fired two signal shots that alerted Howe's entire army.

At once the Second Light Infantry rushed to the front, striking Conway so savagely that he had to call forward his entire brigade to hold his position. Then the Fortieth Light Infantry, under Colonel Thomas Musgrave, a brave and resourceful officer, joined the battle. Conway was stopped. Sullivan then deployed his own troops to the west or right of his route, trying to dislodge Musgrave—but the light infantry held. Sullivan next called upon Wayne, whose men came charging forward yelling, "Have at the bloodhounds! Remember the Paoli Massacre!" For once the Americans used the bayonet effectively. Twice they hurled the redcoats back, twice they withstood their counter-charges. Now the British began to surrender! Their blood up, Wayne's soldiers ran them through, even after they had laid down their arms and "were crying for mercy." Nothing their

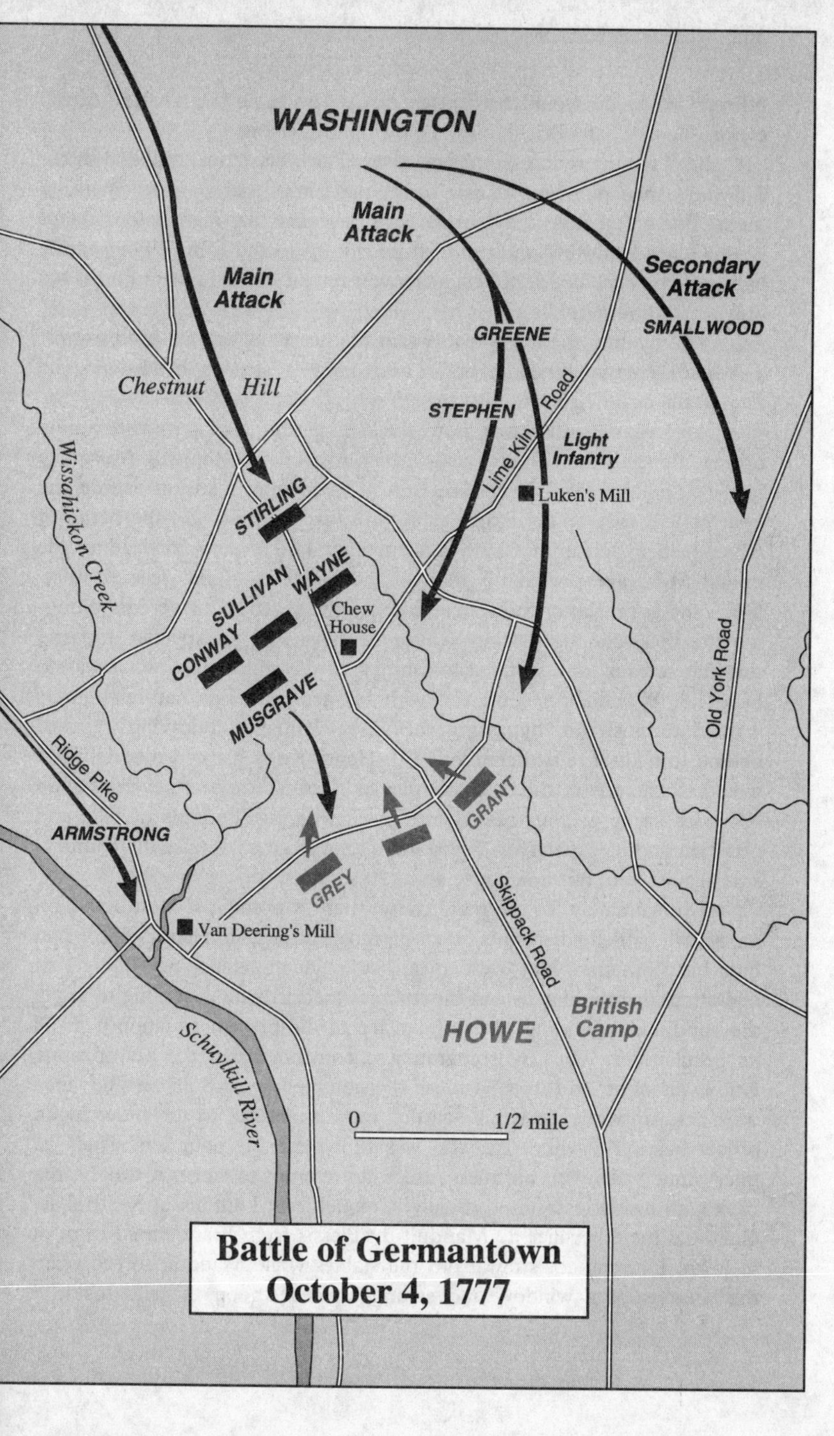
WASHINGTON
Main Attack
Main Attack
Secondary Attack
GREENE
SMALLWOOD
Chestnut Hill
STEPHEN
Lime Kiln Road
Light Infantry
Luken's Mill
Wissahickon Creek
STIRLING
SULLIVAN
WAYNE
Chew House
CONWAY
MUSGRAVE
Old York Road
Ridge Pike
GRANT
ARMSTRONG
GREY
Van Deering's Mill
Skippack Road
British Camp
HOWE
Schuylkill River
0
1/2 mile

Battle of Germantown
October 4, 1777

officers would do would restrain them. At last came the sweetest music ever in Yankee ears: British bugles blowing the retreat.

Back fell the redcoats, making a stand at every fence, wall and ditch. Sullivan's men pursued, tearing down the fences that were fragmenting them. For a full mile they drove Musgrave and his men before them. Now General Howe came riding furiously up to the front. "For shame, light infantry!" he cried. "I never saw you retreat before! Form! Form! It's only a scouting party."

To give him the lie, and to warm the hearts of his maligned troops, a Yankee charge of grape burst over Howe's startled head—and the Americans came charging forward.

The sunrise mist was now thickening into fog, growing rapidly denser. Beneath the cover of its swirling gray billows, the wily Musgrave fed six of his riddled companies into a huge gray mansion astride the east, or left, side of the Skippack Road. The mansion was the home of Chief Justice Benjamin Chew. Closing the shutters and barricading the doors, Musgrave posted his men at the windows of the second story. Upon the approach of Sullivan's reserves, the redcoats delivered a plunging fire that sent the Patriots scattering. It was an unexpected impasse, the first setback of a so-far astonishingly successful attack. What was to be done? Washington conferred with his generals. The natural fighters wanted to push on, bypassing the Chew House and leaving a guard behind to neutralize its defenders. But Henry Knox insisted that doing so would violate one of the cardinal rules of classical warfare: never leave an occupied castle in your rear. Castle, yes, with its hundreds of pike and bowmen and its capacity to withstand a long siege or to raise the countryside against you, but one house and 120 soldiers, no.

Unfortunately for the rebel cause, there is nothing so destructive on an actual battlefield as the "book-larnin'" on which Henry Knox had built his reputation. Not even cowardice or incompetence can unravel an operation as throughly as can the military theorist who is seeking to apply the condition of another time and place to the present situation with all its peculiarities. Thus Washington was convinced that the pontificating Knox was right, and thus all those divisions following Sullivan's advance were held up while, first, the "castle" was summoned to surrender by an officer bearing a white flag who was shot dead; six-pounders struck its thick stone walls with harmless effect; an attempt to storm it was beaten back with heavy losses; and, finally, Colonel John Laurens of South Carolina and the Chevalier de Mauduit du Plessis from France tried to burn it down. Laurens got straw from the stables while Mauduit forced open the shutters of a window and swung himself up on the sill. Inside a

British officer challenged him, and when the Frenchman wryly explained, "I'm only taking a walk," the officer replied: "Surrender, sir!" At that point a redcoat entered the room, fired at Mauduit but hit the officer instead. Meanwhile Laurens took a bullet in the shoulder—and the Chew House remained in British hands.

Now Washington asked himself anxiously: Where was Greene?

With two-thirds of the American army, Nathanael Greene's column had four miles longer to march than did the other columns. Greene had also been led astray by his guide, so that he was an hour late as he drew near to the left of Sullivan's column and the Chew House. At that point Adam Stephen, who was drunk, heard the Chew House gunfire and without orders from Greene, swung his division in that direction. Here was the second unraveling of Washington's plan. Stephen's artillery followed him to join in the futile battering of the big stone mansion, losing another hour.

Greene, with his own division and the brigades of Muhlenberg, McDougall and Charles Scott, pressed forward. Meeting the advancing British at his objective of Luken's Mill on the enemy right, he became engaged in a fierce fight, finally pushing the redcoats back and delivering his planned attack on their right flank. But as the British resisted, they had extended their right so that they threatened to outflank Greene's left. Concealed by the fog now thickened with gunsmoke, the American commander skillfully counter-marched his troops to his left to avoid encirclement. Then he struck the enemy wing so hard that it gave way. Devil Pete Muhlenberg led a bayonet charge so impetuous that his men drove clear through the British camp, taking many prisoners. Victory seemed within Washington's grasp.

Even the major unraveling of the battle plan at the Chew House and the minor one of Stephen's drunken dereliction seemed insufficient to deny Washington the victory, for the British were already debating the wisdom of withdrawing to Chester. Sullivan and Wayne, meanwhile, were driving steadily ahead in the right center, though out of visual communication because of the thick smoke-mixed fog. With visibility at about thirty yards, neither knew where the other was. Wayne, upon hearing the roar of artillery behind him at the Chew House, fancied that Sullivan was in trouble back there. He wheeled around and blundered into Stephen's division, hurrying to overtake Greene. A friendly firefight ensued, until both divisions broke, with their men fleeing in panic. Now the fabric of the battle plan was rapidly unraveling.

★ ★ ★

Sullivan's division, though still fighting, was running out of ammunition. Opposing him, General "No-flint" Grey, on the British left, hurled a brigade at Sullivan's right, while General "Castration" Grant simultaneously struck hard with two regiments at Sullivan's exposed left. Reeling from attacks on their front and flanks, mistaking the sound of gunfire at the Chew House to mean that the enemy was also in their rear, Sullivan's heretofore gallant soldiers began to waver. Their panic was complete when a light horseman rode into their midst shouting that they were surrounded. They broke. Not all at once. At first squads, then companies and battalions, finally en masse. Greene now had no support on either flank, and the British and Hessians who had shattered Sullivan let his fleeing soldiers go while turning to strike at Greene, who had only Scott's and McDougall's brigades with his own division to oppose them, until Muhlenberg, still pursuing the enemy a thousand yards off, turned and made a fighting return with his command.

Now Major General James Agnew's division joined with Grey and Grant to destroy the Americans. But for the skill and tenacity of Greene, the Americans might have perished. Marched out and fought out, they still made a splendid fighting withdrawal, turning to strike back from fences, ditches, walls and houses, stubbornly delaying the oncoming enemy while Greene gradually drew off all his guns. The Americans were so exhausted from their night march and day-long battle that many of them fell asleep standing up or marched like zombies. Muhlenberg, riding at the rear, fell asleep in his saddle.

The retreat became general when it became known that the militia assigned to roll up Howe's flanks had not only arrived at their objective late, but had given such timorous battle that they were easily repulsed. Now Washington sought to stop his army's rearward flow, "exposing himself to the hottest fire." But these beaten men could not be rallied. It was not their fault; they had fought well, but had been undone by the blunders of their leaders. And as they ran past their general, they held aloft their empty cartridge boxes as silent justification of their flight. They had fought until they had exhausted their ammunition. Meanwhile, Cornwallis had arrived from Philadelphia with three fresh battalions. Ordered by Howe to pursue—more likely, given the British chief's obvious relief at having escaped disaster, to make sure the Americans did not turn again—his lordship followed at a respectful distance, exchanging desultory cannon shots with his quarry. After eight miles, he halted. Washington's officers would have halted there also, for as one captain wrote: "We eat nothing and drank nothing but water on the tour." But Washington drove them on, all the way back to Pennypacker's Mill, eight miles farther than the camp they had marched from with such high hopes the preceding night.

Germantown had ended in a tragic reversal of the fortunes of war. Such a complicated plan needs almost perfect execution and completely cooperative conditions of terrain and weather. But the conditions were too hostile and the human errors too numerous. The "ifs" abounded. If there had been easier marching country and no fog, if Stirling and Maxwell in the reserve had not been held up at the Chew House, if Stephen had not gotten drunk (for which he was later cashiered) and disobediently taken his division away from Greene, if Wayne had not mistakenly turned back thinking to help Sullivan and thus collided with Stephen's men and if the militia had marched faster and fought harder—if only a few of these unsettling mistakes or misfeasances had not occurred, Washington might have defeated Howe. As it was, he nearly did—and his troops again showed that when properly led, they could hold their own with anyone.

British casualties were 70 killed and 420 wounded, while the Americans lost 152 killed, 521 wounded and about 400 captured. Clearly a British victory, it was also the fifth time that Howe had failed to destroy Washington's army. The fact that less than a month after losing one army at Brandywine, Washington was able to march with another right up to the brink of victory against the flower of Europe, led by one of the most skillful tacticians of the age, could not have failed to impress France and Spain, already agreeably surprised by what the Americans were doing to the British army at Saratoga, under General Burgoyne.

★ 44 ★

JOHN BURGOYNE

Few ranking commanders on either side of the Revolutionary War possessed a pedigree as long as John Burgoyne's. As the name implies, the family was French, having migrated from Burgundy in the early thirteenth century, settling in Bedfordshire and Cambridgeshire and becoming prosperous farmers. Although untitled at first, the family did have strong connections with John of Gaunt, Duke of Lancaster, in whose mouth Shakespeare placed his splendid salute to his native land—"this precious gem set in a silver sea"—and who, something of a versifier himself, is supposed to have granted some manors to the Burgoynes with this comic rhyme:

I, John of Gaunt
Do give and do graunt
To Johnny Burgoyne
And the heirs of his loyne
All Sutton and Potton
Until the world's rotten.

Although the verse is probably not authentic, it does celebrate the Burgoynes' proclivity for acquiring land, much of which came as payment from King Henry VIII for their assistance in seizing the Catholic monasteries. In 1641 another John Burgoyne was knighted by Charles I, becoming the family's first baronet. The third baronet was Burgoyne's grandfather. This Sir John had seven children, of whom the second, also named John, was Burgoyne's father: a rake and a wastrel, styling himself either "captain" or "major" with no claim to either. His swashbuckling dress and airs secured him the hand of the strikingly beautiful—and equally wealthy—Anna Maria Burnstone, whom he probably married some time in 1713, promptly embarking upon the dissipation of her fortune. Nine barren years were to pass before their only child—a son named John—was born on February 4, 1723.

Thus there entered British and American history that colorful character known as "Gentleman Johnny" Burgoyne, although he was never called that while he lived, and not for another fifteen decades, until George Bernard Shaw introduced him under that name in his play *The Devil's Disciple.* Yet, this son of an old and distinguished family, this famous soldier and politician, poet and playwright, was, almost from the moment of his birth, embroiled in controversy suggesting that he was not all that illustrious, but rather illegitimate.

The story that young John Burgoyne was a bastard is believed to have been started by the wife of Lord Bingley, who had stood as the child's godfather at his christening in the ultrafashionable St. Margaret's Church. Lady Bingley said that her husband was not only the godfather, but the natural father as well. Bingley was not a noble by birth, having been born Robert Benson, the son of an unscrupulous Yorkshire attorney. Handsome, able and unprincipled, he rose to become chancellor of the exchequer under Queen Anne. He also acquired an enormous fortune from the South Sea Bubble, perhaps the most notorious swindle in British history, impoverishing thousands of investors beguiled into buying stock in the company licensed by the government to exploit South America and the South Seas. Bingley was also an inveterate womanizer, living secretively in a huge house resembling an armory, with its tiny windows and soaring walls. It was said it had been designed to discourage would-be witnesses to the sexual orgies conducted inside.

Through the years Lady Bingley's story gained wide circulation, gathering momentum after Burgoyne became famous during the Seven Years' War. The malicious Horace Walpole, that "golden dustman" whose profligate nephew was sharply disciplined by Burgoyne in Spain, put it about that "Burgoyne the Pompous is the natural son of Lord Bingley." By the time Burgoyne died in 1792, this charge was generally accepted. Even the distinguished American historian George Bancroft, without a shred of evidence, baldly stated that Burgoyne sought military glory to bedazzle the dark shame of his birth.

Infuriated, the Burgoyne family commissioned an author to write the general's biography and clear his name. He began by observing that if Bancroft or anyone else had bothered to consult the records, he or they would have encountered two ineluctable facts—the *only* pertinent facts: first, that Burgoyne's parents were married and he was not born until nine years afterward and second, that Burgoyne's mother had a reputation for virtue and that if her similarly straitlaced friends had the slightest suspicion of promiscuity on her part, they would have dropped her, which they never did. This statement seemed to settle the controversy—until another scholar came upon the will of Lord Bingley.

Bingley's will, probated after his death in 1731, was indeed strange, but known only to his beneficiaries. After providing for his wife and two daughters—one legitimate, the other not—Bingley left to Burgoyne's mother two houses, fully furnished and decorated and replete with paintings, plate and jewelry, plus £400 a year for life, while also forgiving her husband's enormous debts. Next, if his legitimate daughter had no heirs and his illegitimate daughter no male heirs, the remainder of his fortune was to pass to his godson, provided he took Bingley's real name of Benson. There were, however, heirs—and John Burgoyne received nothing.

The implications of this curious will were plain: the beautiful and virtuous Anna Maria Burgoyne had slept with the lecherous and wealthy Lord Bingley to pay off her husband's debts. That was the inference generally drawn from these sensational disclosures. But there were other explanations, among them the fact that the Burgoynes were childless and Bingley was without male descendants. Bingley wanted a son and the chance to ravish a beauty, the Burgoynes wanted at least a child and release from debt. This second supposition, without the sort of evidence that a divorce case might have provided, seems more likely. But the truth will never be known.

Doubtless these revelations—or suggestions—had to have had an effect on Burgoyne's character. Mere illegitimacy—common enough in the eighteenth century, especially among the upper classes—would not have troubled him. After all, he fathered four bastards himself, one of them becoming a famous field marshal. But to have been the result of such a sordid deal, and one involving his beloved, virtuous mother, could not have been easy to accept. For his father, Burgoyne had nothing but contempt and hatred. After the elder Burgoyne had succeeded in exhausting his wife's fortune, he was clapped into debtor's prison for failure to pay a debt of £28. At the time his son was rich and influential and could easily have advanced him such a paltry sum, but he did not—and his father died in prison. It is thus possible, as John Burgoyne's career seems to suggest, that Bancroft, not out of anything he knew or for historical ideals of truth or justice, but rather out of mean spite, was right.

★ ★ ★

In 1733, at the age of ten, John Burgoyne was sent to Westminster School in London, then considered second only to Eton among the public schools, and equal to all in the use of the bloody cane. Fortunately for John, he did not board at the school but was allowed to live at home, thus escaping much of this ghastly discipline. The arrival of Dr. John Nicoll at Westminister put an end to most of these horrors, and John Burgoyne probably profited by coming under the tutelage of this most gentle and forbearing headmaster. But Burgoyne's stay at Westminster lasted no longer than four years. At fourteen he joined the Third Troop of Horse Guards as a subbrigadier, the lowest commissioned rank in this most exclusive formation and the equivalent of cornet in the cavalry or ensign in the infantry. The cost of this commission was £1,200, an enormous sum in those days, which did not include the expense of equipping him with the "necessaries to appear as an Officer and Gentleman": to wit, tent and bedding; one full suit of clothes; twenty-four shirts; eighteen pairs of stockings; frock suits; lace; hats and cockades; garters and gloves; a cloak; shoes, boots and spatterdashes, or hip-high gaiters to ward off mud; swords and pistols, with wine, servants and horses thrown in.

Thus accoutered, and with high hopes of glory, John Burgoyne set out on his military career in 1737. But there was no fighting until 1740 upon the outbreak of the War of the Austrian Succession, King George's War in the colonies, and even then, for more than three years thereafter Burgoyne saw no action and was still a subbrigadier. But he had grown into a tall, handsome, courteous and charming man, and upon his transfer into the First Royal Dragoons as a cornet in April 1744, he at last saw combat. This was at Fontenoy in France, where Marshal Saxe defeated the Duke of Cumberland's army. Forever after, Burgoyne had the utmost respect for Saxe, reading his memoirs on the art of war. He was still with the First Royal Dragoons when that regiment was returned to Britain and deployed north of London to meet the anticipated incursion from Scotland of Bonnie Prince Charlie in 1745. He was promoted to lieutenant that same year and to captain three years later, financing the purchase of these commissions from whatever was left of his sale of his Horse Guards commission, augmented by his winnings at the card table, for by then John Burgoyne was an extremely skillful cardplayer.

In 1751 he also overturned the old adage, "Lucky at cards, unlucky at love," by running away with the Lady Charlotte Stanley, daughter of the powerful Earl of Derby, and marrying her on April 14, 1751. He got no money from the infuriated earl, who angrily cut off his daughter without a penny, but did gain a lovely lady: not beautiful but attractive, blessed with a good sense of humor and gentle nature and a will strong enough to disregard all her father's furious threats. At first the marriage followed a rocky road. On a captain's pay Burgoyne was simply unable to support a wife and continue his life as a rake and a gambler, so he sold his commission for a handsome £2,600 and with his wife took ship for France to avoid his creditors. There he befriended the powerful Duc de Choiseul, who would one day be the first minister of France and Pitt's opponent in the Seven Years' War. When Choiseul was sent as ambassador to the Vatican in 1754, Burgoyne and Lady Charlotte followed him to Rome.

In the Eternal City John Burgoyne discovered the sort of cultivation that gratified the creative side of his nature. Among the splendid ruins of Rome or the British colony at the magnificent Piazza de Spagna, with its splendid Spanish Steps, or strolling along the Tiber or in the moonlit gardens where one might accounter cardinals in their broad-brimmed red hats accompanied by retinues of bowing, bobbing monsignori, Burgoyne seemed to find poets and painters, playwrights and prophets everywhere. He had also learned to read and speak French, although he could not write it very well, and had gained a smattering of Italian. Through his friend Choiseul, the protector of the Encyclopedists, Burgoyne and his wife met and conversed with some of the finest minds in Europe. From this experience Burgoyne came home with a breadth of vision far beyond the scope of the ordinary British officer, including many of flag rank with their brains bound in brass. At home Lady Charlotte became reconciled with her father, who granted her £400 annually and busied himself in the interests of his once-despised but now valued son-in-law. Derby pulled strings so artfully that Burgoyne, desponding over the realization that if he returned to the army he would, at thirty-four, remain a very junior captain, eventually saw that thereafter his rise would be rapid. So in 1756 he joined the Eleventh Dragoons in time to participate in some futile—and even disgraceful—raids on the Channel coast of France during the Seven Years' War. From these fiascos he learned how much the army-navy rivalry could cripple the king's armed forces.

On his return to Britain John Burgoyne was overjoyed to learn that his father-in-law had indeed kept his promises: he was promoted from captain to lieutenant colonel, a jump of two ranks. From being among the oldest captains, he was suddenly the youngest lieutenant colonel and was permitted to buy a commission as a captain-lieutenant in the Coldstream Guards. His total costs were about £3,800 or £5,200, but his annual revenue was now £3,000, a princely sum. Even more welcome than this increase in income, was the opportunity to raise his own regiment of a new kind of cavalry, light dragoons.

These troops were modeled on the extremely successful "hussars" of Austro-Hungary. Descendants of the pony-mounted riders of Asia, their mounts were smaller than cavalry horses and hardier, so that the hussars could move rapidly without resaddling for as long as eight or nine days and were unequaled in their ability to gather intelligence. They also fought on foot like dragoons. Such a command was dear to the heart of a soldier who began his military career in the saddle, and its profits would be almost as welcome to a bon vivant with extravagant tastes.

Burgoyne's Sixteenth Dragoons were so surely their commander's creation that they became known as "Burgoyne's Light Horse." They were part of the British-Portuguese brigade that he commanded in 1762 in defense of Portugal against the Spanish. By his bold use of his mounted arm, Burgoyne was able to unhinge the central wing of a three-pronged Spanish attack by storming the town of Valencia with cavalry alone, and again in the fall of that year to make a daring strike at Villa Velha that further delayed the enemy advance. Brigadeiro Burgoyne's exploits had so unraveled the Spanish advance that the enemy went into winter quarters, and when peace negotiations were begun in January 1763, it was clear that he had also saved Lisbon.

Back in London as a full colonel, he resumed the political career he had begun in 1760 by entering the House of Commons as a member from Midhurst, a seat that he held for seven years. But then, anxious to help Lord Strange, his brother-in-law and benefactor, he agreed to try to wrest the borough of Preston from the Tory grasp, and in a campaign so scurrilous, violent and destructive—even by the loose standards of the time—that every window in town and many heads were broken, Burgoyne, who had gone to the polling place accompanied by an armed guard and wielding a pair of loaded pistols, successfully invalidated the Tory mayor's claim of victory and returned to Parliament as the member from Preston. Brought to trial, he admitted these gross violations and was fined a whopping £1,000, but he escaped jail and his victory was upheld, and he remained the Preston member of Parliament until his death.

Burgoyne was never a very active politician except in pursuit of his own selfish ends. He seldom opposed the administration, and his loyalty to the young king soon brought him the governorship of Fort William in Scotland, a lucrative plum seldom given to anyone below the rank of major general. As an orator he was wretched, attempting to ingratiate himself with Pitt, now Earl Chatham, by adopting the "Great Commoner's" hideously pompous and involuted style. Burgoyne's imitative and sham Augustan prose was just as slovenly and unintelligible, although he may be somewhat forgiven on the grounds of insincerity. Actually, John Burgoyne's heart was always with his troops, and when Britain began to reduce its armed forces to a bare minimum after the Peace of Paris, he strove industriously to bring his regiment to such a peak of perfection that the king would not bear to part with it. To do so, he drew up a "Code of Instructions," full of deep insights into the character of the private soldier and what an officer should and should not do. Among the soldiers of Europe, he reasoned, the Prussians were guided by brutal discipline and fear of punishment and the French by a sentimental appeal to honor and glory, making them the worst soldiers of all. For the British he recommended a middle course between the Prussian method of "training men like spaniels with a stick" and the French method of substituting "honor in place of severity." Rather, "English soldiers are to be treated as thinking beings." A commander who cares for his men will be beloved by them and they will do his bidding, he wrote, and in the war to come across the seas Burgoyne would be justified in this attitude by earning the sobriquet "the soldier's friend."

His officers were to follow his example and also be educated. He encouraged them to study French, not only because it would be of great use in foreign service, but also because most treatises on war were written in that language. Officers should be practical. They must saddle and bridle horses themselves to learn why their mounts obeyed or disobeyed them, and should learn the rudiments of veterinary medicine and shoe their beasts themselves like any noncommissioned officer. Finally, an officer should never ask a soldier to do something he would not do himself. Burgoyne also preached forbearance in punishment. Remembering Dr. Nicoll of Westminister, he would say that an officer who was court-martialed and convicted had suffered as much by the shame of his ordeal as any punishment that could be inflicted on him. Conversely, courts that convicted enlisted men should not so readily reach for the whip or the noose. Such common sense was not only farsighted but also revolutionary, today as much as then. As a result, when the Sixteenth Dragoons paraded in 1764 before King George and Queen Charlotte, the king ordered that Burgoyne's Sixteenth should be known as "Queen Charlotte's Dragoons."

Burgoyne's diligence with his regiment did not exclude him from the gay life in London, where he was a regular at all the fashionable clubs, such as Brooks's or White's, or from the gradual acquisition of more wealth and property, or the race track or the gaming table. He had little sympathy for the Americans and had voted against repeal of the Stamp Act. In April 1774, he rose in the House to say, concisely now that Pitt was gone: "We have like an indulgent parent already ruined America by our lenity and tenderness. I am sure that the tax is not the grievance but the power of laying it. That power I shall ever aver exists in the Parliament of Great Britain."

Two months later Burgoyne, the playwright and designer, was presiding at one of the most lavish weddings within the memory of any Englishman, the marriage of the Duchess of Argyll's daughter, Lady Betty, to Edward, Lord Stanley, son of Lord Strange. The reception was held in a magnificent Corinthian pavilion built in the garden of "The Oaks," Burgoyne's home. The centerpiece was a semicircular ballroom, 180 feet long, flanked by two banqueting halls. Every orange tree in London was bought to plant an "orangerie" outside the garden, while groves of trees and shrubs formed an amphitheater. Burgoyne, as the creator and impresario of the gala, had entitled it an idyllic *Fête Champêtre* and there were wood nymphs and shepherds, Punchinellos, Harlequins and Pierrots everywhere, kicking and leaping or swinging from trees, while hidden bands of French horns greeted the arriving guests with fanfares. Throughout the day and night, similarly concealed orchestras filled the air with music, and a choir of cupids and fauns sang to the bridal couple, seated on a throne and dressed as Lord and Queen of The Oaks. Gun salutes announced the serving of dinner, whereupon six tall curtains surrounding the center of the pavilion arose to reveal tables that were spread with an enormous repast of food and drink, set among gleaming silver candelabra, chaste white linen and the finest china beneath chandeliers of Irish crystal glinting blue in the light of their candles. After dinner the tables were whisked away, and the curtains lowered to form a ballroom, and then came the high point of the evening: Burgoyne's comedy, *The Maid of the Oaks,* which was well received. Thus the "good life" among the British well-born in that year 1774. The exact date was June 9, and a year and a few days later, John Burgoyne sailed into Boston Harbor aboard *Cerberus,* one of three generals to whom he had given the pompous name "a triumvirate of reputation." However, Burgoyne did not draw not his sword against the rebels in 1775, but rather his pen, with which, in secret letters to Lord George Germain, he was able to effect the recall of Thomas Gage. Returned to London, he employed his epistolary skill to assassinate the character of Sir Guy Carleton, who, as the senior British officer in America, would certainly have commanded

Germain's cherished expedition into New York from Canada to cut the colonies in two. Burgoyne also demolished the similar ambition of Henry Clinton, who followed him home to plead his own cause, and after Clinton was awarded the consolation prize of a knighthood, John Burgoyne was appointed commander of the northern invasion.

⋆ 45 ⋆

SARATOGA I: TICONDEROGA FALLS

Early in 1777 a new betting book was opened at the exclusive Brooks's Club in London, and the first entry in it read: "John Burgoyne wagers Charles (James) Fox one pony* that he will be home victorious from America by Christmas Day, 1777."

It was thus with a gambler's flamboyant flourish that Burgoyne set out on Lord George Germain's scheme for crushing the rebellion. Burgoyne would lead an Anglo-Hessian-Indian force up the lake-and-river chain from Canada to Albany. A second smaller force, under Lieutenant Colonel Barry St. Leger, was to advance east on Albany from Oswego on Lake Ontario, after which William Howe would either lead or send a third army up the Hudson to that same city, and the junction of the three would not only establish communication between New York City and Albany, but also effectively isolate New England from the Middle Colonies and the South. In the next phase New England would be reconquered, and the other two regions subdued in detail.

Burgoyne arrived in Canada in May and found his troops in fine fighting trim after an unusually mild winter. He had about 7,200 soldiers, as well as excellent lieutenants: Major General Baron von Riedesel, commanding the Hessians, and Brigadier Simon Fraser, the same bold Highlander who had beguiled the French sentries at the Anse-du-Foulon for James Wolfe.

Burgoyne was surprised, though not disagreeably, when an unex-

*Fifty guineas, or £52 5s.

pected and charming recruit joined this quartet of flag officers: the Baroness Frederika von Riedesel, the red-haired wife of the commander of the Hessian troops, a vivacious, intelligent and able woman who refused to stay in Brunswick when her husband went off to war, but followed him with her three little daughters and servants to endure fears of highwaymen, missed ships, months of delay and frustration and a frightening winter voyage not quite as terrifying as the man-eating rattlesnakes and other monsters of the North American wilderness she expected to encounter once she joined her husband. Known to Burgoyne's Cockney soldiers as "Red 'Azel," she was also "Lady Fritz" to her newfound friends or "Mrs. General" to the other troops, to whom she would endear herself through her kindness and concern for their welfare. She would also, through her diary—an astonishing record of the ordeal suffered by Burgoyne's army—inform posterity of the elegance of Burgoyne's equippage and the size of his enormous baggage train as he moved south in June 1777 through the kind of tortuous terrain that no dashing cavalry leader in history had ever before encountered.

That was the great mistake made by Lord George Germain: to select a brilliant, dashing cut-and-thrust cavalryman for such a crawling, exhausting, frustrating miserable operation that required the building of corduroy roads through swamps; the construction of bridges over scores of rushing rivers now swollen and flooding with spring rains; and exposure of the troops to poisonous snakes, clouds of horrible black flies and malarial mosquitoes, drenching downpours and thunder-storms of an intensity seldom experienced in Europe, worse there were no roads over which to transport his huge train of heavy guns—variously estimated at between 128 and 138—or centers of population from which to commandeer supplies or recruit replacements, and the march led through a hostile countryside in which individual parties of contemptible Yankee Doodles worried his flanks with raids, sniping and every form of woodland sabotage possible by men who were more skilled with ax, saw and shovel than with bayonets and muskets. In a phrase, General John Burgoyne knew absolutely nothing about forest warfare. A plodding planner and colorless commander of infantry, such as Henry Clinton, if not exactly accustomed to the difficulties of moving large bodies of troops under such daunting conditions, would have been at least prepared for them.

Riedesel, a veteran infantry general, might have been even better, and though he had no experience of forest warfare either, he had been listening attentively to the accounts of his colonels who had. Among them was an officer named DuRoi, who had this to say of Burgoyne's immense baggage train: "It is almost impossible to get an idea of the excessive amount of baggage carried along with the army. An army which is of any use in these parts, must be almost without baggage, and with no more tents than can be taken in boats." But Riedesel was, after all, a German, and British commanders seldom took counsel from foreigners. Indeed, William Howe possessed a secret commission as a lieutenant general, to be declared only upon the possible appearance of a Hessian general who outranked him. Burgoyne also had to contend with a countryside that was indeed inimical, not friendly and Tory, as King George and Germain imagined.

Both the king and Germain, like most of their generals, still deceived themselves with a false notion of the strength of Tory sentiment. They did so because the British Crown was made up of the king, his nobles and the upper class, whose only contacts in the colonies were among the upper-class people there, and most of these were Loyalists. The British gluttons of privilege had almost no experience of the common people, and this attitude was aped by the American Tories—if they did not actually adopt it as another proof of their Britishness and loyalty to the throne. So they continually assured London that "all substanital men" supported the Crown—which was true—and the Crown took that to mean the generality of the populace—which was not true—as John Burgoyne was discovering as he made his weary, lonely, disheartening way through the cruel northern wilderness of the eastern seaboard.

Unfortunately for Great Britain, both His Majesty and His Secretary fancied themselves brilliant strategists, the king specifying the exact number of men to be employed and the routes to be followed, the secretary insisting on the employment of "corps of savages" to terrorize the American settlements. Neither suspected the extent of how this policy would boomerang to torment Burgoyne, just as neither was yet aware of the extent of the outrage provoked in the colonies by King George's decision to hire German cannon fodder.

Finally, Burgoyne was allowed to believe that Sir William Howe would ascend the Hudson to make junction with him at Albany, while drawing off forces that were blocking his invasion. But Howe had already and long ago informed Carleton that he had "but little expectation that I shall be able, from the want of sufficient strength in this army, to detach a corps in the beginning of the campaign to act up Hudson's River." Carleton said nothing of this to Burgoyne, merely wishing him well—if he did not actually wish him woe, this back-stabber and creature of his implacable enemy, Germain.

So Burgoyne turned his face south at the head of 3,700 British regulars, 3,000 Hessians, 470 artillerymen, 400 Indians and some 250 Canadians and Tories, the Canadians being mostly corvees, that is, laborers recruited under the French medieval *corvée,* or draft, who would build Burgoyne's bridges and roads. Indeed, Carleton was supposed to have furnished one thousand such workmen, but came up with only a few hundred, suggesting again a spectacular lack of interest in the expedition's success. Most of this force of some eight thousand men marched by brigades along the west shore of Lake Champlain, bound for Crown Point and thence Ticonderoga. The rest, with supplies and heavy equipment and the half-naked Indians in war paint, moved by water over the calm clear surface of the lake. Lieutenant Thomas Anbury, for whose diary posterity should also be grateful, recorded the passage of this flotilla of a hundred ships and boats: "In the front the Indians went with their birch canoes, containing 20 to 30 each, then the advanced corps in a regular line, then the Generals Burgoyne, Phillips and Riedesel in their pinnaces; next to them were the second brigade, followed by the German brigades, and the rear was brought up with the sutlers and [camp] followers of the army [mostly women]." Anbury thought the army was "in the best condition that can be expected or wished, the troops in the highest spirits, admirable, disciplined and remarkably healthy."

That was in late June 1777.

John Burgoyne launched his invasion with a proclamation that, for conceit, comical bombast and a sham pretext of clemency, is perhaps unrivaled in military history. He prefaced his polysyllabic and purple prose by listing all his titles, after which he asked his readers to judge "whether the present unnatural rebellion has not been made the foundation of the completest system of tyranny that ever God, in his displeasure, suffered, for a time, to be exercised over a froward and stubborn generation." Next, having recited a long litany of the sins and barbarities of the rebel leaders, he continued: "To consummate these shocking proceedings the profanation of religion is added to the most profligate prostitution of common reason! The consciences of men are set at naught, and the multitude are compelled not only to bear arms, but also to swear subjection to an usurpation they abhor." General Burgoyne, in his infinite compassion even for traitors and rascals, next invited all the repentant to come to him to be comforted and forgiven, yea even unto restoration to the bosom of George the Good. *But,* if they in their hardened hearts reject this merciful offer "in the phrenzy of hostility … the messengers of justice and of wrath await them in the field, and devastation, famine and every concomitant horror … will bar the way."

Ordinarily, such uncommonly putrid prose would not be repeated here except that it offers the occasion to print also the parody of Burgoyne's recital of his titles and commands written by Francis Hopkinson, the American "poet laureate":

By John Burgoyne, and Burgoyne John, Esquire
And graced with titles still more higher,
For I'm Lieutenant-general, too,
Of George's troops, both red and blue,
On this extensive continent;
And of Queen Charlotte's regiment
Of light dragoons, the colonel ...
And furthermore, when I am there,
In House of Commons, I appear
(Hoping ere long to be a peer.)

Next Hopkinson mocked Burgoyne's pompous threats with saltier verse closer to the point:

We'll scalp your heads, and kick your shins
And rip your ass, and flay your skins,
And of your ears be nimble croppers,
And make your thumbs tobacco-stoppers.
If after all these loving yearnings,
You remain deaf as an adder,
Or grow with hostile rage the madder,
I swear by George and by St. Paul
I will exterminate you all.

Next at the point where the Bouquet River empties into Lake Champlain, Burgoyne met with four hundred warriors and sachems of the Iroquois, Algonquins, Ottawa and Abenaki tribes to exhort them in the sacred name of "the great King, our common father," to murder the American rebels without distinction. He cried; "Warriors, you are free—go forth in might and valor of your cause—strike at the common enemies of Great Britain and America, disturbers of public order, peace and happiness, destroyers of commerce, parricides of state." But then, again in that spirit of tenderness and mercy that had characterized his proclamation to the Patriots, he cautioned the Indians against scalping anyone but a certifiably dead Yankee, neither too young nor too old to defend himself. At the conclusion of this tender plea that fell on stone-deaf ears, and perhaps relieved at the end of a speech that none of them understood and in eager anticipation of the orgy of free rum and war-dancing that was to follow, the savages all leaped to their feet shouting the customary word of approbation:

Etow! Etow! Etow!

The American army of the Northern Department, which was all that remained between Burgoyne and his objective of Albany, was, in June 1777, severely demoralized and divided by the quarrel between Generals Philip Schuyler and Horatio Gates. Schuyler, the New York aristocrat, had been the original commander, and it was he who did all in his power to prepare Benedict Arnold for the decisive delaying action at Valcour Island, while Gates, then in command at Ticonderoga, did little to assist Arnold except to befriend him and promise him matériel and men that were never forthcoming.

Gates was a strange man, both in appearance and background. He could claim descent from a family—the name was variously spelled with or without an *S*—dating as far back as the fourteenth century. Among his most illustrious ancestors was a certain Sir John Gate, privy councilor during the reign of Henry VIII. as well as sheriff of Essex County. For his part in Henry's plunder of the church lands, he was given Beeleigh Abbey, where he and his cronies ate, drank and made merry in the halls where the ousted monks had sung hymns and told their beads. But the death of Henry, and then of little Edward, preparing the way for the Catholic Mary, also meant the death of Sir John, who followed the unfortunate Lady Jane Grey to the block and scaffold, after which the family sank into obscurity. It reappeared in association with the name of the Duke of Leeds. According to Horace Walpole: "Gates was the son of a housekeeper of the second Duke of Leeds, who, marrying a young husband when she was very old, had this son by him.... My mother's woman was intimate with that housekeeper, and thence I was godfather to her son, though I believe not then ten years old myself."

The "young husband" mentioned by Walpole was Robert Gates, said to have been a butler for the Leeds family, or a Methodist preacher, although it seems more likely that he was a surveyor. His son, born on July 26, 1727, was named after Walpole. Little is known of Horatio's childhood, although he seems not to have had much formal education. Yet, at the age of twenty-seven he was well enough off to purchase a captaincy for the considerable sum of four hundred pounds. He was with Braddock at the Monongahela and wounded there. Resigning from the army, he married into a wealthy Virginia planter family, and because he had once been a major was made Washington's adjutant general.

Though his biographer, Samuel White Patterson, speaks of him as "handsome and debonair," a portrait of him by Gilbert Stuart shows a long-nosed man in a white wig who looks more womanish than masculine. In fact, his troops always spoke of "Granny" Gates. But then, Stuart also made George Washington look like a fishwife in a wig and may have been a secret soldier hater, eager to do Gates the same disservice. Actually, the two portraits side by side are hilarious, and without an identifying tag, it would be difficult to tell them apart.

Gates was also a confidant of Charles Lee, having joined him like a true-blue British professional in discrediting the amateurish Washington. When Washington at the nadir of his fortunes prepared to cross the Delaware to attack Trenton, he learned from young Major Wilkinson that Gates, without asking permission, was enroute to Philadelphia, presumably to deliver a few more friendly stabs in his chief's back. Having been Charles Lee's aide, "Wilky" was now Gates's most trusted subordinate, a pompous, obsequious twenty-year-old who was loyal to no one but himself, not even to Benedict Arnold, whom he served in a similar capacity for six weeks. He was at least Gates's equal at intrigue and already unrivaled in the sly art of betrayal. Without a moment's combat experience, this sink of ambition became the ranking officer in the United States Army, celebrated as a general who never won a battle or lost a court-martial. Master spy in the pay of Spain, accomplice of Aaron Burr in his conspiracy to create a vast new empire in the lands of the Louisiana Purchase, he reached his finest hour in 1807 when he appeared as the chief prosecution witness in the treason trial of his former friend and co-conspirator, Burr.

This was the pair that sought and received the allegiance of New England's congressional delegation, led by John Adams, in their intrigue against Schuyler. None of these Yankee "levelers" could stand Schuyler's patrician airs, although they allowed themselves to become infatuated with the supercilious Lee and Gates, perhaps because a home-grown aristocrat was infinitely less digestible. At any rate, they were inclined to believe Gates's warnings that Schuyler was incapable of holding Ticonderoga, the fort that guarded the New England west. In March 1777 Congress replaced Schuyler with Gates. But the indignant patroon, a supposed milquetoast, fought back furiously, rallying the New York delegation to his side, and was reinstated. As an olive branch, Schuyler offered the command of Ticonderoga to Gates, who refused with an insolent farewell: "If General Schuyler is solely to possess all powers, all the intelligence, and that particular favorite, the military chest, and constantly reside at Albany, I cannot, with any peace of mind, serve at Ticonderoga." "Military chest" and "constantly reside at Albany," were both true Gatesian touches, as though the honorable and immensely wealthy Schuyler were an embezzler and an absentee general commanding from afar.

Actually when Schuyler resumed command, he did his utmost to strengthen the defenses of Ticonderoga, as well as Fort Edward and the lower positions on Lake George. He was appalled at what he saw at Ti, now commanded by General Arthur St. Clair. Twenty-five hundred Continentals and about nine hundred militia lived in rags and subsisted on salt pork and flour. Only a few hundred bayonets were available for more than three thousand muskets. At a council of war it was decided that the fort could not resist forever against Burgoyne's superior force, but that St. Clair should hang on long enough for reinforcements to arrive. If his position become untenable, he was to retreat with his entire force and all its supplies. But for all Schuyler's organizing skill, loyalty and tenacity in the Patriot cause, he did not possess the true soldier's unerring eye for terrain, and so had failed to notice the big chink in his Northern Army's armor.

Ticonderoga—from the Indian *Cheonderoga*, meaning "clashing waters"—had been built by the French in 1755 and called Fort Carillon from the bell-like sounds of the rapids nearby. It was a classic fortress in the style of the great French military engineer Sébastien Le Prestre de Vauban, star shaped and strong enough to support 144 cannon. Seemingly impregnable and called the "Gibraltar of the North," it had one great defect that Montcalm had observed twenty years earlier. This was Sugar Loaf Hill on the west side of the outlet from Lake George. Rising eight hundred feet in height with nearly perpendicular slopes, it commanded every other eminence in sight and especially Ti and its sister forts. The artist John Trumbull, serving as Gates's adjutant general, saw the danger of Sugar Loaf, but when he tried to warn Gates, Anthony Wayne and others, he was ridiculed "for advancing such an extravagant idea." To convince them, Trumbull fired a six-pounder from Ti and a twelve-pounder from the fort on Mount Independence closer to Sugar Loaf. Both fell near the hill's summit, demonstrating how effective *plunging* fire from Sugar Loaf could be on Ti and the others.

Gates replied that no one could get guns up those steeps. So Trumbull took Wayne and Benedict Arnold up to Sugar Loaf's summit and showed them that a path for hauling artillery could be built on its northwestern slope. With five hundred men and twenty-five guns, he argued,

Sugar Loaf could reduce Ticonderoga and all its sister forts to impotence. No one agreed, and when the incompetent American engineer Jeduthan Baldwin took over at Ti, he repeated the claim that guns could not be mounted up there. Instead of fortifying it, he wasted all his time and the department's money building an elaborate boom across the channel at the head of the lake, intended to block the passage of British ships. It was supported by a fort along the shore and another one on Mount Independence. But after the Polish-born military engineer Tadeusz Kosciuszko arrived at Ti, he was horrified when he looked up at Sugar Loaf and saw that it was undefended.

Kosciuszko, called "Kos" by those who could not spell his name (meaning everyone, including Washington, who spelled it eleven different ways), was the impoverished son of Polish gentry who had to flee his native land after his attempt to elope with a rich nobleman's daughter was broken up by gunfire. He held a captain's commission in the French Army, having studied at the École Militaire in Paris and later at the military engineering school at Mézières. He had laid out the Delaware River forts that so daunted Sir William Howe and was a widely respected expert in designing waterfront defenses. But his suggestion that Sugar Loaf should be fortified was ridiculed by Baldwin, and when Gates endorsed it, St. Clair ignored his order.

So it was left undefended after Schuyler returned to Albany to receive the enormously encouraging news that Washington was sending him Benedict Arnold to help repel Burgoyne. Arnold, as the patroon well knew, was worth at least five thousand men.

Benedict Arnold had just passed through the most humiliating, frustrating and demoralizing experience of his tempestuous life. On February 19, 1777, the Continental Congress, in the first round of the power struggle between civilian politicians and professional generals, promoted five brigadier generals to major general over the head of Arnold, the first in line and, with Nathaniel Greene, George Washington's finest field commander. Thus a Congress that was to be celebrated for the celerity with which, upon the real or imagined approach of the British, would flee Philadelphia for the sanctuaries of Baltimore, York, Lancaster, Annapolis, Princeton and Trenton, had begun its interference in matters military. On the same day that it insulted Arnold, it passed an excusatory proviso called "the Baltimore Resolution" stipulating that it had to consider "the quota of troops raised, and to be raised, by each state," as much as (in actual practice more than) "the line of succession" and the "merits of the persons proposed." In other words preference must go to political hacks in uniform solely because their states had provided more recruits. Like votes, the number of troops supplied counted most, not military skill. Here was the New England leveling principle at its worst, attempting to make a democracy of an army, and it enraged Benedict Arnold to the point where he demanded a court of inquiry. When Washington mistakenly advised against it, he turned for support to Horatio Gates, writing: "I know some villain has been busy with my fame, and busily slandering me." Although Washington had asked him not to resign, he declared: "I cannot draw my sword until my reputation, which is dearer than my life, is cleared up." So he returned home to New Haven, in deep depression and suffering from gout.

Then, at three o'clock in the morning of April 26, there came a loud pounding on his front door from a breathless courier who told him that fifteen hundred British regulars and Tories had sailed up the Saugatuck River, landing at Weston, where they bivouacked for the night, apparently preparing to march the next day on the American supply depot at Danbury. Quickly dressing and buckling on his sword, Arnold mounted a horse and rode wildly through a pouring cold rain and over muddy roads to join the aging General David Wooster in leading a column of six hundred militia—one hundred from New Hampshire, five hundred from Connecticut—in an attempt to intercept the British. But the redcoats and their Loyalist allies had had a head start, reaching Danbury and setting fire to its munition and supply depots. They also burned Patriot houses, and there is a legend that the Tories, like the Children of Israel at the Passover in Egypt who sprinkled lamb's blood on their doorposts, painted black-and-white stripes on their chimneys so that they would be spared the torch.

At eleven that night with the rain still pouring, Arnold and Wooster came within two miles of the enemy at Bethel. Through the rainswept dark they could see the flames of burning buildings. With themselves and their guns drenched, they awaited dawn of the twenty-seventh and clear skies. When both came, they took up the pursuit. Wooster reached the British first and was killed when the redcoats unlimbered six artillery pieces firing grape. His son fought off regulars on foot, refusing to surrender until he was run through with a bayonet.

Now the British, within five miles of their ships, came upon a roadblock between two high ridges held by Arnold and four hundred militia. Enemy drums beat the charge. Three times the British were repulsed with heavy losses. Then they outflanked the Yankee defense, and the militia fled. Arnold was the last to leave. As he turned his mount around, an enemy platoon clambering down a rock ledge fired a volley at him. Nine bullets pierced his horse's body and it went down kicking and screaming, its lips working horribly over its big teeth. As Arnold fell, his pistols flew from his hands. Then he was pinned by his dying horse. Struggling to free himself, a redcoat ran at him with leveled bayonet. "Surrender! You are my prisoner!" Breaking free and seizing a pistol, Arnold cried,"Not yet!"—and shot the soldier dead. Turning, he ran for a fence, vaulted it—and scrambled through a swamp with bullets peening around him.

That night Arnold rejoined his command at Chestnut Hill, a mile from the British camp and within sight of their ships. He now led thousands of militia who had flocked to him during the day. Waiting for the enemy to wade toward their waiting boats, Arnold attacked, supported by artillery. Only the arrival of a formation of Royal Marines saved the redcoats and Tories from destruction. The Marines scattered the militia who had refused to follow Arnold in a charge. Arnold himself had a second horse shot from under him and a bullet through his coat collar, and although the British were able to row to the safety of their fleet, they had lost ten percent of their number—five times more than did the Americans. For this action a sheepish Congress on May 2 finally voted Arnold his second star, but with splendid spite made him junior to the five major generals they had promoted over his head.

To receive his star without his rightful seniority enraged Arnold even more than did the original passover. As he might have suspected, the "villain busily slandering me" was Colonel John Brown, his bitter enemy with whom he had quarreled during the Quebec invasion. Brown had compiled a catalog of charges against Arnold, but when neither Congress nor Gates would convene a court of inquiry to examine them, he resigned in disgust, returning to Pittsfield, Massachusetts, to write a pamphlet maligning Arnold as a greedy incompetent. "Money is this man's god and to get enough of it he would sacrifice his country." Unable to allow such calumnies to pass unchallenged, and thus to certify them by default, Arnold demanded a complete congressional investigation of Brown's charges—and it was granted.

Arnold's bold defense of his honor and his decision to come to Philadelphia to talk to leading legislators so impressed Congress that it almost immediately referred the general's complaint to the Board of War. Fortunately for Arnold, Charles Carroll of Carrollton was one of the board members. Carroll had been in Montreal when Arnold was in command there and could confirm his testimony of how he had struggled to contain a smallpox epidemic, defend a city and feed a starving army. Although Arnold was unable to produce receipts for $55,000 of the

$66,671 Congress had appropriated to him, he explained that during the march to Quebec he had been forced to divide his cash among his divisional commanders, and they had been captured with all their records. His own records of his purchases were lost when the *Royal Savage* was burned at Valcour Island. (Recent research has proved that those records were, in fact, captured by the British and showed that the man Brown accused of embezzlement had kept scrupulous accounts of the money paid to French Canadians.) Arnold also testified that he had spent large sums of his own money and even lent the army money. On May 23, the Board of War reported to a full Congress that Arnold, with the corroboration of Carroll, had given "entire satifaction to this Board concerning the general's character and conduct, so cruelly and groundlessly aspersed in Brown's publication."

Congress approved the report, clearing Arnold of all Brown's charges. But the radicals, led by John Adams, still refused to restore his seniority. They were concerned about the growing power of Washington, fearing that the Revolution might end in a Cromwellian dictatorship. Adams was especially disturbed, declaring: "I have been distressed to see some members of this House disposed to idolize an image which their own hands have molded." *Their own hands?* How about the hands of John Adams, the man who had proposed Washington for the chief command? Actually His Rotundity, himself vainglorious enough to be painted in a conqueror's pose wearing a sword four feet long, was jealous of Washington and would later in life complain: "All the monuments are over the graves of solemn donkeys." Adams, like almost all intellectuals, could not understand that brilliant and erudite minds are not the best fitted for the soldier's hard calling. And Washington, with his scrupulous deference to civilian rule, has come down the ages as the model for the true soldier of democracy. Yet, this was the Congress that spent its time happily hanging general's stars on so many foreign nobles—real or sham—two for the nineteen-year-old stripling Lafayette and two more for an unknown French officer named Philippe du Coudray. No wonder that three of Washington's best commanders—John Stark, Henry Knox and Nathanael Greene—all eligible for promotion to major general, but all passed over, were threatening to resign. Stark did so rather than accept the du Coudray insult.

But even as Arnold's request was denied, Sir William Howe launched his abortive New Jersey campaign to trap Washington, and Congress, falling into its customary flap, begged this man whom they had mistreated to take command of the militia along the Delaware and to defend Philadelphia. He did, and after Howe retreated to Staten Island, he renewed his request and was again ignored. With that, on July 11, Benedict Arnold submitted his resignation, writing: "Honor is a sacrifice no man ought to make. As I received [it], so I wish to transmit it inviolate to posterity."

The day before the resignation was received by Congress, however, a letter from George Washington arrived announcing that Burgoyne had begun his invasion of New York and that it was imperative to send Arnold to the Northern Department to recruit and lead militia against the British threat. "He is active, judicious and brave," he wrote, "and an officer in whom the militia will repose the greatest confidence." Still withholding the seniority that was Arnold's by all the law and logic of military precedence, Congress put the question on hold and directed Arnold to report to Washington. He did, and was sent hurrying north to join Schuyler. By then, Burgoyne had appeared before Ticonderoga.

On July 2 as the British army crept closer to the vital fort, a young lieutenant of Royal Engineers named Twiss informed Burgoyne that he had reconnoitered Sugar Loaf and believed that cannon could be carried up it. They would have to be drawn up with blocks and tackles wound around trees, but it could be done. For two days and nights the British cannoneers worried their guns up the steep slopes from tree to tree, while working parties at Sugar Loaf's summit quietly cleared, leveled and fortified the gun positions. On July 5 the Americans who had passed a quiet and not very exuberant Fourth awoke to find themselves under enemy guns. A plunging fire would make a rubble of their supposedly impregnable fortress, and their own guns could not reach the enemy's.

That night St. Clair conducted an orderly retreat, taking off the men from the new fort on Mount Independence and ordering the works there blown up. Loading his soldiers and supplies aboard two hundred batteaux, he slipped his force down Wood Creek and thence along the west shore of Lake George, heading for Skenesboro. Behind him, four soldiers with lighted matches stood ready to fire the guns on Mount Independence at the British the moment they tried to cross a makeshift bridge in pursuit of the retreating Americans. Instead, they blew out their matches and opened a cask of Madeira, over which they were found sprawled dead drunk when the redcoats burst into the fort. Then Jeduthan Baldwin's sturdy and costly boom, which was to block British passage of the strait between the lakes, was shattered by the first enemy warship to strike it—and the pursuit was begun.

British grenadiers, who had had only four hours sleep in three days, shed their packs and other heavy equipment and, by a forced march, caught up with the American rear guard at Hubbardston, Vermont. A fierce firefight ensued in which the rebels, especially Seth Warner's Vermont militia, surprised their pursuers by showing that they could take heavy casualties and still fight on. The Americans held the British at bay for two hours, until the arrival of Riedesel with his Hessians. After their band struck up a martial air, the Hessians attacked, singing hymns, and shattered the American right flank. Similar defeats were inflicted at Skenesboro and Fort Anne, where the Patriots again fought like disciplined troops. British casualties during the pursuit were 205 men killed and wounded—among the slain, the Yankee-hating General James Grant—while the Americans lost 40 killed and 350 wounded or taken prisoner. But most of St. Clair's force made it safely through the woods to the dilapidated old Fort Edward, where they joined Schuyler.

★ 46 ★

SARATOGA II: FORT STANWIX, ORISKANY, BENNINGTON

John Burgoyne had won the first round in the campaign that has gone into history under the omnibus title of the Battle of Saratoga. He now began to make mistakes flowing from his own personality, his horseman's mentality, his use of Indians and his heavy reliance on artillery.

Two defects—his love of luxury and his inability to grasp the dangers of a march on foot through virgin forests—led him to decide to move on Fort Edward from Skenesboro, rather than to return to Ticonderoga, where he could mount his troops, artillery and baggage on boats and float safely down to Fort George and so on to the Hudson. The first way was the most difficult, over terrain that Burgoyne himself thought "impassable." Yet he chose it. It has been argued that he was persuaded to choose it by the ardent but incompetent Tory Major Philip Skene, founder of Skenesboro, who stood to profit by a new road cut from his colony to the Hudson. But Burgoyne was an honorable and experienced man, who would have instantly seen through and rejected such a scheme. His own explanation was that he feared to encourage the Patriots by a "retrograde motion." More likely he just did not realize what could be done to his progress by axmen rather than riflemen.

Burgoyne's reliance upon Indians would indeed boomerang, and in a way that he would find especially disgusting, but at the moment the very ordeal of his crawling progress toward Fort Edward held the Indians in check. Another mistake, his decision to lug so much artillery through the wilderness—which, of course, would not have been so difficult on the water route—also contributed to his embarrassment. To drag them through the forest required hundreds of teams of horses and wagons, as well as drivers. He would say later that he needed them for bombardment, should he find the Americans dug in behind river fords or on islands, and also for defense of Albany should he be cut off from Howe. But this sounds very much like an afterthought, just as untrue as his report to Parliament that he actually had fewer cannon than were required for an army of his size. The truth was that Burgoyne, like so many other British commanders, had chosen to follow the latest military fashion, the "big-gun" craze so deeply infecting the infantry that Lord Townshend, master-general of ordnance, could complain "that the smallest body of infantry wish not to move without them." Apparently it did not occur to Burgoyne that the delay occasioned in bringing the big guns along might give the Americans time to recover and slow him down further.

From this fixation flowed another error, probably not foreseeable, that he would not need artillery if he chose to send a flying column under a spirited leader, such as Simon Fraser, to seize Fort George and then Schuyler's headquarters at Fort Edward. At Fort George there were only seven hundred frightened militia guarding huge stores, four hundred wagons and sixteen hundred horses. Its capture would have ended Burgoyne's shortage of horses—if it really existed—and given him the chance to move over the road to Fort Edward before it could have been sabotaged. Burgoyne had no excuse for this oversight, although it must be admitted it was raised not by his contemporaries but discovered much later in the diary of a young Lieutenant Hadden. In Burgoyne's defense it may be suggested that he may not have wished to detach such a large force from his main body, already badly depleted by Sir Guy Carleton's refusal to garrison the captured forts with troops from Canada. Carleton was within his rights, of course, but it is also likely that it gave him secret satisfaction to know that now Burgoyne would have to leave 400 men behind at Crown Point and another 910 in Ticonderoga.

So Burgoyne persisted in his obtuse purpose of plodding through the forests, his army coiling and uncoiling, undulating like a great constrictor, his men suffering untold misery while he indulged himself in every luxury. "He spent half the nights," wrote Baroness von Riedesel, "in singing and drinking, and amusing himself with the wife of a comissary, who was his mistress, and who, as well as he, loved champagne."

Benedict Arnold was sunk in gloom as he hurried north to join Schuyler at Fort Edward. American resistance to Burgoyne's invasion seemed to be melting away, and his attempts to recruit militia for the cause had met with depressing failure. All that Burgoyne needed to do, it seemed to him, was to float down Lake George to the Hudson and thence move on to Albany to be joined by St. Leger moving west from Oswego; and then, of course, by Howe. Writing to Horatio Gates, who was hastening to Philadelphia to intrigue once again for Schuyler's ouster and his own elevation, Arnold predicted that the Northern Army would have to retreat to the other side of the Mohawk River fifteen miles above Albany, and there make a desperate stand "to be free, or nobly die in defense of liberty."

But then upon his arrival at Fort Edward on July 24, he was agreeably surprised to learn that Burgoyne had unaccountably decided to move overland against Fort Edward. At once he proposed a delaying action that would give the Patriots time to recover from their losses and perhaps also bring recruits to the cause. Schuyler approved, and Arnold sent hundreds of axmen into the woods to chop down giant trees across the trails, to destroy bridges, to create every kind of obstacle either with rain-filled ditches, felled abattis or piles of brush along the enemy's route. British and Hessian soldiers, weighed down by sixty pounds or more of equipment, toiled in the merciless sun to clear a path or cursed in agonized frustration when the absence of a bridge over a rushing stream compelled them to wade waist- or chest-deep through the water, or the presence of a rain-filled ditch forced them to detour through the underbrush, where they tripped and fell over creepers and vines or floundered through berry patches with sharp briers that bit and scratched. Schuyler, meanwhile, sent out couriers to warn people in the countryside to drive off their cattle and even induced them to burn their harvested grain. Between Schuyler and Arnold they made a labyrinthine hell and a scorched earth of Burgoyne's southward path, and then, as the toiling martial anaconda inched its way toward him, Schuyler wisely withdrew from Fort Edward to Stillwater on the Hudson.

On July 29, three weeks from the day he had landed at Skenesboro, Burgoyne reached Fort Edward. It had taken him three weeks to advance twenty-three miles, seven of which had been over uncontested water. Exhausted, Burgoyne rested—eager for word of St. Leger's progress in the west.

Barry St. Leger, leading a force of eighteen hundred redcoats, Hessian chasseurs and "Royal-greens," or Tories, Indians, Canadian axmen and auxiliaries, had sailed up the St. Lawrence and across Lake Ontario to land at Oswego on the New York shore. Marching southeast, they appeared off Fort Stanwix at the head of the Mohawk Valley on August 2.

St. Leger had been informed by Carleton that Stanwix was held by only sixty men and had no decent defenses. But to his chagrin, the British commander found that the fort had been strongly repaired with glacis, ditches and bastions and was defended by 750 New York militia. He also unwisely paraded his regulars in front of it, thereby suggesting to the Americans that the besieging force was smaller than their own. Moreover, the commander, Peter Gansevoort, a twenty-nine-year-old colonel, was a courageous and intelligent soldier, who was determined to hold his position. In this he was supported by his second, Lieutenant Colonel Marinus Willet, an experienced Continental officer. Holding at all costs was not difficult to impress upon the garrison, once the screeching of St. Leger's savage allies could be heard, and less so after a terrified young girl ran into the fort with an Indian bullet in her shoulder, babbling hysterically of how she and two other girls had been picking berries when a party of whooping, painted Indians fell upon them, killing and scalping her two friends. On August 4 the Indians encircled the fort and ran yelling around it, after which they retreated to the cover of the woods to deliver a steady fire that killed one man and wounded six. But there was no direct assault, and the use of the Indians in the same tactics the next day suggested to Gansevoort and Willet that St. Leger was relying on terror to subdue the fort.

On the sixth three militiamen slipped into Stanwix carrying a message from General Nicholas Herkimer, a veteran militia officer who was at Oriskany, ten miles away, with a relief force of eight hundred men. Herkimer asked for a sortie from the fort to distract St. Leger and cover his approach. He also stipulated that if his message were indeed received, that Gansevoort was to fire a signal cannon three times. This was done, with cheers from the garrison, after which Gansevoort sent Willet sallying from the fort with a command of two hundred militia.

A half mile from Stanwix they came upon a British encampment and attacked it, killing fifteen to twenty of the enemy and putting the rest to rout. Instead of pursuing the fleeing foe and thus providing Herkimer with a more lasting distraction, they returned to camp—probably to bask in the admiration of their comrades and to show off their booty, which included four prisoners, some arms, clothing, money, Indian trinkets and four fresh scalps, two of them from the murdered girls. Unfortunately, this foray had the effect of alerting St. Leger to Herkimer's approach.

That aging worthy had decided to wait until he could hear the sound of battle to his front. But four of his regimental commanders insisted on an immediate advance, taunting their chief for his supposed timidity. Stung, Herkimer moved out—straight into an ambush prepared by St. Leger. He had ordered the Mohawk chief Joseph Brant with four hundred Indians, plus John Butler's Tory Rangers and John Johnson's Royal Greens, to fortify a log road, or causeway, passing through a wide ravine six miles from Stanwix. The Tories were concealed at the head of the causeway, while Brant's redmen were hidden on the sides. Without "eyes"—that is, scouts or "flankers" to the right and left, "pointmen" in advance—the mile-long column, followed by supply wagons, moved onto the causeway into a devastating fire, front, flanks and rear. In the first volley most of the American officers were cut down, and the rearguard regiment fled. Herkimer received his mortal wound, but dragged himself to a tree, lighting a pipe to lean against it while calmly trying to retrieve a disaster his caution might have averted.

After the first shattering blast, the fighting was fragmented into many small groups, and because it was mainly between brothers—the Indians seldom having the stomach for shot-for-shot battle—it was savage, hand to hand and without quarter. When Major John Frey was paraded in St. Leger's camp as a prisoner, his brother, a Tory, tried to kill him, but was restrained by officers. Only a severe thunderstorm saved Herkimer's force. Under cover of it the Americans moved to higher ground to form a defensive position. Upon hearing the sound of battle in the distance—the Willet sally—they took courage and fought on furiously. They were all but undone, however, when John Butler ordered his Tories to turn their bright green coats inside-out and pretend to be a relief force. The Tories were almost inside the Patriot lines when one of them was recognized. Another savage fight ensued, ending when Brant's Indians melted away.

Herkimer's force was badly mauled, with half its numbers dead, wounded or captive. Most of St. Leger's losses were among his Indians, with from sixty to eighty of them casualties. It is believed that the Indians suffered so severely because they were persuaded to join the ambush by gifts of rum and were mostly drunk when it erupted. Nevertheless, with Herkimer's relief force dealt a bloody check, St. Leger next sought to use these Indians as a threat that would induce Gansevoort and Willet to surrender without a fight.

At a parley requested by St. Leger and granted by Gansevoort, Colonel Butler and two other officers were brought blindfolded into Gansevoort's quarters. There with the blinds removed, Butler launched a rambling, convoluted speech that, without specific threats, suggested that if Gansevoort did not lower his flag, St. Leger could not be held responsible for what happened to the fort's garrison and women and children. White with suppressed rage, Willet arose to reply:

"Do I understand you, sir? I think you say that you come from a

British colonel … and by your uniform you appear to be an officer in the British service. You have made a long speech … which, stripped of all its superfluities, amounts to this, that you come … to the commandant of this garrison to tell him that if he does not deliver up the garrison into the hands of your colonel, he will send his Indians to murder our women and children. You will please to reflect, sir, that then their blood will be on your head, not on ours. We are doing our duty. This garrison is committed to our charge, and we will take care of it. After you get out of it, you may turn around and look at its outside, but never expect to come in again, unless you come as a prisoner. I consider the message you have brought a degrading one for a British officer to send, and by no means reputable for a British officer to carry. For my own part, I declare before I would consent to deliver the garrison to such a murdering set as your army … I would suffer my body to be filled with splinters and set on fire, as you know has at times been practiced by such hordes of women- and children-killers as belong to your army."

At the end of this speech, the American officers applauded loudly, and the mollified Butler suggested a three-day truce. Gansevoort agreed, hoping to conserve his meager supply of ammunition. During the lull, Willet and a Major Stockwell slipped from the fort, armed with eight-foot spears and carrying a few crackers and hunks of cheese, to steal past the Indian sentinels. Guiding themselves by the stars, they made for Fort Drayton fifty miles away. They hurried without pause and without eating, sleeping in each other's arms because they dared not light a fire for warmth. Upon arriving at the fort they learned, to their joy, that General Schuyler had already sent a Massachusetts brigade, under General Ebenezer Learned, to the relief of Stanwix. Even better, he had also ordered Benedict Arnold, with the New York Regiment, to the rescue.

At the settlement of Germany Flats Arnold realized that he could not hope to conquer St. Leger with frightened militia. He also realized that the enemy commander's Achilles' heel was his Mohawk Indians. From his long and varied experience with redmen, Arnold was aware that they were credulous and extremely superstitious. They also revered a demented or disturbed person as a being under the protection of the Great Spirit. Thus he thought that the half-wit Tory named Hon-Yost Schuyler, whom he had arrested and condemned to death as a Loyalist plotter, might be a useful means of causing Chief Brant's Mohawks to desert. When Hon-Yost's mother and brother Nicholas came to him to plead for his life, Arnold replied that he would spare him if he agreed to go to St. Leger to spread the story that "Dark Eagle"—as the Abenakis called this dark-skinned white chief—was approaching Stanwix at the head of a huge army. Both the mother and brother agreed, but to ensure Hon-Yost's faithful execution of the scheme, Arnold held the brother hostage. Then he removed Hon-Yost's coat to riddle it with bullet holes to support his story of a wild escape. After Hon-Yost departed, unknown to his relatives, Arnold sent a trusted Oneida to follow him to make sure he went to Chief Brant's camp and to corroborate his story.

Wild-eyed and babbling, his coat in tatters, Hon-Yost appeared among the Mohawks like an apparition. They surrounded him with leveled muskets, listening wide-eyed as he blurted out his story. Asked how many men followed Dark Eagle, he pointed dramatically to the leaves on the trees above him. Brant took Hon-Yost to St. Leger, where he reported that Arnold had two thousand men and was only a day's march away. This last news shocked the Mohawks, who had been complaining of a lengthy siege, productive of little loot and fewer scalps. When the Oneida scout told his friends among them that Dark Eagle sought to punish only the British, not their Indian allies, they began to think of desertion.

St. Leger questioned the Oneida, who not only confirmed Hon-Yost's story but further exaggerated Arnold's strength. Shaken, on August 22 the British commander tried to persuade his departing Indians to stay one more day to attack the fort. They refused, pausing only long enough to plunder St. Leger's supplies and steal his officers' liquor and clothing. St. Leger was compelled to raise the siege, not only by the defection of Brant's braves but by the panicky departure of his own troops, who fled into the woods, leaving behind all their tents, cannon and other equipment. After them came the whooping, laughing Indians, shouting, "Dark Eagle! Dark Eagle!" St. Leger's men did not stop until they had reached Fort Oswego. Those of them who tarried were murdered and scalped by drunken Mohawks, who later staggered into the fort with British scalps hanging at their belts.

On August 24 a delighted Benedict Arnold arrived at Stanwix to discover that his ruse had succeeded beyond his wildest hopes. He was all for pursuing and destroying St. Leger, until heavy rains made it impossible to do so. Still, by his wit this time, rather than by his valor, he had not only saved the Mohawk Valley but had destroyed the western end of Germain's pincers. Burgoyne, still receiving no word from Howe, was experiencing every kind of shortage: in anticipated Tory reinforcements, in horses and in supplies. He was also having difficulty with his own Indians, especially the little band that captured Jane McCrea.

★ ★ ★

Beautiful Jane McCrea was in love with her former neighbor, David Jones. But Jones was a Loyalist serving with Burgoyne. To be near him, Jane came to live with her Patriot brother near Fort Edward. Hungering for news of the man she hoped to marry, Jane often visited the cabin of fat Mrs. McNeil, a cousin of the British General, Simon Fraser.

Because of these connections with Burgoyne, neither woman feared death or violence when Burgoyne's painted Indians broke into Mrs. McNeil's cabin. They were afraid, of course, but not for their lives. So Jane was placed on a horse and taken away to Burgoyne's camp, while other Indians struggled with the difficulty of getting her obese friend mounted. At last Mrs. McNeil went swaying off, clad in her chemise.

To her surprise, Mrs. McNeil arrived at Burgoyne's camp first. She was taken to Fraser. Red faced, the general rushed to cover his huge cousin with his greatcoat. Then Jane's captors appeared.

They were trailing a scalp of long silken hair.

They had quarreled over Jane and had settled their dispute by killing her.

John Burgoyne was shocked. He had already been ridiculed for the high-flown speech in which he had enjoined tenderness upon his savages. He resolved to execute Jane's killer. But his officers, like generations of French and English officers before them, pointed out that to do so would alienate his Indians. Burgoyne reluctantly agreed, and the story of the brutal murder of Jane McCrea—embellished and magnified by Patriot propagandists—soon enflamed the countryside with patriotic anger.

It was white-hot in the hearts of militia gathering across the border in New Hampshire and Vermont.

"I have three thousand dollars in hard money," Speaker John Langdon is supposed to have told the General Court of New Hampshire. "I will pledge my plate for three thousand more. I have seventy hogsheads of Tobago rum, which shall be sold for the most it will bring. These are at the service of the State. If we succeed in defending our homes, I may be remunerated. If we do not, the property will be of no value to me. Our old friend Stark, who so nobly sustained the honor of our State at Bunker's Hill, may be safely entrusted with the conduct of the enterprise, and we will check the progress of Burgoyne."

General Stark said he would lead the brigade. But it would be a New Hampshire Brigade only. He wanted no truck with that Congress which had snubbed John Stark (as it had snubbed Benedict Arnold) by promoting green and untried junior colonels over his head. So Stark gathered nearly fifteen hundred men and marched them toward Manchester, Vermont, twenty miles north of Bennington.

There, General Schuyler ordered Stark to join him in the south at Stillwater. Stark refused. He took his orders from the New Hampshire General Court and no one else. Major General Benjamin Lincoln rebuked Stark, as did Congress later on, but John Stark had already decided that Bennington was the place to be. He marched his men south, leaving word for Colonel Seth Warner and the Green Mountain Boys to join him at Bennington.

Baron von Riedesel did not believe that his Brunswick Dragoons could take the American wilderness much longer. They needed horses. They were ridiculous on foot. Wearing enormous twelve-pound jackboots, they were constantly tripping over the long broadswords trailing from their hips, and their short heavy carbines were not made for forest warfare. Men in great cocked hats with long white plumes might be the envy of the Indians, but they were also unenviable targets as they stumbled along in tight, thick coats; stiff leather breeches; and huge gauntlets nearly elbow length. No, the Brunswickers needed mounts. Riedesel told Burgoyne so, and the British commander, now also in need of cattle for his hungry men, as well as horses to replace the hundred that had perished in this sweltering green hell of a province, decided to send out a foraging expedition to the Connecticut River valley.

A force of about five hundred men, under Lieutenant Colonel Friedrich Baum, was to secure these badly needed supplies. Their expedition was to be a secret one, and therefore, in the curious custom of the day, a German band was going along, plus 150 of those blundering Brunswickers.

The target for the raid was Bennington.

Colonel Baum's "stealthy" advance was so harassed by militia, who were hanging on his front like a swarm of bees, that he became uneasy and sent back to Burgoyne for reinforcements.

Lieutenant Colonel von Breymann was quickly dispatched with about 650 men and two guns. Using parade-ground formations in the woods, Breymann hurried to the rescue at the rate of about one mile an hour.

On August 15, a rainy day, Baum's force nearly collided with Stark's brigade, which was marching down from Bennington along Walloomsac Creek. Baum immediately took a position on high ground and dug in. The next day Stark attacked.

Stark did not launch a headlong frontal assault. Instead, he sent knots of men in shirtsleeves idling forward. They wore the Loyalist white paper badge in their hats. Major Skene, who had accompanied Baum, told him they were Tories. Baum allowed the men to get onto his flank and rear. It was then that Stark is supposed to have uttered his famous battle cry:

"There, my boys, are your enemies. You must beat them, or Molly Stark is a widow tonight!"

Baum's Indians and Tories quickly fled, but his regulars fought on until their ammunition was exhausted. The Brunswickers drew their swords and tried to cut their way out. But the enraged Yankees herded them back into the slaughter pen. Baum fell dying, and only nine of his 374 Germans escaped death or capture. At noon it was all over, which was just when Breymann arrived with reinforcements.

So, too, did Seth Warner with reinforcements for Stark. Between them they fell on Breymann so ferociously that they sent him thrashing backward with casualties of about 230 dead, wounded and captured. Stark lost only 30 killed and 40 wounded during both actions.

The Battle of Bennington stunned General John Burgoyne. Like General William Howe, he seemed to have forgotten Bunker Hill and had underestimated the Yankee capacity for rising to a crisis. Moreover, in a prediction made by Washington after the fall of Ticonderoga, he had encountered the exact kind of reverse that the contemptible General Buckskins had foreseen when he wrote to Schuyler to suggest "that the success he has had will precipitate his ruin." Burgoyne's habit of acting with detachments would undo him, Washington said. Even to cut off and destroy formations of only four or five hundred men would "inspirit the people and do away with much of the present anxiety. In such an event they would lose sight of past misfortunes, and, urged at the same time by a regard for their own security, they would fly to arms and afford every aid in their power." Here was a perfect prescription for what had happened at Bennington. It demonstrated once again the depth of Washington's strategic insights, and it left Burgoyne with about five thousand men, still suffering from severe shortages, and faced by the growing strength of a truly "inspirited people."

★ 47 ★

SARATOGA III: FREEMAN'S FARM, BEMIS HEIGHTS—*FINIS*

Predictably, the fall of Ticonderoga provoked different reactions in different places. In London, King George III was said to have rushed into the queen's bedroom crying, "I've beat them! Beat all the Americans!" All over Britain church bells rang and prayers were read thanking the Almighty for the gift of this great victory and impetrating Him to protect General Burgoyne and his brave lads in their pursuit of the impudent rebels.

In America church bells also rang, but dolorously. Loss of "the impregnable bastion" stunned the Americans. Everywhere, it seemed, there were cries of "Treason!" and demands that Schuyler and St. Clair should be punished. John Adams declared: "I believe we shall never hold a post until we shoot a general." Even George Washington was baffled by the surrender. General Gates, in Philadelphia in quest of Schuyler's command once more, was only too happy to encourage such blindly vindictive nonsense. Forgetting how he had ignored Trumbull's advice to fortify Sugar Loaf, he assured Congress that any patriotic general such as himself could have held Ti with ease. Meanwhile, as the British prayerfully beseeched God to crush the rebels, the ministers of New England implored him to chastise Burgoyne and his Indian allies.

In France, where it was firmly believed that God would never listen to a Protestant, the Comte de Vergennes was having second thoughts. Encouraged by the American performance at Germantown, he had been artfully steering King Louis XVI toward an accommodation with the Americans, even shipping them precious cannon, now emplaced at Stillwater in Burgoyne's path. But the precipitate retreat from the forts on the lakes suggested to him that the American Northern Army was on the verge of collapse, and it might be better to mark time once again.

In the meantime, in Philadelphia it was a new kind of Congress that listened to Gates's second attempt to unseat Schuyler. Many of these delegates had attended the first two congresses, but they were not now the same men. They were as yet far from being, in the words of the French mystic poet Charles Peguy, those "politicians who live off the country that patriots have died for." Nor were they yet like the selfish leeches of our own day, whose order of priorities is themselves; their party; their campaign contributors; and then, if there is anything left, their country. Nevertheless they were not motivated by the same noble and selfless spirit of the First and Second Congresses, when debate was courteous and the objective was the right and proper course to be followed in the crisis dividing the colonies from the Mother Country. But now true patriotism had degenerated into selfish regionalism, characterized by rancor, backbiting and smear. As the war entered its third year the delegates began to look like the professional politicians of our own time, excelling at promoting themselves and their states, overnight experts in whatever subject was scheduled for the following day. Nowhere was this more evident than in Gates's attempt to supplant Schuyler.

At first Gates boasted, whined and even wept by turns, until one delegate suggested that here was a simulacrum of a man "who had manifestly lost his head." But then came the fall of Ticonderoga, and Gates, assisted by the New Englanders led by the Adamses, quickly sought to put the blame on Schuyler. Without a shred of evidence Samuel Adams suggested that the fort's fall had all the "evident marks of design." He said, "Gates is an able and honest officer," who was "always beloved by his soldiers because he always shares with them in fatigue and danger." Gates? Horatio *Gates?* "Granny" Gates? Do soldiers pin a nickname like that on their commander out of any feeling but hilarious contempt? And if Adams the Military Expert had never heard a shot fired in anger, neither had Gates since the Monongahela—let alone had he known a moment of "fatigue and danger" since the war began. But the Gates faction, with their smear tactics, ultimately triumphed, chiefly because, apart from a few infuriated New Yorkers, no one raised a hand to defend Schuyler.

Not a word of praise was spoken for Schuyler's surprisingly successful delaying campaign, probably because it was unglamorous—with no appeal for those New Englanders who were clamoring for that one big battle that would have destroyed the Revolution, while conferring accolades upon a man who would never in his entire career as an American officer come within two miles of the front line. By turning Arnold loose with his axmen and his own scorched-earth policy, Schuyler had compelled Burgoyne to risk a foraging detachment that brought on the stunning defeat at Bennington, breathing new hope into the American cause and sending a flood of recruits flowing into Stillwater. By his despatch of Arnold to Fort Stanwix, he had denied Burgoyne that junction at Albany so vital to Germain's plan for victory, and had gained for America a precious extra month in which to rearm, recruit and regroup.

When Gates faced Schuyler upon his arrival at Stillwater on August 19, the intrinsic differences between the two men that the New Englanders failed to perceive were at once apparent. Schuyler, the gentleman, who had been so generous to Gates when the roles were reversed, nevertheless now offered Gates the boor conciliation and advice, which Gates coldly and arrogantly rejected. Next day, Schuyler resigned, explaining to his friend Gouverneur Morris: "My crime consists in not being a New England man in principle, and unless they change theirs, I hope I never shall be. Gates is their idol because he is at their direction." To Gates, he wrote: "I have done all that could be done ... but the palm of victory is denied me, and it is left to you, General, to reap the fruits of my labors." Gates, the whiner and weeper by turns, the alternately arrogant and unctuous, would certainly lay claim to those fruits, but he would never reap them. That would be done by a true soldier and friend of the betrayed Schuyler: Benedict Arnold.

When Benedict Arnold arrived back at Stillwater, he was shocked to find that a climate that was once warm and friendly had become cold and hostile—and this, from a Horatio Gates whom he also had thought to be his friend. But when comparing notes with other friends of the departed Schuyler, he found that their friendship was their only sin and that until they repented of it to Gates, they were persona non grata. Gates also had remarkable dictatorial powers given him by Congress: for a period of four months he could "suspend any officers for misconduct." Not even Washington possessed such a carte blanche, and Gates was quick to tempt Arnold to defy him and thus enable him to get rid of him.

He began by making John Brown, Arnold's mortal enemy and defamer, a lieutenant colonel under Benjamin Lincoln, one of those five who had been promoted over Arnold's head. Brown was invited to all staff meetings. Some of Arnold's orders were also countermanded at headquarters, but not by Gates but by Wilkinson. When an angry Arnold confronted Gates to ask how the orders of a major general and commander of the army's left wing could be changed by a mere deputy adjutant general, Gates cooly replied that it was his fault and he would correct it—which he never did.

Finally realizing that he was being goaded into an indescretion, the tempestuous Arnold cooled off by horseback rides with Kosciuszko into the country searching for a good defensive position. It was his idea to advance to strike the enemy first to provoke a counter-attack. On September 9 he believed he had found the right spot at a place upriver on the site of present-day Saratoga. This was Bemis Heights, three miles north of the Hudson's confluence with the Mohawk. Gates and his staff rode out to inspect it, while Arnold, from a bluff overlooking the Hudson, outlined his plan for the battlefield. To the west, or his left, as he faced toward the enemy were bluffs and steep hillsides above deep ravines to the north. To the east or right was the Hudson. The ground between them, known as Freeman's Farm, would be a perfect place to fortify, for the British could not get around the American left without stumbling into thick, hilly forests and stump-littered clearings that would immobilize their artillery and mounted troops. Indeed, their European tactics would be useless, and they would be forced to fight American style and be defeated. On the right, proper fortifications above the Hudson would deny them a flanking movement by water. So they would have to come head first against the center.

Gates approved Arnold's plan, and Kosciuszko took paper and pencil from his portfolio to sketch redoubts and earthworks, bivouacs and company streets. Arnold put his most reliable troops on the left: Dearborn's light infantry and Daniel Morgan's riflemen. In the center were New England's finest brigades, Learned's, John Glover's, Enoch Poor's—under Gates's personal command. The right above the river was heavily fortified and held by a scattering of Continentals intended to steady about two thousand untested New York and New England militia. For seven days and nights Freeman's Farm rang to the wham of the hammer and the whine of the saw, the chink of picks and shovels on stone and the cries of drovers shouting at their horses dragging logs. No finer fortifications were ever built by the Americans in the War of the Revolution.

Yet, Arnold seems to have regarded them more as a redoubt from which to "march out and attack" the British, leaving only a small percentage of the army behind the fixed positions while sallying forth with the main body to engage Burgoyne in the forest fighting at which Burgoyne was not adept. If the assault failed, then Arnold would return to the redoubt to receive the enemy there. But a defensive stance, he told Gates, would favor the British, who understood siege warfare and had the big guns to conduct it. At this point Benedict Arnold learned that Gates would accept no more suggestions from him. Gates flatly refused to take the offensive, although he did permit Arnold to use Morgan's riflemen for a reconnaissance-in-force should the occasion arise. But his ear was now closed to Arnold, and he eventually ceased to invite him to staff meetings.

John Burgoyne *had* to attack. He had to brush aside the Americans barring his path to Albany, and had to do it quickly. There were not enough horses to pull his big guns and not enough fodder to feed those he had. He had thirty days' supply of food for his army, with no help forthcoming from either Carleton or Howe. If he did not press on, he would have to return to Quebec, as Carleton had, and produce the same sort of unfavorable reaction in Whitehall. Burgoyne was down to about six thousand men against about seven thousand under Gates. This minimal inferiority did not faze him because he still clung to his low estimate of American fighting prowess. What he did not realize was that Washington's generosity had provided Gates with more experienced regulars than raw militia, a new and reversed composition for the American field forces.

On the morning of September 19, 1777, Burgoyne attacked.

As Arnold had hoped and expected, Burgoyne tried to turn the American left. He had divided his army into three columns. On his left was the bulk of the Hessians, under Riedesel, assigned to guard the artillery train and baggage on the river road and the batteaux on the Hudson itself. In the center were mostly redcoats under his own command, and on the right was Simon Fraser with 2,200 Loyalists, Indians, and British and German regulars. Fraser's mission was to outflank the American left, consisting of Morgan's Virginia marksmen and Learned's New Hampshire veterans.

The morning had dawned chill and foggy, making it difficult for Burgoyne and his staff to get a clear look at the Yankee position. But as the sun rose higher, it burned off the mists, and by eleven o'clock the British host advancing through the forest could make out the long and formidable American lines. Burgoyne ordered three signal guns fired to begin the assault.

A battle seldom develops according to the plan of either side, and it rarely enters history exactly as it was fought. Thus, at the Battle of Freeman's Farm, there are two versions of how the engagement began. The first and the least likely was that Burgoyne's major engagement began as nothing more than an effort to provide cover for parties that had been sent out to collect fodder for the horses and whatever food for troops they might find. Colonel James Wilkinson, hearing that the enemy was on the move, is supposed to have ridden forward from headquarters and seen a foraging party, guarded by a strong detachment, cutting wheat in a field. Reporting back to Gates, he is supposed to have been asked to describe the situation.

"Their front is open," Wilkinson replied, "and their flanks rest on the woods, under the cover of which they may be attacked."

"Well, then, order on Morgan to begin the game."

Another version came from a Continental officer named Ebenezer Mattoon, who was at headquarters when a report came in that Morgan had made contact with some enemy Indians. Mattoon claimed that Arnold said to Gates: "That is nothing, you must send a strong force," to which the understandably irritated Gates replied: "General Arnold, I have nothing for you to do. You have no business here." At this point, Benjamin Lincoln repeated Arnold's advice, and Gates is supposed to have sent reinforcements to Morgan. In a third account Tories and Canadians dressed like Indians began to harrass the American left from the cover of a wood full of fallen timber. Arnold, who had left Gates's headquarters, rode up to Morgan on his big, black horse Warren. Leaning down, the short, stocky general said to the Old Wagoner, a huge man for those days at six feet two inches and two hundred pounds: "Colonel Morgan, you and I have seen too many redskins to be deceived by that garb of paint and feathers. They are asses in lions' skins, Canadians and Tories. Let your riflemen cure them of their borrowed plumes."

Whichever story is correct, or if the true version is an amalgam of any or all of them, it was Morgan who did indeed "begin the game," for Arnold had quickly interpreted the situation as one in which he could utilize Gates's permitted reconnaissance-in-force. At once he ordered Morgan's marksmen and Dearborn's light infantry to strike the advancing British right. He also sent aides to order the rest of his division to support these attacking units.

When Morgan's men reached the southern edge of Freeman's Meadow, a large clearing, they saw British pickets lounging nonchalantly on high ground above them. A single volley from the Virginia marksmen dropped all the enemy officers dead and sent the frightened guards fleeing backward. Morgan's men pursued and ran straight into the center of Burgoyne's army. Volley after volley crashed into them. Black gunsmoke obscured the battlefield. Under cover of it, the stunned Americans turned and raced back across the clearing to the American side of the woods. They gathered around their forlorn leader, who had been standing there weeping openly, believing that his regiment had been destroyed, but still sounding his rallying signal—a squawking turkey call.

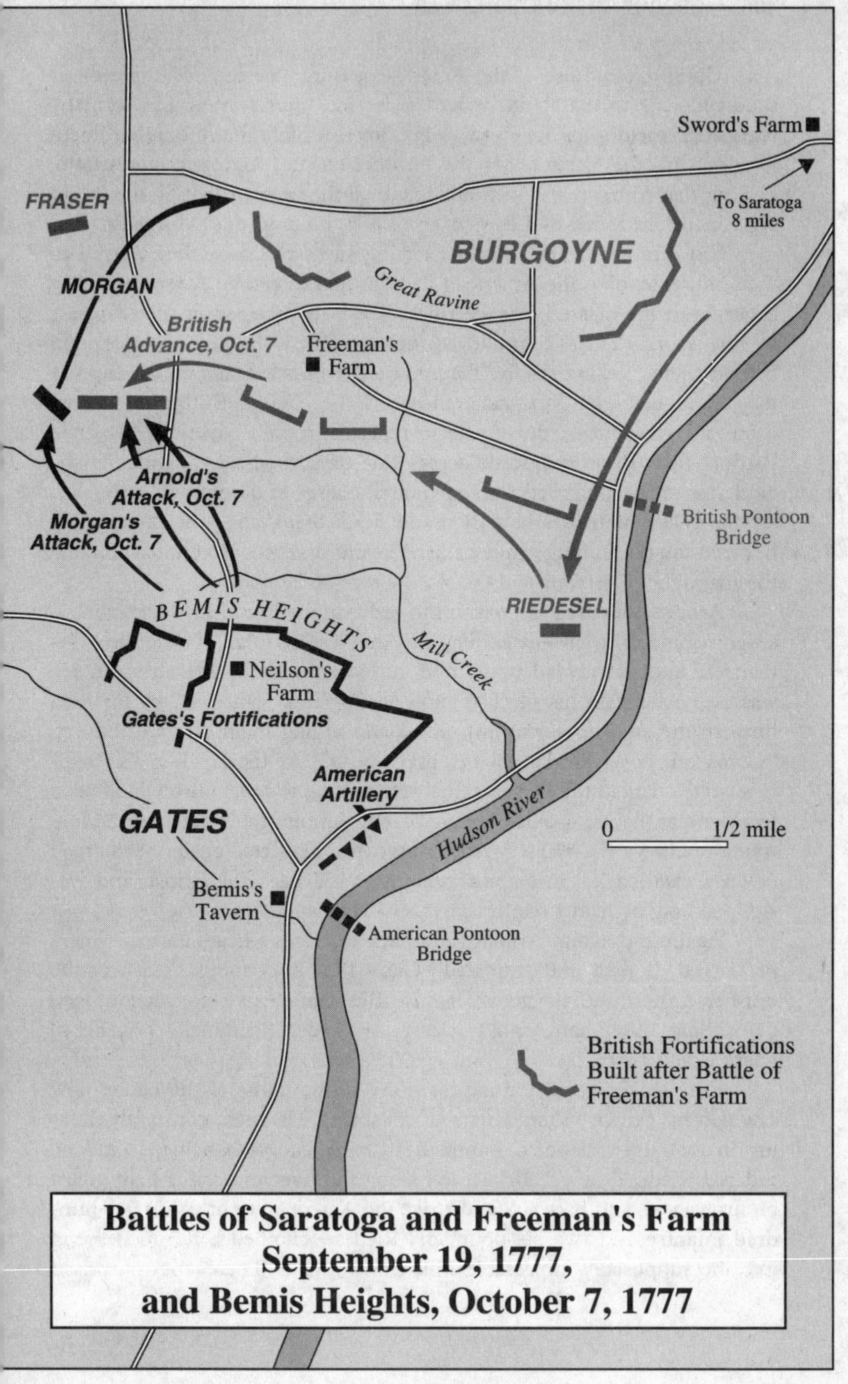

**Battles of Saratoga and Freeman's Farm
September 19, 1777,
and Bemis Heights, October 7, 1777**

Upon this repulse of the Americans, Burgoyne ordered three thousand redcoats to march in perfect order into the clearing and form by regiments. Field guns followed to lay down a preliminary bombardment to soften up the Yankees for the bayonet charge. At this point Arnold, hearing that Morgan was in trouble, had all the warrant that he needed to send in the brigades of Learned and Poor. Finding that Morgan's riflemen had regrouped and were facing the silent redcoats, they moved to their left, extending the American flank in that direction. A terrible volley broke from the massed Yankee rifles. Redcoats dropped in the tall grass by the score. Their comrades turned and fled, leaving their cannon behind them. Yelling wildly, the Americans pursued, hoping to capture the abandoned guns and turn them on the enemy. British grenadiers came charging out of the smoke to repel them with bayonets. Now the Patriots fled. Back and forth across this dreadful field incarnadine the battle raged. It continued for four hours, charge and countercharge, volley for volley, until nearly a thousand dead, dying and stricken men lay between the contending armies, their screams and moans counter-pointing the snapping of muskets and pistols, the roar of cannon.

Arnold now used his warrant to order in the last of his formations—seven regiments in all—extending the American left flank farther and farther left until it crawled uphill and curled around the British right. He was everywhere on his black mount, an inspiring sight seen by his men through the smoke, waving his sword and urging them on with the cry, "Come on, boys! Hurry up, my brave boys!" At the head of five regiments, he charged the British center, attempting to break through. Unable to penetrate, he led a quick countermarch through the woods on the left, trying to chivvy Fraser away from Burgoyne. Thwarted again, he charged down a wooded hill in a third attempt to roll back the British and was stopped only by heavy reinforcements of Hessians.

Again and again, Arnold rode back to Gates's headquarters, where he "urged, begged and entreated" Gates for more troops to deliver the crusher against the staggered enemy. But Gates gave no such orders, demanding only that Arnold release Alexander Scammel's brigade to guard headquarters.

Burgoyne, serenely sitting his horse in the midst of the battle, now saw that his center was in danger of collapsing. His men, constantly moving in that unaccustomed humid heat, were almost exhausted, and he ordered Riedesel on the British left along the river to leave a light guard on his wagons and batteaux and strike the American right. With five hundred infantry and two six-pounders, Riedesel climbed a hill to descend into the supposedly impassable Mill Creek ravine. There, they surprised the weak American force that was depending upon this natural barrier and drove them back. Arnold galloped back to Gates, offering to lead Learned's brigade from the woods on the American left into the Hessian rear. Gates gave the order himself, but without Arnold to lead it. Without him, Learned's men became lost in the woods, blundering into Fraser's light infantry. Hearing that the force that could have smashed Burgoyne at that critical moment was now in trouble, Arnold's self-control broke. "By God, I will soon put an end to it," he cried, spurring his horse toward the sound of musketry. Gates immediately ordered Wilkinson to overtake Arnold and bring him back. Unable to disobey such a direct order, Arnold returned to headquarters, and the battle that could have sent John Burgoyne retreating to Quebec in disarray began to sputter out—ending when darkness fell.

The night of September 19 was horrid with the moans and cries of the wounded and the dying, the horrible howling of wolves and other predators attacking the living as well as the dead. But on the British side no attempts at rescue were made, Burgoyne having forbidden any soldier to go beyond the sentries upon pain of death. With five hundred men and officers killed and another eight hundred wounded, Burgoyne nevertheless resolved to resume the attack at dawn. He believed the Americans were exhausted and demoralized. He was right, for the American soldiers were down to one round of ammunition per man and had no more food. But Burgoyne's troops were hardly better off, Fraser advising his chief that they were too exhausted to deliver another assault so soon. They were also shattered by the surprising courage and tenacity of the Yankees. Lieutenant Anbury wrote a friend: "We are now become fully convinced that they are not that contemptible enemy that we had imagined them." He also wrote that to claim victory because the British remained in possession of the field was but a hollow vaunt. "I am fearful the advantage resulting from this hard-fought battle will rest on that of the Americans, our army being so weakened by this engagement as not to be of sufficient strength to venture forth and improve the victory, which may, in the end, put a stop to our intended expedition."

Burgoyne was aware of this despairing mood, and decided to postpone a second thrust until the twenty-first. But that day dawned wet, cold and foggy, so that he felt compelled to delay once more, probably with a rising sense of futility. He knew that Gates was receiving reinforcements daily and soon might have as many as twelve thousand well-entrenched and well-supplied men opposing his own six thousand with less than a month's supply of food and almost no fodder for the horses, cut off from

Canada and still hearing no word from New York. But that night a message arrived from Sir Henry Clinton in code, suggesting that he was ready to come to Burgoyne's assistance by attacking Forts Clinton and Montgomery in the New York Highlands. With this message, the British commander decided to fortify his position while waiting for further word from Clinton.

In every virtue there is a hole called its vice, and the defect in the strength of audacity is the tendency in an impetuous man to be also a hot-tempered one. No man was more hot-tempered than Benedict Arnold, and because he was also proud and arrogant, he expressed his displeasure in scorn or insulting language. In a word, he could not abide being blocked in his ambition, and ever since his return from the Mohawk Valley, it seemed to him that he had been thwarted and frustrated by Horatio Gates or his contemptible toady James Wilkinson. The day after Freeman's Farm, he sat in his tent, not sulking like Achilles, but simmering, rehearsing in his mind all the insults—some of them exaggerated—that he had endured: Gates reassigning his troops; Gates bringing in John Brown; Gates bluntly rejecting his plan of attack in the presence of both their staffs; and Gates refusing to allow him to lead his troops into action and, when he did, ordering him to return from the front where victory was in his grasp to lead the disgraceful retreat into the redoubt. Then, after the battle, Gates deliberately omitting the name of Benedict Arnold from his official report to Congress, and Gates approving a raid by John Brown on the British positions around Ticonderoga so that—it seemed to Arnold—the fame of this minor exploit might dim the luster of Freeman's Farm. On September 22, Arnold's limited control of his temper snapped when Gates took Morgan's regiment away from his division and assigned it to his own, thus, by stripping him of his best troops led by his old comrade in arms, publicly humiliating him before the entire army.

With this last insult, Arnold charged into headquarters, brushing aside the terrified Wilkinson, who had so artfully contrived this confrontation, and barging into Gates's office to demand an explanation of Morgan's reassignment. None was forthcoming, and after an exchange of accusations couched in forceful—not to say profane—language, Arnold barged right out again. He next asked to be relieved of his command, a decision that caused great consternation in the army. Appalled, Colonel Henry Livingston wrote Schuyler: "His presence was never more necessary. He is the life and soul of the troops. Believe me, sir, to him and to him alone is due the honor of our late victory." Schuyler replied: "Perhaps he [Gates] is so very sure of success that he does not wish [Arnold] to come in for a share of it." Fear of losing Arnold also led General Poor to circulate a memorial thanking him for his services and requesting him to stay that was signed by every line officer except General Lincoln. Arnold changed his mind, but he continued to bombard Gates with his impolitic letters, so that this immemorial military confrontation between Audacity and Timidity ended in the only possible way: on October 1 Timidity, having the authority, relieved Audacity of his command. Gates now commanded both the army and its left wing, while Benjamin Lincoln led the right. Arnold could either leave camp or remain in his tent, a major general without a single soldier to command. Recovering his composure, probably to deny Gates the pleasure of seeing him leave, he remained in his tent.

During the dozen days in which this demoralizing quarrel all but immobilized the Americans, General Burgoyne had been busy fortifying his position at Bemis Heights. It was surrounded by breastworks, and the high ground to the northwest of it was crowned by a formidable redoubt. Breastworks and gun emplacements commanded the left along the Hudson. But even as the defenses grew, an increasing sense of hopelessness—or at least of desperation—seized the British army. Gradually, the Indians disappeared, stealing what they could before departing, and Burgoyne thus lost invaluable scouts who were familiar with the terrain. Rebel raiding parties and snipers harrassed the lines by the hour. Sharpshooters worked their way in close and picked off unwary redcoats. "We are now become so habituated to fire," Anbury wrote, "that the soldiers seem to be indifferent to it, and eat and sleep when it is very near to them. The officers rest in their clothes and the field officers are up frequently in the night."

Burgoyne had by then given up all hope of expecting anything from Sir William Howe—who had indeed informed him in a letter dated July 7: "My intention is for Pennsylvania, where I expect to meet Washington"—but still put his faith in relief from his friend Sir Henry Clinton. To encourage him, he had that coded message received on the night of September 21 promising an expedition up the Hudson. His faith was justified when Clinton, with a force of close to three thousand men, sailed up the great river to capture Forts Clinton and Montgomery, the principle bastions commanding the waterway. By this action Clinton opened the Hudson between New York City and Albany, a skillful strategic stroke that was not actually intended to relieve Burgoyne, whose predicament was not as yet understood. It was not until later that Howe ordered

Clinton to proceed upriver to rescue Burgoyne. But Clinton's attempt to notify Burgoyne of his success was thwarted when his courier Daniel Taylor was captured by the Patriots. Because Taylor was seen to pop something into his mouth and swallow it, American General George Clinton, who was also governor of New York, ordered him dosed with an emetic that caused Taylor to throw up the object. It was a silver-covered musket ball, which, when opened, disclosed a message from Clinton which said: "*Nous y voici,* and nothing now between us and Gates. I sincerely hope this little success of ours may facilitate your operations." Taylor was then hung, and Burgoyne, not receiving this encouraging note, began to take counsel from his desperation.

Even a report received on September 27 that Howe had delivered a decisive defeat to Washington on the Brandywine did not solace John Burgoyne, for it also stipulated that Howe had captured Philadelphia and had paused there. This news meant that he could expect nothing from Howe before winter set in. Burgoyne was now down to fewer than six thousand troops, with Gates commanding twelve thousand to his front and another four thousand operating in his rear. Even so, Burgoyne still believed he could force his way to Albany if a communication could be opened with New York. But nothing was forthcoming from Clinton, despite Burgoyne's frequent messages to him. Even if Burgoyne did get to Albany, he knew that he would have to be supplied through the winter—a most difficult undertaking. If it was not possible to do so, he would have to retreat—just like Carleton—and the movement would have to be begun before the twelfth of October.

Then came more disheartening news: Lincoln's attack on Ticonderoga during which John Brown had shone. Now even Burgoyne's line of retreat was in danger. At once Burgoyne sent a message to Clinton. His food would give out by October 20, and he wanted orders either to attack or to retreat. Still no reply. Soon the October 20 deadline for food seemed wildly optimistic, for the heavy fall rains had destroyed many wagonloads of flour. Sentries were being picked off by American Rangers and the Indians who had now gone over to them. One old backwoodsman who saw his son feeding horses in Burgoyne's camp shot him dead. Each night was made hideous by the howling of thousands of wolves feeding on the rotting corpses. The stench of suppurating flesh hung over the camp like an evil cloud. Desertions, especially among the Germans, were becoming frequent. To stop them, Burgoyne, with a harshness that was unusual in him, let it be known that he had given the Indians permission to kill and scalp any deserters that they caught. But this was a bluff, for Burgoyne also knew that the few redmen remaining now would not venture into the woods alone.

On October 4 with still no word from Clinton, a desperate Burgoyne called a council of war. He proposed holding the camp with the bulk of his army while he led a picked force against the American left in an attempt to turn it. Riedesel, supported by Fraser, suggested a retreat to Fort Edward. Phillips abstained from voting, and no decision was made. But on the sixth, after inspecting the camp to calculate the number of men to be left behind, Burgoyne decided to move the next day.

As with almost everything concerning Saratoga and Burgoyne, there is much controversy over this plan. Riedesel wrote later that it was not a true attack but a reconnaissance-in-force to which a foraging party had been attached. But if this were true, why then did Burgoyne take fifteen hundred of his best men, along with his three generals and the cream of his officer corps, together with two twelve-pounders, two howitzers and six six-pounders? Clearly this was no mere scouting-foraging operation. It is possible that Burgoyne intended to capture a height on the American left to emplace artillery there and enfilade the American line. Hoffman Nickerson, the American authority on Saratoga, insists that no such height existed, when in fact *two* did. Gerald Howson, Burgoyne's British biographer, believes that the heights were discovered by October 5 and that Burgoyne, whose plan was admittedly vague and open-ended, intended to seize one of them for his artillery, waiting there quietly until morning, when his left and center that were held by the men still in camp would launch a frontal attack, so that he, at its peak of fury, could deliver a surprise and shattering blow to the American left. Although Burgoyne admired Gates as an able administrator, he despised him as a timid soldier and probably counted upon his preference for receiving rather than delivering an attack. But he also, as he had done at Freeman's Farm, left the presence of Benedict Arnold out of his calculations.

Burgoyne did not move at daybreak, as was customary in such operations, but deliberately waited until ten o'clock in the morning of October 7, 1777, so that if his attempt failed, he would be able to retreat under cover of darkness. Here, at the outset, was a suggestion of doubt in Burgoyne's mind. But he was the old brave and bold Johnny Burgoyne as he rode jauntily at the head of fifteen hundred regulars, followed by their artillery and forage wagons carrying servants and women camp followers, making slowly for the American left. After covering two-thirds of a mile, they entered a rising field of cornstalks, where Burgoyne ordered a halt. While his troops formed a thousand-yard red line, the servants and camp followers jumped from their wagons to fill them with fodder for the horses. Burgoyne then ordered the column to re-form and move to higher ground ahead of him. By then word of his movement had been received at Gates's headquarters. Wilkinson rode out to Morgan on the left, carrying back the Old Wagoner's request to attack the British. At this request, Gates is said to have exclaimed once again: "Order on Morgan to begin the game." So freed, Morgan deployed his three hundred marksmen to work around the enemy right. As they did, General Poor's brigade moved toward Burgoyne's left.

At half-past two both formations were in position, taking losses from shells lobbed into them by enemy howitzers, but standing firm. Between them was a hill occupied by Major Dyce Acland's Grenadiers, firing high with musket and artillery. Then the Grenadiers came yelling downhill in a bayonet charge. Poor's Yankees stood rock still until the redcoats were within range, then opened up in a shattering volley that struck them to the ground. Turning, the Grenadiers fled, abandoning their cannon and their commander, shot through both legs. A boy who wandered onto the battlefield prepared to shoot the commander dead until Wilkinson rode up to intervene.

On the left Morgan's riflemen were engaged with Fraser's Canadian Loyalists, who had strayed from the main body. Passing through and around them, these demons in fringed buckskin and coonskin caps struck savagely at the light infantry under young Lord Balcarres. As they turned to face the backwoodsmen, Dearborn's light infantry appeared on their left to join Morgan in a crossfire that forced the British to break and run. The brave Balcarres rode among his men trying to rally them, but to no avail. Now Burgoyne saw that soon all would be lost and sent his aide Sir Francis Clerke forward to order a general withdrawal from the cornfield into the fortifications. But one of Morgan's sharpshooters shot Clerke from his horse, and he fell to the ground.

Back at Gates's headquarters two miles to the rear, Benedict Arnold fumed and fretted outside his tent, listening in agony to the battle that he was forbidden to join, anxiously watching the curling black smoke toward which he was enjoined not to ride. At last he could no longer endure his confinement and leaped aboard his big black charger Warren, riding around the encampment "betraying great agitation and wrath." He saw Gates outside his tent nonchalantly receiving messages, saw Gates look up and see him—and then see through him—and that tore his restraint like a piece of paper. Shouting, "Victory or death!" he plunged his spurs into Warren's sides, hauling back on the reins to clear a sally port—and went galloping toward Morgan and Dearborn, his favorite fighters and their beloved men. Behind him Gates called for Major John Armstrong to order Arnold back. But for some mysterious reason, though mounted on an extremely fast horse, Armstrong did not overtake Arnold.

Following a wagon trail winding through tall trees, Arnold began rounding up stragglers, drawing his sword and pointing it toward the enemy. At the edge of a clearing he found some of Learned's men drinking at a brook and washing the black powder stains from their faces. "Come on, brave boys, come on!" he shouted, leaping the stream to lead them up a hill toward the Hessians. But as the Germans opened fire, Arnold turned in the saddle to find himself alone. Riding back he reformed the Americans and led them uphill again, and this time it was the Hessians who fled—sprinting through the cornfield and hurdling the bodies strewn throughout it. Wilkinson, who appeared just then, described the cornfield: "In a square space of ten or fifteen yards lay eighteen grenadiers in the agonies of death and three officers propped up against the stumps of trees, mortally wounded, bleeding and almost senseless."

Arnold next rode toward Morgan, directing his men opposite Fraser. The Loyalists were fighting savagely while Fraser rode up and down on a big, steel-gray mare, shouting at his men, forming them in a new line. Arnold pointed to him and yelled to Morgan: "That man on the gray horse is a host in himself, and must be disposed of!" The Old Wagoner nodded, and called for Tim Murphy, a legendary marksman and veteran Indian fighter. "That gallant officer is General Fraser," he said, pointing to him. "I admire him, but it is necessary that he should die—do your duty!" Murphy climbed a tree and lifted his double-barreled rifle.

His first shot creased the crupper of Fraser's horse. The second parted his horse's mane, and Fraser's aide urged him to take cover. But the brave Highlander shook his head. "My duty forbids me to fly from danger," he said, just before Murphy's third shot struck his chest, mortally wounding him. Fraser died that night in the home of Baroness von Riedesel, who had been preparing supper for him, supposedly crying: "Oh, fatal ambition! Poor Burgoyne! Poor Mrs. Fraser!"

Now Burgoyne, with bullet holes in his collar and coat, led a retreat through a sally port into his encampment, telling Lieutenant Anbury: "Sir, you must defend this post to the very last man." Anbury's reply was drowned out by the blasting of British cannon firing at an American column approaching the British right. Obviously the jubilant rebels planned to attack the British position. Remnants of Fraser's light infantry also hurried through the sally port, taking position with about two hundred Hessians manning Breymann's redoubt in front of the main British fort.

Now Benedict Arnold galloped over the battlefield like a mad wraith, so exhilarated that at one point his waving sword accidentally struck a rifleman on the head, but did him no harm. Coming upon one formation of troops, he shouted: "What regiment is this?"

"Colonel Latimer's, sir."

"Ah, my old Norwich and New London friends. God bless you! I am glad to see you. Now come on, boys! If the day is long enough, we'll have them all in hell before night!"

Spurring his black charger again, he rode out of the forest and into Freeman's Meadow, finding a narrow path through the enemy's abattis outside the British forward trenches that had been left there for British patrols. Galloping through it, he led his cheering men toward Breymann's redoubt. Racing its length, he passed like an avenging angel through the shot and shell flying forth from both armies, his own head and shoulders visible to the men of both sides, but not to the men following him. Coming to Breymann's, he yelled for his men to follow him around the position and into its rear through a sally port. They followed, many falling under the fire poured down upon them from the Hessians on the walls. Inside Colonel Breymann slashed wildly with his sword at his panicking soldiers, before falling to the ground dying, believed to have been shot by his own men. Now German musket balls pierced Warren's side, and the stricken horse fell kicking and screaming, throwing Arnold clear. Arnold jumped erect with drawn sword, just as a wounded Hessian rolled over and fired at him. Arnold went down. His men lunged at the German with their bayonets. "Don't hurt him!" Arnold yelled. "He's a fine fellow. He only did his duty."

Morgan, Dearborn and other officers rushed toward Arnold, but he waved them away, shouting encouragement to his men firing American rifles and captured British cannon to beat back the last fierce enemy counterattack. And that was the last gasp of the Battle of Bemis Heights, the final round in the decisive Battle of Saratoga—the turning point of the American Revolution.

Benedict Arnold's triumphant troops made a litter out of ridgepoles and tent cloth to carry their idolized leader gently back to the American camp. Here as he lay gasping in agony, Major Armstrong at last overtook him and ordered him to return to his quarters lest he do something rash. A gasp—something akin to a laugh—broke from Arnold's twisted lips. Dearborn asked, "Where are you hit?"

"In the same leg," Arnold whispered hoarsely. "I wish it had been my heart."

Burgoyne's gamble had cost him another five hundred men, half of them captured. Among those were his beloved aide, Sir Francis Clerke, who lay dying in Gates's headquarters tent while that coarse creature lectured him on the justice of the American Revolution. Upon Clerke's feigning a smothered yawn, Gates snapped: "Did you ever see such an impudent son of a bitch?"

The day after the Battle of Bemis Heights, General Fraser was buried in a ceremony of which Anbury wrote: "The enemy with an inhumanity peculiar to Americans cannonaded the procession as it passed and during the service over the grave." It is likely, however, that the rebels had no way of knowing that the formation they saw forming was a funeral cortege. There was some brief skirmishing that day, and that night Burgoyne decided that his position was no longer tenable, withdrawing during a heavy rain and abandoning his wounded and baggage. Baroness von Riedesel and her daughters moved with the army. She was dismayed when they stopped for the night, sitting disconsolately by a fire after putting her children to bed.

"I am amazed at you!" General Philips cried. "Completely wet through, have you still the courage to go further in this weather? Would that you were … our commanding general! He halts because he is tired, and intends to spend the night here and give us supper."

Eventually the retreating army reached Saratoga, where Burgoyne, in an act inexplicable in a man of such courtesy and generosity, ordered Schuyler's fine home burned to the ground. Then he made an attempt to push farther upriver, but was halted by Poor's and Learned's brigades, which had moved above the British and occupied high ground to the northwest. Burgoyne was in the bag, and the string was being drawn tight. Inside was an entire British army, frazzled indeed and down to only thirty-four hundred effectives, with about another two thousand unfit for duty for various reasons. But with it were all its paraphernalia—all its splendid equipment, its guns, wagons and horses—its ancient regiments rich with traditions and laden with battle flags, its three generals. Rations were down to three days' supply, with the men already subsisting on half issues. A makeshift hospital, a converted mansion near the riverfront, was already filling up. The Baroness von Reidesel lived there in the cellar with her children, working by day in the hospital. Thinking it was a headquarters, the Americans shelled it. "Eleven cannon balls went through the house," the Baroness wrote, "and we could plainly hear them rolling overhead. One poor soldier, whose leg they were about to amputate, had the other leg taken off by another cannon ball in the middle of the operation." By then she had given up all hope of escaping the American trap.

But not Burgoyne, preparing one more attempt to break free. A double agent was sent to Gates to inform him that the British had left for

Fort Edward. Without bothering to scout the enemy position, Gates sent Morgan, Glover and John Nixon in pursuit. Just as Morgan's and Nixon's troops had crossed Fishkill Creek and were climbing a hill, a deserter appeared to inform them that so far from being in retreat, the British were waiting for them with loaded cannon and muskets. Morgan and Nixon at once withdrew, after which, on October 12, Burgoyne and his staff sorrowfully concluded that there was nothing else to do but surrender. But when Burgoyne asked Gates for terms, Gates curtly replied that Burgoyne must surrender unconditionally. Infuriated, refusing to submit to such a disgrace, Burgoyne threatened to fight to the last man—whereupon Gates relented, and conditions were agreed upon.

Under these the British troops marched out of their encampment with full honors of war, drums beating, fifes squealing, to stack arms. But even the usually stirring strains of "The British Grenadiers" failed to halt the flow of tears or lift sunken chins. Then they were to march to Boston and there await transportation to Britain. By this condition, said Burgoyne, trying to put the best possible face on his disastrous defeat, he had "saved" the army. These returning troops would be able to relieve those on duty at home, who could then be shipped to America.

When the surrender took place at two o'clock in the afternoon of October 17, 1777, Burgoyne seemed far from downcast, actually appearing to be the conqueror in "costly regimentals bordered with gold and a hat with streaming plumes," while Gates, in a plain blue overcoat without insignia or braid, might have been the conquered. When they met, Burgoyne, looking "like a dandy rather than a warrior," removed his plumed hat with a flourish, bowed—and said: "General, the caprice of war has made me your prisoner." Bowing in reply, Gates replied: "You will always find me ready to testify that it was not brought about through any fault of your excellency."

Thus ended the Battle of Saratoga, the campaign that turned the tide of the American Revolutionary War against Great Britain.

⋆ 48 ⋆

AFTER SARATOGA/THE FRENCH ALLIANCE

After the surrendered British-Hessian troops marched off to Boston, Philip Schuyler took both John Burgoyne and the Baroness von Riedesel and her children under his protection in his handsome Albany home. Unaware of her benefactor's identity, she said to him: "You are certainly a husband and a father, since you show me so much kindness."

Schuyler was equally courteous to Burgoyne, even though it was he who had burned his Saratoga mansion, and this astonished the defeated general, who exclaimed: "Is it to *me,* who have done you so much injury, that you show so much kindness?"

"That is the fate of war," the American replied. "Let us say no more about it."

Burgoyne's imprisoned soldiers were not so generously and cordially treated. After their long, debilitating march to Cambridge, they spent almost a year in miserable quarters waiting for the homebound ships that never came, for Congress repudiated the article in the Saratoga convention that permitted them to be returned to Britain and Germany. So they were compelled to march another six hundred miles to barracks in Charlottesville, Virginia. Their passage through the towns and villages along the way was greeted either with warmth or hostility, depending upon the politics and personalities of the residents. But they suffered horribly either way, from lack of food, from rotten clothing hanging in tatters from their emaciated bodies, from worn-out shoes. Those who fell sick almost invariably died. The most fortunate were the deserters, usually the youngest who, not too firmly bound to home and hearth, dropped out to become American farmers, blacksmiths or mechanics.

The Hessians had looked forward eagerly to their passage through the "Pennsylvania Dutch" country, but when they reached it, they were disappointed and dismayed. "The inhabitants are very wealthy," DuRoi wrote. "They came as poor people from all parts of Germany. The houses are very clean inside and the way of living is exactly like that in Germany. Our hopes of being received ... by our countrymen were cruelly deceived.... On the whole, we were ashamed of being Germans, because we had never seen so much meanness in one spot from our countrymen."

It is from DuRoi also that there comes the most penetrating insight into how this rabble in arms overcame a proud and formidable British army: "The British came over to fight the Rebels, and the Rebels can always select the best places from which to defend themselves. Whenever an attack proves too serious, they retreat, and to follow them is of little value. It is impossible on account of the thick woods to get around them, cutting them off from a pass, or force them to fight. Never are they so much to be feared as when retreating. Covered by the woods, the number of enemies with which we have to deal can never be defined. We think ourselves victors and follow them; they flee to an ambush, surround and attack us with a superior number of men and we are defeated. These are drawbacks which the Royal Army cannot avoid.... The scouting parties of the Rebels ... go out in small troops without baggage and little provisions. In case of need they live on roots and game. They are fit to undertake the longest incursions of all around the Royal Army, while we have no troops who can do so." Thus the American soldiers in 1777, hardy irregulars and forest fighters. This description of them can accurately describe the foes of another generation of American soldiers, two centuries later, the Communist irregulars of Vietnam.

John Burgoyne could have profited immensely from the insights of this Hessian officer, if he had been able to shed his unshakable faith in the superiority of trained European professionals. Indeed, this was the common error of the entire British nation, from commanders, such as Burgoyne, Howe and Clinton—that ill-starred "triumvirate of reputation"—down to young Lieutenant Anbury; from King George to Lord North and his ministry and among all those loyal Britons who nourished the illusions of the American barbarians poised for flight at the first flash of a scarlet coat, the ever-impending large-scale Tory uprising and the handful of rabble-rousers, such as the Adamses, who held a million-and-a-half Americans spellbound to satisfy their own craving for power.

Burgoyne was much maligned when he arrived back in London in April 1778. After all, he had done the unthinkable: surrendered a splendid British army to a contemptible crowd of farmers in homespun. In this, so thought so many Britishers, from the king down to a chimney sweep, he had violated the will of God. Burgoyne was indeed crestfallen, "sunk in mind and body," and he may well have remembered the words of Charles James Fox after he entered that flamboyant wager in the new betting book at Brooks's: "Be not oversanguine in your expectations. I believe that when next you return to England you will be a prisoner on parole."

And he was—a crushed and petulant one, demanding a court-martial to clear his name, which was not granted, and defending himself in Parliament in a long and actually persuasive speech—even publishing his apologia in book form. Saratoga was certainly not his fault alone—although the invasion was according to his own plan—but a scapegoat was needed, and it was Burgoyne upon whose head were placed all the sins of that ill-fated campaign before he was sent stumbling pitifully into the wilderness.

He never received another command.

The consequences of Saratoga were enormous, and from the American point of view both for good and evil. First, this crushing blow did not do what the Americans desired of their armed rebellion: convince the Mother Country that she was embarked on a costly and impossible campaign. After Saratoga, Gates wrote prophetically to his wife: "If old England is not by this lesson taught humility, then she is an obstinate old slut bent upon her ruin." To the contrary, Saratoga stiffened the British resolve to fight on to ultimate and inevitable victory. "The majority both in and out of Parliament," said the Duke of Grafton, "continued in a blind support of the measures of the Administration. Even the great disgrace and total surrender of General Burgoyne's army at Saratoga was not sufficient to awaken them from their follies." Lord Chatham's motion to repeal the most oppressive acts of Parliament since 1763 was brushed aside, while thirteen million pounds stirling were voted to continue the conflict.

Saratoga also lifted the stubborn jaw of King George III. When a despairing Lord North attempted to resign, the king would not hear of it. "I should have been greatly hurt at the inclination expressed by you to retire, had I not known, however you may now and then be inclined to despond, yet you have too much personal affection for me, and a sense of honor, to allow such a thought to take any hold on your mind." Both men knew full well that with North gone, the only man in Britain who would be able to form a new government would be William Pitt, Lord Chatham, at whose very name the Hanoverian jaw rose higher. "No advantage to this country, nor personal danger to myself, can ever make me address myself to Lord Chatham, or to any other branch of opposition. Honestly, I would rather lose the crown I now wear than bear the ignominy of possessing it under their shackles." Lord Chatham might enter North's cabinet—to which he would never consent—but as George's personal Lord Anathema, he would never head a government.

Another evil effect of Saratoga, from the American standpoint, was that it made a hero of Horatio Gates. It would take Gates's cowardice at Camden three years later to reverse this misplaced adulation and to give to the eventual traitor Benedict Arnold the credit that was due him. It was actually disgusting to see how Gates basked in this misdirected glory, and how it raised his popularity and prestige, which is only to say his inexhaustible capacity for making mischief. Here was another cross that George Washington, already entering that dreadful winter at Valley Forge, was forced to bear.

Even as Saratoga hardened the Hanoverian heart, it sent the spirits of the Patriots soaring. The summer and early fall had been gloomy with defeat and retreat: the Brandywine … Germantown … Ticonderoga … Skenesboro … Fort George and Fort Edward … Washington's ragged veterans marching wearily toward the grim hills around Valley Forge to be caught in the cold white clutch of a despairing winter. But now Saratoga, bright with glory! Bennington … even Oriskany … Fort Stanwix … Freeman's Farm … Bemis Heights … *Surrender!*

How could France now fail to side with America?

The Comte de Vergennes, in his policy of doing all possible to weaken Britain, had to be careful not to involve his sovereign King Louis XVI too deeply or openly in assistance to the Americans lest Britain quickly crush the rebellion, and then, in vengenace and covetousness, fall upon France to complete the destruction left undone in the Seven Years' War. Vergennes's policy was completely practical and cynical, motivated by neither a sentimental love of the Americans nor an unsettling hatred of the British. He sought to serve his master the king and could do so best by keeping the Americans in the field against Britain until that propitious moment when it appeared to him that George III would not achieve a quick victory. Then he could move openly, perhaps even toward an alliance.

George Washington, of course, had been delighted when ships

loaded with munitions began arriving from the Bourbon allies. Not all members of Congress, however, felt entirely grateful for these gifts or even approved of a French alliance. After all, as the archenemy of Great Britain, France had been the enemy of the British colonies throughout their history. The Catholics of New France in Canada had been the mortal foes of the Protestants to the south. Were they now to fly into each other's arms? This, of course, was the thinking of the idealists, delegates who, if they were not actually absolutists, could not adopt a cause without making it a crusade. Expediency was to them a kind of betrayal, and if such a course were adopted, they must wrap it in a standard of nobility. Patrick Henry and Richard Henry Lee were like that, as indeed are most Americans, even to this day. But there were the pragmatists like John Adams, who understood that in foreign policy today's foe can be tomorrow's friend. These are marriages of convenience that end when the union no longer serves the purpose of one or both parties. Fortunately, most of the delegates agreed with Adams's belief that "it was the unquestionable interest of France that the British continental colonies should be independent," just as it was obvious to them—and to George Washington as well—that Britain could not be defeated without outside help or the distraction of another major European war. So Silas Deane in Paris was instructed to pursue this course.

Other delegates were concerned about the nature of the arrangement with Beaumarchais. He had said that Hortalez et Cie. had been created to send help to the Americans "in the shape of powder and ammunition in exchange for tobacco." Was the tobacco to be payment for the supplies Beaumarchais was providing? If so, it was woefully inadequate. Or were the munitions—or the money to buy them—the outright gift of the French crown? Or was it possible that Beaumarchais and Deane were actually lining their own pockets? Some delegates thought so, with the result that Benjamin Franklin and Arthur Lee had been sent to France to check up on them.

No more fortuitous accident could have overtaken the American cause than the arrival of Benjamin Franklin in Paris. He became at once the darling of the French intellectuals, who saw in him the apotheosis of Rousseau's confection of the natural man. No matter that Franklin—editor, scientist, inventor, author, diplomat, roue and "Immoral moralist"—was easily as sophisticated as any decadent French aristocrat and just as shrewd, devious and subtle as Vergennes himself, he was taken to be that simple farmer whom Crevecour had discovered in the American wilderness, with a touch of his own delightfully wise and witty "Poor Richard" thrown in. And Poor Richard loved it, even wearing a beaver cap while promenading the boulevards to bask in the admiration and salutations of these corrupt Parisians. The loveliest ladies competed for his favor, and he received them every morning—these elegant countesses and marquessas—while lying in bed. John Adams has recorded the extraordinary if not ludicrous tableau enacted when Franklin and Voltaire met at the Academy of Sciences, the Valhalla of French intellectuals. A "general cry" arose that the two philosophers should be introduced to each other. "This was done," Adams wrote, "and they bowed and spoke to each other. This was no satisfaction. There must be something more. Neither of our philosophers seemed to divine what was wished or expected; they however, took each other by the hand. But this was not enough. The clamor continued until the explanation came out. '*Il faut s'embrasser, á la Francaise.*' The two aged actors upon this great theater of philosophy and frivolity then embraced each other, by hugging one another in their arms, kissing each other's cheeks, and then the tumult subsided. And the cry immediately spread through the whole kingdom, and, I suppose, all over Europe, '*Qu'il etait charmant de voir embrasser Solon et Sophocle!*'"

Adams believed that Franklin had no peer in the nascent art—if it was then even recognized as a skill—of publicizing himself. He was probably right. Poor Richard's fame was universal and, as Adams said: "He was considered as a citizen of the world, a friend to all men and an enemy to none." Such popularity may not have won any battles against the British at home, but it certainly made many friends for America in many places, in church and state, court and kitchen, so that, like a fertilized field awaiting the sun and the rain, the way was prepared for the good news from Saratoga.

Franklin's other important contribution was to dissuade the indiscreet Silas Deane from adopting an "unless" position, that is, "Unless you help us, we'll make peace with Great Britain." It sounded too much like a bumptious ultimatum from a suppliant to a patron and, as Arthur Lee observed, might cause the French to cut off the flow of munitions. It was then agreed that the best possible course was to maintain that flow and even try to increase it.

The American commissioners were very much aware of the fragility of Vergennes's allegiance to the American cause. It was not just a possibility that this flow of munitions might be cut or cease: it had already dried up twice. In the summer of 1776 Washington's defeats had led Vergennes to forbid the supply ships to sail to America. The French foreign minister was so discouraged that Lord Stormont, the British Ambassador, could gleefully write home that "our neighbors will let us finish our business in our own way." Again in July 1777, after the fall of Ticonderoga,

Vergennes had second thoughts about Hortalez et Cie. Moreover, he was constantly afraid that the common blood and faith shared by the British and Americans, and the memory of the wars they had fought together against the Catholic French, would remain strong enough for them to settle their differences amicably and to resume a united front against France.

Vergennes above all wanted a fighting ally. As Beaumarchais said: "America says succor us and we will never make peace. France says prove to me that you will never make peace and I will succor you." The only proof possible was an American army that was still in the field against Britain. Vergennes, meanwhile, did everything within his power to assist that army and still retain his status as a neutral. In 1777 no fewer than eighty ships set sail from Bordeaux alone laden with supplies for the rebels, while many other vessels departed for ports in the French West Indies from whence their cargoes were transshipped to Charleston, Boston or Philadelphia. The British did indeed protest that these were the acts of a belligerent, not a neutral, but Vergennes was adept at answering hard questions with soft answers. He said it was true that some supplies reached America from France, but only in the ships of merchants acting illegally. He earnestly assured Lord Stormont that he would do all possible to discourage this traffic.

Although France opened its ports to American vessels, it did not allow war supplies to be sent to America in French bottoms. Capture of such contraband by British cruisers would leave France powerless to deny this violation of neutrality and thus provoke the war that both nations still dreaded. Nevertheless, it soon became apparent to Britain that the American flag became "a mask for all the nations in the world ... to plunder the British trade." In the West Indies French ships flew the American flag and under the guise of privateers attacked British shipping. Moreover, because the American ships flew the French flag for protection, British warships began to board all ships flying those colors, taking them all—willy-nilly, French or American—into British courts to be sold as prizes. In response, France began arming her merchant ships—and once again a powder keg had been stuffed waiting for a spark.

Having greatly strengthened its navy, France accidentally conferred another gift upon the American cause: the French fleet kept forty British ships of the line in home waters. When Lord Howe requested more warships for the American station, the Admiralty replied that it could not detach them without gravely weakening the Home Fleet against the rising naval power of the Bourbons. Conversely, with most of the fast cruisers and frigates in American waters, these leviathans, manned by five hundred men or more and heavily armed, were simply too slow and ponderous to suppress the growing number of small, fast and highly maneuverable American privateers that were gnawing on the British merchant fleet like schools of barracuda. To send first-raters against them was like sending whales after minnows. These actual pirates, made legal by their letters of marque, often operated in British territorial waters so successfully that it was not unusual for them to take as many as thirty prizes in a single cruise. Indeed, it was admitted in the Admiralty that if American and British naval power were to be measured by the number and worth of sea prizes, the Yankees would have a clear superiority. And the number of rebel privateers was growing, both through the hospitable welcome given them in French ports—where they could be resupplied and rearmed—and because privateers could be outfitted in French ports with French crews sailing under the American flag. Indeed, with insufferable arrogance, some of these American privateers deliberately hoped to provoke a war between France and Britain. One captain boasted: "Our late cruise has made a great deal of noise and will probably soon bring on a war between France and England, which is my sincere wish." Just a little of this was much too much, even for the deliberately thick-skinned policy adopted by the British, and Lord Stormont minced no words in telling Vergennes that His Gracious Majesty had had enough.

Dismayed, Vergennes let the American commissioners feel his displeasure. In the fall of 1777, deeds followed words, with all shipments to America halted, all ports closed to American privateers, all captured British ships in French ports returned to their owners and the entire crew of one American privateer sent to prison in Dunkirk. The French court turned so hostile that one American diplomat feared that all Americans would be expelled from the kingdom, while the gloomy Silas Deane was heard to remark that "it was a pity that Great Britain did not bring about a reconciliation with the colonies, and jointly make war against France."

Poor Richard, however, merely changed his tactics: from wooing France, he began flirting with Britain, hoping thereby to shake Vergennes with a salutary case of anxiety. He spread the report that he would soon leave Paris for London in the role of a peacemaker. The maneuver worked, for the fear of an American-British reunion was like a hairshirt that the French minister could never quite shed. Repenting of his harshness toward the trio of Yankee commissioners, he nevertheless adopted a waiting game, knowing as he did through his agents that Lord North's ministry was counting heavily on crushing the rebellion in the summer of 1777. Failure to do so, the Crown realized, would mean a protracted war and almost certain intervention by France and Spain. Thus while the news of Burgoyne's surrender burst like a hell bomb in Whitehall, shaking

North so thoroughly that he remained sunk speechless in a chair for hours, remarking how much he envied Howe his Philadelphia snuggery, for if he were only half that secure in Parliament, he would be well content, it came to Vergennes like a blessing from Heaven. All was now well and clear. When a last-minute attempt by British agents in Paris in December 1777 to seduce the American commissioners, by offering them an armistice and peerages in the new American nobility that would be created was flatly rejected by them, Vergennes realized that the time had come to join the Americans or lose them forever. "There is not a moment to lose," he observed. "Events have surprised us, they have marched more rapidly than we could have expected."

Nevertheless, with the American diplomats eager for the meeting—knowing full well that they now held all the cards—Vergennes still had to deal with Spain and Louis XVI. As the world's largest colonial empire, Spain had no wish to encourage rebellion and republicanism in the Western Hemisphere. She had much to lose, while France risked almost nothing, having been stripped by Britain of most of its colonial possessions in the Seven Years' War. Spain's policy was to give the Americans just enough aid to keep them in the field against Britain, but never enough to produce complete victory, for a protracted war would weaken Great Britain, just as the War of Dutch Independence had drained Spain. To this end, the Spanish used the house of Garoqui and Sons, their equivalent of Hortalez et Cie, but smaller. Unlike Hortalez, Gardoqui required payment for all supplies shipped. Despite this difficulty, Spain did assure France that if war were declared on Britain, it would stand by its ally—albeit with reluctant bad grace.

King Louis's objection to an alliance was that it would provoke an expensive war and thus ruin the policy of economizing, which he pursued so passionately. He yearned to go down in history as one of the few French sovereigns to balance the budget. But he was also fond of glory and inclined to depend upon the advice of his uncle King Charles III of Spain. So Vergennes placed before him a vision of how an alliance with the Americans would be an act of magnanimity that would glorify his reign, while reminding him that King Charles stood ready to support his ally. Having thus overcome the reluctance of the Spanish court and his own sovereign and having been informed by his spies that Lord North was preparing a conciliatory offer to the Americans when Parliament reconvened in mid-February 1778, the Comte de Vergennes was now more eager for the treaty than were Franklin, Lee and Deane. Because he also sought it as soon as possible, negotiations began in December 1777.

Such was the enthusiasm on both sides, however, that there was little difficulty in forging this historic and revolutionary pact between a nascent republic and the oldest monarchy in Europe. It was agreed that the Franco-American alliance would go into effect only if war erupted between Britain and France. When war occurred—and both sides were certain that it would—the United States was bound to defend the French West Indies and not to make peace with Great Britain without the consent of France. For its part, France guaranteed the independence of the United States and would continue the war until that objective was obtained.

In a treaty of commerce also negotiated, France did not demand exclusive control of American commerce in the style of mercantilist Britain or her own mercantilist policy for her own colonies. Instead, France would "give America to the whole world." Actually, she could do no other, for America did not intend to exchange British economic shackles for French mercantilist chains, nor did Vergennes desire to alienate the powers of Europe he was organizing against his mortal foe by hogging the American market. In this spirit, the agreement upheld the cherished American ideal of freedom of the seas. Here, of course, was a menace to mercantilism fully as grave as the republican threat to monarchy. Vergennes realized this fact full well, convinced in his own mind that once free, this young republic would become one of the great carrying nations of the seagoing world. He foresaw that the United States might become a danger to all Europe, that it might build a navy that would be more than a match for the combined seapower of the entire Old World, while dominating all North and South America and stripping the European powers of their colonies there. With rare candor he described this to the British ambassador, emissary of his archenemy, remarking: "All these consequences would not, indeed, be immediate. Neither you nor I should live to see them, but for being remote they are not less sure."

By this treaty monarchic France also subscribed to the American doctrine that oppressed people everywhere had the right to rise against tyrannous rulers, but all French subjects—especially those overjoyed intellectuals, such as the Encyclopedists—were warned that this concession was only for foreign consumption and was not to be enjoyed at home.

Although the treaties were signed on February 6, 1778, they were not proclaimed because the Spanish treasure ships had not yet made home port and France feared that Britain might retaliate by attacking Bourbon shipping. It was not until March 20 of that year that the American commissioners were formally received at Versailles by King Louis XVI, and amid the elegance and splendor of the most brilliant court in Europe, the United States of America joined the family of nations.

★ 49 ★

THE FALL OF THE DELAWARE RIVER FORTS

Sir William Howe was determined to reduce the American forts on the Delaware River below Philadelphia. They blocked his supply line over the water route that was both easier to traverse and to defend, compelling him to adopt the landward route that was open both to attack and to the difficulty of movement created by storms, especially in winter.

The forts had been built under the expert supervision of the French engineer, the Chevalier du Plessis—one of the few foreign volunteers commissioned by the foreigner-fawning Congress who proved to be of value in the Revolutionary War. Plessis had constructed an interlocking system based upon two forts—Mifflin and Mercer—and supported by lesser fortifications at the village of Billingsport on the New Jersey shore plus two small adjacent isles in the river known as Billings Island. Fort Mifflin was on Mud Island, close to the mouth of the Schuylkill River. It was heavily fortified, as was Fort Mercer, slightly higher upriver at Red Bank in New Jersey. Plessis's defensive system relied heavily on the use of cheveaux-de-frise, that is, "iron horses," which were constructed of a long horizontal baulk of timber or an iron barrel to which iron spikes five or six feet long, sharpened at either end, were affixed. Used in water, they were towed to a channel and then sunk with loads of stones, so that their spikes were not visible above water. A ship sailing into one would founder on it. On land they were used to block narrow passes or breaches, most often against cavalry. Galleys and floating batteries, under Commander John Hazelwood, also supported the forts' defenses, and beyond Mercer's cheveaux-de-frise were the frigate, *Delaware,* 28 guns; *Province,* 18; thirteen galleys each with one 18-pounder; seventeen fireships; and numerous fire rafts loaded with powder and dry brush. Compared to the leviathans commanded by Lord Richard Howe, these naval defenses were puny, indeed, but they represented much of the strength of the fledgling United States Navy, especially their precious cannon. Without foundries of their own, the Americans had been heavily dependent on either captured ordnance or the light field pieces provided by Beaumarchais.

About four hundred men of two Rhode Island regiments held Fort Mercer under the command of Colonel Christopher Greene, a cousin of Nathanael's, a "stout and strong" man, good-humored, beloved of his soldiers. Greene had distinguished himself at Bunker Hill, and again at Quebec. Against him came Colonel Carl Emil Kurt von Donop, who had commanded the chain of Hessian posts in New Jersey when Rall was overwhelmed at Trenton by Washington. In Donop's mind that unfortunate raid was a stain upon his reputation, and to remove it, he requested that Howe grant him the honor of attacking Mercer. It was done, and Donop collected a force of about two thousand Hessians, among them grenadiers and chasseurs both mounted and dismounted, together with eight field pieces and two British howitzers. Donop asked for more artillery, a request that Howe denied with the remark that if Donop thought that his Germans could not take the fort, then a British force would. Stung, Donop told the aide who brought the message: "Tell your general that the Germans are not afraid to face death." To his officers, he said: "Either the fort will soon be called Fort Donop, or I shall have fallen." Some of the Hessian chief's resentment of Howe's gratuitous insult was dissipated, however, after Howe sent a British formation across the Delaware to seize the unfinished fort at Billingsport, thus making Donop's approach to Mercer easier.

Inside that fort, meanwhile, Plessis advised Greene to withdraw from his outer defenses to concentrate inside a five-sided redoubt at the center of the works. Greene agreed, but decided not to do so until the enemy appeared, perhaps because this would give the appearance of a retreat. Meanwhile, inspired by a dispatch from Washington reminding him that if he held out, Howe would have to evacuate Philadelphia, he raised his flag on a high hickory tree inside his lines.

The flag was visible on October 22 to Colonel von Donop as he led his superior force through the woods that ended four hundred yards short of the fort. Hoping to capture the position by summons, he sent an officer forward under a flag of truce and preceded by a drummer boy "as insolent as his officer." Donop's message declared: "The King of England commands his rebellious subjects to lay down their arms, and they are warned that if they wait until the battle, no quarter will be granted." Greene rejected the demand with scorn.

Meanwhile, Donop lost more time by his methodical preparation for the assault, so that it was four o'clock in the afternoon before the oboes blew and the Hessian lines moved forward. That meant only an hour of daylight remaining in which to take the fort. Nevertheless, Donop exhorted his officers to fight like Germans, watching proudly as they dismounted with drawn swords and led his men forward, marching in parade-ground formation over the intervening four hundred yards and following sappers carrying fascines to bridge the ditches of the enemy's outer works.

At this point, Greene ordered his withdrawal. Seeing the Americans back-pedaling, assuming that they were fleeing, the jubilant Hessians shouted, "*Vittoria!*"—and rushed forward, throwing their hats into the air. Reaching the abatis outside the redoubt, they were halted by its sharpened branches, and as they gathered there in bunches, a dreadful fire broke from the unseen Yankees. Greene had instructed his men to fire low and aim at the broad white belts of the enemy's uniforms, and they did so with devastating effect. The sight of so many comrades down unnerved Donop's men, and many turned to flee. Brought back by officers beating them with the flat of their swords, they still milled about among the abatis branches they sought to cut with their bayonets—and many more fell.

Retiring and regrouping for a second assault, Donop's men were struck by a savage flanking fire from the American galleys and floating batteries on the river. In this onslaught Donop fell mortally wounded by a musket ball in the stomach. Twenty-two of his officers, including all the battalion commanders, were either killed or wounded—and with this, the entire attacking force turned and fled, leaving almost a third of their number, almost seven hundred men, either killed, wounded or captured. American casualties were fourteen killed and twenty-three wounded. Two British warships, *Augusta* and *Merlin,* also were lost. So complete was the Hessian rout that Donop's men dumped their cannon into the river so that they could use the gun carriages to take off their wounded.

When the dying "No-Quarter" Donop was carried into the fort, American soldiers began baiting him, one of them exclaiming: "Well, is it settled that no quarter is to be given?" To this, the Hessian commander replied: "I am in your hands. You can avenge yourselves." Plessis appeared to rebuke the Americans, prompting Donop to ask who he was. "A French officer," the engineer replied, whereupon Donop, with the eighteenth-century soldier's fondness for the studied line, remarked: "I am content. I die in the arms of honor itself." But he had three more days to live, and by then was ready with an even more flamboyant farewell: "This is finishing a noble career early, but I die the victim of my ambition and the avarice of my sovereign."

Victim of his own vanity and William Howe's insulting indifference might be more correct, for there is little doubt that Donop, to save his honor, attacked with panache but without artillery, suffering a resounding defeat in one of the most striking American victories of the war, minor though it may have been.

It is also possible that the defeat shocked the lethargic Howe into activity of which, though not endeared, he was eminently capable, for his preparations to take Fort Mifflin on Mud Island were masterful. On November 10 he opened his bombardment of the fort with four 32-pounders from *Somerset,* six 24-pounders on *Eagle* and one 13-inch mortar, together with the artillery he had already emplaced at the mouth of the Schuylkill. The effect might have been devastating but for the presence of another capable French engineer, François Louis Teissedre de Fleury. He was a descendant of one of the noblest families in France, and though hardly more than a boy so skillful an engineer and so brave a soldier that he quickly won the respect and affection of those Americans with whom he served. If his requests for fascines and palisades to shore up the fort's defenses, as well as for a heavy chain to be stretched to the Pennsylvania shore to block the passage of British warships, had been granted, it is likely that Mifflin might have held out indefinitely. Fleury himself was undaunted, declaring: "The fire of the enemy will never take the fort. It may kill us men but this is the fortune of war. And all their bullets will never render them masters of the island if we have courage enough to remain on it."

The ragged, footsore, hungry Yankee Doodles did indeed possess that courage, among them Joseph Martin, who wrote: "Here I endured hardships sufficient to kill half a dozen horses." He and his comrades had not "a scrap of either shoes or stockings to my feet or legs." And again: "The British batteries in the course of the day would nearly level our works, and we were, like the beaver, obliged to repair our dams in the night. As the American defenders made repairs, a soldier would stand guard, and when he saw the muzzle flash of a British artillery piece, he would call out—'A shot!'—upon which everyone endeavored to take care of himself, yet they would ever and anon, in spite of all our precautions, cut up some of us."

"Ever and anon" those casualties were mounting, and when the dead and wounded were evacuated at night to Fort Mercer, replacements were sent into Mifflin bringing timber, tools and other supplies for repairs. But Fleury, acting as a commander in the absence of Lieutenant Colonel Samuel Smith, was still determined to hold out. "Our ruins will serve us as breast-works," he said. Unfortunately, the tenacity and courage of Fleury and Mifflin's four hundred defenders—most of them Marylanders—had already been undone by the treachery of an engineer named Robert White. He was a secret Tory, and when he was placed in charge of sinking a line of cheveaux-de-frise to bar the river to British warships, he deliberately left open a passage on the Pennsylvania side. Again and again enemy warships penetrated this line of sunken obstacles to come within pistol shot of Mifflin. Even so, the stubbornness of the rebel defenders had begun to discourage Howe's troops, until White deserted to them and, by his reports of the Americans' dire circumstances, persuaded them to renew the assault.

Washington, meanwhile, in his eagerness to hold the Delaware forts, was all for reinforcing and resupplying the garrison. Remote from the battle itself, however, he had to depend upon the reports of staff officers, who advised evacuation. It was done, and among those survivors taken off Mud Island was the badly wounded Fleury, as well as Joseph Martin, who, having been ordered to destroy hogsheads of rum, had the American private soldier's customary good sense to fill his own canteen with the delectable liquid before he closed his eyes and swung his ax.

The fall of Fort Mifflin seriously crippled the defense of Fort Mercer, not so much materially as morally. Mercer's defenses were still in the hands of the capable Plessis, and Nathanael Greene had been sent by Washington to take command in New Jersey and to repel Lord Cornwallis in Howe's second attempt to take the fort. Moreover, whereas Fort Mifflin had been undone chiefly by the fire from shore batteries on Province Island and the treachery of Robert White, Fort Mercer had been reinforced—including a command led by the Marquis de Lafayette, recovered from his Brandywine wound—and still possessed the gunboats and galleys that had sunk *Augusta* and *Merlin.* Yet when Cornwallis landed at Billingsport on the New Jersey shore on November 18 with two thousand men, the fort was abandoned without a shot and all its buildings and supplies were burned.

Why remains a mystery to this day, except the possibility—if not actually the probability—that its defenders were demoralized and Greene did not dare rely upon them for another siege. They had behaved splendidly in beating back Donop's force, but then, night after night they had witnessed the arrival of casualties from Fort Mifflin and day after day they had seen that fortress taken apart shot by shot. The prospect of having to face the same sort of bombardment, heavier now that the British could sail upriver unimpeded as far as Red Bank, may have sapped their moral strength. Indeed, Yankee Doodle never could match the disciplined stoicism of the European professional under artillery fire, and so the Delaware forts fell to the British, enabling Sir William Howe to spend a snug and safe winter in the City of Brotherly Love, basking in the adulation of Tories now happily thronging its streets, as well as the favors of Mrs. Loring—or "the Sultana," as the young officers called her—while George Washington, with a heavy heart, marched his weary veterans off toward the grim and gloomy hills of Valley Forge.

⋆ 50 ⋆

VALLEY FORGE/VON STEUBEN

Valley Forge lay at the junction of the Schuylkill River and Valley Creek. Actually, it was not a valley but high ground—a thickly wooded slope two miles long overlooking the Schuylkill. Another capable French engineer named Duportail had laid out the camp's fortifications so skillfully that Lieutenant General Charles Grey—the villainous "No-Flint" Grey—after a thorough reconnaissance reported that Valley Forge was virtually impregnable. The lines ran from a promontory in the middle called Mount Joy to the Schuylkill on the left and Valley Creek on the right. Knox's artillery was emplaced on the high ground, while Washington's headquarters, with its blue flag with thirteen white stars, occupied the triangle formed by the junction of the river and the creek.

When Washington decided to march his army to this encampment about twenty miles from Philadelphia, many Patriots criticized him bitterly for failing to attack Howe in the Quaker City. Their discontent proceeded from a mistaken assumption that his army was twice the size of Howe's—a superiority that the American commander never was to possess—and the Pennsylvania Assembly, with the politicians' customary conviction that armies move on maps, rather than on earth, chided him so unjustly that for one of the few times in his career, he lost his temper and replied: "The gentlemen reprobate the going into winter quarters as much as if they thought the soldiers were made of sticks or stones. I can assure these gentlemen that it is a much easier and less distressing thing to draw remonstrances in a comfortable room, than to occupy a cold bleak hill, and sleep under frost and snow without clothes or blankets. However, although they seem to have little feeling for the naked and distressed soldiers, I feel superabundantly for them, and from my soul I pity their miseries which it is neither in my power to relieve or prevent."

Surgeon Albigence Waldo of the Connecticut Line, an extremely dedicated and cultivated physician and a great favorite with the troops, was also outraged by this ignorant and unfeeling censure, writing: "Why don't His Excellency rush in and retake the city ...? Because he knows better than to leave his post and be caught like a damned fool cooped up in the city. He has always acted wisely hitherto. His conduct when closely scrutinized is uncensurable. Were his inferior generals as skillful as himself, we should have the grandest choir of officers ever God made."

In choosing Valley Forge, Washington rejected advice to winter farther from Philadelphia in comfortable quarters west of the Schuylkill at Lancaster, Reading or Allentown because it was his experience that armies in soft billets usually deteriorated. Like Napoleon, he believed that "Adversity is the school of the good soldier." He had listened when the bellicose Wayne argued that to winter far away might suggest to the enemy that the Continental Army was afraid. Moreover, Valley Forge was well chosen, for it protected a considerable area of rich country against British foraging, while covering Lancaster and Reading from an enemy offensive. Finally close enough to watch Howe, it was far enough away to guard against surprise. Of course, George Washington, having spent one trying winter striving to form an army in Cambridge and another near-disastrous one from which his daring strokes at Trenton and Princeton rescued him, now expected that in this, his third winter, he would have the opportunity to preserve his exhausted force and mold it into a tough, professional army. Fully expecting to be armed, fed and clothed from the well-stocked bases at Lancaster and Reading, he had no way of knowing that at Valley Forge he was embarked upon one of the most miserable quarter years of privation and pitiless suffering ever endured in the annals of modern arms.

As a foretaste of what was in store for the Continental Army as it stopped at Gulph on its march from Whitemarsh to Valley Forge, the men were jubilant to hear that Congress had authorized a Day of Thanksgiving. Private Martin wrote: "We must now have a sumptuous Thanksgiving to close out [this] year of high living.... Our country, ever mindful of its suffering army, opened her sympathizing heart so wide ... as to give us something to make the world stare.... It gave each and every man *four ounces* of rice and a *tablespoonful* of vinegar!"

Bitter and sour vinegar was indeed the portion of those indomitable scarecrows marching into camp in that chilly mid-December of 1777. It was not the severe cold that was to make the Continentals so miserable, for the winter of 1777–78 was actually a mild one. It was rather a bungling quartermaster department and the avarice of American merchants and farmers that made the name Valley Forge stand forever as a synonym for suffering soldiers. Troops there went hungry because nearby farmers preferred to sell to the British in Philadelphia for hard cash, rather than for those worthless Continentals; because New York's grain surplus was diverted to New England civilians and the British soldiery in New York City; and because Connecticut farmers refused to sell beef cattle at ceiling prices imposed by the state. Soldiers went half-naked because merchants in Boston would not move governmental clothing off their shelves at anything less than profits of from 1,000 to 1,800 percent. Everywhere in America there was a spirit of profiteering ("expanding" it was then called) and a habit of graft that made George Washington grind his teeth in helpless fury. In response to his appeals for supplies, Congress passed the buck by authorizing him to commandeer them from the countryside. This he was reluctant to do among a people supposedly engaged in throwing off a tyrant's chains, even though his army, after arriving at Valley Forge on December 19, "decreased two thousand from hardships and exposure in three weeks." Only 8,200 men were fit for duty.

At first the winter camp did not appear to be the cold, starving hell that it would become. Orders went out immediately to divide the men into parties of twelve to build their own huts. Because so many of Washington's soldiers were farm boys, they were familiar with axes and saws and fell to with enthusiasm—encouraged by their commander's offer of a prize of twelve dollars for the best-built and soonest-completed hut in each regiment. Because the British had burned the local sawmill, there was no lumber, but the ingenious Yankees cut and trimmed their own building material out of the timber growing on the wooded slopes, using mud or clay to fill the chinks between the logs.

The huts were sixteen feet long by fourteen feet wide and six and a half feet high. Into each corner were built tiered bunks. Washington had hoped to overcome the lack of boards for roofing by offering one hundred dollars for the best substitute, but with only sapling poles and a compound of straw and dirt available, the replacements leaked like a sieve after a few hours of rain or during a thaw. There were fireplaces with chimneys of wood lined with clay, but with only green wood to burn in them, they smoked horribly. Split slabs of oak were used for doors and oiled paper for windows. It was not long before this two-mile double row of wretched log huts became a veritable Misery Road, and it is Surgeon Waldo again who gives the best description of life inside of them, even for an officer:

"Poor food—hard lodging—cold weather—fatigue—nasty clothes—nasty cookery—vomit half the time—smoked out of my senses—the Devil's in it—I can't endure it—why are we sent here to starve and freeze? What sweet felicities have I left at home. ... Here all confusion—smoke and cold—hunger and filthiness—pox on my bad luck! Here comes a bowl of beef soup, full of burnt leaves and dirt, sickness enough to make a Hector spue—away with it boys!—I'll live like the chameleon upon air."

As early as December 23—two days before Christmas—Washington reported ominously to Congress that there was so little food that a "dangerous mutiny" had only barely been averted. There was "not a single hoof of any kind to slaughter and not more than twenty-five barrels of flour." Each night from these filthy, verminous, leaking huts there issued the dolorous croaking cries: "No bread! No bread—no soldier! No meat! No meat—no soldier!" The common diet shared by both officers and men was a paste of flour and water, cooked upon hot stones called "Firecake." Thus the sardonic plaint arose twice daily: "Firecake and water for breakfast! Water and firecake for supper!" Even water was scarce, for there were no springs on the high hills of Valley Forge. Water had to be carried up from Valley Creek in buckets. Sullivan's men found some clams, but when he passed a group huddled around a stone boiling in a kettle and asked why they were doing it, he was told: "They say there's strength in a stone, if you can get it out."

In their appearance the Continentals might have been wild bipeds, and again it is Waldo who describes them: "Here comes a soldier, his bare feet are seen through his worn-out shoes, his legs nearly naked from the tattered remains of an only pair of stockings, his breeches not sufficient to cover his nakedness, his shirt hanging in strings, his hair dishevelled, his face meager. His whole appearance pictures a person forsaken and discouraged. He comes and crys with an air of wretchedness and despair: 'I am sick, my feet lame, my legs are sore, my body covered with this tormenting itch' (an affliction common in the camp)."

Blood on the snow was their sign—and this was no exaggeration. Washington himself reported that the path of his army's march from Whitemarsh to Valley Forge could be traced by the splotches of red in the snow.

In such rags, and with blankets so scarce, many soldiers sat up all night beating themselves for warmth, rather than risk freezing to death. When the young Lafayette arrived in camp, he was horrified to see soldiers whose legs had frozen black being carried from their huts and piled on wagons taking them to hospitals that were often no better than charnel houses—there to have their limbs amputated. Nothing was feared more than a Continental Army hospital. To be ticketed to one was like a passport to suffering and death. Dr. Benjamin Rush, the physician general of the Medical Department, who had resigned in disgust at a situation he could not correct, reported that most hospital rooms that were large enough for six or eight well men were crammed with twenty or more sick soldiers, all lying a few feet apart in shirts or blankets they had been wearing or using for five months and on beds of straw that were seldom changed. Most of them suffered from dysentery or pulmonary diseases, but because they were in such close proximity to one another, they were also vulnerable to those twin terrors: "jail" fever and "putrid" fever. Nine out of every ten cases of fever ended in death. Out of forty patients in a Virginia regiment, only three survived.

In most hospitals discipline was merely a word. With no guards or military police to enforce it, the patients did as they pleased: dirtied their quarters, fought among themselves, sold their clothes for rum and bullied or robbed the local inhabitants. Conversely, many soldiers were robbed or relieved of their clothes by hospital personnel.

None of these dreadful conditions was deliberate, but, rather, the result of an inefficient service of supply, graft and theft. Actually there was enough of everything, if only it could be delivered. In France and the West Indies huge supplies of clothing were held up by squabbles between local agents. Dishonesty was compounded by its more disruptive twin: stupidity. When Anthony Wayne dipped into his private fortune for a whopping £4,500 to provide new uniforms for his men, the clothier-general refused to supply them because the transaction was "irregular." Congress, as might be expected, was to blame for most of the confusion. Rather than accept Washington's advice to place the supply departments under the command of an able general, it made the Commissary Department directly responsible to one of its own committees, where it was quietly strangled in red tape.

Transportation of supplies was a macabre fantasy that might have been based on a short story by Franz Kafka. Wagons, horses and drivers were all in short supply, while contractors who demanded forty-five shillings a day for a wagon, driver and four horses received only thirty shillings from Congress. Experienced drivers, fearing fines for absence from militia duty, refused to lift the reins, and their replacements were an abomination. Predictably, if they did not lighten their loads by draining the brine from casks of salt meat, thus causing it to become spoiled, they ruined flour or other perishables by clumsily spilling it on the ground or by unloading the barrels in the rain or on washed-out roads where they had become bogged down. Or they simply drew their pay and quit the job, leaving wagonloads of every sort of badly needed supplies to rot or be stolen.

A network of bad roads, deep snows and the constant flooding of the Susquehanna River also contributed to delays, and the absence of grain and hay for the Continental Army's horses made a bad transportation situation worse. Washington might save his light horses by sending them across the Delaware to subsist on the abundant produce of the New Jersey farms, but in Valley Forge the work animals of the artillery and the wagon trains died by the literal hundreds. In a thaw the stench of putrifying horse flesh, combined with the ever-present reek of unwashed human bodies and the manifold odors of the huts, made even outdoor life at Valley Forge stink like the inside of an abattoir. Twice a week, work details were assigned to burying the dead horses.

Daily, meanwhile, the cemetery carts, known as "meat wagons," rattled through the camp with creaking wheels. Each time a wagon halted before a hut, men of the graves detail leaped down to fetch the body of a soldier who had either starved or frozen to death during the night. Eventually the meat wagons would be piled high with carcasses. The dead men's skins were blackened and wrinkled, and their limbs no bigger than sticks. Half of them were naked, for the ghouls of the graves detail were always careful to strip the bodies of anything useful, especially shoes, which, if they didn't fit, could be boiled and eaten. Sometimes the grave ghouls fought the dead men's comrades for possession of articles of clothing. To deal daily with ungainly death had also made the ghouls less than gentle or respectful, heaping the corpses onto the wagons helter-skelter and with calloused indifference. Some of the dead lay on their backs with sightless eyes upturned, their mouths drawn back from shriveled black gums. Other lay with their faces resting on the bare behinds of others or with their heads hanging over the side of the carts, their tongues lolling from their mouths. Should a cart rolling downhill go jolting over a bump, it might dislodge not only a carcass but one or two bloated rats that had been feeding there.

Such, then, was the ordeal of Valley Forge, a place of pain and horror, a hellish place like a painting by Hieronymus Bosch, to which George Washington had marched his men in high hopes of forging anew another army. But then there also arrived in Valley Forge in February 1778, like an Angel from Heaven come to rescue the Continental cause, another one of those counterfeit German barons.

He called himself Lieutenant General Friedrich Ludolf Gerhard Wilhelm Augustin von Steuben, aide-de-camp to King Frederick the Great of

Prussia, the greatest soldier of the age. Decorations blazed on his stout chest, among them the Order of Baden, a patent of knighthood. He arrived in a horse-drawn sleigh with an Italian greyhound at his side. Around him, on horseback and in a carriage, were five grooms and drivers, three servants, a cook, and three French aides: De Pontiere, Du Ponceau and L'Enfant. Pierre Etienne Du Ponceau acted as the general's interpreter—for Steuben spoke no English—and would become in later years a leading citizen of Philadelphia. Pierre L'Enfant was a gifted artist and engineer and would one day design the capital city of Washington, his very own "city of magnificent distances." De Pontiere's first name and background are unknown. All three gave great deference to this noble general, dressed in a brand-new buff-and-blue American uniform. Though stout, he stood ramrod straight, and it was perhaps this military bearing that made American soldiers believe he was much taller than his five feet nine and a half inches. He had a large nose and ruddy cheeks, twinkling gray eyes and an expressive mouth. But there was a startled look on his face when he stepped from his sleigh to hear that croaking cry: "No bread, no soldier!"

Friedrich von Steuben of course, was in no way entitled to the ennobling "von" of the German Junker, nor the "de" of the French noblesse, which, like that other genial fraud, de Kalb, he preferred. But he was neither noble nor a general. Born in Magdeburg, Prussia, in 1730, the son of an army engineer, he had been educated at Breslau by the Jesuits and had become, at seventeen, an officer in the Prussian Army. But he never rose higher than captain and probably never spoke to Frederick the Great, although he did serve in the Seven Years' War on Frederick's staff. Because it was the great Frederick who invented the modern military staff, Steuben (actually Steube) may be said to have passed through the finest military school in the world. Discharged in 1762, he served as chamberlain to the court of Hohenzollern-Hechingen, where, like most other courtiers, he sank heavily into debt. Eager to retrieve his fortune, he heard of the war in America and went hurrying to Paris, where he met Benjamin Franklin. That worthy, always a shrewd judge of human flesh, was deeply impressed, as was the French minister of war, and thus, with a nice loan from Beaumarchais, he was able to arrive in Philadelphia in style. Courtly, with a bluff Germanic charm—and a basic if not actually crude Teutonic sense of humor—he also impressed the delegates. He was not boastful of his military prowess or knowledge, like Charles Lee, but carried his credentials in his brain. So it was that John Hancock provided him with servants, a sleigh, a carriage, horses and uniforms and sent him on to Valley Forge.

Steuben—he had as yet no rank—was shocked at the appearance of the American soldiers. He had found an army almost without hope. "The men were literally naked," he observed. "The officers who had coats had them of every color ... made of an old blanket or a woolen bedcover. With regard to their military discipline, I may safely say no such thing existed." No unit was at full strength. Desertions—especially among the foreign born—disease and death had depleted every unit. One company had shrunk from a hundred men to only one—a corporal. One regiment could muster only thirty soldiers. Their muskets were "in a horrible condition, covered with rust, half of them without bayonets," and those who had them used them chiefly as spits on which to cook their meat. Each regiment had its own idea of how to drill, camping as its colonel decreed without any sense of standard or order. There were more supply officers in the Continental Army than in all the armies of Europe, but no one actually kept records of arms, clothing equipment or ammunition. In the American belief that with no battles to fight, camp was an utter and useless bore, many officers and men went home for the winter. Men who had completed their service, carried their weapons and clothing home with them, contrary to army orders. Incredibly, quartermasters were paid a percentage of the supplies they purchased—a license to steal if there ever was one! Such waste inevitably contributed to inflation and an unstable currency.

Steuben marveled that Washington's army had not melted clean away. No European army could have survived under such conditions. Yet, as he deplored the attitude and appearance of these ragged and undisciplined troops, he was deeply moved by the sardonic jocularity with which they made light of their miseries, and the depth of their devotion to the cause of freedom. He had never encountered such spirit before.

Steuben had insisted that he desired no command until he learned "the language and the genius and manners of the people"—in itself an insight of genius—and he saw at once that the whole problem was one of discipline: and that meant drill. If that fierce spirit of independence could be controlled and harnessed like wild horses, what soldiers would emerge! But it was a month before he was able to compose a standard drill, chiefly because of the language difficulty. First he would write it in French, which would be translated into English by Du Ponceau and then into American, as it were, by Nathanael Greene and Alexander Hamilton. As Steuben remembered: "I dictated my dispositions in the night; in the day I had them performed." His drill squad was a model platoon of picked soldiers who would become the drillmasters for their own units in the Continental Army's fourteen brigades. Though all these men had been in battle, and therefore had the right to be considered veteran soldiers, Steuben began as though he were welcoming recruits at a "boot camp" of the United States Marines. The presumption was that they knew absolutely nothing about soldiering and were no better than civilians, and thus he started—oh indignity of indignities!—by telling them how to stand. Head up, chin in, shoulders back, chest out, stomach (or what was left of it) in, arms and hands rigid at the side. Next he demonstrated the twenty-eight inch stride and how they must step out left foot first upon the command, "Vorwaarts, march!" Then how to stop upon the command, "Halt! Vun-doo!" Then the various commands and changes of direction: "Doo der rear, march!" "Left oblique, march!" "Right vlank, march!" "Golumn left, march." As they marched he chanted cadence, "Vun-doo-dree-four," which they took up themselves—some of them deliberately mimicking Steuben's guttural accent, to his delighted surprise—that sing-song chant with its rhythmic power to bind men together as a unit sensitive to nothing but their leader's commands.

This was exactly what Steuben was doing, in the way of every drillmaster since Agamemnon: he was stripping his soldiers of every vestige or shred of individuality, making automatons of them, taking them apart by denying every trait or like or dislike; then, once he had dissembled them as human beings, putting them together again as soldiers by instructions in the manual of arms, a much more complicated procedure in those days with twelve different motions involved in loading and firing a musket. Here was the basic unlearning-learning process that still takes place at recruit depots all over the world, and though it did take time and patience, it did at last have its rewards, as these shoeless men stepped out smartly or snapped their naked heels together with a soft thump, rather than a sharp click; swerved left on the oblique or right on the column pivoting off the right foot; or changed direction in a body to either flank.

Steuben was a born impresario, a show in himself, attracting hundreds of soldiers and officers drawn by his colorful polyglot combining three languages that made them roar with laughter. Best of all, he was making the parade ground—so often a citadel of boredom—a place of fun and laughter, with his infectious grin and his outrageous ability to curse fluently in three languages. Thus to Captain Walker: "*Viens, Valkaire, mon ami, mon bon ami! Sacre!* Goddam *de gaucheries* of *dese badouts. Je ne puis plus.* I gan gurse dem no more!"

Within four weeks, the baron had worked a transformation. The rabble in arms could now march like any European soldiers and, best of all, could deploy and change formation under combat conditions. Steuben was himself surprised, and wrote: "My enterprise succeeded better than I had dared to expect, and I had the satisfaction ... to see not only a regular step introduced in the army, but I also made maneuvers with ten and twelve battalions with as much precision as the evolution of a single company." He also discovered the difference between the European and American soldier. "The genius of this nation is not the least to be compared with that of the Prussians, Austrians or French. You say to your [European] soldier, 'Do this,' and he doeth it. But [to an American] I am obliged to say, 'This is the reason why you ought to do that, 'and then he does it." Unknown to the baron, while he was making soldiers out of free spirits, they were converting a Prussian autocrat to democracy.

Thus when his French aides, with his permission, invited a number of young officers to dine at his quarters, the condition, according to Du Ponceau, was that "none should be admitted that had on a whole pair of breeches." In this, he continued, all those he invited "were very sure not to fail." Each guest brought his own ration to the "feast," and in the way of jolly comrades in arms of all wars, "we dined sumptuously on tough beefsteak and potatoes, with hickory nuts for dessert. Instead of wine, we had some kind of spirits with which we made 'Salamanders,' that is to say, after filling up our glasses we set the liquor on fire and drank it up, flame and all. Such a set of ragged and at the same time merry fellows were never brought together!" The baron called the guests his "sans-culottes," thus using for the first time the sobriquet made famous by soldiers of the French Revolution. When an American officer who spoke no French inquired its meaning, his host with the customary impish grin and twinkling gray eye, replied: "Mittout pants."

George Washington had expected much from Steuben, but the miracle that Steuben had wrought was beyond his wildest hopes. In gratitude, when Thomas Conway resigned as inspector general, he recommended the baron as his replacement with the rank of major general. Also, as the winter turned to spring and the supply problem began to ease, recruits began to come in, perhaps drawn by the new spirit of professionalism animating the Continental Army.

But these improvements could not end the food shortage, so that Washington, seeing absolute disaster in the sunken eyes of his starving soldiers, at last and with great reluctance availed himself of his authority to commandeer food. He did so also upon receipt of reports that the British were about to launch a second great foraging expedition among the concentration of Tories along the Brandywine, and he decided that if the inhabitants were to be plundered, it might as well be by Americans. But when the Patriots, under Greene, got there, they found the area stripped nearly bare. Suspecting that much provender might be found hidden in the woods, Greene, told his men: "Harden your hearts. We are in the midst of a damn nest of Tories." Merciless, Greene seized livestock and wagons without payment of any kind and brought them back full of produce while imprisoning their owners. Anthony Wayne was equally ruthless in New Jersey, where he found the Tories even more loyal to the Crown than those in Pennsylvania. He became so proficient at driving off cattle that he earned another sobriquet: Wayne the Drover. By this means, and by this alone, the Continental Army averted starvation.

Much of the pitiless seizure of Tory property and produce was provoked by the dreadful Patriot-versus-Tory guerrilla warfare that broke out in Pennsylvania and New Jersey. British and Hessian soldiers burned and looted savagedly in both states, while the area around Philadelphia became a no-man's-land. Gangs of Tories and civilians pretending to be Patriot militia seized upon the reigning anarchy to commit what Greene called "the most villainous robberies imaginable."

Irregular warfare also raged between Howe's and Washington's troops. Actually, the Americans gave better than they got. On the Germantown front Captain Allen McLane's picked force of cavalry and infantry made the area dangerous to any enemy force smaller than a brigade, while Captain Henry ("Light-Horse Harry") Lee—who would one day become Washington's favorite commander—routed more than two hundred British dragoons near Darby. Yet the indolent Sir William Howe made no effort to mount a concerted campaign against Washington in Valley Forge. As much as his critics might importune him or impugn him for failing to take advantage of the rebels' obvious vulnerability, he still occupied himself with balls and galas and Mrs. Loring. Washington could not believe that Howe could display the same supine folly that had saved him at the Delaware in '76, at Morristown in '77 and now at Valley Forge in '78. Though his fortifications were strong, his men were weak, and the horses he needed to move his guns or conduct a retreat westward were all dead.

But as the food supply improved, the recruits poured in and the yokels became a professional army, Washington's fears subsided. By spring he was in a jovial mood, actually joining his officers in a game of cricket. A pageant or Grand Parade was held, complete with Maypoles for every regiment and dogwood blossoms sprouting from every soldier's hat. The commander in chief was not only encouraged—he was exhilarated. As an officer wrote in the New Jersey *Gazette:* "The army grows stronger every day. It increases in numbers … there is a spirit of discipline among the troops that is better than numbers. Each brigade is on parade almost every day for several hours. You would be charmed to see the regularity and exactness with which they march and perform their maneuvers." Washington had been an almost daily observer of Steuben's reforms. His policy had always been to be with his troops, but at Valley Forge, because of the ordeal they endured, he had made his presence felt by his soldiers even more. Just to see their big commander riding about on his chestnut sorrel was an inspiration to them. And yet, perhaps because their relationship was more like sons with their fathers than soldiers with their general, they were unafraid to speak their minds. No incident attests more to this easy affinity than the exchange that occurred one spring day when Washington rode past a group of laughing soldiers and saw that they were drinking precious and probably stolen wine and were already a bit tipsy. One of them, named John Brantley, boisterously invited him "to drink some wine with a soldier."

"My boy," Washington replied gently, "you have no time for drinking wine." Then he rode on with his staff.

"Damn your proud soul!" Brantley called after him. "You are above drinking with soldiers?"

Turning his mount, Washington rode back. "Come, I will drink with you." He received Brantley's jug and swung it up to his lips, taking a deep swig before returning it to the astonished soldier. Pointing to his staff, Brantley proffered the jug again and said: "Give it to your servants." This was done, the staff officers drank—and once again Brantley reclaimed his jug.

Looking up at his commander in chief with tears in his eyes, the brash young soldier declared:

"Now, I'll be damned if I don't spend the last drop of my heart's blood for you!"

⋆ 51 ⋆

THE CONWAY CABAL

Probably the most humiliating and infuriating ordeal that George Washington had to endure as commander in chief of the American War for Independence was the so-called Conway Cabal, a loose coalition—or, rather, coalescing—of disaffected generals and discontented members of Congress who were at first united in their determination to dismiss Washington and then, later, in their hopes of replacing him with Horatio Gates.

Thomas Conway, who gave his name to the conspiracy, if such it really was, was Gates's coadjutor. Born in Ireland, he had served in the French Army for thirty years and had been commissioned an American brigadier general. Like Gates, Charles Lee and some native-born generals, he considered Washington to be a bungling amateur and did not hesitate to say so either in conversations or in letters. Conway had distinguished himself at the Brandywine, and Sullivan said of him: "His regulations in his brigade are much better than any in the army, and his knowledge of military matters far exceeds any officer we have." Conway, evidently a conceited and boastful officer, would have supported that opinion, while those in Congress who shared his disdain for Washington were John and Samuel Adams and Richard Henry Lee, together with Dr. Benjamin Rush and General Thomas Mifflin, both of whom had resigned from the army.

Except for John Adams, they circulated an anonymous pamphlet entitled *Thoughts of a Freeman,* which criticized Washington's generalship and warned of a growing cult to deify him. "The people of America have been guilty of making a man their God." In this they could count upon the allegiance of John Adams, who sincerely—but without evidence—

feared that Washington would use his power and popularity to make himself a military dictator. In that insane jealousy that often possessed him, Adams could suggest that Washington's men were barefoot because they had worn out their shoes in useless marching. As Benjamin Franklin wrote of Adams: "He was always an honest man, sometimes a wise one, but ... about some things absolutely out of his mind." Among those "things" was comprehension of matters military. Samuel Adam's distrust of the commander in chief sprang from the same conviction, as well as from fear of a threat to his secret ideal of an American theocracy.

Dr. Benjamin Rush was no more competent to judge a general than was either Adams. He had resigned as physician-general of the Medical Department ostensibly because of the deplorable condition of the hospitals, but actually during a dispute with his superior. He spoke openly of "the weak conduct of General Washington." He warned that "a cry begins to be raised for a Gates, a Conway, a de Kalb." Obviously to him no native-born American could aspire to chief command, a suggestion given credence by his attacks on Washington's leading officers. Greene was a "sycophant," Sullivan a "weak vain braggart," Stirling a "lazy ignorant drunkard" and Hamilton a "paltry satellite," whatever that is. It was by this shabby company that Washington was to be judged.

General Mifflin seems to have been the chief conspirator. Once devoted to Washington, he had held his stirrup for him when he mounted his horse in 1775 to ride to Cambridge. But his jealousy of Greene soured him, and he told all who would listen that Washington's numerous failures were all due to his listening to Greene's advice. As far as Fort Washington is concerned, this criticism was true—but no further. To Mifflin, Washington's latest and biggest blunder was in not attacking and liberating Philadelphia—where Mifflin had made his fortune as a merchant. As is often true of discontents, he disguised his disappointment at not regaining his extensive Philadelphia holdings in the nobler language of high moral purpose. Thus, when he resigned from the army, he said it was because as a Patriot he was unalterably opposed to Washington's policy of avoiding decisive battle with a superior foe. Rather, Washington should actively seek it.

Such abysmal military ignorance, as well as sheer civilian folly, characterized the thinking of *Thoughts of a Freeman* as it was widely circulated in December and January. All the woes besetting the nation and the army—commissary and quartermaster failures, desertions, dreadful hospital conditions, even inflation and a depreciated currency—were blamed on Washington. Traditional distrust of a standing army—a cardinal tenet of the New England democrats' creed—induced the writers to insist that a nation fighting for its life should entrust the defense of liberty to the militia, those peerless marchers to the rear. The militia, not the Lines of the Continental Army, had been responsible for every victory! There was also something "mysterious" about the fall of the Delaware forts. Among the recipients of *Thoughts* was Henry Laurens of South Carolina, president of the Continental Congress then meeting at York. Laurens forwarded his copy to his son John, an officer on Washington's staff, expecting him to put it into the hands of his chief—as he did. Washington was thus warned of the movement against him, but with that unshakeable equanimity that was one of his noblest qualities, he did nothing—until he realized that Congress seemed to be siding with his two bitterest enemies: Horatio Gates and Thomas Conway.

In the winter of 1777–78 Congress had degenerated even further from the first two assemblies. Many of the earlier leaders had either gone into the army or become officials in their home states. Often the sessions in York drew no more than sixteen or seventeen delegates, sometimes as few as nine or ten. As it shrank in numbers and excellence, the Congress seemed to grow in jealousy of its power and prerogatives and in a mindless mistrust of military power—the one true guardian of its cherished liberties—as exemplified by the slovenly thinking of *Thoughts*.

Thus Congress was most receptive to Thomas Conway when, after the Brandywine, he began badgering the members for his second star. Conway bombarded York with boastful letters setting forth his qualifications. His remark that Washington was a gentleman and a brave man, "but as to his talents for the command of an army, they were miserable indeed," was well known and eminently acceptable to many of them. So many members of Congress began to consider Conway one wing of a two-part plan to emasculate Washington's authority. Conway would be made Washington's inspector general, and the moribund Board of War was to be revived with Horatio Gates as its chairman, his toady Wilkinson as its secretary with the rank of brevet* brigadier general and Thomas Mifflin as its most influential member. Thus Washington's two worst enemies would have him in a cross-fire, for Conway as the new inspector general was to be independent of Washington, reporting only to Gates. The Board of War side of this two-edged sword of decapitation would come later, but Conway as his unbridled inspector general was a dangerous challenge so immediate that Washington dropped his reserve and went over to the counterattack.

To Richard Henry Lee, Washington wrote: "General Conway's

*A brevet commission confers the rank but not the pay.

merit as an officer and his importance in this army exists more in his imagination than in reality. For it is a maxim with him to leave no service of his untold, nor to want any thing which is to be obtained by importunity." Here was a surprising Washington, brief and pungent as a Julius Caesar, his prose as short and deadly as a Roman short sword. Next: "It will be impossible for me to be of any further service if such insuperable difficulties are thrown in my way." To this unvarnished threat to resign, he appended a prediction that promotion of Conway would produce wholesale resignations among his officers, of which he had received twenty in the past six days. Lee replied somewhat plaintively that he did not think the Congress would risk such evil consequences, but it did: on December 13 Thomas Conway became Washington's inspector general with the rank of major general.

The storm of indignation that Washington had predicted would erupt at Valley Forge if Conway was promoted was far fiercer in actuality. And when Wilkinson's appointment to brigadier as Gates's secretary was announced, it was so thunderous that Gates's wily aide-de-camp hastily resigned his new rank.

But Wilkinson did not—could not, granted his vaulting ambition—put aside his vision of glory as the deputy of the general who seemed certain to replace Washington. Wilkinson had conceived this perception of power when, at twenty years old, he had come south from Saratoga with Gates's report to Congress on his great victory over Burgoyne. With typical arrogance, Gates had chosen not to make his report to Washington, as was proper, but to go over his head to the kingmakers at York. While there Wilkinson was invited to tea with Mifflin and two congressmen and was startled at the venom with which Washington's "misfortunes" were openly discussed. A few days later he wrote gleefully to Gates of "dissensions, jealousies, calumnies and detractions," all concerning you-know-who. He was careful to add that Gates's insult to Washington had not passed unobserved.

While at York Wilkinson met General Stirling, who was recovering there from a fall from his horse. He dined with Stirling and his aides, and the general's always-excellent wine seems to have loosened his tongue, for he babbled of a certain highly damning sentence that Conway was supposed to have written to Gates. Supposedly a drunkard, Stirling was not so inebriated that he could not remember the sentence, which he loyally reported to Washington.

After York, the odious Wilkinson moved on to Reading, where he heard the same seditious gossip, and thence to Whitemarsh, where the army lay, fancying that he heard it again, when, callow youth that he was, he mistook the customary grumbling of young officers to be disloyalty to their chief—to whom, in fact, they were devoted almost to a man.

In the meantime, Washington sent this note to Conway on November 9: "A letter which I received last night contained the following paragraph: 'In a letter from General Conway to General Gates, he says, "*Heaven has been determined to save your country, or a weak general and bad counsellors would have ruined it.*"'"

There was no immediate reply, but when Conway did come to Valley Forge, Washington made plain his destestation of him, receiving him coldly but correctly, with proper respect for his rank and duties. Thereafter Conway's letters to Washington were characterized by a singular insolence and mendacity, all of which the commander in chief received with contemptuous silence.

But the false step for which Washington had been patiently waiting had been made: Wilkinson's tipsy babbling in York had set the flimsy stage on which the timid Gates would venture on tiptoe, finger to his lips, and thus bring the entire conspiracy crashing down. Conway, to his credit, was a bold conniver, if not an admirable one. His eventual reply to Washington's damning note was an attempt to bluff his way through. Why, my dear general, he protested in his haughty, superior style, there is not a subaltern in Europe who would not fill his letters with complaints about his chief, without exciting the least suspicion. "Must such an odious and tyranical inquisition begin in this country?" Washington gave no answer, for his fish had already been hooked.

Granny Gates had lost his nerve. Where he might have written to Washington suggesting that Washington was certainly much too fair-minded to hold Gates responsible for anything written to him by some malcontent, he wrote instead to both Washington and President Laurens for help in unmasking the wretch who had revealed his correspondence. He also asked Laurens for what amounted to a congressional investigation. With this request, Washington had the opportunity to bring the entire intrigue out into the open, and he seized it.

Washington sent to Congress Conway's letters of complaint on the manner in which he considered himself to be ill received at Valley Forge, together with this comment: "If General Conway means by 'cool reception' that I did not receive him in the language of a warm and cordial friend, I readily confess the charge. I did not, nor shall I ever, till I am capable of the arts of dissimulation." He also expressed surprise that Gates had sent copies of his letters to him to Congress. With beautiful ingenuousness he blandly stated that some high purpose must have been intended, but he now felt compelled to return his answers through the same channel. He had not known that Conway was one of Gates's correspondents until Stirling's letter reached him. He had thought Stirling's information had actually come from Gates as a friendly warning to himself. "But in this, as in other matters of late," he concluded, still starry eyed, "I have found myself mistaken."

Gates had been an excellent stalking horse for Washington's enemies, but in the glare of publicity he wilted. He wrote to Washington that the paragraph quoted was a wicked forgery, and then turned on the faithful Wilkinson with such ferocity that this unhappy young man of high rank lost his temper and challenged Gates to a duel "with pistols tomorrow morning behind the English church." Gates did show up, but with the indulgent smile of a forgiving father. He apologized for his rudeness and said the entire affair was a plot against him masterminded by Alexander Hamilton. So there was no duel, which might have been a pity for posterity—not to know which of these two sly schemers would have been the first to shoot the other in the back.

Conway's response to the glare of publicity was to make a baldfaced denial that he had ever written such words and then, with a perverse touch of the pixie present in most Irishmen, to warn Washington gravely against flatterers and sychophants. But President Laurens, who had seen the letter, told John Fitzgerald, an aide of Washington's, that although it did not actually contain the sentence quoted by Wilkinson, it said ten times more, including the lament: "What a pity there is but one Gates!" Gates's reputation was peeled further when Daniel Morgan and his riflemen arrived at Valley Forge to tell everyone that the true hero of Saratoga was Benedict Arnold. When Morgan was approached by Gates's supporters, he swore angrily that he would serve under no one but Washington, and Conway's attempt to make use of de Kalb's criticism of his chief induced that officer to protest to Laurens: "I look upon him as the sole defender of his country's cause."

With indignation rising against them everywhere, the plotters scattered like cockroaches running from the light. Dr. Rush strove strenuously to have his name removed from authorship of *Thoughts of a Freeman,* Mifflin left York in disgust and Wilkinson resigned as secretary of the Board of War. Both Adamses remained conspicuously silent, although John, who had relieved Silas Deane in Paris, was still, according to Tom Paine, a supporter of Gates. That worthy, along with Conway, made one more insidious attempt to discredit Washington. The Board of War had proposed an "irruption" into Canada led by Lafayette. Unaware of the true nature of the operation, the idea that for the young marquis to liberate the French Canadians from British yoke would surely undermine

Washington abroad, the young general accepted—until he joined Gates in the north and discovered that Conway was to be his second in command, doubtless expecting to be the actual chief. Lafayette insisted on substituting de Kalb, thus ousting Conway, and in regarding himself as answerable only to Washington. But he soon learned that with only twelve hundred men available, the operation was impossible and was only too happy to be recalled to Valley Forge, with de Kalb.

Conway thereupon resorted to offering his resignation, a maneuver that had worked for him once before, but this time it was accepted. Charles Carroll told him bluntly that anyone who did not support Washington should leave the army. Conway did, while Gates remained in nominal command of the Northern Department, his mouth now firmly closed. But Conway could never keep still, badgering Congress again for reinstatement, still criticizing Washington—until an indignant General John Cadwalader challenged him to a duel, "stopping his lying mouth" by sending a bullet through it and into his neck. Thinking that he was dying, Conway wrote to Washington saying that he was sincerely sorry for having written or said anything disparaging about him. But he did recover, returning to the French Army as governor of the French colonies in India, commanding a Royalist army in the south of France in 1783, whence he was driven into exile and died seven years later.

Thus ended the so-called Conway Cabal, a spurious, selfish disaffection that, in the end, only strengthened the authority of the long-suffering George Washington.

★ 52 ★

THE BRITISH LION PURRS

The first fruits of the Franco-American alliance sprouted not in France or America but in Britain, where Lord North made a determined effort to bring the Americans back into the empire. It was now or never, for the earthquake of Saratoga had produced many aftershocks: new lows on the London stock market; a refusal by the German princes to provide more cannon-fodder, having lost so many men in Burgoyne's disastrous campaign; Britain's own manpower reserves at the bottom of the barrel; and North's majority in Parliament diminished. As a condition of his remaining in office, North had received from his friend the king permission to make new offers of conciliation to the Americans.

During the Christmas holidays, rumors of an impending alliance had stimulated North to bring an end to hostilities before the alliance treaty could be signed. Benjamin Franklin in Paris had been approached by his "dear old friend" James Hutton, who had been empowered by North to explore the possibility of peace. Hutton told Franklin that he wished to see him and his countrymen "secure in your liberties" and that "anything short of absolute independency ... could take place." Franklin's reply showed Poor Richard at his best:

"You have lost by this mad war, and the barbarity with which it has been carried on, not only the government and commerce of America, and the public revenues and private wealth arising from that commerce, but what is more, you have lost the esteem, respect, friendship and affection of all that great and growing people, who consider you at present, and whose posterity will consider you, as the worst and wickedest nation upon earth. A peace you may undoubtedly obtain by dropping all your pretensions to govern us; and to your superior skill in huckstering negotiations, you may possibly make such an apparently advantageous bargain as shall be applauded in your Parliament." But, he went on, almost nothing after all this bullying and barbarism would regain the affection of the American people. In recompense the Mother Country in atonement should grant not only independence but cede Canada, Nova Scotia and east and west Florida to America as well!

Such a reply staggered North and had as much to do with his Conciliatory Propositions as did the king's permission to offer them, and thus, on February 17, 1778, they were introduced in a House of Commons consisting of stunned Tories and jubilant Whigs. Three days later, in North's certainty that they would be approved, they were despatched to America.

North began by relinquishing Parliament's right to tax the colonists. He said he had never believed it was practicable to tax them and prided himself that as prime minister he had never proposed such a levy. He even conceded the colonies' right to tax themselves and that any such revenue raised by them should be spent by them on themselves rather than be transferred to the British exchequer. Clearly, he was granting in 1778 everything that, if offered in 1775, would almost certainly have averted the war. North did not speak to the rebellious colonists like the prime ministers of old—a parent chastising an unruly child—but as an equal depending upon the blandishments of sweet reason to bid the prodigal to return to the bosom of the Mother Country.

Yet, he was actually granting nothing, for he did not retract a single jot or tittle of the apparatus of British mercantilism. American manufacturing and commerce would remain under the strict regulation of Britain. Thus the British would resume their lucrative practice of exploiting the rich resources of America while monopolizing the equally profitable policy of supplying her growing millions with manufactured goods. In fine, he was renouncing the unobtainable—colonial tax revenues—in the interests of retaining the true fruits of empire: mercantilist control of the American economy. As he had told the king: "to give up the levying of positive taxes here is to give up in effect nothing as it is practically certain that none will for the future ever be levied by the British Parliament."

This was essentially the position taken by the opposition Whigs during the earlier debates on the American question. But the Whigs, sincere in their concern for the Americans, and not, like North, acting out of the duress of military defeat and an American treaty with detestable France, were not so two-faced. Not even the Adamses, in the years preceding the firing of the shot heard round the world, would have been so fatuous as to have expected the Mother Country, alone among the world's exploitative colonial empires, to have abandoned gratuitously its mercantilist policy.

Yet the Whigs were indeed jubilant to hear themselves vindicated by a Tory prime minister, and it was said that they were overheard to be "publicly congratulating themselves on the excellent acquisition which they had just made in the person of Lord North." But the Whig policies, alas, they well knew, had been adopted after it was too late. As Edmund Burke ruefully observed, "the pride of men will not often suffer reason to have any scope until it can no longer be of service."

Because there had been rumors of an impending Franco-American alliance, many Whigs suspected that North's Conciliatory Propositions were not sincere efforts at peace adapted to the terms they had been supporting for years, but rather an attempt to wreck this alliance. Thus Charles James Fox arose to ask the direct question: was it true that a treaty between France and the colonies had been signed recently? North remained silent in his seat. After Burke arose to remind the prime minister that his proposals were an exact replica of those he had himself made two years earlier, only to hear them condemned and see them rejected by the Tories, North still remained at a loss for words. He came to his feet only after an irate Whig jumped erect to threaten impeachment and shout: "An answer! An answer! An answer!" But North's replies were so halting and evasive that it became evident to all present—Tory as well as Whig—that a treaty had, in fact, been negotiated.

Now North's duplicity and his true intentions became clear: he sought to torpedo the Franco-American alliance by confusing and demoralizing the Americans, by appealing for peace, not to the American leaders, but to those who were neutral or secretly loyal to the Crown or simply weary of the war. With gleeful indignation the Whigs went over to the attack. Isaac Barré denounced the propositions as "a shameful imposture" ... a "scandalous deceit ... a cheat of the most gross kind ... a trick upon the public to divide, distract and sow divisions."

Probably the most shattering denunciation of the prime minister was delivered by Burke, who castigated him as a hawk in dove's plumage and warned him that his proposals had not the slightest chance of being accepted by the Americans. "To leap at once from an obstinacy of five years," he concluded, "to a total concession of everything; to stoop so low without hopes of being forgiven—who can understand such a transformation?"

Even the great William Pitt, Lord Chatham, arose from his deathbed to enter the fray, appearing on crutches in the House of Lords, swathed in flannel, supported by his son-in-law and son, who would soon rival his father as a great British leader. In a breaking voice he expressed his sorrow that America, the jewel of the imperial crown, the colonies that had always been at the center of his policy that had brought France to her knees during the Seven Years' War, had now, as he lay dying, turned for succor from North's misdirected policies to that same hated kingdom. After the reply of the Duke of Richmond, Chatham again attempted to rise in rebuttal, but fainted and was carried from the chamber. Within a month he would be dead, grief stricken in the knowledge that his very triumph over the French had led to the discontent that was now surely about to sever America from the Mother Country.

Just as the Whig opposition had acted with predictable rage and contempt, the Tory majority was stunned and confounded at this absolute reversal of policy. "Astonishment, dejection, and fear overclouded the whole [Tory] assembly." Was the British lion such a tabbycat, they asked, that it must lie down and purr and "crouch to the vipers and rebels in America?" Narrow-minded and implacable enemies of the insolent Yankees though they might be, they were still true Britons, whose "hearts of oak" would not quiver at the prospect of fighting both France *and* America. Some of them began to talk of replacing North with a more acceptable prime minister in the true-blue British mold, but all of them knew—just as did the Whigs—that for all the denunciation and the bluster, even though three-quarters of the House for diametrically opposite reasons opposed the Conciliatory Propositions, most of them would swallow their pride and vote their approval. As the Tories maintained, this alone would demonstrate "the affection of the indulgent, injured mother even to her most degenerate, refractory, guilty children." It was with that noble, self-sacrificing sense of coming to the side of the Americans as a mother to her child, that the Tories sullenly accepted a rare union with the smirking Whigs. The Conciliatory Propositions were accepted, and a Peace Commission, under the Earl of Carlisle, "a young man of pleasure and fashion, fond of dress and gaming," was authorized to negotiate with Congress.

Before the members of the Carlisle Commission boarded ship for America, they were entertained at a farewell by Lord North. To their puzzled disquiet, these gentlemen, all well known to the charming and affable prime minister, were treated with a strange reserve. It was not as though they were total strangers but, rather, an embarrassment to His Lordship, in the way that the jovial boss at the office suddenly finds himself thrown in socially with his employees. They discussed this reserve during their transatlantic crossing, but it was not until they sailed up the Delaware to the heart warming boom of saluting British guns that they came in deep dismay upon the explanation of Lord North's reserve.

Philadelphia was being evacuated!

They had expected to arrive under the protection of a victorious army and to be offering peace from a conquered capital to a chastened country whose armed forces, despite this one brilliant stroke at Saratoga, had been soundly and repeatedly beaten and that, even then, by all accounts of the ordeal at Valley Forge, was dissolving under the duress of misery and privation.

North had deliberately withheld from them the vital detail of his approval of Lord George Germain's order to evacuate Philadelphia. When they sailed up the great wide river in early June 1778, they had beheld with enthusiasm and patriotic pride the great chain of warships anchored at frequent intervals along the watercourse. It was not until they had landed that they realized these warships were not intended to support some new campaign against the rebels but to protect General Howe's supply ships from Yankee raids, which, in spite of the fall of the Delaware forts, had continued unabated throughout the winter and spring. Lord Carlisle lamented: "As long as we had the army to back us, we had hopes of success; but this … will certainly make them reject [our] offers." All the military bustle and movement with bands and bright bayonets and loaded wagons were not in preparation for the final crushing campaign, but in compliance with the orders of the singularly obtuse Germain to leave Philadelphia by sea and proceed to New York. Why, is not clearly known. Because Britain had declared war on France and the Comte d'Estaing had already sailed for America with a fleet that could trap the British Army there? Possibly. But that was a military decision that absolutely negated the diplomatic mission of the Carlisle Commission.

Even worse for the British commission was the news that word of the French alliance had beaten them to America, that Congress had ratified the alliance and that receipt of the Conciliation Bills had enraged the country and set it seething as it had not done since the days of the Stamp and Townshend Acts. Congress, fearing like Washington that the people might be war weary and inclined to accept the proposals, had launched a campaign of denunciation against them, while having copies of them made and widely circulated through the states. The result was an explosion of wrathful indignation, culminating in Providence, Rhode Island, where the bills were burnt beneath the gallows.

The inept North government had simply gotten the carrot and stick of diplomacy and war backwards: it had offered the carrot without the stick to back it up. A frustrated Lord Carlisle was aware of this when he complained of his mission as "the appearance of supplication for mercy from a vanquished and exhausted state," and the perceptive Commissioner George Johnstone vowed, in bitter chagrin, that there was nothing "more contemptible than a retreating army or a supplicating prince." Yet, in their anger and choice of words, it was apparent that no matter how conciliatory North might have been, these commissioners were still coming to the Americans "as a mother to her child." Therefore, there does not seem to be much validity in the claims of some historians that poor timing and slovenly planning had once again unraveled British policy, that if the Conciliatory Proposals had been made two or three months earlier before the French alliance and had been supported by a proper show of force, the Americans might have accepted them. If they had been made in 1775 or 1776, of course, they undoubtedly would have been received with favor—but not in 1778. Henry Laurens spoke for all patriotic Americans when he said: "If all the fine things now offered had been tendered some time ago, admitting their solidity, there can be no doubt that the people of America would joyfully have embraced the proposition, but now what answer can be given but that which was returned by the foolish virgins—'the door is shut!'"

★ 53 ★

THE BRITISH IN PHILADELPHIA/HOWE GOES HOME

In November 1777 a Frenchman in Paris reported to Benjamin Franklin that Howe had captured Philadelphia, to which, with twinkling eyes and an impish smile, Franklin replied: "I beg your pardon, sir, Philadelphia has captured General Howe."

Undoubtedly. Nowhere in the British Empire had any British Army passed a winter as comfortably and pleasurably as Sir William Howe's officers and men had in Philadelphia. And this delightful sojourn, of course, was simply a case of like general, like troops. Add to this the city itself, so pleasantly established with its three-story brick country houses rising among groves and hills, ponds and gardens, and fronting on paved streets, well-lighted at night, over which rumbled smart coaches whose panels were decorated with heraldic devices. Philadelphia became an unrivaled sanctuary for campaign-weary soldiers seeking what today is called "rest and rehabilitation": that is to say, an unbridled and unrestricted round of gaiety and license.

The doors of all the best Tory homes were opened wide for British officers. Inside elegant and opulent drawing rooms, Quaker ladies tried desperately to keep everyone entertained without benefit of dancing, drink and cards. Some succeeded, but most found that conversation was not enough. Skating on the Delaware or merry sleighing parties were sometimes acceptable substitutes, but, for the most part, the occupying soldiery found these recreations tame in comparison to the gaming tables, the taverns, the dance halls—and even the theatricals organized by Captains John André and Oliver Delancy, as well as the dashing twenty-three-year-old brigade major, Banastre Tarleton—he of the long green plume.

Although the British officers were invariably courteous and circumspect in their relations with the townspeople, the free-swingers among them preferred club dinners at the Indian Queen or even wilder supper parties at the Bunch of Grapes, topped off by a boisterous night of singing and perhaps female entertainment at the Cockpit. There was, of course, a faro bank run by a foreign officer, a favorite stop of General Howe and a disastrous one for young officers, who were so badly "plucked" that they had to sell their commissions and sail home penniless. Mistresses were kept openly, even in billets rented in the homes of decent people. Handsome black bondswomen were also available, escaping slavery by answering the unblushing advertisements for young women "who can occasionally put her hand to anything." One Major Williams kept a beautiful English girl, whom he paraded in front of his artillery regiment in an open carriage with fine English horses and an English coachman and footman. She looked lovely wearing the regimental colors with matching plumes.

With their officers blithely jumping on the Ten Commandments, the men could not be expected to be "regulation." Except for occasional forages in force and the inevitable burden of guard duty, there was little to occupy them, so that they became slovenly and insolent, turning to their own forms of amusement, which included looting and chopping down fences, fruit trees and even vacant houses to keep their barracks warm and their kitchen fires burning. But the British Tommy was no match for the Hessian Hans in the ungentle art of plunder. Under the jolly and crude General von Knyphausen, who used his thumb to butter his bread and who cared as little for off-duty carousing or looting as he did for table manners, the German troops did as they pleased. They robbed Tory and Patriot alike, and what they could not carry off they destroyed, usually by burning. Stabling their horses in fine homes with gross Teutonic indifference to beauty or elegance, they disposed of their mounts' manure by shoving it through holes they cut in the floor to lie festering in the basement. Sanitation, where it existed, was basic—and by the time the thawing breezes of spring arrived, the city stank like a livery stable. Libraries were also plundered, by both Briton and German, while even the customarily correct Captain André did not scruple to leave Philadelphia with many of Benjamin Franklin's finest books in his luggage.

Only Sir William Howe, so indolent and so fond of pleasure himself, could have indulged such indiscipline. Indeed, he set the style for it.

A regular at the faro table, he was soon joined by the lovable Mrs. Loring, of those carefree Boston and New York days, accompanied, of course, by her husband. For his complaisance in this mênage à trôis, Mr. Loring was rewarded with the post of commissioner of prisons at a handsome salary of thirty thousand dollars a year. Betsy meanwhile captivated the younger officers, and it was an unwise hostess who sought to lure Sir William to her drawing room without also inviting Mrs. Loring. The poet Francis Hopkinson, who had so deliciously lampooned John Burgoyne, had a try at Howe after a rebel attempt to blow up British warships with floating kegs of powder:

Sir William he, snug as a flea,
Lay all the time a'snoring,
Nor dreamed of harm as he lay warm
In bed with Mrs. Loring.

Despairing Loyalists, indignant at their humiliation by the Hessians, were furious to see their city turned into a military fortress. The State House yard became an artillery park filled with cannon, limbers, caissons and wagons, while the gunners, together with the Highlanders, were quartered close by. The government was completely military. Even Joseph Galloway, loyal to the despairing end while his fortune of seventy thousand pounds was gradually whittled away, received only a minor post under the authority of the provost marshal. Under "Sir Billy" there was so much corruption—clipping, cutting and graft—that it was widely believed that Howe was in secret partnership with an unscrupulous merchant named Coffin, who always seemed to be abundantly stocked in whatever was in short supply. Upon Howe's return to London, Horace Walpole wrote that he was "richer in money than in laurels."

Under Howe the hospitals were pesthouses and the prisons floating hells on water and graveyards on land. The abominable Provost Marshal Cunningham treated prisoners of war with a cruel indifference that would have shamed an Iroquois. Washington's appeals and threats were steadily rejected by Howe, who ignored the facts and insisted that the Americans were receiving proper care. In truth, the American prisoners were crowded by the hundreds into poorly ventilated rooms and while they slept, their guards picked their pockets. Needless to say, there was a steady procession of coffins to the potter's field that is now Washington Square.

Howe's lethargy was the despair of the Tories of Pennsylvania and New Jersey. His failure to appreciate what their loyalty to the Crown was costing them infuriated them, and their offers to raise military units of their own fell on the unhearing ears of a disdainful British professional. Most disturbing of all was Howe's indifference to their entreaties to drive Washington across the Susquehanna, so that an unknown versifier wrote:

Awake, arise Sir Billy,
There's forage on the plain.
Ah, leave your little filly,
And open the campaign.

But there would be no more campaigns for Sir William Howe. He had written repeatedly to Germain asking to be relieved from "this painful service." In April he was notified that his wish had been granted and was told to turn his command over to Sir Henry Clinton. Before he sailed home in May, his officers bade him farewell in an astonishingly lavish and, in many ways, ludicrous gala called the *Mischianza.*

Mischianza is the Italian word for medley, and an extravagant mixture it was, indeed. Its only redeeming feature was that it was paid for by wealthy field officers, rather than through the customary "borrowing" of Crown funds. It consisted of a tournament of knights for the favor of their ladies fair and a grand ball. Its theme was a kind of roccoco medievalism with Turkish accents, or at least what its authors believed to be thus, and took place in Mrs. Thomas Wharton's fine mansion fronting the river.

Captain John Montresor's unit of engineers constructed the lists and barriers, as well as two pavilions for the British and American Queens of Beauty at either end of the beautiful four-acre lawn. Each of these pavilions was attended by six damsels of honor in Turkish costumes. Twelve champions were to joust for the favor of these beauties. They were divided into Knights of the Blended Rose, wearing crimson-and-white silk and riding gray horses, and Knights of the Burning Mountain, in orange and black mounted on black steeds.

Captain André designed the ladies' dresses: incredibly extravagant costumes with soaring headdresses sparkling with pearls and jewels, polonaises—a sort of three-quarter drapery over a short skirt—of white silk with spangled pink sashes and spangled shoes, stockings and sashes for the Blended Rose and for the Burning Mountain, similar outfits except that their polonaises and sashes were black.

At four o'clock in the afternoon of May 18, under the protection of British warships on the Delaware River, the queens and their knights and all the notables, headed by Sir William Howe, the guest of honor, boarded decorated barges serenaded by military music and were rowed from Knight's Wharf to the landing place at Old Fort. From there they proceeded along an avenue one hundred yards long, lined with soldiers in gay regimentals and underneath two triumphal arches, also designed by the indefatigble André, each of which bore a figure of Fame star spangled like the beauty queens and blowing from her trumpet the motto in French: "*Thy laurels are immortal.*" A herald then presented a laurel wreath to Howe and declaimed verses of praise—again by André—that, though perfect in rhyme and scan, were without pith or point.

Next there ensued the clash of arms as the knights started sham jousting with lances, swords and pistols. Subalterns in herald's tabards proclaimed the victors, and the queens blushingly bestowed their favors. At this point the audience—variously thrilled or bored according to their mentality—was denied the pleasure of seeing Miss Peggy Shippen, the seventeen-year-old daughter of wealthy Judge Edward Shippen, and said to be one of the most beautiful girls in America. But the straitlaced Judge Shippen would not have his daughter parading in Turkish bloomers, and so, brokenhearted, she stayed home.

Next the assembly re-formed and proceeded to the mansion, where dancing began in the ballroom at six o'clock. André and his associate Oliver Delancy had made this splendid room gorgeous by painting garlands of roses against a blue-and-gold background. Nearly one hundred mirrors were fastened to the walls to reflect the brilliance of the scene, and as night fell servants in livery lighted a thousand glittering candles to magnify it. At ten there were magnificent fireworks above the lawn, and two hours later supper was served: a repast of four hundred covers and twelve hundred dishes, borne by twenty-four black slaves with silver bracelets around their muscular arms and silver collars around their necks—an unintended allusion to their chains noticed by no one—and toasts were proclaimed by the heralds to everyone of consequence, beginning with their majesties the king and queen. Finally, dancing was resumed until four o'clock in the morning.

Not everyone was enchanted or enthralled by the *Mischianza*, especially not the veteran officers, who were mortified by such an expensive and foolish extravaganza blossoming among suffering, privation and death. When a small boy asked a grizzled artillerist what was the difference between the two orders of knights, he replied gruffly: "Why, child, the Knights of the Burning Mountain are Tom Fools and the Knights of the Blended Rose are damned fools. I know of no other difference between 'em." And then, in an aside to his peers: "What will Washington think of all this?"

The answer came the following night, when Lafayette sallied forth from Valley Forge with a formation of Continentals to take up a position at Barren Hill midway between Philadelphia and camp. Sir William, eager to catch "the boy," issued his last order, sending Clinton himself out to capture him. What a trophy the boy would make to take home: a French marquis, the first captive of consequence in this old war that was now a new one between France and Britain. But Lafayette, maneuvering with the precision conferred upon the Americans by Steuben, got clean away.

A few days later, on May 25, 1778—three years to the day since his arrival in Boston aboard *Cerberus*—Sir William sailed for home.

To the end of his long life, Sir William Howe maintained, in the face of bitter criticism, that the failure to crush the rebellion during those frustrating three years was not his fault. But he was never able to demonstrate why it wasn't. A Parliamentary investigation, which left him a bitter and aggrieved man, was inconclusive, as was his reply to Joseph Galloway's relentless accusation that by his indolence he had lost the war. Howe also could not escape the direct charges in the following indictment of him, found in the paper of Sir Henry Clinton and believed by most historians to have been written by Clinton himself:

> Had Sir William fortified the hills around Boston he could not have been disgracefully driven from it; had he pursued his victory at Long Island he had ended the rebellion; had he landed above the lines at New York not a man could have escaped him; had he co-operated with the Northern Army [Burgoyne] he had saved it, or had he gone to Philadelphia by land he had ruined Mr. Washington and his forces; but, as he did none of these things, had he gone to the Devil before he was sent to America, it had been the saving of infamy to himself and indelible dishonor to his country.

Some critics then and now seem to believe that Sir William was a poor tactician, but he was not. Except for Germantown, in the six major battles in which he defeated Washington he was always able to turn the American's flank and get into his rear: the orthodox tactic for a skilled and veteran professional up against an amateur. But his movements after these victories were always slow and ponderous, even timorous, and showed no inclination to take advantage of a vulnerable foe. At the conclusion of each of these six engagements, he had his enemy staggered, but he never once moved in for the kill. Is it possible that he had no killer instinct? War is not like boxing, in which, failing a knockout the opponents are awarded points by judges and the match is won by a "decision." There are no judges or decisions in war, and thus "Mr." Washington always got away, after which, like the proverbial phoenix arising from his ashes, he appeared once more with a new army. Washington's army *was* the American Revolution: its surrender or decisive defeat never to appear again meant the end of the Rebellion. But Sir William Howe was unable to achieve this. Again why? There is a temptation to compare him to the Union General George McClellan, who by his own timidity and lack of the killer instinct may be said to have prolonged the American Civil War by at least two years; but prior to the Rebellion there is no hint of the timorous in William Howe.

Charles Lee was not exactly fair in depicting Howe as a lethargic libertine. Easygoing Howe certainly was, but not to the detriment of his duties, and if he is to be judged as a prisoner of his lusts, than so, too, must almost every Britisher of consequence in that abandoned age. But Lee was right in suggesting that here was an excellent subordinate being overwhelmed by the duties of commander in chief: In the modern phrase Howe had reached his "level of incompetence." One of Howe's officers, Allen Maclean, also attested to this failing:

> It would not be unjust to say that General Howe is a very honest man, and I believe a very disinterested one. Brave he certainly is and would make a very good executive officer under another's command, but he is by no means equal to commander-in-chief.

There is, of course, another explanation of Sir William's failure, a highly popular one put about at the time by embittered Tories, such as Joseph Galloway: that his failures to exploit a victory were all the result of his preference for ending the Rebellion by conciliation, rather than by force. Galloway said that because of Howe's fondness for the Americans, he "succeeded as far as he chose." But this charge is as false as it is fatuous. It is not begging the question to suggest that no professional soldier eager for glory and promotion—and in Howe's case the dazzling prospect of a peerage should he succeed—would so risk his career just because he had once been fond of the enemy. Howe himself insisted that he never permitted the hope of conciliation to control his conduct, and he must be believed. His failure to deliver the crusher sprang not from his character, but from his military training and the military doctrine of the day. During the inquiry of 1779, he explained it himself, though in a convoluted sentence:

> As my opinion has always been, that the defeat of the rebel regular army is the surest road to peace, I invariably pursued the most profitable means of forcing its commander to action under circumstances the least hazardous to the royal army; for even a victory attended by a heavy loss of men on our part, would have given as fatal check to the progress of the war, and might have proved irreparable.

This was a surprising contradiction of his repeated assertions that he always considered the Continental Army his true objective and constantly sought to bring it to decisive battle. Here he maintains that rather than risk Pyrrhic victories, he preferred to occupy territory and cow the Patriot population while encouraging the Tories. In November 1776, he wrote that such operations "would strike such terror through the country that little resistance would be made to the progress of His Majesty's arms." Indeed, his strategic campaign for 1777 called for the deployment of almost forty thousand men—including Burgoyne's eight thousand—not only in the Northern states but in the South as well. It was only abandoned after he was denied such large reinforcements. Even so, such a strategy would explain his incredible indifference to a defeated Washington slinking away to some not very remote lair, there to recruit, rearm, re-form—and take the field again. Washington's army simply didn't enter into his calculations. As Professor Maldwyn A. Jones stated in his study of Howe's American campaigns, Washington's army "was simply to be prevented from interfering with the triumphant march of the British."

Given the military doctrine of the day—the "rosewater war," aghast at risking the king's expensive soldiers—Jones's statement does seem to explain Howe's behavior. Occupying territory or taking enemy capitals captive, these were the true objectives, to be obtained—not by bloody pitched battles—but by maneuver.

Such was the mode of the limited wars of Europe in the eighteenth century, a school of warfare absolutely disqualifying its students from conducting the savage forest warfare of this first ideological war. Sir William Howe, then, could no more conform to this new method of warfare than his contemporary Mozart could have composed heavy metal music. Although Howe is certainly to be faulted for being a fine subordinate officer who was beyond his depth, it is not fair to blame him for the loss of the Revolutionary War because he did not possess the insights of a military genius.

The sad truth is that there was no better commander available, and that includes Sir Henry Clinton. No Marlborough, who had come and gone; no Wellington, who was yet to appear; and of these two great British captains, it is useless to speculate how either would have fared against Washington, fighting his kind of war on his own grounds with themselves at the end of a supply line three thousand miles long. In America the man and the hour had met; in Britain there was no man, and the hour was already past.

★ 54 ★

THE BATTLE OF MONMOUTH COURTHOUSE

There had been little, if any, rejoicing in the British Army at Philadelphia when Sir Henry Clinton succeeded Howe in the chief command. Although Sir William had failed to crush the Rebellion, he was still popular with the younger officers and especially the men, who were conscious of his bravery and his concern for their welfare. But Clinton, the cold, colorless careerist, could never have been popular in such a way. Thus it was remembered more against him that he had failed at Charleston than that he had succeeded at Forts Clinton and Montgomery and, with any help from Howe, might have saved Burgoyne.

In truth Sir Henry Clinton did not inspire loyalty. Judge Thomas Jones, the Tory chronicler, spoke of him as "haughty, morose, churlish, stupid and scarcely ever to be spoken with." William Franklin carried the uncomplimentary caricature further: "The commander in chief is gallant to a proverb, and possesses great military knowledge in the field, but he is weak, irresolute, unsteady, vain, incapable of forming any plan himself, and too weak, or rather too proud and conceited to follow that of another." Short and stout, with a full round face, large nose and tight and disdainful little mouth, he quarreled with his senior officers while keeping subordinates at a distance and sought solace in the bottle and the arms of easy women.

After Howe's departure, Clinton had to face two difficult problems: what to do with the three thousand Philadelphia Tories who would become destitute refugees once he had evacuated the city and whether to obey Germain's orders to proceed to New York by sea. On the first count, he knew that he certainly could not take all the Loyalists aboard the transports, and because he was not a very sympathetic man he was inclined to regard them as a nusiance, now that their comfortable homes and great estates were no longer of any use. He also seems to have considered advising them to make their peace with the rebels, now that Washington had proposed to Congress an amnesty through which they could swear allegiance to the new nation. Such was Clinton's lack of understanding that he could not comprehend the Loyalists' fierce rejection of such a course. They well knew that an official pardon would be but a fragile shield against the hatred of their neighbors. At the utmost, they would be tolerated, and if the war ended in a Patriot victory, they would be scorned as supporters of a traitorous cause.

But Clinton's solution of this first problem of the Tories was made for him by his response to the second: whether to proceed to New York by land or by sea. The water route would expose Britain's only army in America not only to storms or calms, but also to the Comte d'Estaing's fleet, which was approaching America with twelve ships of the line, a squadron of frigates and four thousand infantry. A storm could scatter Clinton's ships so that Admiral Lord Howe could not possibly defend them all; a calm could so delay them that Washington might be free to attack New York. In the end Clinton decided to move his army by land across New Jersey by way of New Brunswick, while the ships carried his great guns and the Tories with their possessions.

Thus for the third time in nineteen months the sidewalks of Philadelphia were heaped high with the property of refugees: furniture, china and silver, clothing, paintings, even the equippage of the carriage houses, all to be transported to the waterfront or sold at auction. Every available wheeled vehicle was pressed into the service of this traffic of sorrow moving woefully to and from the wharves and warehouses. Although these unfortunate people, whose costly loyalty to the Crown never was fully appreciated, had been granted ample space for their goods and chattels, they were still confined to quarters below decks, and as the loaded transports dropped one by one down the river, there to anchor and await completion of the loading operation, they suffered from the mosquitoes and heat of a typical American tidewater summer. Once the evacuation fleet was in movement, Clinton's march by land began.

With the thoroughness and organizational skill that were Sir Henry's chief abilities, he had prepared carefully for the departure. Redoubts were built at Cooper's Creek, on the New Jersey side of the Delaware, to hold a beachhead to protect the troops arriving on that bank. From five to six hundred sailors spent a week ferrying the army's five thousand horses and their wagons across the river, followed by the siege guns left in their fortifications until the night before the evacuation. Two nights earlier the shipyards were set afire, consuming nearby houses as well.

Each soldier carried four days' cooked rations in his pack, while the wagons were loaded with twenty days of supplies. Although the distance to New York was only about ninety miles, it was over difficult terrain—what is called "cross-hatched" with highly defensible rivers and hills—occupied by what was now an almost totally hostile population. Progress as slow and careful as five miles a day could well consume all their supplies. There would also almost certainly be the danger of Washington hovering on Clinton's flanks, looking for that moment of unrivaled military opportunity: a fatal gap or confusion in the line of an army on the march.

Washington's army now numbered about 11,800 men, including the sick, wounded and otherwise disabled. His estimate of Clinton's strength at about ten thousand was much too low. Clinton's forces were close to twice that number, although the disaffection of deserters at the departure of Howe had seriously depleted his ranks. Two battalions of Germans from Anspach were considered so unreliable that they were put aboard the transports, and many of the Hessian and British soldiers who had married local girls—especially the Germans, with their fondness for Pennsylvania Dutch belles—had "gone over the hill." When the army marched to the embarkation point on the morning of June 18, 1778, Clinton commanded about fifteen thousand men.

This amphibious withdrawal—another highly dangerous military movement—was handled skillfully by Admiral Howe's fleet. A year before at Head of Elk, Admiral Howe had efficiently and with high hopes landed his brother's army; now, with the same skill but with some regret, he was withdrawing it from abandoned Philadelphia. By ten o'clock the last redcoat had reached the New Jersey shore, not too long before Light-Horse Harry Lee and his cavalry galloped down to the landing on the Pennsylvania side. That night Colonel Daniel Morgan rode through the Quaker City proclaiming a curfew: all persons found abroad after midnight would be arrested. Next day, Benedict Arnold, still on crutches and unable to ride, entered the city in a coach to take command as military governor. On June 20 George Washington set his army in motion for the New Jersey hills, convinced now that New York, rather than the South, was Clinton's objective. As he left Valley Forge, surrounded by a guard of fifty troopers with drawn sabers, his head was still visible above theirs.

★ ★ ★

Washington had good reason to hold his head high. He rode at the head of a transformed army. In pride and discipline—the twin forces that forge true soldiers out of civilians—his troops had been molded anew in the cold crucible of Valley Forge. Even their dress was more soldierly, their filthy rags left lying in the dismal cabins of that dreadful winter. Although some units of the Continental Army could afford to dress themselves in the regulation buff and blue, most of Washington's men wore what he called "rifle dress": a hunting shirt with ruffles at the neck, shoulders, elbows and wrists; long breeches and leggings, warmer and more durable than stockings; a round dark hat turned up in three places and decorated with a cockade or sprig of green; a black stock; hair in a cue; and a white belt over the left shoulder to hold cartridges. In this dress they did not rival the military splendor of European soldiers, but what they wore was neat, comfortable and far more suitable to forest warfare. The Continentals, as well as a few militia formations, also marched with brisk precision, although even Steuben's magic could not straighten the slouching stride of the farmer or frontiersman. Yet, by mid-May training had produced such effective results that there was no drill on Friday afternoons, the men taking to the river or the brook instead. The camp no longer stank, for a new encampment of tents had been erected a mile in front of the old bivouac, which reeked of buried carcasses and accumulated filth.

Washington also was pleased with the army's reorganization, with the strength of an infantry battalion fixed at 477, artillery battalions at 336 and cavalry regiments at 342, with an engineer company of 60. Cavalry had been much improved, and for the first time Washington could rely upon his mounted troops for reliable intelligence, while General Knox had made good the artillery's losses in guns and men. Moreover, the dispute between Washington and Congress over the retirement pay for officers and men once the war was over had reached an amiable compromise: half-pay was to be granted all officers for seven years—although generals would receive no more than colonels—and each soldier would be given a bonus of eighty dollars.

If George Washington had been a boastful man, as he was not, he would have been entitled to plume himself on having entered winter camp under general opprobrium for having failed to attack and recapture Philadelphia and beneath the growing shadow of the Conway Cabal, and was now leaving it after clearing New Jersey of the enemy without a battle, thwarting his Conway traducers, while not only keeping his army together but reinvigorating it, so that by its remaining merely a force-in-being so close to Philadelphia, it had compelled the enemy to evacuate the city without firing a shot.

No wonder he could afford to be magnanimous when Congress, in a move plainly intended to humiliate him, ordered Thomas Mifflin and Horatio Gates back to his command. Loyal Continental officers who had remained at their posts, suffering financial as well as physical privation, were furious at this insult, but Washington said nothing publicly, writing dryly in a letter that he knew would be quoted: "[Mifflin's] stepping in and out, as the sun happens to beam forth or become obscure, is not *quite* the thing, not *quite* just, with respect to those officers who take the bitter with the sweet." So he ignored Mifflin, and because he admired Gates's administrative ability, sent him off to take command at Peekskill. Why not, since Congress had ordered both generals to resign from the Board of War, now sinking back into desuetude, and placed both under his direct command? Why not also, when the unspeakable Charles Lee was exchanged for Major General Richard Prescott, greet him also with a smiling face?

Major General Charles Lee had spent fifteen months as a British captive because no British officer of equal rank had been taken prisoner until July of 1777, when Major William Barton of Rhode Island led a daring raid in which Prescott was captured. In the spring of 1778 Lee was exchanged—unchanged. He was still, as Mrs. Mercy Warren wrote about him early in the war, "without religion or country, principle or attachment; gold was his deity and liberty the idol of his fancy; he hoarded the former without taste for its enjoyment, and worshiped the latter as the patroness of licentiousness rather than the protectress of virtue." He was still, worst of all, convinced that he should be the American commander in chief and still sneering at Washington as "not fit to command a sergeant's guard."

Nevertheless, Washington welcomed him to Valley Forge "as if he had been his brother," according to Elias Boudinot, the Commissioner of Prisoner Exchange, riding out four miles from camp to greet him and leading him back to a reception of general officers over a route lined with cheering soldiers. That night there was an elegant dinner with music in Lee's honor, and Washington assigned to him a cozy room "back of Mrs. Washington's sitting room, and all his baggage was stored in it." In the morning, while Washington patiently waited to breakfast with him, Lee did not appear until very late, looking, in Boudinot's words, "as dirty as if he had been in the street all night." Boudinot also learned that "he had brought a miserable dirty hussy with him from Philadelphia (a British sergeant's wife) and had actually taken her into his room by a back door and she had slept with him that night."

Still, Washington treated Lee with incredible deference, even though he was aware of Lee's contemptuous criticism of him. He saw to it that Lee was reunited with Mr. Spada and his pack of poodles, which he had been careful to protect against the hunger of a starving army, and studiously ignored Lee's belittling of the marvelous improvement in the Continental Army (he now, like many New England Congressmen, argued that militia were superior to regulars) or the miracle of the French alliance. Lee had also gone straight to York, after a brief stop at Valley Forge, to resume his intrigue for the chief command, and was effusively welcomed by a Congress that was still infatuated by foreign officers. Such tolerance seems to suggest that Washington, like Congress, was still overawed by this ugly, rude, selfish, cantankerous and artful officer. Or is it possible that the American chief, having seen how a patient waiting game disposed of Gates, Mifflin and others, was now convinced that plotters such as Lee were best given all the rope they needed to hang themselves. Washington survived character assassination only too well for posterity to persist in that mistaken belief of George the Good, too trusting and naive to use his authority to quell a challenge.

Perhaps, if Washington had known of Lee's treason in captivity, he might have given him a different reception. Lee's capture had chastened his Patriotic ardor, and he had quickly discovered that he was now a devoted advocate of peace. He went so far as to propose to his friend Sir William Howe a plan for a quick victory over the Americans and had written to the Carlisle Commissioners: "It appears to me that by continuance of the war, America has no chance of obtaining its ends." His plan to crush his former comrades was based on a belief that if Maryland were conquered, "the people of Virginia are prevented or intimidated from marching aid to the Pennsylvania army [and] the whole machine is divided." Howe, disposed as always to reject suggestions, did not adopt this one—although it might have influenced his decision to move on Philadelphia via the Chesapeake. Some historians offer this change of plan as evidence that Lee was an outright traitor, but it really is more suggestive of his insufferable paranoid behavior. He had no sooner arrived in York than he proceeded to scold Congress for promoting other generals over him while he was in captivity, after which he wrote an arrogant letter to Washington suggesting that since Americans could never hope to beat British regulars in battle, he should construct a huge redoubt in Pittsburgh as a sanctuary for the American treasury and all the old men, women and children in the country! Next, Congress should be sent for safety down the Mississippi into Spanish territory! Finally, Washington should move south, for that was where Clinton was bound.

Is it possible to construe these insane proposals, as a few historians have done, as attempts to demoralize the Patriots and to send Washington blundering into a trap or to draw him away from Clinton's true objective of New York? Actually, it seems more reasonable to see in them the vapors of a disturbed mind that is convinced that the cause is lost and offering itself as the agent of reconciliation. Whatever the cause of Charles Lee's erratic behavior, his return to the Continental Army—though without any ulterior motive on the part of the British—may be compared to the decision of the German General Staff in World War I to grant V. I. Lenin safe passage to his homeland and there to commence the revolution that would draw Russia out of the war. Such was the "reinforcement" that George Washington received in that hopeful, aspiring spring of 1778.

While Washington prepared to cross the Delaware to follow Clinton, he sent Maxwell's brigade of militia to strike the enemy's advance guard. Among Maxwell's troops was Joseph Martin, who has left a vivid description of how thoroughly the British and Hessians could devastate the countryside through which they marched, as well as explain Benjamin Franklin's furious denunciation of a British policy of atrocity and why New Jersey's numerous Tories could turn so solidly Patriot: "We had ample opportunity to see the devastation they made in their rout; cattle killed and lying about the fields and pastures, some just in the position they were in when shot down, others with a small spot of skin taken off their hind quarters and a mess of steak taken out; household furniture hacked and broken to pieces; wells filled up and mechanics' and farmers' tools destroyed. It was in the height of the season of the cherries; the innocent industrious [British] creatures could not climb the trees for the fruit, but universally cut them down."

Maxwell's brigade collided with the British at Haddonfield, but Clinton used his light infantry to drive them back to Mount Holly. Here while the brigade re-formed, some of the hungry rebels went foraging, among them Martin, who had not eaten for almost two days. Finding a half-empty barrel of salt—"as valuable as gold"—he filled his pockets with the precious white substance and went searching for something to sprinkle it on. He found it in a farmyard filled with geese, ducks and turkeys. To lure his prey, he gathered corn that was scattered about the yard and drew the clucking, hissing, gobbling fowl within reach. Seizing one, he wrung its neck, plucked it and washed it in a stream and "stalked into the first house that fell in my way, invited myself into the kitchen, took down the gridiron and put my food to cooking upon the coals. The women of the house were all the time going and coming to and from the room. They looked at me but said nothing. 'They asked me no questions and I told them no lies.' When my game was sufficiently broiled I took it by the hind leg and made my exit from the house. … When I got into the street I devoured it after a *very* short grace." Thus refreshed, he rejoined his company as Maxwell resumed his harassment of Clinton's flanks.

Washington, meanwhile, had marched his main body north to cross the Delaware, about forty miles above Philadelphia. He moved warily, fearing that Clinton was deliberately trying to draw him into full-scale battle. By June 24 the Continental Army was near Hopewell, ten miles east of the Delaware and six miles northwest of Princeton. Unlike their enemy, European troops unaccustomed to such enervating heat, the Americans had made good time, even though they were delayed by thunderstorms that had spared the British. Nathanael Greene had chosen the line of march and resting places with skill. The rebels had marched forty-seven miles since they left Valley Forge, while the British had covered only thirty. Nevertheless, Clinton still possessed the advantage in distance. New Brunswick was fifty-eight miles from Philadelphia and sixty-six miles from Valley Forge. By the night of the twenty-fourth, Clinton was at Crosswicks, about eighteen miles south of Washington. It was clear that by two or three days of rapid marching, Washington could throw his army across Clinton's path and compel him to fight. It was a precious opportunity, and that night Washington called a council of war.

Since Lee's capture, the American chief had deferred less and less to the advice of his generals, rather asking them to discuss what he planned to do and then making the decision himself. But this time, he allowed the council to be dominated by Lee, once again a baleful influence. Although Lafayette, Greene and Wayne had argued for immediate attack, Lee opposed it with a startling vehemence. Resuming his inveterate praise of the British Army, he forgot how he had predicted that Philadelphia would never be abandoned, and how he had insisted, once Clinton crossed the Delaware, that this maneuver was a faint intended to draw the Patriots into New Jersey, so that the enemy could about face and sail downcast to Maryland. Now that the French alliance was a reality, he argued, what was the use of seeking useless victories? Finally, to challenge British regulars was to awaken the sleeping lion. With these excuses—for there was no cogency in anything he said—he gave the majority of the generals present the opportunity to take refuge in their natural timidity, for as Napoleon Bonaparte would say out of long and bitter experience: "Councils of war never fight." They voted against attacking, and Washington inexplicably assented—much to the consternation of his bravest and ablest leaders.

This decision, Alexander Hamilton wrote mockingly, was worthy of "the Most Honorable Society of Midwives," while Nathanael Greene retired to his tent to allow his anger to cool before putting his objections in writing. His telling sentence, "The people expect something from us, and our strength demands it," as well as the sight of his eager, earnest face, changed Washington's mind, and he gave orders for the attack. Planning to ask Lafayette to lead it, he realized that Lee was senior to the French marquis, so he offered the command to Lee, making it plain that he preferred Lafayette. Lee demurred, deferring to Lafayette. But then he decided to accept, finally stepping aside again because "he was well pleased to be freed from all responsibility for a plan he was sure would fail." So Lafayette prepared to take command of a force of about 2,500 men that had already begun a cautious pursuit of Clinton.

When Washington received word that the enemy was making for Monmouth Courthouse (present-day Freehold), he correctly divined that Clinton's objective was Sandy Hook, from where Admiral Howe's fleet would ferry the British to New York City. So he sent Wayne with another thousand men to join the advance force. Lafayette went along with Wayne as the overall commander. Next day—June 25—Lafayette, now leading about four thousand men, pushed on to Cranford, while Washington, with the main body, marched to Kingston. On the twenty-sixth Lafayette, in a series of encouraging messages, indicated to Washington that the entire Continental Army was now in an enviable position to strike Clinton's left flank. At this point, Lee, hearing that his youthful rival was poised for the knockout blow, wrote Lafayette a shameless letter of entreaty begging him to relinquish command to him, declaring: "It is my fortune and my honor that I place in your hands. You are too generous to cause the loss of either." Lafayette was indeed "too generous," for he replied that if Washington wished to send General Lee with a few thousand more soldiers, he would be happy to serve under him. Lee immediately took the letter to Washington to demand, as senior to Lafayette, his right to command the entire detachment. Washington, once again inexplicably, consented—and Lee with two brigades joined Lafayette the next day at Englishtown to take command of a force now numbering about five thousand men—a little less than half the Continental Army.

Here was George Washington's first mistake: he had placed command of a major operation, perhaps even a decisive one, in the hands of a general who had argued passionately against it and had repeatedly declared in public that it would fail. Worse, he compounded this error by sending Lafayette a vaguely worded letter stating that he had obtained from Lee a promise that upon receiving the command "he will request you to prosecute any plan you may have already concerted for the purpose of attacking or otherwise annoying the enemy." Washington later declared that this was his only possible way of reconciling the vacillating Lee's determination to secure the command with Lafayette's obvious ardor for an immediate and bold attack. But why any attempt to reconcile opposites, which, by definition, is simple sentimentalism? After all, *he* was the chief, not Lee or Lafayette, with the right to ignore seniority, even if it meant relieving Lee. Or he could have solved the dilemma by taking charge of Lafayette's force himself and assigning the main body to Lee. His only objective was success in battle, and he could not—should not—allow sentimentalism or the fear of dissension or the mysterious deferral to this erratic or disturbed, if not actually demented, glory seeker to interfere with that trust. Wasn't the memory of Lee's contemptible dismissal of the miracle of Valley Forge—wrought in despair while he wined and dined with the enemy at Philadelphia—or of his council-of-war performance, which bordered on the treasonable, recent enough for Washington to have serious reservations about Lee's trustworthiness? Did he really expect, by this ambiguous note to the Frenchman, that Lafayette would gladly direct Lee's army or Lee permit him to do so? Here, in truth, was George Washington at his worst: normally a strong man, there seemed to be in him a hidden doubt of his own competence, which appeared only in the presence of an arrogant British professional. But the decision had been made, and it was perhaps fortunate for Washington that he was not present in Lee's camp that night when General Scott came to inquire of his plans. "He said that he had none," Scott wrote.

To understand the confused and confusing Battle of Monmouth Courthouse a clear comprehension of the terrain is necessary. The road from Englishtown passed first through Freehold Meeting House and thence in a southeasterly direction to Monmouth, ending at a right angle against the road running northeast to Sandy Hook, the route of the British retreat. Three ravines were the other main features. The first of these, the West Ravine, was a morass through which ran a branch of Wenrock Brook. It was crossed by a bridge about two and a half miles west of Monmouth on the road to Freehold. A mile southeast of it, or down the road, was the Middle Ravine, another morass through which ran the main stream of Wenrock Brook. A causeway crossed it. The third morass, or East Ravine, was parallel to the road from Monmouth to Sandy Hook.

June 27 was a day of rest for Sir Henry Clinton's exhausted British and Hessian soldiers who were encamped at Monmouth Courthouse. For nine mornings in succession they had been under arms and marching by three o'clock in the morning. For the first few hours the cool dark was a blessing and the hundred pounds or more of equipment that each soldier bore were not yet a curse. But then the early summer sun rose, and by nine o'clock they found themselves struggling through an alternating scourge of heat and thunderstorms of tropical violence. While it rained and the black skies growled and flashed overhead, they slipped and slogged through narrow sandy roads that quickly became quagmires of mud so deep that it sometimes sucked their shoes off. After the rain stopped and a blistering sun shone once more, raising temperatures to ninety-five degrees or higher, the roads steamed and the humidity set the perspiration streaming from their bodies, so that their thick wool uniforms became dark with sweat. Everywhere along the line of march lay soldiers who had been struck down either by heat exhaustion or sunstroke. Among the Germans who were accustomed to the cool summers of Central Europe, were clothed in thicker wool and were bearing heavier equipment, the casualty rate was an appalling one out of three. Nor was there any rest for the afflicted, for the ground was sodden or scorching by turns. As they lay gasping, clouds of mosquitoes tormented them. Under such conditions ten miles a day was considered a good rate of march, but usually the rate was less.

During the first few days, Clinton's right flank had been covered by the Delaware River, but after reaching Crosswicks and turning east toward New Brunswick and Amboy, his columns were subject to relentless enemy harassment and his route to sabotage. Interminable delays were caused by blown bridges in their path, which had to be repaired by Montresor's engineers, or by the gaps opening in Clinton's enormous baggage train compelling the troops to wait until they were closed. Always this train of baggage and provision wagons, rolling bakeries and blacksmiths' shops, pontoon trains for river crossings and fodder wagons for the thousands of horses, together with innumerable private carriages and wagons carrying fugitive Tories, stretched out for a distance of no less than eight and sometimes ten miles. Any one sizable vehicle that was overturned by shying beasts or was sunk in the mud brought the whole struggling column to a halt. Camp followers were another problem.

Most of the camp women had been put aboard the transports, but they jumped ship to be with their men, distracting them by their very presence while inciting them to plunder. Looting was common, again especially among the Hessians, and Clinton's threat to hang anyone caught in the act was no great deterrence. Clinton had hoped by this attitude to gain the friendship of the inhabitants, but the army marched through a scorched earth in which the farmers burned what they could not carry away, filled their wells or cut the ropes, scattering behind them warnings that the British were going to be "Burgoyned." Clinton did hang two soldiers for burning a house and another for trying to desert, but once again his threats and exemplary punishment failed to block a backward flow of deserters to Philadelphia. Finally, the detachments that Washington had sent out to harass Clinton were singularly effective. Morgan's riflemen shot up stragglers on Clinton's right flank, while Cadwalader's Pennsylvanians hung on his left. General Philemon Dickinson, with his New Jersey militia, sniped away at his rear guard or delayed the advance with frequent skirmishing and ambuscades that were so ferocious that they had to be driven off by artillery fire, and once by the elite dragoons, grenadiers and light infantry. The Americans also felled great trees across the road and blew up so many bridges that Clinton had to assign eighty pioneers with their tool wagons to the advance guard.

The British commander was far from anxious to draw Washington into a decisive battle, as the American chief believed. Rather, he wanted only to behold the welcome sights of the sails of Howe's fleet waiting for him at Sandy Hook. That was why, having received incorrect intelligence that Gates was marching from Peekskill to join Washington, he changed his line of march from New Brunswick–Amboy as his objective to the New Jersey coast. At Allentown he also reversed his order of march. Up to that point he had kept his most reliable soldiers—mostly British picked troops—in the van. But when he departed Allentown on June 25, he moved out "by the left," sending Knyphausen and his Hessians, strengthened by a few British brigades, out to the head of his column and placing most of the British troops at his rear, which he now regarded as the point of danger. He did so because he wished to put Washington to his rear, rather than let the American operate against his flanks. This maneuver was also motivated by his belief that Washington sought to capture his baggage train rather than to engage in decisive battle. It also took some time and effort, and that was why, after the column's safe arrival at Monmouth Courthouse on June 27, he felt that his army needed a day of rest.

On that same June 27 Washington rode over to Englishtown to consult with Lee, Lafayette, Wayne and Maxwell. Before he left, he issued orders

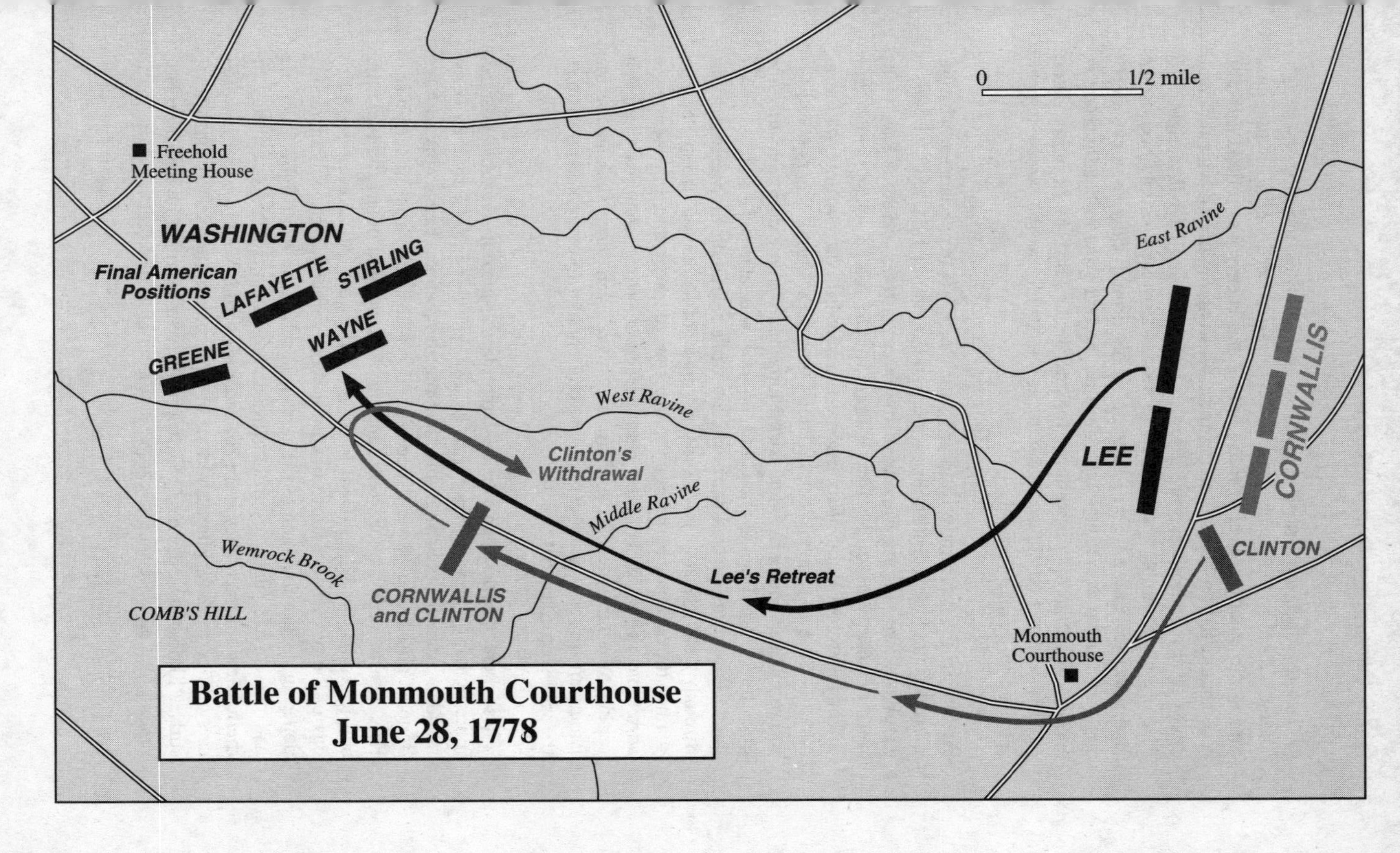

Battle of Monmouth Courthouse
June 28, 1778

to Lee to attack the British rear guard the following morning at daylight should Clinton resume his retreat. This was to be done, no matter how strong the enemy appeared to be, and if the enemy was indeed difficult, Lee should fight a holding action until Washington arrived with the main body. These oral orders were given to Lee in writing later that night. But Lee did not assemble his generals to discuss his plans, simply because he had none—as Lafayette was to learn to his dismay early the next morning. Concerned at not hearing from Lee, he had gone to headquarters to inquire about troop dispositions for the attack. But, as he wrote later: "Lee thought it would be better to act according to the circumstances, and had no plans."

At four in the morning of Sunday, June 28, 1778, Knyphausen, with his Germans and two British brigades, moved out on the road to Sandy Hook, followed by the wagons of the baggage train. An hour later Clinton's redcoats were under arms waiting for the road to clear so that they might follow. As usual, it took some time, and it was not until well after sunup—close to eight o'clock or later—that the waiting soldiers heard firing from their outposts. Such skirmishing had become common since the departure from Philadelphia, and no one was alarmed—until an hour later Clinton's astounded staff officers, while searching the westward hills through field glasses, saw a dense mass of American troops appear against the skyline, marching rapidly toward them and in surprisingly admirable order. When they next perceived strong columns marching briskly to either side of the road, they were even more shaken, for the American troops seemed certainly strong enough to overtake and capture the vital wagon train.

These were Charles Lee's troops, blundering into an enviable position more by happy happenstance than by any skillful maneuver by their commander. Actually, that morning and the day before, Lee seems to have done all possible to prevent success, and it is difficult for a modern historian, as it was for Wayne, John Laurens, Morgan and others, to avoid the suspicion that he did not want to succeed. First, he had allowed the entire day of the twenty-seventh to tick by without sending out scouts or reconnoitering parties to examine the terrain in which he must fight. Then he had passed that night reshuffling his commanders, so that few if any of them knew the men they were to lead into battle. When one of his officers offered to show him a shortcut to Monmouth, he rejected him with a surly, "I know my business." Next, on this very morning he had been late sending out an observation party, as Washington had requested the night before. Thus, without plans or reconnaissance and with an army shorn of the familiarity between men and officers that produces the cohesiveness so necessary to success in combat, he blundered into battle.

At five o'clock in the morning Philemon Dickinson, who was watching Clinton's wagons, reported the enemy on the move, but about the same time Steuben, with the rear guard in view, sent word that the British were still in bivouac. With this seeming contradiction from two generals observing two different forces, Lee lost his temper and his head. According to the disgusted Laurens, orders burst from his lips "with a rapidity and indecision calculated to ruin us." Conversely, no orders at all were sent to Daniel Morgan, three miles away on the British left flank, with the result that this veteran formation of riflemen and its valiant and able leader missed the entire ensuing action. Thus it was not until half-past nine—not daylight at five, as Washington had ordered—that Major General Charles Lee swung his army of five thousand men north of the road a mile from the courthouse and deployed them against the left flank and rear of Clinton's rear guard. Lee's dispositions cannot be cited with exactitude if only because of the difficulty of following this chaotic battle in detail. Broadly put, the Americans occupied the part of a field lying between the East Ravine and the road to Sandy Hook. At this point Charles Lee appeared to be the soul of confidence. Jubilant to see that Cornwallis's covering command was only fifteen hundred to two thousand men, he conceived the idea of cutting them off, sending a message to that effect to Washington. As one of his aides said to Lafayette: "The rear guard of the enemy is ours." In this spirit the attack began.

Sir Henry Clinton was still obsessed by his fear of losing his immense baggage train, and had hurried on ahead with it and with most of his rear guard, leaving about fifteen hundred to two thousand men to dispute the American advance. But they were commanded by the redoubtable Lord Cornwallis, and as the Americans deployed, the British struck at them in a series of attacks designed to give Clinton time to hurry his rear guard back to the point of danger. The first attack was made by British dragoons, charging valiantly but riding into an ambush that routed them. Next the Rangers struck, but were driven back. Now, with Washington hurrying to Lee's side, Clinton faced disaster unless he could drive Lee from the field. Yet, his method of counter-attack actually invited disaster, for in the time it took him to hasten each of his formations back down the Sandy Hook road to the widening battle, each of them could be defeated in detail.

Anthony Wayne perceived this almost immediately. Already beyond the courthouse, he called for support with this intention in mind. Lafayette, seconded by Captain l'Enfant of the engineers, also urged immediate assault, reminding Lee that his command of five thousand men and ten field pieces outnumbered Cornwallis's force. Lee replied: "Sir, you do not know British soldiers. We cannot stand against them. We shall certainly be driven back at first. We must be cautious." Lafayette was appalled. The golden moment was passing! He again beseeched Lee to go over to the offensive, but could obtain no more than permission to strike at the left of the line Cornwallis was forming. Happy to be away from this strangely disquieted general, Lafayette rode off with an aide. As they approached the front, the aide was killed by a cannon ball. Lafayette, conspicuous on a white horse, might also have fallen had not Clinton, with that incredible class prejudice of the day, forbidden his gunners to fire on him.

Now, simply and ineluctably because Charles Lee had neither a plan of attack nor a general grasp of the situation, there ensued that chaos that disarmed the rebels. There was movement and counter-movement like the scurrying over a huge anthill. Brigades and regiments advanced and withdrew. With no orders from on high, everyone gave orders—sometimes obeyed, sometimes ignored. If it was not actually every man for himself, it was every formation for itself, and a measure of this perfection of confusion was that when Lafayette moved forward on the American right, he saw to his amazement that the Patriot troops on his left were retreating. Within another few minutes he received Lee's direct order to retreat.

For all this confusion the retrograde movement was at first orderly. There was no terror in the eyes of the men but, rather, anger. Everywhere unit commanders were asking, "Where is General Lee?" One who found him was dismayed by being told: "Take your men any place where they will be safe." With Lafayette covering, there began what Laurens called "a senseless retreat without firing a musket over ground which might have been disputed inch by inch." Eventually the vanguard of this unseemly flight reached all the way back to the West Ravine and began to flow over the bridge there. It was here that they were met by an infuriated George Washington.

Washington had been marching to Lee's side with his main body, slightly larger than the advance force. He had received Lee's message about cutting off Cornwallis, and had stopped at a house for a late breakfast. Aware of Lee's superiority of nearly three to one over Cornwallis, he was confident of initial success. He was therefore incredulous when a gentleman of the vicinity informed him that Lee was retreating. Mounting a splendid white horse given to him only that day by Governor William Livingston of New Jersey, he rode hard to overtake his troops. Putting himself at their head, he advanced, with Greene commanding the right wing and Lord Stirling, the left. Now he reached the bridge over the West Ravine to plunge into the human backwash of a general retreat: first a frightened farmer on horseback, then a terrified young fifer. Next came a major who said: "They are flying from a shadow." With some relief Washington, who could never forget Kip's Bay, saw that there was no terror in their faces—only the sullen look of soldiers seeking someone to blame for their shame. But the American war chief also was aware of what would happen if enemy artillery began to flash and crash among them. Again and again he rode anxiously up to officers to ask who gave the order to retreat. Private Martin, who was among those trudging over the bridge, heard an officer reply: "General Lee." With that, Washington swore. Martin was not close enough to hear what he said, but his comrades said it was an uncharacteristic "Damn poltroon!"

At last Washington saw Lee, and his face went white with rage. Sitting his magnificent horse like the splendid equestrian figure that he was, Washington came galloping down on Charles Lee with all the wrathful countenance of the God of Battles. "I desire to know, sir," he roared, "what is the reason—whence all this disorder and confusion?"

"Sir?" Lee stammered. "S-s-sir?"

"What's all this confusion for?" Washington continued furiously. "And what is the cause of this retreat?"

It was at this point that Washington is supposed to have called Lee a "damned poltroon" and ordered him to the rear. There are so many different versions of this exchange, including a full page of dubious dialogue from Washington Irving, that it is unwise to choose a specimen. But few historians have resisted the colorful account given by General Scott when he was asked if he had ever heard Washington swear. "Yes, sir, he did once. It was at Monmouth and on a day that would have made any man swear. Yes, sir, he swore that day till the leaves shook on the trees. Charming! Delightful! Never have I enjoyed such swearing before or since. Sir, on that memorable day he swore like an angel from heaven!"

It has been said that Washington next ordered Lee to the rear, but if he did, Lee did not go; pulling himself together instead and with incredible cheek reminding his chief that the operation "was contrary to his opinion, that he was adverse to an attack, or general engagement, and was against it in council—that while the enemy were so superior in cavalry we could not oppose them." Why, then, Washington asked, had Lee taken the command and since he had, why had he not obeyed orders? To this question, there was no answer, and yet Washington, once more inexplicably, offered Lee command of the defensive line he was forming while he organized the rest of the army in the rear. Lee assented with a flourish, saying that he would be the last to leave the field, whereupon Alexander Hamilton, who was there, swung his sword and cried: "That's right, my dear General, and I will stay and we will all die here on the spot!"

With this remark, Washington rode forward to stop the retreat. He stopped it by his magnificent presence, riding easily among the men, re-forming them, inspiring them by his calm courage. Galloping down the road to Monmouth, he halted two retreating regiments and ordered them to turn and hold off the enemy. They did so with great bravery and many casualties, including their commanders. But their delaying action gave Washington the time to form a defensive line on high ground behind the causeway crossing the Middle Ravine. He put Greene on the right, himself in the center and Stirling on the left. Behind him Lafayette commanded the second line, while Wayne held an outpost behind a hedge in Washington's front. There is no record of Charles Lee appearing in the ensuing engagement.

Cheering and charging with typical elan, the British struck first at Stirling's men on the left. They were among Clinton's finest formations—the famed Black Watch, light infantry and Forty-second Foot—but they were met by a rattling and devastating roll of musketry. An artillery duel ensued after Washington's guns, flanking the British to either side, took a terrible toll of the oncharging redcoats and Clinton responded by bringing up his own artillery. A savage hour-long battle raged in hundred-degree heat. Everywhere soldiers of both sides fainted from heat exhaustion. In this roaring martial symphony, the pounding of the guns like percussion instruments counterpointing the higher rattle of rifles and muskets and the screams of the stricken, it was impossible to hear orders. Yet, as Steuben watched in satisfaction, Washington was at last able to maneuver like an eighteenth-century general. Stirling's position was saved when American regiments wheeled into line under fire "with as much precision as on an ordinary parade and with the coolness and intrepidity of veteran troops." Alexander Hamilton remarked afterwards that until he had seen soldiers deploy and fight as they did, he had never "known or conceived the value of military discipline."

Having failed at the American left, Clinton now struck at the Yankee right held by Greene, sending against it a force composed of "the very flower" of his army and led by Cornwallis himself. As usual they came forward in dressed ranks, and were raked horribly by the six-gun battery to their left on Comb's Hill, commanded by the Chevalier du Plessis. The battery was directed with such accuracy that one round shot struck the muskets from the hands of an entire squad. Meanwhile, Greene's muskets were blazing. Taking casualties, the British pressed forward, but the combined onslaught of muskets and artillery was too much to bear—and they fell back.

While this assault was being repulsed, Clinton simultaneously tried to evict Wayne from his forward position behind the hedge. Again it was the elite troops who came on with such spirited swiftness that they were within reach of the rebel line before the first volley tore into them, forcing them back. Re-forming, they charged again—and Wayne coolly waited until they were close enough for musket balls and grapeshot sent them reeling back a second time. A full hour passed before a third assault was mounted. It was led by the gallant Lieutenant Colonel Henry Monckton, again composed of picked troops. Monckton formed his men so close to the Patriots that they could hear him giving orders. Crying, "Forward to the charge, my brave grenadiers!" he led them toward the hedge at top speed. "Steady!" Wayne called to his men. "Steady! Wait for the word, then pick out the king-birds!" Wayne's men did, and when the order "Fire!" was given at a distance of forty yards, they unleashed a fearful volley that shattered the charge and left the field dappled with scarlet coats. Monckton fell so close to the hedge that the Americans ran out to seize his body and his colors.

Still a fourth charge at Wayne was organized, this one with such an overwhelming number of troops that Wayne was outflanked on both sides. Wisely, he withdrew, again in good order. He had fought his position well, and it is to Washington's credit that he had chosen that singular outpost behind the hedge. Stirling and Greene, to either side, and Washington himself between them were simply too well posted for Clinton to risk another costly assault.

But Washington was not satisfied. He wanted the major victory for which he had been yearning for three years. Fresh troops were brought forward to strike the enemy on both flanks, but by the time they were formed, darkness had fallen and the attack was canceled.

That night the Americans slept on their guns, confident of victory the next day. Washington lay under an oak tree covered by his cloak, with Lafayette beside him. But when he awoke at daylight, there was no enemy to strike. Just as silently as "the Old Fox" himself had slipped away from Cornwallis at Trenton, Clinton had put his army on the road at midnight and caught up with Knyphausen by dawn. On June 30 his entire army and baggage train were at Sandy Hook, and by July 5 they were safely in New York.

At the Battle of Monmouth Courthouse the Americans reported their casualties to be 69 dead, 161 wounded and 130 missing, of whom all but a few returned to their units, and the British reported theirs to be 65 killed, 160 wounded and 64 missing. But American burial parties counted hundreds of unburied enemy corpses, and for weeks afterward more were found in the surrounding woods. Washington, never prone to exaggeration, emphatically stated that Clinton's casualties were no less than two thousand men, or 15 percent of his entire command, a devastating loss in an era when 10 percent was considered disastrous. Moreover Clinton also lost 136 British soldiers who deserted on the march from Philadelphia and 440 Hessians, as well as thousands of horses that had to be put to death on the shores of Sandy Hook because there was no way to get them aboard Howe's ships. And there was also an unusual entry in the British casualty report: "3 sergeants, 56 rank and file died with fatigue," meaning, of course, heat exhaustion. Perhaps only a half dozen rebels perished the same way, if only because they were accustomed to torrid summers and had removed their coats and packs before they went into action. Because of that horribly enervating heat, a heroine entered the young nation's brief history. She was Mary Ludwig Hayes, wife of a Pennsylvania artillery private. Twenty-two, illiterate, smoking and chewing tobacco and swearing "like any trooper," she endeared herself to her husband's comrades by rushing back and forth from a stream with pitchers of cool water, for which she received the undying sobriquet "Molly Pitcher." Joseph Martin, who seems to have been almost everywhere in this war, saw her in action. "While in the act of reaching for a cartridge and having one of her feet as far before the other as she could step, a cannon shot from the enemy passed directly between her legs without doing any other damage than carrying away all the lower part of her petticoat. Looking at it with apparent unconcern, she observed that it was lucky it did not pass a little higher, for in that case it might have carried away something else." Molly Pitcher also served her husband's cannon, and when he fell dead at her feet, she fired it.

Both sides could have claimed success at Monmouth with equal justice, for both sides remained upon the field, the customary criterion of victory. But Clinton did not want the field, but wanted rather to get to New York, which he did. Washington, who wanted Clinton, or at least a part of him, and was thus on the offensive, was compelled by Lee's blunders to adopt a defensive stance, at which his troops excelled. Actually, Monmouth was a stalemate, for Clinton's successful retreat from Philadelphia to New York was more than offset by Washington's immense satisfaction at seeing his men hold their own against the best professionals of Europe. A new spirit now informed the American Army. But Monmouth, the longest battle of the war and the last major engagement in the North, also had an unpleasant aftermath.

Lee, as might be expected, could not be quiet, and a few days after the battle, he wrote a pair of insulting and insolent letters to Washington, demanding a court-martial to clear his name. The court-martial was rapidly convened, only five days after the battle, and Charles Lee was found guilty of ordering "an unnecessary and, in some few instances, a disorderly retreat." He was sentenced to a year's suspension from the service, but when Congress reviewed the verdict, the desperate Lee hurried to York to begin a campaign to vilify those who testified against him—Alexander Hamilton, for instance, was "the son of a bitch" who perjured himself in Washington's behalf—and to gain support among his old admirers. But the number of his admirers had shrunk to Richard Henry Lee, Samuel Adams and a few others, so that the sentence was approved by a vote of fifteen to seven.

If anything, the sentence for such a dereliction of duty was far too light, perhaps because by then most Americans of consequence realized that Charles Lee was indeed not just a little mad. Elias Boudinot, who knew Lee well, wrote: "General Lee had considerable military knowledge and did very well on a small scale, but I have no doubt that whenever anything on a very large scale struck him, that a partial lunacy took place." *Partial?* Entering battle without a plan is about as lunatic as a general can get. He might as well do so without weapons. True enough, few battles are ever fought according to plan, and sometimes the opposing generals have the same plan, say, each intending to strike the other's right so that a kind of revolving-door ballet may ensue. But even in such a case, victory usually goes to the general who is quick thinking enough to sense what is happening and adjust to it or to the one who strikes first.

Most surprising is the extent to which Lee was able to influence ordinarily practical and perceptive Patriots, not the least of them George Washington. Some of this self-hypnosis was due to his genuine ardor in the Patriot cause before war erupted, and more to his superior airs as a military professional once hostilities had commenced. Among powerful persons who were ignorant of military matters, he spoke constantly in military jargon in the way that a wine expert will discuss a vintage before fanciers of the grape whose untrained taste buds can tell them only that the wine is good or bad. In a word, Charles Lee was a snow job. A mad one, indeed, but madness does not ordinarily "exercise a strong influence on normal people," as one historian has suggested. In backward or primitive societies that are dominated by medicine men, it does indeed, as witness how the Mohawks, with their reverence for the unbalanced mind, were tricked by the half-wit Hon-Yost whom Benedict Arnold sent to them. It seems more likely that Patriots, such as the Adamses or Thomas Mifflin, ignored Lee's erratic behavior—his slovenly dress, his pack of yapping poodles, his attempts to persuade troops by cursing them—because they wanted to ignore it, and they wanted to do so because they either distrusted Washington as a potential military dictator or envied Washington his glory. They chose Gates as a replacement because Lee was a British captive, but if he had not been, they would probably have gone to him first. His occasional penetrating insights may be explained by Dryden's remark: "Great wits are to madness sure allied." But he also knew his audience, yearning for the great captain that the Cause needed, and was aware that when he discoursed among them so knowingly, he was dumping an intellectual blizzard upon people who knew as much about matters military as a pig knows about Sunday.

The Battle of Monmouth Courthouse, while establishing Yankee Doodle as a formidable fighting man, also had the perhaps more fortunate consequence for the United States of ridding George Washington of the hairshirt of Charles Lee. Washington was now truly and forever more the American commander in chief, and his authority was established beyond question. "Never," wrote Lafayette of Washington's conduct at Monmouth, "was General Washington greater than in this action. His presence stopped the retreat; his dispositions fixed the victory; his fine appearance on horseback, his calm courage roused to animation by the vexations of the morning, gave him the air best calculated to excite enthusiasm. ... I thought then as now that never had I beheld so superb a man." By giving Lee command, rather than Lafayette, of the advance force, Washington had indeed compromised his own plan of cutting off Clinton's rear guard. But he redeemed all, not by some stroke of that brilliance of mind so cherished by intellectuals, but rather by those more modest qualities that are the true traits of a great captain: courage, of course, the sine qua non that Charles Lee also possessed, but then resting upon that courage like a cathedral upon a cliff, steadfastness and calmness in adversity.

The final paragraph on the American career of Charles Lee is a sad one. After Congress approved his sentence, he wrote a bitter and vituperative letter denouncing the action, for which he was dismissed from the service. Retiring to Virginia, he lived with his dogs in that filth and squalor that he found so amenable—and which should have been the surest sign of his derangement—in a big, barnlike house without windows or rooms except those chalked out hypothetically on the bare floor. He continued to attack Washington until John Laurens challenged him and wounded him in a duel. When he died in 1782, it was widely believed that he had killed himself. If he had, he had also, after Congress approved his sentence, written his own epitaph—crying aloud in anguish:

"O that I were a dog, that I might not call man my brother!"

★ 55 ★

THE FRENCH ARRIVE/NEWPORT FIZZLE/SAVANNAH LOST

After Monmouth, Washington gave his army a day of rest. The men bathed in a brook, washed their clothes and cleaned their arms and equipment. Some of them took to plundering the local inhabitants, and when the inhabitants complained, Washington ordered a search of knapsacks and issued a threat of death to any man found guilty of looting. Meanwhile, Molly Pitcher's gallantry was rewarded with a sergeant's warrant, small solace for the loss of her young husband, and yet an indication of Washington's surprising tolerance in an age when women of her class were generally kept inside the kitchen and the bedroom and away from school.

Next Washington made for New York State, moving his army by "easy marches." Breaking camp at three in the morning, the men marched about ten miles until the July heat compelled them to halt, when they made camp in the late morning or early afternoon. Even so the heat was intense enough to prostrate many men with heat exhaustion, while killing a few of them, as well as more horses than could be spared. Halting on the cooler banks of the Raritan River opposite New Brunswick, the troops rested a few days before marching on to Paterson, where Washington and his staff picnicked on cold ham and biscuits beside the Passaic Falls, enjoying its thunder and delightfully cool mists. From there they crossed the Hudson to join Gates's command at White Plains. Here Washington established himself in a strong defensive position, waiting to see what Clinton, holding New York City, Staten Island and Newport, would do next. He was quietly jubilant, writing: "It is not a little pleasing, nor less wonderful to contemplate that after two years maneuvering ... both armies are brought back to the very point they set out from." Here was a solid achievement that has generally gone unnoticed in the history books: for three years, beset by every privation and shortage; inhibited by dissent, disorder, desertion and discontent; outnumbered and outgunned and more often than not outmaneuvered, the American Cunctator had fought the enemy to a standstill, and as vindication of his often-criticized policy of delay, there came the welcome news that the Comte d'Estaing's fleet, led by the mighty *Languedoc* mounting ninety guns, had arrived in American waters. True, the comte's incredibly lengthy voyage of eighty-seven days—which he attributed to bad weather and "practice maneuvers"—had brought him off the Delaware ten days too late to intercept Howe's fleet carrying Clinton's big guns and much of his baggage or to prevent Howe from ferrying Clinton's army to the safety of New York. With at least double the firepower of Howe's fleet, now in New York Harbor, it is almost certain that if d'Estaing had arrived in time, he would have defeated the British at sea, and with his four thousand infantry to thicken Washington's army, probably would have helped to recapture New York.

Such a British defeat could have ended the war in the summer of 1778. As it was, after Sir Henry Clinton wrote a report of Monmouth wearing rose-colored glasses, the victory bells began pealing again throughout Britain. Not the first general to achieve "victory" by sheathing the sword to seize the pen, he wrote that except for the sabotage of bridges, his masterful retreat had passed "without interruption." Monmouth was dismissed as a minor rearguard action. Clinton exaggerated Washington's losses and minimized his own, saying nothing of his six hundred desertions. He also put Washington's main body at twenty thousand men and Lee's advance guard at twelve thousand, meaning that he, with fifteen thousand, had easily repulsed a force of 32,000. But the report was effective: King George was transported with delight, while Lord George Germain assured Clinton of His Majesty's "highest approbation of your whole conduct."

Even so, when Sir Henry laid aside his pen, he still looked down the muzzles of d'Estaing's menacing cannon across the bar in Sandy Hook. If the French admiral could get across the bar and into New York Harbor, all could be redeemed for the Patriot cause. He could destroy Howe's fleet and make Clinton's situation untenable. Cut off from all reinforcements and supplies, threatened by Washington in White Plains, surrounded by a hostile countryside and isolated on an island with so many accessible streams and estuaries, Clinton could be starved into submission. But d'Estaing did not cross the bar. He spent ten days cautiously taking soundings, finally offering an enormous reward of fifty thousand crowns to any pilot who could get his deep-draft monsters into the harbor. "All refused," he wrote, "and the particular soundings which I caused to be taken myself too well demonstrated that they were right." D'Estaing's best opportunity appeared on July 22, when wind and a high tide raised thirty feet of water over the bar, but d'Estaing bowed to the warnings of his pilots and stood away to the south.

New York, the very hub of British power in America, had been spared. Perhaps it had been spared because the French admiral was not too eager to end the war with a single blow and thus free Britain to turn all her power against his own country. History does not say, but the fact remains that the Franco-American alliance was, at its outset, put to a severe strain.

Washington was disappointed at the missed opportunity, and within the next few days reports of British-led Indian massacres of western settlers increased his dismay. On July 4—to mock American independence—Colonel Sir John Butler struck at the Wyoming Valley in Pennsylvania. Hundreds perished. Men were burnt at the stake or thrown on beds of coals and held down with pitchforks while their horrified families were forced to witness their torment. Others were placed in a circle while a half-breed squaw called Queen Esther danced chanting around them to chop off their heads. Soon the entire frontier was in flames, with Washington unable to come to its rescue.

All the commander in chief's resources were at that moment directed toward recovering Newport from the British. Sullivan, with about ten thousand men divided between Greene and Lafayette, had marched north of the vital port city to rendezvous with d'Estaing's four thousand French soldiers. But Clinton and "Black Dick" Howe acted quickly to discomfit them. Clinton collected a force of five thousand to come to the aid of General Pigot, who held Newport with about three thousand troops, while Admiral Howe, now reinforced, crowded on all sail for Rhode Island.

Hearing of Howe's approach, d'Estaing reembarked his troops and sailed out to meet him. Sullivan was furious, but the Frenchman would not change his mind. On the night of August 11 the ships of both fleets were scattered by a violent storm, and both had to sail away for repairs—Howe to New York and d'Estaing to Boston.

In the meantime, the French withdrawal had so disgusted Sullivan's militia that more than five thousand of them went home. Sullivan had to backpedal furiously away from the eagerly pursuing Pigot, and the Newport expedition ended in a fiasco. Sullivan was openly critical of his allies, and there were some tense moments in Boston after a French officer was killed during riots between sailors and soldiers of both nations—but tempers eventually cooled, especially after d'Estaing sailed for Martinique on November 4.

A week later Walter ("Hellhound") Butler, the bloodier son of Sir John Butler, ravaged the patriot settlement of Cherry Valley in western New York. Assisted by Joseph Brant, Butler put the town to the torch. Then, with the American frontier being pushed back and ravaged, the British moved south.

In November 1778 Clinton sent about 3,500 regulars and Tories, under Lieutenant Colonel Archibald Campbell, against Savannah, a port that not only offered entrance into the most southern colonies but also linked these colonies with the West Indies. Campbell was to be assisted by General Augustine Prevost, marching up from St. Augustine in Florida.

Opposing them was Major General Robert Howe, with about one thousand Georgia and South Carolina militia. Howe took position to the east of Savannah, with his right resting on a swamp and his left on rice paddies. Campbell feinted through the paddies, while another column, led by a black slave, slipped through the swamp and turned the Americans' right. At that juncture Campbell converted his feint into a strike, and both columns closed on the Patriots, putting them to rout and inflicting about five hundred casualties against a handful of their own lost.

The date of Savannah's fall was December 29, and after that the British, now under Prevost, set about clearing Georgia.

Up north, both Washington and Clinton had gone into winter quarters, the British in and around New York, Washington in a great arc beginning in Middletown, New Jersey, not far from Monmouth and stretching through West Point and Fishkill in New York and then east to Danbury, Connecticut.

It was a mild winter, and the troops were relatively comfortable, a small blessing for which the harried Washington found it difficult to be thankful after having seen the campaign of 1778 begin so brightly only to fizzle in the end.

★ 56 ★

THE BORDER WAR/JOHN PAUL JONES

While the chief commanders and their armies wintered in the North, fighting flared in the South and on the western border.

In Georgia, the capture of Savannah had been tantamount to conquest of the state. After the arrival of General Prevost the state was once more subjected to the Crown, and as 1779 began, Georgia's inhabitants "flocked by hundreds to the King's officers, and made their peace at the expense of their patriotism."

Soon Prevost moved against South Carolina, where he was opposed by Benjamin Lincoln, commanding about three thousand ragged Continentals and untrained militia. There ensued a series of marches and countermarches, skirmishes and small pitched battles, clashes between Tories and Patriots marked by brutality and depredations on both sides, and although the British regulars certainly could claim most of the victories, the net result of the campaign was that Prevost withdrew to Georgia, and South Carolina remained in the rebel camp.

In the West a dashing frontiersman named George Rogers Clark struck a sharp blow at the British. Acting for Virginia, which was anxious to nail down its old claims to the Northwest, Clark had begun clearing the Illinois country during the previous summer by capturing posts at Kaskaskia and Vincennes. But then the British, under the unsavory Colonel Henry Hamilton—the "Hair-buyer," who paid Indians for American scalps—recaptured Vincennes. Hearing of this, Clark rushed to Kaskaskia, about 150 miles to the southwest. In early February he led a tiny force of 130 men, half of them French, against Vincennes. Few marches in American history have equaled the ordeal that awaited Clark's men. Torrential rains and floods barred their path. Much of the time they floundered through icy water up to their chests. Men who sank beneath the surface were fished up and placed in canoes. But Clark urged them on, ever onward, until at last they debouched before Vincennes. Here Clark deceived Hamilton's superior force by marching his little band back and forth to create the impression of a thousand men approaching. That was enough for Hamilton's Indians, who quickly deserted. Then, after Clark's sharpshooters began picking off the fort's defenders, Hamilton asked for talks. To make up Hamilton's mind, Clark had five Indians, who had been captured with scalps in their possession, tomahawked in full view of the garrison. Hamilton surrendered Vincennes.

Although Clark had given British power north of the Ohio a severe check, he had not destroyed it—if only because he could not capture Fort Detroit. As a result, warfare of the savage border kind was to be renewed in the Illinois country.

Meanwhile, with the advent of summer, General Washington moved to retaliate against the British and Indians who had ravaged the Wyoming and Cherry valleys the year before. He sent General Sullivan and about five thousand men to destroy Iroquois towns and to capture Fort Niagara, the base for their raids. Niagara, however, was not taken, although the Indians were severely scourged by Sullivan, leading one column up the Susquehanna from the Wyoming Valley, and General James Clinton, pushing up the Mohawk Valley with another. No fewer than forty Iroquois towns were destroyed, and the People of the Longhouse were struck a blow from which they never completely recovered. Standing crops were ruined, granaries were burned and orchards were cut down. In the cruel winter of 1779–80 that followed, hundreds of Indian families starved to death. Still, the British and Indians were not completely suppressed, and it remained for the kingdom of Spain to deal Britain her severest blow in that summer of 1779.

On June 16, 1779, Spain declared war on Britain, and at once seriously complicated the problem of subduing the American colonies.

The British fleet, already spread thin over the vast new empire, now found it necessary to reinforce Gibraltar and Minorca. The West Indies came under the threat of a Spanish fleet at Havana and a French fleet and army at Santo Domingo. D'Estaing began to take island after island away from Britain, with the result that Sir Henry Clinton had to send eight thousand regulars from New York to the West Indies.

Clinton was so gravely weakened that he began to consider the evacuation of New York. He did not do so, but Newport, which had resisted both the French and the Americans the year before, was abandoned without a shot.

Then, in August, the Mother Country herself came under the guns of a Franco-Spanish fleet. For the first time since the Spanish Armada was routed in 1588, the "island set in a silver sea" was threatened with invasion. In his alarm, King George III tried to rally the people by reminding them how valiantly the subjects of Queen Elizabeth had met the same threat two centuries previously. His oratory was not needed, however, for the vast enemy fleet turned out to be only a "huge mob of ships." On August 16 as the combined fleets came in sight of Plymouth, a storm drove them out of the Channel never to return. The Bourbons "talked big, threatened a great deal, did nothing, and retired."

The only sailor who really twisted the British lion's tail in that year of 1779 was a renegade Scots captain named John Paul Jones.

John Paul Jones had been born plain John Paul in 1747 in Galloway, Scotland, the son of a gardener. Like his father he might have been drawn to the soil, but the sight of the great bay called Solway Firth that was visible from his home and the tangy smell of salt in the air drew him instead to the sea. As soon as he could walk, little John toddled into the tiny nearby port of Carsethorn, to clamber over the moored ships and talk to the sailors about life at sea and the sights of the romantic ports over the horizon. He and his playmates in their rowboats pretended to be great ships of the line of battle, and when they divided into fleets and struck at each other with their oars, above the squeals and high cries of these diminutive warriors could be heard the voice of John Paul shouting orders. After the "battle" was over, he would sink back into silence, walking quietly home to dinner. John Paul would always be a person of these two conflicting moods: in repose quiet, his voice soft and still, his hazel eyes as gentle as a deer's; in action, fierce and murderous, thirsty for the kill, those eyes now flashing like a hawk's when falling on its prey, his voice rising to a piercing shriek. Like most small men who were accustomed but never submitted to the bullying of the bigger boys of his youth, John Paul would reach manhood notorious for his terrible temper, which could prove to be a tremendous strength in war, but a weakness in peace.

At the age of thirteen John was apprenticed to a local shipowner, agreeing to sail and work for seven years at minimal pay to learn the hard sailor's trade. In the beginning he served aboard those dreadful, stinking African slavers, floating cesspools that carried black bondsmen from

Africa to Europe and America. Eventually he sickened of this "abominable trade" and quit it in disgust. Upon the death of his master—a bonanza for John—the young apprentice was free.

In 1768, when he was twenty-one, John Paul had matured physically. He stood five feet, five inches tall and had brown hair and bright hazel eyes. He was thin, wiry, extremely active, with a rather foxlike face: his nose sharp and belligerent, his chin cleft and jutting and his cheekbones high. At this time, just like the for-him fortunate death of his master, the captain and mate of a small ship he was sailing on died of fever at sea, and John Paul, now the only man aboard who could navigate, took command and steered her home. In gratitude the owners made Paul her captain, and thus, at an unusually young age, he began his career as a sailing master.

It was hard and demanding work, and the responsibility was heavy. He needed not only to care for his ship and his crew, but to navigate by the sun and stars, maintain discipline and even stand a watch himself. In port he tried to sell his cargo for the highest profit and take aboard a cargo for the home voyage at the lowest price. But he persevered and made his employers happy.

Captain Paul showed early in his career that he was not an amiable skipper. He expected his orders to receive instant obedience, and when it was not forthcoming he exploded in wrath. At twenty-three that temper got him into trouble. A lazy seaman named Mungo Maxwell refused to obey his orders, and Paul had him tied to the rigging and flogged. After the ship reached port, Maxwell went to the authorities there, displayed his scars and brought charges against Paul. Although a court cleared Paul, the death of Maxwell shortly afterward was attributed to the flogging, and Paul was imprisoned. He was freed only after proving that the sailor had actually died of a fever.

Eventually, at twenty-six, having shown himself to be an excellent seaman, navigator and trader, Captain Paul was made part owner and master of a much larger, square-rigged ship named *Betsey*. It seemed that he was now on his way to wealth, until his crew, chafing at his strict discipline, mutinied on the island of Tobago and chased Captain Paul into his cabin. Drawing his sword, he awaited their attack—killing their leader, who struck at him with a club. Paul was considering going ashore to give himself up for trial, until his friends convinced him that he could never receive true justice on Tobago. Instead, he fled to another ship and sailed for America.

Arriving there—he had taken the precaution of concealing his identity by adding "Jones" to his name—John Paul Jones seems to have dropped out of sight, although he did visit a brother living in Virginia and spent some time in North Carolina. Upon hearing "the shot heard round the word" fired at Concord bridge, Jones immediately applied for and received a commission as lieutenant in the nascent Continental Navy. He was the first to receive that rank, and he served under Ezek Hopkins of Rhode Island, the first chief of naval operation of that tiny navy of four converted merchantmen. It was John Paul Jones who first threw the new American flag to the breeze: a standard of "thirteen stripes, alternate red and white, (with) thirteen stars ... white in a blue field." That was when he was aboard the *Alfred*, commanded by Captain Dudley Saltonstall of Connecticut. He was still aboard her in early 1776, when, with the fleet now consisting of seven ships, Hopkins led his bantam navy on a raid to the British West Indies, capturing badly needed cannon and powder in the Bahamas. Returning home, the fleet attacked and severely damaged the British *Glasgow* near Block Island on the Connecticut coast.

In May 1776 John Paul Jones became a captain with his own ship, the sloop *Providence*, with twelve guns and seventy-three sailors—the best crew he ever commanded. Skilled seamen were rare in the navy in those days, when the lure of prizes aboard American privateers had drained the United States of most of its competent seamen, and only the refuse of the ports could be persuaded to join the Continental Navy. With such men discipline was but a word, and when in port Jones and his fellow officers had to stand watch day and night to prevent the men from deserting. But John Paul Jones was to change all that. On his first cruise he took sixteen British ships, sending eight into port "and sank, burned or destroyed the rest." Eventually he was to become on the sea the legend that Benedict Arnold had become on land. Actually, he was Arnold's seagoing duplicate, though somewhat smaller: fiercely ambitious, with a natural aptitude for combat, his tactics not always scrupulous, his thirst for gold and glory unquenchable. It was this last characteristic that led him to end the privateers' monopoly on able-bodied seamen, recommending to the influential Philadelphia financier Robert Morris that Congress should authorize a naval policy of giving all captured prizes to the men and officers who took them. This policy was necessary and immediately needed, he said, because "the common class of mankind are actuated by no nobler principle than that of self-interest. This, and this only, determines all adventurers in privateers, the owners as well as those they employ." Thus John Paul Jones, a fiery, dapper little warrior, tough enough to run a pirate ship, was just the man Benjamin Franklin was looking for in his desire to punish the British for their atrocities in America.

★ ★ ★

Jones had met both Adams and Franklin in Paris, impressing both of them, especially Adams, who seems to have had more than his share of the Boston intellectual's fascination for men of action. Franklin remembered Jones as he proposed to burn English and Scottish cities in retaliation for the scorching of the Patriot countryside, especially his adopted Pennsylvania and New Jersey. He had also asked Congress to authorize expeditions to set fire to London and burn Buckingham Palace to the ground. In the early years of the war, however, the privateer captains were too busy taking profits to listen to such patriotic nonsense; and, in fact, they were so successful in their raids on the British merchant marine that a disgusted Franklin in 1777 could declare that American shippers had grown richer through legalized piracy than they had by commerce. Meeting Jones and hearing about his exploits, by his influence with Congress he turned Jones loose in the enemy's home waters.

In 1778 in command of the *Ranger,* Jones attacked the English town of Whitehaven and burned ships in port. He also invaded Scottish soil and he so terrified the British coast that Lord North planned to send a special squadron against him as soon as Britain was free of the fear of a Franco-Spanish invasion. After the Franco-American alliance, Jones began to use French ports as sanctuaries, and he quickly put together a small, marauding fleet. His flagship was the *Bonhomme Richard,* named for Franklin's famous *Poor Richard's Almanac.* She was a clumsy old veteran of the tea trade with India, converted by the French into a forty-two-gun third-rater. Most of her officers were American, with French Marines in her fighting tops, while her crew was a motley of Scots, Englishmen, Swedes, Norwegians, Portuguese and Swiss, as polygot as any pirate ship that sailed the Spanish main. In September 1779, Jones put out from France for the North Sea. With him sailed the 32-gun frigates *Pallas* and *Alliance* and the 12-gun brigantine *Vengeance.* Captain Jones was proud of his fleet as he paced the *Bonhomme Richard's* quarterdeck, resplendent in a fine new blue coat with white lapels and gilt epaulets on the shoulders. As he walked he sipped at a glass of limeade.

At dusk of September 23 Jones's ships were sailing off Flamborough Head on the coast of northeast England. It was a calm evening. There was almost no wind, and the darkening blue sea was like glass. Through his glass Jones sighted a convoy of merchantmen escorted by two warships. At once he guessed correctly that only a British convoy would be in such waters, and ran the Union Jack up his masthead. He was right. The warships were the *Serapis,* a brand-new ship of the Royal Navy mounting fifty guns, and commanded by Captain Richard Pearson, and the *Countess of Scarborough,* 20. Jones at once signaled his ships to form line while he made for the heavier *Serapis.*

Like the land warfare of the eighteenth century, naval combat of that period was based upon shock. On land it was the bayonet charge; at sea it was the broadside, usually fired within pistol shot of the enemy ship, a shock so devastating that neither stout human hearts nor stout wooden ships could long endure it. Because a fighting ship's armament was arrayed on either side of the ship at from one to two or even three levels, ships almost never fired at each other from the few guns mounted fore and aft; rather, they fired from their sides, with as many as thirty or forty-five heavy-caliber guns fired by each ship in a single salvo. Thus from sixty to ninety projectiles, weighing as much as fifty pounds apiece, might be flying back and forth in a single exchange of broadsides. The effect was staggering and awful to behold. Heads were shot away, limbs were torn off and great oaken planks were shattered to fill the air with flying splinters as deadly as the cannon and musket balls. Decks of the fighting ships sometimes were literally awash with blood. Stricken men were carried into makeshift surgeries, where, in the absence of anesthetics, rum was poured into their throats, after which they clenched their teeth on a leaden bullet, and where the screams of the afflicted were counterpointed by the whining of the bone saws. Often a ship's own guns were as destructive as the enemy's, for they sometimes burst under pressure, killing or maiming the gunners or sending the wheeled cannon caroming wildly over the decks. Nothing was more terrifying than a loose cannon on a ship that was rising and falling in the swells. Some ships fired shrapnel to clear the enemy rigging of sharpshooters, or chains intended to tear the enemy's sails and lines to shreds. This, then, was the combat that ensued after an outgunned John Paul Jones boldly challenged the enemy.

For some reason, *Alliance* stood off at a safe distance, while *Pallas* went after *Countess of Scarborough,* eventually capturing her. Undismayed at this lack of support, Jones engaged the heavier *Serapis.*

The *Bonhomme Richard's* first broadside resulted in disaster: two of the three heavy guns on her engaged side burst, killing the crews and blowing up the deck above them. For fear of a repetition, the third gun was abandoned. Still undaunted, Jones put himself alongside *Serapis* and lashed both ships together. There they lay in the moonlight for two and a half hours, pounding each other at point-blank range.

At first it seemed that *Serapis* would prevail. Her guns splintered *Richard's* rotten timbers and sent them flying. She scored numerous waterline hits and set *Richard* to leaking badly. And one by one she knocked out Jones's main battery of twenty-eight twelve-pounders. Jones had only three nine-pounders left. All around him fires were breaking out and the pumps were falling behind the leaks. Still, he fought on. When one of his gunners called out to *Serapis* for quarter, he broke the man's skull with his pistol. When the captain of *Serapis* shouted for verification of the gunner's appeal, Jones bellowed back: "I have not yet begun to fight!" And when the British attempted to board him, he led the fight that repulsed them.

Yet, as badly as *Richard* had been hurt below, she had begun to conquer aloft. Under the direction of American officers, French marines in *Richard's* fighting tops had cleared the enemy rigging of British seamen and had begun to pour a heavy fire into *Serapis*. Sniping, hurling grenades and combustibles, they cleared the Britisher's upper decks. Then a grenade thrown into a pile of cartridges on a lower deck set off a chain of explosion that racked *Serapis* from bow to stern. A half hour later *Alliance* appeared and took up a raking position off the Britisher's bow. Some of *Alliance's* shells struck *Richard* by mistake, but enough of them landed on *Serapis* to force the British captain to strike his colors.

By then *Bonhomme Richard* was a floating wreck, and Jones was compelled to transfer to *Serapis*. Nevertheless, he had won. By his refusal to submit, the indomitable John Paul Jones had humbled British naval pride, given the Continental Navy its greatest victory and bequeathed to the United States Navy one of its most cherished traditions. After his triumph, however, except for privateering and a few sea skirmishes, the American battle for freedom was fought exclusively on land.

★ 57 ★

STONY POINT/SAVANNAH REPULSE/INFLATION

During 1779 the most that Sir Henry Clinton had been able to do in the North was to launch a series of destructive raids into Connecticut and to seize the Hudson River forts at Verplanck's Point and Stony Point. His objective in Connecticut was to lure Washington out of his new headquarters at West Point in New York. But Washington, though angered by the frightfulness of the British raids, refused to budge. Instead, he sent Mad Anthony Wayne out to retake Stony Point.

Wayne led about twelve hundred men of the American Light Infantry, the Continental Army's new elite. Remembering what "No-Flint" Grey had done to his own troops at Paoli's Tavern, he ordered most of his men to attack with bayonets only. On the night of July 15 all the inhabitants in the Stony Point area were taken into custody. Dogs on the line of march were destroyed to prevent their barking.

Moving along the river bank, wading through two feet of water, Wayne's men moved out silently. Just after midnight, under the guns of the fort, they parted into three columns and moved to the attack.

British sentries spotted Wayne's column on the right and opened fire. Wayne fell, stunned by a ball that grazed his skull. He got up on one knee and shouted to his men to go forward. Angered by his fall, the Americans went yelling against the fort. They overwhelmed it and had to be restrained from using their bayonets to avenge Paoli.

It was a perfect little victory. Against American losses of fifteen killed and eighty-three wounded, the British suffered sixty-three men killed, about seventy wounded and 543 captured. Only one man got away, and Wayne's triumph—even though Washington eventually evacuated Stony Point—forced Clinton to abandon his intention of a campaign in New Jersey.

Instead, Clinton also evacuated Stony Point, and Verplanck's as well, sending the garrisons south to help defend Savannah against the French.

Washington hoped that Count d'Estaing would help him capture New York, and he daily awaited word that the French fleet had been sighted off the Delaware capes. But d'Estaing thought differently. Turning from his West Indies plunder, spurning the most valued prize, Jamaica, he sailed with his troops to recover Savannah from the British.

On September 12 about 3,500 French soldiers sailed up the Savannah River, came ashore and took up positon south of the town. Three days later they were joined by Count Casimir Pulaski's mounted legion of two hundred horsemen. On the sixteenth Benjamin Lincoln appeared with six hundred Continentals and 750 militia. D'Estaing now had about five thousand men against about 2,400 British, of whom the vast majority were Tories. If he attacked immediately, he would undoubtedly overwhelm Prevost. Instead, he tried to take Savannah by summons. The wily Prevost asked for a truce, which he used to strengthen his position and await the arrival of Lieutenant Colonel Maitland from Port Royal to the north.

Maitland's march seemed hopeless. The French held the sea and Lincoln's army blocked him by land. Still, though ill of malaria himself, he led eight hundred regulars through a swamp, crossing the Savannah River under cover of a fog to make a most welcome addition to Prevost's fighting force. And then d'Estaing delayed further, deciding to try to take the town by regular approaches.

The first trenches were opened September 23, and on October 3 nearly fifty land guns, plus those of three ships in the river, began battering the city. Savannah's fall seemed inevitable, and yet d'Estaing could not wait for it. Reports that Admiral "Foul-Weather Jack" Byron* was en route to Savannah with a British squadron made him fear for his ships. Storms of the season might scatter them. So he decided to attack Savannah.

Three columns were formed. One, under General Count Dillon, was to march to the British right rear and try to enter the town through the Sailor's Gate. A second, under General Isaac Huger, was to make a feint at the British left, while a third, the main blow, under both d'Estaing

*Grandfather of the poet.

and Lincoln, struck at the British right on the Spring Hill Redoubt.

Unfortunately for the Franco-Americans, Sergeant Major James Curry, of the Charleston Grenadiers, overheard the plan and revealed it to the British after he deserted. Prevost at once sent Maitland and a force of regulars to strengthen the Spring Hill Redoubt.

Early in the morning of October 9 Dillon's men began moving toward the Sailor's Gate. They blundered into a swamp, came out into the open and were repulsed by British fire. Dillon ordered a retreat. On the British left Huger made his appointed feint, and Prevost calmly ignored it. Thus when d'Estaing and Lincoln sent the main body hurtling toward the Spring Hill Redoubt, the British were braced to receive them.

This they did with a dreadful hail of musketry and interlocking artillery fire that tumbled the American spearheads in heaps. On came the South Carolina Continentals, led by the "Swamp Fox," Lieutenant Colonel Francis Marion. They reached the redoubt's parapet. Two officers raised their flag and were shot down. Another officer met a similar fate, and Sergeant Jaspar, who had bravely rescued the flag at Fort Moultrie, attempted it again at Savannah and was killed.

With Americans and French now milling wildly about outside the redoubt, Maitland launched a counterattack. The redcoats rushed from their fort and fell upon the enemy with fury. But they could not break them. A savage hand-to-hand fight raged for an hour, until the allies were finally driven back.

On their left, Count Pulaski and his legion tried to save the day with a cavalry charge. But a crossfire broke them up, and the gallant Polish nobleman was killed. That was the end of the attempt to storm Savannah. D'Estaing refused Lincoln's plea to continue the siege operations. Stunned by losses of about 250 dead and 600 wounded, against British casualties of about 150, he reembarked his troops and sailed away.

The French had failed a second time, to the great delight of the British and growing numbers of Southern Tories, and to the deep dismay of Washington, who was entering winter quarters at Morristown for a second time.

Nothing in the history of the trials of the Continental Army, not even the ordeal of Valley Forge, compares to the cold white crucible of that second winter at Morristown. It was so cold that New York Harbor froze over. Howling blizzards lashed Morristown. Often officers, as well as men, were buried beneath deep drifts after the wind had blown their pitiful ragged tents away. Other soldiers without tents or blankets, barefoot and half-naked, struggled to build rude huts out of the oak and maple trees around them.

"We have never experienced a like extremity at any period of the war," Washington wrote, and soon he was complaining that his men lived off "every kind of horse food but hay." Another day he wrote: "We have not at this day one ounce of meat, fresh or salt, in the magazine."

Food supplies grew scantier. And once again, while the Continentals suffered and died, the countryside waxed fat and flourished. Washington's only choice was to commandeer supplies, and just as he feared, he was hated for it. The situation was summed up by Alexander Hamilton, who wrote: "We begin to hate the country for its neglect of us. The country begin to hate us for our oppressions of them."

As the Continentals suffered, Congress struggled with the evil that was the chief cause of their misery: runaway inflation.

On the one hand, there was a shortage of goods because of the British naval blockade and a boycott of British manufactures. On the other, there was a demand for goods, aggravated by the requirements of the armed forces. Into this situation came unscrupulous merchants and speculators: the one raising prices again and again, the other "cornering" articles in short supply and controlling the market for them. Washington hated these wreckers of the American economy with a white-hot ferocity, and he once wrote: "I would to God that one of the most atrocious of each State was hung in Gibbets upon a gallows five times as high as the one prepared by Haman. No punishment in my opinion is too great for the man who can build his greatness upon his Country's ruin." But there was no way that Congress could check profiteers from amassing huge private fortunes. In rage, the Continentals blinked at the opulence of bloated rich men; starving, they heard of dinners in Philadelphia at which as many as 169 different dishes were served. Paid in Continental dollars, the army might have found it cheaper to wear or eat that near-worthless paper.

Paper currency was perhaps the chief cause of inflation. Not only Congress, but every one of the thirteen states had its own issue. The states refused Congress's plea to cease printing, and some even passed laws protecting their paper money. As a result, the paper printed by Congress became less and less acceptable. Congress had to print more and more currency in larger and larger denominations. Because there was little gold to back up this paper blizzard, the value of the Continental dollar fell. In 1776 four Continental dollars were worth one in gold, but by the end of 1779 the ratio was as high as one hundred to one, and the phrase "not worth a Continental" was born.

In desperation, Congress repudiated the dollar, declaring on March

15, 1780, that forty Continental dollars equaled one in gold. By this step Congress wiped out $200 million in debt, but it worsened the plight of the small wage earner and the Continental soldier, who was paid in Continental paper.

If the Continental soldier had unwisely hoarded his meager pay, he was ruined. If he tried to buy anything with such money, he was rebuffed by farmers and merchants, who demanded hard coin or twice as much as he thought his money was worth. Thus, as Washington wrote, "The long and great sufferings of this army is unexampled in history," and a Loyalist poet could confidently predict:

> Mock-money and mock-states shall melt away, And the mock troops disband for want of pay.

As the campaign of 1780 opened, he looked like a true prophet.

⋆ 58 ⋆

THE FALL OF CHARLESTON

Sir Henry Clinton had decided to open the campaign of 1780 by an all-out attempt to subjugate the South. He still believed with Lord George Germain that the South was Toryland. With Georgia—or at least its populous eastern half—now restored to the Crown, he would use Savannah as a base to conquer the Carolinas and then Virginia, after which, with his army augmented by a huge influx of Tories, he would move to reduce the North in similar detail. If he failed there, he would at least have saved the huge southern region for King George. The centerpiece of this campaign was to be the capture of Charleston, with its great port and strategically vital rivers.

Sir Henry had been meditating long and hard on the failure at Charleston in 1776 and had concluded that it was due to three mistakes, all by Sir Peter Parker, of course, not by himself. The first was to have landed him on the Isle of Palms, rather than on Sullivan's Island where Fort Moultrie stood, and thus wasted his army in a foolish attempt to ford The Breach; the second was Parker's unwise decision to fight a fort with wooden ships; and the third was Parker's serious underestimation of the Charlestonians' will to fight. None of these would recur with himself in complete command.

Every circumstance seemed favorable to the project. Clinton's strength in December 1779 stood at twenty-five thousand men and would allow him to spare a sufficiently large body of troops for the operation. Washington's army, wintering in New Jersey, was too small to attempt to save the city and was too far away to make a winter's march through New Jersey, Delaware, Maryland and Virginia, where the weather could also be cruel. Further the Patriots of the Carolinas were much disheartened by the loss of Savannah and the disappearance of the French. General Benjamin Lincoln's garrison at Charleston was also woefully weak, and the Carolinas were resentful of the fact that they could expect little help from the North, even though Virginia and North Carolina had sent their Continentals north to save Washington's army in 1777. Finally, winter in Charleston would provide excellent campaigning weather.

So eager was Sir Henry to try Charleston again that he cut the Christmas holiday revelry short by turning his command over to General Knyphausen on December 26, 1779, and setting sail south in a fleet of ninety transports carrying eight British regiments, five Hessian and five Tory corps—8,500 soldiers in all—plus detachments of cavalry and artillery. The troops convoy was protected by five ships of the line and nine frigates mounting 650 guns and commanded by Admiral Mariot Arbuthnot. Naval crews and Marines numbered five thousand men.

As might be expected that time of year, the weather was stormy. Off Cape Hatteras, North Carolina, shrieking gale winds approaching hurricane force struck and scattered the mighty fleet. Giant waves battered the ships so savagely that the legs of all the artillery horses were broken and the terrified beasts had to be destroyed. Many cavalry mounts also perished. One ship loaded with Hessians was driven all the way across the Atlantic, landing at Cornwall on the coast of England. It was a full month before the last of the dispersed ships could assemble at Tybee Island at the mouth of the Savannah River. Here the damaged ships were repaired, supplies were replenished and the fleet changed course to north for Charleston, dropping anchor at Seabrook Island, thirty miles below the target city, on February 10, 1780. On the following day, Clinton's troops began going ashore.

Charleston occupied the narrow end of a low-lying peninsula formed by the broad Ashley River on the west and the equally wide Cooper on the east. These two streams converged at the tip of the peninsula to flow into Charleston Harbor, which was bounded on the north by the mainland and Sullivan's Island—scene of the 1776 repulse—and on the south by James and Morris islands. Two forts constituted the harbor defenses: Moultrie (formerly Sullivan's) on Sullivan's Island and Johnson on James Island. Fort Moultrie had fallen into disrepair and Fort Johnson was in ruins, so the harbor was undefended against enemy warships.

Charleston was also vulnerable on the land side. Its peninsula was connected to the mainland by a long and narrow isthmus called the Neck. Obvious to anyone but a commander as inept as Benjamin Lincoln was the fact that all that a besieging force needed to do was blockade the harbor and seize the Neck and thence to advance on the city by digging siege parallels. Obvious also but to Lincoln, Governor John Rutledge and the South Carolina Assembly was that other ineluctable fact: Charleston simply could not be held. Yet the assembly voted unanimously to defend the city "until the last extremity." Here, if not bluster, was a misplaced resolution when the equally valuable virtue of discretion was required. It may have been that this decision was born of a fear that a general decline in Southern morale would ensue if the city were abandoned without a fight. Yet, better to suffer lowered morale than to lose an army. Morale, incidentally, was very low among the mainland militia because of the severe epidemic of smallpox that had broken out in Charleston. Many of the militiamen refused to come to the city's assistance for fear of the disease, openly declaring that "they dreaded that disorder more than the enemy." Also the South Carolina Line of Continentals, through death, wounds, desertion and the expiration of enlistments, had dwindled from 2,400 men to about 800.

Along with the 800 Continentals, Lincoln at first commanded about 3,600 men, to be augmented later by 1,450 North Carolina and Virginia Continentals whom Washington sent south from his New Jersey encampments. Eventually Lincoln's strength would rise to well over 5,000 soldiers.

Clinton had brought about 6,000 soldiers with him from Georgia, and this number would be more than doubled in the spring, when Lord Charles Cornwallis and Lord Francis Rawdon would arrive with strong reinforcements, so that his ultimate command numbered 13,500 men supported by a strong fleet.

Immediately after entering the broad waters of Edisto Inlet to land unopposed on Seabrook, Clinton sent part of his fleet to blockade the harbor, but then, having acted with celerity on the foreign element of water, he moved with tortoise-like speed on his own element of land. Even Howe on Long Island and at White Plains, or Cornwallis at the Assunpink, moved more rapidly than Clinton did at Charleston. First Clinton seized the Stono River Ferry connecting Johns Island with adjoining James Island; then he occupied Johns Island itself, bridging the narrow but rapid strait or creek known as Wappoo Cut that separated James Island from the mainland. Then he crossed the cut to erect artillery batteries on the west bank of the Ashley menacing the town. These were all the right moves, but they were made at that languid pace so characteristic of the British Army in America, and thus it was not until March 29 that Clinton's guns were safely emplaced on the peninsula itself.

Yet this delay worked to the disadvantage not of its author, but to that of the defending Americans, who mistakenly counted it as a heaven-sent opportunity to make their defenses impregnable. The legislature having invested Governor Rutledge with dictatorial powers, this energetic gentlemen impressed six hundred slaves for work on the fortifications. Under the direction of two French engineers—the Chevaliers de Cambray and de Laumoy—the bondsmen dug a "wet ditch," or water-filled moat, across the Neck, emplacing a tightly packed barricade of abatis to its front and formidable redoubts mounting artillery to its rear. At the center of these positions stood "the Citadel"—a "horn-work" built of stone and considered invincible. In all, some sixty-six guns stood on these new lines. At the town's southern tip was a redoubt mounting sixteen cannon, six small forts with four to nine guns each guarded the Ashley River side on the west, on the Cooper side were seven of these little works with from three to seven guns apiece. A flotilla of nine medium or small ships—some bought from Admiral d'Estaing—was assigned to protect the waterfront. But their 244-gun armament could hardly challenge the firepower of Arbuthnot's monsters, with their 650 cannons. These reinforced defenses, rather than securing the city, were to prove to be its undoing, for the Americans now believed themselves strong enough "to hazard their lives and fortunes upon the event of a siege." Much faith was also placed in an emissary sent to Cuba to beg the help of the Spanish governor there. Now that Spain was also an enemy of Great Britain, it was naively assumed that such succor would be immediate, but the governor, with no authority to weaken his own defenses, declined the honor.

It was this seemingly iron ring that induced the Charlestonians and their Southern allies to enter Cloud Cuckoo Land. They did not or would not see that their defenses were a ring within a ring. The Almighty was not on their side, as they thought, but rather, as the always cynical Napoleon would say, "On the side of the big battalions," and these belonged to Clinton. Worse, the American commander was a general in name only. A fat and fatuous failure wherever he had "fought," he did not have the wit to see that he could neither retreat nor reinforce his army unless he kept open some safe route into or out of the city, what is called a "line of communications." He relied upon a mixed force of the new and untried Continental cavalry, the remnants of Pulaski's dragoons and similar detachments under General Isaac Huger and Colonel William Washington and a "body" of raw militia to hold Monck's Corner at the head of the Cooper River, about thirty miles to the north. In all, Huger's command numbered less than a thousand men.

In the meantime, Clinton began to move with more speed. After crossing the Ashley in force, he broke ground a little more than a mile above the American positions across the middle of the Neck and began to dig parallels, that is, trenches cut into the ground parallel to the enemy fortifications for the purpose of covering the besieging force. While thus closing the gap on land, he also sealed off the city by water.

On April 11 eight British frigates, under Admiral Arbuthnot, upped anchor in Five Fathom Hole at the mouth of Charleston Harbor, spreading their sails to a favoring wind and making for Fort Moultrie on Sullivan's Island. Because Moultrie was thought to be invulnerable, crowds of spectators lined the Battery at the tip of the Charleston Peninsula to watch the discomfiture of the British, while the shore of James Island was packed with British redcoats and Hessians in black and green cheering the fleet onward. It was a holiday scene—to be repeated nearly a century later with the opening shots of the Civil War on Fort Sumter—with the white of the enemy's billowing sails standing stark against a blue sky reflected in the wind-whipped harbor waves or blotched by the puffs of cannon smoke shredded by the wind. But it was no contest, except for a lucky shot from Moultrie that toppled the mainmast of the *Richmond,* killing or wounding twenty-seven sailors and Marines.

Many Charlestonians were shocked by the ease with which the British fleet slipped past their most formidable fort to take possession of the harbor and thus seal the city off by sea. Soon small boats, loaded with passengers and their personal possessions, could be seen crossing the Cooper to the sanctuary of the mainland. But in another three days that route would also be slammed shut by probably the two most successful British leaders of the war: Colonel Banastre Tarleton and Major Patrick Ferguson.

Banastre Tarleton was born on August 21, 1754, one of seven children of the wealthy John Tarleton, mayor of Liverpool and descendant of a family founded in the middle of the sixteenth century. He was a healthy and extremely active boy, red haired, hot tempered, excelling far more on the playing fields than in the classroom—although he did in his childhood and youth display a proficiency in Latin that led his father to register him in the Middle Temple of London's Inns of Court. But Banastre's love of Latin could not be translated into a fondness for Coke or Blackstone. Rather he became enamored of the theater and an ardent admirer of the painted beauties of Drury Lane. He was by then physically mature, short but powerfully built, proud in bearing and already attractive to women. Banastre also thought of following a military career, having become friendly at University College, Oxford, where he began his law studies, with Francis Rawdon, a thin, gangling youth who was the son of Sir John

Rawdon of County Down, Ireland. Francis left Oxford to join the British Army, and after his father was created Earl of Moira, he assumed the courtesy title of Lord Rawdon, while earning the unsought distinction of being perhaps the ugliest man in the British Army. Rawdon's choice of a military career was to have an influence on Banastre Tarleton, but not until after Tarleton had exhausted a handome legacy of five thousand pounds left him by his father. By 1775 Tarleton had just enough money remaining to purchase a cornet's commission in the First Regiment of Dragoon Guards, after which he sailed for America.

Under Cornwallis he proved himself an able commander of dragoons. He was bold, shrewd and quick to strike. Like many such resolute commanders, he was arrogant, insolent and domineering, and in battle coldly calculating, cruel, hard-hearted and vindictive. As a cavalry leader he was probably unmatched on either side, and he made his name a bloody anathema in the South, so that by the time Clinton sent him up to Monck's Corner, he was feared and detested as "Bloody" or "Butcher" Tarleton. His British Legion, better known as "Tarleton's Tories," was composed of American Loyalists who were famous for their dashing green uniforms and their thirst for Patriot blood. It was like all legions of the era—a mixed formation of dragoons and infantry, although the foot soldiers were also mounted at times or rode behind the dragoons.

Major Patrick Ferguson had similar antecedents of wealth and birth, though he was not Tarleton's equal in fame. He was a Scots officer who had joined the British Army at the age of fifteen. Coming to the American war at thirty-six, he was celebrated for his gallantry and courtesy and for his fame as the inventor of a breech-loading rifle that could fire up to six rounds a minute from a stationary position, and four at a marching pace. Such a weapon could have been almost as revolutionary as the invention of gunpowder itself. In 1776 Ferguson gave two demonstrations of his remarkable rifle: one to a board of generals and another to King George III. All who witnessed them were astonished. In place of the heavy, clumsy, inaccurate Brown Bess, here was a weapon as accurate as the American frontier rifle, but one that fired far faster using a new pointed bullet, rather than the old round one, and could even fire while wet! It weighed half as much as the nine-pound Brown Bess, which had been issued seventy years earlier, and because a Ferguson rifle could be loaded lying down, rather than standing, it was much safer. Yet because of the glacial speed of the Board of Ordnance, its production was limited to two hundred. If manufactured in the tens of thousands, it might have crushed the American rebellion and made the British redcoat the master of European warfare.

Ferguson was of medium height, slender, but strong and athletic. His serious square face earned him the sobriquet "the Bulldog" from his admiring troops. He was also a dead shot with either a rifle or a pistol, as well as a formidable swordsman, even though he had shifted to his left hand after being wounded in the right at the Battle of the Brandywine. During that battle, he had another opportunity to change the course of history. With his snipers all armed with the Ferguson rifle, he was on the edge of a wood when he saw two American officers riding about a hundred yards away. One of them was a big man "dressed in dark green or blue, mounted on a bay horse, with a remarkable large hat." Ferguson ordered "three good shots to steal near to them and fire at them, but the idea disgusted me. I recalled the order." The horsemen disappeared, but the big man returned. Ferguson stepped out of the wood, a crack shot carrying the great rifle he had invented. He did not want to shoot the man in the back, but thought that he might take him prisoner. Then:

> On my calling, he stopped; but, after looking at me, proceeded. I again drew his attention, and made signs to him to stop, but he slowly continued his way. As I was within that distance at which, in the quickest firing, I could have lodged half a dozen ball in or about him before he was out of my reach—I had only to determine [what to do]. But it was not pleasant to fire at the back of an individual, who was acquitting himself very cooly of his duty. So I let him alone.

The big man, of course, was George Washington, and when Patrick Ferguson later learned this, he remarked, with typical gallantry: "I am not sorry that I did not know at the time who it was." Like Tarleton, Ferguson hated Yankees with a fierce venom and was almost as infamous for his relentless plunder of American civilians. His American Volunteers were also Loyalists, a corps of trained riflemen, although they did not carry his fearful rifle.

Both these units were joined by about fourteen hundred British light infantry under Colonel James Webster. They outnumbered the Americans of Huger and William Washington by about three to one and were seasoned veterans, infinitely better trained.

On April 13, 1780, as Tarleton's column trotted north toward Monck's Corner, his advance guard saw a black slave dart into the woods beside the road as though in fright. Giving chase, they captured him and searched him, finding on his person a letter from General Huger to General Lincoln. The letter gave the disposition of the American troops in detail, while the slave, "for a few dollars," was also helpful. Huger's cavalry had been posted on the Charleston side of the Cooper, with the rest of his forces on the other side. His militia was stationed at Biggin Church commanding Biggin Bridge. With this lucky bit of intelligence, Tarleton decided to make a surprise night attack.

Commanding his legion to strict silence, Tarleton proceeded slowly up the road. With dark, his dragoons dismounted to walk. At three o'clock in the morning of April 14 they encountered Huger's mounted sentries, driving them before them and pursuing them right into the American camp, where they charged the stunned Yankee horse with such ferocity that the Americans broke and fled on foot into a swamp. General Huger and Colonel Washington were among the fugitives, preferring to risk the jaws of snakes and alligators than the wrath of Ferguson's rifles and Tarleton's sabers. Major Paul Vernier, commanding Pulaski's Legion, and a few other officers and men who stood their ground were killed or wounded, while Vernier, horribly mangled by those same sabers, was carried dying into a nearby house and laid upon a bare wooden table. There, gasping and cursing, he condemned his comrades for their cowardice and damned the British for sabering him after he had asked for quarter. But that, of course, was Banastre Tarleton's policy: he never gave quarter if there was a chance to slaughter terrified men.

After this skirmish, known as the Battle of Biggin's Bridge, three of Tarleton's green-clad dragoons broke into the plantation home of the ardent Tory Sir John Colleton where local women had taken refuge. Singling out the beauties, they prepared to rape them. A physician who sought to defend them was slashed several times. During this scuffle, the women escaped, seeking the protection of British officers. Even the chivalrous Major Ferguson demanded that the miscreants be instantly executed. But Colonel Webster, the overall commander, sent them back to Charleston instead, where they were convicted and subjected to a flogging so prolonged and bloody that death by comparison would have been indeed merciful.

In this skirmish the British had only three soldiers wounded, while the rebels suffered fifteen killed, seventeen wounded and another hundred taken captive. More important to Tarleton was the acquisition of eighty-three fine horses, for so many of his mounts had been lost in the storm that many of his troopers were riding little "tackies" that were barely stronger than ponies. Although Tarleton had indeed cut Lincoln's line of communications, the British force was not sufficient to patrol all "the forks and passes" of the Cooper River area. But then Lords Rawdon and Cornwallis arrived with reinforcements, and Clinton ordered Cornwallis to occupy and hold the quarter between the Cooper and the Atlantic Ocean. The British besieging army now stretched from the Edisto to the Ashley to the Cooper, and from the Cooper to the Atlantic. With Tarleton's Tory dragoons patrolling the countryside to the north, Benjamin Lincoln's army was effectively bottled up. Nothing or no one could leave or enter Charleston.

On April 10 the first of Clinton's parallels was completed, about six hundred to eight hundred yards above the American lines on the Neck. On the twelfth his big siege guns were emplaced: fifteen twenty-four-pounders and a huge mortar. They began a heavy fire on the city while sappers, working during the nights, began a second parallel. The use of carcasses, those perforated iron balls stuffed with burning pitch that had burned down Charlestown, Massachusetts, during the Battle of Bunker Hill, likewise set fires burning in Charleston, South Carolina. By April 19 the approaches were within 250 yards of the town. Hessian riflemen could now exchange shots with the Yankees, although little damage was done. But the constant bombardment was taking the town apart, street by street, steeple by steeple.

Now an acrimonious debate ensued between the townspeople, who were anxious to hold the city, and Lincoln and his officers, who were finally convinced that it was indefensible. The civilians accused the soldiers of a "cowardly" intent to leave them "to the mercy of an enraged enemy." If there were to be an evacuation, they argued heatedly, they wanted to be brought off along with the troops—a manifest impossibility to anyone able to take a calm and reasonable view of the situation. Meanwhile, the faint hearts and the secret Tories did everything possible to widen the gap between the two factions.

For their part, Lincoln's field officers, aghast at their chief's timidity and ceaseless vacillation, attempted to stiffen his spine by urging him "to take absolute command over every person in this garrison," by which they meant every able-bodied person in Charleston, white as well as black, to be impressed into service on the works or to relieve the exhausted Continentals. They also suggested that the numerous officers without commands be allowed to escape so that they might be useful elsewhere, and pleaded with him to be firm and to "accept the advice of such military councils as you may think proper to be called upon." But Lincoln was not firm. He even allowed Lieutenant Governor Christopher Gadsden to be admitted to his councils of war—an anomaly if ever there was one—at which he vehemently opposed evacuation of the military. Why there should have been such a furor over "evacuation" is unclear, inasmuch as it must have been plain to everyone that no numerous body—of soldiers or civilians—could now get out of Charleston. Even escaping officers would have to attempt it singly or in twos. Yet the debate continued, arousing such mutual animosity and recrimination that one of Gadsden's councillors swore that if the soldiers attempted to withdraw, the townspeople would burn their boats, open the city to the enemy and join them in attacking American troops.

On April 21, Benjamin Lincoln at last bit the bullet, proposing to Clinton a capitulation on incredibly naive terms: an unmolested withdrawal by American troops with full honors of war, allowing them to march up the Cooper's east bank to whatever destination they chose. Clinton curtly refused, and the so-called battle continued—small action by minor skirmish.

Two hundred Continentals wielding bayoneted muskets attacked the British parallels on the Neck, killing and wounding a few and taking a few prisoners. The British overran a small fort on Hadrell's Point on the mainland across the Cooper. Arbuthnot landed a party of sailors and Marines below Fort Moultrie, and the garrison of two hundred men surrendered without firing a shot. Tarleton attacked the remnants of Huger's cavalry at Lenud's Ferry, on the Santee, scattering them while killing or capturing thirty or forty of them. By May 8 the British approaches were so close to the American lines on the Neck that the soldiers on both sides could exchange shots and insults and British sappers were able to drain the "wet ditch" dry. Obviously prepared for the final assault, Sir Henry Clinton again demanded a surrender.

Lincoln was trapped and he knew he was trapped, but he still stalled—asking for a truce to discuss terms. But neither Clinton nor Arbuthnot would consent to Lincoln's reiterated demands.

Then for some unknown reason, the American garrison renewed hostilities. Some two hundred guns on the Neck opened fire simultaneously. Shells that collided with each other burst so that "it appeared as if the stars were falling to the earth." It was an aimless and admittedly futile exhibition. An American cannon firing low-trajectory shot could not possibly drop a shell inside the approaches. Only vertical fire mortars could do so, and even they, only with luck. It was an outburst of sound and fury truly signifying nothing except the relief of the frustrated feelings of the beleaguered garrison. In return, the superior British ordnance responded with a cannonading that set many houses and buildings on fire and made the night so hideous for the townspeople that on the following morning they dropped all opposition to submission and actually demanded it.

General Lincoln then accepted Clinton's terms, which were a little more generous than those given to Burgoyne at Saratoga. The militia were to be allowed to go to their homes, being regarded, along with the civilians, as prisoners on parole. At eleven o'clock in the morning of May 12, the Continentals marched out with colors cased and their drums beating a *Turkish* march!—probably to forfend against any European military air being misconstrued as a violation of the terms—after which they piled their arms beside the Citadel. The militia followed them later in the day, and General Moultrie, already incensed at being made captive, was outraged to see that there were actually three times as many militia as had served on the line—suggesting that they had been in hiding throughout the siege.

So Charleston fell to Sir Henry Clinton, along with about 5,500 imprisoned Continentals, 391 guns, about 6,000 muskets, 33,000 rounds of small-arms ammunition, over 8,000 round shot, 376 barrels of powder, all the American ships in the harbor and a great quantity of other military stores. The siege had cost the British only 76 men killed and 138 wounded, against 89 Continentals killed and 138 wounded, and about a dozen casualties in the militia. The Siege of Charleston, then, could not properly be called a battle—yet it was the most disastrous defeat in the history of American arms and would remain so until 1942, with the fall of the Philippines to Japan. It remains, however, the most shameful. Benjamin Lincoln simply did not fight. His apologists, such as David Ramsay, have written of his "judicious and spirited conduct in baffling" Cornwallis for more than three months so that "British plans were deranged, and North Carolina ... was saved for the remainder of the year 1780." But this statement implies that Charleston was a delaying action, which it never was; and Lincoln's defense of the city, so far from being spirited or energetic, was actually lethargic. Cornwallis certainly did not lose time because of anything or anyone but his own decision to employ eighteenth-century siege tactics in order not to lose soldiers who were attacking Americans when they were the most dangerous: inside fixed positions.

Instead of constantly harassing Cornwallis's sappers by repeated night attacks against them and constantly using mortars to drop shells into their trenches and thus compelling the British commander, if not to change his tactics completely, at least to risk one major assault on the Neck, the repulse of which would greatly diminish the glory of his victory, Lincoln contented himself with one brief and halfhearted sally of two hundred men, after which he sat still while Cornwallis's approaches crawled steadily closer. He also should not have let stronger personalities, such as Governor John Rutledge, dissuade him from saving his army in the interests of holding the indefensible city. He paid far too much attention to the entreaties and threats of the townspeople, instead of listening to his officers who urged him to abandon the city and save his army, and although it is, in part, understandable because of the inevitable storm of criticism from Southerners that such a decision by a New Englander would arouse, to lose both the city *and* his army was absolutely inexcusable.

Lincoln's one great error, of course, was not to do all possible to keep a line of retreat open. To expect Monck's Corner and environs to be held by only five hundred men simply reflects the timorous nature that was his undoing at Savannah and again at Charleston. Thus, by omission, rather than by commission, he departed unconsciously from Washington's stated policy of attrition, a steady assault upon the British will to fight while avoiding decisive battle with a superior foe. So the enemy victories at Savannah and Charleston seemed to have detached Georgia and South Carolina from the rebel cause, although it may be said that they also served it by detaching Benjamin Lincoln from the Continental Army.

Clinton made wise use of his victory, ignoring Hessian entreaties to be turned loose among the Yankee captives, whom they blamed for an enormous explosion that killed more than fifty British soldiers and that occurred because of the careless handling of captured loaded muskets. He also disappointed the Tories who were clamoring for rebel blood by adopting instead a conciliatory policy of granting pardons and paroles. His clemency was so successful that no fewer than two thousand Patriots volunteered to fight for King George if they could oppose French or Spanish soldiers, rather than their countrymen. But then Colonel Banastre Tarleton reinvigorated the spirit of mutual hatred in South Carolina.

Through spies Tarleton learned of the presence of a force of about 500 men—380 Virginia Continentals and the remnants of William Washington's cavalry—who were encamped at the Waxhaws, a district near North Carolina, under the command of Colonel Abraham Buford. Buford had been making for Charleston until he heard of the city's fall. Turning, he had headed for the North Carolina line. Warned of the approach of the Tarleton's Tories under their redoubtable and legendary leader, he halted and formed his soldiers in an open wood to the right of the road he was following. He gave orders not to fire until the enemy dragoons were only ten paces away, an incredible command, since the mounted survivors of the first volley would be upon them with slashing sabers before they could reload! That is exactly what happened. Some Tory saddles were emptied, but the main body, with fierce cries and yells and slashing, flashing sabers, fell in fury upon these effectually disarmed Americans and began to slaughter them.

Buford at once knew he was beaten and sent an aide forward waving a white flag of truce. He was shot down while Tarleton, whose horse had been shot from under him—an excuse for not having seen the white flag—allowed his aroused Loyalists to continue the massacre of defenseless men begging for mercy. This was "Tarleton's Quarter," a byword for the slaughter of surrendered men. In this merciless episode the British lost only five men killed and fourteen wounded against more than a hundred Americans slain, probably double that number either wounded or running for life and two hundred taken captive. Among the prisoners was thirteen-year-old Andrew Jackson. Commanded by a Tory officer to clean his boots, Jackson calmly replied: "Sir, I am a prisoner-of-war and claim to be treated as such." With this, the Tory struck at him with his sword, and as the boy instinctively threw up his arm to deflect it, he was slashed on his arm and head. But he was later released on his mother's plea of his extreme youth.

The Waxhaws massacre and the Tories' open revenge upon those Patriots who had abused them when they were in the ascendancy gradually began to unravel Clinton's work of conciliation. Clinton believed before he sailed for New York, leaving Lord Cornwallis in charge, that he had pacified South Carolina. But the Palmetto State soon erupted into what was nothing less than a civil war. Tories and Patriots shot at each other in the woods and on the streets of towns. It was almost always death by ambush, rarely by confrontation or a shoot-out. Long after the war was over a rebel magistrate boasted of how he had shot down ninety-nine Loyalists in cold blood and was disappointed when the advent of peace prevented him from rounding out the score.

South Carolina especially became a cockpit of murder, arson, rape and robbery. In an eighteenth-century South that was fully as violent and lawless as the "Wild West" was to become after the conquest of Mexico, the Palmetto State was inhabited by perhaps the hardest, cruelest and most bloodthirsty Americans, eager to kill and torture without restraint once the fact of civil war had made chaos of what had been at best the barest law and order. Patriots and Loyalists fought each other with a ferocity that is possible only between brothers and former friends and neighbors. Individually, it was conflict of both shoot-out confrontation and the sly art of bushwhack. But there was also group warfare between disciplined and well-organized bands of irregulars. Around the old Cheraw district civil war was especially vicious, and the Loyalist Colonel William Cunningham was probably the fiercest and most murderous leader on both sides.

Cunningham did indeed deserve his sobriquet "Bloody Bill." It was said that his implacable hatred of Patriots sprang from the brutal murder of his crippled and epileptic brother John. It is also said that because he did not have a horse, Cunningham, to avenge his brother, walked 160 miles from Ninety-six to Savannah to kill Captain William Ritchie, the reputed murderer. The slaying was all the more suggestive of the fratricidal fury inflaming both sides in that Ritchie and Bloody Bill had once been comrades in arms in the Cherokee War of 1776. For this crime his cousin Patrick Cunningham rewarded him with the gift of Ringtail, one of the state's most famous horses.

Mounted on this splendid steed, Bloody Bill, with three hundred Tories at his back, surprised a body of only thirty Patriots under Captain James Butler in November 1781. The Patriots, holed up in an unfinished log cabin, were so badly outnumbered that they surrendered unconditionally. They should have known Bloody Bill better, for he butchered on the spot all but two escaped rebels. Some time later Colonel Joseph Hayes and fifteen men also gave themselves up. Another Patriot mistake, for Cunningham murdered all the surrendered rebels but Hayes and another man, whom he hanged. When the gallows broke, Bloody Bill drew his saber to hack both the half-strangled Patriots to death.

As British power in South Carolina waned and American strength grew, Cunningham was at last defeated, fittingly by rebels under Captain William Butler, the son of the murdered James Butler. But Bloody Bill managed to escape, surviving the war to become one of the leading Yankee haters in exile.

Terror and atrocity, however, were not the exclusive tactics of the Tories, for the Patriots also showed themselves capable of slaughtering both the innocent and the defenseless. Their leaders were only somewhat less ruthless, three of them rising to the rank of brigadier general: Thomas Butler, Andrew Pickens and Francis Marion—the last having entered American history under the well-earned and romantic sobriquet "the Swamp Fox."

Francis Marion was born in midwinter 1732, at Goatfield Plantation in Berkeley County, South Carolina, the descendant of a Huguenot family that fled France in 1685. He was a puny baby, so frail that he was not expected to live. "I have it on good authority," said Peter Horry, his comrade in arms, "that this great soldier at his birth was not larger than a New England lobster, and might easily have been put in a quart pot." At fifteen, still dwarflike, Francis went to sea, encouraged by his parents, who thought that a sea voyage might stimulate his growth. Oddly enough they were right, but Francis had to endure shipwreck, five days in an open boat without food or drink except the flesh and blood of a little dog, watching two of his shipmates die before their craft reached land. From this ordeal, wrote Horry: "His constitution seemed renewed, his frame commenced a second and rapid growth, while his cheeks, quitting their pale, suet-colored cast, assumed a bright and healthy olive." At maturity, Francis Marion was wiry, swarthy and short, with a long aquiline nose, a strong chin, a high forehead and piercing, steady black eyes. During the Cherokee War, he was known as a brave and skillful soldier and a superb horseman.

Marion was forty-eight when the war began, yet he was among the first to take the field, proving himself a born partisan leader. His men were seldom-paid volunteers, untrained in formal warfare, wielding crude weapons, such as sabers hammered from wood saws or hunting muskets or what they could capture from the enemy. They were nevertheless children of the swamp forests and watery labyrinths of the South Carolina low country. Tough and resilient, they needed none of the logistical support required by a large, conventional army, but lived and fought on a diet of cornmeal, molasses, sweet potatoes, hominy and hominy grits, augmented by fish and game taken in the swamp forests or the stringy flesh of the wild cattle and pigs that roamed the woods. There is a famous story of a British officer who came under a flag to Marion's headquarters on Snow's Island. Accepting an invitation to dinner, the officer was dismayed to sit down to a meal consisting solely of sweet potatoes roasted in the ashes of a fire. Returning to Charleston, he is said to have refused to serve any longer against such a dedicated enemy.

For his men, Marion deplored the absence of such amenities as rum, wine or other spirits, even though he himself drank nothing stronger than water mixed with vinegar, the refreshment of the Roman armies and the eighteenth-century soldiers of France. Marion always believed that his drink's purifying qualities kept him healthier than his troops. They were devoted to their selfless leader, who always rode into battle at their head, never entering it, preferring instead to sit his horse calmly, his black eyes keenly searching for the moment of opportunity when he would signal the attack, or warily watching for the first sign of hesitation among his men when he would call for a withdrawal. Though he was fearless in combat, he had so little taste for drawing blood himself that on one occasion, being engulfed in the melee of battle, he tried to draw his short infantry officer's sword and found, to his dismay, that it had rusted to its scabbard.

Although Marion was in the forefront of the give-and-take of the constant raiding warfare raging between Patriots and Tories, his great reputation as a commander of irregulars was won against Cornwallis's regulars. His favorite tactic when pursued by redcoats was to retire at his own pace until he reached the ford or bridge of a stream. Concealing his men near it, he would wait for the enemy to arrive. The first glimpse of a scarlet coat through the underbrush produced a murderous volley, followed by the cries of the stricken mixed with the high, yipping fox-hunter cries of Marion's men retreating even deeper into the swamps. It was thus that he earned his famous nickname, given to him by a frustrated Banastre Tarleton, who, finally wearying of his fruitless pursuit of a phantom, declared that "the devil himself could not catch the damned old fox."

Lord Cornwallis suffered similar frustration. Nevertheless, he remained undaunted, for this able and ambitious commander had at last received what he desired with all his heart: independent command.

★ 59 ★

LORD CHARLES CORNWALLIS

On December 31, 1738, Charles Cornwallis was born into one of the oldest noble families in Britain. For four centuries the Cornwallises had been prominent peers and probably went even further back in time to Norman or even Saxon England. The family name itself, plus the appearance of Cornish choughs, or crowlike birds, on the Cornwallis coat of arms, suggest that it had its roots in the county of Cornwall in southwestern England. But at some point in the unlighted past, some unknown ancestor must have journeyed east to settle in Suffolk, and it was there that Thomas Cornwallis, onetime sheriff of London, established his estate in the village of Brome some time before his death in 1384. It is from him that the family took its lineage.

Two centuries later one of its most famous sons, Sir Thomas Cornwallis, scandalized the family by serving the Catholic Queen Mary and adjusting his faith to suit his service. He built a manor called Brome Hall. Another pair of centuries passed before the first marquis emerged, and during that interval the Cornwallises established a reputation as sober barons who were devoted to their soveriegn and had returned to the Church of England, despite the appearance every generation or so of some troublesome "sport," who, by engaging either in political controversy or marital infidelity or quarreling with his neighbors, attached an unwelcome notoriety to Brome Hall.

The name Brome, incidentally, appears in the family title after one Baron Cornwallis rose two steps in the peerage in the eighteenth century, taking as new titles Viscount Brome and Earl Cornwallis. Thereafter the oldest son of each successive Earl Cornwallis received the courtesy title Viscount Brome. Actually, when Charles Cornwallis, Viscount Brome, was born, the family no longer lived at the manor of that name but at Culford, a less imposing estate that had been inherited through marriage. The Cornwallises, always short of money, were unable to improve it.

It was at Culford that Charles grew up, learning to ride almost as soon as he could walk and to shoot not long after. The woods around Culford abounded in grouse and pheasants, as well as fox, which Charles exuberantly pursued when he was riding to hounds. In his boyhood he showed promise of the mature man of strength, will and stamina that he would become. At Eton he learned that he belonged to a privileged group: the peers of the realm, some two hundred of them who, by birthright, held a special claim to the high offices of the country and those financial rewards—usually more eagerly sought—that went with them.

In the eighteenth century Eton was Britain's outstanding public school. Founded in 1440 by Henry VI, its original purpose was to train local poor boys for the clergy. After Henry VIII broke with Rome, it shifted to secular education, and although it continued to instruct youths from lower- or middle-class families, it emerged in the seventeenth century as the fashionable school for children of the aristocracy. As such, the school carefully fostered class distinction. As an aristocrat, young Lord Brome ate and lived in town, not on campus, and on the days of their patron saint—either St. George of England, St. Patrick of Ireland, St. Andrew of Scotland or St. David of Wales—the English, Irish, Scots and Welsh noblemen had the privilege of dining with the headmaster. They also could bring their own tutors to Eton, another custom that cultivated their sense of superiority, so that they looked down on the assistant masters who taught at Eton, actually defying them when they sought to restrain them from bullying the younger boys.

Much as the sanctity of rank might be revered, Eton was far from being an incubator for the coddling of young nobles. Rank there was indeed in the various "forms" or grades, but within each rank life at Eton was a jungle. Those "playing fields of Eton," made famous by Wellington's remark that it was on them that he had won his victories, were not for the faint-hearted. Here the students fought each other or tried to maim each other while playing cricket, football or hockey, and here Lord Brome was struck so forcefully in the eye during a hockey game that it left the lid permanently puffed and raised, conferring on him a lifelong quizzical expression. Punishment at Eton, as elsewhere in the public schools, was corporal and brutal, and it was a rare student—noble or no—who escaped a caning.

How young Lord Brome fared is not known, although before he left he had a reputation for being a "very military" youth. When the passion for the glory of arms seized him is also not known, but it might have occurred as a boy at Culford when he would be enchanted by tales of foreign campaigns told by his uncle, General Edward Cornwallis. Thus after Eton he did not go on to Oxford or Cambridge; rather, a few weeks before his eighteenth birthday his father purchased for him a commission as an ensign in the First, or Grenadier, Guards. Almost immediately this high-hearted youth—physically mature now, with a medium height and heavy build that would become corpulent over the years—decided that in the absence of British military schools, he would seek instruction in foreign academies when he took the customary Grand Tour of the Continent. Through his father's friendship with the Duke of Cumberland, he obtained the king's permission to travel abroad before joining his regiment, and he crossed the Channel in 1757, accompanied by one Captain de Roguin, a veteran of the War of the Austrian Succession (King George's War).

Brome settled at Turin, Italy, to attend the famous military school there, enrolling after an audience with the king of Sardinia. His instruction included dancing, German, tactics, mathematics and fortifications. It lasted for about three months, more than enough to give him a military education superior to other youths of his rank. Thereafter he would avidly steep himself in military history. Now hoping to join his regiment, he found, to his dismay, that it had been sent to Germany to help Frederick of Prussia defend King George's Hanover lands against the French. Hurrying to Germany, he attached himself to Prince Ferdinand's army as a volunteer, and after his regiment arrived became an aide-de-camp to the marquis of Granby, then a lieutenant general in His Majesty's forces. Brome remained in Germany for four years, rising to the rank of lieutenant colonel in the Twelfth foot. An admirable staff officer, he never received the active command he desired so hungrily. But he showed himself to be brave, determined and self-reliant, as well as hardy and healthy in the extreme. His service ended in July 1762, when, learning that his father had died, he returned home to become the second Earl Cornwallis. In November he took his seat in the House of Lords.

Lord Charles Cornwallis seems to have made a smooth transition from the life of a soldier to the civilian career of a peer, charged with providing for his brothers and sisters and overseeing the estate that he had inherited. At first, he seems to have felt obliged to attend the endless round of balls, masquerades and private parties that were the obsession of his neighbors, but then, having no fondness for either cards or dancing or the bottle, he gradually withdrew into a valued domestic tranquillity enlivened by his passion for fox hunting. In 1768, as he neared the age of thirty, he married Jemima Tullekin Jones, the daughter of an army colonel. She gave him a son, another Charles and Lord Brome, and a daughter, Mary. It was a close family, with Cornwallis so devoted to his wife that in the year of their marriage he retired from active politics.

During his brief career in the House of Lords, he voted mostly as a Whig, to the dismayed surprise of his friend King George III, opposing the Stamp Act and voting for its repeal and, along with only five other peers, against the accompanying Declaratory Act by which a pouting Parliament declared that if the abhorred tax had been a mistake, it had still possessed the *right* to impose it. Generally, Cornwallis showed himself in sympathy with the colonists, yet inexplicably remained within the king's good graces, receiving from him such profitable offices as chief justice in Eyre, vice-treasurer of Ireland, privy councillor and constable of the Tower of London. Perhaps this seemingly paradoxical friendship continued to flourish simply because for all Cornwallis's Whiggery, King George *liked* him. Both men were sober, dignified, temperate and devoted to their families, although the humorless sovereign was not as understanding and good-natured as was Cornwallis. Thus His Majesty was agreeably surprised when, early in November 1775, Lord George Germain informed him that Cornwallis thought it his duty to help suppress the rebellion. In the following month Major General Cornwallis hurried to Ireland to take command of the Charleston expedition, knowing full well that when he arrived in North Carolina, he would have to relinquish command to his friend and senior officer, Major General Henry Clinton.

After the Charleston repulse and the failure to catch Washington in New Jersey, the friendship between Cornwallis and Clinton seemed about to founder on the rock of mutual dissatisfaction with the other's generalship. But then Cornwallis, already chafing at perpetually being second in command, received word of his wife's illness and asked Clinton for leave to return to Britain. Sir Henry, now a knight, saw this as an opportunity to use Cornwallis's influence with the king and Germain to plead for reinforcements and granted his request. Sailing on November 27, 1778, in the company of the king's disappointed peace commissioners, Cornwallis arrived in London about a month later. But he did not speak to George or Germain; he only submitted his resignation and hurried to his wife's bedside. He found her so ill that he had no time to press Clinton's appeal for more troops, never once venturing from Culford until she died on February 14, 1779.

Her death shattered Cornwallis. His conviction that his prolonged absence had broken her heart made him inconsolable. "The separation proved too much for her weak nerves to bear," he wrote in his memoirs; "She literally fell a prey to love, sunk beneath the weight of her grief, and died." Now, everything he loved—his home, his young family, the Suffolk countryside—became abhorrent to him. He had to get away from all that reminded him of his beloved wife, even if it meant returning to America and again accepting subordinate command. Both the king and Germain gladly reinstated him as a major general, even bestowing on him a dormant commission as a full general in the event that Clinton was recalled or died. After joining Clinton again in Charleston and replacing him as commander of the Southern army when Sir Henry returned to New York, Cornwallis continued Clinton's systematic plundering of the Patriot plantations along the Ashley and Cooper rivers, while, in a series of small skirmishes from the Waxhaws to Ramsour's Mill, he scattered the Patriots, driving Francis Marion and Thomas Sumter into the swamps and so thoroughly pacifiying Georgia and South Carolina that they appeared to be forever restored to their loyalty to the Crown.

Prepared now to do the same to North Carolina, Cornwallis—like Howe and Clinton before him—was astonished to discover that a new rebel army had risen from the ashes of the old one and was even then, in August 1780, marching toward the vital strong-point and supply depot held by Rawdon at Camden.

★ 60 ★

THE BATTLE OF CAMDEN

After General Washington had sent fifteen hundred Continentals from Virginia and North Carolina marching south to reinforce Charleston—where they, too, were surrendered by the timid Lincoln—he learned that in April 1780 Rawdon and Cornwallis had sailed for the besieged city with reinforcements of their own. To counter them, the American war chief ordered the Maryland and Delaware lines to give "further succor to the Southern States." These were probably the finest troops in the Continental Army, "distinguished for valor" and "represented on nearly every battlefield." They were joined by the First Artillery with eighteen fieldpieces. To command them, Washington chose Baron de Kalb.

Major General Baron Jean de Kalb had no more right to the French aristocratic particle "de" than he had to the German "von" he had adopted early in his military career. Like "von" Steuben, he was a military adventurer, born Johann Kalb, the son of a Bavarian peasant. In 1737 at the age of sixteen he left home to become a soldier. Nothing more is known of him until 1743, when he reappeared as Jean de Kalb, a lieutenant in a French infantry regiment. He had ennobled himself, not out of the dishonest instincts of an imposter, but because he had quickly realized that no commoner might rise to a commission in a European army. And Jean de Kalb, an excellent enlisted man, did rise. By 1747 he was a captain. During the Seven Years' War, he rose to major and lieutenant colonel. After the peace he met and married Anne van Robais, daughter of a wealthy French manufacturer. Upon the death of her father, Anne inherited his estate at Courbevoye, together with his fortune. Somewhere during these years Kalb had made himself a "baron."

De Kalb soon came to the attention of the canny Duc de Choiseul, who sent him to America in 1767 to study whether it would be worthwhile for France to come to the aid of the rebelling Americans. De Kalb toured the colonies extensively, returning to Paris with an exhaustive report, only to find Choiseul preoccupied with European problems. But then when the Americans did revolt, he hurried to Paris in 1776 to obtain a major general's commission, and it was there that he met Lafayette and sailed with him to the New World.

De Kalb had a commanding physical presence, being more than six feet tall and powerfully built. His countenance was cheerful, as well as shrewd. He had a high forehead, clear and searching hazel eyes, an aristocratic nose and a belligerent chin. He was also something of an ascetic, arising before dawn to work until nine, when he ate a slice of dry bread and drank a glass of water, his only drink. At noon he partook of a bowl of soup and a bit of meat, washed down by more water, and for supper, he consumed a replica of his breakfast. Such abstemiousness in food and drink may have accounted for his remarkable stamina. He would walk twenty to thirty miles a day because he preferred that exercise to riding and when on campaign, he suffered every hardship with good-natured resignation. At night he would "arrange his portmanteau as a pillow and, wrapping his great horseman's cloak around him, stretch himself before the fire" to fall almost instantly into a sound sleep. As a soldier, General de Kalb was the soul of gallantry and bravery.

He needed such virtues to lead his force of fourteen hundred Continentals on their long journey—mostly by foot—to South Carolina. Breaking camp at Morristown on April 16, de Kalb soon discovered that he was woefully short of every supply required for such a long march: food, horses and wagons, fodder and tenting equipment. As the little army moved south, the weather turned hotter, and the men became thinner. At Petersburg in southern Virginia, de Kalb was shocked to hear of the fall of Charleston. His mission had been to succor that city, but now he did not know what to do next. He had hoped that as he marched through the southern states he would attract recruits to his command, but there were few volunteers in Virginia and fewer in North Carolina when he arrived at Charlotte. Evidently, the Old North State would care only for its own.

Major General Richard Caswell, with a large force of militia, declined de Kalb's invitation to join him, preferring an independent command and local fame as the scourge of the Loyalists. All the requisitions and requests that de Kalb sent to the governor went unanswered.

In still rising heat, without regular supplies of food, his men, forced by the shortage of transportation to carry their own baggage, grew still thinner and sicker. They were living off the country, foraging as they went, but they found little grain in the granaries of the abandoned farms they passed, and the pens and coops were empty of pigs or chickens. Fearing this hungry army of alien Continentals like a plague of locusts, the farmers had vanished—taking their produce and livestock with them. For meat the Continentals had only the sour and stringy flesh of half-starved cattle that were running wild in the woods or the green corn and unripe fruit of the fields. No prescription for diarrhea or dysentery could be more effective.

Meanwhile, in the North the problem of who should replace the imprisoned Benjamin Lincoln as commander of the Southern Department arose. Though de Kalb was indeed a foreigner, a "rank" that Congress always seemed to find irresistible, he had never cultivated the friendship of the gentlemen in Philadelphia and thus was ignored by them. Washington for his part might have suggested de Kalb, but with Congress obviously unwilling to accept de Kalb, he chose Nathanael Greene, who, with Benedict Arnold still physically unfit for campaigning, was probably his ablest general. Without even consulting Washington, still refusing to believe that the true hero of Saratoga had been Benedict Arnold, Congress selected Horatio Gates.

Gates was at his Virginia plantation when he received word of his appointment. His friend and neighbor Charles Lee warned him: "Take care lest your Northern laurels turn to Southern willows." Ignoring it, Gates hurried south, replacing de Kalb at Rugeley's Mills on July 25. Their meeting was without rancor. Gates was polite, and de Kalb was cheerful and without regrets. While assuming command of the Southern Department, Gates continued de Kalb in command of what he called "the grand army": those pitiful nine hundred remaining of the fourteen hundred Continentals who had left Morristown three months earlier, plus Colonel Charles Armand's Legion—formerly Pulaski's—of sixty horse and sixty foot.

Gates, in his own words, now had "an army without strength, a military chest without money." His was also commanding an alien army surrounded by hostile Tories, facing a victorious enemy strongly posted throughout South Carolina and preparing to march north. Among these posts was Camden, which de Kalb had already selected as his objective, in which decision Gates concurred. Thereafter Gates practically ignored his second in command, and although he seemed to have taken hold with the energy and decision of a military genius, his bustle actually changed nothing for the better. One of his great blunders was to inform his starving troops that they must be prepared to march "at a moment's notice," when, in truth, the only place they were capable of reaching so rapidly was the latrine. Next, Gates disagreed with de Kalb's line of march.

De Kalb's line was about fifty miles longer than the route Gates proposed, but it ran through counties populated by patriotic Scots-Irish, and magazines and hospitals could be provided there. Moreover, it offered the assurance of a friendly country through which to retreat if the attack on Camden failed. But Gates insisted on marching the direct way, even though it possessed every disadvantage: thinly populated and infertile pine barrens, a wilderness of deep sand and swamps calculated to delay wagons, crisscrossed by streams liable to swell and overflow within an hour of heavy rains, while already scoured clean of food and fodder by the enemy and probably the most hostile Tory region in the entire South. When Gates gave the order to march this hard and hungry way, "men and officers looked at each other with blank amazement." What was worse, they were to march immediately "with only a half-ration for today and not even a half-ration for tomorrow."

General de Kalb was stunned and prevailed upon Colonel Otho Williams to remonstrate with Gates. Williams was one of the most respected and revered officers in Gates's army. A full colonel at thirty-one, he was tall and gracious, even elegant. He had been marching with the American army since 1775, having joined Washington in front of Boston. Captured at Fort Washington, he was exchanged in January 1778, when he was named to lead the Sixth Continental Regiment of his native Maryland.

Highly educated and persuasive, he hastened to point out to Gates all the advantages of the longer route, which was the old trading road between Philadelphia and Charleston by which supplies from the north could be received. In support of his argument he presented a paper signed by the leading officers suggesting that this route should be followed. Gates replied that he would call a council of war to discuss the matter, but he never did. On July 27—two days after he took command—his grand army moved out on its nightmare march, the men assured by General Gates that they would receive large issues of rum and rations en route.

It was a lie. There were no such issues. Sergeant Major William Seymour, of the Delaware Line, wrote in his diary that during fourteen days of marching, the men received one half-pound of flour that had to be augmented with unripe fruit that produced the customary stinking results. On August 6 Gates received word from General Caswell that he was about to be attacked by Rawdon, and asked for help. With Williams,

Gates rode to Caswell's camp to find complete confusion and disorder among the militia but a profusion of "wine and other delicacies" on Caswell's table. Still, he accepted Caswell's troops and with this, "the grand army" was joined by 2,100 North Carolina militia who might better have been left behind. On August 14 seven hundred Virginia militia, under General Edward Stevens, also joined Gates's army. But on the same day this augmentation was reduced by four hundred veterans who were sent to Thomas Sumter who was planning to raid a supply train from Charleston to Camden. But these goods could be had for the taking if the Americans triumphed at Camden. Why detach a company of artillery, two guns, three hundred North Carolina militia and, most foolish of all, one hundred seasoned Marylanders for a mere raid?

Apparently Horatio Gates believed that he had troops to spare, putting his army at seven thousand strong in comparison to the 2,240 commanded by Cornwallis now at Camden. Colonel Williams realized that this was a count as dishonest as the promise of rum and rations, but when he demonstrated to Gates that only about three thousand men were fit for duty, he was told: "Sir, there are enough for our purposes!" Ah, one could almost hear the sound of bugles in that epigrammatic reply. If it had been spoken by Washington or Greene or Arnold or even the ignored Jean de Kalb, Colonel Williams might have been confident of a matching victory to engrave upon the pages of history. But this was Granny Gates speaking, so he ignored it. He could not—nor could anyone else—ignore the incredible order for a night march on Camden to begin at 10 P.M. August 15. A *night* march! By mostly raw troops with even the veterans dog-tired, without a moon but only faint starlight over unfamiliar roads through alternating swamp and sloughs of sand, and this to be led by *cavalry?* Colonel Armand protested that for his horsemen to lead the way made it impossible to approach the enemy unheard. But Gates dismissed the demurral with an airy wave of his hand and is supposed to have said: "I will breakfast tomorrow in Camden with Lord Cornwallis as my guest."

Worse, while Granny Gates was coining epigrams again, his men were fed a meal based upon a menu that might have been provided by Lord Cornwallis. Some meat and cornmeal had been secured, but instead of the promised but unavailable rum usually issued to warm hearts and stimulate the flesh, Gates decided to enrich the bill of far with *medicinal* molasses: in a word, a physic. So these weary soldiers gorged themselves on half-baked bread and half-cooked meat, to be followed by a desert of cornmeal mixed with this molasses, which, Sergeant Major Seymour wrote, "served to purge us as well as if we had taken jalap." Throughout that nightmare march, Colonel Otho Williams reported, Gates's weary scarecrows kept breaking ranks to relieve themselves and were, as Colonel Williams reported, "certainly much debilitated before the action commenced in the morning."

Actually, the fighting began before daybreak. Four hours after Gates's army started marching—at about 2 A.M. August 16—Colonel Armand's cavalry collided with the horsemen of Banastre Tarleton. Cornwallis, hoping to surprise Gates in the morning, had marched from Camden at the same hour that Gates had departed Rugeley's Mills. At first, Tarleton's Tories forced Armand's troopers back. But they were, in turn, struck by the American flanking parties to either side of the road and repulsed. Both sides hastily formed for battle, but after fifteen minutes of desultory musketry in the dark, the woods became quiet again. Neither side wanted to fight at night.

Horatio Gates now called together his generals and regimental commanders in a council of war. There was still time to withdraw, and Jean de Kalb was prepared to urge it, for when Otho Williams appeared to summon him to the conference, he asked; "Well, has the general given you orders to retreat the army?" But when the council met, no one—not even de Kalb—advised retreat, probably because of a reluctance to be the first to recommend it. There was a pained silence, broken only when the brave but rash Edward Stevens cried: "We must *fight!* It is now too late to retreat. We can do nothing else. We must *fight!*" There was another silence, while Gates and his officers glanced at Edwards and then at each other.

"We must fight, then," Gates said quietly. "To your commands, gentlemen."

The two armies had collided in an open forest, sparsely populated by towering pines. This narrow space, which would permit the passage of horses, was flanked on either side by wide swamps that were somewhat narrower behind the British, widening so much behind the Americans that they could be passed by turning movements. Otherwise the Americans had the advantage of holding higher ground with a clear avenue of retreat. Conversely, the British rear was blocked by Sander's Creek, a full two hundred feet wide.

Gates formed his line by daybreak. Brigadier Mordecai Gist's brigade, composed of one Delaware and three Maryland regiments, held the right flank; Caswell's North Carolina militia, the center; and Stevens's Virginians, the left with Armand's horsemen on his left flank. Brigadier General William Smallwood's Maryland brigade was in reserve in the

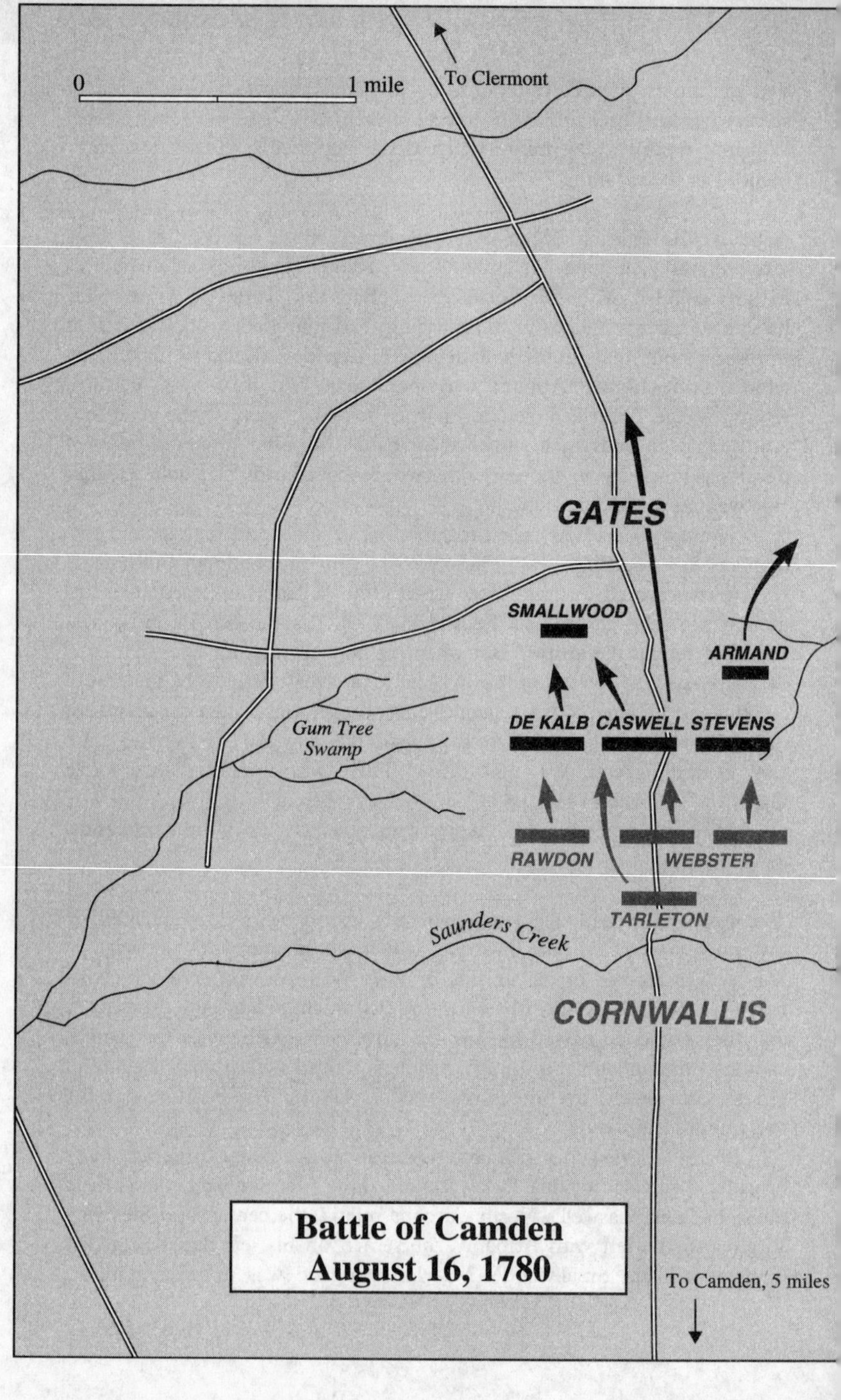

Battle of Camden
August 16, 1780

rear. Between them was Gates's headquarters, about six hundred yards behind his front line. De Kalb, in command of the right wing, attached himself to Gist's right flank. In front of the center were Gates's six fieldpieces.

Cornwallis's left, commanded by Rawdon, comprised Tarleton's infantry, the Volunteers of Ireland, the Royal North Carolina Regiment and Colonel Morgan Bryan's North Carolina Tories. On the right was Lieutenant Colonel Webster, commanding about twelve hundred regular redcoats. To the rear with Cornwallis were the dead Simon Fraser's Highlanders as a reserve. Like Gates, Cornwallis had posted artillery to his front, rather than to the rear as was customary, suggesting that both commanders might have been expecting the battle to start with an enemy charge. Two six-pounders, however, were in the second line with the Highlanders, while still farther back was Tarleton with his mounted Tories in column on the road. The flanks of both armies were anchored on the swamps.

Dawn came in hot and hazy, and the veterans of both armies—especially the British in their thick wool uniforms—realized with an inward shudder that they were going to have to fight in the scorching humidity of a Carolina August. Colonel Williams, straining his eyes, could just barely see the redcoats of the enemy advancing in columns. Riding to Captain Anthony Singleton of the artillery, he shouted: "Open on them at once!"—and galloped to the rear to report to Gates. Singleton's guns boomed, and the British replied. Black powder smoke mingled with the haze, and the atmosphere became befogged.

At headquarters, Williams told Gates: "The enemy are deploying on the right, sir. There's a good chance for Stevens to attack before they're formed."

Gates nodded. "Sir, that's right. Let it be done." It was Horatio Gates's last order as an American general. Williams rode off to find Stevens and give him the command to advance. The Virginians moved forward with slow reluctance and in ragged groups. Williams watched them with narrowed eyes that quickly filled with dismay. It was too late! The British were already formed. At once Williams called for volunteers to charge the enemy with him and thus draw their fire too early. Forty or fifty men responded, running toward the surprised foe.

"Take trees, men!" William yelled. "Choose your trees and give them an Indian charge!"

But by then the red lines were striding steadily forward with such fearsome precision that Williams and his volunteers fell back to their own positions. The canny Cornwallis had been studying the American right flank through his glasses and had seen the hesitation of Steven's Virginians. At once he ordered Colonel Webster to charge with the bayonet. With loud "Hurrahs!" the dreaded Welsh Fusiliers and the West Riding Regiment, with Webster leading, came on in a scarlet mass, their blades gleaming in the sunlight. Firing a single volley, they charged out of the smoke with outthrust bayonets. To the terrified Virginians it was like a horrible apparition. First the muskets flamed and men fell, then the foe was obscured by the gunsmoke only to reappear running at the double, horribly. A few rebels fired a faint and ragged volley, but most of them fell back in disorder.

"We have bayonets, too!" Stevens shouted encouragingly. "We can charge! Come on, men! Don't you know what bayonets are for?"

Hardly. They had never even held a bayonet until the day before, when the bayonets were issued in time to be used as spits to roast their meat on, let alone had they spent a single second in the thrust-parry-thrust-up-with-the-butt movements of bayonet fighting. The sound and sight of that yelling scarlet-and-steel mass turned their hearts flabby with fear, and they turned and ran—throwing away their muskets to speed their going. On their right—the American center held by Caswell's North Carolina militia, seeing the fainthearted flight of the Virginians on their left—broke and ran themselves without firing a shot. In all, some 2,500 Americans—more than Cornwallis's entire army—their terrified silence a contrast to the exultant cries of the pursuing British, went flowing backward "like an undammed torrent" that burst through the First Maryland Brigade in reserve, scattering it—and ran "raving along the roads and bypaths toward the north."

One regiment alone among all those North Carolinians—Colonel Henry Dixon's—stood firm, probably under the steadying influence of Gist's rocklike Marylanders and Delawares on their right. But the American left and center had been swept clean away. Only this stunned American right, under Gist and the dauntless de Kalb, held the field against the relentless blows of the fiercely attacking enemy left wing under Rawdon. Turning to face the enemy with the swamp to their backs, these Americans held firm while de Kalb ordered the scattered First Maryland Brigade to join him. Though recovered from the confusion caused by the collapse of the Patriot left and center, this fine formation was without a commander, for General Smallwood had left the field. Brave Colonel Williams took charge, bringing the brigade forward to reinforce the embattled Yankee right. He sought to form on its left. But Rawdon's men could not be dislodged, holding a gap of about two hundred yards between the American formations.

Seeing his chance, Cornwallis ordered Webster to strike at the front and flank of Williams's brigade. The First Maryland's soldiers gave ground, rallied, were driven back, rallied once more—but at last were overcome and driven from the field.

"Firm as a rock, the phalanx of de Kalb and Gist remained."

They had fought like lions, repeatedly holding off Rawdon's mostly Tory left. Scenting the kill, thirsting for the blood of their fellow Americans, the Tories drove forward—a thousand to six hundred. But their Yankee cousins held them off—at one point launching a bayonet charge of their own to break through and take fifty prisoners. But the Tories counterattacked to recover lost ground and turn the Patriot left. De Kalb reformed his scattered left. Again the Tories charged but were once more driven back—only to attack again.

It was at this point that the other brigade was swept away. But in the confusion of battle and the smoke-filled haze that reduced visibility to less than fifty feet, neither de Kalb nor Gist was aware that they stood alone against Cornwallis's army. They knew only that they were holding their own. If they had realized their predicament, they probably would have ordered a retreat, rather than sacrifice more men uselessly. So a savage fight ensued: hand to hand, clubbed muskets swinging blindly in the maze, sometimes missing, sometimes crushing skulls; slashing sabers doing the same. Now Cornwallis committed his reserve: screeching Highlanders in their kilts, "ladies from hell" swinging their dreadful Claymores, two thousand British now against whatever remained of the original six hundred Americans.

Almost surrounded de Kalb called for the bayonet once more. Without hesitation his men surged forward, their huge leader at their head. They burst through the astonished enemy, turned and struck their rear. No braver fight was ever fought by the Continentals. Marylanders and Delawares and Dixon's men rallied around the indomitable de Kalb. But then de Kalb's horse was shot from under him. He fought on foot. A saber laid open his head. He battled on.

As he did Horatio Gates made a halfhearted attempt to halt and rally the fleeing men of his left and center. He failed, and fled himself. De Kalb and his remnant still struggled. Ball after ball struck the giant general. With the last stroke of his sword, he cut down a British soldier and then fell dying with eleven wounds. It was Cornwallis himself who rescued de Kalb from the plunging blades of his enraged soldiers, and such was the immense vitality of this noble and valiant soldier that he lived for three more days.

But the fall of General Jean de Kalb ended the Battle of Camden. Those of his broken-hearted men who could saved themselves and went staggering north. Far, far ahead of them rode their commander, galloping madly from Camden and clear out of the Continental Army on one of the fastest and most famous mounts in America. He stopped that night in Charlotte, 60 miles away, but continued his flight until he reached Hillsboro, 210 miles from the battlefield. No general ever fled faster and farther from the scene of his defeat, and in the words of a jeering Alexander Hamilton: "It does admirable credit to the activity of a man at his time of life." Some kindly disposed historians speak of Gates as having been "swept away" by his fleeing militia; however, it would seem that 210 miles is rather a long sweep.

Camden, then, was another British victory that seemed to assure the final success of British arms in the South. In casualties, it was cheaply bought: 68 killed, 245 wounded and 18 missing against a much larger American total that could only be estimated. It was believed that 650 Continentals were killed or captured and an unknown number of men wounded among those imprisoned; about one hundred North Carolinians were killed or wounded and another three hundred were captured; and, as proof of the virtue of rapid decampment, only three Virginians were wounded. This totaled 1,053, a full third of Gates's army.

More lopsided losses were to follow at the Battle of Fishing Creek, which was fought two days later—on the eighteenth—between Thomas Sumter's irregulars and Banastre Tarleton's Tory Legion. Sumter, with his own troops and those detached to him by Gates, had made good on his proposal to capture that British wagon train. On the fifteenth he had surprised the enemy column, taking prisoner one hundred British soldiers and fifty Tory militiamen, together with forty wagons with their loads. At noon of the eighteenth, encamped at Fishing Creek with arms stacked, some of his men bathing, other sleeping, himself napping under a wagon, he was surprised and overwhelmed by Tarleton, who killed 150 Yankees, capturing more than 300 and putting the remaining 300 to flight at a loss of only 16 men killed or wounded.

Everywhere, it seemed, the reports flowing over the Atlantic Ocean to Lord George Germain and his master King George III were most encouraging. They were badly needed, indeed, after the traumatic shock that shook the kingdom during the Lord George Gordon Riots in London.

★ 61 ★

LONDON RIOTS PROLONG THE WAR

Lord George Gordon, "the whimsical and eccentric" son of the third Duke of Gordon in Ireland, had, by 1780, emerged as the leader of all those Protestant groups that had organized to oppose religious toleration for Catholics in Britain. In 1778 Parliament had unanimously approved an act relieving "His Majesty's subjects professing the Romish religion from certain penalties and disabilities imposed on them in the reign [1689–1702] of William III ... it being the general opinion of liberal-minded men of all parties that the laws against the Papists were abundantly too rigorous and that in an enlightened age, in which the principles of toleration so much prevailed, they were a disgrace to our statute-books."

Since then Lord George had tirelessly denounced the Toleration Act as a betrayal of Protestantism, deliberately fanning the London populace's traditional hatred of papists. On June 2, 1780, he led a crowd, estimated at more than sixty thousand people, from St. George's Fields to the houses of Parliament, presenting a petition for repeal of the act. The petition's rejection transformed Gordon's followers from a peaceful gathering into a howling, cursing mob, bent on destruction of all things and persons Catholic and, by extension, anyone who supported toleration of the Catholic faith. Not only Catholic property—churches, chapels, schools and convents, as well as private homes—was destroyed, but Catholics and their friends were assaulted, with the resulting murder of an unknown number of innocent subjects.

No one was safe from the anger of the rioters. For almost a week they held the city of London—the greatest metropolis of the empire and probably of the entire world—hostage to their hatred. Members of Parliament who were besieged in the House of Commons had to be rescued by soldiers carrying loaded and bayoneted muskets. (There was no police force in London then, and restoration of law and order fell to the army.) The home of Sir George Savile, who had introduced the Toleration Act, was systematically wrecked, while peers and prelates who were known to favor the abominated act were attacked and savagely beaten. For days on end civil authority was powerless to cope with the uprising.

The Earl of Sandwich, First Lord of the Admiralty, detested for his unwavering support of the unpopular war in America, was dragged from his coach while en route to Westminster. His carriage was destroyed and he was badly beaten until he was rescued with difficulty by the Horse Guards. The home of Lord North was attacked and had to be defended by a troop of light horse.

Next the mob descended upon Newgate Prison, abominable symbol of the Crown's repressive policies. With surprising military discipline, its members produced scaling ladders and sledge hammers and axes. Breaking into the chief jailer's house, they piled his furniture against the prison gate, setting it ablaze to burn the gate off its hinges. With howls of delight, they poured into the prison to tear open the cell doors and free their incarcerated brethren—uncaring whether they were habitual criminals or not, seeking only to demonstrate their resentment of their despised stations, a displeasure that began to emerge with a bitterness equal to their hatred of the Catholic Church. From Newgate, parties split off to burn and pillage the homes of Catholics, as well as the powerful peers who supported them. One of them attacked the home of the Earl of Mansfield, revered dean of British jurisprudence. While Lord and Lady Mansfield escaped out a back door, their magnificent furniture was hurled through plate-glass windows and burned in the street, along with precious paintings and his lordship's extensive law library and priceless manuscripts. Next, in the way of mobs everywhere but in abstemious Islam, the rioters made for the earl's wine cellars, only to be deterred in their hopes of quenching their thirst and refueling their hatred by the arrival of a party of soldiers. The Riot Act was read to them, and when they refused to disperse, the soldiers opened fire, killing six men and a woman and wounding others.

By the fourth day of the riots, troops had been mobilized to defend the principal public buildings. But then, while Newgate continued to smolder, another mob assaulted and plundered the sessions house of Old Bailey, another prison. Dr. Samuel Johnson, riding by in a carriage, observed: "They did their work at leisure, in full security, without sentries, without trepidation, as men lawfully employed in full day." Now rumors flew about that the mobsters intended to let loose the lions in the Tower of London and the lunatics in Bedlam. That night Fleet Prison, the King's Bench Prison, Bridewell Prison and St. George's Church were set ablaze. Growing bolder, the mobs overran the artillery grounds to arm themselves for an attack on the Bank of England and the Pay Office. Here the soldiery returned their fire, killing and wounding many, who were left lying in the streets while others were carried off by their comrades.

Gradually, the centers of the uprising were closed off to the riotors by heavy chains protected by soldiers. But fires still raged unchecked all over London, so far beyond the capacity of the city's firemen to control them that at one point they threatened to engulf the entire city. Frequently the rioters fought the firemen, actually cutting their hoses and cheering maniacally when they could drive them off. As was probably inevitable, an unguarded distillery was found near St. Andrew's Church. Now there ensued what the historian William Lecky called, "Such a scene of drunken madness as had perhaps never before been exhibited in England." Men and women actually killed themselves by drinking huge gulps of denatured alcohol that was gushing into the gutters. Soon the fiery liquid caught fire and burned to death many of the mobsters who were lying senseless in the street.

Before the Lord George Gordon riots could be contained, four jails and seventy-two houses had been destroyed, while 285 rioters lost their lives. The number of their innocent victims is not exactly known. Of all this destruction and death, pillage and plunder, the historian Edward Gibbon wrote mournfully: "Our danger is at an end, but our disgrace will be lasting, and the month of June, 1780, will ever be marked by a dark and diabolican fanaticism which I had supposed to be extinct."

It was not only fanatical religious hatred that sent these raging multitudes hurtling over the edge of reason, but also a deep, burning and less deplorable resentment of the status quo in Britain. Certainly begun in a spirit of religious prejudice that was whipped into a frenzy by the unscrupulous and unspeakable Gordon, by the mob's sudden shift from its original targets of Catholics and Catholic property to the persons and possessions of unpopular politicians and to prisons and public buildings, it became clear that their dissatisfaction with the government was far greater than their hatred—however ignorant and mindless—of fellow citizens professing a once-prescribed faith. The riots were the only way in which the depressed common people of London could express their outrage at their condition in life. The common people might despise Catholics, but they hated the government, its agencies and policies and, most of all, its detestable war in America with a foaming frenzy.

Unfortunately, riots have a melancholy history of counter-production. Like American blacks, similarly enraged by their low position in society, burning down their own neighborhoods, the Gordon rioters put a definite damper on popular meetings of the future called to discuss "the redress of grievances," as it says in the cherished First Amendment. Those same small-shopkeepers, mechanics and merchants, who frequented the sort of discussion clubs that had made Tom Paine, were so appalled by the spectacle of drunken, screeching, lawless mobs roving the city to loot and burn at will—often to the destruction of their own property and menace to their own persons—that their zeal for constitutional reform went up in the flames that consumed the prisons and houses. So also all hope for an early end to the war in America turned to despair as black as the charred walls of Newgate Prison. Fear of the Franco-Spanish enemy, so far from discrediting the government, served only to rally the upper classes to support the throne on which George III sat in adamantine disdain. "I can never suppose," the king wrote, "this country so lost to all ideas of self-importance as to be willing to grant American independence." And again: "The giving up the game would be total ruin." British naval successes during the winter had already hardened the king in his resolve to stay on his ruinous course, and the capture of Charleston and the Lord George Gordon riots lifted the Hanoverian jaw still higher.

It would be a pleasure to report that Lord George came to some satisfyingly ignoble end for his cynical skill in arousing the baser emotions of the poor and suffering people of London. But he was cleared of a charge of treason, and after he was excommunicated from the Anglican Church, he became converted to Judaism. Finally convicted of libel upon the person of Marie Antoinette in 1787, he spent his remaining years in his elegant quarters in Newgate Prison, where he gave dinners and dances until his death in 1793 at the age of forty-three.

Although his deluded followers had succeeded only in strengthening the king's resolve to continue the war, as well as to block the Catholic Toleration Act, the good news from Camden suggested to George and his ministers that the war could not last much longer. Better news—much, much better news—might soon follow, for Sir Henry Clinton had begun negotiations with Benedict Arnold for the sale of West Point and the Hudson River to the Crown.

★ 62 ★

TREASON I: ARNOLD'S DISAFFECTION

On June 19, 1778, Benedict Arnold rode into Philadelphia as the military commander of the city and its environs. Still unable to mount a horse or to move erect except with the use of crutches, his wounded leg two inches shorter than the other, he had been compelled to come in a coach with his foot propped up on a pillow. Such confinement did nothing to detract from the splendor of his entrance, for his magnificent coach-and-four was easily the most elegant in the city as it rolled over the streets behind a parade of Massachusetts Continentals. Surrounding it were the high-spirited horses of his aides, resplendent in their braided uniforms, while other coaches containing his liveried servants followed.

Such display somewhat startled the thousands of ecstatic Patriots who lined the streets to welcome their liberators. Most of them had always associated elegance and luxury with those treacherous Tories, who, now that Clinton's army was gone, were deliciously at their mercy. It would be more seemly for a true Patriot to ride in a plain and open carriage. What they did not know, of course, was that for all this appearance of the luxury that Arnold cherished, he was at that moment badly in need of money. Congress had still not reimbursed him for the thousand pounds he had spent in raising an artillery company in New Haven, nor for the £2,500 owed him for his expenditures in Canada. Nor had he received any pay for three years, and the privateer *General McDougall*, in which he had invested, had been captured. It cannot, of course, be stated with any certainty that as he entered what was now the capital city of the

United States, the thought of milking this vast metropolis occurred to him. Yet, speculation was always in his soul.

Arnold was himself startled to see that the faces of many of the welcoming Patriots were pinched with hunger. Then he was appalled at the devastation he beheld. The city's neat squares and commons had been churned into a mixture of mud, horse manure and debris. Whole blocks of houses in neighborhoods on the southern, western and northern edges of the city had been knocked down for firewood, and almost all fences had been similarly consumed. In the cemeteries, where horses had been exercised, the turf was torn up and gravestones were overturned, while churches were stripped of their pews and pulpits to heat both barracks and billet. All the furnishings of Independence Hall had been burned to warm the bodies of five companies of artillery stationed there, while above them all windows and shutters were nailed shut to contain American prisoners of war, and in the basement below, others were confined behind locked doors. In the now-infamous potter's field nearby were the long, shallow mass graves of some two thousand of the miserable Yankees who had died in captivity. Every street, it seemed, was lined with abandoned, broken-down vehicles standing among the rotting carcasses of horses that were still yoked to their traces.

But then, this horrid scene of sights, sounds and smells offensive to those three senses suddenly changed as though an angel's wand had been waved over it. Arnold's coach had entered what might be described as Torytown: a square mile enclave of handsome mansions, many of them built of red-and-black brick with classic pediments over the windows, surrounded by formal gardens and orchards and "commodious" living quarters that were once occupied by the slaves and indentured servants of the wealthy Quakers and Loyalists who lived there. One of these houses was occupied by Judge Edward Shippen, IV, scion of one of the oldest families in Pennsylvania, hereditary allies of that William Penn who had founded both the colony and its capital city.

On June 11, 1760, a baby girl named Margaret was born to Judge Shippen. She was the fourth member of that "worst sex" born to him and his wife, and there was also a ne'er-do-well son. Two later sons died in infancy, so that pretty little Peggy very early became the spoiled darling of the family and the apple of her doting father's eye, and, at eighteen, this remarkable young woman—reputed to be one of the prettiest ladies in America, with her blond hair, gray-blue eyes and dainty features and figure—possessed unusual understanding of human beings and business. Though her distinguished ancestors founded institutions of learning, filling their private libraries with the best of French and English literature, as well as the classical ancients in their original tongues, while decorating the rooms of their lavish homes with paintings by many of the old masters of Europe, the conversation and letters of Peggy Shippen rarely mentioned art or music or literature, speaking almost exclusively of society and business.

Feminine to the core, she also took a deep interest in politics, seated in the drawing room with her father, studying him with her calm gray-blue eyes while he discoursed quietly on the terrible turn the colonies were taking under the mob rule installed by those horrid levelers of New England. Under his tutelage she became a thoroughgoing Tory and a devout Anglican—to which her father had turned from his own father's Presbyterianism—looking down from her eminences of favored faith, privileged birth and inherited wealth upon those insolent and ignorant, coarse and penniless creatures who dared to challenge the rectitude of royal rule.

When Major General Benedict Arnold rode into town in a coach worthy of the Prince of Wales and she learned that he had begun life as an apothecary clerk, her pretty lips curled in contempt.

If one of George Washington's greatest mistakes was to make Benedict Arnold military commander of Philadelphia and its environs—including parts of New Jersey—then Arnold's most grievous error was to have accepted it. In so doing, he had inserted himself into a political crossfire between the Congress and the radical Supreme Executive Council of Pennsylvania led by Joseph Reed, the commonwealth's eventual president and virtual dictator. Arnold also soon became the object of the implacable hatred of Reed, a lanky, querulous Calvinist absolutist, who seemed to believe that any departure from a life of sackcloth and ashes was a sin against the Almighty. Reed had earlier shown his lust for power and his capacity for conspiracy, when, as Washington's adjutant general,* he had entered into a secret and disloyal correspondence with Horatio Gates and Charles Lee. There was no color or degree of gradation in this man's outlook: only black and white, the former for Tories, the latter for Whigs such as himself; the first an enemy, the second a friend. A man's talents or a woman's charms were either commendable or condemnatory to the degree with which they coincided with Reed's. Thus, when Arnold sought to enforce Washington's order and Congress's resolution against the molestation of any citizen or confiscation of his property because of

*An adjutant general is the chief administrator of an army.

political beliefs, Reed proposed that five hundred Tories of all ranks and stations should be hung and their property seized.

Arnold's efforts to protect these people so infuriated Reed that he openly accused him of being a Loyalist lover. Arnold's next false step was to fall in love with Peggy Shippen, the daughter of the well-known Tory, Judge Edward Shippen. The general had given a ball in honor of Count Conrad Alexander Gerard, ambassador to the United States from the Court of King Louis XVI. Peggy had been invited because her inadvertent absence from the *Michianza* had qualified her for the Patriots' criterion of social acceptance. But the sight of Arnold's ornate carriage parked so often and so openly before the Shippen mansion enraged Reed and his followers, such as Timothy Matlack, secretary of the Supreme Executive Council.

There were other sins feeding Reed's rancor: Arnold's loyalty to General Schuyler, the enemy of Reed's idol, General Gates; his friendship with the rich and powerful New York conservatives, such as Robert Livingston, John Jay and Gouverneur Morris, who were frequent guests at his table, along with Robert Morris, the wealthy Philadelphia financier. Reed regarded these men as profiteering leeches who were battening on the misery of the war. He could never accept Robert Morris's defense of free enterprise by declaring that if there were profits to be made in war, there were also losses to be taken—proof of which would be his own impoverishment. To preclude profiteering, Reed, upon Arnold's arrival, had drawn up a proclamation closing all shops and ordering all merchants to report their stock so that the needs of the military might first be served. At Reed's insistence, Arnold signed it as military governor, after which he executed a secret agreement with Clothier General James Mease, whereby Mease would buy at cost goods in great demand to be sold at profit after the shops were reopened. Reed considered this ploy to be unfair to the merchants, but did not then accuse Arnold of dishonest speculation.

Of all Reed's grievances against Arnold, it was Arnold's life-style that most annoyed this self-anointed John the Baptist. Without question, Arnold loved luxury, adoring wealth with an ardor that almost justified John Brown's charge that money was "his only God." He believed that both wealth and luxury were the rewards due a brave and able soldier such as himself, who had suffered so grievously and served so successfully in his country's cause.

Without hesitation he had chosen for his headquarters the grand and venerable Penn mansion, only lately vacated by Sir William Howe, and there had established a household that was even more ostentatious than his predecessor's. Although the mansion had been stripped by the British, Arnold refurbished it in even more lavish style, purchasing china, silver, furniture and furnishings from a merchant named Joseph Stansbury, while hiring a housekeeper, coachman, groom and seven lesser servants. He rode in his fine chariot behind four beautiful horses and would pay a staggering thousand pounds for two casks of wine. At his table, where congressmen and other leading Philadelphians dined, an empty plate was instantly replenished and a drained bottle was replaced. Inevitably, such a show of affluence provoked charges that he was living miles beyond his means—and where did the money come from?

He was indeed living well above an officer's pay, but Benedict Arnold had gone off to war a wealthy man, even though the British blockade strangled his shipping business. More, he had consumed much of his personal fortune to feed his army in Canada and had financed that artillery company in New Haven; yet, two years after his return from Canada, his accounts were still buried beneath a blizzard of audits and hearings conducted by the congressional Board of Treasury. Nevertheless because of his high station he was expected to maintain a headquarters and household out of his own pocket. No wonder that he eventually pursued a series of business adventures that, if not illicit or illegal, were only so because neither Washington nor Congress had expressly forbade them. Exposure of these unsavory deals would also bring him into conflict with Joseph Reed and his council. Meanwhile, he was also having difficulty persuading his prospective father-in-law to approve his marriage to the charming and beautiful Peggy.

When General Arnold's ostentatious chariot drew up at the Shippen front door and the wounded warrior came hobbling into the parlor on his crutches, Peggy Shippen's face lighted up and her heart beat faster—as there began nothing less than a contest for possession of that heart between Father and Suitor, Age and Youth, Position and Ambition, Discretion and Flamboyance. Seated in their worn wing chairs, the symbol of her father's failing fortunes that so embarrassed Peggy, the two men conversed, with every word actually directed at Peggy and all four eyes fixed on her. When Peggy spoke, both men abruptly ceased to speak, listening with delighted surprise to this girlish voice ticking off points like a trial lawyer in a courtroom. When they resumed their conversation and the discussion turned to politics, the difference between the suitors became more evident: Shippen speaking quietly and with confidence, Arnold with a rising voice so insistent that had he not been crippled and his bad leg stretched before him on a footstool, it is certain that he would have paced the floor. They were both handsome men: Shippen, with his abundant iron-gray hair and his fine, suave, aristocratic features, was a sharp contrast to Arnold's hawkish, swarthy radiance, with those hard blue eyes and flashing white teeth—the face of a pirate captain. It was clear to Peggy, even at her young age, that her father did not want to surrender the daughter whom he loved above all others and that Arnold sought this conquest more ardently than he did the capture of Quebec or the defeat of Burgoyne. As he had fought—headlong—so he made love, charging madly at her heart.

Edward Shippen did not like Benedict Arnold. He might have objected to his being twice his daughter's age, but such unions were common in those days, and eighteen year olds regularly married older men—usually widowers—without exciting comment. No, Judge Shippen's distrust sprang from the immemorial conflict between the old and the new, the established order defending itself against the pretensions of the adventurer soaring high on the wings of war and revolution. More, Shippen was a thoughtful man suspicious of men of action, "men of blood," as it says in the Bible. It distressed him that his favorite child was thrilled to be courted by a professional murderer, and to him, this was also a sorrowful measure of how far she and he had drifted apart.

Benedict Arnold was not attracted to Peggy Shippen just because she was young and beautiful, blessed—if that is the right word—with enormous sex appeal. True enough, Arnold was the sort of radiant and vital man who could lose his head over such a seemingly simple creature and, in turn, attract one. But Peggy was also intelligent and strong (Arnold did not learn until much later of her frequent fits of hysteria), possessing by birth and breeding the social position he sought for himself and his children. He could judge by the shabbiness of the Shippen home, and had learned from discreet inquiries, that Judge Shippen's fortunes had ebbed. But it did not bother Benedict Arnold that the Shippens were no longer wealthy; he might even have been pleased by it, so that he could provide Peggy with all the money she needed to share with him a love of luxury.

Judge Shippen also suspected this motive, and though he realized that Arnold was probably a good match, he was too much a man of his own class to accept him—and so he opposed their marriage. Here the man of the mind had woefully misjudged the man of action. Rather than retire, Arnold pressed the suit even harder. Himself misjudging his opponent's motive, this man of action decided that he was disdained because he was a cripple and immediately sought to transform himself into a healthy man. "With the assistance of a high-heeled shoe and cane he begins to hop about the floor and in great measure dispense with his crutches." Peggy was enchanted. Her lover did indeed desire her! Unconsciously, Benedict Arnold had chosen the right approach. Though never voicing it, Peggy's only reservation had been that Arnold was a cripple—and so she began to use all her wiles to overcome her father's objections. Meanwhile, Arnold's reincarnation did not pass unnoticed in high society, Tory or Patriot. Mrs. Robert Morris wrote: "I must tell you that Cupid has given our little general a more mortal wound than all the host of Britons could … Miss Peggy Shippen is the fair one."

Arnold was so passionately in love that he was probably not aware that his romance with Peggy was drawing him deeper and deeper into Tory society. His enemies, led by Joseph Reed, were openly denouncing him as the friend and protector of the enemies of America. Conversely, Arnold's failure to persecute the Tories may have been a factor in Judge Shippen's decision to withdraw his objections, so that Benedict Arnold and Peggy Shippen were at last united in matrimony on April 9, 1779.

Not long afterward, General Arnold realized that while he had been busy romancing, Joseph Reed and his council had been collecting evidence to bring about his disgrace and downfall.

Joseph Reed's hatred of Benedict Arnold did not spring from disagreements of a political or military nature, but, rather, from General Arnold's refusal to join him and his Jacobins in a Tory pogrom. With the same ferocity with which the French revolutionaries would make the streets of Paris run red with noble blood a decade later, they sought a harvest of Loyalist heads with the concomitant confiscation of their property. In this, Arnold had frustrated them. It also seemed to them that he was the leader in the steady corruption of sturdy American republican virtues. He had always been a dandy, but now, as military governor of Philadelphia, he indulged in every luxury while surrounded by a crowd of fawning aides, such as the foppish Major David Franks, a relative of the wealthy merchant of the same name, and dozens of pretty Tory girls wearing the latest gowns with mounds of white hair piled atop their heads in the enormous headdresses that John André had designed for his *Michianza* and were now the height of fashion.

Because all bitter rivalries seem to need a symbol expressive of what divides them, in Philadelphia it was dress. Reed's followers abominated the ladies of Peggy Arnold's circle, with their haute coiffure, or officers like Franks, with his powdered wigs and and effeminate manners. They despised Americans who wore high conical hats similar to the miters of Hessian soldiers, wide ones with brims "the size of my tea-table" or long greatcoats with skirts down to the ankles. In protest, they put away their own wigs, cropped their hair short and wore suits of sober black or gray with plain white shirts. Thus simply dressed, they launched their attack on the bewigged and dandified Arnold on the second anniversary of the Fourth of July.

Reed's followers paraded down Second Street hauling a cart carrying a toothless, barefoot old black woman wearing a huge wig to whom they bowed and curtsied while a band played the "Rogue's March." Watching them from City Tavern was Colonel Jack Stewart of Maryland and the sharp-tongued Becky Franks, niece of the aforementioned merchant David Franks and Peggy Shippen's best friend.

Smiling, Colonel Stewart remarked: "The lady is equipped altogether in the English fashion."

"Not altogether, Colonel," Becky replied. "Though the style of her head is British, her shoes and stockings are in the genuine Continental fashion."

The remark was given wide circulation, provoking a storm of derisive laughter or angry denunciation—and it was in effect the opening gun in the war between Reed and Arnold. Through the columns of the Pennsylvania *Packet* and the vitriolic pen of Timothy Matlack, Reed now sought to discredit Arnold through charges of using his high office to reap enormous profits in commercial speculation. He published an account of how Arnold had twice attempted to obtain from his council an illegal pass into New York for Hannah Levy, another relative of the merchant Franks, ridiculing Arnold's "explanation" that the lady was on a military errand too secret to be disclosed. To all of these charges, Arnold wrote indignant denials, but in verbal duels with Matlack he proved to be as ineffectual with pen and paper as he was formidable with sword and pistol. Arnold was now beside himself, so that he blundered badly in the most trivial of the growing list of charges against him.

Sergeant William Matlack of the Pennsylvania militia, the son of the artful Timothy, was on duty at Arnold's headquarters when the fastidious Major Franks discovered, to his horror, that his wig was improperly powdered. Franks ordered a maid to tell Matlack to fetch his barber. Matlack went, did not find the barber in his shop and left word for him to come to headquarters. Distraught at being kept waiting in such a crisis, Franks sought out Matlack and cried angrily: "Sergeant, I thought I had ordered you to go for my barber."

"I told him," the youth remembered, "I had received no such order. He then asked me why I did not go. I told him that I waited his orders. He then told me to go, and I told him, with his orders, I would go, and did go. Major Franks, on my return, asked me If I had been. I told him I had, and left the same orders as before." Matlack said that when he complained to General Arnold the next day, he "gave me to understand, not in an abrupt manner, that if I did not like such duty, I should not have come here."

When young Matlack reported this exchange to his father, Timothy jumped on it gleefully, lecturing Arnold on the nobility of the militia, and declaring: "Freemen will hardly be brought to submit to such indignities." Arnold, in turn, lectured the senior Matlack on the necessity of military discipline, when he might simply have ordered Franks to explain to young Matlack that he had no intention of treating him like a servant and thus have precluded the furor that ensued. By his failure to rebuke Franks publicly or order him to apologize, he fulfilled the fears of all freemen in uniform that the senior officers of the Continental Army hoped to perpetuate themselves as an aristocracy, and that by their own struggle to abolish one tyranny, they were to be made subservient to a new one. This theme, skillfully played upon by Matlack, finally succeeded in convincing many Pennsylvanians that Arnold had opposed their government in its every attempt to create a fair and democratic nation. With this and other accusations, Joseph Reed and his council were ready to make their formal eight-point indictment of the military governor.

The eight points were these: (1) While Arnold was still at Valley Forge, he had granted persons of "disaffected character," that is, suspected Tory merchants, an unjustified pass to get the schooner *Charming Nancy* loaded with hoarded goods, in both of which Arnold had a fourth share, out of British-held Philadelphia and into a United States port; (2) On his arrival in Philadelphia, Arnold had deliberately closed all the shops so that he could buy up goods in great demand at an unfair price to make a tremendous profit; (3) He had imposed "menial" duties on a militiaman and stubbornly defended his right to do so; (4) He had interposed in a prize case—the seized vessel *Active,* in which he also had an interest—the cargo of which he had illegally purchased at an inadequate price; (5) He had used public wagons to transport his private property; (6) He had tried illegally to slip an "improper" person [Hannah Levy] into New York; (7) When questioned about the wagons, he had returned "an indecent and disrespectful refusal"; (8) His "discouragement and neglect" of patriotic persons and his "different conduct toward those of another character [Tories] are too notorious to need proof or demonstration." The council closed these charges by stating that while Arnold remained in the Pennsylvania command, they would pay none of its costs and would call out the militia only under "the most urgent and pressing necessity."

This proclamation, sent to all governmental bodies and published in all newspapers, exploded like a bomb in Philadelphia. Tongues wagged incessantly, and gossip reached such heights of fantasy that a merchant could write in his diary, like a grim harbinger of the future: "News of the day is that General Arnold has left Philadelphia and gone over to the enemy."

Arnold, of course, was indeed gone—not to confer with Sir Henry Clinton, but rather with George Washington at Valley Forge and from there to New York State, where his conservative friends planned to reward him for his services in the north by giving him forty thousand acres on Lake Champlain to colonize with his former troops and thus provide a buffer against Canada. Arnold, weary of his endless battles with his detractors in the Philadelphia papers, planned to resign his commission and to buy the land at an extremely low price. But the scheme came to naught, and instead he returned to Philadelphia to defend himself.

Arnold had demanded a court-martial to clear him, believing that he was safer in the hands of soldiers than in those of politicians, but Reed and his council prevailed upon a deeply divided Congress to refer the charges to a committee headed by William Paca of Maryland. At this point the council members were so embarrassed by their inability to provide any real evidence and because there was no law or rule anywhere—either in Congress or in the Continental Army—that specifically prohibited profiteering, that they lost their balance and resorted to vilification in place of facts. Reed and Matlack dug up John Brown's little booklet of calumnies and published it, knowing full well that Congress had already exonerated Arnold of all these charges while excoriating Brown. But Matlack insisted that Arnold had massacred an entire Canadian village and plundered Montreal. In the end Paca's committee cleared Arnold of all six of the charges they considered civilians capable of trying, while forwarding to Washington the two military matters—abuse of a militiaman and use of the wagons—for a court-martial to decide.

Benedict Arnold was overjoyed, confident that the soldiers would clear him, and so he resigned his command and became a major general without an assignment.

So far from calming the conflict raging between Reed and his council and the United States Congress, the Paca Report turned it into a political tornado. Reed was infuriated to see his prey escape him. He accused congressmen from other states, particularly Arnold's friends from New York, of being the general's dupes and toadies. Having already warned Congress that if it sided with Arnold it would incur the undying enmity of Pennsylvania—a threat, in effect, of eventual secession—he now brought such pressure to bear that a majority of its members came to regard justice for Arnold as tantamount to dissolution of the union. So a new committee was empowered to reach a "compromise" with Reed: in effect, surrender. Two of the civilian charges—the pass for the *Charming Nancy* and speculation when the shops were closed—were restored and joined to the two military accusations.

Arnold was outraged. He knew, of course, that he was guilty of these two resurrected charges. What infuriated him was that he had been acquitted and then placed in jeopardy again. What else was this but double jeopardy! So he appealed. A mollified Congress wavered, and as it did, a movement arose to do the wounded hero justice. With that movement, the president of Pennsylvania, in the most flagrant and unilateral abuse of the power invested in him, wrote Congress that if any action favorable to Arnold were taken, then the people of America faced "a melancholy prospect of perpetuated disunion between this and the other United States."

Here was an open threat—not a veiled hint—of secession! Here was a crowd of radical absolutists threatening to pull down the entire Union unless the head of the general who offended them was given to them on a tray. And Congress meekly bowed its head and acquiesced. Arnold's appeal was buried in committee. No wonder his embittered soul now turned toward thoughts of treason.

Shortly after Benedict Arnold and Peggy Shippen were married, the union flowered in the ugly weed of betrayal. There seems to be no doubt that the first words suggestive of treason came from Peggy's lips. She had good reason to wish to change sides. The British evacuation of Philadelphia had made of her and her friends de facto exiles: Tory islands set down in a Patriot sea. They might flaunt their headdresses and their superior breeding, but they lived in terror, just like the aristocrats of Revolutionary France. If there had been no Congress or George Washington to restrain the lust for blood and power of Reed and his council, many of their men would have been hanged and their property confiscated, and their impoverished women would have been reduced to begging or worse. Peggy had learned to dread such a fate from the example of her relative, Joseph Galloway. He had given both himself and his fortune to the British cause, and the only result was that his wife now lived in squalor.

Peggy had really begun to live after Howe conquered Philadelphia. She had been enchanted by the round of balls and cotillons, dazzled by dashing young officers, such as John André and Oliver Delancey. How well they danced, and how easily compliments or droll quips or beautiful poetry flowed from their lips! Oh, to live in luxury again without having it thrown up to you by a crowd of barefoot peasants that you were a scarlet Jezebel or one of "the mistresses and whores of British officers." Her husband, she knew, shared her love of privilege, and she played skillfully upon his apprehensions that Congress would never pay him the £2,500 pounds it owed him. Her softly feminine beauty exciting him and so masking a strong will and a subtle intellect, she renewed in him the bitterness he felt at the indignities and injustices he had suffered at the hands of Congress, and was artful enough to make him feel that her resentments and fears were actually his own. Gradually, she brought him to realize that if the United States would not pay him his due, the enemy might be interested in doing so. Besides the money from Congress, Arnold owned his house in New Haven, and he had just bought Mount Pleasant, the mansion on the Schuylkill that John Adams called "the most elegant seat in Pennsylvania." Both homes and the money owed him could be lost if his treason—the word had not yet been spoken—became known. Peggy's penetrating mind had seen long ago that the Crown's chief error—at least as far as she was concerned—had been its failure to create an American aristocracy. But to be introduced everywhere one day as "Lord and Lady Arnold" was another enducement she held out to him. Perhaps it was this consideration that would lead Arnold in his early correspondence with the British to sign himself "Monk," the name of the Cromwellian general who brought about the restoration of Charles II, for which treacherous service he was created Duke of Albemarle.

Yet Benedict Arnold did not immediately submit to the sophistries of his wife, for he was still the man of action who abhorred the thought of betraying his "brave boys." It was too much for him to think of himself their hero turning to them the face of a traitor. He had to be persuaded into thinking that what Peggy proposed, onerous as it might appear, was actually for their own good. Those who might scorn him now and seek his life, she argued, would one day thank him for being the savior who delivered them from the anarchy of a devilish democracy that was imposed upon them by a pack of power-hungry, squabbling lawyers who never heard a shot fired in anger, while restoring to America peace and prosperity under a benevolent monarch. She well knew how deeply he despised politicians, as well as how poignantly he had regretted being unable to solve his problems with sword or pistol, to make the nobility of his soul plain to all by leaping once again on some splendid charger and go charging down the enemy line to victory—as he had done at Saratoga. This was the state of mind to which Peggy Arnold had brought her anguished and embittered husband just before the finding of the Paca Committee, and from which he seemed to deliver himself with joy and jubilation upon being informed by Washington that his court-martial would begin on May 1.

But then, unknown to Arnold, Reed wrote to Washington that if the military court dismissed the charge that Arnold had misused public wagons, the state of Pennsylvania would never again supply the Continental Army with transport. He also demanded postponement of the trial, to give him time to collect witnesses. Washington had no choice but to inform Arnold that for reasons he would explain later, he was indefinitely postponing Arnold's court-martial. Benedict Arnold's hands trembled as he read that letter, and his blue eyes lifted to stare into Peggy's with an anguish that told her she had won.

Together they would now search for a safe way to join the enemy.

★ 63 ★

TREASON II: ARNOLD'S BETRAYAL

In the beginning of the Arnolds' quest for the right road to treason, there was no notion in either mind of their betrayal of some vital post, the loss of which might ruin the Continental Army, if only because Benedict Arnold was a general without a command. Their purpose, then, was merely to sell Arnold's services to Sir Henry Clinton for a sum that would compensate them for the loss of their property and the money owed by Congress. Aware that Clinton was unapproachable, Peggy immediately thought of her old friend, John André, on whom in her first blush of beauty she seems to have had a crush. Arnold was delighted, but then: that was all right for the British side, but who would be their go-between? At this point, in the very beginning of their duplicity, the Arnolds showed how unfit they were for conspiracy. Why not Peggy herself? So many people were slipped in and out of New York and Philadelphia for so many different reasons that there should be no difficulty for a disguised Peggy to find sanctuary at the home of her numerous Tory friends. There would then be no need of an outsider, who, rather than risk himself in carrying messages safely to Clinton, could easily gain fame and money by taking them to Washington instead. Peggy could bargain directly with André, who was now a major and chief of British intelligence, thus obviating the additonal risk of written messages that a go-between would have to carry. But neither Arnold nor his wife seems to have considered this possibility, and it seems likely that if Peggy had suggested it, he would have shrunk from such a course in horror. Out of grief and bitterness he had chosen a dishonorable road, but his sense of chivalry was still too strong for him to implicate his wife in his treason.

So the china dealer Joseph Stansbury was selected, probably

because of his secret pro-British sympathies. Because of her intimacy with British officers, only Peggy would have known that Stansbury, while taking the oath of allegiance to Pennsylvania, had done so solely to avoid being driven into exile, and was actually the author of comic verse lampooning leading Patriots. His heart really belonged to the Britain in which he had been born and educated. Smooth and obsequious, he seemed just the man to be Arnold's courier. He was not, of course, if only because he was a coward, eager only for a large reward if the plot succeeded; but he was so distraught after he slipped through the British lines into New York without a pass that he immediately violated his vow of secrecy by including another man in the conspiracy: the Reverend Jonathon Odell, a former British officer who was now an Episcopal minister in New York, and also an agent in André's intelligence system. Like Stansbury, an amateur poet, Odell had no trouble arranging a meeting with André, another devotee of the muse.

The charming major rose to his feet with a smile when the two poets entered his office, perhaps anticipating a pleasant literary chat. But once the true nature of their visit became known, he rushed to his door and locked it. Reading Arnold's message, he then hurried to Clinton's office. Both men were astonished. Seeking secret allies among the Patriots was a routine of André's intelligence section, but no one had dreamed that Benedict Arnold—the best of the rebel generals—would *volunteer* his services! André was still excited when he returned with Clinton's reply, but after the two poets departed he became so ill that he had to go to his quarters to rest. Meanwhile, Stansbury, terrified once more, slowly made his tortured way back to Philadelphia.

The Arnolds were not overjoyed by André's phlegmatic reply. He had not the slightest interest in Arnold's changing sides, a blow to the traitor's self-esteem if ever there was one. He would only be of value if he could secure an important command, at the moment a distinct impossibility now that Arnold's wound had been complicated by an extremely painful attack of gout. André would be happy to receive useful intelligence, of course, but did not specify what or for how much money. Arnold was almost apoplectic with rage. Crumbs from the table! Here he was risking his neck—he, who had twisted the British lion's tail at Ticonderoga and with the barest luck would have torn Canada away from the Crown, who had stopped Carleton at Valcour Island and ruined Burgoyne at Saratoga—and they spoke to him as deprecatingly as though he were the unctuous courier Stansbury. Yet, the Arnolds had opened the door and they wished to keep it open, so they sent André some intelligence, hardly more than gossip, and in the meantime General Arnold prepared to journey to Morristown for his court-martial, which was scheduled to begin June 1, 1779.

Although the trial did begin as scheduled, it was postponed indefinitely once more by the appearance of a British army advancing up the Hudson. While Washington hurried to the defense of the Hudson, Clinton, with a force of 3,700 men, "conquered" no more than a garrison of seventy-four soldiers at Verplanck's Point and Arnold made his painful return to Philadelphia. At once Arnold resumed his correspondence with André, who suggested that if Arnold could rejoin the army and be able to surrender "a corps of five or six thousand men [he] would be rewarded with twice as many thousand guineas." Here, at last, was more than a nibble on the hook of treason, but Arnold still found the fish to be a bit too cautious. Why should he be paid only if his treachery were successful, he replied, and then, through Stansbury, demanded to be indemnified "for any loss he may sustain in case of detection, and ... that ten thousand pounds shall be engaged him for his services." André's reply was to ask for "an accurate plan of West Point" with information on the American naval power in the Hudson, together with the complete "order of battle" of Washington's army. Arnold, again answering verbally through Stansbury, complained that it would be unjust to his family to trade "a certainty for an uncertainty," and with that the correspondence came to a close. Both sides had bargained like fishwives, André and Clinton beginning to doubt that their correspondent was truly Benedict Arnold, the American general disgusted with the devil's attempt to buy his soul by deferred payment.

After the 1779 campaigning season ended, the court-martial of Benedict Arnold resumed in Morristown on December 23. By then Arnold's spirits had risen. His gout had disappeared and the pain in his leg had subsided so that, using his high heel, he could limp about with almost all his old vigor. In June on his journey to Morristown, he had had to be lifted into his carriage, but this time he clambered aboard himself. Confident that he would be exonerated, he saw himself setting out anew on his career in the Continental Army. Perhaps it was fortunate that the British had been so indifferent to his offer. Now, vindicated, his health regained, restored to his cause and his comrades, his name would shine again in glory.

Arnold's confidence issued from his conviction that Reed had been unable to unearth any new evidence. This belief turned out to be true, once the trial was renewed. On the *Charming Nancy* pass there was no proof that the euphemism "disaffected characters" meant enemies of America, and on the accusation of using his office for speculation, there was again no evidence. There was really nothing to the "abuse of a militiaman" charge, which actually should have been laid against Franks, not Arnold, and again the use of military wagons for private purposes could be upheld only if the wagon master, Colonel John Mitchell, testified that he had been ordered to provide them. Instead, he said Arnold had "requested" them and that he felt it his duty to do so.

Arnold might have been acquitted on all counts had he handled himself like a lawyer attacking the plaintiff's credibility, rather than as a soldier parading his past glories. If he had *prepared* his case, as any competent attorney would, he could have scoffed at the notion that he, revered and respected by every militia formation that had served under him, could actually so demean a militiaman. He could have observed that it was Major Franks, not General Arnold, who had seemingly offended Sergeant Matlack and that he was in court this very day to say that he had had no such intention and to apologize if he had given that impression. As for the wagons, he could have relied on Mitchell's testimony, as well as his own claim, that he had been prepared to pay for their use until the wagoners, at the instance of Reed, had refused to accept it.

Instead he paraded his victories, his honors and his service to his country. He read letters from Washington and resolutions from Congress praising his patriotism. He contrasted his loyalty to the cause to the perfidy of Joseph Reed, who had conspired with Gates and Lee while serving Washington as his adjutant general. "I can say I never basked in the sunshine of my general's favor and courted him to his face when I was at the same time treating him with the greatest disrespect and vilifying his character when absent." With bluster, then, rather than logic, he sought to clear himself of all charges—and failed. The court, dismissing the militia and speculation charges, found him guilty on the charges regarding the *Charming Nancy* and the wagons, sentencing him to be reprimanded by Washington. If the verdict was cruel, the sentence was kind—and Washington's eventual censure could not have been gentler.

But Benedict Arnold had been wounded where he was most sensitive—his pride—and when he heard the verdict with unbelieving ears, he was instantly once again the embittered general ready to betray.

He had come limping into the courtroom, but he went hobbling out.

In the months that followed this conviction, Benedict Arnold toyed with wild schemes to recover his fortune and his glory. He proposed that the Board of Admiralty authorize him to raise a fleet of privateers to prey upon enemy shipping, asking Washington for four or five hundred soldiers to man his ships. Washington's answer—no—was prudently dispatched to the Admiralty Board. Next he besought the new French minister—Anne Cesar La Luzerne—to obtain for him a French loan that would keep him in the field against Britain, but was politely—if not wryly—refused. Then he dreamed of organizing a great Indian confederation beyond the frontiers, until he realized that Peggy and his newborn son Edward Shippen Arnold could never survive in buckskin and in feathers. In despair, he remembered André's request for "an accurate plan of West Point," and it dawned on him that perhaps if he were in command there, he would have a real commodity to sell. In May 1780, he began trying to convert his immovable assets, such as Mount Pleasant and his house in New Haven, into cash, while shifting his movable ones to London, and reopened his correspondence with the British. This time, distrusting the smooth Stansbury, he used one of André's secret agents, a militia colonel named Samuel Wallis. Through him, pretending that he was now commanding West Point, he demanded £10,000 for his past services, an annual stipend of £500 and £20,000 for "West Point, the garrison, etc. ... I expect a full and explicit answer."

Now excited, but still not sure it was Arnold that he was dealing with, Clinton allowed André to agree to this proposal only in part: about £500 for past intelligence and the £20,000 for West Point, provided three thousand soldiers and vast military stores went with it.

Arnold did not receive this reply immediately, having gone to Washington's headquarters to press his campaign for the West Point post. The commander in chief was mildly perplexed. Why should a valorus soldier such as Arnold seek such an inactive command? Arnold replied that his leg was still not properly healed and that he could neither walk nor ride. To his dismay, Washington instead offered him command of the left wing of his army as he moved to the assistance of a French army in Newport, menaced by six thousand men under Clinton. Arnold was crestfallen, and Washington amazed, later writing: "Upon this information, his countenance changed, and he appeared to be quite fallen." Returning to camp, Arnold began to hobble about to impress everyone with his disability. Nevertheless, on August 1, general orders put him in command of the left wing. But then Clinton abandoned his expedition to Rhode Island, and on August 3, 1780, general orders declared; "Major General Arnold will take command of the garrison at West Point."

At West Point Benedict Arnold established himself in a gloomy mansion on the opposite side of the Hudson from the fort. It had been confiscated from Beverly Robinson, now a Loyalist colonel in New York. Its isolation suited Arnold's plans to betray the fortress, but he was troubled by the prolonged silence of André, unaware as he was that in Philadelphia Peggy was having difficulty forwarding his letter agreeing to Arnold's price for control of the Hudson River.

Also unknown to him, Sir Henry Clinton was now on fire to close a deal on the fort. His spies had informed him that Washington was prepared to attack New York City, assisted by the French marching down from Long Island. "It is beyond doubt," Clinton wrote, "that the principal Rebel depot must [be] made at West Point." To take the fort, then, would not only give him control of the Hudson, but also would wreck the Franco-American expedition by compelling Washington to retire into New Jersey, whereupon the unsupported French army would fall "into our hands." Clinton now asked André, whom he had raised to the position of adjutant general, if there were news from Arnold.

There had been none, but Clinton would have been overjoyed to learn that the new West Point commander was feverishly complying with Washington's order to put the post "in the most defensive state which is possible." Arnold was shocked at first by this command, until he realized that to fill the post with men and munitions would only make it that much more valuable to the enemy. And he did so with his customary energy that belies two centuries of claims that the traitor sent away his troops and skimped on his requisitions. He might have done so earlier, but not after the express order from Washington. Instead, as surreptitiously as possible, he spread out his reinforced garrison in such a way that battalions could be cut off piecemeal. Actually, twice three thousand American soldiers could not have held West Point, for Arnold had found it in an earlier inspection "totally neglected" and "most wretchedly planned." His attempts to rectify its condition failed, chiefly because there was simply not enough time or material, engineers and equipment, to do so.

As September approached, Benedict Arnold was in an agony of suspense: both for the arrival of his beloved Peggy and little Edward and for an opportunity to speak personally to André, for he now realized that nothing could be concerted by message but only in consultation. His chance came when a woman named Mary McCarthy, the wife of a captured British soldier, appeared at West Point with a pass from Governor Clinton. Upon her return she carried a letter from Arnold, written "in mercantile style," asking André, in the guise of a trader named John Anderson, to meet him at Dobbs Ferry.

This hasty and uneven scheme, distrusted at once by General Clinton, who did not wish his favorite officer to act as a spy and thus risk the gallows, was fraught with every conceivable danger, including the inconceivable appearance of a British gunboat intercepting Arnold's barge as it was rowed downriver and driving him off. Arnold's dismay at this unexpected intervention was dissipated, however, when he returned to his headquarters to find Peggy and Edward there. But he was still at his wit's end as how to rearrange a meeting with André—until Sir Henry Clinton took a hand.

Clinton was convinced that now—September 1780—was the time to take West Point. The fear of a Franco-American attack upon New York had faded upon the arrival there of British naval reinforcements under Admiral George Rodney, together with news that the expected French reinforcements had been blockaded in the port of Brest. The French in Rhode Island would now have to stay there with no possibility of any campaign against Clinton until the spring of 1781. But if West Point were his, there wouldn't be any campaign *ever.*

The rebel cause had never seemed blacker, not even in 1775. Cornwallis's victory at Camden had all but ensured the fall of the entire South, and the Continental Army was washing away like sand with the ebbing tide. Few militiamen were willing to enlist in it, and the introduction of the death penalty had failed to discourage desertion. Washington himself openly feared that his officer corps would resign in a body. The loss of the famous fort that had cost three million dollars and three years to build, together with the great river it guarded, would force the French out of America and crush the rebel will to continue to fight. Yet, with all this to gain, the ever-cautious Clinton still wanted to be sure that André's correspondent was indeed the West Point commander. He feared a trap, that his army moving against the fort would find not a white flag fluttering up the flagstaff, but a determined resistance, with Washington suddenly appearing in his rear to block his retreat. Clinton had to be *certain* "both as to the person being Major General Arnold commanding at West Point; and that in the manner in which he was to surrender himself, the forts and the troops to me ... should be conducted under a concerted plan between us, so that the King's troops sent upon this expedition should be under no risk of surprise or counterplot."

With this impetus from the only man who could say yea or nay, it was quickly arranged that Major John André, accompanied by Colonel Beverly Robinson, whose confiscated mansion was now Arnold's headquarters, should, on September 20, take ship aboard the sloop *Vulture,* from which André would be rowed ashore to a meeting with Arnold.

André would be dressed in full regimentals so that if captured, he would never be mistaken for a spy, although the uniform would be covered by a long blue coat. Clinton had told his adjutant general that he must never put on civilian clothes, and André had promised that he would not. It is not clear whether or not he expected to meet Arnold that night, but Arnold himself had decided that André should spend the night in the home of his agent, Joshua Hett Smith.

Joshua Hett Smith lived in a mansion overlooking the Hudson River crossing of King's Ferry and near the village of Haverstraw, where there was a landing. Locally he was suspected of Tory sympathies, inasmuch as his older brother William was the chief justice in British-held New York City. Although he was not exactly a cretin, he was extremely stupid, sly, self-esteeming and childishly fond of intrigue to the extent that he was forever pestering Arnold's predecessor with useless "intelligence." He was not so ardently enamored of the Crown that he would risk a hangnail in its service; rather, he was so disdainful of the bucolic clods who made up the hostile Patriot population surrounding his mansion that he secretly wished for their ultimate defeat. Actually his only true allegiance was to himself and his bottle, and so, when the new commandent, on the lookout for agents, did him the honor of visiting his home—soon to be known as "Treason House"—he popped a succession of corks that soon had him boasting like the simpleton he was of how well he had served the former commandant and wished to do the same for Arnold. But Smith did have the advantage of knowing the river and the area, together with owning the mansion that one day might be used as a safe house. His stupidity, it seemed to Arnold, made him the perfect dupe to carry out missions he could not comprehend. That was why Arnold chose Smith to row "Mr. Anderson" ashore and put him up for the night.

On September 20—the date set for the rendezvous—Major John André rode to Dobbs Ferry to board a small vessel that carried him to *Vulture* out on the river. In his eagerness for his mission, he forgot to deliver to the ship's captain a note from Clinton ordering him to return to Dobbs Ferry once André had disembarked. Instead, the ship remained at anchorage off Teller's Point, irritating Colonel James Livingston, commander of the Yankee outposts in the area. Livingston quickly began collecting cannon and shot to disabuse *Vulture* of its security. At midnight, the time set for the appearance of Arnold's agent, André came on deck. He was still excited, his head lifted skyward as though to drink in the beauty of that glittering heavenly bowl above him. He paced the deck, listening anxiously for the sound of splashing oars. But all he heard was the gentle splash of an occasional fish breaking the water. Dismayed, fearful that by his continued presence above decks he might arouse the curiosity of the sailors, he went below—finally retiring in disappointment.

Earlier that night, Smith had asked one of his tenants, Samuel Cahoon, to row him down the river, thus widening the circle of conspirators. Smith should have rowed the boat himself, but considered such a menial task to be beneath his station. Cahoon demurred, and Smith did not press him. Instead Smith asked Cahoon to carry a message to Arnold explaining the interruption. Again Cahoon objected, but the hectoring Smith insisted, and the sleepy farmer clambered aboard his dray horse and went shambling off to West Point. Just before sunrise the next day, he delivered the note to an aide who said that General Arnold was still asleep. When Arnold awoke, he was infuriated by Smith's letter. Deciding to rely on him no longer, he ordered out his barge and was rowed down to King's Ferry, ostentatiously inspecting outposts along the way. Colonel Livingston thought him strangely "reserved."

Finding Smith, he swallowed his disenchantment with him and told him to prepare to fetch "Mr. Anderson" that night. Then he went straight to a bedroom on Treason House's second floor. As much as he disliked this disruption in his plans, he would have to carry on. He sensed that there could be no third attempt at a meeting without unmasking the plot.

André thought the same when he awoke. He was too well known in camp to disappear a third time without arousing suspicion. Nor could he stay too long aboard *Vulture.*

That night Smith brought Cahoon to see General Arnold. Though obviously awed to be in such an exalted and famous presence, he again demurred when Arnold pleasantly informed him that he was expected to row out to *Vulture* that night to pick up a secret American agent. He did not openly object, but his body language—lifting one foot after another, plucking at his coat, removing his hat to scratch his head and then twisting the cap—did not suggest enthusiasm. Then he said he could not row that far alone, and Smith told him to get his brother Joseph. Samuel soon returned to say his brother's wife had forbidden him to go. Enraged, Arnold smashed his fist on a table and threatened to arrest both of them. Now Samuel agreed to fetch Joseph, and Arnold relaxed—until Smith returned to say that both brothers stood in the yard like balky mules refusing to move. Hurrying downstairs, Arnold sought to persuade them by offering them a gift of flour and saying, "It must be done for the good of the country." With slow reluctance, they then agreed to go.

Now Smith discovered that the rowboat he had ordered had not arrived. He sent his black slave to investigate, while a distraught Arnold went back upstairs. Joseph came up to inform him that the rowboat was on the way, and Arnold relaxed again. But then Joseph, more mulish than his brother, began to fidget. Finally he blurted out that it was too late, and he would not go until morning. Now Arnold exploded, pretending to summon the guard to arrest Joseph and his brother. With this, Smith took the Cahoons downstairs, fixed them a stiff drink and at last induced them to go, so informing Arnold. Elated, Arnold limped downstairs to clap the sullen Cahoons jovially on the back, and then watched them narrowly as they disappeared in the darkness moving toward the landing. His nerves frayed to the snapping point, Arnold listened to the balky Cahoons protesting Smith's order to muffle their oars in sheepskins, but then sighed again in relief when he heard no more.

Underneath *Vulture* Joshua Hett Smith was shaken to hear an officer cursing him in a volley of seagoing oaths, threatening to hang him at the yardarm—but was chastened when a cabin boy appeared above to say, "The captain orders the man below."

Inside the captain's cabin he was surprised to see his erstwhile neighbor—Beverly Robinson—dressed in a British colonel's uniform, but he said nothing. Robinson fetched André, and was prepared to leave the ship with him until it was discovered that Arnold's passes provided for only one male adult in addition to Smith and the Cahoons. With regret, Robinson had to stay behind. André would meet Arnold alone, and he would be returned by Arnold under another pass so that the British made no provision to pick him up. So Smith and André in his long blue coat left the cabin, going over the side to clamber down a Jacob's ladder into the rowboat. In silence the boat set out for the return journey to Haverstraw, where Benedict Arnold awaited Mr. Anderson inside a stand of fragrant firs. It was there that Major John André, adjutant general of the British Army in North America, groped through the murky dark to seize the hands of Major General Benedict Arnold, commandant of West Point.

Arnold was miffed when André offered him only £6,000 for betrayal of the fort, win or lose, insisting that he receive the stipulated £10,000. André then promised to persuade Clinton to pay that amount. Next they discussed the possibility of capturing Washington with the fort and thus making doubly certain that the Rebellion would be crushed. But this, they quickly realized, was but a wild chance that could boomerang: if Washington returned to the fort from Hartford at the time of the assault, he would assume command and override all Arnold's orders. To try to pick him off in a raid was also risky, an outside chance that might warn the Americans and thus ruin the entire scheme.

Then they began to exchange information: Arnold describing the terrain, the fortifications and the disposition of the garrison, André enumerating the ships, men and artillery that Clinton would command. In effect, they put together a military ballet. Each step of Clinton's was to be counterpointed with a counterstep by Arnold, seemingly to blunt the enemy's moves but actually to complement them. It was a conference of two or three hours' duration, passing so swiftly that before it was finished the pale light of dawn filtered through the riotous autumn foliage and the eastern mountains gradually took shape.

It was then that Arnold asked Smith to have the Cahoons row Mr. Anderson back to *Vulture*. But when he did, the brothers said they were too tired and feared the Rebel guard boats. Neither Arnold nor André protested, probably because they still had much to discuss, and the American traitor had papers he wished André to see. Arnold had not brought them with him because he feared to light a lantern in the woods. So they mounted their horses—one had been provided for André—and rode slowly toward Treason House. A sentry challenged them, and Arnold gave the password. They were now inside an American position, a violation of Clinton's orders, but André made no protest. Instead he gazed in silent awe at the mighty river—four miles wide at Haverstraw Bay—glowing salmon pink in the light of a new blue day. Then they heard cannon fire. Looking downriver, they saw *Vulture* off Teller's Point taking hits from Colonel Livingston's artillery. Unfortunately for André and Arnold, a veteran artillery officer had advised Livingston that to fire his puny four-pounders at that range would be "a waste of powder." So Livingston had obtained a six-pounder and a howitzer, and shot and shell were now hulling the British ship and damaging its rigging.

Vulture quickly upped anchor and sailed downstream, anchoring off Sing Sing a few miles below. One effect of this exchange, witnessed by Smith and the Cahoons, was to convince Arnold's faint-hearted agent that the river was no place to be after dark. So the Cahoons were dismissed, trudging back to their farms, while inside Treason House, Arnold showed André the papers he had prepared: a detailed list of the garrison's strength of three thousand, the number needed to defend each position, the caliber and quantity of the fort's ordnance, the artillery commander's plan of defense and Washington's military intentions. André was deeply impressed, so much so that he persuaded a reluctant Arnold to allow him to take the papers to Clinton. André said he would hide the documents inside his stockings, promising Arnold that if he were in danger of being captured, he would destroy them. As Arnold prepared to return to West Point, André later recalled, there was "some mention of my crossing the river and going [back] by another route, but I objected much against it, and thought it was settled that the way I had come, I was also to return."

But it wasn't.

That night, with Arnold safely returned to West Point, Joshua Hett Smith informed Mr. Anderson that it would be too dangerous to row back to the *Vulture*. It would also be too dangerous for Mr. Anderson to wear the British army uniform. Rather, he should appear in the civilian clothes proper to a merchant, and then they would cross the river together and proceed toward the British lines. André objected vehemently, but Smith merely smiled his stupid smile and eventually André found himself once again disobeying Clinton's orders by exchanging his scarlet uniform coat for a claret-colored coat with gold-lace buttonholes lent to him by Smith. A round civilian hat replaced his tricorne. Beneath his long blue coat, his boots, nankeen breeches and waistcoat, though military, would not be conspicuous.

At sunset the two men mounted horses and rode away from Haverstraw, bound for Pine Bridge across the Croton River and the British lines on the other side. Along the way André, with a sinking heart, realized that his guide was a fourteen-carat fool. Rather than move quietly along, he invited attention: pausing at the ferry crossing below Stony Point to share a bowl of grog with a group of rebel officers, waving gaily to everyone he passed, boasting openly of his intimacy with Arnold, even calling to their side as a companion an officer who had been present when André dictated the terms of surrender for Stony Point. But André felt some relief after they had clattered aboard the ferry and the oarsmen shoved off, until Smith—now half drunk—began clowning at the rail for the amusement of the boatmen. Upon reaching the farther bank, Smith actually paid a call on Colonel Livingston. André's heart sank when he heard Livingston in his tent invite Smith and his companion to stay for dinner and drinks. Here, however, Smith's ballooning self-esteem came to the distraught Britisher's rescue: oh, no, my dear colonel, our business is much too important to permit delay.

So they rode on, into a lonely and empty countryside filled with abandoned homes. This was border territory, dominated by bands of robber ruffians, the Tory Cowboys and Rebel Skinners, whose allegiance to either side was usually just a cover for their lawless looting. Here they were halted by a sentry at a Yankee outpost commanded by Captain Ebenezer Boyd, one of those doubting and eternally suspicious officers who question the slightest departure from routine. For a quarter hour Boyd argued with Smith over the validity of his pass from a man of such high rank and fame as Benedict Arnold. At last, he relented, insisting, however, that the two men stop somewhere for the night to avoid a band of Tory Cowboys in the area.

Nothing would have pleased André more than to have fallen into their hands, but Smith took heed and led André down the road to a cabin. Smith knocked on the door. There was no answer. André's spirits rose. Perhaps the cabin was empty and they would have to continue on their way. But then the bolts were drawn, and a surly man named Andreas Miller, his cowering family silhouetted against a blazing fireplace, motioned them inside. Miller pointed silently toward an open bedroom. The two travelers went inside, and the door slammed and there was the sound of a key turning in the lock.

At dawn they remounted, making for Pine Bridge. Suddenly the silent André recovered his customary loquaciousness. Shining out of the mists ahead was the Croton and the bridge. Journey's end! Success! At the end of the road at least a lieutenant colonelcy! Smith stared at his companion in astonishment as the vision of the end of the war and his own leading part in it loosened André's tongue. He spoke of everything: of the war, of music and poetry and painting and the wild beauty of the Hudson Valley. At last they were at the bridge, and Smith prepared to say good-bye. André was glad to be rid of Smith, first borrowing a few Continental dollars before they parted. He rode onto the bridge, listening happily to his horse's hoofs clattering in the still silence. Soon he was near Tarrytown—and there, barring the way with a shout, stood three ragged ruffians with raised firelocks.

"Gentlemen," André said with a charming smile, his eyes upon the leader, an awkward giant of a man named John Paulding, "I hope you belong to our party."

"What party?" Paulding growled.

"The lower party," Andre said, and the big man nodded. André continued: "I am glad to see you. I am an officer in the British service, and have now been on particular business in the country, and I hope you will not detain me." To show that he was a gentleman, he pulled out his gold watch.

Paulding replied by ordering André to dismount. With a laugh and a shrug intended to demonstrate his patience and good will, André handed Arnold's pass to the giant. Paulding read it with slowly moving lips, glancing now and then at his companions, David Williams and Isaac van Wart. Again he ordered André to dismount. André did, once more feigning indifference and saying: "Gentlemen, you had best let me go, or you will bring yourselves into trouble, for, by your stopping me, you will detain the general's business."

At this Paulding shouted: "Damn Arnold's pass! You said you was a British officer. Where is your money?"

Thus the account of the dialogue given later by Major André. Paulding, however, differed, declaring: "I told him I hoped he would not be offended, and I told him we did not mean to take anything from him, and told him there were many bad people going along the road, and I did not know but perhaps he might be one, and I asked him if he had any letters about him."

It is not possible to accept either version with certainty, if only because both men were under duress by then: André fearing execution as a spy, Paulding not wishing to be charged as a thief. But then, having been asked for his money, André said he replied:

"Gentlemen, I have none about me."

"You a British officer, and no money! Paulding shouted in disbelief. "Let's search him!"

With a sinking heart Major John André was led into a thicket, where he divested himself of his clothes, one by one, his captors finding in them his gold watch and chain and Smith's dollars, which they confiscated. Standing naked in his boots, André thought for a moment that his tormentors were satisfied, but then, according to Williams: "We told him to pull off his boots, which he seemed indifferent about, but we got one boot off, and searched in that boot, but could find nothing; and we found there were some papers in the bottom of his stocking, next to his foot, on which we made him pull his stocking off, and found three papers wrapped up." Paulding, the only one of them who was literate, grabbed the papers and began to read, his lips again moving with painful slowness.

"This," he shouted in a voice of doom, "is a *spy!*"

André was delivered to Lieutenant Colonel John Jameson, commander of the American outpost at Northcastle. Jameson was puzzled. True, he had been notified by Arnold that a trader named "John Anderson" would be coming his way, and he did have a pass from Arnold, but the man was captured going in the wrong direction and bearing suspicious papers. Could the fighting hero of the Revolution be a traitor? If not, and Jameson had acted as though he were, he would suffer the gravest consequences. So the colonel compromised by telling a relieved André that he was returning him to Arnold, while sending a messenger with the incriminating papers post haste to meet Washington on the Danbury Road bound for West Point. Then he sent André toward West Point under a guard.

Jameson had acted on the side of his suspicions, but with a subtlety calculated to disarm both André and Arnold. Danbury and West Point were about equidistant from North Castle. However, the messenger to Danbury and Washington left in the afternoon on a fast horse, while André departed at night on foot. Four soldiers marched before and behind him and to either side of him, while Lieutenant Solomon Allen, on horseback, threatened with drawn sword to run him through should he attempt to escape. André had no such intention. Rather, to be delivered to Arnold was like a passport to freedom! He was unaware that Washington had entered the drama or that Lieutenant Allen carried a letter from Jameson describing the documents found on André's person. A three-cornered race now ensued.

If André, with or without the letter carried by Allen, were delivered to Arnold in time, both conspirators could escape. If André were delayed on the road and Allen's letter reached Arnold ahead of him, then Arnold could flee. But if Washington received the incriminating documents first, both the traitor and the spy would be caught. But then, like fickle fate, the era's agonizingly slow speed of communications, either oral or by message, on horseback or on foot, began to complicate the race.

First, Washington did not go toward West Point by way of the lower route to Danbury, but chose instead the upper way through Fishkill, fifteen miles above the fort. En route with Lafayette, Knox, Hamilton and other aides, he encountered the French ambassador La Luzerne, and the party turned back to dine and sleep at Fishkill. When Jameson's messenger, mounted on his fast horse, reached Danbury, he could not find Washington, and he turned about heading for South Salem.

André, to his dismay, was also headed that way, for Jameson had changed his mind. He had conferred with Major Benjamin Tallmadge and both concluded that Arnold, if not actually a traitor, had much explaining to do. They also agreed that not to send Mr. Anderson to West Point, as Arnold had ordered, would risk a charge of insubordination. To protect themselves, they concocted a story of enemy patrols on the road above them, sending a courier galloping off to overtake André with the explanation that for his own safety, he must return. Allen was to deliver him to South Salem, and then Allen was to turn about and ride with the letter to Arnold. Allen obeyed this new order, and when he informed André of the change, André turned away from sanctuary with a sinking heart and walked instead toward a prison cell at South Salem.

At West Point, meanwhile, Joshua Hett Smith had informed an elated Benedict Arnold that he had escorted Mr. Anderson to the very edge of British-held territory. Arnold broke the good news to his beloved Peggy, and the overjoyed couple fell soundly asleep in their feather bed, perhaps dreaming of the peerage that awaited them across the river. Smith, meanwhile, had gone on to Fishkill, where he joined Washington at table. Because he did not suspect the true character of the mission he had carried out, he was not upset when Washington casually remarked that he and his staff would breakfast in the morning with General Arnold and his wife.

While the Arnolds and Washington slept, a weary John André was delivered to Lieutenant Joshua King at South Salem. King locked André in a small bedroom with mounted guards at the door and window. André looked frazzled. He had not shaved for two days, and there was a stubble of black beard on his face. When he asked King if he might have his filthy clothes washed, the lieutenant consented and graciously lent him a suit of dry ones. The two men then walked together in a spacious yard surrounded by sentries. André was sunk in thought. He saw clearly that the plot had failed. Arnold could no longer help. Now, he must do what he could to escape the odious imputation of spying! Turning to King, he announced that he was not Mr. John Anderson, an American agent, but rather Major John André, adjutant general of the British army. He asked for pen and paper, and the astounded King complied. André then sat down and composed a letter to Washington requesting clemency. He had entered an enemy post in uniform but against his will, he wrote, and was thus a prisoner of war—and a prisoner of war had the acknowledged right to try to escape in civilian clothes. Thus, he was not a spy and could not be so charged. André's letter was added to the other incriminating documents intended for Washington, and the horseman who had failed to find him at Danbury now set out for West Point, where Washington was expected next day.

This courier was far behind Lieutenant Allen, who had set out for the same destination hours earlier, although his pace was slowed to the walk of the foot soldier who accompanied him. The late starter thus could have moved more quickly, if his speed had not been reduced by a friendly glass or two at a tavern along the way or a flirtatious chat with a comely lass who waved at him as he passed. Allen, denied such solace by the presence of an enlisted man, was therefore able to maintain his lead when both messengers stopped for the night. More than thirty-six hours had elapsed since the capture of André, and still no ranking American officer was aware of what had happened.

In the morning Washington and his party made for West Point, pausing along the way to inspect fortifications. When Lafayette reminded him that Mrs. Arnold was waiting breakfast for him, he replied jokingly that all his young officers were half in love with pretty Peggy. But he did despatch two aides—Majors James McHenry and Samuel Shaw—to ride ahead to tell Mrs. Arnold to begin the meal. They found Peggy still in bed, so they sat down at the breakfast table with General Arnold. Arnold rose a few minutes later to enter the buttery. Inside he met Lieutenant Allen and his soldier. Allen silently handed him Colonel Jameson's message. Arnold opened it, glancing vaguely around the buttery as though wondering what he had come there for. He began to read, his blue eyes beginning to glitter, the color draining from his swarthy face:

"I have sent Lieutenant Allen with a certain John Anderson taken going into New York. He had a passport signed in your name. He had a parcel of papers taken from his stockings, which I think of a very dangerous tendency. The papers I have sent to General Washington."

Arnold glanced quickly at the second message, which explained that Mr. Anderson had been returned to South Salem. Thrown "into great confusion," according to Allen, Arnold told him to wait for an answer and limped rapidly into the yard to order his horse saddled, sending a servant down to the river to tell his barge crew to stand by. Then, still in "unusual agitation," he limped through the breakfast room and quickly upstairs to his bedroom.

Peggy was sitting up in bed, hungrily awaiting the arrival of some young officers with fresh peaches. In a desperate whisper, Arnold informed his beloved that all was lost. Peggy cried aloud in anguish. There came a low knock on the door and a deferential voice declaring, "His Excellency is nigh at hand." Peggy fell back on her pillow in a faint, and Arnold rushed out the door, almost bowling over the informant, clattering rapidly downstairs on his high heel and making for the stable yard at a limping run. Springing into the saddle from his good leg, he rode around the barn and almost cannoned into a quartet of Washington's dragoons. At once, his hand dropped to his horse pistol—but the horsemen reined aside deferentially, and Arnold galloped recklessly down a steep incline to the river bank and his barge. There, inexplicably, though he was leaving everything he possessed behind him and could expect pursuit momentarily, Arnold, just as he had done when he left Canada, wasted valuable seconds unbuckling his saddle and tossing it onto the barge. Then he went limping aboard and ordered his boatmen to shove off, hoist their sails and make for Stony Point. Arriving there, he told them to change course and head for *Vulture,* where he had "particular business of His Excellency." Confused, they hesitated—and in his alarm, Arnold, quickly persuaded them to obey by promising them two gallons of rum.

Aboard *Vulture* its skipper Captain Andrew Sutherland and Colonel Robinson stood at the rail watching the approach of Arnold's barge, joyfully anticipating the return of André. Instead only Arnold came climbing up the Jacob's ladder, followed by his boatmen. In consternation, they heard him report that the plot had failed and—worse—that André was a prisoner. Both were frightened at the prospect of facing a wrathful Clinton, and they reproached Arnold for not having returned André by water, as he had promised. Crestfallen, Benedict Arnold chose that most unpropitious moment to show these doubters what a great hero and soldier had come to their side, what a flow of American deserters would follow him! Going up to his nine bargemen, he told them that he had found the Revolution an evil cause and was now a British general empowered to raise a Tory brigade. "If you will join me, lads, I will make sergeants and corporals of you all, and for you, James," he said to the coxswain, "I will do something more."

"No, sir!" James replied in a biting bitter rage. "One coat is enough for me to wear at a time." Feeling the loathing in their eyes, Arnold tried to argue with them, but then, in a helpless fury, turned to Sutherland to demand that these faithful Patriots be thrown in chains into the brig. Then he went limping slowly down the ladder into the cabin once occupied by Major John André.

George Washington was somewhat dismayed not to find the Arnolds awaiting him at the breakfast table, until Colonel Richard Varick, Arnold's secretary, explained that the commandant had hastened across the river to prepare a reception for him. This explanation mollified the commander in chief, who began conversing with his staff. Upstairs, a revived Peggy Arnold heard his clear, calm voice and she almost burst into a hysterical scream. No! No, no, no! She must not. She must give her husband time to escape! With her and her precious baby now in rebel hands, no one must be allowed to suspect her part in the conspiracy. She lay quivering on her bed with her face sunk in pillows lest her hysteria betray her, until she heard Washington departing for West Point. Then she erupted: screaming, shrieking, raving, dashing about her bedroom with disheveled hair clad only in her scanty, revealing nightgown. A horrified Colonel Varick came rushing to her side. He knew the source of her hysteria, having learned from Lieutenant Allen of Arnold's treachery. He sought to soothe her, but "She seized me by the hand with this distressing address and a wild look: 'Colonel Varick, have you ordered my child to be killed?'"

Thus there began a performance by Peggy Shippen Arnold that would have done credit to the famous Perdita—the darling of the London stage. By her feigned hysteria, she deceived everyone who came near her, including Dr. William Eustis, who begged Varick "for God's sake" to send for Arnold "or the woman would die." Having thus diverted attention from her escaping husband, Peggy next begged to see General Washington. There was a hot iron on her head that could be removed only by His Excellency. But Washington was across the river, surprised not to receive a welcoming artillery salute, and even more startled not to find any reception prepared or Benedict Arnold there in person.

But then Alexander Hamilton handed him the packet delivered by the Danbury courier, and when he broke it open and read the contents, he knew why. When Lafayette appeared, Washington cried out in a voice of anguish: "Arnold has betrayed us! … Whom can we trust now?" His voice still breaking, he ordered Hamilton and McHenry to gallop to King's Ferry in the hope of capturing the traitor. Then he returned to Arnold's headquarters, where he was taken to see Arnold's hysterical wife. Such was the nobility of this man that in the midst of the most despairing moment of his life, he tried to comfort the raving woman. But when Varick told her that Washington was there, come to take the hot iron from her head, she exclaimed: "No! That is not General Washington. That is the man who is going to assist Colonel Varick in killing my child!" Unable to console her, obviously upset, Washington left the bedroom, and Peggy Arnold sank back upon her pillow, convinced, now that she had seen the commander in chief's anguished visage, that her husband had indeed reached safety.

That night a silent and reserved Washington dined with his staff. "Never was there a more melancholy dinner," Lafayette wrote. Later a courier from Hamilton arrived bearing three letters sent ashore from *Vulture.* One was from Robinson, defending André against the suspicion of spying, and the others were from Arnold to his wife and to Washington. Ever the gentleman, Washington sent Peggy's letter unopened upstairs, together with a note explaining that though it was his duty to capture her husband, he was happy to tell her that Arnold was safe. His own letter from the officer whom he had loved and trusted spoke hypocritically "of love to my country." Then he begged Washington's protection for his wife "as good and as innocent as an angel and incapable of doing wrong."

Washington now began to act. He had known for three hours of Arnold's treachery, but had done nothing except to send Hamilton and McHenry on their vain errand. He had delayed probably because until he received these letters, he could not have known for sure if Arnold had actually fled, or was merely absent on some unexplained errand; or of how many accomplices Arnold had besides André. But now, in his eagerness to make West Point defensible against a possible attack by Clinton, he confirmed Hamilton's earlier suggestion to Nathanael Greene that he put the Continental Army on marching alert, relieved Colonel Livingston of command of the outposts just on the chance that he might have been a party to the plot, summoned all troops from the surrounding countryside to West Point and notified Arnold's second in command to prepare for an attack.

In the meantime Peggy Arnold's hysterical deception went shrieking to its successful end. Although it is possible that her original hysteria might have been genuine, she seems to have been able to suppress it to gain time for her husband's escape and then permit it to flow unchecked to conceal her own guilt. Moreover, Peggy's history of hysteria shows her always recovering from her fits with her health unharmed and whatever secret she sought to shield unrevealed. Yet so effective was her performance that Alexander Hamilton, admittedly an incorrigible swain hopelessly susceptible to a woman's wiles, could write: "One moment she raved, another she melted into tears. Sometimes she pressed her infant to her bosom and lamented its fate occasioned by the imprudence of its father, in a manner that would have pierced insensibility itself. All the sweetness of beauty, all the loveliness of innocence, all the tenderness of a wife and all the fondness of a mother showed themselves in her appearance and conduct.... It was the most affecting scene I ever was witness to."

Affecting indeed: even *effectively* affecting, for with her friend André in durance vile, her husband in disgraced exile, every heart in the headquarters mansion, from Washington on down to the lowliest scullery maid, beat with love and pity for poor, pretty Peggy—the mastermind of the entire plot.

⋆ 64 ⋆

TREASON III: ANDRÉ'S END

Few tragic figures in history have encountered as many mischances as those that overwhelmed Major John André—from the gunboats that chased Arnold's barge on the first attempt at rendezvous, to being forced to stay overnight in Treason House, to the cannonade that drove *Vulture* downriver and so terrified Joshua Hett Smith that he refused to return André by the safer water route, to the selection of this feckless fool as his guide, to the encounter with that trio of oafish Cowboys within a few scant yards of sanctuary—but none worked so terribly against him as his failure to inform his friends of the line that he had adopted in his own defense. In his letter to General Washington, André had argued that he had "fairly risked his person" on a military mission, but Colonel Robinson, after questioning Arnold, had written the American commander that André had gone ashore under a flag of truce. Whereas André claimed that he was forced (by Arnold) behind American lines, becoming a prisoner of war, Robinson insisted that André had willingly placed himself under Arnold's orders. When André argued that as a captive he was entitled to use any means of escape, including putting on civilian clothes, Robinson stated that in all his acts—assuming a feigned name, wearing civilian clothes, carrying those damning papers—André had been acting in obedience to the orders of the authorized American commander in the area. "Under these circumstances," Robinson concluded, "Major Andre cannot be detained by you without the greatest violation of flags.... I must desire you will order him to be set at liberty and allowed to return immediately."

Washington made no reply, probably because he did not wish to dignify Robinson's illogical arguments. The American chief, together with the seven generals convened on the board that would try André, certainly did not take André's own line of defense seriously: that he was "forced" inside an American post and was therefore a prisoner of war. But now Robinson was insisting that André came ashore under a flag of truce (which he did not, and which he did not claim) and subsequently obeyed the orders of Arnold. But for what did he come ashore, and what were Arnold's "orders?" No officer is obligated to obey an enemy officer's orders, no matter how high his rank, nor is such obedience a defense against spying. Moreover, a flag does not cover the suborning of treason. If André had been acting legally—once again his purpose was never described in either version—he would have had no need for an assumed name. The instructions Washington gave André's captors indicate that he regarded André as a spy. These instructions were: "I would not wish Mr. André to be treated with insult, but he does not appear on the footing of a common prisoner of war, and therefore he is not entitled to the usual indulgences they receive, and is to be most closely and narrowly watched." André was finally moved to Tappan, near Washington's headquarters. His bedroom was a shed under a sloping roof, although his living room was spacious. He was not permitted outside, but was kept under the constant surveillance of American officers, who watched him in pairs.

Throughout the Continental Army headquarters there was universal sympathy and affection for this charming, handsome and gracious man, regarded by everyone as the unfortunate victim of circumstance and of the perfidy of the unspeakable Arnold, who had chosen to save himself while his accomplice blundered into captivity. Even Washington, whose duty it was to remain sternly aloof, spoke of him as "a gallant and accomplished officer." Everyone marveled at André's calm bearing, unaware of his conviction that it was absurd to suggest that he could be tried as a spy. John André, well born, well bred, well educated—the adjutant general of the British Army—to be tried in the "mean character" of a common spy? Preposterous! Moreover, General Clinton held many leading rebels who had been taken under similar circumstances, whom he would gladly exchange for Major André. So he calmly awaited his return to New York.

In that British-held city Sir Henry Clinton was beside himself with anguish when he heard that his favorite officer and closest friend had been captured and was being held as a spy. To Germain he wrote: "The general has escaped to us, but we have lost—how shall I tell it to you—poor André. I am distressed beyond words to describe." In his agony that he might never see André's beloved face again, Clinton treated Arnold with a cold contempt that at least concealed his hatred. He kept his part of the bargain—but maintained the original offer of six thousand pounds, not the ten thousand André would not now be able to obtain for him—and created him a brigadier general in the provincial service with the right to wear that uniform but the true rank of only a colonel in the British Army. Arnold would, of course, never receive an independent command of any importance, and would always be held on a leash by a superior general. Having boasted that his fame alone would attract thousands of rebel deserters to the brigade he proposed to raise and command, Arnold received barely forty. From the Tories, whom he expected to acclaim him, he received sneers, frowns and turned backs, for these aristocratic exiles in their own country considered this low-born adventurer in an evil cause to have been motivated more by greed than by principle. So did most of the British officers, many of whom vowed that they would refuse to serve under him.

Meanwhile, Benedict Arnold frantically besought his beloved Peggy to join him with their little son. But Peggy had opted to return to the bosom of her father. Journeying across New Jersey, she stopped in Paramus at the home of Mrs. Theodora Prevost, the widow of a British officer. There, in the only recorded instance of her telling the truth about the conspiracy, she told Mrs. Prevost that she was "heartily sick" of the "theatrics" that she had been compelled to assume. She said that she had always been an enemy of the Patriot cause and that it was only "through great persuasion and unceasing perseverance" that she had convinced her husband to offer himself to the British. Resuming her journey, she was shocked by the hatred shown her whenever her carriage stopped. Everywhere, it seemed—in press and pulpit from the oceans to the mountains—her husband was being vilified in the vilest terms. Everywhere also, it seemed, there arose demands that Washington exchange André for Arnold—and these demands frightened her.

George Washington did indeed try to get the traitor in his clutches. At first Sergeant Major John Champe, of Light-Horse Harry Lee's famous dragoons, was sent into New York as a "deserter" to Arnold's brigade. The traitor was delighted to receive him, elevating him to a post of trust. When his chance came, Champe wrenched the palings from Arnold's fence, tacking them back so lightly that they could be easily removed when he dragged the general bound and gagged down to the waterfront and a waiting boat. But the chance of finding Arnold alone and unarmed never appeared. Washington's next attempt was more subtle. Unable in his exalted position to make a formal request for such an unthinkable exchange, he had a subordinate hint, during an exchange of letters, that should Clinton "in any way suffer General Washington to get within his power General Arnold, then Major André should be immediately released."

Clinton was sorely tempted by this suggestion, for he was doing all possible to secure André's release. He had appointed a delegation of prominent Tories to protest his friend's detention as "illegal," and even proposed that the foreign generals—Rochambeau and Knyphausen—be named as mediators, but neither of these actions moved Washington, who could never forget Howe's summary and cruel treatment of Nathan Hale. Sir Henry could not agree to such an exchange, even though he detested Arnold, for it would inhibit any further attempts to attract deserters. That is why he said: "A deserter is never given up." He uttered that refusal with a broken heart, for in the exchange of letters had come a message from Washington stating that André had been taken in activities that flags "were never meant to authorize or countenance in the least degree"; that his friend had confessed that he had not been under the sanction of a flag; and, finally—oh, dreadful phrase!—that a board of general officers had convicted André of spying and sentenced him to be hanged. This horrifying communication caused Clinton to lose his balance, for he now resorted to threats, not by himself, of course, for his position, like Washington's, forbade such a direct approach, but by Arnold, who wrote to his former chief and friend that unless Washington released André, Arnold would be bound to execute any American soldiers "as may fall within my power" and that Clinton held forty South Carolinia gentlemen "to whom clemency can no longer be extended" should André be hanged. To this threat there was no reply, and on October 2, Major John André was informed that on that very day he would hang by the neck until he was dead.

George Washington had no choice but to hang André. Arnold's treason had shaken the Patriot cause like no other event in the Revolutionary War. Civilians and soldiers alike were joined in a common distrust of the army. Congress, already fearful of a military dictatorship, became even more suspicious, while the common soldiers—learning how Arnold had betrayed his boatmen into captivity—felt more certain than ever that the kind of hectoring officers they hated were conspiring to form a postwar aristocracy. These were also the black days that had convinced Clinton that the moment to take West Point was propitious. Should a British spy, however manly and charming, receive any punishment less than death, it would be construed as softheartedness in the high command and provoke a reaction that would be furious and bitter enough to sink the rebel cause forever. Washington, then, having ordered so many young American soldiers to die for an ideal, simply could not spare André. Nor could he change the mode of execution, as much as André might plead with him to be shot as an officer and a gentleman. Again, he had no choice: André had been convicted of spying, and the mode of execution for spies in those days was the noose.

At noon of October 2 John André was ready. He spoke quietly to his guards, who could barely control their sorrow, and rebuked his batman for breaking into sobs. "Leave me until you can show yourself more manly!" Breakfasted and shaved, he carefully clothed himself "in the rich uniform of a British staff officer." To his guards he said calmly: "I am ready at any moment, gentlemen, to wait on you." At that moment music sounded and a large detachment of troops formed outside André's place of confinement. At once André linked his arms with his guards and pulling them after him, ran out the door, down the steps and into the center of the square of soldiers. The fife and drum corps struck up the death march, and as André marched in step to it, he said in a loud clear voice: "I am very much surprised to find your troops under such good discipline, and your music is excellent." Under such circumstances, no compliment could have been more gallant—and yet, to the very end, it was the deprecating remark of the superior and supercilious British officer to his buckskin inferiors.

All in step, the procession marched up a hill and into a field packed with spectators held in check by lines of soldiers. Upon sight of André, the mob surged forward, but then, impressed by the victim's composure, shrank back again. Many of the churchgoing pious among the spectators were scandalized that a man could both refuse the consolation of a clergyman and walk so calmly to his death as though defying the Almighty. Others were awed "to see a man go out of time without fear, but all the time smiling." When André caught sight of the knot of the mounted general officers who had convicted him, he bowed graciously to each of them, as though absolving them of any blame, but when he looked up and saw the gallows standing on a little rise ahead of him, he paused, stepping back as though in horror, and asked:

"Must I then die in this manner?"

Told that it was unavoidable, he said: "I am reconciled to my fate, but not to the mode." Head erect, he strode purposefully toward the gallows and the little horse-drawn cart standing beneath it. At first he made as though to spring onto the cart, but then he put his knee on the tailboard and clambered up. His fine figure in its gorgeous uniform was now in full view of the mob, and a murmur arose. André seemed to shrink back from the dangling rope, but then straightened and said: "It will be but a momentary pang."

Taking off his hat, he gave it to his sobbing batman, revealing "a long and beautiful head of hair" bound with a black ribbon and hanging down his back. Colonel Alexander Scammel read the death sentence to him, and he listened quietly with his hands on his hips. After Scammell asked him if he had anything to say, he straightened and replied: "I have nothing more to say, gentlemen, but this: you all bear me witness that I meet my fate as a brave man." With this reply, a melancholy wailing arose from the crowd, and the frightful figure of the hangman jumped onto the wagon. His face was unshaven and blackened with soot taken from the outside of a grease pot. André would not have been other than appalled at this apparition, and when the hangman sought to put the noose around his neck, he snatched it from his filthy fingers and placed it over his own head, securing the knot on the right side of his neck. Then he tied a white handkerchief over his eyes, but when Scammell shouted, "His hands must be tied," he undid the bandage, gracefully drew another handkerchief from his pocket and handed it to the hangman. After André had blindfolded himself again, his hands were tied behind his back. Then this foul creature jumped down from the cart to go shinnying up a gallows post and secure the loose end of the rope to the crossbeam. Dropping nimbly to the ground, he ran toward the horses with a whip in his hand. As the crowd began to moan and yell hysterically, he struck the horses, the cart moved—and the gallant Major John André did indeed "go out of time."

★ 65 ★

THE BATTLE OF KING'S MOUNTAIN

After Cornwallis's victories at Charleston and Camden, Sir Henry Clinton had instructed His Lordship to hold fast to what he had—South Carolina and Georgia—and not to risk losing them by some bold and perhaps rash adventure. Clinton's plan was to subdue Delaware, with its numerous Tories, in the following summer of 1781, and thus, holding that state with New York, South Carolina and Georgia, he could commence a war of attrition against the rebels that would so whittle them that he could at least save a vast territory, if not all the colonies, for the Crown.

But then, as Cornwallis consolidated his hold on Georgia and South Carolina, Clinton began to look favorably upon an expedition into North Carolina. This incursion was eminently acceptable to the aggressive Cornwallis, who was panting for an offensive war. He had already induced Clinton to allow him to make his reports directly to London, rather than to his chief in New York, and had thus secured for himself what amounted to an independent command. He now wished to drive farther north than the Old North State, into Virginia, and to consolidate the entire South clear up to Pennsylvania. This plan was forwarded to Germain, who instructed Clinton to support it.

Cornwallis marched north from Camden in mid-September 1780 in two divisions: the main body under himself and a secondary force led by Banastre Tarleton. En route to the border, both columns were harassed by bands of mounted American riflemen, a particularly fierce skirmish erupting on September 12 at Wahab's Plantation between a detachment of Tarleton's Tories and Colonel William Davie's light dragoons and two companies of riflemen led by Major George Davidson. In this skirmish, Tarleton lost 60 men killed or wounded, together with ninety-six completely equipped horses and a stand of 120 arms. Davie's loss was but one man wounded. In another flare-up near Charlotte, however, the British Legion took its revenge upon Davie, inflicting casualties of thirty killed and wounded on the Americans, while receiving losses of exactly half that number themselves. Shortly afterward, Cornwallis sent orders to Major Patrick Ferguson at Ninety-six in South Carolina to march to North Carolina.

At Ninety-six the fierce and resolute Ferguson had drawn an enormous number of South Carolina Loyalists to his command, so that eventually he commanded a formidable force of four thousand well-trained soldiers divided into seven regiments. With these soldiers he held the district of Ninety-six in absolute subjection, sending out detachments to punish and plunder the rebels and to encourage the "overlies," or young Patriots hiding across the mountains, rather than take the oath of allegiance to join the king's army. His orders from Cornwallis had been to take a force of Tories into Tryon County west of Charlotte to secure the western half of North Carolina. If this could be done, a flood of Crown sympathizers would flow into his army, so Cornwallis thought, and secure his flanks from rebel strikes.

Ferguson moved into North Carolina with a thousand militiamen and a hundred men from his American Volunteer regiment, an elite corps of Tory riflemen. Why he did not take more of his command at Ninety-six is not clear, unless he was afraid to leave it too reduced to cope with the constant threat of American guerrillas, such as those under Francis Marion, Thomas Sumter and Andrew Pickens. Whatever his reason, to divide his force and take the lesser formation north was not a happy decision. A second mistake was to send a captured American militiaman over the Blue Ridge into what is now east Tennessee with a message to Colonel Isaac Shelby that if he did not surrender, Cornwallis "would come over the mountains and put him to death, and burn his whole country." It was not the sort of threat to which these "over-mountain" men were accustomed to submit. So they reached for those wicked long Deckland rifles above the fireplace and saddled up.

No breed of frontiersman existed in America hardier than these settlements of mostly Irish and Scots-Irish along the Watauga River. Fiercely independent, hunters, Indian fighters, deadly shots with those rifles to which they had given such names as "Sweet Lips" or "Hot Lead," they could campaign for days on their horses with no other equipment than a blanket, a hunting knife and a bag of parched corn sweetened with molasses or honey. When the corn gave out, they lived off fresh-killed game. Mostly illiterate, with few of their leaders familiar with any book other than the Bible, none of them could have quoted a line from Tom Paine's *Common Sense* and the phrase *Declaration of Independence* meant about as much to them as it did to their livestock. But they did sympathize with the Patriots and they did hate Patrick Ferguson with a bitterness born of his thorough ravaging of the Carolinas, and they sincerely believed that if any fighting and destroying was to be done, it should occur in the enemy's country, rather than in their farms and homes along the Watauga.

So when Colonel Shelby received Ferguson's infuriating message, he summoned his own riders to meet at Sycamore Shoals on the Watauga and sent out emergency calls to similar bands of mounted riflemen in North Carolina and Virginia. By September 25 about one thousand of them were gathered at Sycamore Shoals, under leaders such as Colonel William Campbell, a huge man at six foot six inches, who was renowned as a marksman and a fighter. Campbell was married to Patrick Henry's sister, and he brought four hundred Virginians to the shoals. A pair of militia colonels—Charles McDowell and Benjamin Cleveland—arrived with about three hundred men from both the Carolinas. To these forces were added five hundred "over-the-mountain" men under Shelby and Colonel John Sevier. At first there was the usual touchy question of which of these tough, aggressive leaders should command the combined force. Campbell, Shelby and Sevier were the chief candidates, but since they could not agree on any single officer, it was decided that a council of war would meet each night to decide the next day's movements, to be executed by a permanent officer of the day. Next the Reverend Samuel Doak ascended a makeshift pulpit, which was erected in a meadow, to blister the assembly with a marathon, fire-and-brimstone sermon based upon Gideon's uprising against the Midianites. When he concluded by suggesting the battle cry, "*The sword of the Lord and Gideon,*" a mighty cheer arose, which was probably due as much to the end of the sermon as to approval of the slogan, for these hardy and profane Christian soldiers would shortly substitute for it a cry somewhat less printable. Then they mounted their horses and rode off in pursuit of Ferguson.

Patrick Ferguson soon heard they were coming, in numbers at least equal to his own. So on September 27 he turned south, feinting in the general direction of his former headquarters at Ninety-six, swinging east again and moving along the Carolinas border to come closer to Cornwallis at Charlotte. His plan was to march to Charlotte if he needed protection or to send for help if he needed it. Meanwhile, he could search for good defensive positions if he decided to turn and fight. Hoping for reinforcements, he also sent out this proclamation to the Tories along the Broad River:

> Unless you wish to be eaten up by an inundation of Barbarians ... if you wish to be pinioned, robbed and murdered, and see your wives and daughters, in four days, abused by the dregs of mankind—in short, if you wish or deserve to live and bear the name of men, grasp your arms in a moment and run to camp.

This taunting appeal, typical of Ferguson's character, moved almost no one, and the Tory commander began to worry as he moved along, hearing that more Carolinians had joined the shabby army that was pursuing him. That army now numbered fourteen hundred men, but it was decided that for speed, nine hundred of them with the best horses should push ahead. Ferguson soon realized that he was in trouble, but made no move to seek the sanctuary of Cornwallis, at Charlotte with his heavy artillery. By October 5 he did begin marching toward Cornwallis, requesting, meanwhile, "three or four hundred soldiers, part dragoons." But this dispatch was delayed, and even if it had not been, the one cavalry leader who could get such a force to him quickly—Banastre Tarleton—was too sick with malaria to ride. Still worrying in the mistaken belief that he was outnumbered, Ferguson rode steadily toward the safety of Charlotte, and he was only thirty-five miles from that tiny hamlet of twenty homes when he realized that his pursuers were too close to him to risk being caught on open ground. So he stopped and prepared to fight atop King's Mountain, a high point in a long chain of hills just south of the North Carolina border.

King's Mountain was an exceptionally strong natural position. Its level summit was about 500 yards long and 70 to 80 yards wide, broadening to about 120 yards at its northeast end, where Ferguson set up camp. Its steep, heavily wooded sides rose about 60 feet from the plain below. In shape it resembled a turnip with the top in the northwest and the narrow bottom in the southeast. Around the rim of the wide northeast end, Ferguson arrayed his thousand Tory militia and his hundred riflemen of the American Volunteers. All were as well trained and experienced as were regulars, especially in the use of their crude bayonets, actually a long blade jammed down the muzzle of their muskets. When in use, of course, the musket could not be fired.

With a battle approaching, Ferguson's fidgeting was replaced by a true warrior's calm. Mounted on a splendid white horse, he rode around his perimeter talking cheerfully and confidently to his men as they erected their tents. He had a hunting shirt over his uniform, and around his neck he wore a silver whistle with which he would sound his orders. Apparently no effort was made to fortify the hilltop, perhaps because the steep wooded hillside seemed to be a perfect barricade against any enemy force's attempt to march up it. But these American woodsmen had never marched in their life, and when they saw the steep slopes studded with tall pines, from which they could fire and flit, fire and flit, they realized that here was terrain made for their own style of Indian fighting, not for the immobile defenders on the top.

That moment was on the afternoon of October 7, 1780.

Upon reaching King's Mountain, the Americans surrounded it, leaving only the bottom of the turnip open, perhaps hoping to turn any attempt to escape through it into a slaughter pen. Their sudden appearance cut off a large party of foragers whom Ferguson had sent out that morning, thus reducing his army to about a thousand men. How many Americans opposed him is not exactly known, if only because such irregular armies do not keep exact muster rolls. Nor is it known how many of the five hundred riflemen left behind had caught up with the nine hundred who were sent ahead. Probably the forces were nearly even, and of these two thousand men, Patrick Ferguson was the only British soldier among them. All the rest were Americans, and the fight would be brother against brother, Tories against Patriots, many of whom knew each other. There is no deadlier formula for savage, merciless battle.

The Americans were in a particularly vicious mood. They had heard of the massacre at the Waxhaws and "Tarleton's Quarter" and had ridden all night through a torrential rain. Revenge was uppermost in their minds as they dismounted and moved on foot in four columns to ring King's Mountain at its base except for that narrow avenue of escape. There was no signal for an attack. It just began as five different coalesced phalanxes, one at the top and two on either side, began climbing up the slopes. The hilltop flashed with muzzle blasts, but the Tories were firing high. Excellent marksmen that the Tories also were, it was difficult to hit these attackers who were moving from tree to tree, firing as they climbed. And they did reach the crest almost intact, whereupon the giant Campbell roared at his Virginians: "Here they are, boys! Shout like hell and fight like devils!"

They did. Both sides did, and when Ferguson ordered a counterattack with bayonets, the yelling Loyalists drove the frontiersmen down the slopes. One sixteen-year-old rebel was not quick enough. As he cocked his rifle, a screaming Tory bayoneted him through the hand and thigh. The impact triggered the fallen youth's rifle, and the mortally wounded Tory and the Patriot fell tangled together. Another rebel pulled the blade out of the fallen youth's thigh and kicked it free of his hand.

Thus the seesawing rhythm of the Battle of King's Mountain had been established. Whenever the attacking riflemen, who had no bayonets, clawed their way to the summit, Ferguson ordered one or another of his companies to charge them with their bayonets and drive them down the slopes. Four times this happened, and in the intervals the sharpshooters of both sides picked one another off. Ferguson's marksmen, who had been firing high at first, at last lowered their sights, and the exchange became almost even. As testimony to the accuracy of both sides, most of the dead men at King's Mountain had been shot in the head. Some of them were found to have one eye open and the other shut: they had been squinting over their sights when hit. One frontiersman, who carried the rifle called "Sweet Lips," recalled: "I recollect I stood behind one tree and fired until the bark was nearly all knocked off, and my eyes pretty well filled up with it."

Finally, in their fifth ascent the rebels remained in possession of the hilltop. They began to herd the retreating Tories into an ever-shrinking circle. One of the Tory officers approached Ferguson in despair and shouted that it was time to surrender. Ferguson shouted back that he "would never surrender to such damned banditti." Calling for his fifth bayonet charge, he started downhill on his white horse, a stirring figure with his sword upraised in his left hand, shouting "Huzza, brave boys, the day is our own!"—but also an unbelievable target. Rebel rifles puffed smoke in unison, and the brave Patrick Ferguson fell down dead under a shower of bullets, one of his feet still caught in the stirrup. "Seven balls had passed through his body, both his arms were broken and his hat and clothing literally shot to pieces."

With his death, the terrified Tories tried to surrender. But the vengeful rebels would not let them. A Loyalist who was riding toward them with a white flag was shot down. A second, making the same effort, was killed. The rebel blood was up, their vengeance fed by the memory of the Waxhaws. "Buford! Buford!" they shouted. "Tarleton's quarter! Tarleton's quarter!" They pursued their frightened victims as they ran to a hollow place on the hilltop and cowered there in horror. One by one, the frontiersmen cut them down, sometimes singling out neighbors by name before they fired. Many of the Patriots thirsted to revenge themselves on the deaths of relatives and friends who were murdered by the Tories. Their eyes glittered maniacally as they loaded and fired ... loaded and fired.... At last Major Evan Shelby called on the Loyalists to throw down their arms. They did, but the rebel rifles still blazed.

Colonel William Campbell rode among his bloodthirsty Virginians shouting: "For God's sake, quit! It's murder to shoot anymore!" Captain Abraham de Peyster, who took command of the Loyalists after Ferguson died, rode up to Campbell pleading with him to stop the slaughter. At last Campbell ordered the Tory officers to detach themselves from their men and told the men to sit down and take off their hats. They did so, but sporadic shots were still fired until they finally ceased. Even so, the enraged Patriots gathered four deep around their crouching prisoners, glaring at them, hurling insults, calling out the names of those who were known for their atrocities. With restoration of order, the captives' arms were collected and confiscated, and they were confined under guard. Ferguson's personal effects were divided among the officers as souvenirs, and his body was wrapped in an oxhide and buried.

The Battle of King's Mountain had lasted exactly an hour. Except for the 200 men Ferguson had sent foraging in the morning, every one of his soldiers was killed, wounded or captured. Of about 1,000 men, 157 were killed outright—most of them murdered after the first white flag appeared—and 167 were so badly wounded that they were left on the field to die or to suffer horribly while recovering. The less seriously wounded were included among the 698 who surrendered. Rebel losses were 28 killed and 62 wounded.

Marching their prisoners to Gilberttown, the still-aroused Patriot troops demanded retaliation upon them to avenge Tarleton's massacre, as well as for the execution of forty Patriot prisoners by the British in battles at Camden, Augusta and Ninety-six. One Patriot officer claimed to have seen eleven of his friends hanged. A kind of impromptu court was convened, and from thirty to forty captives were convicted of assisting the enemy in raiding, looting and burning homes in the Carolinas. Of these forty, only twelve were condemned to death, but one of them escaped and two others were pardoned. Of the nine who were hanged, one was the elderly Colonel Ambrose Mills, a kindly man of character and reputation.

As so often happens in war—especially among armies on the march—the problem of what to do with the prisoners arose. Understandably, no one in this hastily raised and loosely organized army had given thought to such a delightful difficulty. Nor did anyone desire to guard the prisoners. The over-the-mountain men and the Virginians wanted only to go home, and they did. So the prisoners were entrusted to Cleveland's North Carolina troops, who eventually marched them to Gates at Hillsboro. Gates asked Thomas Jefferson what to do with them, but this dedicated pacifist, who spent the war in his Williamsburg snuggery, made the absurd recommendation of turning them over to the civil governments of the Carolinas, when, in fact, Cornwallis had effectively destroyed both. So they were eventually loosely guarded, and within a few months, all but sixty escaped. Yet those who returned to their homes brought with them a dire tale of death and defeat so chilling that the Battle of King's Mountain, small as it might have been in numbers and brief as it was in duration, had an enormous effect on Cornwallis's campaign in the South, if it did not effectually wreck it. It instantly halted—like a sluice gate suddenly raised—the flow of Loyalists to the cause of the Crown.

At Charlotte Cornwallis was shocked by the totality of the defeat and anguished by the loss of Patrick Ferguson and all those trained and experienced Tories who were to have been the nucleus of the army of ardent Loyalists whom he expected to join his triumphant march to the Pennsylvania border. For months His Lordship had been receiving assurances that this march would happen, but now he realized with a sinking heart that it was ended for 1780 at least. There was also distressing news from South Carolina, where Francis Marion, with only sixty men, had routed a force of Tories, sending them into a rapid retreat of twenty miles that unmasked the important coastal city of Georgetown. Sumter's troops, who had been at King's Mountain, rejoined their commander and were again raiding areas that Cornwallis had pacified, while his commandant at Ninety-six was in a panic lest the victors on the hilltop turn south to destroy him. Neither he nor Cornwallis had the slightest notion that the ragged rebel army had disbanded even quicker than it had assembled. Reports from the big base at Camden were also bad: a flour shortage arose there, followed by an epidemic of defections among the Loyalist militia. At Charlotte Cornwallis became aware that the supposedly Tory countryside was turning Patriot again and that his couriers who were riding south were under constant sniper fire. Finally, malaria and other unknown fevers were ravaging his own army.

Most shattering to this confident commander was the blow struck against his policy of seeking out Camden after Camden to smash the regular troops of the Continental Army so decisively that the rebels everywhere, under Washington as well as Gates, would lose heart and quit the war. But then all these uncouth frontiersmen in hunting shirts came riding out of the back of beyond to go climbing up King's Mountain in another demonstration of the chilling truth that if the armies of the Americans could be easily beaten, there was no way of preventing them from raising another one. So Charles Cornwallis reluctantly decided to return to South Carolina, where he would await reinforcements from Clinton while preparing to try again in 1781.

On October 14, the earl headed back the way he had come. Almost immediately he succumbed to a fever so severe that for two weeks he could not hold a pen to sign an order. Rawdon took command. Then rains drenched the marching columns and turned the roads into troughs of mud. The men went on half-rations while enduring a steady sniping fire from wooded hillsides. Tarleton had recovered from his own attack of malaria, but in one jolting wagon six officers lay groaning in the oven of high fever, their bones aching in its viselike grip. Only one of them survived: the unpredictable cavalryman Major George Hanger, who put himself on the improbable but delightful diet of opium and port wine. By the end of the month Cornwallis and the survivors of the army that had routed Gates at Camden and then set out so confidently to conquer North Carolina had reached Winnsboro, South Carolina, between Ninety-six and Camden, and gone into winter quarters.

⋆ 66 ⋆

MUTINY/GREENE AND MORGAN/COWPENS

The year 1780 had ended in dishonor and near-disaster, but the year 1781 began with mutiny. For years this had been George Washington's greatest fear. Again and again he had warned Congress that if his beloved, faithful troops were not properly fed, clothed and paid—in specie, that is, not in worthless Continentals—they would mutiny or just plain go home, and that would be the end of the American Revolution. As often as he issued the warning, Congress ignored it—for Congress, in truth, had neither the money to finance these basic needs nor the means of raising it.

The soldiers of the Pennsylvania Line, quartered at Mount Kemble near the old encampment at Morristown, had suffered cruelly. They were half-naked and starving and had not been paid for twelve months. They were convinced that they had been tricked by Congress. Although they had enlisted for three years or the duration of the war, these men believed (or said they had been told) that this meant that they would serve for three years unless the war ended *before* then, when they would be discharged. Thus when their three years were up—and for most of them that was on New Year's Day, 1781—they would be given a choice of discharge or the chance to reenlist and gain Pennsylvania's generous bounty of eighty-one dollars in silver and two hundred acres of land after the war. This was what was being paid to new recruits, some of whom were convicts who were freed on their promise to enlist. It infuriated these loyal, starving, freezing troops in threadbare clothing to realize that common criminals, who had not yet suffered as much as a headache or heard a shot fired in anger, should have their pockets filled with hard money while theirs were empty.

Their complaint was certainly a just one, and their commander, Anthony Wayne, openly sympathized with them and placed himself staunchly on their side. This was not true of most of their junior officers, many of whom were unfit to carry a private's musket. Thus, as the year 1780 neared its close and both Congress and Joseph Reed's council took no notice of their misery, they decided to mutiny. On New Year's Day, with huzzas and random firing of muskets, they burst out of their wretched huts to form on the parade ground. Next they broke into the magazine and began firing off cannons. Throughout this display, there was neither drunkenness nor indiscipline. Under the direction of their sergeants, they maintained a remarkable order—much more precise than under their detested officers—and promised to harm no one. However, when cannon and muskets go off at random, someone is bound to be hurt—and one officer was unintentionally killed and two others wounded.

Hearing of the uprising, General Wayne cut short his own holiday celebration to mount his horse and attempt to quell the mutiny by persuasion. The men told him their quarrel was with Congress and the council. When he persisted, they fired over his head. In anguish Wayne tore open his coat and dared them to kill him. They repeated their pledge not to harm any officer and marched off toward Princeton with guns and baggage.

Mutiny in the Continental Army had long been the dream of both the Tories and the British commanders. Sir Henry Clinton at once sought to take advantage of it, alerting a strong force of British and Hessian troops for a possible landing at South Amboy "to favor the revolt and keep the militia back." He also assured the mutineers "that if they will lay down their arms they will be pardoned for all past offenses, be paid all the pay due them by Congress, and not be required to serve [in the British army] unless they chuse [*sic*] it." In indignation, the Pennsylvanians rejected Clinton's offer, and when he sent two spies or agents provocateurs among them, they seized them and handed them over for trial and execution. From Princeton the mutineers marched on Trenton, where they were met by Joseph Reed. Their elected Board of Sergeants negotiated with dignity and without threats, but also with acumen. They knew that their cause was just and they were not to be dissuaded by promises.

Washington, meanwhile, was faced with an agonizing decision. Mutiny, of course, is anathema to any military organization and cannot be tolerated. Like any commander, he would rather suppress the rebellion by force than end it by negotiation. No matter how unjustly they have been treated, to talk to disaffected troops can be taken as a sign of soft-heartedness—and the malaise can spread. But if he used force, he might provoke an adverse chain reaction among the other units of the Continental Army. Washington, had he not known of the suffering of his soldiers and sympathized with the men deeply, might have been distracted enough by this dilemma to opt for the rod, rather than reason. In the end he refrained from calling upon other Continentals to quell the uprising of their mutinous comrades, standing wisely by while the problem was solved by a firm promise to pay part of the back pay and the discharge of all those who claimed their three-year enlistments had expired.

Yet when the smaller New Jersey Line, quartered at Pompton, mutinied over similar injustices, Washington used force. A strong body of Massachusetts Continentals, under General Robert Howe, surrounded the New Jersey mutineers, compelling them to parade without arms and seizing the ringleaders. Two of the ringleaders were executed by a firing squad of twelve of the most flagrant mutineers, and the uprising was quelled.

A week later there was at last good news from the South, where Washington had sent his most trusted and able general: Nathanael Greene.

In human activity, as in physics, there seems to exist a rule that every action has a reaction. But in human activity, so prone to the forces of accident and irrational behavior, the results of the action cannot be exactly calculated, and the reaction may even be counterproductive. Thus, in World War II Hitler's victory in Norway caused the downfall of the incompetent Prime Minister Neville Chamberlain of Britain and brought into the field against Der Führer the indomitable Winston Churchill. In the American Revolution Lord Cornwallis's victories at Charleston and Camden removed from the Continental Army two of its most inept generals—Benjamin Lincoln and Horatio Gates—and brought into the field against him Washington's ablest commander: Nathanael Greene.

No more unlikely prospect for military glory has existed than this slender, pleasant, bookish ironmaster, who was bound by the pacificsm of his Quaker faith never to take up arms. Even if he had fancied a military career, a pronounced limp of unknown origin would seem to have precluded such ambition. ("You dance stiffly," a young lady had once complained to him, and he replied with his wry humor, "Very true, but you see that I dance strong.") Like another ironmaster of Civil War notoriety—Thaddeus Stevens—he had a rough charm bordering on the scatological and could do a rollicking imitation of *Tristram Shandy's* Doctor Slop that would collapse his dinner guests with laughter. Avid reader that he was, it never influenced his spelling, which can only be described as original and that probably encouraged Noah Webster, his fellow New Englander and Patriot, to do something about standardizing it.

Prior to the Stamp Act and the successive injustices imposed upon the colonies by the Mother Country, Nathanael Greene was satisfied with his life, running the family iron forge and drinking "deep of the Pierian Spring." It never occurred to him to question one of the central tenets of his Quaker religion: doctrinal pacifism. But in 1773 at the age of thirty-one, he and one of his numerous cousins turned out to watch a militia parade, for which the Meeting of Friends to which they belonged demanded that they "make satisfaction for their misconduct." Instead, they broadened their study of things military and were summarily read out of Meeting. In reply Greene calmly announced that war to destroy injustice and evil was of the essence of morality.

Greene's thirst for learning and his retentive memory were thereafter fixed on military history and the study of tactics, so that he became a regular customer at Henry Knox's Boston bookstore. He helped to rewrite his colony's militia regulations and was sent by the Rhode Island Assembly with another man to concert with the Connecticut Assembly "upon measures for the common defense of the New England Colonies."

But then his limp made him stumble. He had joined a new militia company near his home as a private, and when his name was put forward as an officer candidate, he was mortified to hear fellow militiamen complaining that his limp not only disqualified him for command but made it impossible for him to march properly—so they wanted him out! Humiliated, Greene wrote to his friend the company commander—who had threatened to resign if Greene were ousted—to tell him that he accepted his expulsion but was still anxious to pay his share for equipping the company. He also urged his friend not to resign. He didn't, and Greene was permitted to remain in the company as a private. But when the militia marched and Greene's musket bobbed up and down in rhythm with his limp, the men beside and behind him were sorely tempted to look the other way.

After Lexington-Concord—no longer a private but actual commander of the Rhode Island Army of Observation—Greene led fifteen hundred men to Cambridge. There George Washington quickly discovered the qualities that had prompted the Rhode Island Assembly to pass over scores of men who were better qualified in military experience in favor of

Greene. These qualities were keen intelligence, determination, energy an even temper, but above all, the ability to perceive what was wrong and to correct it. As Greene rose in Washington's estimation, he also rose in rank. He was a major general when Congress, having chosen Lincoln, who lost both Charleston and his army, and Gates, who had lost the South and his army, at last acknowledged in effect not only its inability to pick a winner but its myopic failure to judge a soldier and asked General Washington to select a successor to Gates. Without hesitation, the commander in chief wrote immediately to Greene at West Point: "It is my wish to appoint You."

Just as welcome to Greene as this appointment to command all troops from Delaware to Georgia was the congressional instruction to report only to the commander in chief. Gates had reported directly to Congress over the head of Washington, a procedure that was productive of much mischief. But Greene's elation gradually subsided under a steady stream of denials of his requisitions. Although Quartermaster General Timothy Pickering did promise to send him two companies of "artificers," Henry Knox could pledge only a single company of artillery with but four small fieldpieces and two light howitzers—puny ordnance indeed with which to challenge Cornwallis's massive artillery park. When Greene reached Philadelphia and asked Joseph Reed for four or five thousand stands of muskets, he got only fifteen hundred. Calling on Congress for clothing, he received none. Appealing to the city's merchants for five thousand uniforms to be billed to France, his request was politely declined. Reed, however, did promise one hundred "road wagons" and Pickering forty "covered wagons" in badly needed transport. Though not much, it was still something. From Congress came a whopping $180,000 in Continental currency, a gift of printed paper if there ever was one. As he proceeded south through Maryland, Delaware, Virginia and North Carolina, appeals for clothing, arms and "any measures for giving effectual aid" produced impassioned pleas of poverty. Governor Thomas Jefferson of Virginia told Greene, "The situation as to clothing is desperate." It was, indeed; the South had been so thoroughly impoverished that neither Maryland nor Virginia could provide forage for Greene's horses. Undaunted outwardly, though certainly discouraged inwardly, Greene pressed doggedly deeper into the South until, on December 2, 1780, he arrived at Charlotte, to meet Gates and replace him as commander of the Southern army. The meeting was cordial: Greene was respectfully sympathetic, Gates dignified and polite. Leaving Charlotte, Gates returned to his life as a Virginia planter.

Behind him Major General Nathanael Greene might have been forgiven a sardonic smile at his title of commander of "the Grand Army of the Southern Department of the United States of America." The grand army consisted on paper of 2,307 infantrymen, of whom 1,482 were present for duty; of that number, only 949 were Continentals and the rest militia, 90 cavalrymen and 60 artillerists. Of the entire force, a pitiful 800 were properly clothed and equipped. All were on starvation rations; all were demoralized; all had lost their discipline; and all, it seemed, were "so addicted to plundering that they were a terror to the inhabitants." On hand were but three days' provisions and no promise of more. The countryside surrounding Charlotte had been stripped clean by this scarecrow army, with its wretched service—or *unservice*—of supply, and especially by the North Carolina militia that—in the way of militia almost everywhere—did its hardest fighting in henhouses, orchards and barns. Greene saw at once that he needed a new camp to rebuild a new army, "a camp of repose," he called it, where in safety from Cornwallis he could repair wagons and equipment, obtain food, collect horses and hammer the steel of discipline into the sagging spine of his troops.

To find this safe and smiling place, he called upon Tadeusz Kosciuszko, the great engineering general of the Revolution whom he much admired. Kosciuszko began exploring the territory where the Carolinas met, and upon his return he reported that he had found an excellent location at Cheraw Hill on the Pee Dee River, just across the border in South Carolina. Greene decided to go there. But first he had to come to an even more difficult decision, perhaps the most important, daring and dangerous of any made by any commander in the entire war. This decision was to divide his army.

With such demoralized troops in such wretched condition, Greene could not possibly give battle to Cornwallis. He must wait until the troops were reinforced, retrained and refitted. Yet he must not appear to be retreating before the advance of his enemy, which was then around Winnsboro, South Carolina, lest he encourage him and dishearten his men and the whole country. In war, Napoleon would say, morale is to the material as three is to one. Greene could not risk lowering morale either in his soldiers or in the local civilians, upon whom he must depend for supplies and sanctuary. But because Cheraw Hill was farther from the foe than was Charlotte, a removal to that place would look like a retreat and certainly be proclaimed as one by the public-relations-conscious British. For the moment he must carry on harassing operations that were not likely to bring on the general engagement that would if not destroy both him and, if not the Rebellion, at least would lose the South. This meant nothing less than guerrilla warfare, partisans menacing or munching on Cornwallis's flanks, severing his communications, seizing his supplies, and to do so while the experienced irregulars Francis Marion, Thomas Sumter and Andrew Pickens were waging the same kind of warfare.

By dividing his inadequate army, Greene would be violating probably the most inviolable rule of war: do not divide your forces in the face of a superior foe, for such is to invite him to destroy you in detail. Certainly the Revolution already abounded in horrible examples of what befell commanders who ignored this axiom: Washington, in August 1776, dividing his army at Long Island and New York; Howe, in December of that year, scattering his Hessians along his "chain of posts" in New Jersey; Burgoyne, in August 1777, sending his ponderous Hessians into defeat at Bennington; even Washington allowing Lafayette to take that risky position at Barren Hill the day after the *Mischianza* in May 1778. True, Lafayette was able to escape because his troops had been well trained by Steuben, but in the most recent example, Patrick Ferguson had lost both his life and the battle at King's Mountain. Nathanael Greene had the depth of mind to see that he risked disaster, but he also had the flexibility of mind—the mark of a true general—to understand that the dictates of military doctrine apply only to so-called normal situations. Like any true craftsman, from a carpenter to a commander of troops, he realized that the time had come to break the rules.

He saw that if he divided his army into two parts, he would make it easier for both to live off the land, and by subsisting on the same regions that supplied the British, they would reduce the enemy's portion. If Cornwallis moved to return to South Carolina, each of these forces could hang on his flanks like terriers in a bullring. If Cornwallis turned against the force on his left, or west, he would expose Charleston to a dash by the right-hand, or eastern force. If he turned to his right, he would unmask Ninety-six and Augusta, Georgia, to the western unit. If he remained in place, he invited constant harassment. Greene did not especially fear that Cornwallis could attack and defeat each of his divisions one by one, for he relied on superior American mobility to escape the slower, equipment-heavy British. For these cogent reasons, Nathanael Greene planned what was nothing less than the most audacious operation of the war. Greene would accompany the eastern force, led by Brigadier General Isaac Huger, while the western unit would be commanded by Daniel Morgan.

The parents of Daniel Morgan were said to have been of Welsh extraction, but little is known of them or of Morgan's boyhood, except that he was born in Huntington County, New Jersey, either in 1735, 1736 or 1737. At the age of seventeen, when he was already a huge man standing six feet two inches and weighing 210 pounds, Daniel and his family moved to Jefferson County, Virginia, where he worked on a farm. During the French and Indian War, he was a teamster in Braddock's army, gaining the nickname "the Old Wagoner" and the friendship of young George Washington.

In 1757 for some unknown reason a British officer struck him with the flat of his sword, and Morgan promptly knocked him down. For this, he was court-martialed and sentenced to five hundred lashes, which he endured with incredible stoicism. His tormentor, aghast at this barbaric punishment, begged his forgiveness, which was promptly given, together with the dry advice that since he had really received only 499 lashes, they should find a sergeant major who could count. Later, at the head of a party of woodsmen, he defeated a force of French and Indians, for which feat he received an ensign's commission. But in another engagement with them, all his comrades were killed while he received a ball in the neck. Near fainting, fearing to fall into the hands of the Indians, he fell forward on his horse's withers, grasping its mane and digging his spurs into its side so that it bolted forward along a forest trail pursued by screeching Indians. But Morgan drew away, and his foremost pursuer, in a cry of baffled rage, uselessly hurled his tomahawk after him.

After the war Morgan received a grant of land east of Winchester, Virginia, and married Abigail Bailey, said to be a great beauty. He built a home called "Soldier's Rest," but there was to be no rest for Daniel Morgan, for he was soon called into service during Pontiac's War. A civilian again after that war, he prospered as a farmer, acquiring much land. After Lexington-Concord, he raised a company of ninety-six Virginia sharpshooters and led them as their captain to Cambridge, where he renewed his friendship with Washington. He was with Arnold on that fearful march to Quebec and was captured there after Montgomery was killed and Arnold was wounded. Proof of the British admiration for his fighting prowess soon came, when an officer visited him to offer him a commission of colonel in the British Army. Enraged, the hulking Morgan jumped to his feet to bellow his rejection of an offer "that plainly implied that he thought him a rascal."

Exchanged, Morgan distinguished himself at Saratoga, rejoining Washington's army in the campaigns of 1777 and 1778. In June 1779, like Greene, Knox and Arnold infuriated at Congress's penchant for ignoring excellent commanders and promoting incompetent bunglers, he went into retirement. A year later, when Gates urged him to return to action, he refused, saying he could not serve as a mere colonel under the orders of amateurish militia generals. After Camden, however, he swallowed his pride, and when Greene relieved Gates, Greene was overjoyed to find that Daniel Morgan, at last a brigadier general, was awaiting him at Charlotte.

On December 20, 1780, Morgan left Charlotte at the head of eleven to twelve hundred men, bound for "the camp of repose" at Cheraw Hill. He arrived there six days later after a gruelling and miserable march through the slop and mud and torrential cold rains of a Carolina December. At Cheraw he was in position to assist Francis Marion as he harassed Cornwallis at Winnsboro or to threaten Camden. He was even closer to Charleston than Cornwallis was. The day before, Huger's eastern detachment, accompanied by Greene, had gone into camp along the Pacolet River after a five-day, fifty-four-mile march through deep swamps and high hills.

While at the Pacolet, Greene was pleased to receive a valuable reinforcement: Light-Horse Harry Lee's famous legion of 100 horse and 180 foot. Washington had sent him his favorite commander leading his favorite formation, and Greene was grateful. Lee's men were "the most throughly disciplined and best equipped scouts and raiders in the Revolution." Like Tarleton's Tories, they wore short green jackets, and the dragoons were mounted on handsome, powerful, well-groomed horses furnished by the "horse-proud" Lee. On the march, they often took the infantryman up behind them to speed their progress.

Both Greene's detachments rested for three weeks in their camps, waiting for Cornwallis to make a move.

Cornwallis had also been reinforced: Clinton had sent Major General Alexander Leslie with 2,500 men south from New York. Fifteen hundred joined Cornwallis at Winnsboro, while the remaining thousand remained at Wilmington, North Carolina. Cornwallis's superbly trained, disciplined and supplied army now numbered four thousand men, certainly much more than enough to destroy and scatter Greene's three thousand tatterdemalions, who were short on everything except devotion and durability. Yet His Lordship was dismayed. Greene's decision to divide his forces had so shocked him that he began to rethink his own situation. At first he had shared Tarleton's belief that had Greene known of the Leslie reinforcement, he would not have made such a blunder and that now was the time for a rapid return to North Carolina. But then Cornwallis saw clearly that Greene had indeed compromised him. If he attacked Huger and Greene in the east, the way to Charleston lay open to Morgan; if he struck at Morgan, Huger and Greene would advance on Ninety-six and Augusta. Like a canny chess player, he countered by dividing his own army, but into three rather than two parts. Leslie went south to hold Camden against a possible attack by Huger and Greene, while Tarleton was sent galloping out of Ninety-six westward to crush Morgan. Cornwallis, with the main body, would move cautiously and slowly back up into North Carolina to intercept and destroy the Americans who were defeated and scattered by Tarleton. To do so, the famous (or infamous) "Green Dragoon" led his own legion, together with regular batallions of fusiliers, Highlanders, light dragoons, Tory militia and artillery—a force of about eleven hundred men, just about equal to Morgan's force, although in trained regulars, Tarleton outnumbered the Old Wagoner three to one.

On January 17, 1781, the two small armies collided in a place of sandy hills where cattle wandered in open cowpens, which was thus given the name Cowpens.

Daniel Morgan chose to fight in what looked like a trap. He held a plain dotted with widely spaced trees in which Tarleton's superior horsemen could easily maneuver, and he had his back to the Broad River. But the Old Wagoner knew his men. If he secured his wings on swamps, as he said later, his militia would have vanished through the bogs, and if he crossed the river, half of them would have abandoned him. He wanted no hope of retreat, so that his men would fight the dreaded Tarleton with the desperation of the doomed, and he was certain that his dashing enemy would charge straight ahead, rather than nibble at his exposed wings.

So Morgan put about 150 picked riflemen forward in a skirmish line. About 150 yards behind them were about three hundred militia, under Andrew Pickens, and back another 150 yards, on the crest of a hill, was Morgan's main line of about four hundred Continentals, under John Howard. Again to the rear, behind another hill, were about one hundred horse, under the fat but capable William Washington, the cavalryman who had been wounded at Trenton.

The sharpshooters in front were not to open fire until the enemy was within fifty yards, and then they were to aim at "the men with the epaulets." They were to deliver two volleys, and then fall back on Pickens's militia. The militia were then to fire only two volleys, before retiring around the American left to the rear of the main line on the hill, there to re-form as a reserve. Morgan promised them they would be perfectly

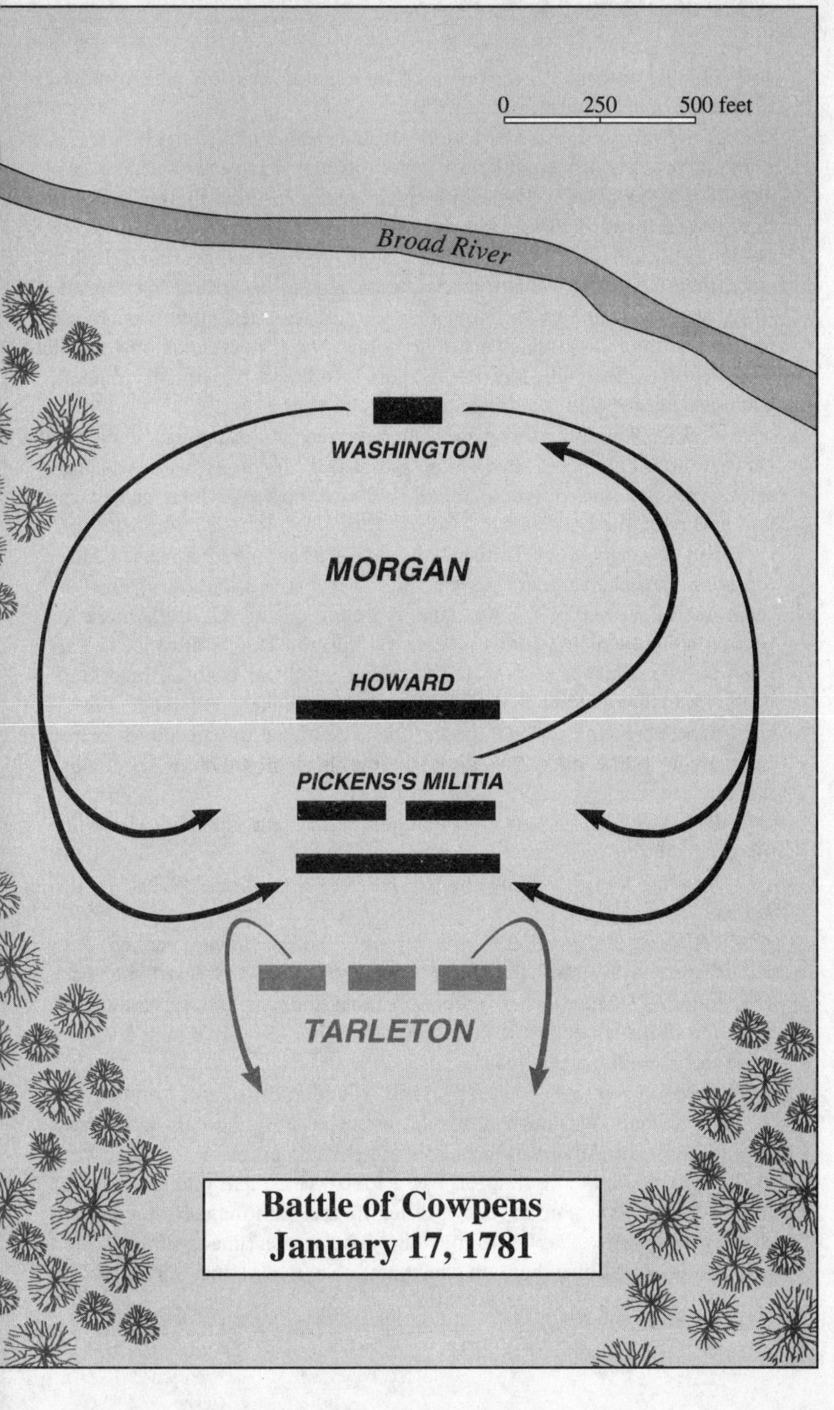
0
250
500 feet
Broad River
WASHINGTON
MORGAN
HOWARD
PICKENS'S MILITIA
TARLETON
Battle of Cowpens
January 17, 1781

safe. He also informed every man of his plan, so that no one would be alarmed at the withdrawals.

Tarleton came on. His legion cavalry rode at the sharpshooters. A scathing fire sent fifteen riderless horses off the field, and the Tory cavalry fled, never to be induced to reenter the battle. Now the main British line moved forward, dragoons on either wing. Here was the crux of the battle. If the militia showed their customary reaction to bared British steel, they would flee. But Pickens's men stayed, firing and loading and firing again to send two volleys into the scarlet line. Then they began running to the left as planned, to get behind the Continentals on the hill. The militia on the right had the farthest to go, and the British dragoons came thundering down on them.

Suddenly, out of the American right rear Washington's horsemen came riding. They fell upon the astonished dragoons with whistling sabers, routing and pursuing them, while all Pickens's men gained the rear and re-formed.

But the impetuous British had taken Pickens's retirement to mean the start of the customary retreat, and they came shouting against the main line of Howard's Continentals. Kneeling on the hill, the Americans poured a plunging fire into the enemy. Still, the British advanced. Tarleton put his Highlanders on his left. They stretched beyond the American right. Howard saw that he was being outflanked. He called for his right-hand company to face about. Then they were to wheel and form a right angle to the main line and face about again to blunt the British flanking movement.

But they faced about and marched to the rear, and the whole line followed suit.

Morgan came rushing up to Howard, shouting, "What is this retreat?"

"A change of position to save my right flank," Howard replied.

"Are you beaten?" the Old Wagoner yelled, and Howard shot back scornfully: "Do men who march like that look as though they were beaten?" Morgan nodded, and dashed off to find Howard's men a second position between the two hills.

Tarleton, sensing victory, pursued. His men broke ranks and rushed forward. William Washington, whose pursuit of the dragoons had carried him ahead of the American lines, saw the British confusion. He sent word to Morgan: "They're coming on like a mob. Give them one fire, and I'll charge them." Morgan gave the order to the Continentals; they faced about and blazed away from the hip. The scarlet line crumpled, and Howard cried: "Give them the bayonet!" So it was that an American cheer and American blades went forward, just as Washington's cavalry burst upon the enemy flank and rear like a tornado. After that charge, Pickens's re-formed militia struck the Highlanders down, and the Battle of Cowpens was over, but for an individual and inconclusive mounted skirmish between Tarleton and Washington.

Banastre Tarleton himself rode off, his brilliant plumed helmet drooping in a defeat that was nearly total: nine-tenths of his force had been killed or captured, against only twelve Americans killed and sixty wounded.

Cowpens was the American Cannae, it was the glittering small gem of the Revolution, and it was brought off by an American backwoodsman, who, like the great Hannibal himself, was merely adapting himself to men and terrain. Moreover, Cowpens made the way of the wary Nathanael Greene easier as he waged his war of attrition against Cornwallis.

★ 67 ★

THE BATTLE OF GUILFORD COURT HOUSE

On the evening after Tarleton's defeat at the Cowpens, Lord Cornwallis, encamped with his main body at Turkey Creek about twenty-five miles away, confidently awaited news of Morgan's "rout," so that he might move rapidly to cut off Morgan's "retreat." Instead, a hard-riding courier on a lathered horse rode into camp bearing tidings of disaster. It is doubtful that the earl ever received a more shocking report. He now found himself in exactly the same position as he had been when the unbelievable news from King's Mountain had compelled him to abandon North Carolina.

But this time he could not again give up his plans for conquest of the Old North State because, even then, Leslie was marching toward him with reinforcements and his heavy equipment for the forthcoming campaign. Therefore, he delayed his departure from Turkey Creek until the nineteenth, giving Morgan ample time to make good his escape. When he did move in pursuit, it was slowly and in the wrong direction. Thinking that Morgan might make a strike at Ninety-six, he marched northwestward toward the Little Broad River, when his prey actually was making straight for Sherill's Ford by way of Ramsour's Mills. At Turkey Creek Cornwallis and Morgan had been equidistant from Ramsour's Mills, and Cornwallis might have despatched a brigade of fast-moving light infantry to intercept the Old Wagoner there, holding him at bay until the main body could come up. But when Cornwallis changed direction and headed for Ramsour's Mills, he did not arrive there until the twenty-fifth, dismayed and infuriated to find that the canny Yankee with his typically hard-marching troops had put two days and two rivers between them. Nathanael

Greene's conviction that the Americans' extraordinary mobility would thwart every effort of the equipment-laden enemy to bring them to decisive battle had once again paid handsome dividends. Morgan, marching to join Huger and Greene, had covered one hundred miles and crossed two rivers in fewer than five days. Any other British commander but Cornwallis might have been discouraged enough to drop the North Carolina venture for a second time. But His Lordship, just as he had earlier divided his own forces to counter Greene's original maneuver, now decided that, having lost all his light infantry at Cowpens, he would make light troops of his main body simply by destroying all his heavy equipment.

It was a daring—even a unique—decision. Cornwallis spent two days at Ramsour's Mills consigning all of his superfluous baggage to the flames. To set an example, he put his own possessions to the torch, and his officers did likewise. All the wagons except those needed to carry ammunition, salt and medical stores, plus four others to carry the sick and wounded, also were reduced to ashes. The tents were burned as well, and all the food that the men could not carry in their haversacks. Finally, to the immense resentment of the troops, the rum casks were stove in. In this Cornwallis and his officers acted out of the British upper class's typical indifference to the happiness of their men. Quick to discipline their soldiery with whip and noose, they rarely, if ever, sought to humor them. If each man had been allowed to fill his canteen with the delightful liquid before it all ran out upon the ground, there might have been some drunkenness and disorder before the march was resumed, but not enough disruption to compare to the generally sour discontent and the 250 desertions that succeeded the smashing of the casks. Thus, without his heavy equipment and with unhappy troops—two fatal disadvantages that, in the end, were never to be redeemed—Lord Charles Cornwallis began his pursuit of Nathanael Greene.

Greene was with Huger at Cheraw Hills anxiously awaiting news of Morgan. When it came on the twenty-fifth, he was overjoyed. He immediately ordered his commissaries at Salisbury and Hillsboro in North Carolina to move with their prisoners and their stores to Virginia. He directed his energetic quartermaster Lieutenant Colonel Edward Carrington to seize all boats on the northern rivers and station them along the Dan River at the North Carolina–Virginia border, just in case he might be compelled to retreat. Next he ordered Huger to prepare to march his division to join Morgan on the Catawba, while he, alone but for an aide, a guide and a sergeant's guard of dragoons, set out through a Tory-infested wilderness to reach Morgan, 125 miles away. Had he been captured or killed, the Revolution most probably would have foundered. Because of this great risk, Greene's decision has been criticized as most imprudent. It has been said that to guarantee his own safety, he should have accompanied Huger's division. But time was of the essence. He had to reach Morgan as soon as possible to discuss with him his own plan for a daring game of martial cat and mouse that would lure Cornwallis farther and farther away from his base in South Carolina, while drawing him closer to Greene's base in Virginia. Traveling light, he could be on the Catawba in two or three days.

With Huger it would have taken much longer, for his progress turned out to be a march of incredible hardship made by men, subsisting on a pittance of flesh and flour, moving over roads that were frozen after sundown and muddy by the noon thaw, fording icy streams and whipped by freezing rains; some of the men were barefoot, and all of them were shivering in rags and without tents. Although they staggered on without a single desertion, they were still too late to join Morgan before he left the Catawba.

Long before then Greene had reached Morgan in an incredible two-day ride. He astonished the Old Wagoner by his boundless enthusiasm, and when he heard that Cornwallis had destroyed his baggage and was marching north in pursuit, he cried aloud in joy: "Then, he is ours!" Greene immediately sent a courier to Huger urging him to hurry to overtake Morgan at Salisbury and another to recall Lee's Legion from Marion to Georgetown. "Here is a fine field and great glory ahead!" he wrote. All this jubilation at being pursued by Cornwallis and his superior army puzzled Morgan, who was eager for a quick retreat into the sanctuary of the rugged western mountains that would thus make pursuit impossible. But here was Greene *inviting* it! Greene was, indeed inviting pursuit, as he explained to the Old Wagoner: he would spurn the inaccessible Appalachians and move through easy country, leading Cornwallis on like a will-o-the-wisp, just far enough ahead to be kept in view, but never too close to be caught and brought to decisive battle. He would lure His Lordship north, ever northward, until at last they were in Virginia, with Greene close to his own supplies and reinforcements and Cornwallis out of reach of his. Marching north, Cornwallis would have to cross many small streams and four major rivers: the Catawba, Yadkin, Deep and Dan. Where he could, Greene would oppose him at the fords, hoping to whittle him, to douse his ardor and drown his dreams. The Old Wagoner shook his head. It was a plan born of desperation, too bold, too risky—too fraught with danger and unhappy happenstance. If it were attempted, he, Morgan, could not answer for the outcome. "Neither *will* you!" Greene cried. "For I shall take the matter upon myself."

★ ★ ★

On January 28—the day that Greene rode out of the Cheraw and Huger began his march—Earl Cornwallis departed Ramsour's Mills, marching north toward Beattie's Ford on the Catawba and Morgan's camp on the east bank. Finding the river so swollen by rains as to be impassable, he stopped four miles short of the ford, waiting two days for the river to subside.

In the meantime General William Davidson, of the North Carolina militia, had about eight hundred men holding the four Catawba fords. About three hundred held the likeliest crossing at Beattie's, while a lesser number was posted at the more difficult Cowan's or McCowan's Ford. Cornwallis's plan was to feint at Beattie's with a small force under Lieutenant Colonel James Webster, while he and General Charles O'Hara took the main body across Cowan's to turn the Yankee flank. It was Cornwallis's favorite maneuver, and on January 31, with the river falling, he was ready to execute it.

What his lordship did not know was that Cowan's Ford, about five hundred yards wide and in that great width not exactly an easy crossing, also had the peculiarity of splitting in two about halfway across the river. The straight course, used by wagons, was about three or four feet deep and swift and turbulent over a rocky bottom. The one diverging to the right, used by horsemen, was shallower and smoother, although longer. It reached the east bank about a quarter mile below the wagon course. Here Davidson had posted most of his remaining guard, with only twenty-five pickets opposite the wagon course. Cornwallis's Tory guide knew of these divergent courses, but no one else did—least of all the gallant Colonel Hall, who was to lead the spearhead crossing there.

Just before the dawn of a dark and rainswept morning, General O'Hara ordered his advance guards into the wagon course of Cowan's Crossing. In waist-deep icy water, their cartridge boxes high on their shoulders, their bayoneted but unloaded muskets high above their heads, they struggled four-abreast through the swirling black water. They had advanced a hundred yards before the smaller rebel force became aware of them, opening fire. Their bullets took a terrible toll among Colonel Hall's first three ranks, and the column halted. Then the men struggled forward again, taking more hits, stumbling over the rocky bottom, some soldiers being swept downstream—but still advancing. At this point the Tory guide took fright and fled—without warning Hall of the easier horse course to the right. So the British column splashed doggedly through the uneven, deeper wagon course. Now men and horses were swept off their feet. Hall's horse was shot from under him. Cornwallis's horse was wounded, but did not fall until it reached the farther bank. Both Leslie and O'Hara were unhorsed. Still the British advanced, now clearly visible as the thin light of dawn crept across the swirling black water.

Down at the horse course General Davidson heard the firing above him and rushed with his men toward the sound. He arrived in time to take a bullet in the heart from the sodden redcoats, who had routed the American pickets, loaded their muskets and opened fire. With Davidson's death, the American defenders broke, but not before the Colonel Hall was killed as he rode ashore.

It had been a costly crossing for Cornwallis, and it gained little more than the death of Davidson—for Morgan and his division had broken camp, marching all night until they were thirty miles away on the road to Trading Ford on the Yadkin. Continued rain made the roads impassable for pursuit. Drenched like his soldiers by rain and river, mounted uncomfortably on a strange horse, his wig plastered against his flesh, Lord Cornwallis stared glumly north, where, as he well knew, another probably difficult and defended river had to be crossed.

Meanwhile Nathanael Greene, in whose innovative brain just such discomfiture had been planned, had narrowly escaped capture. After Morgan departed, he had remained behind near Salisbury to arrange for Davidson's militia to join him and follow Morgan once their ford duty was done. Below him as he sat his horse, he heard the sound of musketry. It was Tarleton's cavalry scattering mounted Tar Heels at Tarrant's Tavern. Greene stayed where he was, still waiting for Davidson—until a messenger arrived to tell him that the general was dead and Cornwallis was over the Catawba. Dismayed, Greene rode on alone to Steele's Tavern in Salisbury. There a friendly voice came out of the darkness: "What? Alone, Greene?" "Yes," he replied softly, "alone, tired, hungry and penniless." Then he went inside, where Mrs. Steele prepared him a hearty breakfast. As he ate, she came to his table bearing two little bags of hard money. "You need them more than I do," she said, placing them in his hands. Greene looked up at her with tears of gratitude shining in his eyes. He had come to her hungry, penniless and forlorn, but now he had been fed, and in his hands he held—a pittance though it might be—the renewed war chest of the Grand Army of the Southern Department of the Continental Army.

His confidence restored by this touching act of patriotism and generosity, Greene quickly wrote to Huger, instructing him to change his line of march to the northeast to meet Morgan at Guilford Court House. Then he mounted his horse to overtake the Old Wagoner. On the nights of February 2 and 3, thanks to the efficiency of Carrington, who had been joined by Kosciuszko, Morgan's division, accompanied by Greene, was able to cross the swollen Yadkin with the cavalry swimming their horses across and the men rowing in boats.

On February 6 Morgan and Greene reached Guilford Courthouse and met Huger's exhausted soldiers there. Proud though their commander was of their loyalty and endurance, they were a pathetic sight, and Sergeant Major Seymour reported they were "in a most dismal condition for the want of clothing, especially shoes, being obliged to march … barefoot from Cheraw Hills. Here, however, the men were supplied some shoes, but not half enough." At Guilford Nathanael Greene also had come to a crossroads. Had he not whittled and discouraged his opponent enough and drawn him far enough away from his base to turn and fight him here? Guilford seemed to offer a good defensive position. Lee's Legion had joined him, and he expected reinforcements from Virginia. Also he had sent to Hillsboro for ammunition. His whole army numbered about 2,000 men, of whom there were no more than 1,400 reliable Continentals. Cornwallis still led 2,500 to 3,000 excellent regulars. Even so, if as many as 1,400 Virginia militia rallied to Greene's side, he would still give battle because he feared that continued retreat might discourage recruitment of the militia and encourage the Tories. But no militia appeared, and so it was decided at a council of war to continue the retreat to the Dan.

Before the retreat began, Greene formed a light corps of about seven hundred of his elite troops to cover the retreat of the main army. It consisted of all the cavalry under William Washington, the infantry from Lee's Legion, a battalion of 280 Continental veterans and 60 Virginia riflemen. Command of this corps was offered to Daniel Morgan. But the Old Wagoner was too sick to continue the campaign. Recurring fits of malarial chills and fever, together with constant rheumatism had made him unfit to carry on, and he retired to his home in Virginia to fight no more. In his place command was given to Colonel Otho Williams, an admirable choice. It was Williams's mission to harass and delay Cornwallis, to blow bridges in his path and to keep constantly visible to the enemy so as to draw him away to the upper fords of the Dan, while Huger and Greene, with the main body, made for Boyd's and Irwin's ferries on the river's lower reaches.

The importance of William's mission cannot be exaggerated, for the contest between Cornwallis and Greene was now the centerpiece of the War of the American Revolution. If Cornwallis could overtake Greene's little army and destroy it, he could move into Virginia to join forces with Philips and Arnold there. He would be able to free the Saratoga prisoners and those taken at Cowpens, while seizing and fortifying Richmond, as well as strong posts at Hillsboro, Ninety-six and other points in the Carolinas. He would thus have subdued the South, except for irregular detachments such as Marion's, and these eventually would be crushed or melt away. Thus Georgia, the Carolinas and Virginia—four great states constituting a vast region—would have been conquered for the Crown. In America both Patriots and Tories alike held their breath, for they knew what was at stake, and so did King George and Lord George Germain in London and King Louis XVI and the Comte de Vergennes in Versailles.

On the night of February 8, 1781, the picked force, led by the brave and able Colonel Williams, left Guilford, turning west to follow a road between the British and the roads that Greene and Huger took two days later with the main body, making for the lower Dan. Cornwallis, hoping to draw Greene to the east, made a feint at his Hillsboro base—until he became aware of Williams's corps, which he mistook for the advance guard of the entire American army. As Greene had planned, Cornwallis turned to march directly for the upper Dan, hoping to arrive there before Greene did.

The race for the Dan, seventy miles away from Guilford, was now on. Because it was still midwinter and snow became more frequent with the movement north, progress was slow. The red-clay roads, although frozen at night, were turned to soft mud by the daylight thaw. Horses sank in it knee-deep, and men with shoes sometimes had them sucked off. Wagon wheels, enmired up to their hubs, had to be pulled free by hand. Moving on parallel roads, Williams and Cornwallis were never far apart. But the American detachment, so much smaller, had to be careful not to be overtaken or surprised—for then the deception that it maintained would end. Williams also had to take care that Cornwallis did not get between his formation and Greene and Huger. To do so, he had to send out numerous patrols and establish so many pickets that half his force was on night guard. He halted for only six hours a night, and each man had only six hours sleep in forty-eight hours. Traveling light, the men had no tents and would not have dared to set them up if they had. Each day began at three in the morning, when they hurried forward to get them far enough ahead of the enemy to give them time to pause for breakfast—their only meal—before renewing the march. Cornwallis pursued with such rare speed that a troop of Tarleton's horse overtook Lee's Legion in the rear guard. A fight ensued in which eighteen Tories were killed and the rest were put to flight. After it, with Cornwallis still snapping at his heels, Williams decided that His Lordship had been misled far enough to give Greene and Huger time to reach the Dan, so he swung to his right, followed by Lee, to try to catch up with them. Cornwallis detected the maneuver and changed direction himself—still coming on fast.

At last, on February 13, Williams received a message from Greene: "Irwin's Ferry, 12 past 5 o'clock. All our troops are over and the stage is clear.... I am ready to receive you and give you a hearty welcome." The great news ran backward through the American column. Cheer after cheer rose into the sky, so loud and clear that O'Hara, in the British van, heard them and realized that the race to the Dan was over.

The Americans had won.

To Charles Cornwallis it might have seemed that if the Americans had won the race, they had lost the campaign: the South, from Virginia to Florida, was now free of any organized Yankee army. In a sense, he had achieved his objective. Yet, Greene's army was still unconquered, and until it was destroyed, His Lordship's subjugation of the South was not complete. Moreover, Cornwallis could not move against Greene because he had no boats to cross the Dan and could not attempt the river's upper fords without finding Greene there to oppose him. Finally, he was 230 miles away from his base and had no way of obtaining supplies to replace those so rashly destroyed at Ramsour's Mills, and was stalled in a hostile countryside with American irregular forces hanging on both his flanks. Obviously, he had no alternative but to go back the way he had come, much as that might discourage the Carolina Tories who had cheered his pursuit of Greene. And that was what he did, resting his army for one day before about-facing to march back to Hillsboro, where he issued a proclamation thanking God for helping him "in driving the rebel army out of this province" and calling upon all loyal Tar Heels to rally to the cause of the Crown.

Nathanael Greene, meanwhile, was hardly better off. True, his retreat had been masterful, both in concept and in execution. True also, a successful retreat in front of a superior foe is the most difficult of all maneuvers, worthy of military genius, and it had indeed lifted the hearts of Patriots everywhere. But though he had drawn Cornwallis far from his base and whittled his army as planned, he had not found himself strong enough to turn upon him to destroy him in decisive battle. That, of course, had been the coup de grace of the entire plan—and because it could not be attempted, the plan may be said to have failed. Nor was it now possible to strike that death blow at the enemy, who was still so far from his base, simply because the reinforcements he had expected to find—especially those Virginia Continentals being enlisted by Steuben—

had not appeared. Not a single man. With the Dan falling rapidly, it now seemed likely that Cornwallis—not he—might be able to cross and deliver the death blow. That was why he was relieved—not disappointed—when he received word that the British Army was retiring south. But he still realized that he must return to North Carolina, if only because his objective remained the destruction of Cornwallis, whom he could not allow to grow stronger by trumpeting his "victory" among the Tories. So on February 18 General Andrew Pickens led a force of Marylanders and Lee's Legion across the Dan with orders to harass Cornwallis, cut off his foraging parties and—above all—make life unpleasant for Tory activists.

Almost immediately, Pickens was amazingly successful. He had at first attempted to surprise Tarleton, but then, failing to find him, he heard of a force of four hundred mounted Loyalists who were hurrying to join the Green Dragoon. The information came from a pair of Tories who were picked up by Lee's men. Mistaking Lee for Tarleton because his troopers wore identical short green jackets, they told him that the Loyalists were commanded by Colonel John Pyle and were on the same road a short distance ahead of him. The wily Lee sent one of them ahead to Pyle with "Colonel Tarleton's" compliments, asking him to draw up his men beside the road to allow Tarleton's Tories to ride by without hindrance. Pyle complied, and the Patriots, with drawn swords and cocked pistols, rode by the Loyalists, who were armed only with rifles and muskets—too clumsy for use at close quarters—held over their shoulders. Lee halted his men to shake hands with Pyle, intending, as he said later, to advise him of his predicament and to order him to send his men home. But just then some of Pyle's men spotted Pickens following with the Maryland infantry and opened fire on them. With this Lee's troopers wheeled to their right, with slashing sabers and blazing pistols, to fall upon the startled Tories. It was a terrible massacre. Unable to bring their unwieldy shoulder weapons to bear, Pyle's men went down among the hooves of terrified, screaming and kicking horses. Of Pyle's four hundred, ninety were killed and almost all the rest were wounded. Not one of Lee's men was hurt.

News of this slaughter, together with the depredations of Williams's light corps in Tory country, had a disastrous effect on the flow of recruits to Cornwallis's command at Hillsboro. The flow of recruits was shut off just as suddenly and completely as Cowpens had done, and His Lordship, already upset by a countryside made hostile by his house-to-house forcible requisitioning of food, complained to Lord Germain that he was "amongst timid friends and adjoining to inveterate Rebels." The Tories were growing fewer, and the Patriots more numerous. This dearth of recruits, joined to the growing scarcity of food around Hillsboro, prompted Cornwallis to evacuate the town in search of more amenable quarters. On February 27 he crossed the Haw River to a defensible position on Almanace Creek, at a junction of roads leading to Hillsboro, Guilford, Salisbury or Wilmington that provided him with a choice of routes for maneuver. Greene, who was now across the Dan, together with Williams, spent the next ten days moving from place to place to keep Cornwallis guessing as to the American intentions. Greene's movements so annoyed His Lordship that he crossed the creek on March 6 to bring on a skirmish in which both sides suffered casualties of about twenty apiece. Afterward, Williams's light corps rejoined Green's army, which had been receiving reinforcements so steadily that by mid-March it stood at 4,400 strong—the most powerful American force yet assembled in the South—against Cornwallis with about 2,000. Greene was now strong enough to challenge his British opponent, and he knew exactly where to do it: at Guilford Court House, which he had reconnoitered six weeks earlier on his retreat north. He arrived there on March 14 and went into line intending to fight the next day.

Of Greene's host only about fifteen hundred were Continentals, and of that number only about five hundred—Marylanders and Delawares—were tough and savvy veterans of combat. The rest were militia, the Virginians considered good, the Tar Heels not so good. Greene could remember what Daniel Morgan had written him about these militia: "If they fight, you beat Cornwallis; if not, he will beat you." Morgan had advised Greene to put the militia "in the center with some picked troops in the rear to shoot down the first man that runs." This was done as Greene formed his army in three lines: The first was of North Carolina militia across the main road leading through a clearing uphill to the courthouse and behind a rail fence, and obliquely behind this to either side, were Washington's cavalry, plus sharpshooting riflemen on the right and Lee's Legion of both horse and foot and more riflemen to the left. The second line, three hundred yards farther back, was composed of Virginia militia with sharpshooters posted at intervals behind them, as Morgan had suggested. Five hundred and fifty yards farther back and curving around the brow of the courthouse hill was the third and principal line, with Greene and Huger, Virginia and Maryland Continentals and artillery.

Marching against the Americans on this March 15, 1781, a cold, clear day with a high sun suggesting the end of the Carolinas winter, came Cornwallis's army in two wings: the right, under General Leslie, and the left, led by Colonel James Webster with General O'Hara behind him with the supporting guards. From about a mile away the foremost

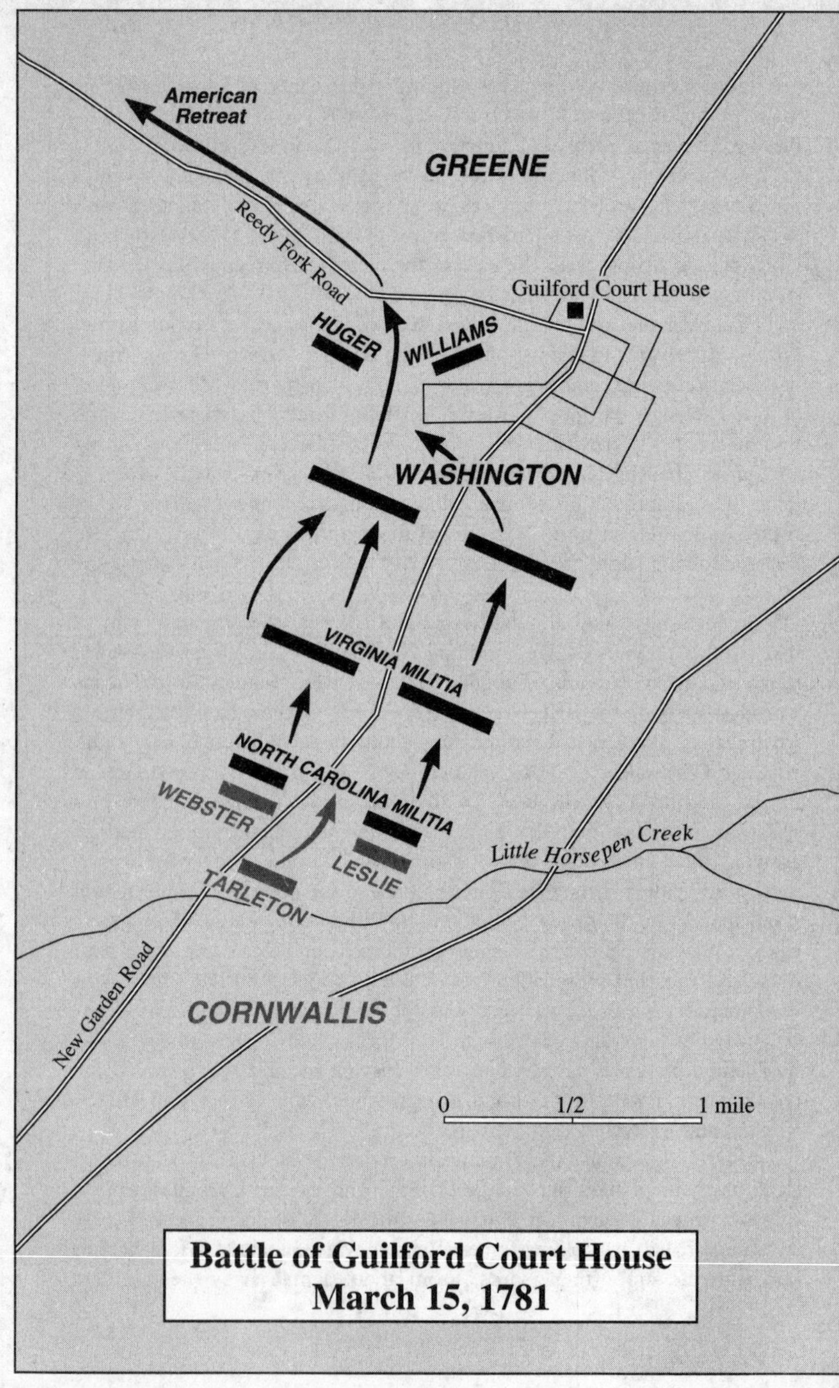

Battle of Guilford Court House
March 15, 1781

Americans could see that sun glinting on burnished blades, falling on bright scarlet and green jackets, while the sound of rattling drums and squealing fifes came faintly on the wind. These were nervous Tar Heel riflemen to whom Greene had said, just as Morgan had asked his first line at Cowpens: "Two rounds, my boys, and then you may fall back." About half-past one they were ready, squinting through the sights of rifles laid in rows across the zigzag rail face, as the British line came gradually within range, marching precisely as though on parade, its wings invisible in the woods enclosing the clearing. The enemy line was two-thirds of the way across the clearing when a thousand rifles spoke in a ragged volley that sounded like a string of firecrackers. Gaps appeared in the red-and-green line, but it still came forward. Coming to within musket shot of the fence, it halted, and the British delivered a volley of their own—but with markedly less effect—striding forward again. Once more there came a volley of American rifles, but this time with much, much greater effect—actually staggering the enemy. At this point Webster rode forward, waving his sword with the cry, "Come on, my brave Fusiliers"—and with a wild yell the British left charged with outthrust bayonets.

At once the North Carolina militia turned and fled. They did not bother to reload, for they had delivered the promised two volleys and now it was time to flee that wickedly gleaming steel. With more yells both British wings pursued, coming to a second fence with no opponent visible. Yet bullets were keening among them, and stricken men were screaming and falling. An oblique fire was coming from the wings of Washington's and Lee's mixed forces stationed in the woods to either side and ahead of the British. It was a particularly deadly and "most destructive fire," for the bullets coming at an angle might miss soldiers on one side but would almost surely strike some on the other. To remove it, the British sought out their tormentors face to face. But to do so, they had to enter the woods, in which they were seldom adept, while the Americans, firing and flitting from tree to tree, though forced back, were actually never destroyed. Those under Washington on the right at last formed an oblique position to the right of Stevens's Virginians, while Lee, on the oblique left, though forced up to a height and was never conquered, remaining a factor in the battle.

Now the British line, solidly re-formed with Webster and O'Hara leading the left and Leslie on the right, swept forward once more to reach the second line held by the Virginians. Webster's men struck at the right of Stevens's brigade, forcing it to give way, to pivot on its left flank like a gate swinging backward until it was ultimately swept away. What was left of Stevens's troops fought valiantly against repeated British attacks, repulsing three consecutive bayonet charges and standing firm. But then Webster, on the far British left, finding no one opposing him, drove ahead to strike at the right wing of the third American line without waiting for the rest of Greene's second line to be finished off. Unwisely, he sent his men charging forward with the bayonet straight into the best troops Greene had: Maryland and Delaware Continentals supported by untried but valiant Virginian regulars, all under Colonel John Gunby. They waited until Webster's blades were within a hundred feet before triggering a terrible volley that stopped the British cold. When Gunby called for the bayonet, they charged the staggered enemy and drove them down into a ravine and up the opposite side in great disarray.

The critical moment of the Battle of Guilford Court House had come. Lee's force, on the height to the right, was still holding firm against a Hessian assault, while the Virginians, on the second line, were still standing firm against Leslie on the right, supported by O'Hara to Leslie's left. Webster was beaten and in disarray. If at that moment, Greene, again emulating Morgan at Cowpens, had thrown Washington and Lee against the demoralized and disorganized Webster, while charging O'Hara and Leslie with his whole third line of Continentals, he might have destroyed Cornwallis, just as Morgan, by making that very same maneuver at Cowpens, had overwhelmed and routed Tarleton. But then, of course, Morgan was leading only a detachment of the Southern Army and could afford to risk defeat. Greene, in command of the whole, could not afford to risk all-out battle because it could mean all-out defeat and, at the least, the loss of the South. So he gave no such order; Gunby was recalled and Webster was allowed to recover and re-form and Cornwallis's entire line straightened. Except for the contingent fighting Lee in the woods, Cornwallis's entire army was free to assault the third American line.

The British surged forward into combat that was fierce and bloody. O'Hara was wounded, and Colonel Stuart was killed, and even though a green Maryland regiment was driven from the field, the two armies were so closely engaged and the British were apparently getting so much the worst of the struggle that Cornwallis made a desperate move. He ordered his artillery to fire grape upon the melee, high enough, of course, to pass over the British before exploding above the Americans. But grape—clusters of balls scattered from inside exploding shells—cannot be aimed with accuracy. Once the balls burst from the shells, they strike everything within range. It is said that Charles O'Hara, lying wounded beside the guns, begged Charles Cornwallis not to sacrifice his own men. But Cornwallis grimly—yet with justification—kept to his purpose of shattering that ominous melee that looked like it would reel backward in his direction at any moment. The grape was fired, and its effect was bloody among both sides. But most of all, it struck the Americans, forcing them to withdraw so that the British line could be re-formed.

Webster, on the far left, was the first commander to put his troops back in battle array, and he launched a furious assault against what remained of the American third line. But the Yankees held and drove Webster back. There now ensued a lull in the battle, during which Greene pondered his situation. All of his militia—Virginian as well as North Carolinian—had vanished clean away, and the Fifth Maryland Continentals had been scattered. But he still had his remaining Maryland and Delaware regulars, together with Lee's and Washington's detachments, still fighting forest warfare on those oblique flanks. Cornwallis, however, was just as badly staggered, if not more so—and he had begun the battle heavily outnumbered. If Greene had known Cornwallis's situation, he might have delivered the death blow. But he did not even suspect it, and furthermore he was not an ardent warrior in the cast of Daniel Morgan. Probably Greene's discretion was all to the good in the American cause, for the defect of the virtue of ardor is recklessness, and Greene wisely decided not to risk decisive defeat but to keep to his plan of preserving his army. At half-past three he ordered a retreat to his old encampment on Troublesome Creek. He would fight again another day.

Lord Charles Cornwallis would not be able to do so—at least not in the Carolinas. Although he had won the battle, it was a Pyrrhic victory: he had got more than he gave. Of the approximately nineteen hundred British troops who entered the battle, more than a quarter were casualties: 93 dead and 439 wounded, and many of the wounded were mortally stricken, some of them breathing their last many days later. Twenty-nine of his officers had been killed or wounded, among the latter two generals—O'Hara and Howard—while the gallant Webster received his death wound. Greene's casualties were much lighter: 78 killed and 183 wounded, not including the thousands of militia who ran away and might technically be counted "missing."

As a brave soldier himself, Cornwallis could take solace in the performance of his troops. Of these valiant soldiers Sir John Fortescue, historian of the British Army from Crecy in the middle of the fourteenth century to the middle of the nineteenth, wrote: "Never, perhaps, has the prowess of the British soldier been seen to greater advantage than in this obstinate and bloody battle." What Sir John did not mention was how these veterans of the set-piece battles of Europe had adapted themselves to the rigors and misery of forest warfare in America. From those noble Guards who obeyed O'Hara's order to plunge on a freezing day into the waist-deep icy waters of the Catawba River to those same Guards who, with the Welsh Fusiliers, were torn to pieces at Guilford, the British regulars had learned to endure. Drenched with the torrential rains that struck them on the night of the battle, they awoke on the morrow to find fifty more of their comrades dead of wounds, and still no food or water for themselves since they had supped forty-eight hours earlier. At the end of that period each man received just four ounces of flour and the same weight of beef.

There were simply no supplies to be had by the British Army at Guilford, an alien island stuck in a hostile sea. No foraging party dared leave camp, and no boat or wagon could pass over roads or rivers now dominated by jubilant Patriots. Nor could Cornwallis, like a wounded lion that has lost too much blood, risk another battle. His only recourse was to withdraw to Wilmington, his nearest food magazine, but still a melancholy two hundred miles away. Two days after the battle, on March 17—another sad St. Patrick's Day similar to the one on which Howe evacuated Boston—Cornwallis turned south again, finally limping into Wilmington twenty days later. Wilmington was about all that he possessed in the entire Old North State, although South Carolina was still controlled by Rawdon at Camden. To fight Greene again was out of the question, for Cornwallis, even after resting and refitting his army, still commanded only a few dozen more than fourteen hundred men. News that Greene had begun marching south from Ramsey's Mill convinced him that he was bound for Camden. Should he hurry to Rawdon's side? No. It was too risky. The distance was too great, and there were too many rivers to cross where he might find Greene waiting in ambush. Besides, Greene was already en route and would get to Camden before him. Thus there was nothing he could do: if Rawdon were defeated, he could not help Cornwallis; if Greene lost, he would not be needed.

It was this consideration that decided General Charles Cornwallis to take the fatal step of invading Virginia. He reasoned that to keep the South, "a serious attempt upon Virginia would be the most solid plan, because successful operations might not only be attended with important consequences there, but would tend to the security of South Carolina and ultimately the submission of North Carolina." In other words, conquest of the Old Dominion would guarantee subjugation of the South. Cornwallis thus resolved "to take advantage of General Greene's having left the back door of Virginia open and march immediately into the province, to attempt a junction with General Philips."

Nathanael Greene may have lost the Battle of Guilford Court House, but he had won his campaign to force Cornwallis to abandon the Carolinas.

★ 68 ★

GREENE RECONQUERS THE SOUTH

By his retreat to the Dan and the Battle of Guilford Court House, Nathanael Greene had done in the South what Washington had accomplished in the North by his retreat across New Jersey and his raids on Trenton and Princeton. Unaware that he had also forced Cornwallis to take that first fatal step toward a little tobacco-trading port in Virginia named Yorktown, he wrote to Washington after Guilford: "I am determined to carry the war immediately into South Carolina." His first objective would be Camden, held by Lord Francis Rawdon with about nine hundred men.

Greene himself was down to about fourteen hundred troops, but all of them were battle-blooded infantry, while in the troopers of William Washington and Light Horse Harry Lee he possessed a fine corps of cavalry. His militia might be gone, but he really didn't want them back, although a few hundred Tar Heels did return to prove themselves decent soldiers. On April 6 at Ramsey's Mill, Greene detached Lee's Legion with a company of Maryland Continentals to march to Fort Watson on the Santee, linking Camden with Charleston. First, however, Lee was to move along the Cape Fear River as though he was bound for Cornwallis at Wilmington. On the following day Greene broke camp with his main body, also feinting at Wilmington, before changing his course to the west, bound for Camden. His men were in good spirits, for April in the Carolinas is a balmy time, with the leaf-bearing trees green again and the azaleas and camellias bursting into riotous bloom. There was plenty of food and rum and little hardship as the Yankee columns moved along at the brisk rate of eighteen miles a day.

As they approached their objective, Lee, joined by Francis Marion, moved against Fort Watson, held by eighty British regulars and forty Tories. It was a small, stout stockade standing on a level plain. It was also a tough little nut to crack, especially without artillery or entrenching tools. But then Colonel Hezekiah Maham suggested building a "rifle tower" above the level of the fort. For five days the woods rang to the sound of axmen cutting down trees and notching logs. On the night of April 22 the tower was erected, and a platform with a protective parapet was built on it. At dawn riflemen on the tower took the fort under fire, while two small forces attacked its abatis. Unable to protect the abatis without exposing themselves to sniper fire from the tower, the garrison surrendered. At a loss of two killed and six wounded, Lee and Marion took 114 prisoners and captured Rawdon's communication link with Charleston.

Camden was not so easy. Arriving there on April 19, Greene found the town strongly fortified, although a settlement within a mile of it was taken by a company of those valiant Delawares, under the veteran and able Captain Robert Kirkwood. Greene saw that he could not hope to storm a position protected by the Wateree River, Pine Tree Creek and a formidable system of redoubts. So he withdrew to Hobkirk Hill, about a mile and a half north of Camden. A sandy ridge of little height, it sloped down between swamps to a level plain. Picket guards were stationed on the plain while Greene pondered his next move, a decision that was made for him by Rawdon after a deserting Maryland drummer boy gave him an accurate description of the Yankee position. At once Rawdon decided to attack.

On the morning of April 25 the quartermaster Colonel Carrington arrived with promised provisions, and the delighted Americans stacked their rifles and began cooking breakfast. As they ate, they were startled by musket fire coming from the pickets' vicinity. The fire rose in volume, and Greene sent Kirkwood with his Delawares to support the guards. He did so with skill and bravery, even though he was facing the advance units of Rawdon's attacking force. Once His Lordship brought his entire strength to bear against the American outpost, its members retired in good order to the main body, by then thoroughly alarmed and in position to receive an attack.

On April 25, 1781, Rawdon approached Hobkirk's southeastern slope where the ascent was easier. He had almost all his troops in column, advancing in good order, but Greene saw almost instantly that the enemy front was remarkably narrow and vulnerable to a double envelopment. His own troops were emplaced in a line of four regiments peculiarly adaptable to such a maneuver. They were, from right to left, the Fourth and Fifth Virginia and the First and Fifth Maryland. Greene's plan was to strike the enemy with artillery before this entire line charged down the hill. In the center Samuel Hawes's Fifth Virginia and Gunby's First Maryland could hit the enemy head-on with the bayonet, while the other two regiments on the wings struck Rowdon's flanks and thus held his entire force in a deadly embrace.

The battle began when the American center stepped a few paces to the right and the left to present Greene's artillery with a field of fire. Once the cannons opened up, the rebels charged with a cheer. The effect on the British was disconcerting, until Rawdon quickly realized his predicament and ordered his own troops extended in a phalanx so wide that it outflanked the Americans at both ends. Nevertheless, the Yankees attacked with élan—the center penetrating with the bayonet, the wings closely engaged. In the meantime Washington's dragoons were sweeping around the British right in an effort to get into their rear. But then Gunby's First Maryland paused to deliver a volley instead of driving straight ahead with the bayonet. A British volley in reply killed Captain William Beatty, Jr., in command of the right-hand company. Beatty's soldiers faltered and fell back. So did an adjoining company, whereupon Gunby, rather than moving to rally these two wavering formations and bring them back into line, ordered his entire regiment to retreat to the base of the hill, there to be re-formed and realigned.

Now it was Rawdon who saw his chance. With loud cries his redcoats made for the gap in the American line, and all the Marylanders broke and ran. Gunby and Otho Williams strove frantically to halt them, but when Colonel Benjamin Ford, of the Fifth Maryland, was wounded and carried from the field, his regiment also broke and headed rearward. Their panic infected the men of the Fourth Virginia, who likewise began sprinting for safety. Only Hawes's Fifth Virginia remained unbroken, and Greene quickly ordered its men to cover their fleeing comrades. They did so with great bravery and spirit, not only checking the British pursuit but actually driving them back. Nevertheless, it was now not possible for Greene to reorganize his demoralized army in the face of the enemy. He could only gather his regiments together for a less disorderly retreat. Meanwhile his gunners had also fled, and his artillery was in danger of being captured, until about fifty young Irishmen from the Maryland Line volunteered to rescue them. Led by Captain William Smith, they seized abandoned ropes with one hand and their muskets with the other and tried to tow the guns to safety. At that point a company of Tory dragoons, led by Captain John Coffin, came galloping forward. Dropping the ropes, Smith's soldiers opened a deadly fire that drove the horsemen back. Returning to the attack, the Tories were again repulsed—but were then reinforced by friendly infantry. In the ensuing seesaw fight Smith was wounded and every one of his gallant little band either killed, wounded or captured. Greene's cannon seemed hopelessly lost. But then William Washington's dragoons came trotting back from their fruitless attempt to turn the enemy rear. Loaded with non-combatant prisoners, they dumped these captives by the roadside, to charge Coffin's cavalry and drive them from the field. With that the guns were hitched to horses and towed safely away.

Greene was now able to lead his reorganized army, recovered guns and reluctant prisoners on an orderly withdrawal, while sending Washington with Kirkwood's Delawares back to the battlefield to rescue his wounded and take more captives. Because Rawdon had retired by then into Camden, Washington found only Coffin's men at Hobkirk Hill, immediately charging them and once again driving them off. Thus he and Kirkwood were able to collect all their wounded and bring them back to their new camp at Sanders Creek, the scene of Gates's disgraceful defeat.

American losses at Hobkirk Hill were 19 killed, 108 wounded and 136 missing, the latter probably those who ran away and returned; the British casualties were 258, of whom 38 were killed and the rest either wounded or missing. Because Greene had retreated, Rawdon must be accounted the victor, although his victory, like Cornwallis's, was Pyrrhic, for his casualties represented almost 30 percent of his command—again like his chief far too many to endure. Greene, meanwhile, was furious to have been deprived of what could have been a signal triumph, and he angrily placed the blame on Gunby with this report to Joseph Reed: "We should have had Lord Rawdon and his whole command prisoner in three minutes, if Colonel Gunby had not ordered his regiment to retire. ... I was almost frantic with vexation at the disappointment." Yet, he remained undaunted. As he wrote to La Luzerne, "We fight, get beat, rise and fight again."

Despite Hobkirk Hill, Nathanael Greene was still confident of achieving his heart's desire: the mop-up of the entire South. Even though his anticipated reinforcements of about 2,500 militia from Virginia and the Carolinas never appeared, especially a veteran thousand irregulars under the independent—not to say arrogant—General Thomas Sumter of South Carolina, he was not especially depressed. "You see," he said to his staff officer Colonel William Davie, "that we must again resume the partisan war. ... You observe our dangerous and critical situation. The regular troops are now reduced to a handful and I am without militia to form the convoy or detachment service. ... Congress seems to have lost sight of the Southern States and have abandoned them to their fate, so much so that I am even as much distressed for ammunition as for men."

Yet, as bleak as Greene's outlook certainly was in May 1781, Lord Rawdon's situation in Camden was even worse. Although not actually besieged, he was nevertheless deprived of food and forage by the numerous bands of Patriot irregulars that were buzzing around him like swarms of bees in a rose garden. Moreover, there was a kind of mutiny spreading among his troops, begun by American deserters who had joined his forces and were now—having heard that Greene had hung five such traitors—visibly disturbed and terrified. Finally, Rawdon's losses at Hobkirk Hill had not been replaced. So he decided to abandon Camden, and on May 10, having burned the jail, the mills and a few private houses, he marched from the town hoping to overtake Greene and bring him to battle again, or even to come upon some of those American formations that were now so busily nipping off British outposts after Greene had commenced his southern mop-up.

In exactly twenty days Greene's detachments, such as Light-Horse Harry Lee's—together with those of the irregular commanders Pickens, Sumter and Marion—had broken six links in the enemy's imposing chain of posts in the South: Camden, Watson, Motte, Granby, Nelson's Ferry and Orangeburg. Their loss had the effect of isolating Charleston and Savannah, while only Ninety-six and Georgetown in South Carolina and Augusta in Georgia remained in British hands. So Greene next assigned Augusta to Pickens, assisted by Lee's Legion with some Tar Heel militia under Major Pinketham Eaton, while he would personally take his main body against Ninety-six. Georgetown was to be taken by "the Swamp Fox"—Francis Marion.

Lee moved on Augusta with his customary speed made possible by his practice of mounting his foot soldiers behind his dragoons. Nearing the city, he learned that the king's annual gift to the Indians—a mass of useful material—was on temporary deposit at Fort Galphin (Dreadnought), about twelve miles below Augusta. Leaving Eaton to follow with his militia and artillery and again mounting his infantry behind his troopers, Lee made for the little fort, reaching it on May 21. There he assigned the raw Georgia and South Carolina militia with him to make a sham attack on what was little more than a stockaded farmhouse. The men were instructed to appear in full view and then to run. They did, whereupon most of the garrison sallied forth in pursuit, so that Lee could rush the fort with almost no opposition. Thus a great store of small arms, ammunition, medicine, blankets, clothing, rum, salt and other supplies fell to the Americans.

Lee next hurried back to join Pickens in Augusta. In the center of town stood the formidable Fort Cornwallis, with 250 Tory militia and 300 Creek Indians under Lieutenant Colonel Thomas Browne. A half mile distant was another smaller position, Fort Grierson, held by a Tory colonel of that name with eighty Georgia Loyalists and two guns. An American attack on Grierson prompted the garrison to try to escape to Cornwallis, but they were intercepted and slaughtered with the ferocity familiar to those Patriot-Tory encounters. Grierson was himself murdered by a Georgian who hated him. Only a few Americans were killed, among them Major Eaton.

Lee and Pickens next went after Fort Cornwallis. But Colonel Browne was alert and not easily dislodged. American approaches were attacked by sallies from the fort. Remembering Fort Watson, Lee suggested building a "Maham tower." It was done, despite Browne's attempt to knock it down with cannon shot. Erected during the night, its guns raked the fort incessantly while the approaches crawled closer. On the day the assault was to be launched, Pickens and Lee decided to summon the position to surrender again. To their surprise, their terms were accepted—and one more British position fell to the rebels. The next day Lee set out to join General Greene at Ninety-six.

The village of Ninety-six received its unusual name because it was believed to be that many miles from the old frontier fort of Prince George on the Keowee River. Besides being one of the most important British posts in the Carolina chain, it served to protect the Tories in the countryside and to maintain communication with friendly Indian tribes. Its defenses had been vastly improved since the evacuation of Camden through a rectangular stockade surrounding the village, which was itself protected by a deep ditch with an abatis, and all were encircled by a high bank formed by the excavated earth. East of the main stockade was the Star, a roughly circular fort provided with sixteen angles for exit and entering, and also ditched with an abatis. To the west there was a large spring from which a rivulet of water ran inside the stockade. This was the village's only water supply. To protect it, the jail on the stockade side had been fortified, while on its other, or western side, was Holmes's Fort, a strongly palisaded position containing a pair of blockhouses. Holding Holmes's Fort were about 550 veteran Tory soldiers under Lieutenant Colonel John Harris Cruger, probably the best of a mostly inept corps of Loyalist officers.

When Greene arrived at Ninety-six with something less than a thousand war-wise veterans, he saw "a very respectable work ... so well furnished that our success is very doubtful." Without cannon of sufficient weight to knock it down, he decided to try to take it by siege approaches. At once Kosciuszko, ignoring the customary courtesy of summoning the fort to surrender, began digging approaches about two hundred feet from the Star. To be so rudely denied the opportunity to make a disdainful rejection of enemy terms so angered Cruger that he at once opened fire on the parallels with his trio of three-pounders, after which about thirty of his soldiers sallied forth from the fort to rout the working party and seize its tools. Sobered, Kosciuszko renewed his digging 1,200 feet from the fort. By June 3 a second parallel was completed, and the fort was properly summoned. After Cruger rejected the terms, Greene's artillery began a heavy cross fire. But the fort still held out, so another Maham tower was erected, from which blazing arrows were fired at the barracks' roofs. Without hesitation, the resourceful Cruger ordered the roofs torn off all the buildings, uncaring that the garrison was thus exposed "to all the pernicious effects of the night air."

On June 8 Lee and his legion arrived. At once the perceptive Lee saw that Greene was attacking Ninety-six from both the wrong and the strongest side. The vulnerable spot was on the west, where the water supply began, and it was also less heavily defended. So parallels were begun there. Three days later came the bad news that Rawdon had been reinforced by the arrival of troopships in Charleston. Rawdon now had two thousand regulars to command—including 150 horsemen—and he was marching to the relief of Ninety-six. Thus Greene was left with three alternatives, all unwelcome: quit the siege and retire; march to fight Rawdon and defeat him; or attack the fort immediately before Rawdon, thirty miles away on June 17, could arrive with his relieving force. Greene chose the third course, and at noon of the eighteenth a signal gun launched a two-pronged assault on both sides of the fort. On the west, at Holmes's Fort and the spring, Lee's Legion and Kirkwood's veterans drove the Tories out of the fort and then sat down to await developments against the Star on the eastern side.

But on the other side a bloody and bitter battle was raging. Greene's guns began with a cross fire on the bastion, followed by volleys of musketry and a raking fire from the marksmen atop the Maham tower. While bullets and balls poured into the Star, a pair of "forlorn hopes"—squads of soldiers on a perilous mission—led by Lieutenants Duval and Seldon, raced down the third parallel, leaping up from it to attack the abatis. Axmen quickly cut a path through the fallen trees, and hook men next began pulling down the sandbags that were protecting the position's parapet. Cruger's Tories were unable to fire down on the attackers without exposing themselves to the sharpshooters on the tower, and it appeared that if the hook men could fill the ditch with sandbags, Greene's veterans could clamber over them into the Star for a final hand-to-hand struggle. At that point British Major Green commanding the Star, decided that only a counterattack could save Ninety-six. Two parties of thirty men each slipped out of a sally port to the Star's rear, turning in opposite directions to come running around the fort and to fall on Greene's forlorn hopes. When both Duval and Seldon fell, the Americans fell back—and Ninety-six held.

On June 20 Nathanael Greene began his retreat. He had lost 57 killed, 70 wounded and 20 missing, while Cruger's casualties were 27 killed and 58 wounded. Greene had fought and "got beat" once more. But he would also "rise and fight again," for as long as he continued to challenge British control of Georgia and the Carolinas, the hearts of the Patriots in those three states would still beat for final victory, while the hopes of the Tories were plunged in gloom.

After relieving Ninety-six, Lord Rawdon marched to Orangeburg, where he was joined by Lieutenant Colonel John Stuart, who arrived from Charleston with more troops, including the famous "Buffs" regiment, bringing Rawdon's strength to about two thousand men. This was where Greene found him. Studying the British position, Greene thought it too strong to attack, even though he outnumbered Rawdon. So he began moving north toward the Carolinas border, seeking fresh food as a substitute for the frogs and even alligators on which his starving men were subsisting, as well as surcease from the merciless South Carolina sun that scourged them or the clouds of mosquitoes that were infecting them with malaria. He found what he wanted at the High Hills of Santee, a hill chain along the Wateree. Here was a salubrious campsite where the suffering Grand Army of the Southern Department rested for six weeks, free of both sunstroke and malaria and where the pure air, clear water and friendly countryside restored health to the sick and bestowed recovery on the wounded.

The British had no such blessings. As Tarleton wrote: "During a renewed succession of forced marches under the rage of a burning sun, and in a climate at this season peculiarly inimical to man, they were frequently when sinking under the most excessive fatigue not only destitute of every comfort, but almost of every necessary which seems essential to his existence." When the food ran out, "their only resources were water and the wild cattle which they found in the woods." Lord Francis Rawdon himself succumbed to this debilitating ordeal, sailing home in broken health. Taken prisoner at sea by the French fleet, he was carried to Brest, from which he was eventually exchanged. Colonel Stuart replaced him in command of the British army. It was Stuart who opposed Greene when the tenacious American finally found the enemy at Eutaw Springs, South Carolina, in September 1781.

The two Eutaw springs were actually the first and second surface appearances of a strong subterranean stream. Eutaw Creek flowed from the lower of the two basins alongside the road to Charleston and thence into the Santee River. Between the creek and the Charleston road stood a fine brick house fronting on a clearing penetrated by the road. On the morning of September 8 Greene, with 2,400 men, came marching up this road, while Stuart, with about 2,000, learning of his approach, put his own force across the road at an oblique angle below the clearing. One of the curiosities of this approaching battle was that many of Stuart's regulars were American deserters and about as many of Greene's Continentals were British deserters. As Greene was to say: "At the end of the war, we fought the enemy with British soldiers; and they fought us with those of America." In quality, experience and valor they were about even, which explains the ferocity peculiar to this final battle of Greene's incredible campaign.

Stuart believed himself so secure from enemy attack that he had that morning sent out a "rooting party" of one hundred unarmed men under a small guard to gather sweet potatoes. Afterwards he ordered Coffin with 140 foot and 50 horse to scout the road. Marching toward these two formations was Greene's army in four columns: the first, under Lieutenant Colonel John Henderson, which included Lee's Legion and the South Carolina militia; the second, composed of Carolinas militia under Marion; the third, made up of the Continentals led by General Jethro Sumner; and the fourth, comprised of Washington's horse and Kirkwood's light infantry. Ahead of the army was a scouting party under Major John Armstrong. A mile from the enemy line, Armstrong sighted Coffin, falling back to Henderson with his report. Henderson put Lee's troops in the woods to the right and the Palmetto militia on the left. Into this trap came the bold but reckless Coffin, charging with his horse only to be met with a shower of bullets from an unseen enemy. Coffin's infantry was "destroyed, several killed and about 40 taken with their captain," while his cavalry escaped by precipitate flight. Stuart's rooting party, drawn to the scene by the sound of gunfire, also was captured.

Halting to partake of a welcome ration of rum, the Americans came on again—just as Stuart finished arranging his line of battle. His last move was to put a force of three hundred redcoats, under Major John Majoribanks, into a dense thicket of blackjack to his line's right rear. Coffin, with a smaller force of horse and foot, was to Majoribanks's left rear. As the Americans advanced while the British held firm, the field artillery of both sides dueled each other, with the Americans losing two guns and the British only one. Repeated volleys were exchanged, so that even before either side had caught sight of the other, a bitter and obstinate battle had begun.

Henderson's militia amazed Greene, advancing steadily at the enemy and firing constantly as they went. They got off no less than seventeen rounds each, so that Greene could say that their conduct would have gratified "the veterans of the great King of Prussia." At this point Lee's Legion tried to get around the British left, just as the Carolinas militia in the front of Greene's center began to weaken. At once Stuart ordered a charge against them, and the Tar Heels broke and ran. Yelling wildly, the redcoats made for the gap, just as Greene filled it with Sumner's North Carolina Continentals. These Tar Heels not only halted the enemy, but drove them back. As the British withdrew, Stuart brought up Coffin's detachment. That detachment staggered the Palmetto, who then recovered and held firm—even under the fire from Majoribanks's troops in the thicket to their left.

At this point the Tar Heels on the right front began to bend back under the weight of Coffin's reinforcements. Then they withdrew, but in good order. Shouting again in anticipation of victory, the redcoats charged once more—and Greene hit them with his Continentals, his best and freshest troops. Washington and Kirkwood followed. Now it was the Yankees who were yelling, pausing at a distance of forty yards to fire a volley, coming on again at the double with outthrust bayonets.

"Assailed on flank and front," the entire British line fell backward. First the left, then the center, then the right—all turning to flee in utter disorder and confusion, a struggling back-pedaling mass that did not halt until its members entered the clearing. Only Majoribanks remained on the field. Washington's horse charged his men with a reckless and fatal abandon, only to find that their mounts could not penetrate the thicket of blackjack. Washington saw an opening and tried to force it, his sections galloping straight across the British line of fire. A terrible slaughter ensued. Stricken men fell beneath the hooves of screaming horses. Washington's horse fell, pulling him down with his foot in the stirrup. A redcoat bayoneted him and then took him prisoner. His second and two lieutenants also fell. Fully half his command was either killed or wounded. Nevertheless, they rallied to charge Majoribanks once more—only to be repulsed. Now it was Kirkwood's veterans who came to their rescue, entering the thicket in a furious rush that drove the British back and down into a ravine and up the other side before they halted to re-form with their backs to the creek.

Yet Majoribanks's gallant stand and Washington's frightful losses did nothing to deter the British retreat. Rushing through their own camp in the clearing, they went up the Charleston Road in a pell-mell mass. Here was the great opportunity of Nathanael Greene's campaign: the culminating victory that he sought. All he needed to do was consolidate his advance, overwhelm Majoribanks, pursue Stuart trying to rally his troops on the road and seize Stuart's brick headquarters before it could be occupied and fortified by Cruger's Tories. But at that golden moment Greene's men betrayed him. Entering the enemy camp, the Americans halted to loot it, to gobble the enemy's rations and gulp his rum until so many of them became so thoroughly drunk and sated that it was impossible for their officers to reorganize them. This disgraceful breakdown in discipline disarmed not only the militia—as might be expected—but the supposedly reliable Maryland and Virginia Continentals. Greene, apparently unaware of the disorder that was to deny him the victory, still struggled to sweep Majoribanks aside and seize the brick house from which the British were now firing upon Lee's and Kirkwood's infantry. But to no avail. Moreover, Stuart, having rallied his fleeing men, returned to that position. But not to give battle. Three hours of fighting in that enervating heat had exhausted his men, and Greene's as well. While the British commander held the field, the American withdrew his troops into the woods.

Most historians regard the Battle of Eutaw Springs as another defeat for Nathanael Greene. Actually it was a standoff. In casualties, the British got much more than they gave—a total of 866 soldiers divided among 85 killed—including the gallant Majoribanks who died of his wounds—351 wounded and 430 missing—against American losses of 139 killed, 375 wounded and 8 missing, for a total of 522. Even though Greene had once again failed to triumph, he had achieved a favorable result once more. Eutaw Springs drove the British back to Charleston, from which, together with Savannah, they would not emerge until the war ended, and King George held no more territory in the South. Meanwhile, the state governments of these three former colonies were reestablished and continued to function without hindrance.

Greene's southern campaign was indeed incredible. In ten months—

from December 2, 1780, when he took command of the Southern army, to the end of September, after he had fought his last major battle—Greene and his army marched an unbelievable 2,600 miles; from Charlotte to the Catawba to the Dan and from the Dan back to Charleston and Augusta. They fought five major battles—one of them Morgan's major victory at Cowpens—and scores of minor skirmishes, raids and ambuscades. They crossed as many streams, some of them the typically great rivers of America, many of the others large enough to be considered major in other parts of the world. Greene and his soldiers were nothing less than magnificent.

For all practical purposes, Nathanael Greene, because of the vast distances between himself and Washington in New Jersey, was completely on his own. Every tactic, every maneuver, line of march or order of battle sprang from his own brain, just as he chose every position on which to attack or defend. In a sense, while being his own strategist and tactician, he was also his own quartermaster, for he had to supply the necessary logistics—food, clothing, shelter and arms—for his own troops.

And the troops, again, in their endurance, doggedness and loyalty were a kind of soldier perhaps unrivaled in military history. They could be beaten, of course, and were, for they were up against the splendidly trained and equipped and equally brave British redcoats with their German allies. But they were nevertheless unconquerable. A lost battle to them was a familiar reverse from which they made the likewise-customary rapid recovery. Shoeless and in rags; often tying masses of Spanish moss around their bare hips and shoulders to prevent their muskets and cartridge boxes from rubbing them raw; trying to subsist on a daily cup of flour and a morsel of moldy beef—which they had to supplement with green corn and unripe fruit, just enough to produce dysentery but not sufficient to keep them from fainting on the march—tramping through mountains and over malarial plains in alternating hells of heat and cold and over roads muddy, frozen or dusty by turns; sleeping without tents on ground that was similarly inimical, they were even invincible in death, for their accomplishments lived on, so that these noble soldiers were, in a real sense, indeed, stronger than death. And if their commander is criticized for having never won a battle because—not possessing the ardor of a Morgan or a Wayne or even a Benedict Arnold—he would not risk the final, all-out blow, it may be said, as has been suggested before, that neither could he risk all-out defeat and thus doom the Revolution or at least lose the South. His were not the glamorous or flamboyant martial virtues—dash, élan, daring—but, rather, the less showy but more solid strengths of, in Fortescue's words, "patience, resolution and profound common sense, qualities which go far towards making a great general." And the limping, little ironmaster from Rhode Island—the amateur who outwitted the professional Cornwallis and Rawdon at almost every turn—was indeed a great general. Again to quote Fortescue: "Greene, who was a very noble character, seems to me to stand little if at all lower than Washington as a general in the field."

His modest report to La Luzerne—"We fight, get beat, rise and fight again"—would forever be cherished as a motto of the United States Army to be. More important, he forced Lord Cornwallis to take the fatal step of invading Virginia and so lose a war, which—though certainly not among the bloodiest or fiercest in military history—was, by its results, the most momentous event since Columbus discovered the New World.

★ 69 ★

YORKTOWN I: FRANCE DELIVERS

In February 1781, the Comte de Vergennes began to have reservations about the Franco-American alliance. He had gambled upon the success of a limited effort in America—to the chagrined Americans a *very* limited effort—and it seemed to him that he had lost. King Louis XVI's treasury was distressingly low, and the economy-minded monarch was, to say the least, dismayed. King George III had no such misfortune to endure: Britannia still ruled the waves and thus remained the commercial mistress of Europe and the world. It seemed to the secretive, scheming, calculating French foreign minister that the time had come to cut his losses.

So he dictated, for his own eyes only, a private memorandum outlining the way to end the war. A summit of European powers was to be held in Vienna, with Russia and Austria-Hungary as mediators, and the ministers of the Netherlands and probably Sweden—ever dependent on France for financial and military aid—also in attendance. Next would come the belligerents: France, Britain, Spain and the American colonies. On the surface the conference would be the customary European power feast, with much ado about trading islands, cities, duchies, principalities, colonies, fishing and mining rights and so on. Each minister would expect to win a little, lose a little—except the Americans, for they had no interest in the European balance of power but wanted only independence. This—the real reason for the assembly—they were not going to get. Rather a truce was to be arranged between the colonies and the Mother Country based on the status quo in America at the beginning of 1781. At that point, the British were in virtual possession of Georgia and the Carolinas, as well as New York and Long Island, while they controlled the area to be known as Maine with garrisons in Lake Champlain, Niagara, Detroit and elsewhere, establishing their dominion in a huge area embracing the modern states of Wisconsin, Minnesota, northern Illinois, northern Indiana, Michigan, northern Ohio, northwestern New York and northern Vermont.

Vergennes was not at all disturbed by this betrayal of the pledge made in the alliance of 1778. It was rather an "adjustment" that had to be made because, in the euphemistic language of diplomacy, his attempt to redress the balance of power between France and Britain had not been entirely successful. Neither was it perfidy or desertion, but, as he put it: "One may presume to say that the King would be lacking in delicacy, that he would be somewhat violating his engagements, that he would be giving the Americans just cause for complaint or at least distrust, if he should propose to Congress to sign a truce leaving the English what they possess on the continent. Therefore only the mediators, bound by no such ties, could make a proposition so painful to the Americans."

Would the Yankees rebel? Would they challenge the combined power of Europe? Perhaps, if the belligerent character of John Adams, the American plenipotentiary in charge of such negotiations, was any indication. So Vergennes cooly had the suave La Luzerne, French ambassador to the United States Congress, which he seemed to have in his satin-lined pocket, bring about a change in Adams's instructions, together with formation of a new and pliant peace commission that sailed for France in June 1781. Next Vergennes sent out feelers to the ministers of George III, inquiring if Britain would be amenable to such a conference. When the answer was an emphatic yes, the French foreign minister was content.

George Washington was far from content in that spring of 1781. He had heard rumors of an impending peace conference, but knew nothing of what the agenda was to be, still less that American independence was up for sale. All he knew was that the great French ally seemed to be dragging her feet, that Admiral d'Estaing's captains had sailed backwards at Newport in 1778 and that the admiral himself had repeated the maneuver at Savannah. It seemed to the American war chief that the revolutionary cause in that doleful spring of 1781 was about to die of inanition.

The people everywhere were weary of a war that had dragged on for six long, miserable and bloody years. Few young men could be induced to enlist for any long term of service, let alone for the duration. In the towns the citizens believed that somehow, through someone, peace and independence would come. In the country the farmers wanted only to be left alone at seed and harvest times and to be able to sell their produce for hard money. There was actually no centralized government, and Congress—a rope of sand—had no real power over the states other than to suggest, not order, what they should do. Finances were a total wreck, and the treasury was empty. So were the military magazines, and Washington's reluctant but necessary seizure of food had soured the populace.

In the Continental Army there was little coherence or concentration and no prospect of combined operations. At and around West Point Washington had about 3,500 regulars, mostly from New England. New York's regiments were scattered along its western frontier, and New Jersey's guarded the Garden State alone. Pennsylvania's best were with Wayne and Lafayette in Virginia, while the southern Continentals were with Greene in the Carolinas. Rochambeau, with about 4,800 French troops in Newport, had yet to prove himself. The war chests everywhere were empty, the army's credit was exhausted and even Rochambeau's supply of money was dwindling. On May 1, 1781, a desponding Washington wrote gloomily in his journal: "Instead of having the prospect of a glorious offensive campaign before us, we have a bewildered and gloomy defensive one, unless we receive a powerful aid of ships, land troops and money from our generous allies." All he could do was to hope that the personal emissary he had sent to Versailles would impress upon the French that without a healthy injection of gold, guns and gunpowder, the ailing Revolution would expire of undernourishment.

The bearer of this warning was Colonel John Laurens of South Carolina, son of the former president of Congress, who, having been captured at sea while en route to Holland in quest of a loan, was even then languishing in the Tower of London facing possible execution as a traitor. At twenty-six, John, though a tall, extremely handsome, poised, cultivated and charming young man, seemed hardly more than a boy to send on such an errand to the sophisticated court of Versilles, when the venerable, shrewd and immensely popular Benjamin Franklin was already there. But if Franklin had captivated the French, then the French, with their elaborate courtesy, unrivaled culture, splendid architecture, exquisite cuisine and beautiful ladies, had perhaps to a comparable extent conquered Franklin. Moreover, Franklin was the agent of Congress and a civilian, while Washington wanted his own emissary: a soldier, and one in whom six straight years of defeat and retreat had failed to quench his patriotic ardor. Moreover, John Laurens was not for a moment awed by the grandeur of Versailles. Rather, he launched nothing less than a thundering cavalry charge against the king's ministers, starting with the Marquis de Castries, the minister of marine, whom he met by chance on the road to Paris. Collaring the astonished nobleman in his carriage, he actually demanded—not requested, demanded—that a powerful French fleet be sent to America. In high disdain, the marquis replied that he had already decided to send his ships to the West Indies, not to the United States.

Undaunted, Laurens spent the ensuing six weeks besieging Vergennes for an immediate loan of 25 million livres. At last in desperation, and perhaps also to rid himself of this importunate young gadfly, the French foreign minister promised a mere 6 million livres. Laurens was unimpressed, for he was aware that this amount had already been pledged to Franklin. He also knew that by 1781 France had already expended more than 100 million livres—about $25 million—in American aid; nevertheless, he reiterated his demands, as though to say, "Yes, but what have you done for us lately?" Exasperated, Vergennes complained to Franklin, who warned Congress that "the best friends may be wearied by too frequent and unexpected demands." Franklin was undoubtedly correct, and so was Vergennes—if their conduct is to be judged objectively. But Laurens was desperate. He could remember only the last words of Washington's last letter: "... in a word, we are at the end of our tether and now or never our deliverance must come." In his mind's eye he could also see the bloody footprints in the snow ... sick soldiers dying without medicine ... fighting each other with bayonets over scraps of food.... How could he be objective with these dreadful tableaux at the back of his brain?

So for six weeks he fought for the money like a tiger, until Vergennes, still courtly, smiling and deprecating, at last declared: "Colonel Laurens, you are so recently from headquarters of the American Army that you forget that you are no longer delivering the orders of the Commander-in-Chief, but you are addressing the minister of a monarch who has every disposition to favor your country."

"*Favor,* sir?" Laurens shouted, leaping erect. "The respect which I owe my country will not admit the term. Say that the aid is mutual, and I cheerfully subscribe to the obligation. But, as the last argument which I shall use with your Excellency: the sword which I now wear in defense of France as well as my own country, unless the succor I solicit is immediately accorded, I may be compelled to draw against France as a British subject!"

Vergennes was shocked almost speechless, and then horrified when the outraged young American informed him that his next step would be to go directly to King Louis XVI. Benjamin Franklin was similarly shaken when Laurens spoke of approaching the king, flatly refusing to have anything to do with such a brash petition. Nevertheless, at a levee the next day Colonel John Laurens approached Louis, seated on his throne and surrounded by his glittering retinue of ministers and courtiers. Clad only in his buff-and-blue uniform, as plain as a sparrow among a flock of brilliant tropical birds, the tall young American bowed and handed the king a small scroll containing his appeal. Startled, the king stared at it, and then handed it without a word to his minister of war, the Comte de Segur. Laurens moved on, despairing once more.

But the next day, to his great joy, he received a summons to the office of Jacques Necker, director of finance, where he was promised generous material and financial aid. In all, he received supplies worth 2.3 million livres and the same amount in cash, together with a loan of ten million livres from Holland guaranteed by France. It was not quite as much as the 25 million livres he had hoped to procure, but at least it was something. Better than the money and supplies, as he sailed from Brest for home in May 1781, he was elated to know that the great French fleet bound for the West Indies would also visit America during the summer. With this support, small though it might be, and this report, great news that it was, George Washington again prepared to attack New York, assisted by his French counterpart, Lieutenant General Jean Baptiste Donatien de Vimeur, the Comte de Rochambeau.

At fifty-five Lieutenant General Rochambeau was one of the most experienced and battle-seasoned commanders in the French army. A kindly man, called "Papa" by his adoring troops, Rochambeau looked the part: of medium height with a substantial paunch, full and rosy cheeks, friendly smile and twinkling eyes. Yet, his mind was a balanced and incisive military instrument, always on guard against rash adventures or the calloused expenditure of troops. He showed these qualities shortly after his arrival at Newport, Rhode Island, when the impetuous Lafayette came to him with a plan for an audacious assault upon New York City. The young marquis—a general only slightly older than the count's own son, a captain—prefaced his proposal with a tearful description of the suffering of the American soldiers, together with an angry denunciation of France's limited support of the Revolution. Another general might have been indignant, but Rochambeau ignored this obvious attempt to stampede him into undertaking such a risky operation, politely pointing out that New York could not be conquered without a superior fleet. He also had only four thousand men, although another division was then preparing to take ship at Brest. It would be wiser to await the division's arrival, hopefully with a protecting fleet.

Lafayette returned to White Plains, where he prepared a twelve-page plan for an even more extravagant expedition against New York, which he despatched to Rochambeau with another declaration that the French were not doing enough to win the war. "Papa" Rochambeau replied, a bit sharply this time, that he intended to stay in Newport and that the young marquis, though a major general, was not running the war. To this reply, Lafayette, with that humility that did so much to endear him to Americans, responded with an apology: "If I have offended you, I beg your pardon for two reasons: first, because I am earnestly attached to you; and secondly, because my purpose is to do everything here that I can to please you." Rochambeau's was the last word, a paternal lecture on the importance of an officer's having the confidence of his troops and of giving no orders out of "personal and selfish ambition." By the time Lafayette left for Virginia to take command of a ragtag-and-bobtail army of about a thousand men charged with harassing Cornwallis, the two noblemen from the Auvergne were fast friends. Meanwhile, Washington and Rochambeau had received the depressing news from Paris that there would be no second French division sailing from Brest and that the American chief's request for another ten thousand soldiers could not be taken seriously.

Next, however, came the joyful news that "superior naval forces" were indeed on their way, under Admiral Comte François Joseph Paul de Grasse. De Grasse had twenty men-of-war and would pick up ten more in the West Indies. Together with the eight vessels in Newport under Admiral Comte de Barras, he would command a formidable fleet of thirty-eight vessels. He would arrive off the American coast either in July or August and would be available for joint operations.

Washington at once proposed that the powerful French fleet join him in the recapture of New York. Rochambeau, however, being in constant communication with Lafayette, was for going to Virginia and hoped to do something there to help "the poor Marquis." He even offered to lead an army there himself. But Washington was adamant. Admiral Barras had already refused to transport troops south because of the power of the British fleet patrolling the sea lanes off New York. His refusal would mean a landward movement in the heat of summer with wagons in short supply and his mostly northern troops reluctant to enter that moist and sulphurous southern climate, which, they were convinced, was hard on their health. Washington realized that on such a march literally half his army might vanish through disease and desertion. What he left unsaid, of course, to himself probably as much as to anyone else, was that only a reconquest of New York City could assuage his wounded pride. Three times he had been defeated there—at Long Island, White Plains and Fort Washington—and now with France finally delivering substantial military aid, he had it within his power to avenge those losses. He also was eager to achieve a great victory before the approaching peace conference assembled, and in a letter to La Luzerne in Philadelphia, he begged him to beseech de Grasse to add "a body of land forces" to his "naval armament" so that by "one great, decisive stroke the enemy might be expelled from the continent, and the independence of America established at the approaching negotiation." So Rochambeau agreed to the New York operation—but only on the surface.

Wily and tenacious as any Auvergnat, Rochambeau realized that the American war chief had no control over Admiral de Grasse. He began writing to de Grasse urging him to make for the Chesapeake. "The southwesterly winds and the state of distress in Virginia will probably make you prefer Chesapeake Bay, and it will be there where we think you may be able to render the greatest service, whereas you will need only two days to come from there to New York. In any case, it is essential you send, well in advance, a frigate to inform Barras where you are to come and also General Washington." In another letter Rochambeau urged de Grasse to bring troops and money and informed him how close to disaster the American cause was. "I must not conceal from you, Monsieur, that the Americans are at the end of their resources, that Washington will not have half of the troops he is reckoned to have, and that ... at present he does not have 6,000 men."

Washington, still obsessed by his desire to capture New York and thus redeem his reputation, disagreed emphatically with Rochambeau's choice of the Chesapeake as the suitable area in which to defeat the British. He persisted even in the knowledge that Clinton commanded 14,500 splendidly supplied and trained regulars in New York, while Cornwallis in Yorktown had only a little more than five thousand, and that Admiral Arbuthnot's fleet outnumbered Admiral Barras's, while Cornwallis had no ships and would soon come under the guns of de Grasse's mighty armada. It could be that his decision was made in the light of a message from the ministry of marine that de Grasse would spend only a short time on the American coast, and thus he would have to prepare hastily to do something in a hurry before Vergennes's dreaded peace conference would have time to convene. Therefore he proposed to surprise all the British forts on the northern end of Manhattan Island.

On the night of July 1 a force of about eight hundred men, under Benjamin Lincoln, who had been exchanged, was secretly landed below the heights of Fort Knyphausen—formerly Fort Washington. Lincoln was to take the fort in a surprise attack, after which, reinforced by Washington's main army and a French force commanded by the flamboyant Duc de Lauzun, he would join them in reducing Fort Tryon, Fort George on Laurel Hill, the works on Cox Hill at the mouth of Spuyten Duyvil and those at Kingsbridge. It was a much too complicated plan ever to succeed, which Lincoln realized the moment he viewed the enemy fortifications from Fort Lee on the opposite shore and saw that they could not be stormed. So he tried the secondary effort at Spuyten Duyvil and failed there also. The next day, Washington's army fell back to Dobbs Ferry, where it was joined on July 6 by Rochambeau's main body.

Now General Washington turned cautious. Though still planning to attack Manhattan Island, he decided to make a thorough reconnaissance of Clinton's defenses. For four days—from July 21 through 24—screened by a force of five thousand soldiers and guarded by 150 Continentals, he, Rochambeau and two other French generals made a complete study of the British positions. In the end they concluded that they could not be forced, and Washington's thinking turned toward the South. If he sent a force marching in that direction in a feint, it might compel Clinton to send reinforcements to Cornwallis and so weaken his own garrison. Or if Clinton called on Cornwallis for troops, Washington might combine with Lafayette against the British in Yorktown—or even go farther south to join Greene in South Carolina to invest Charleston.

As he marked time considering the alternatives, there arrived from de Grasse perhaps the most momentous message of the entire war. On August 13 de Grasse would sail from Santo Domingo directly to the Chesapeake with twenty-five to twenty-nine warships carrying three regiments of regulars numbering a total of three thousand men plus one hundred dragoons and one hundred artillerists with ten field pieces, as well as siege cannon and mortars. He would stay in the Chesapeake until October 15, when he would return to the West Indies with his troops. Washington was electrified. It was all there! A powerful fleet, troops and guns! Even a timetable! All his, to be at his service for a month and a half! No longer did he hesitate: Cornwallis or Charleston was now the true objective. On August 15, the day after the message arrived, Washington wrote to Lafayette directing him to prevent Cornwallis from returning to North Carolina. On the seventeenth he sent General Duportail hastening to meet de Grasse with a letter saying that Rochambeau and as large a part of his own army as could be spared would meet him in the Chesapeake for operations either in Virginia or at Charleston—depending on the circumstances—and requesting the movement of frigates and transports to the Head of Elk to carry the Franco-American forces down the bay. Finally, a message was sent to Admiral Barras in Newport to load his eight ships with the French siege guns there, as well as all the provisions left behind by Rochambeau, and to make for the Chesapeake—sailing a wide circuit to avoid the British patrol ships and to give de Grasse enough time to arrive with his protective fleet.

On August 21, 1781, the march south began.

★ ★ ★

The French and the Americans marching south toward destiny in that memorable summer of 1781 were as different as the Old World and the New. The French were a riot of color, like a moving flower garden. Their coats and long waistcoats were as white as the flag fluttering above them emblazoned with the golden lilies of France, but their coat lapels and collar bands seemed to be in every color of the rainbow: crimson, sky blue, pink, green or yellow. Most of the sergeants had white plumes stuck in their hats, while those of the grenadiers had red, and the chasseurs—the French light infantry—had green. When the French marched through Philadelphia in full parade dress, with their big bands seemingly complete with every instrument but a piano playing martial music, the throngs of spectators crowding the sidewalks were ecstatic. They were particularly taken by the couriers in embroidered jerkins and emblazoned headdresses, holding the gold-knobbed canes that were the symbol of their speciality as they dashed from unit to unit, thinking that they were generals, and that when they paused to take orders, they were actually giving them. Moving with precision, these gorgeously attired French were a dazzling array indeed, but their battle flags suggested that they were something more than parade-ground soldiers.

Rochambeau's regiments were among the finest in the French Army. The Soissonais, in which Lafayette's brother-in-law, the Vicomte de Noailles was second colonel, traced its lineage to 1598, and its motto was the words of a sergeant killed at the moment of a victory: "What does it matter? We have won the battle." "*En avant sur les canons*"—"At the cannons' mouth"—was the motto of the Bourbonnais Regiment formed in 1600. Rochambeau's son commanded the Saintonge, also two hundred years old, an ancient regiment of Navarre, while the Royal Deux-Ponts Regiment came from the Saar Basin, and its men spoke only German. The Deux-Ponts was a "proprietary" formation commanded by the Duke of Deux-Ponts. Its colonel was Count Christian Forbach de Deux-Ponts and his second, Count William Forbach de Deux-Ponts. Unlike the rulers of the German principalities who hired their troops out to the British, the dukes of Deux-Ponts remained fiercly loyal to the French crown.

Some of Rochambeau's officers were dismayed when they saw the American troops. After six years of war they still had no uniforms, although most of the officers now wore the buff and blue prescribed by Washington a year earlier. Young Baron Ludwig von Closen, an aide to Rochambeau, was among those who were shocked. "It is really painful to see these brave men, almost naked, with only some trousers and linen jackets, most of them without stockings." But then, on closer examination, the baron and his skeptical comrades were astonished by the physical size, lean strength and proud bearing of the Americans. "Would you believe it?" Closen wrote. "[They are] very cheerful and healthy in appearance." At a later inspection he was even more impressed. "Their arms were in good condition; some regiments had white cotton uniforms. Their clothing consisted of a coat, jacket, vest, trousers of white cloth, buttoned from the bottom to the calves, like gaiters." He had special praise for the Rhode Island Regiment, three-quarters black. It was "the most neatly dressed, the best under arms, and the most precise in its maneuvers."

The French were also incredulous at the durability of their allies. Abbé Robin could not believe that in the ragged tents occupied by three or four Continentals there was hardly a mattress and "not over 40 pounds of baggage." In their march from Newport, where "the army left its heavy equipment," each French regiment had fourteen wagons and the men were "bent under the weight" of the gear they carried. Closen, though only an aide, had four horses and several servants. What the French did not realize was that Washington's men were the survivors of six years of misery and privation, and that they were witnessing a lesson in the sacrifices that can be called forth by devotion to a noble cause, as well as the truth of another axiom of Napoleon: "Adversity is the school of the good soldier."

Most of all, the French admired George Washington. Another aide of Rochambeau, Major General François Jean de Chastellux, a member of the French Academy and one of Europe's leading men of letters, wrote of him: "Brave without temerity, laborious without ambition, generous without prodigality, noble without pride, virtuous without severity, it will be said of him at the end of a long civil war, he had nothing with which he could reproach himself." Whenever the American war chief rode by, the French soldiers—officers as well as men—would gaze enraptured at "*le grand Washington.*" So it was that this coalition army, so disparate in so many ways—in race, religion and language, the one half struggling for independence and self-rule, the other to do an ancient enemy a disservice—were bound together by a spirit of good will and good cheer, as well as by the common objective of bringing the British lion to bay.

In great measure Washington's daring decision to cut loose from his base and march hurriedly south had been forced upon him by de Grasse's definite, fixed and limiting plans. But the plan was still fraught with danger and to succeed had to be conducted in total secrecy. Clinton, reinforced by 2,500 Hessians, now commanded nearly 17,000 men, and if he should learn early of Washington's departure, it would be no great effort for him to overwhelm Heath's rear guard of perhaps 2,500 men and seize control of the Hudson. The control of the great river, together with a failure at Yorktown, would irretrievably sever New England from the South and would thus cause the collapse of the Revolution. So the Franco-American army did indeed slip stealthily away, crossing the Hudson by King's Ferry to Stony Point, then marching under cover of the New Jersey Palisades through Newark and New Brunswick. Washington paused in New Jersey to erect an extensive encampment that was intended to appear as a staging area for an assault on Staten Island. Roads toward that apparent objective were improved, and at nearby Chatham bake ovens, large enough to feed a formidable force, were constructed. Thirty flatboats on wagons suggested a pending amphibious operations against New York. Clinton was completely deceived, and it was not until the allies were across the Delaware and making for the Chesapeake and Yorktown that the British commander realized that the Old Fox had once again outwitted him.

By then, there was not much he could do about it except to count upon the customary supremacy of British sea power either to extricate or reinforce Cornwallis. Even so, he did not earn the admiration or affection of His Lordship through the welter of conflicting orders and counter-orders that he sent him. Clinton's first order had been in July, when, fearing an attack on New York, he had asked Cornwallis to send him three thousand men. Marching for Portsmouth to embark them, the earl had encountered Lafayette at Green Spring Farm on July 6. Hoping once again to "catch the boy," he very nearly did, but darkness saved Lafayette. Thereafter Cornwallis received five different orders, each contradicting the previous one. First, Clinton told him to ship the troops to Philadelphia, rather than to New York; second, to send them to New York after all; third, to retire to Yorktown on the peninsula between the James and York rivers; fourth, to go to Old Point Comfort instead, but to fortify Yorktown if necessary; and fifth, to keep all his troops for himself if he thought he needed them, but to hurry to New York as many as he could spare. Feeling somewhat like a weather vane, Cornwallis went to Old Point Comfort and inspected it, but decided that Yorktown could be more easily defended, and that was where he went in August 1781.

Cornwallis considered himself secure at Yorktown as long as the British Navy still controlled the sea. British ships entering the Chesapeake between the Virginia capes at the great bay's lower mouth had easy access to Yorktown. They could supply him, reinforce him or evacuate him. French warships, of course, could seal off the Chesapeake and thus make Yorktown vulnerable to siege by land. But neither His Lordship nor Sir Henry believed that this possibility was likely.

In the meantime, the incoherence and confusion crippling the British command on land was being duplicated, if not exceeded, at sea.

The British knew that Admiral de Grasse had sailed for the Chesapeake, but were unaware of his objective. Nevertheless, the aggressive Admiral Sir Samuel Hood, suspecting that de Grasse might be headed there, had sailed from the West Indies with fourteen "liners" hoping to intercept him. Because Hood had taken a more direct route, he arrived off the Virginia capes at the great bay's lower mouth three days ahead of the Frenchman. Poking cautiously inside them, seeing nothing, he withdrew and made for New York, arriving off Sandy Hook on August 28. There he received a typically lethargic message from the inept Admiral Sir Samuel Graves, then in conference with Clinton. It said:

> No intelligence of de Grasse. Accounts say that he has gone to Havana to join the Spaniards. A little time will shew us. All the American accounts are big with expectation and the army has lately crossed to the Southward and appears in motion in the Jerseys as if to threaten Staten Island....

Alarmed at what appeared to be his superior officer's incredible unconcern over the French fleet's whereabouts, Hood had a small sailboat put him ashore on Long Island, where he burst in upon Graves and Clinton in a leisurely conference. At once he urged the senior admiral to put to sea. "You have no time to lose," he cried. "Every moment is precious." Graves was unmoved by Hood's plea—until a patrol ship arrived with the news that Admiral de Barras had sailed from Newport with Rochambeau's big guns and provisions. This news at last alarmed Admiral Graves. Still, there were delays. Five of Graves's ten big ships were not seaworthy, and it was not until the morning of August 31 that Graves and Hood, with nineteen warships, joined forces on the Atlantic. The combined forces headed for the Chesapeake because it seemed the logical place to go, although Graves still had no clear picture of what was going on or any suspicion of the gravity of the situation. He hoped only "to fall in with one of the enemy's squadrons." If he meant de Barras, he was disappointed. Because the Frenchman had sailed on a wide circuit and because his ships were not sheathed with copper bottoms like the British and thus were not their equal in speed, he had fallen far behind his enemy.

On September 5, Graves's fleet at last entered the Chesapeake, expecting to find it empty and thus enable his ships to block the approaches to Yorktown. At midmorning, however, a lookout aboard HMS *Solebay* reported sighting many masts about ten miles up the bay. The *Solebay's* captain was incredulous. "It must be the charred pines you see," he said. "They burn them for tar and leave the trunks standing."

But they were not charred trees.

Sir Samuel Graves was astounded. He had been on the hunt for de Barras's little fleet and when he received reports of enemy masts to the north, he had concluded that he had found it. But then came word of at least twenty-seven warships—big ones! It was de Grasse!

It was, but the French admiral's ships were *inside* the bay, not outside it like the British. To give battle, the French must sail slowly out to the open sea—ten miles because of the nature of the bay—tacking repeatedly—a line of plodding ducks approaching the guns of the enemy. No matter that the British were outgunned and outmanned, 1,700 guns to 1,400, 19,000 sailors to 13,000—or even that they had five fewer ships. They were already in battle position, they had the wide Atlantic for maneuver and they held the enormous advantage of the wind. But they also had Sir Samuel Graves in command, one of those numerous bungling "Blimps" who had risen in rank while the British Navy had sunk into desuetude with the unsteady hand of the corrupt and luxury-loving Earl of Sandwich at the Admiralty's helm. If command had been held by Sir Samuel Hood, an aggressive and decisive seaman—typical of that indomitable "band of brothers" that was to revive the glories of the British Navy a few decades later under Horatio Nelson—Britannia might not have rued that day of September 5, 1781, when the climactic Battle of the Capes was fought. Hood would have fallen on those slow-moving, incredibly vulnerable enemy ships and torn them to pieces, just as earlier, doughtier British sea captains had done at Quiberon Bay a few decades before, and with the same decisive results. But Graves was in command, and Graves was a slave to naval doctrine, the hidebound "Fighting Instructions" that specified that in fleet-to-fleet engagements ships were to form in a precise line to give each other support and thus reduce the danger of any one of them being cut off and destroyed.

Warlike admirals, such as Hood, were aware that line tactics were—like most "doctrine" on land or at sea—the outmoded tactics of another age that almost always resulted in drawn battles because each ship engaged an opposite ship, taking and giving hits and eventually hauling off. Moreover, Graves was well aware of what had happened to admirals who ignored the "Fighting Instructions": Thomas Matthews drummed out of the service in 1744 and John Byng executed by a firing squad on his own quarter deck in 1757. In Graves's defense, the wretched state of British signaling, so bad that many commanders refused to signal, seemed to leave him no alternative. He had only two signals to choose from as he approached de Grasse: "general chase," used only to pursue a fleeing fleet, or "line ahead" to oppose a fleet preparing to give battle. So he remained in line of battle while de Grasse, to his own amazement, was permitted to come straggling out of the bay to form opposite him.

Here was Admiral Graves's first and greatest mistake: to have allowed de Grasse to sail unmolested from Lynnhaven Bay and to form in battle line opposite him. More mistakes were to be made by de Grasse as well as Graves—and by an unusually timorous Hood—but all the British errors flowed from this opening and enormous blunder. And so the opposing fleets sailed in parallel lines.

The British van was commanded by Hood in *Barfleur,* the center by Graves in *London* and the rear by Admiral Francis Drake in *Princessa,* and among the French, the leading squadron of five ships was led by Commodore Louis Antoine de Bougainville, the same man who had surrendered Canada to the British after the death of Montcalm and then gone to sea to cure his asthma, leaving behind him in the Pacific a Solomons island named after him and bringing back a brilliant tropical plant also bearing his name. Following Bougainville in *Auguste* was de Grasse in his towering triple-decked flagship *Ville de Paris,* the largest warship in the world, and the rest of his fleet.

Although the chance to destroy the French ships as they emerged from the bay had been lost, there was still an opportunity for what Hood called "a rich and most delightful harvest of glory," for Bougainville's leading ships, perhaps because they were among the few French vessels with copper-sheathed bottoms, had drawn far ahead of the main body and easily could have been cut off and sunk. Even Graves recalled that they were "very particularly extended," and yet, he still flew the signal "line ahead at cable length." Worse, he allowed his own flagship *London* to stop dead in the water while the incredulous Bougainville closed the fatal gap! *London*'s log read: "Brought to in order to let the center of the enemy ships come abreast of us." An hour and a half passed before this occurred.

Now only the leading ships in both fleets were in position to fight each other, and at this moment Graves raised a blue-and-white checkered flag meaning "Ships to bear down and engage close." However, he neglected to lower the white "line ahead" flag, and this confused many of his captains. Confusion was compounded when Graves, in the center, turned *London* abruptly to starboard to bear head-on against the French line, and other captains followed him—thus effectively scrambling the British line. Next Graves bore off before reaching the French line, firing a broadside that fell short into the sea, and then, trying to untangle the muddle he had made, ran up more signals, creating more confusion. But by then—four-fifteen—the great leading ships were within a hundred yards of each other and almost simultaneously opened fire.

As was their policy the British fired on the downward roll of their ships to destroy the enemy vessels, while the French fired on the rise to riddle the foe's rigging and make it impossible to maneuver his ships and thus lay them open to capture. As a result the French hulls were holed and their seamen killed and maimed, while the sails of the British ships were shredded and their spars and masts splintered or sent crashing to the decks with a heavy loss in Marine sharpshooters. Drake's foremost ship, the seventy-four-gun *Shrewsbury,* was battered in that first blast. Shots from the *Pluton* tore off her captain's leg and killed his first lieutenant and thirteen seamen. Twelve more sailors fell dead and forty-eight were wounded under *Pluton's* continuing fire, while *Shrewsbury* took five hits below her waterline and had her topmast broken in three places. She fell out of line while *Intrepid* hastened to cover her, only to be battered so badly by *Marseillais* that she, too, withdrew with sixty-five holes in her starboard side. But Drake's *Princessa* responded with a shattering broadside that forced *Reflechi* and then *Pluton* and *Caton* out of the battle.

With the sun of September 5 beginning to sink beyond the Virginia shore, it appeared that Bougainville in the van was again in danger. Inexplicably, de Grasse, throughout the battle, had remained too far in the rear to be of assistance. Bougainville, with four ships, came under the fire of seven to eight British vessels. *Diademe* was so fearfully scourged that only thirteen of her guns could fire, and she might have been pounded beneath the waves had *Saint-Esprit* not come to her rescue, her guns roaring so rapidly "that the gentlemen of Albion could not stand and had to haul their wind." Aboard *Auguste* Bougainville received so many hits that he had to sail close to Drake's *Princessa* for cover. Within pistol shot the two warships traded broadsides, punctuated by the clearly audible yells and screams and shouted orders of their opponent's crews. When *Princessa* bore off to uncover *Auguste* to British fire, Bougainville turned his guns on the seventy-four-gun *Terrible* of Hood's division. Already leaking badly before she entered the battle, *Terrible* was so badly shattered by *Auguste's* broadsides that she would eventually be abandoned and blown up—the only ship totally lost in the Battle of the Capes. But *Auguste* with ten sailors already killed and fifty-eight wounded, was also taking shots. Twice her topmast bowline was shot away, making it impossible to trim her mainsail. Brave sailors who climbed the rigging to repair it were dropped into the sea by *Princessa's* sharpshooters. When Bougainville called for volunteers, none stepped forward—until the commodore held up his purse as a reward. A sailor quickly scrambled up the mast and out on the yardarm. "General," he called down, "we do not go there for money" and repaired the line with musket balls whispering around him.

It was now half-past five, and the ships of the rival center divisions were at last in position to attack one another. Hood in *Barfleur,* aware that Graves's signal "engage the enemy" was still flying, turned to starboard with two other ships to attack the French rear, firing broadsides as they approached. Most of their guns were aimed at *Citoyen,* but almost all their cannon balls fell into the sea. At six o'clock Admiral Graves hauled down his "engage the enemy" flag, and the Battle of the Capes came to an end.

As sea fights go, it might have been a standoff: six of Graves's ships badly damaged, one of which—*Terrible*—would eventually sink; four Frenchmen also battered, but not quite so severely. But the French warships, because of the British policy of firing low, were not so badly crippled in sailing capability, their holed hulls being much more easily repaired than the delicate and intricate rigging and masts of a ship's upper works. In casualties the French had lost 209 men killed and wounded, the British 336, of whom 90 had been killed. But the Battle of the Capes had not really been fought for victory at sea, as the subsequent maneuvering of both fleets was to demonstrate.

Throughout September 6 and 7 the two fleets remained within sight of each other, sailing steadily south toward Cape Hatteras on the coast of North Carolina. During this time, while the mutual recrimination so common between Graves and Hood mounted into open hostility in a blame-fixing debate that was to continue for a decade, de Grasse proved himself the master of the situation and showed that he alone—with the possible exception of Samuel Hood—knew what he was doing.

De Grasse's mission was to prevent the British fleet from reinforcing, supplying or evacuating Cornwallis's beleaguered army. To do so, he need not defeat Graves, but only prevent Graves from defeating him. Although he had handled his own fleet only somewhat better than Graves had led his, and had actually been saved by the gallantry of Bougainville, to whom he generously gave all the credit; he had accomplished his mission. By sailing south, he was also luring Graves farther from the Chesapeake and guaranteeing the safe entry there of de Barras's smaller fleet carrying those precious guns and provisions. Once these ships were unloaded, de Barras might sail south to join de Grasse and give the

British fleet the coup de grace. But it still would be better for de Grasse to slip away from Graves under cover of darkness and join de Barras *inside* the bay. This is what de Grasse did on the chill and windy night of September 9, crowding on all sail and heading north, a maneuver observed with satisfaction by Hood, who had already warned Graves that it might occur. Thus when a frigate notified Graves on September 13 that de Grasse had joined de Barras in Lynnhaven Bay and now commanded thirty-five battleships, Graves, in distress, asked Hood what he should do about it. Hood replied: "Sir Samuel would be very glad to send an opinion, but he really knows not what to say in the truly lamentable state we have brought ourselves." Upon receipt of this message, Graves sailed back to New York.

In that sentence Hood wrote the epitaph for the British attempt to suppress the American rebellion. British bungling had made American good fortune. Clinton and Howe had hated each other, and so had Carleton and Burgoyne, and then Cornwallis and Clinton. With similar rancor Hood hated Graves. All of them hated the war in which they were serving with such painful reluctance. With the least cooperation or interest in victory, some of them might have brought the Revolution to a different end. But because they merely went through the motions—in effect, did nothing—George Washington, alias General Buckskin, was on the verge of beating them, and that was because *he* always did *something*.

It has been said that Washington was lucky, and he was indeed; there are at least a dozen "ifs" in the decisive Battle of the Capes that, if just one of them had backfired, would have landed Graves and Hood, rather than de Grasse and de Barras, in Lynnhaven Bay. But Washington was lucky because he took chances, because he did things—and action usually creates luck. Lady Luck does not wave her wand over the lazy or inert. The harder a man works, the luckier he gets, and of a general it may be said that the more he takes the initiative, the more likely he is to succeed.

So the Battle of the Capes, negligible though it might have been in ships lost and men killed and wounded, was big with consequence. Just as Nelson's great victory at the much, much fiercer naval Battle of Trafalgar prepared the way for the decisive Battle of Waterloo that ended the Napoleonic Era, so the Battle of the Capes was the climactic sea fight that cut off Cornwallis from all help from the British Navy, leaving him at the mercy of the Franco-American army on his landward front and making possible the final, determining battle of the Revolutionary War that—even more significant than Waterloo—culminated in the birth of the new American nation.

⋆ 70 ⋆

YORKTOWN II: THE END

Like the lull before the storm, Sir Henry Clinton in New York and Earl Charles Cornwallis in Yorktown spent almost the entire month of August 1781 in mutual moods of lassitude that were remarkable for their indifference to the noose being drawn slowly tighter on the Chesapeake. It was not until August 22 that Cornwallis, who, for some inexplicable reason, had chosen to spend the earlier weeks fortifying the Gloucester side of the York River, began to work seriously on the Yorktown defenses. Meanwhile, he persisted in refusing to send a single soldier to Clinton's side in New York. Clinton, meanwhile, as late as August 27, wrote Cornwallis that Washington was then encamped in New Jersey, adding: "I cannot well ascertain Mr. Washington's real intentions by this move of his army. But it is possible he means for the present to suspend his offensive operations against this post, and to take a defensive position at the old post of Morristown, from whence he may detach to the southward." It was not until September 2 that he was able to notify the earl that Washington and Rochambeau were marching south to attack him. It was two weeks before Cornwallis received this warning, during which de Grasse had entered Lynnhaven Bay and won the Battle of the Capes. On September 4, the day before that battle, Cornwallis wrote Clinton: "Comte de Grasse's fleet is within the Capes of the Chesapeake." Alarmed, Clinton replied: "I think the best way to relieve you is to join you as soon as possible, with all the force that can be spared from hence. Which is about 4,000 men."

But Clinton made no move, if only because he couldn't—Graves and Hood having sailed with their ships from Sandy Hook on August 31—and because he had already launched Benedict Arnold on a raid against his hometown of New London, one of those "desultory expeditions" that were Sir Henry's favorite mode of making war.

Arnold arrived off New London on the morning of September 6, attacking with his customary zeal. Most of the forts surrounding the town fell almost instantly, but the position held by 140 Connecticut militia under Lieutenant Colonel William Ledyard held out stubbornly. Twice Lieutenant Colonel Edmund Eyre ordered frontal assaults that were repulsed with heavy losses. In the second attack Eyre was carried dying from the field, and a third charge went forward under Lieutenant Colonel van Buskirk of the New Jersey Volunteers. It succeeded, but when Ledyard proffered his sword to van Buskirk, the vengeful Tory seized it and ran Ledyard through. That was the signal for a general massacre of the Americans, a scene of horror in which pleading defenseless men were bayoneted on their knees or beneath bunks and gun platforms where they had taken cover. Inside the town, Arnold was busy entertaining his old friends by setting fires to warehouses and ships. One of the warehouses contained gunpowder. When it exploded, the fire became general, and 140 buildings were burned to the ground before it burned itself out.

Professing to be horrified at such barbarian tactics, Clinton, who had ordered Arnold to New London to get rid of him, now sent him south to Virginia to join General Phillips. There the traitor enjoyed himself in ravaging his former countrymen, burning whatever he could not carry off as plunder.

Cornwallis had at last begun to fortify Yorktown. The town was on a bluff on the south, or right, bank of the York River as it flowed into the Chesapeake. In its main course the river was two miles wide, narrowing to about a half mile as it passed between Yorktown and the village of Gloucester on the opposite bank. Above the town on the British right, a ravine had worn its way halfway across the peninsula, while on the left was Wormley Creek. These were the anchors of the British line, extending in a six-mile curve around the town and consisting of seven redoubts and six batteries connected by entrenchments. In the center was an impassable swamp not needing to be fortified. On the river side there was another line of batteries, one of which, the Grand Battery, mounted eleven heavy guns commanding the narrows between Yorktown and Gloucester. These were the main fortifications, inside another line of six redoubts and a battery. Gloucester was defended from landward attack by a short line drawn across Gloucester Point to the rear of the village. In the river lay the large frigates *Charon* and *Guadaloupe,* forty-four guns each, and three big transports. Cornwallis had garrisoned Gloucester with seven hundred regulars under Lieutenant Colonel Dundas and Tarleton's British Legion. His Yorktown defenses were held by six thousand British and Hessians with himself in command.

While these defenses were being constructed, His Lordship was the soul of confidence, believing, as he did, that he held all the cards. First, he was confident that Clinton was coming to reinforce him; second, he believed that the British navy would, as always, make short work of the French fleet; and third, as he repeatedly informed his officers and men, the Franco-Americans were simply incapable of maintaining a siege without heavy artillery. Unaware that de Barras had departed Newport with Rochambeau's big guns, he believed that with only field artillery at his disposal, Washington's cannon balls would bounce harmlessly off his redoubts like tennis balls. So he calmly—nay, hopefully—awaited the appearance of General Buckskin.

Marching south against him was Washington's army of about 8,800 men and Rochambeau's of 7,800. All the way down to the Head of Elk, where Lord Howe had landed his brother's army four years previously with such high hopes, Washington pondered the question: where is de Grasse? He had not heard from him since receipt of that letter in mid-August. Gambler that he was, Washington well knew that so many things could go wrong, as they usually do in any coordinated land-sea operation, and because he didn't know where de Grasse was or what he was doing, he actually underestimated the number of risks.

First, if after the Battle of the Capes, Graves had renewed the battle the next day on September 6 with his faster ships and what was his customarily superior British seamanship, he might still have saved the day. Or if he had merely hurried back to the capes and posted himself at the entrance of the bay, he could have contacted Cornwallis while destroying de Grasse's supply ships and transports that were already inside the bay. Or if he had left de Grasse still heading south, he might have arrived in the Chesapeake in time to destroy de Barras. Or de Grasse could have been delayed by as much as a week by the autumn storms that usually lash the coast of southeastern America or by unfavorable winds—and any delay favored the British. It was no wonder, then, that a worried Washington could write Lafayette: "I am distressed beyond expression to know what is become of the Count de Grasse, and for fear the English fleet, by occupying the Chesapeake ... should frustrate all our flattering prospects in that quarter."

He still had no word as his Americans—mostly Continentals with about three thousand militia—reached the Head of Elk and began embarking in boats for Williamsburg on the James. The French followed. As Rochambeau and his elegant aides neared the landing on the Virginia shore, they saw a strong, tall figure in blue and buff waving his big hat wildly, and almost capering for joy. Rochambeau stepped ashore, and a beaming George Washington rushed up to embrace him. Then French hats went soaring into the air, for Washington had informed them that de Grasse had met the British fleet off the Capes, driving it back to New York, that he now held the Chesapeake and had completely cut off Cornwallis and had already put ashore three thousand more French regulars under the Marquis Saint-Simon. As one of Washington's generals was to write of Cornwallis: "we have got him handsomely in a pudding bag."

Among those jubilant Americans who had marched south with Washington was the ubiquitous Joseph Plumb Martin, now a sergeant in the miners and sappers. At Head of Elk he and his men boarded the schooner *Birmingham* for the trip down the bay. Also aboard were six or seven junior officers and a supply officer, who had in his keeping a small store of provisions and a hogshead of rum. Naturally, Martin and his men coveted a mug of "the creature" as much as did the officers, but they in the selfish way of all officers in every army since Agamemnon went ashore at Troy, wanted it all for themselves. So they had the hogshead placed in a cabin walled off by a bulkhead. Crowding into the cabin, chuckling over how they had outwitted the stupid enlisted men, the officers became so loud in their revelry that they did not hear the sound of bulkhead boards being removed, or of Martin fastening his own tap to the now-exposed hogshead. Aware that they were in a consumption-contest, as the officers were not, Martin and his buddies began to swallow the creature in great gulps. By the time the still-sober officers discovered, to their dismay and amazement, that the hogshead was empty, Martin and his buddies were quite unsober, but never to the extent that they neglected to nail the bulkhead boards back in place. Singing the ballad "The World Turned Upside-down," they went staggering back to their bunks, while the officers were thoroughly mystified as to how their men had managed to get drunk while they couldn't.

So the *Birmingham* continued to sail south. In the words of Martin, that prince of foragers in whom there was much guile: "We prepared to move down and pay our old acquaintances, the British at Yorktown, a visit. I doubt not that their wish was not to have so many of us come at once as their accommodations were rather scanty. They thought, 'the fewer the better cheer.' We thought, 'the more the merrier.' We had come a long way to see them and were unwilling to be put off with excuses."

On the morning of September 17 Washington and Rochambeau sailed aboard the captured British ship *Queen Charlotte* to a meeting with Admiral de Grasse aboard *Ville de Paris*. With them were Generals Knox and Duportail. Climbing up the ladder, they were pleased to see de Grasse in his uniform of blue and scarlet lavishly decorated with gold lace, the flame-colored sash of the Order of St. Louis across his chest, standing among his resplendent officers while the ship's guns boomed in salute. De Grasse was a giant of a man, with a physique a proportionate match to his massive flagship. He advanced upon Washington with a friendly smile, embracing him and bestowing enthusiastic Gallic kisses upon his cheek. Washington, unaccustomed to looking up at other men, was further startled to hear the Frenchman murmur affectionately: "*Mon petit general.* My little general." It is said that at this point Henry Knox burst into laughter, but this is definitely doubtful. Perhaps later in the privacy of his home with his plump wife, Lucy, the equally chubby and jolly Henry might have chuckled, but never at that very moment in the presence of his chief.

Except for this faux pas, which the discreet Washington chose to ignore, the meeting proceeded in a spirit of cordial cooperation. De Grasse was amenable to all Washington's requests, except to send ships above Cornwallis's position on the York to block any attempt to escape. It seemed to the admiral that the river was not wide enough to permit the maneuvering of large warships, and although he did not mention it, he also feared fireship attacks that could not be easily avoided in such narrow waters.

Finally, as a gesture of good will and a symbol of the friendship of the two nations, de Grasse took his guests on a tour of his great ship. The Americans were impressed, not only by its firepower of 110 guns, but by the beautiful tropical flowers the gunners were growing among their cannon. After the tour "the little general" and his correspondingly diminutive retinue climbed back down the ladder for a return trip that was delayed four and a half days by contrary winds. Upon his arrival at his headquarters in Yorktown, Washington was dismayed to see that Cornwallis had been busy erecting a second line of fortifications outside his inner ring. This meant that the outer works could delay the attack upon the inner works with its main body for at least a week—seven days that could permit the arrival of a British rescuing fleet. But then, on the morning of September 30, Washington discovered, to his great joy, that his opponent had abandoned his outer works, leaving them empty after silently withdrawing their garrisons during the night.

His Lordship's seemingly inexplicable withdrawal had an apparently logical explanation. On the September 29 Cornwallis had received from Clinton the following message:

> My Lord: At a meeting of the General and Flag officers held this day, it is determined that above five thousand men, rank and file, shall be embarked on board the King's ships, and the joint exertions of the navy and army made in a few days to relieve you, and afterwards cooperate with you.
>
> The fleet consists of twenty three-sail of the line, three of which are three-deckers. There is every reason to hope we start from hence the 5th October.

Aware that relief would be on the way, Cornwallis quite reasonably decided to strengthen his main position by shortening his line. Concentration would thus make it more difficult for the enemy to overwhelm him. He was, he thought, trading land for time. Also, he was avoiding an engagement in which some of his forward formations might be cut off and lost. To this retrenchment was probably added his indestructible confidence in the fighting prowess of the Royal Navy. Apparently His Lordship did not consider that twenty-three ships against the thirty-two now commanded by de Grasse would not seem to be an equal battle, especially since the presence of British troop transports would require detailing some of Graves's warships to protect them. And if the French were to prevail, those transports carrying five thousand soldiers might be sunk or captured and the War of the American Revolution would be irretrievably lost. Actually, Cornwallis was not actually trading land for time, but quite the reverse. Those outlying redoubts with their single battery could have delayed the American assault for some time: probably a week. In abandoning them with no attempt to blow them up, he was conferring on General Buckskin the gift of a Trojan Horse.

Because all these works but the battery were enclosed, they were immediately useful against Yorktown, and the battery was enclosed that night. Meanwhile on the morning of October 1 the French drove in the pickets at the Fusilier's Redoubt near the river. On the same day Colonel Alexander Scammel was lost to the Americans. While he was on a scouting detail, he was captured by Tarleton's men, and one of the Tories deliberately murdered him by shooting him in the back.

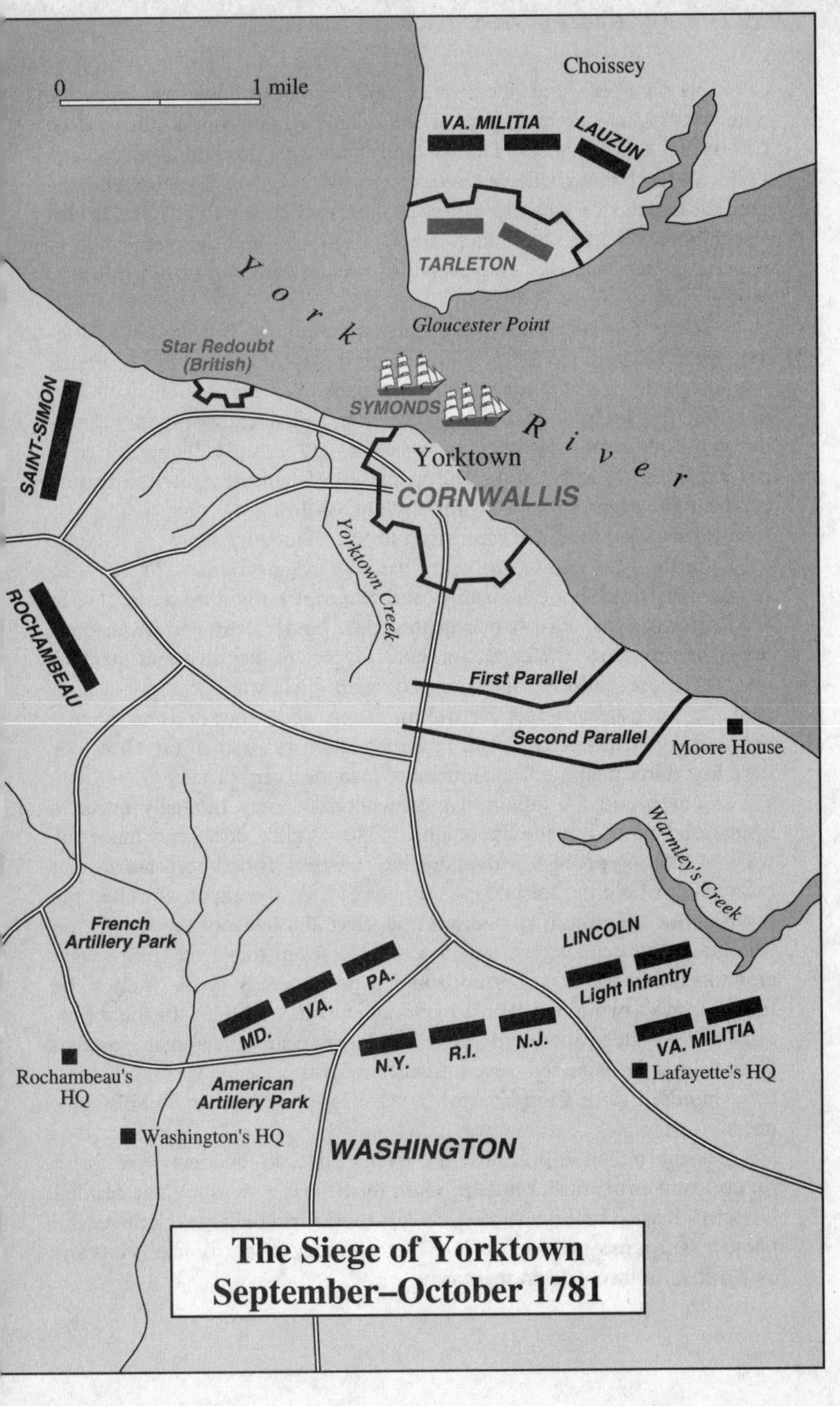

The Siege of Yorktown
September–October 1781

On October 3, as the French and Americans were readying the outer works for bombardment of the enemy's main works, General de Choisy led a force against Dundas and Tarleton's position at Gloucester Point. A brief though fierce firefight ensued in which Tarleton and the Duc de Lauzun very nearly met each other saddle to saddle. The British lost thirteen soldiers, the Franco-Americans none—and the main result of the engagement was that Dundas and Tarleton were pinned down for the duration of the siege.

Three days later work was begun on the first of Washington's parallels, about six hundred yards from the lower end of the town. The trench was to run down to the water's edge. Diggers toiled throughout the night, sweating profusely in that moist heat that had already spread sickness through both camps. Heavy guns were dragged into place, and on October 9 a French battery on the left opened up. Then the American battery on the right began blasting, with Washington firing the first shot, and a British frigate on the York was driven to the Gloucester shore.

On the next night two bigger batteries began roaring. The French set another frigate hopelessly afire, and two transports were destroyed. In all, fifty-two guns were battering the town, and Cornwallis wrote ominously to Clinton: "We have lost about seventy of our men and many of our works are considerably damaged; with such works on disadvantageous ground, against so powerful an attack we cannot hope to make a very long resistance. P.S. 5 P.M. Since my letter was written (at 12 M.) we have lost thirty men. ... We continue to lose men very fast."

Clinton and the admirals, meanwhile, had only belatedly begun a rescue operation. But the limitations of New York's dockyards made the work of refitting proceed with agonizing slowness. It had been hoped that the repairs would be finished by October 5, then the eighth and then the twelfth. But the twelfth passed, and the fleet still had not sailed. Clinton was beside himself. At last, on October 17, seven thousand troops were embarked, and the ships began dropping down Sandy Hook—only to be forced to wait two more days for favorable winds and tides. In the meantime, some sixteen thousand French and Americans drew ever closer to Cornwallis's beleaguered seven thousand, and a second parallel, only three hundred yards from Yorktown, was begun by Steuben and his engineers.

As the trench approached the river's edge, its builders were raked by fire from two British redoubts close to the water. Washington decided to storm them. The French took the left in a stirring charge, climbing the parapet with cries of "*Vive le Roi!*" and forcing its garrison of Hessians and British to throw down their arms.

Alexander Hamilton led the Americans against the one on the right. Now grown fond of the bayonet, the Patriots went at it with unloaded muskets, clawing their way through the abatis, crossing the ditch and leaping over the parapets. From all the British lines came a storm of shells and musket balls. Washington, watching the assault, was cautioned by his aide: "Sir, you are too much exposed here. Had you not better step a little back?"

"Colonel Cobb," Washington replied gravely, "if you are afraid, you have liberty to step back."

And so both redoubts were won, the second parallel was extended down to the river and the second nail driven into the British coffin. On the morning of October 16, Cornwallis sent out a force of 350 men to capture and destroy the batteries in the second parallel. In a brave charge, the British succeeded in entering both positions and in spiking some guns, but they were eventually driven back, and the guns were restored to service.

So desperate now that he was losing his judgment, Cornwallis attempted a wild escape across the river through Gloucester. He expected to burst through the Franco-American force there and proceed to New York by forced marches. That midnight he began embarking his troops, but a violent storm broke upon him and forced him back into Yorktown.

That was the end.

In the morning of the seventeenth, two days before Clinton's relief force made the open sea, the allies opened on the town with a dreadful cannonade. One by one the British works collapsed. There was no answering fire, for the British had exhausted their ammunition. Soon a redcoated drummer boy strode onto a parapet and began to beat a parley. He could not be heard in all that thunder, but he was seen. The guns fell silent, and a British officer advanced to be blindfolded and led to Washington.

He asked for a twenty-four-hour armistice. Washington granted him two hours. The officer returned with Cornwallis's surrender terms, including a condition that his army be paroled to Britain. Washington insisted that the enemy surrender as prisoners of war, and Cornwallis submitted.

At noon of October 19, 1781, the gay military music of the French sang out, and for the last time the vivacious white-coated soldiers of France went into line on American soil. Into line opposite them, moving proudly across trampled fields to the Celtic lilt of fifes and drums, went the tall Americans in brown or hunting shirts and here and there in blue and buff. George Washington rode up on a great bay horse and stood at their right. Across from him Rochambeau and Admiral de Barras sat their horses. De Barras was there because Admiral de Grasse was uncomfortable aboard a horse. His deputy was hardly better. As his mount stretched to void itself, he cried: "My, God—I'm sinking!" To the right of them Yorktown's main sally port was flung open. Faint on the wind came the mournful beat of drums and the melancholy squeal of fifes. Out rode Brigadier General Charles O'Hara. With stupefying bad grace, Cornwallis, pleading illness, had sent a deputy to surrender for him.

Bewildered, O'Hara rode first toward Rochambeau. But the count, by a gracious inclination of the eyes, directed him to Washington. Slightly flustered, O'Hara approached the tall Virginian. Washington indicated General Benjamin Lincoln, after himself the senior American officer present. Deputy must surrender to deputy.

Here was the supreme irony of the war: Benjamin Lincoln, the obese champion of lost battles, one of those politicking militia generals that a meddling Congress had promoted over the heads of Greene, Arnold, Knox and John Stark, was to receive the enemy commander's sword symbolizing surrender! But Washington, a stickler for protocol, could do no other. Certainly he would have preferred the gallant and able Nathanael Greene, except that Greene was too valuable where he was: campaigning in South Carolina with his customary skill. So O'Hara handed Cornwallis's sword to Lincoln, who returned it while calling for the surrender to begin.

Out they came, the scarlet-coated British and their Hessian allies, brilliant in blue and green. Out came the German mercenaries, striding briskly, stacking their arms neatly, then the British, moving along slowly, their faces sullen, some of them already weeping. Down went their arms in a disorderly crash. Drummer boys stove in their drums, infantrymen smashed their musket butts and stomped on their cartridge cases. Officers pouting like schoolboys avoided the eyes of their captors.

Above the clatter of grounded arms and the hoarse cursing of brokenhearted soldiers rose the music of the British bands, bringing the War of the American Revolution to its effective close with the prophetic notes of "The World Turned Upside-down."

EPILOGUE: A NEW ORDER OF THE AGES

News of the surrender of Cornwallis at Yorktown was received by a Congress so penniless that some of its members had to pay a dollar out of their own pockets to pay the expenses of the courier who brought it on October 22. A watchman who had conducted that messenger to the home of President Thomas McKean began to cry through the streets of Philadelphia: "Past three o'clock and Cornwallis is taken!" Two days later Washington's official reports arrived, and the entire Congress walked in a procession to the Lutheran Church for a service of Thanksgiving. As the joyous word spread through the states, there was great rejoicing and jubilation, especially among those members of the Continental Army, such as Joseph Plumb Martin, who now knew that they would go home alive and well instead of inside a pine box. Fear, hunger, privation—their constant companions for six long sacrificial years—had been replaced by an infinite joy elate.

The bad news arrived in London on November 25, when Lord George Germain brought it to Lord North, who received it, according to Germain, "as he would have taken a ball in his breast, crying out wildly as he paced to and fro, 'Oh, God, it is all over!'" King George III was also shocked, but took news of the disaster with more composure, promising to carry on the war "though the mode of it may require alteration." For a time the traitor Benedict Arnold became his chief adviser on the alteration of that mode, urging relentless prosecution of the conflict, telling His Majesty what he wanted to be told: that the American people universally detested Congress and the French—his own personal bêtes noires. But even though there were still British troops in New York, Charleston and other places, the war eventually was not fiercely continued, especially after the North government fell and Parliament voted in early 1782 to authorize King George to seek peace.

Peace commissioners were appointed by both sides. On November 30, 1782, they signed provisional articles, but it was not until September 3, 1783, that a definitive treaty acknowledging the independence of the United States of America was formally signed.

With that treaty, a new age appeared in the history of humankind. For the first time since civilization dawned in the light of written language, a nation was born, based on freedom and justice for all and the belief that all men are created equal. Here was an even greater revolution, and it had been born and bought in human blood—as all new orders must be. And that was the motto of this new nation, with its remarkably mild restraints on human conduct, all based on the rule of law rather than of men. Its founders with their love of Latin called it *Novus Ordo Seclorum*—A New Order of the Ages—an ideal of perfection in representative government that, though not always attainable among imperfect human beings, nevertheless challenged, as it still does today, all the cruelties and injustices of fixed societies and despotisms everywhere.

SELECTED BIBLIOGRAPHY

Adams, James Truslow. *The Living Jefferson.* New York: Scribner's, 1936.

Alden, John R. *A History of the American Revolution.* New York: Alfred A. Knopf, 1969.

———. *George Washington.* New York: Dell, 1984.

Allan, Herbert S. *John Hancock.* New York: Beechhurst, 1953.

Andrist, Ralph K., ed. *George Washington, A Biography in His Own* Words. New York: Harper & Row, 1973.

Bailey, Rev. J. D. *Some Heroes of the American Revolution,* Easely, S.C.: Southern Historical Press, 1976.

Bailyn, Bernard. *The Ideological Origins of the American Revolution.* Cambridge, Mass.: Harvard University Press, 1967.

Bass, Robert D. *Green Dragoon, The Lives of Banastre Tarleton and Mrs. Mary Robinson.* New York: Henry Holt, 1957.

———. *Swamp Fox, The Life of Francis Marion.* Orangeburg S.C.: Sandlapper, 1959.

Beach, Stewart. *Samuel Adams.* New York: Dodd, Mead, 1965.

Bill, Alfred Hoyt. *Valley Forge.* New York: Harper & Row, 1952.

———. *The Campaign of Princeton.* Princeton, N.J.: Princeton University Press, 1948.

Billias, George Athan. *George Washington's Opponents.* New York: Morrow, 1969.

Bolton, Charles Knowles. *The Private Soldier under Washington.* New York: Scribner's, 1902.

Bowen, Catherine Drinker. *John Adams and the American Revolution.* Boston: Little Brown, 1950.

Callahan, North. *Henry Knox.* New York: Rinehart, 1958.

Cary, John. *Joseph Warren.* Urbana: University of Illinois Press, 1964.

Commager, Henry Steele, and Richard B. Morris. *The Spirit of Seventy-Six.* 2 vols. Indianapolis: Bobbs-Merrill, 1958.

Curtis, Edward E. *The Organization of the British Army in the American Revolution.* New Haven, Conn.: Yale University Press. 1926.

Dann, John C. *The Revolution Remembered: Eyewitness Accounts of the War for Independence.* Chicago: University of Chicago Press, 1980.

Davis, Burke. *Heroes of the American Revolution.* New York: Random House, 1971.

Dos Passos, John. *The Men Who Made the Nation.* Garden City, N.Y.: Doubleday, 1957.

Dull, Jonathon R. *Diplomatic History of the American Revolution.* New Haven, Conn.: Yale University Press, 1985.

Dwyer, William M. *The Day Is Ours!* New York: Viking, 1983.

Ellsberg, Commander Edward. *Captain Paul.* New York: Literary Guild, 1941.

Emery, Noemie. *Washington.* New York: Putnam's, 1976.

Esposito, Colonel Vincent J., ed. *The West Point Atlas of American Wars.* Vol. 1. New York: Praeger, 1959.

Fay, Bernard. *George Washington.* Cambridge, Mass.: Houghton Mifflin, 1931.

Fehrenbach, T. R. *Greatness to Spare.* Princeton, N.J.: Van Nostrand, 1968.

Fleming, Thomas. *Beat the Last Drum.* New York: St. Martin's, 1963.

———. *Now We Are Enemies.* New York: St. Martin's, 1960.

———. *1776: Year of Illusions.* New York: Norton, 1975.

Flexner, James Thomas. *The Traitor and the Spy.* New York: Harcourt, Brace, 1953.

Flood, Charles Bracelen. *Rise, and Fight Again.* New York: Dodd, Mead, 1976.

Foner, Eric. *Tom Paine and Revolutionary America.* New York: Oxford University Press, 1976.

Forbes, Esther. *Paul Revere.* Boston: Houghton Mifflin, 1942.

Fowler, William D. *Rebels under Sail.* New York: Scribner's, 1976.

Freeman, Douglas Southall. *Washington.* 6 vols. New York: Scribner's. 1948, 1951, 1952, 1954, 1957.

Gelb, Norman. *Less Than Glory.* New York: Putnam's, 1984.

Gerson, Noel B. *Lafayette, Statue in Search of a Pedestal.* New York: Dodd, Mead, 1976.

Griffith, Samuel B. *In Defense of the Public Liberty.* Garden City, N.Y.: Doubleday, 1976.

Guttmacher, Manfred S., M.D. *America's Last King: An Interpretation of the Madness of George III.* New York: Scribner's, 1941.

Handlin, Oscar, and Lilian Handlin. *Liberty and Power, 1600–1760.* New York: Harper & Row, 1986.

Holbrook, Sabra. *Lafayette.* New York: Athenaeum, 1977.

Holbrook, Stuart H. *Ethan Allen.* Portland, Oreg.: Binfords & Mort, 1958.

Howson, Gerald. *Burgoyne of Saratoga.* New York: New York Times Books, 1979.

Ketchum, Richard M. *The Winter Soldiers.* Garden City, N.Y.: Doubleday, 1973.

Kline, Mary-Jo, ed. *Alexander Hamilton, A Biography in His Own Words.* New York: Harper & Row, 1973.

Lancaster, Bruce. *The American Heritage Book of the Revolution.* New York: Simon & Schuster, 1958.

———. *Lexington to Liberty.* Garden City, N.Y.: Doubleday, 1943.

Leckie, Robert. *Forged in Blood.* New York: New American Library, 1982.

———. *Great American Battles.* New York: Random House, 1968.

———. *The World Turned Upside Down.* New York: Putnam's, 1971.

———. *The Wars of America.* New York: Harper & Row, 1981.

Loth, David. *Alexander Hamilton.* New York: Carrick & Evans, 1939.

Lumpkin, Henry. *From Savannah to Yorktown.* New York: Paragon House, 1986.

Mackesy, Piers. *The War for America.* Cambridge, Mass.: Harvard University Press, 1965.

Maier, Pauline. *The Old Revolutionaries.* New York: Alfred A. Knopf, 1980.

Manceron, Claude. *Winds from America.* New York: Alfred A. Knopf, 1978.

Martin, Joseph Plumb. *Private Yankee Doodle.* Boston: Little Brown, 1962.

Meigs, Cornelia. *The Violent Men.* New York: Macmillan, 1950.

Miller, John C. *Triumph of Freedom.* Boston: Little Brown, 1948.

Mitchell, Broadus. *The Price of Independence.* New York: Oxford University Press, 1974.

Montross, Lynn. *Rag, Tag and Bobtail.* New York: Harper & Row, 1952.

———. *The Reluctant Rebels.* New York: Harper & Row, 1950.

Morgan, Edmund S. *The Challenge of the American Revolution.* New York: Norton, 1976.

Morris, Richard B. *The Peacemakers.* New York: Harper & Row, 1965.

Nelson, Paul David. *Anthony Wayne, Soldier of the Early Republic.* Bloomington: Indiana University Press, 1985.

Nelson, William H. *The American Tory.* Oxford: Clarendon, 1961.

Parmet, Herbert S., and Marie B. Hecht. *Aaron Burr.* New York: Macmillan, 1967.

Patterson, Samuel White. *Horatio Gates.* New York: Columbia University Press, 1941.

———. *Knight Errant of Liberty: General Charles Lee.* New York: Lantern, 1958.

Randall, Willard Stone. *Benedict Arnold.* New York: Morrow, 1990.

Roberts, Kenneth. *The Battle of Cowpens.* Garden City, N.Y.: Doubleday, 1958.

Royster, Charles. *A Revolutionary People at War.* New York: Norton, 1979.

Seymour, George Dudley. *Documentary Life of Nathan Hale.* New Haven, Conn.: By Author, 1941.

Smith, Page. *A New Age Now Begins.* 2 vols. New York: McGraw-Hill, 1976.

Stille, Charles J. *Major General Anthony Wayne.* Port Washington, N.Y.: Kennikat, 1968.

Swigget, Howard. *Forgotten Leaders of the American Revolution.* Garden City, N.Y.: Doubleday, 1955.

Thane, Elswyth. *The Family Quarrel.* New York: Duell, Sloane & Pearce, 1959.

Tharp, Louise Hall. *The Baroness and the General.* Boston: Little Brown, 1962.

Valentine, Alan. *Lord George Germain.* Oxford: Clarendon, 1962.

Van Doren, Carl. *Mutiny in January.* New York: Viking, 1943.

Vaughan, Alden T. *America Before the Revolution.* Englewood Cliffs, N.J.: Prentice-Hall, 1967.

Vulliany, C. E. *Royal George: A Study of King George III.* New York: D. Appleton, Century, 1937.

Wagner, Frederick K. *Robert Morris.* New York: Dodd, Mead, 1976.
Wallace, Willard M. *Traitorous Hero: The Life and Fortunes of Benedict Arnold.* New York: Harper & Row, 1954.
Ward, Christopher. *The War of the American Revolution.* 2 vols. New York: Macmillan, 1952.
Whitridge, Arnold. *Rochambeau.* New York: Macmillan, 1965.
Wickwire, Franklin, and Wickwire, Mary. *Cornwallis.* Boston: Houghton Mifflin, 1970.

INDEX